The Greatest Lie Ever Told

W H Uffington

Published by **Workhorse Publishing**

Published 2011

Copyright © W H Uffington, 2011

The moral right of the author has been asserted

All rights reserved
Without limiting the rights under copyright reserved above, no part of this publication may be reproduced, stored in or introduced into a retrieval system, or transmitted in any form or by any means (electronic, mechanical, photocopying, recording or otherwise), without the prior written permission of both the copyright owner and the above publisher of this book, nor be otherwise circulated in any form of binding or cover other than that in which it is published and without a similar condition being imposed on the subsequent purchaser

Every effort has been made to fulfil requirements with regard to reproducing copyright material
The author and publisher will be glad to rectify any omissions at the earliest opportunity

A CIP catalogue record for this book is available from the British Library

ISBN 978-0-9567980-0-8

to Jane Talbot

In the beginning you appeared within a halo of dazzling sunlight. I saw and I felt and my journey was now to begin: I was cast down into the darkness of the Duat to experience. Through experience is found knowledge and so blessed will come the return out of the darkness — not into the light, but as light.

Contents

	Acknowledgements	iii
	Introduction	v

Part One
The Torah Tale of Arrogance Oppression and Genocide

1. Abraham — the Wandering Star — 3
   the origins of Ur and the true significance of the area in which Abraham's story was set

2. Digging the Dirt on Abraham and Isaac — 13
   the archaeological evidence for the story of Abraham and the lack of morality shown by his family

3. Orion and the Patriarchs — 25
   Judean scribes of seventh century BCE create a past for their people, disguise their Egyptian links and encode sacred secrets

4. Moses — One More Basket Case — 35
   the story that revives an old Babylonian legend to boost Judean supremacy and the historical evidence that tells us no Exodus ever took place

5. David and Solomon — Superheroes — 49
   the comic book kings created to glorify a psychopathic God and an imaginary Israelite Empire in an arid land; neighbours call it 'home to hilltop farmers and bandits'

6. The Seventh–Century Propagandists — 59
   King Josiah's scribes create a God who makes his people racially superior, orders ethnic cleansing on an unprecedented scale and writes laws that bind the people to the state forever

7. Holy Book of Horrors — 77
   the scribes enslaved by the Babylonians encode their Egyptian links and return home to a country soon to be Hellenised; attempting to oust Alexander's religions, the Judeans turn the fictitious genocide of earlier times into a nightmare reality and the Romans intervene

Part Two
And in the
Beginning
— Egyptian
Monotheism

8 The Egyptian God of Creation   95
   the myth, theory and supporting evidence that explain
   Ancient Egyptian beliefs, question assumptions about the
   people and show why their religion is relevant today

9 Uncovering the One God   127
   after the story of Thutmosis and the Dream Stele a new
   dawn lights the path of Atum–Ra, it leads away from
   Amun and moves towards the Aten

10 Akhenaten The Man Who Gave Us God   133
   Spirit of Aten brought one God and one religion; his
   Holy City was built in the exact centre of Egypt with the
   same precise measurements used in the Great Pyramids

11 The Pharaoh In Gods' Image   145
   Akhenaten chose to be portrayed in a stylised and
   elongated form in order to look like the Elohim described
   in the Book of Enoch

12 From Egypt to Exile   161
   Ay, Divine Father of the Aten Temple, restores stability
   in Tutankhamun's reign, the Atenist priests have to go,
   taking their monotheistic religion with them, to Canaan

13 Akhet–Aten to Eden   169
   Akhenaten's legacy is revealed and some baffling Bible
   stories start to make sense at last

Part Three
New Testament
— The Jesus
Myth Corruption

14 Out of Egypt Once More   185
   from the earliest records of Egyptian religion through the
   Greek philosophers to the Druids, the story of Man and
   God has been told, Alexander helped spread the stories
   and teachings of Jesus under his changing names

15 From Mystery to Mayhem   207
   Pythagorean Jews create their own Mysteries but when
   Jerusalem falls their followers, enslaved in Rome, lose
   their priests and corrupt their religion

16 The Gospel Truth   219
   Literal Christians in Rome have no teachers,
   misunderstand the allegories, and believe the Jewish
   Mystery stories are tales of real people

17 The Man Who Never Was   233
   the evidence presents the mythological Jesus and what
   contemporary writers said about the Jews

18 Isis — The Real Mary   239
*from Mary Magdalene and Black Madonnas to the
Blessed Virgin, the stories all lead to Isis*

19 He Who Points The Finger To Orion   249
*Druids, Cistercians, Knights Templar, Priory of Sion
and John the Baptist, all pointing to a distant star*

20 Some of Our Apostles Are Missing   257
*searching for evidence that the Apostles ever existed
and showing what they really represent*

21 Paul — Dangerous Heretic   261
*why we know he was initiated into the Mysteries, what
happens when you 'look through a glass darkly,' where
the road to Damascus led and when his work was forged*

22 Pearls Before Swine   277
*tell Roman Jews a truth that they don't want to hear,
from the Commandments to the Psalms and Miracles,
Christianity enslaves those the truth would set free*

23 Tall Tales of Mystery Martyrs   287
*Roman religious tolerance and sense of justice outweigh
the perversion of Christian leaders who invent the fate
of thousands in their history, evidence shows few were
punished and none for holding a belief*

24 Buy Me a Bishop   301
*the rift between Gnostic and Literalist Christians widens,
the popularity of the latter amongst the uneducated leads
to exploitation and ruthless money-making*

25 For Mine Is the Kingdom, the Power and the Glory   309
*civilisation is at its peak until the death of Marcus
Aurelius, then political squabbling takes its place,
Constantine takes control and the greed and corruption in
the Roman Church become his tool, for the next thousand
years civilisation is buried beneath the slaughter and
oppression of a ruthless and mindless religion*

26 The Prince of Peace & His Reign of Terror   327
*Christianity official religion of the Roman Empire, pagan
practices of washing and discussing religion banned;
Christians slaughter pagans, bands of monks torture, loot
and burn books; brutes in the pay of bishops and dead
thugs sanctified, as they all go about Christ's work*

27 The Mystery to Misery Millennium   337
*Christianity in its true form survived in rural outposts and
the Celts spread it far and wide, the Roman Church found
Kings and Princes to support it and after a thousand year
struggle endorsed its mission with the Holy Inquisition*

Part Four The Truth, The Way, The Light —The Future	28 From Inquisition to Inspiration *after two hundreds years the printing press severs the shackles on the intellect, science and philosophy replace hell and damnation*	373
	29 Isis Unveiled *Rosicrucians and Freemasons keep the ideals and moral teaching alive, they give us the Royal Society, Académie Française, the French and American Revolutions as the covert movement attempts to create a perfect New World*	399
	30 Quo Vadis? *Where are you going, once you've read this book? The churches may help you but the path will be your own. If you get it wrong, you won't see God in the afterlife, but neither will those who get it right. We'll all see God, when we learn we are one. Hope you can wait, Consensus could take an Eternity.*	433
Appendix 1	Islam — The Prophet Rolling in his Grave *the influence of Gnostic exiles on Mohammed who wanted an end to Arab greed and infighting and a return to their traditional caring society*	443
Appendix 2	The Templars, Their Cathedrals and Their Cistercian Friends *sacred geometry and unprecedented engineering of the Gothic cathedrals, their Druid and Cistercian links*	461
Appendix 3	Holy Grail *its history and origins, what it isn't and why, what it is and where you'll find it*	463
Appendix 4	Lessons from the Afterlife *a group of lawyers assess the evidence for the Afterlife and reveal what they have learned*	467
	Bibliography	475
	Index	485
	Map of Middle East and Timeline	back

Acknowledgements

"They have a right to censure that have a heart to help."
William Penn

This book was a long time in its gestation as the seed of the idea grew into something resembling a large ungainly tree, its branches spreading everywhere, but once felled and trimmed and sculpted, a coherent shape began to form. The rough edges were chiselled away by my assistant Gabrielle Elrond and I am indebted to my editor Andy Charlesworth for his thorough and painstaking sanding down.

John Anthony West, Daniel Harnam and Victor Zammit sustained me on the journey and I thank them for giving me their time.

My deepest thanks go to those who take the time to read through the final work. Don't feel disheartened, as I did at what you discover within these pages, but use what you learn about the greatest lie ever told to build a more honest world of your own.

THE GREATEST LIE EVER TOLD

Introduction

"We have all examined our past critically and are very much aware of even the unpleasant things. Now, we need to look at what we plan to do with the lessons we have learned from the past."
Heinz Fischer

Christianity has become the dominating world force not only in religion, but politics, history, art, social behaviour and the way people think. Its influence has been profound, but what if it were false, based on a misconception, built on a lie. Would that not be the greatest lie ever told?

If that were so, would we ignore the truth and continue to accept the lie because the truth is too hard for us to deal with. The coward will turn from the truth, the brave will face it and want to know more. Perhaps what existed before the lie was something wonderful. To search for the truth takes courage, but you find a light that shines on the world that no-one can ever extinguish. All it takes to find the truth, is to let the greatest lie unfold.

My discovery of the scandalous truth was traumatic, though it really should not have been so. I had always had uncomfortable reservations, but they were ones that I pushed away — the easy option is always to bury one's head in the sand. I had always thought of myself as a good Christian, though I had never been devout or a regular churchgoer. Besides doubting the integrity of the Old Testament, I was repelled by the ritual and the subservience that the congregation gave to the priesthood and to God. The latter may appear shockingly blasphemous, but as I did, in time you may come to understand that this is not so; that eventually it makes perfect sense for what I learned was that the point of our existence is a reunion with God, where we become one and equal.

Church buildings assailed me with another problem; I loved the exterior architecture, but could never feel comfortable inside. Churches were cold soulless places where I was always conscious of an invisible dark shadow pressing down heavily upon me. Eventually I discovered the reason why: virtually every ancient church was constructed over a pagan holy site that had been a place of healing using the earth's energy. Christian missionaries had capped these energy vortices with stone altars; the Christian structure now laid on top, with its unskilled and uneducated priests within unable to use the energy to heal their miserable congregations.

THE GREATEST LIE EVER TOLD

Despite my unease and reservations, I still called myself a Christian, but I awoke with a jolt at the end of the 1990s. I had started research for a novel based on the historical King Arthur. I wanted to open the story with Joseph of Arimathea bringing the young Jesus to Britain, so that I could show how Celtic beliefs might have influenced Jesus, whose in turn eventually influenced Arthur. I began by immersing myself in Celtic history and mythology but once I widened my research to early Christianity I found something that shook me to the core. In 1999, I came across a new book, *The Jesus Mysteries* by Timothy Freke and Peter Gandy, two philosophers who had apparently aspired to write a biography of Jesus, but had instead exposed a minefield full of facts that showed there was no-one for them to write about, and that the original Christianity was not unique, but just another version of the widespread Mystery religion. The revelations in this book hit me hard when perhaps I should have been prepared, instead I was shocked and stunned and even worse, I felt betrayed. I felt a rage at the Church's deliberate lies, for many obviously knew the truth, and even worse, I felt fury at the way these unscrupulous people had used religion to control — frightening children with threats of eternal torture by demons in hell for committing sins is appalling spiritual, mental and emotional abuse.

Eventually I overcame my anger and the feeling that I had been cast adrift. Now with no God and no afterlife, I returned to my research, not for a novel, but to unearth the truth that could expose that greatest lie. I discovered that the Jewish religion was a political concoction of myth, legend and history designed to hide its true origins in Egypt. I discovered that Christianity was a shallow distortion of the original Egyptian Mysteries. I discovered that the Church hid its origins by persecution and slaughter and created a fictional history to portray itself as the upholder of the one true faith; it had been run by people who were morally corrupt, who lusted after wealth and power, who unhesitatingly resorted to lies and forgery, who undertook the destruction of civilisation and indulged in the mass slaughter of rivals with a psychopathic enthusiasm. Yet it had always been opposed by a secret organisation which kept the true Mystery alive. More surprisingly I discovered that the original deceivers are now at the cutting edge of scientific research that proves beyond doubt the eternal soul. In the early years, the uneducated Christians of Rome were considered pariahs; by chance they rose to power and destroyed their critics, destroyed evidence and invented a new fictional history for themselves. They turned religious allegories into real history, now they have the opportunity to make a better world, but first they must admit that theirs was the greatest lie ever told.

WH Uffington,
January 2011

Part One

The Torah Tale of Arrogance Oppression and Genocide

Chapter 1

Abraham — the Wandering Star

"Truth is a pathless land, and you cannot approach it by any path whatsoever, by any religion, by any sect."

Jiddu Krishnamurti

Our quest to uncover what's hidden beneath the mantle of religious history must start with one man. The Jewish and Christian Bibles and the history of Islam, all take us back to the time of Abraham.

When we read the story of Abraham, the characterisation, plot and exploits seem familiar and we start to recognise the ingredients of a modern day pot–boiler. Our hero is a simple man, with humble beginnings and grand ambitions, who strives to create a family dynasty. The plot overflows with jealousy, lust, ambitions, intrigue and brotherly rivalry, that in their turn fuel the dynastic progress. No one tires of the tales that built a nation's self–confidence and sense of belonging, evoking stirring tales of its people's hard struggles and ultimate success.

Create a local hero, recount his daily hardships and familial infighting: have him fight political bigwigs and win, and see him rise to power and influence over his family and friends and former enemies too. The recipe works for TV soaps today and Abraham repeats have been running for synagogue audiences for the last 2,500 years. If pride in their ancestors' achievements fails to impress us, then we have the pointed reminders that Abraham's descendants have been singled out for special treatment; for all time; by no other than God himself. Those Bible scriptwriters crafted a history that the Jewish people would all want to hear about, talk about and would love to retell.

As popular fiction, the story of Abraham might make the best sellers and even a box office hit, but as a historical document, it is badly flawed. The authors, Judean scribes, who started writing in the 7th century BCE, had no inkling of life a thousand years previously, yet they tried to write a book giving the history of their tribe. The scribes had an additional problem — during their exile in Babylon, they had to protect important information about their religion, but disguise its origins from their captors.

The first historical anomaly relates to where Abraham came from. This chapter reveals the real relevance of Abraham's homeland and explains how misunderstanding arose about its location.

The Bible story records that Abram — his original name — lived in Ur of the Chaldees and there is a common assumption that this is the prosperous Mesopotamian city on the Euphrates River — near Basra in southern Iraq — that flourished for 2000 years before Christ. Many reference books confirm this; adults remember that trick question they were asked as a child, "Where did Abraham come from?" When they answered "Err…" they were told "That's right," and so Ur maintains its status in common belief.

The renowned American scholar, Professor W F Albright,[1] claims this assumption is incorrect. Ur on the Euphrates is not the home of Abraham. Albright points out that in the Greek translations of the Bible, Ur is never mentioned alone. In the Greek translations it says 'Ur of the Chaldees' which means Ur *in the land of the Chaldeans*. So Abraham's birthplace was changed to 'Ur' and 'in the land of the Chaldeans omitted after the Bible was translated from Greek to Latin not when the story was first documented, but six hundred years later, in the fourth century CE.

More evidence that Ur was a careless misrepresentation comes when Genesis indicates that Abraham's original homeland was much further north. In Genesis 24, Abraham sends his servant from Canaan to Nahor to find a wife for his son Isaac. The Bible calls *Nahor* "Abraham's country, his father's house and the land of my kindred": Nahor lies in the *northwest* of Mesopotamia, near Haran. The city of Ur, on the other hand, is in the south.

In Joshua 24, we get another clue to the true geographical location. Joshua says, "Your fathers dwelt on the other side of the flood in old time, even Terah, the father of Abraham and the father of Nahor". Mesopotamian Ur stands on the side of the Euphrates nearer to Canaan, whereas Nahor is on the *other* side, on the *other side of the flood,* which is the biblical term for the River Euphrates. The Bible stories seem to negate the southern city of Ur, but by shining some new light onto some old archaeological evidence, an even more significant detail begins to emerge.

When the 4,000-year-old Mesopotamian city of Mari was unearthed in the 1930s, archaeologists discovered many thousands of clay tablets. The records preserved on those clay tablets gave the names of towns that lay

---

[1] Albright, W F *Archaeology and the Religion of Israel*

within the domain of this city–state. To Biblical scholars, these names will be familiar: Haran, Nahor, Peleg, Serug, Terah. All these places lie within the area bounded by the Euphrates and Tigris rivers on the northern plain called Aram. Mari, with its biblically linked towns, lies roughly halfway up the Euphrates, whilst Ur lies in the far south by the Persian Gulf delta.

As the tablets were deciphered, Christian theologians were overcome with joy, for here at last was proof that the Old Testament stories were based upon historical fact. In Genesis 11, we read, "These are the generations of Shem" and the verse goes on to name Peleg who begat Reu, who begat Serug, who begat Nahor, who begat Terah, who begat Abram, Nahor and Haran. Astonishingly, the clay tablets, unearthed in Mari, have the names of Abraham's ancestors on them. However, what appears to be conclusive evidence of his forebears' existence is not quite as it seems.

To any rational person, it should seem extremely odd that the names of Abraham's forefathers are identical to the names of the towns in the north-western region of the kingdom of Mari. Is it also coincidental that the name, Abram is very similar to the name of the area, Aram? A character out of legend having the same name as a historical town can indeed occur: the Ptolemaic Greeks named Herakleopolis after one of their gods, Herakles (the Roman Hercules). But a town name cannot be used as proof that a character of the same name actually existed. One can prove that a town was named after a known historical person: Byzantium was renamed Constantinople when it became the seat of the Emperor Constantine and history proves many such examples. When there is no evidence whatsoever that any of the Biblical forefathers of Abraham, nor even the man himself, ever lived, it is impossible to argue that the towns were named after the men.

For argument's sake, we cannot say we have evidence that they didn't exist, but we are able to ask which might have come first, town or man. The answer to this question lies in the name Haran. Haran, we are told, is the name given to Terah's third son, but the story also states that Terah moves *his family* to the *town* of Haran. In this particular case, the town was already called Haran, before the son was named, so clearly the town did not derive its name from the Biblical character, but Haran was given his from it. The same is almost certainly true for the other sons, for it is totally unknown for one single family–line, particularly one with no regal or political connections, to give its names to a group of towns.

To understand if the town's name might also be a Jewish given name, we need to look at how Jewish families describe themselves. For thousands of years, the practice among Jews has been to use *ben,* the Hebrew word for son, followed by the given name of the father, to indicate the family. So Terah's sons would be known as Abram ben Terah, Nahor ben Terah and

Haran ben Terah. The names only reflect the child's given name and who his father was, Jewish names unlike Arab ones, do not use a place to denote the person.

The *son of* naming system was common amongst Jews until the sixteenth century, when the more affluent Jews, who settled in Gentile lands, adopted a fixed family name. By the end of the eighteenth century, when registration of town dwellers for tax purposes became common, the practice of using a family name was established in Central and Eastern Europe. Family names were usually derived from the traditional one, but changed to reflect the local language, so we get variations with Jacob *Ben David* changing to Jakob Davidovitch or Jacob Davidson, depending on where Jacob eventually lives.

The traditional form of naming, as son–of–the–father, continued until very recently amongst some groups of Jews. Only when they migrated to Israel, in the 1980s and 1990s, did the Jews of Ethiopia adopt a fixed family name. So we can reasonably assume that it would have been much the same at the time of Abraham— the son is named from the father — unless external influences forced a change and in no case have we found a Jewish name derived from a town.

Let's now consider what likelihood there is that the place name was added on in those days — a practice now common amongst modern day Arabs. Could these people have been named after their place of origin, as for example a name like the King of Jordan's, Abdullah *ibn* Hussein *al* Amman, Abdullah son of Hussein from Amman? To add in 'from the town' is possible, but then if that might be the case, it explains any *fixed family name*, but not what a particular *given name* is. With the Abrahamic dynasty, we have a Bible that uses a single given name for each person and archaeological evidence of a coincident place name and therefore historians have assumed that the latter confirms the actual existence of the former. This is, to say the least, very peculiar and in the extreme, vague and anonymous.

We are left to conclude that the names used in the Bible were, for some reason, deliberately meant to be impersonal. Perhaps the reason was much more esoteric and it was always the intention, that the geographical nature of the names be covert arcane guides for 'those with the eyes to see' who were 'seeking the truth'. The only rational conclusion we can reach at this stage is to recognise that even if the Bible scribes did not appreciate the fundamental significance behind the ancient Abraham legends, the original author, or authors, whoever they were, had a connection with this area and chose to give the characters names which had important links to it. Their reasons may be obscured at present, but will become clearer as the book moves on.

ABRAHAM — THE WANDERING STAR

Many Biblical scholars currently believe that the early stories were actually a conglomeration of separate localised tribal myths and legends. When the Hebrew Bible was being compiled in written form, the authors realised the political advantage of combining all the disparate, unrelated tribal tales into one cohesive and linear story that would bind together the fractious Israelite tribes into a people with a shared written history. The story of Abraham is one of these localised legends, but it is one whose great significance is little known. If the compilers of the Hebrew Bible had understood this significance, they would certainly have concealed it and there is some indication that this in fact may have happened.

But what *is* the undeclared significance of Haran and of the puzzling Ur? The answer lies in their connection with Egypt. This claim may appear both surprising and unlikely, but over the course of this book, the reader will discover that Egypt underpins the core of the Bible. It is important here to look at the history of these towns and their origins, but first of all we need to look at that place called Ur from another point of view.

Islamic sources have long held that Abraham was born in a town called Ur that was near to Haran. The Qur'an states that he was born in the kingdom of Namrood, the Nimrod of Genesis. These days, most academics and theologians agree with them and believe that the Biblical *Ur of the Chaldees,* is the Turkish town of Urfa, which stands on a tributary of the northern Euphrates, just a few miles northwest of Haran.

Originally, Urfa's name was *Urhay,* town of the Chaldees. According to legend, the Biblical character, King Nimrod built the town of Urfa: Nimrod is described as, 'a mighty hunter before the Lord'[2] and later in the book, I show the significance of this designation. A story told to the modern day tourists in Anatolia, tells of Nimrod casting Abraham off a cliff into a water pool: Urfa is renowned for its natural spring that feeds the pools. Though clearly a fictional fantasy, this legend has an arcane astronomical message, which is discussed in Chapter 3.

Urfa, according to Greek sources, was ancient before Alexander the Great invaded the region in the third century BCE. The Greeks renamed this strategically important town Edessa. As a heavily fortified citadel–town, Edessa expanded and prospered under the Greeks and Romans, then finally the Byzantines. During the Christian period, Edessa became an important theological centre with churches said to rival those of Constantinople. Likewise, its great libraries rivalled those of Athens, for the town was strategically placed to become the melting–pot for the exchange of ideas and philosophies between east and west, not only amongst the various

---

[2] Genesis 10:9

Christian sects, especially the Gnostics, but also numerous eastern belief systems such as Zoroastrianism, Hinduism and Buddhism.

There was another religious doctrine with a base in Edessa that had its origins in Egypt. Academics believe that the essence of the archaic Mystery religion of the Ancient Egyptians, was translated into the Greek language and written down in Alexandria; this possibly occurred around the end of the first century BCE and into the early years of the first century CE.[4] These profound works became known as the Hermetica — they were attributed to the Egyptian god Thoth, whose Greek counterpart is Hermes. The hidden philosophy of the Hermetica is widely held to be just the mere kernel of the Egyptians' religion; the real meanings had inevitably been lost in translation. Many Egyptian words have a variety of meanings and as was common practice in sacred texts, these had been employed deliberately, in order to disguise the true sense and importance of the scripts. This deliberate disguise would never be a problem as long as there were initiated masters of the philosophy, who could interpret the teachings for new acolytes.

In the third century CE, Clement of Alexandria, whilst head of the Christian Church, wrote about the works of Hermes and in particular the importance of cosmology and measurement.[5] Although this might seem like an odd subject for a *literalist* orthodox Christian and forerunner of the Roman Popes to discuss, it would be entirely understandable if Clement had been a Gnostic Christian, as his writings have led many academics to believe. Unfortunately, by the next century, another Bishop of Alexandria, Theophilus, in 391 CE, arranged the destruction of all pagan temples as well as the great Library of Alexandria. With that, thousands of crucially important books were lost forever. This barbaric act was typical of the atrocities perpetrated against civilisation and humanity as the rampaging literalist Christians of the Church of Rome suppressed any opposition. Reputedly, a few works escaped the holocaust and were safely hidden away, including copies of the original Hermetic works, preserved and guarded in places such as Haran and Edessa.

Edessa was the home of the world-renowned School of Persians. The most famous were, of course, the astronomer wise-men known as the Magi. A star-worshipping sect, known as the Sabians, became guardians of the Hermetica in Edessa. The name Sabian derives, according to some linguists, from the Egyptian word, S'ba, meaning star.

---

3 Brandon, S G F *Religion in Ancient History*,
4 Grimal, N *A History of Ancient Egypt*
5 Richardson, A and Bowden, J eds *The Westminster Dictionary of Christian Theology*

Egyptologist Selim Hassan thought that inscriptions on numerous votive stelae show that during the Hyksos occupation of Egypt circa 1730–1575 BCE, Semitic-speaking people from Haran founded a new town named Haran near Giza.[6] It would be reasonably safe to assume that when they left the Great Pyramids, the descendants of these people from Haran, were those same people known in Edessa as the Sabians. After the Hyksos expulsion from Egypt, records show that the Sabians made regular pilgrimages to the Great Pyramids and, according to Arab Historian Yaqut al Hamawi, were doing so as late as the eleventh century CE.[7]

The Sabians and their philosophical teachings later exerted great influence on Muslim mystical sects, such as the Sufis. In the same manner, the Sufis' influence extended to the south of France and further on in this book, we see how they affected the beliefs of the Cathars and the Knights Templar and why this provoked such a violent reaction from the Christian Church of Rome.

The Sabian name is still found amongst the Marsh Arabs of southern Iraq. Known as the Mandaeans, they have an alternative name Sa'Ba (sometimes written Sabba) but however it is spelled, it derives from S'ba and they are sometimes referred to as the Sabian Mandaeans. The Mandaeans record that their ancestors came to Haran and after a short stay moved north east, to the Lake Van region of modern day Turkey — settling in a place they called the Mountain of the Madai — though they claim that their true ancestral home is Egypt. Indeed, within a religion which appears to be a confused mixture of Gnostic Christianity, Old Testament Judaism and Iranian dualism, the Mandaeans hold important clues to the origins of Christianity; clues that are investigated in Chapter 8.

A measure of scepticism is necessary when considering the likely veracity of any ancient account, burdened inevitably by a confusion of time and place; coloured by exaggeration and propaganda and diminished or enhanced by failed memory, depending on which facts one forgets. A significant aspect of the Mandaean legends is that they do not claim that their ancestors returned to Haran, but that they came there. These were not the Semitic people who settled in northern Egypt, at a time when its power was weak and moved back to Palestine after the Hyksos expulsion. The Mandaeans instead seem to be referring to an extremely archaic migration that occurred before the supposed rise of the middle-eastern civilisations. The telling factor is that Haran was only one step on the Mandaeans' forebears' path as they moved to dwell in the northern mountains.

---

[6] Selim Hassan *Excavations at Giza Vol 6 Part 1*

[7] Yaqut, Jwaideh, Wed/tran *The Introductory Chapters of Yaqut Mu'Jam Al-Buldan*

Whatever the cause of their journey, it is clear that in Haran there was an Egyptian connection and that some knowledge attributed to the supposed mythological god of teaching, Thoth, came to Haran from Egypt. The great Hermetic works were derived from Thoth and for a long time, pilgrims from all over the Middle East — India, Persia, and even Egypt itself — were attracted to Haran to study them.

The importance of this region — the so-called Abrahamic homeland — is that it predates the rise of the accepted ancient middle-eastern civilisations. Amongst academics, this area is presently favoured as the region in which man first changed from hunter-gatherer to farmer and smith and took up the harvesting of crops, domestication of animals and metallurgy. The area, which these days extends from eastern Turkey and northern Iraq into Armenia and around the giant Lake Van, through the mountains just to the north of the Rivers Tigris and Euphrates, is commonly referred to as the 'Cradle of Civilisation'.

In these northern lands, we find the earliest known permanent centres of habitation, established up to 5,000 years before the Sumerian cities of the Fertile Crescent of Mesopotamia emerged. These early towns were situated around the outer edges of this region: Catal Huyuk, a Neolithic town in eastern Anatolia; the enigmatic settlement at Nevali Cori, by the upper Euphrates; and much further south in Canaan, we find the renowned Jericho.

The library at Haran gives us the first Egyptian link to this area and the Mandaean legend points to the second. There is a strong argument to suggest that there was some kind of mini exodus out of Egypt and it could have taken place around 9,000 BCE to the Lake Van area — just as the Mandaean legend insists. Archaeological finds indicate that in Egypt a farming and tool-making culture existed which predated the developments around Lake Van. A full account of this theory of the flight to higher ground, during the floods at the end of the Ice Age, is contained in Andrew Collins' works *From The Ashes Of Angels*[8] and *Gods Of Eden*.[9] Though I profess to differ in opinion over certain details, the Egyptian connection is clearly confirmed.

Drawing upon the findings of other scholars, ancient Akkadian records and old Kurdish tribal legends, Collins also promotes the claim for the mythological Garden of Eden being the memory of a real historical place inhabited by the Egyptian exiles of 11,000 years ago, a place he identifies as being Lake Van. At this stage, I do not wish to pursue the idea — its importance becomes apparent later in my proposal for the origins of

---

[8] Collins, A *From The Ashes Of Angels*
[9] Collins, A *Gods Of Eden*

religious beliefs — its relevance here is solely to support the importance of this region to the ancient people of the Middle East and to show why it was essential to locate Abraham and his family there: to give him prestige and gravitas. The fictional Abraham was not just an important symbolic character, but one meant to secure the basis for the lore of the stellar religion that was covertly recorded in the Biblical texts.

The area has prominence too as the post–flood landing place for survivors of Akkadian and Babylonian legends. The Biblical Noah lands in the mountains immediately north of Lake Van, whilst in the Kurdish legend he lands south west of the lake. Regardless of whether the Noah story be fact or fiction, one can relate this landing place after a destructive catastrophe, to the site of a new beginning for mankind — a site from which man had to make a start on the road to, or possibly back to, civilisation. If there had been a historical Noah, or various individuals amalgamated into a single character, it is important to remember that he or they would not have been Hebrew. No Hebrew race existed at that early date, thus it makes no sense to attach Noah to a much later god who was exclusive to the Hebrews. Neither can one accept as truth the notion that, out of the whole world population, this god saved just Noah's family, for there are similar legends from which recount the same tale. A merciful god picks a local leader and saves just his family while the rest of the world is drowned, but it happened almost simultaneously, in dozens of places, all over the world!

So here, in the homelands of the legendary Abraham, we have groups of wise men that, right through to the eleventh century CE, sought to preserve ancient works that originated in Egypt. They also made frequent unexplained pilgrimages to their sacred place by the Nile. Was it a mere chance of fate that these ancient philosophical and scientific works should end up in Haran and Edessa/Urfa — or was there already something that linked Egypt and these two distant lands?

There was indeed something, something exceedingly ancient — but before investigating what this extraordinary link might be, it would be beneficial to consider the somewhat more mundane topic of whether a historical Abraham and his rapidly growing family migrated into Canaan.

THE GREATEST LIE EVER TOLD

Chapter 2

Digging the Dirt on Abraham and Isaac

"Man is a credulous animal, and must believe something; in the absence of good grounds for belief, he will be satisfied with bad ones."
                                                                Bertrand Russell

Archaeology led us to discover that Abraham's relatives had the curious names of towns. So what more does archaeology have to reveal about Abraham, his family's journey into Canaan and the growth of the Hebrew people? Before we ask the questions, we need to learn more about the people we expect to give us the answers: the archaeologists.

The University of Tel Aviv carries out most modern archaeological work, done in the 'Holy Land'. Whenever they uncover any antithetical findings, as Jews, these academics are effectively destroying the validity of their own sacred books, both on a religious level as well as a historical one. If the Jewish Bible is shown to be seriously flawed and inaccurate, then those other two religions, Christianity and Islam, will have their shared foundations undermined and discredited too. The solid Jewish foundation has always been of great concern to the Christian Church, for everything it believes is built upon God's promise to Abraham, Isaac and Jacob. It gave the Jews their birthright and the Christians their prerogative.

It became imperative to Christians to find proof that the Biblical stories were indeed historical fact and that the Patriarchs had actually lived. For that reason, many Biblical archaeologists in the past were trained clerics and theologians, on a critical mission. As an inevitable result, their zealous searching replaced open–minded objectivity with tunnel vision and expectant bias. *Awkward* finds could be subjected to *remoulding* so that the square pegs fitted the round holes. Amongst fundamentalist Biblical academics, criticism of their dubious conclusions would engender virulent defensive attacks and angry accusations of heresy. The very purpose of archaeology in Palestine was to find the proof that would confirm the traditional belief — anything else was unacceptable and heretical.

Much of the early research was carried out under these unscientific conditions, in the certainty that everything that the Bible recorded was true. Within this restrictive mindset, the archaeologists and theologians concocted a chronology, going backwards in time. The Bible, in 1 Kings 6:1, states that the Exodus occurred 480 years before Solomon built the Jerusalem Temple. Prior to that, according to Exodus 12:40, there had been a period of 430 years of Israelite slavery, in Egypt. Two hundred years were added on here, to allow for the overlapping lives of the Patriarchs — they cause historians problems with their longevity — this then afforded a working date of roughly 2000 BCE for Abraham's migration from Haran into Canaan. But is this date going to be accurate, is it to be trusted, can it be considered valid? Well, if one is supposed to accept the contents of the Bible as being historically credible, then this date, allowing reasonable flexibility, has to be the one we must use to evaluate the archaeological evidence presently available.

On the surface, it seemed that the Bible, with its detailed background information, confirmed the historical authenticity of the stories and many scholars sought to verify their beliefs by promoting unsound theories backed by seemingly sound data. Christian academics shared the opinion of the acknowledged founder of the Biblical archaeology movement, William F Albright, that "as a whole, the picture in Genesis is historical, and there is no reason to doubt the general accuracy of the biographical details." Yet one of his peers, Burke Long, points out another flaw that encourages the bias. In *Planting and Reaping Albright: Politics, Ideology, and Interpreting the Bible*,[1] Long describes Albright and his students as being on a crusade, with the intention of seeking and retaining the political and ideological dominance of American biblical scholarship. Not only do they want to accept a foregone conclusion that the Bible is a historical document, they want to ensure that they are considered the undisputed experts in this academic discipline.

Although Albright had convinced himself and his students, that the Bible gave sufficient evidence to show that Abraham led an Amorite migration out of northern Mesopotamia, modern research has shown conclusively that no such large-scale movement of people ever took place.[2] Moreover, the research indicates that the inhabitants of Canaan, at this time, were solely Canaanites, and there is no evidence of an Amorite population living in Canaan. The *historically crucial* background information that the Bible provides is far from sound. It is so vague that it could apply to almost any period of middle-eastern history and to a wide range of tribal groups.

---

[1] Long, B *Planting and Reaping Albright*
[2] Finkelstein, I and Silberman, N A *The Bible Unearthed*

DIGGING THE DIRT ON ABRAHAM AND ISAAC

Alarmed and frustrated, Christian academics attempted to move the Canaan goal posts, or rather the supposed time of Abraham, to make their model fit the facts. They first tried moving Abraham forward by some 500 years, but couldn't find what they needed, so they tried 1000 years on — no shred of evidence there. Some attempted to move Abraham the other way by finding a much earlier date, but none of them succeeded in establishing anything significant, that linked him to any particular period. Conclusive evidence eluded them. Because they believed and still believe in the reality of Abraham and the Patriarchs, they could not bring themselves to widen the scope of their research and accept the possibilities of another scenario — the only truth that mattered to these scholars was the one that they believed in. As a consequence, they still frantically continue a fruitless search to find a proof that doesn't exist because the man they seek never existed either. They hold on hard to disproven beliefs; not quite telling outright lies, but certainly circumventing the truth.

Modern archaeology has failed to provide any evidence of an Amorite migration of nomadic pastoral shepherds into Canaan. In Bronze–Age Canaan, circa 3500–2200 BCE, life was characterised by a mainly urban existence. Numerous city–states controlled the outlying rural areas and farming communities. These large, strongly fortified towns and cities — some covering up to 50 acres — with several thousand inhabitants, reflected a sedentary, well–organised society. The evidence shows they were ruled by local kings, with tiered strata of temple priests, court officials, warriors, merchants and artisans. Towards the end of the third millennium BCE, this urban culture went into decline and many cities and towns were destroyed and abandoned. Some scholars have attempted to put Abraham and the Amorite migration into this earlier period.

Unfortunately for the Biblical scholars, the facts did not fit the theory. Archaeological evidence shows that the urban society did not fall to outside invaders.[3] The reality was that it went into a gradual decline following a steady deterioration in the economy of the region. As the economy worsened, the new experience of deprivation caused social upheaval in the cities. With the financial collapse, the citizens could no longer purchase the food brought in from the outlying rural areas. The inevitable result was a breakdown of law and order with food riots, civil strife, looting and pillaging. As a consequence, the disaffected populations of the urban centres abandoned them, one after another. In numerous cases, the lawless remnants of the population who stayed behind caused the wanton destruction of the cities. This collapse did not hit every city at the same

---

3 ibid

time, but there was a progressive domino effect, the decline taking place over several decades.

Gradually the urban population drifted back to its old ancestral villages, adopting an enforced rural lifestyle in order to survive the famine. Though there was some nomadic pastoralisation, for most people, life continued to be a sedentary one, now focused upon village life. Then as now, a nomadic life would have been totally alien to a city dweller. Was there any evidence to indicate that the cities fell to foreign invaders and not because of an economic slump? The answer is a definite no: there is no evidence of a foreign influx, either peaceful or aggressive.

All the archaeological finds: settlement patterns, architectural styles, pottery, artefacts and strata indicated that there were no outsiders and no changes. The finds also showed that the population of Canaan was made up of its own indigenous people for thousands of years.

The cycle reversed after several hundred years of village subsistence; a surplus of crops, together with an accumulation of saleable home manufactured goods, led to increasing trade and the inevitable realisation that a centralised trading base was better suited to expansion. So the same Canaan natives, the descendants of those old original city dwellers, gradually returned to live in an urban environment and became the new merchants and artisans in the rebuilt cities.

The evidence shows that the inhabitants of Canaan were a static gene pool, allowing for their brief urban–rural–urban fluctuation. There was no sign of an influx of nomadic Amorite migrants from outside their lands. Crucial to this, archaeologists also discovered that the name Amorite was not restricted to the nomadic pastoralists of northern Mesopotamia, but that it also applied to the sedentary communities living in what is now northern Syria. The fact that the Amorites were already well-established residents in the towns and villages further to the north pulled the rug from under the theory that a large-scale migration of Amorite nomads moved into the area of Canaan. All archaeological evidence suggested that the people living within the area bounded by the Mediterranean and the eastern highlands remained the same, with no augmentation from outsiders.

So, if Jewish people cannot trace their roots back to the migrating family of Abraham, who appeared to wander around southern Canaan and even into Egypt, then where exactly are the beginnings of the Jewish people to be found? The answer is simply — where they have always lived — in the hill country along the River Jordan, on the eastern fringes of Canaan. In other words, the Jews are Canaanites and always were!

Intensive archaeological studies of this area have revealed that the first occupation of the highlands occurred in the period known as the Early Bronze Age, which approximates to around 3500 — 2200 BCE. Along the central ridge of this region, the settlers constructed around a hundred towns and villages. Don't be tempted to wonder if this could have been Abraham. Remember that at 3500 BCE, as the first people settled in, it is far too early for the supposed Abrahamic period and the archaeological evidence indicates these people were Canaanites. Refitting the achaeological pieces of the Abrahamic jigsaw, to get the desired picture, has already been tried and failed. The image on the box shows that the Canaanites always lived there, and the individual pieces of the jigsaw show that Abraham's don't fit.

Around 2200 to 2000 BCE, the period of the urban decline, their inhabitants deserted most of these sites. Not long afterwards, a new settling took place. Small scattered villages grew until there were just over 200 sites, including a few small towns, some of which were fortified. In the much later period of Israel and Judea, these places would be known as Jerusalem, Hebron, Bethel, Shiloh and Shechem, but in this Middle Bronze Age era, these places were basically Canaanite. Abraham and his entourage would have been far too small a group to have filled an area this size. They would not have had enough people to fill around two hundred villages; besides which Abraham supposedly led a nomadic life, not a sedentary one, as the evidence about the area's inhabitants revealed.

The area was abandoned a second time around 1500 BCE and this time remained desolate for some 400 years; with only about 25 sites left occupied. In the Iron Age, around 1200 BCE, a third wave of settlement took place. Just like before, in the first phase, the villages grew in number to around 250 sites and by 800 BCE, they reached around 500 individual locations. The settlements included medium-sized market towns and a few small cities, with the total population of the region expanding fourfold, from 40,000 to 160,000.

It was during the earlier part of this period, approaching the first millennium BCE — the era of David and Solomon's kingdom — that one can finally declare that the population has taken on a distinct Israelite identity. But even then, there was no physical evidence to show that the early Israelites were ethnically, culturally and religiously different from the Canaanites and indeed unique. When comparing all the archaeological finds unearthed in the highland villages, with those unearthed in the village sites east of the Jordan river — which later Jews came to consider the enemy territory of the Moabites, Edomites and Ammonites — there was no physical evidence of any ethnic differences except one: a uniqueness that did not appear until the time of the early Israelite kings around 930 BCE.

The only difference, starting some time during the first millennium BCE, was that the Israelite villagers stopped eating pork. Unlike their surrounding neighbours, these early Israelites of the Davidic period no longer kept or ate pigs. Yet oddly, pigs made a re-appearance towards the end of the Iron

Age, when the Israelites separated into the two kingdoms of Israel and Judea. Other than this single oddity, there was no detail to distinguish the early Israelite from any one of his neighbours.

So why did this occur when the reality of a fairly harsh existence tends to deter a hungry person from turning his nose up at any kind of food, especially something which was so readily to hand and easy to keep. The only answer to the conundrum is that someone told the Israelites to stop eating pigs and the only people likely to have done that would have been their priests. Who these priests were and where they came from, is discussed in detail when we consider the origins of the Abrahamic religions.

By studying animal bones in the highland area, palaeontologists and anthropologists identified how the highland villages developed and how an independent kingdom, formed of native Canaanites eventually emerged, from these small beginnings. Archaeologists found that during the periods of settled occupation of the highland villages, cattle were numerous. However, during the periods of decline, sheep and goats predominated and there were few signs of any cattle. This evidence supports a change from intensive farming to a semi-nomadic pastoral lifestyle, since for a nomadic and even semi-nomadic lifestyle in such hilly areas, the keeping of cattle was and still is, impractical.

What the experts realised from all of this was surprising. It was apparent that during periods of economic wealth and security, the highland farming villages were abandoned. The reason, they deduced, was that the city-states obtained their supplies from local farms. This left the highland farms with a grain surplus for which they had no customers, causing the inhabitants to migrate down to the cities, towns and villages of the coastal plain. Those people who stayed in the highlands took up a semi-nomadic pastoral existence. They were able to trade their sheep-meat, wool and hides in the cities of the lowland plain, for the grain that nomadic pastoralists were unable to grow their own crops.

The survival of the nomads was dependent on the wealth of the cities, so when the city-states collapsed, the market for the nomads' goods also collapsed, leaving them unable to obtain the vital grain that they needed to survive. This, in turn, meant that the nomads were forced into settling in one place, so that they could start to grow their own grain. The wheel had turned once more and the highland farming village communities grew.

This reversed cyclic system surprised the archaeologists, but was clearly evident after the three centuries of Egyptian occupation of Canaan. Once the strong trading economy was established, the farming villagers deserted the highlands and the nomadic pastoralists again took their place. When Egyptian control collapsed in the twelfth century BCE — because of

DIGGING THE DIRT ON ABRAHAM AND ISAAC

Akenaten's lack of foreign policy — the highland farming communities suddenly sprang up again.

It is within this second period of political and economic collapse of the city–states that the early Israelite kingdom emerged. The people started to forge a new ethnic identity, which would give strength and unity to its fledgling kingdom, though it's another 500 years before anyone refers to Judea and Israel as separate states.[4] The oddest thing about this new identity was that whereas there had been pigs in the highland villages before their collapse, when they were re-established, no pig bones were found. This was the only thing that differentiated the lifestyle of the new highland Canaanites from their lowland compatriots. The migration gave the highland settlers their own political break, freeing the communities from their dependence upon the lowland cities. Independence from the cities on the coastal plain afforded them stability and permanence in their pig-free world.

In contrast to the belief propagated by the Bible, the emergence of the Israelites as a distinct group and their formation of a nation kingdom was simply a result of the collapse and fragmentation of the Canaanite urban-oriented society. The Israelites were nothing other than a breakaway group of Canaanites, who did not eat pork. They were certainly not an invading force of outsiders, but rather were they the descendants of the people who had occupied the highlands throughout their periods of settlement from the early Bronze Age on.

As I will shortly show, there was no Israelite conquest of Canaan — it was merely a self-glorifying myth of late invention, to draw a definite distinction between the Jews and everyone else. Without conscience, the inventors of the Bible histories denied their true birthright and reviled and demonised as idol worshippers their pig-keeping Canaanite brothers. The Judean scribes repeated the shameful scenario after Solomon supposedly died; treating their pork-abstaining brethren in the rival northern kingdom of Israel, in the same denigratory fashion.

With a sleight of hand — the one holding the pen — a new history, a new beginning was invented. And to ensure that no one dared question its authenticity, we are told that God himself had guided this hand. Fear turned the lie into unquestionable truth.

All the archaeological evidence shows that the people residing within the lands of Canaan were and always had been Canaanites. There is no evidence at all for outsider migrations or significant invasions until the far-later influx of Philistine settlers from the western sea. There are no grounds for the argument that Abraham infiltrated the area around 2000 BCE,

---

[4] Grant, M *The History of Ancient Israel*

because an Abrahamic incursion at this date would put him squarely into the period when the city–states of Canaan had re–established themselves. Oddly, yet for our purposes, significantly, the Abrahamic story fails to mention any important cities, such as Hazor, Meggido, Gezer and Shechem, which all wielded substantial power and influence, militarily, politically and economically. This is a strange and seemingly inexplicable omission.

The answer is, of course, straightforward: rather than true and accurate eyewitness accounts of history, carefully passed down through the generations, the stories were just vague tribal myths and legends, eventually cobbled together by politically–motivated priests and scribes who were entirely ignorant of any real historical knowledge.

Christian Biblical scholars still insist upon the Bible's historical authenticity, even pointing out that it is the accurate historical details in the stories which prove that they are genuine: an odd claim when the Bible is so full of historical inaccuracies. Surely, if the proof is in the detail, then inaccurate detail will undermine the whole foundation. We find such an example of this small detail, in Genesis 24, that talks of camels being taken through Mesopotamia; women, children and servants riding on camels and indeed, camels repeatedly crop up in the patriarchal stories. Yet we find that camels were supposedly, first domesticated at least 200 years after Abraham's time and they were not used at all as beasts of burden until about 1000 years later. Excavations of camel bones indicate that camels were used extensively in the seventh century BCE and became a common sight around the Middle East, including Palestine. The camel became a preferred means of transport just around the time when the first Biblical stories were compiled.[5]

The next anomalous detail is the reference to shekels as a means of payment: it is out of its historical era by a considerable margin. The shekel was not Canaanite but Hebrew; nor was it a coin, but a unit of weight, much later used as a silver coin. According to Herodotus[6] the coin first appeared some time after 550 BCE. It may seem trivial and irrelevant, but it is the Biblical scholars themselves who seek to use this kind of minor detail as proof of authenticity. If the details are proven false, then they have no grounds for complaint when the same details are used to dispute their claim.

Another story that must raise doubts about its historical accuracy starts in Genesis 14. It recounts the tale of a powerful alliance of four Mesopotamian kings, under the command of a character called Chedorlaomer, King of Elam. The alliance supposedly attacked a

---

5 Bright, J *A History Of Israel*
6 Herodotus, *The Histories*

confederation of five rebellious subservient kings, which included the Kings of Sodom and Gomorrah. Chedorlaomer's army apparently defeated the rebel kings and with his loot and captives, Chedorlaomer went on his way. Lot was among the captives, so Abraham collected 318 of his men and set off to rescue his relative. We are then told that Abraham, with 318 men of undetermined background and fitness, defeated the combined armies of the four powerful kings and affected great slaughter — an achievement that had just proved to be beyond the capabilities of the combined armies of the five rebellious kings. Such a feat points to literal exaggeration and is evidence of another historical impossibility.

John Van Seters points out, in Abraham in History and Tradition,[7] that there was no historical period when this allegiance of kings could have taken place. There is no record of an Elamite king called Chedorlaomer and no Elamite king controlled a vast empire at that time. In the 23rd and 24th centuries BCE, Sargon established the kingdom of Elam in southwest Mesopotamia and expanded it from the Persian Gulf to the Mediterranean. His grandson King Naram–Sin undertook conquests into Syria; this too was well before the supposed time of Abraham. After Naram–Sin died, nomadic raiders gradually eroded his descendants' control and eventually took over the region, ruling it very badly for another hundred years — and made no mention of Abraham in their early history of Babylon, I'm afraid.

Once again we find that the places mentioned in this particular story relate only to the seventh century BCE. "En–Mishhpar, that is Kadesh" — Genesis 14:7 — is Kadesh–barnea, a site which reappeared in the Exodus stories. Excavations, at this large oasis in eastern Sinai, have revealed an occupation mainly in the seventh and sixth century BCE.[8] One of the other named places, Tamar, has been identified as present–day Ein Haseva, north east of Kadesh, below the Dead Sea. The late Iron–Age fortress found there shows, yet again, an occupation date that centred around the seventh century BCE. Once more we find a date contemporary with when the Judaean scribes, who knew nothing of the area's history, were putting the Bible stories together and writing them down.

The flaw in the detail comes to light again when we find Abraham in Gerar. The Bible refers to it as a Philistine city. The Philistine migrants, however, did not cross over from the Aegean to establish settlements along the coast of Canaan until after 1200 BCE, eight hundred years after Abraham and Isaac's time. Excavations at Gerar have revealed that, during the early period of Philistine occupation, it was not even a city, it was nothing more than a small village and certainly not the capital of a king.

---

7 Van Seters, J *Abraham in History and Tradition*

8 Cohen, R *Excavations At Kadesh-Barnea: 1976-1978*

Once more we find that it was in the seventh century BCE that Gerar grew to some importance as an Assyrian stronghold.[9]

In Genesis 10:11 there is mention of the Assyrian capitals of Calah and the later Nineveh, the capital in the seventh century BCE. In Genesis 15:10 and 23:10 there is mention of Hittites. Yet the Hittite Empire was not established until the seventeenth century BCE and reached its zenith around 1350 BCE. Had there been any earlier Hittite invaders coming down from the north into Anatolia, there would have been nothing to bring them to Egyptian–controlled Palestine, at such an early date. It was far far too distant in the south, so there was never a Hittite near Hebron for Abraham to have had dealings with.[10]

In the stories concerning Jacob's marriage, the Arameans take centre stage and yet this ethnic group was not recorded until around the start of the first millennium, some eight hundred years too late. The Arameans only became important around 900 BCE, when a number of Aramean kingdoms arose in southern Syria, on the northern border of the post–Solomon kingdom of Israel.

The story of Jacob and his twin brother Esau tells us that Esau was cheated of his birthright and pushed out into the hinterlands where he founded the kingdom of Edom. Another example of incorrect history: Assyrian records prove that Edom did not come into existence until around the eighth century BCE, one hundred years before the Judean scribes wrote about it.

Having shown how the historical evidence is seriously flawed, we need to look more closely at the stories themselves to see that things really don't make sense. In Genesis 12:10, 20:1 and then in 26:1, we have the bizarre tales of Abraham and Isaac pretending that their wives were their sisters. Not only is this a peculiar thing, for a man in Abraham's position, to do whilst on a mission from God, it is dishonest and despicable. That he is dishonest once, according to the story, when he is in Egypt, we can possibly allow, though he compounds his deceit by letting the Pharaoh take his wife Sarah for a bride. God having intervened to restore Sarah to her husband, many years later, showing no remorse for his earlier misdemeanour in Egypt, Abraham repeats the deception when visiting the city of Gerar. There, to save his own skin, he perpetrates the same shameful ruse by allowing the Philistine king to take Sarah as his wife, believing her to be Abraham's sister. As if this shocking behaviour of Abraham's is not disgraceful enough, years later Isaac comes to Gerar and commits this very same crime all over again.

---

9 Oren, E D *Gerar*
10 Bruce, FF *The Hittites and The Old Testament*

These sordid acts raise various issues, which need to be considered. Firstly, it would be a matter of great honour for a man to protect his wife, even unto death. Secondly, concern about his personal safety should not have been a problem if he were the one human singled out for special consideration by God. Thirdly, since it had never been a concern when he had travelled anywhere else, why should Abraham suddenly worry that his wife would be coveted and he himself put to death. Fourthly, Abraham was supposed to be a nomad, who had come to Egypt, with no doubt thousands of other refugees, to escape famine — so why should the Pharaoh, hundreds of miles south in his capital, be told about one foreign refugee's wife, albeit a supposedly beautiful one. Fifthly, Egyptian royalty did not marry commoners and at that alleged period, neither did they marry foreigners. Sixthly, when Abraham repeats the same act at Gerar, why would the king be interested in lusting after a woman who was in her nineties. Seventhly, someone who, with only 318 of his men, took on and defeated the powerful army of four Mesopotamian kings might have been wary of taking on the Egyptian army, yet surely he should have considered the King of a small city such as Gerar, as easy meat; such a hero as Abraham, with an impeccable ally, being afraid for his life is starting to sound quite ridiculous.

His son, Isaac then repeats the unsavoury behaviour, inexcusable in Abraham. With presumably even more men at his disposal to protect him than his father had, why should Isaac have repeated the same shameful self-centred act as his father. If Abraham and Isaac carried such extreme anxiety for their own safety, then why go to the lion and put their heads in its mouth. If each man had a wife of such profound beauty, one who even kept her looks until ninety, surely their worry would have been a constant one and they should both have been continually passing a wife off as a sister. Why wasn't every man they encountered harbouring avaricious lust and murderous intent?

This whole scenario is sordid, dishonourable and totally bizarre, but it is nothing but a fantasy. When the scribes concoct such an ignominious tale, we have to assume that they have some purpose, something particular to relate; these stories were meant to glorify God's special people. The reason this story was related in this bizarre format was to highlight the importance of a different piece of information. The real story was encoded within it and the three accounts of the same act ensured that its importance would be recognised. It didn't really matter that the story seemed to form an immoral tale, that was never the point of its telling. The real story is about the history of the Hebrew religion that began in Egypt. The full explanation, which will astonish and shock many readers, is revealed in a later chapter.

In Genesis, the Bible is constantly making reference to things out of their correct time setting, things that were not contemporary. The full list of flaws is long and as we shall see in the forthcoming chapters, the list gets even longer. Despite all of this, many theologians and those scholars deeply ingrained in the Christian faith, seek to pick and choose what truths to believe and which to cast aside. They have attempted to dismiss the uncomfortable incompatible details as later irrelevant insertions — in other words, admitting that numerous things within the Genesis histories are wrong. But if some of the information is known to be false, then what about the rest, can we really accept it as the Gospel truth?

The whole acceptance of historical truth lies in its detail; the information given about the places, the peoples, the dates. Once these are shown to be untrustworthy and even worse, false, then it is no longer history, but mythical folk-tales — tales cleverly woven together to create a unique history, intended to unite a number of small disparate warring tribes, threatened by powerful dangerous neighbours.

It was first and foremost, a political tactic to employ a religious theme with the Hebrew people under the exclusive protection of the one and only true God. In the seventh century BCE, the Judaean priesthood began writing the texts that would become the Bible, but the work of inventing a history was crucially flawed when they inserted contemporary facts. Indeed, when one reads their accounts of events prior to their own time, rather than finding the unique and detailed historical record one would expect, there is an acute and obvious lack of historical knowledge of any kind. Probably, in the limited world that they knew, an age where virtually nobody was literate, when people could not differentiate between mythology, legend and fact; it would simply not have mattered. However we live in different times: we know the power of knowledge and propaganda, the corruption of prejudice and lies. Those details, which for fundamentalists are undisputed, which for so long gave the patriarchal texts their supposed historical truth, are now the very same details which have shown the Bible history to be lies.

There never was a Garden of Eden and Abraham wasn't the man the Bible describes. We have seen the falsehood that is Genesis. What more lies have we been told? What is the truth, how was it all lost? We visit Moses and Exodus in Chapter 4 to find out, but first, within the encoded scriptures, we find the key to what the Abrahamic religions really mean.

Chapter 3

Orion and the Patriarchs

"Tell your friend a lie. If he keeps it secret, tell him the truth."
Spanish Proverb

The story of Abraham that unfolds before us in the Jewish Bible, is a crass attempt at one–upmanship, which also encodes vital information about the true religion of the Jews. The Judean priests of the seventh century BCE had a dual task: they have religious secrets to record and they need a story to sell to *all* Israelites that confirms the Judeans' superior status over the rest.

The Israelites first appear in Egyptian records just before 1200 BCE. At this time they were referred to as "the people of Israel": a tribal group inhabiting a loose collection of villages, in the hills of Canaan to the west of the Galilee lake. These *Israelites* had a lifestyle identical with the Canaanites, except that they didn't keep pigs. The *Judeans* were a group of Israelites centred in Jerusalem. They wanted religious authority and used their invented history and the knowledge of their esoteric religious background, to encrypt the truth into a history that confirmed their superiority over the Israelites in the north. The scribes started to record Judean religious history around 700 BCE. By this time, as the archaeological records show, the Judeans had made significant changes in their thinking, beliefs and lifestyle.

As it seems there was no *historical* Abraham, he was probably an invention of the Jewish scribes, to give a *starting point* to their history. There are strong reasons to conclude that the patriarchal *history* is not one sequential story, but as the German Biblical scholar, Martin Noth points out,[1] a compilation of several disparate tribal legends, with each tribe having its own ancestral leader or *Patriarch*. When we look at what the stories contain and how they were composed, the Judean political agenda becomes

---

[1] Noth, M *The Deuteronomistic History*

apparent. The scribes of the Judean priesthood, in their power base of Jerusalem, took mythological stories from the Israelite tribes, interweaving them into a single genealogy and gave a Judean the starring role.

The Judeans located Abraham in the hill country of southern Judea. It is politically significant that they place him around the area of Hebron, the earliest Judean royal city. His son Isaac is placed in the desert fringes of southern Judea, at Beersheba, whilst his grandson Jacob, later called Israel, is sited far away in the hill country of the north. Jacob receives a further demotion when his son Joseph *deserts* his homeland, albeit involuntarily, and joins the *enemy* Egypt. Martin Noth argues that the first patriarchs were quite separate *ancestral* characters taken from different tribal regions.

The Judean scribes make another unequivocal statement when they recount that Abraham established the first altars to Adonay, a name they used to mean God, at the important cult centres of Shechem and Bethel, in what later became the northern kingdom of Israel. Not only does this serve to make Abraham the *father* and the uniter of the two kingdoms but more importantly, it underlines Judean supremacy. The scribes give us another tell-tale sign in the account of how the ageing Jacob pronounced his son Judah, to be the leader of his people, (Genesis 49: 8–10) where there is even a mention of the lion, the symbol of Judah. It is curious that Jacob did not choose his old favourite, Joseph, who was supposed to be the second most important man in all Egypt and thus, the whole world. By making Judah Jacob's heir, the scribes make an emphatic statement about Judean seniority and superiority in the kingdom of Israel. The prime aim of the seventh century scribes was to compose a history that united the Israelite tribes and ensured that the Judeans were perceived as their natural and historical leaders, appointed by God.

As the scribes were compiling their history, in 720 BCE, the Assyrians were destroying the homeland of the northern Israelites, forcing some to flee south, though many remained in the invaders' control. The historical writings made it clear that Judea had the right to rule over its fallen northern brothers, whilst giving some slight solace to those Israelites who had been displaced. The kings of Judea, from their capital Jerusalem, were promoting themselves as the sole and rightful rulers of a new pan-Israelite kingdom. The story of Abraham pursuing, then defeating, the Mesopotamian alliance of kings, who had taken Lot as a prisoner, was in reality a seventh-century tale which encoded Judea's political ambitions: to stake a claim over the kingdom of Israel, after its fall to the Assyrians. By inventing a story of Abraham liberating his kinsman from the Mesopotamians, the Judeans were announcing their ambition to liberate their kinsfolk, the Israelites, from the Assyrian yoke, just as their ancestor had done before.

ORION AND THE PATRIARCHS

Associated with this ambition, is the patriarchal insistence that the people remained pure and avoided marriage with those from other lands. This is another contemporary, seventh–century concern as the Assyrians were settling foreigners into the captured land of Israel. The Judean scribes transformed Abraham into a real person, who gave a historical starting point and unity to the disparate tribes. With Abraham, they were now glorified and afforded heavenly protection, even in times of great peril, by their exclusive connection to the one true and all–powerful God, Adonay. Like all desperate people, in times of great peril, they are primed for heroic legendary nonsense, to which they will clutch fiercely, as if it were a sacred security blanket.

There was though, another more arcane reason to choose the Abraham portrayal. He was an adaptation of a specific character who had long been represented in this eastern Mediterranean area under various guises. Later Biblical characters too, were cast to represent the same mythological personification — that of Orion the Hunter. It is at this juncture, that the reader must suspend all beliefs and prejudices that they may hold on the subject of ancient Egypt. One must understand that it is only the beliefs of the ancient peoples of the middle–east which count here — be they right or wrong — the important thing is what they believed and they considered the stars to be meaningful and sacred. To the people of the day, Orion held a prominent role and astronomy was important in their religious beliefs. The detail and significance are discussed in Part Two.

These days, there is a general, if somewhat muted and in many cases begrudging acceptance amongst Egyptologists, that the Giza pyramids are a ground plan of the stars of Orion's Belt. It must be said too, that there is a hard core of Egyptologists who continue to refuse to accept the weight of evidence that shows it to be so. They display an irrational insistence that the ancient builders were too primitive and ignorant to construct a star ground plan, yet are happy to promote the notion that these same people could have the astonishing technical ability to construct the wondrous Great Pyramids! The problem lies in the fact that there are many uncomfortable questions about the ancient Egyptians' knowledge and building skills, which Egyptologists seek to gloss over, yet when pushed, they proffer the most inadequate and often inane explanations.

This part of the book is concerned with establishing the historical perspective to the Jewish Bible, so I do not wish to become embroiled here in the wider and often controversial subject of present–day Egyptology, but it is important to point out that a great deal of guile, deceit, skulduggery and concealment takes place. When scientific and geological experts find evidence that runs contrary to long–accepted beliefs, they find themselves banned from further investigations. One such disagreement resulted in the banning from Giza, of Boston University geologist, Dr Robert Schoch.[2] His team's stunning scientific survey conservatively dated the Sphinx far beyond the Dynastic times, to an absolute latest date of 4,500 BCE, when the last heavy rain period ended, but the monument's severe rain weathering suggested it was more likely to be thousands of years older still. The first person to point out what caused this weathering had been French mathematician R A Schwaller[3] who, between 1937 and 1952, had been studying advanced mathematics in ancient Egypt. As he was 'only a mathematician', Egyptologists 'knew better' and chose to ignore his observations. When Schoch came along, they had to take notice of a geologist, but to minimise the amount of evidence he could use to support his argument, they refused him a licence to investigate further. Numerous other licences have been refused or revoked by the Supreme Council of Antiquities, which fears that the orthodox history of ancient Egypt will be turned upon its head.

Unfortunately, amongst established academics, there is a great deal of virulent self-protectionism and a fierce desire to maintain the status quo of traditional beliefs: new finds are fine and acceptable as long as they are small and reinforce orthodox history. Geologists, scientists and engineers have made many significant discoveries, which established academia steadfastly continues to ignore. Much of the work, which has thrown new light onto the taboo areas of Egyptology, has been carried out by people whom the jealous academics dismiss derisively as psuedo-archaeologists and cranks. Though the experts have not been able to prove new findings wrong, the virulent attacks continue, giving rise to accusations that the more virulent the attacks, the more the attackers are trying to hide. It was the so-called amateurs and cranks who first drew attention to the Giza-Orion link. More recently, another amateur historical investigator, Ralph Ellis[4] recognised that the two great pyramids at Dahshur, referred to as the Bent and Red, belonged to the same expanded Orion ground plan. Ralph Ellis's book *Thoth, Architect of the Universe* explores this proposition.

I, and other researchers are deeply troubled by the fact that access to the site of the Bent and Red pyramids is permanently barred. The Egyptians have built a large army camp in the area surrounding these two important pyramids. This is in itself a bizarre thing to do at a site of such immense historical importance, and in addition, the authorities have imposed a complete ban on anyone, even academics, from visiting this site. There are no exceptions and the ban is a permanent one. At the risk of

---

[2] Schoch, RM & West, J A. Redating the Great Sphinx of Giza, Egypt
[3] Schwaller de Lubicz, R A. *The Temple in Man*
[4] Ellis, R. *Thoth, Architect of the Universe*

initiating another dreaded conspiracy theory, one must ask, what do the pyramids contain that the Egyptians don't want anyone to know. It is highly unlikely that there is any military or national security reason to deny access to everyone, to whom the pyramids are of historical, scientific or cultural interest. If there is nothing to hide, then exactly what is going on?

Though there is no access to two of them, the Orion ground plan has at least five pyramids marking significant stars, so we know that the Orion star system held great importance to the ancient Egyptians. Orion was a stellar representation of Osiris, the 'dying–resurrected' son of God, whom they called Ra. The Egyptians believed that upon death, the soul was carried on an astral ship along the 'River of Heaven', the Milky Way, to a star held in the 'outstretched hand' of Orion. This point in the starry night sky, was their door to Heaven: a Stargate that opened up onto the eternal afterlife with God. The inner sanctum of the Ra Temple at Heliopolis, the Holy of Holies, was called the 'Star Room' or ' Star Chamber', and the high priest held the title of 'Chief Astronomer'.

Though many people have some knowledge of the Osiris myth, fewer people know that the Osiris Mystery cult of Egypt was the forerunner of the numerous Mystery religions, which sprang up around the Mediterranean in the last four centuries BCE, and that Christianity was the Jewish version of it. Osiris/Orion was of great significance to the Egyptian priesthood and to its foreign disciples. This meant that the symbol of Orion passed down through the ages and through different cultures in an iconic representation, based on local religious or heroic figures.

Abraham was one of these 'Orion men' and this symbolic facet of his persona, can be located in the ancient Chaldean city of Urhay, later called Edessa. It was in Edessa that the renowned School of the Persians preserved the ancient teaching of the Egyptians. In time, the Persians formed much of the ancient Egyptian teaching into what is now known as the Kabbalah. The School was located at the foot of a cliff, beneath a citadel, next to what are considered to be holy pools or fishponds, known locally as the 'Pools of Abraham'. The local legend has a character called Nimrod who arrests a man named Abraham. Abraham was taken up to the citadel and tied between two large stone columns on top of the sheer cliff face. When Abraham refused to do Nimrod's bidding, Abraham was cast over the cliff, but miraculously, pools of water opened up beneath him and broke his fall. Nimrod is mentioned in the Bible in a much earlier age, well before Abraham, just after the time of Noah. Nimrod was probably the original local hero of the Orion story in Edessa. In Christian times the reinterpretation of the local story gave Abraham the superior role, by using him to replace Nimrod as the Orion personification.

Naturally, the story is a fanciful invention with no foundation in historical fact — it was meant to be understood symbolically. It has to be significant, that the mythological event occurred at the spot where the school of learning, which protected the Egyptian secrets, once stood. Taken in isolation, the legend of the Pools of Abraham is of no real significance and without any point — plus one might be wondering what possible link there could be to Orion. However, the story proves to have a very strong Orion link. Exploration of this site above the 'Pools of Abraham' led investigative author Adrian Gilbert[5] to a revelation concerning the Orion constellation, that he discloses in his book Signs in the Sky. Gilbert discovered that the stone columns, which were actually erected by Agbar the Great, around 200 CE, are aligned so that the north/south meridian exactly bisects at right angles, the imaginary line between the two tall edifices. From below, down by the pools, perhaps viewed from a stepped platform looking south, Orion would have been observed moving between the pillars. If for no other reason, the pillars had a practical use as a very accurate chronometer that marked the beginnings of the seasons, though they would have had other more esoteric and religious significance as well.

Without doubt, the mixed-up legend is making a reference to Orion. In their book Hamlet's Mill, Giorgio de Santillana and Hertha von Dechend[6] expose the link between the precession of the equinoxes and the various stellar mythologies exemplified by such characters as Orion the Hunter. In Greek mythology, Orion was a great hunter, an invincible hero-strongman, until that is, he fell under the wiles of a woman named Merope. He was then blinded, but had his sight restored by the sun god, Helios. His end came when he was slain by the moon goddess, Artemis. Orion was then turned into a constellation and accompanied by his two dogs, Canis Major and Canis Minor, for the rest of eternity, hunted the great bull Taurus.

In this story, one can see the clear parallels with the Biblical Samson: the hero is tied to columns like Nimrod/Abraham, then, like Orion, he is beguiled by a woman and blinded. There are several stellar connections inside of the Samson myth: the lion which Samson kills, represents the constellation of Leo, that rises close to Orion; Samson's weapon, 'the jawbone of an ass', mirrors the jawbone-shaped Hyades star cluster, part of the Taurus constellation which lies on the ecliptic, closer to Orion than is Leo.

Santillana and von Dechend identified the Bible's Nimrod the Hunter as another representation of Orion. Later Biblical characters seemed to have been shown in the same form, such as the prophet Elijah, portrayed as a

---

5 Gilbert, A. *Signs in the Sky*

[6] v Dechend, H & de Santillana, G. *Hamlet's Mill*

'wild strongman', who, like Orion and Samson, wore rough garments tied with a belt — an allusion to Orion's belt. In the Elijah story, he sacrifices a bull. This was a common way of referring to the passage of the age of Taurus the bull into the newer age of Aries the ram. The covertly ambiguous, John the Baptist is portrayed in a similar manner. In Matthew 11:10–15, Jesus declares that John is Elijah, unequivocally identifying him as another 'Orion' man. I have much more to say about John the Baptist, when discussing the New Testament characters later.

The mythological St Christopher is yet another allegorical variant of the rough–living strongman. Though the Roman Catholic Church rightly agreed that he never lived and removed him from its list of saints, the eastern church continues to celebrate him on May 9th. On this date, during the period of the Egyptian Old Kingdom, the sun would have been over the outstretched hand position of Orion, 'midstream' in the Milky Way — the Egyptian's River of Heaven. Astrologically, Jesus was associated with the sun, so the St Christopher story of the strong man carrying the 'creator of the world' across the river, is clearly a later allegorical version of Orion encoded into Christian mythology.

The story of Jacob has stellar links too. Jacob spent fourteen years with his uncle Laban in the city of Haran, which, with its close neighbour Urhay, shared the Orion star cult. In the Bible story, God honours Jacob by renaming him Israel, a name to be passed down to his people. This is interesting because the nation's symbol is the lion, which is drawn from the star Regulus in Leo. Leo is also a crucial component in the star–inspired ground plan of the Giza pyramids. 'Jacob's Staff' is an alternative designation given to Orion's Belt — both staff and belt being euphemisms for phallus. 'Jacob's Ladder' is also a possible *alias* for the Milky Way, or the Egyptians' 'River of Heaven'. Another interpretation of the ladder is found in an Egyptian hieroglyphic inscription of a ladder with six rungs, which probably translates as the six trials or tests to be undergone by a dead pharaoh when seeking to elevate himself to the heavenly cosmos.

Throughout the Bible, there are encoded stellar references, in both the Old and New Testaments. Jewish Gnostics, for instance, understood the Twelve Tribes of Israel to be a representation of the twelve signs of the zodiac, later echoed by Jesus choosing twelve disciples. This latter usage is evident in the story taken from the Acts of John, 97–102, which describes the twelve disciples — the constellations — dancing around Jesus — the pole star. This initiation dance was long used in the Pagan Mystery religions, where the dancers wore masks to represent the twelve zodiac constellations and an initiate representing the Son of God, or God made man played the central pole star. The timelessness of this theme can be found once more in ancient Egypt. In the King's Chamber of the Great

Pyramid, there are narrow shafts. Egyptologists still insist that they are airshafts, despite the fact that they do not penetrate the outer wall. Genuine scholars, however, have discovered that these shafts align to the northern pole star — to an accuracy within one degree — and the southern shaft aligns to Orion. It was to the pole star that the souls of the pharaohs ascended, to be reunited with the Eternal God.

The reason why the Judeans encoded references to the Egyptian religion was to disguise its source from the Babylonians. The Judeans compiled the story of the patriarchs just before the Babylonians captured Jerusalem in 597 BCE and readjusted it during the time they were exiled in Babylon. The story of Abraham going to Egypt seems fairly unimportant, but it must be significant if it was deemed necessary to include it and risk the wrath of their Babylonian masters, who despised any notion of Egyptian links.

The task of the Judean scribes was to document their religion, which was based on the Egyptian beliefs, in a way that would be innocuous to their Babylonian captors, whose enemy the Egyptians were. Yet the tale of Joseph's rise to power, to become the Pharaoh's grand vizier, remains. In Egyptian records, there is nothing to indicate that a foreigner was elevated to such a lofty and powerful political position. Indeed, for a foreign nomad and former slave to be given the second position of power over all Egypt, on the strength of interpreting dreams, is beyond belief. Certainly the tale of Joseph advising the Pharaoh to store food supplies against a coming famine is fantasy, as the Egyptians had long practised storing grain. Joseph seems to have been a fictional addition like Abraham.

It is certainly possible Joseph could have been a vizier under one of the foreign Hyksos kings, but there is no evidence to confirm it, despite the proliferation of inscribed information which abounded within Egypt. The Hyksos people themselves are still something of a mystery, and even their name continues to be controversial. Some academics think it means 'Shepherd Kings', but many now believe that the name means 'rulers of foreign lands'.

The general opinion, held amongst historians, is that the Hyksos were migrant Canaanites and archaeological studies definitely indicate that they did not come into Egypt as invaders. Any newcomers appear to have dribbled in, over a long period of time and eventually, around 1670 BCE, their increasing numbers, coupled with a decline in Egyptian power, allowed them control in northern Egypt. The Hyksos stayed in charge until the Pharaoh of southern Egypt finally expelled them in 1570 BCE.

If Joseph was alive during the Hyksos period, he was not an Israelite as there is no mention of them, or Hebrews, in Egyptian records for another 300 years. His masters would not have been Egyptian, they would have been Canaanites. Using Bible chronology, its date for the Exodus is 480 years before Solomon built the Temple, between 950 — 1000 BCE. This would put Joseph around 1440 BCE; around 130 years after the Hyksos were driven out of Egypt.

The Bible mentions the city of Harnesses, known as Pi–Rarnesses; scholars think that Rameses II built the city between 1279 to 1213 BCE — too late for the Exodus account. Undeterred by the date given by the Bible, Christian scholars shifted the time of Moses' Exodus 200 years and pronounced Rameses II the unnamed pharaoh of the Exodus story. It seems everyone else is expected to believe in Biblical authenticity, but Christian scholars are exempt if it does not suit them.

Once more, the historical detail, which is lauded by theologians and Christian scholars, is proving to be totally wrong. These historical inaccuracies appear throughout the Bible time and time again. The extremely extensive Egyptian records, though they name many different peoples, give not a single mention of Hebrews or Israelites throughout this time period. This is enough surely to condemn the Bible to the dustbin as a historical document. The first mention of Israel comes from an Egyptian stele, which relates the campaigns at the end of the thirteenth century, conducted by the Pharaoh Merneptah, the son of Rameses II. The stele describes the Egyptian's destruction of Canaanite cities, as well as boasting that 'the seed of Israel is not'. The report of this campaign suggests that the Israelites were ranked in importance below that of the Canaanite city–states and that that they were militarily small and weak. This then is a strange contradiction: the Bible and its supporting scholars, claim huge numbers and military might for the Israelites, who supposedly just a short time before, invaded and wrought havoc in Canaan. If this were true, then why did the Egyptians rank them beneath the Canaanites whom they had conquered and why did the Egyptians wipe them out so easily. Clearly the population size, power and great exploits of the Israelites are nothing other than wishful fantasy. All the evidence shows, as demonstrated already, that the emergence of the Israelites from amongst the Canaanites was gradual and as a distinct social, rather than ethnic, group, they only emerge at the end of thirteenth century and there is definitely no evidence of their being in Egypt before this time.

Had Joseph existed, then whomever he had served, even the temporary Hyksos regime, he would have had to be inducted into the Egyptian religion. Whilst the Egyptians did occasionally promote foreigners who became civil servants and even priests, they would never have accepted a lowly–born foreigner who worshipped a foreign god.

When we examine the Joseph story, we find a number of names belonging to Egyptians: Potiphar, Zaphenath–paneah, Potihera and Aesath, but they were not contemporary with this era, only becoming popular in the seventh century BCE — the time of the Judean scribes. It becomes apparent, as we analyse the history, that like Abraham, the Judean scribes invented Joseph to emphasise the importance of the Jewish people, even over the all powerful Egyptians; but they had a second more serious purpose, to keep alive their religious connection to Egypt.

By the time that the Old Testament came to be written, the Judean priesthood had reasons to hide the fact that they were Canaanites and to disguise their Egyptian links. Yet because the beliefs, which they 'exported' through Abraham, Jacob, Joseph and Moses, originated in Egypt and were the foundations of their own hybrid religion, the truth had to be left in. The solution was to record a complex allegory, so heavily disguised that only those initiated by oral tradition would have 'the eyes to see'!

Chapter 4

Moses — One More Basket Case

"The man who promises everything is sure to fulfill nothing, and everyone who promises too much is in danger of using evil means in order to carry out his promises, and is already on the road to perdition."

Carl Jung

The story of Moses forms the real bedrock upon which the Jewish religion is built. Moses' meeting with God moves things along, so that now, God is no longer known only to the Patriarchs in their private revelations. Moses introduces God to the people and God is known by the new sacred name, 'I am who I am'. The four Hebrew letters Yod Heh Vau Heh were used to represent the name and are more commonly seen as YHWH referred to frequently as Yahweh and finally mistranslated in the sixteenth century from ancient Jewish texts as Jehovah.

This is Jehovah, the God of the Christians, the God of Jesus, the God of the young Mohammed. From Moses came Judaism and the Laws, laws which were given by God for his 'chosen people' to follow and to live their lives by; laws which were later adopted by the Christian church. It is a powerful, moving and very human story, which despite its epic scope and supernatural miracles, seems so very real and steeped in historical fact. The account of Moses' life is filled with great detail and numerous specific geographical references, making it easy to authenticate — or in this case disprove.

The story of Moses and the Exodus from Egypt is a well-known one. The Pharaoh, that his Hebrew slaves would become more numerous than the Egyptians, decreed that all the first-born of the Hebrews be killed. The mother of Moses hid her new baby in some bulrushes, he is then found by an Egyptian princess, who takes him home and rears him as her own. Thus Moses is brought up as an Egyptian prince.[1]

---

[1] Exodus 1-2

One day Prince Moses kills an overseer who is attacking Hebrew slave workers and then, fearing for his life, flees to the Sinai desert to live with a Bedouin tribe. During this exile, God announces himself to Moses and tells him to remove his people from Egypt and to return them to the 'Promised Land'. Moses returns to Egypt and joins up with his brother, Aaron.[2] Having failed to persuade the Pharaoh to release his Hebrew slaves, Moses inflicts various plagues upon the Egyptians. Moses then leaves with the Hebrews, but with the Pharaoh's army in pursuit. The Hebrews are saved by a miracle, when the Red Sea parts offering them an escape route; the Egyptians follow, but the sea closes back in and drowns the whole army.[3] The Hebrews then flee into the Sinai desert. Whilst Moses goes off up a mountain to communicate with God and bring back the stone tablets of 'The Law', the Hebrews resort to worshipping a golden calf and as punishment for this offence, they are forced to wander the desert for forty years.[4] Finally, Moses leads his people to the 'Promised Land,' carrying with them the Ark of the Covenant. God does not allow Moses, now very old, to enter the 'Promised Land' and it is his successor, Joshua who leads the Hebrews into Canaan as an invading army and by use of extreme force, they annex the land for themselves.[5]

This is a stirring, heroic tale, but is it true: the hard historical and archaeological evidence conclusively says, no. When the story is studied carefully, convincing details are found to be anything but; where there should have been specific references, there are none; the geographical references also prove to be false. Put the tale into its contemporary historical setting and the result is that it could not have possibly happened and archaeology proves this. However, an exodus did take place, but it was not one of 600,000 Hebrew slaves fleeing the Egyptians. Rather, it was an exile of what was mainly Egyptian nobility, priests and civil servants and a large entourage — all passionately devoted followers of a banished Egyptian religion. But first let us consider whether it was possible that there could have been a large-scale escape out of Egypt in the claimed time of Ramesses II.

The first problem we encounter is a direct result of the Hyksos expulsion in 1570 BCE. The Egyptians were now wary and had no intention of letting foreign immigrants drift into their land again. They set up a line of garrison forts along the Nile delta's eastern border and were strict to monitor and

---

[2] Exodus 3-6
[3] Exodus 7-15
[4] Exodus 16-24
[5] Exodus 25-40

limit those who wished to enter. Along the main highway into Canaan and within Canaan itself, they built more forts. At this period, Egypt was the world's most powerful kingdom and it had total control over all the middle-eastern lands through into northern Syria as far as the River Euphrates.

The Egyptian administrators kept records of all who came and went; yet on the Canaan borders, they made not a single reference to the Hebrews or Israelites. Elsewhere in Egypt, where they kept meticulous records of all manner of things, there is not a single mention of the Israelites, even though the Bible states their numbers had grown to rival those of their captors. How could such an extraordinarily huge ethnic group have gone unrecorded — archaeologists have found no traces of the Hebrews being resident in Egypt[6] — the truth must be, that they were never there.

Despite the total absence of any record, even if the Hebrews had been there, for an enormous group of people to attempt to leave Egypt, would have been virtually impossible. If there were 600,000 men and up to 2,000,000 in total with women and children, that would have meant half of Egypt's population, attempting to leave *en masse*. From the chain of forts, there not just to control immigrants, but manned to repel invaders, someone would have noticed a large body of people trying to slip out unseen. Once the alarm was raised at one fort, others would have sent their soldiers in support. In little time, there would have been formidable heavily-armed forces coming at the large body of moving Hebrews from in front and behind, blocking any escape.

The only possible way to escape from Egypt was south-eastward, into the desolate wastes of the Sinai Peninsula desert, provided that the enormous mass of people could evade the Egyptian forces for long enough to get that far away. The fanciful story of the Red Sea parting and then drowning the Pharaoh's army is just that. Christian theorists who attempted to authenticate the story, have relocated it to the northern delta's 'sea of reeds' and have proposed ideas which range from the Egyptian chariots getting bogged down in the mud, to a tidal wave caused by the eruption of Santorini's volcano doing the damage. Even were one Egyptian force lost, there would have been many others stationed in the vicinity who would have been mobilised, now with a powerful desire to extract an immediate and bloody revenge.

But let's address this unlikely story of some 600,000 or more Israelites fleeing into the Sinai desert, with no more supplies than those that they could carry. They were, supposedly, wandering about the desert for forty years. How did they manage to achieve this feat, when surviving in a desert environment for even a few days is extremely difficult? The amount of food

---

[6] Finkelstein, I & Silberman. N. *The Bible Unearthed*

and water required for a vast number of people is enormous and for such a region to accommodate this wandering nation, without them getting separated is impossible. Even if the figures had been wildly exaggerated, the number of Israelites — if they were sufficient to invade Canaan — were still far too large to live in the desert. Survival in this desolate environment, is wholly dependent upon the scattered oases, however none of these could have sustained more than a small tribe of Bedouin.

Archaeology has also dismissed any notion of there having been any large number of people occupying the Sinai.[7] Even if the Israelites had been just a hundred people, the teams of archaeologists who have scoured the peninsula for so long would have found their remains. The Exodus story gives specific sites that Israelites occupied, during their forty-year sojourn. All the places that the Israelites stopped at have been named in the Jewish texts and as a consequence, they have been searched extensively, including the Mount Sinai area, but without any evidence coming to light.

Remains of pastoralists have been found going back to the third millennium, as well more substantial remains from the subsequent millennia, but no traces of the Israelites have been found anywhere in the peninsula. We are told that the historical truth of the Bible stories comes from the historical authenticity of the details they give. The lack of any historical evidence to support the stories must condemn their claims to the realm of fantasy.

The fact is that all the places where the Israelites claim to have resided during their desert wanderings were not occupied at any time during the flexible period of Exodus, which falls into the Bronze Age. At Kadesh-barnea, for instance, a site reputedly lived in for thirty-eight of the Israelites' forty-year wanderings, there are no Bronze Age remains at all, only evidence of a late Iron Age fort and despite extensive searching by archaeologists, not even a single pottery shard has been found which could have belonged to the Israelites. Considering how many of them were said to be wandering about, this total lack of evidence leaves only one conclusion to be inferred: the Israelites were never there.

When one studies the places mentioned in the Exodus story, most of them were not occupied at all, until the seventh century BCE, which again clearly shows that the story had no historical authenticity, but had been given a backdrop which was contemporary with the time of writing. Once more, we find the hand of the seventh-century scribes in the writing of this tale, just as they had been the authors of the story of Abraham.

Further evidence to suggest the period when the Exodus story was compiled, comes from place names in Egypt. *Migdol*, for instance, was a

---

7 ibid

MOSES — ONE MORE BASKET CASE

common Egyptian name for a fort, but in the seventh century, in the eastern delta of the Nile, there was an important *Migdol,* the eminent city of Pithom, supposedly built by the Israelites for the Pharaoh. Yet, it wasn't built until the seventh century. Goshen, the region where the Israelites dwelt in the Nile delta, could not be an authentic name, since it is not Egyptian, but Semitic. There would only have been Egyptian names, when the Hebrews went there, but significantly, as Egyptologist, Donald Bedford[8] pointed out, the name Goshen derives from a dynastic name Geshem, which belongs to the royal family of the Qedarite Arabs, who settled in the Nile delta in the sixth and fifth centuries BCE. Again, this is around the time the Judean scribes would have written the Exodus story; we need to remind ourselves that these Biblical stories were constantly being revised and added to in the two or three centuries after the written record started.

During the Israelite wanderings, the Bible describes how the Canaanite king of Arad in the Negeb, raided and took captives. Many years of work by archaeologists have revealed that there had been a large city at Arad in the early Bronze Age, but the site and indeed the whole region had been completely deserted during the *late* Bronze Age, the alleged period of Exodus. Other locations must also be called into question, namely those relating to the regions to the south–east and east of the River Jordan.

In the Exodus story, when at Kadesh–barnea, Moses sent emissaries to the king of Edom, requesting permission to be allowed passage through his kingdom. However, at that time, such a kingdom did not exist, it was a barren region occupied only by a few nomadic pastoralists. All the archaeological evidence indicates that Edom came into being, with the aid of Assyrian patronage, in the seventh century.

East of the River Jordan, the Israelites, on their way to Canaan, met with resistance in Moab and Ammon, yet these kingdoms did not exist at that time and the whole area was sparsely inhabited by nomads. But yet it is written, that the Israelites were forced into battle by the Amorite king at Heshbon. This site has been investigated over twenty years[9] and it was found that during the late Bronze Age, the period of the Exodus, Heshbon did not exist in any form, not even as a village, let alone a city.

Strangely, given all the wealth of detail in the Exodus story, one of the leading characters throughout it is never named. That character is, of course, the Egyptian Pharaoh. This is a bizarre omission, especially when other Pharaohs are mentioned by name in other stories of far lesser significance. There is an obvious explanation for this mysterious anomaly: the name was never mentioned, because it would have placed Exodus into

---

[8] Redford, DB. *Egypt, Canaan, and Israel in Ancient Times*
[9] Ibach, R D Jr, La Bianca, O S ed. *Archaeological Survey of the Hesban Region*

an exact historical time frame. This, the Judean priesthood and scribes, did not want, for to have named the Pharaoh would have exposed their story as a lie — not only that, the whole of Jewish history would be thrown into dispute along with the story of Moses.

When we approach the end of the Moses story, the Judean scribes certainly give the plot their best, building up the pathos and the heroic climax to events, as the Israelites fight for God's precious gift of a homeland. For some bizarre reason that isn't too clear, but may have something to do with the Israelites squabbling amongst themselves, God would allow none of the generation who had left Egypt into their 'Promised Land'. Our hero Moses himself was denied entry on account of his petulant behaviour when he was supposed to be drawing water from a rock, though God did at least allow him to look at the 'Promised Land' from across the river on Mount Nebo. After showing Moses the place he would not be allowed to reach, God instructed Moses to assemble his followers and pass the leadership on to his aide and second in command, Joshua ben Nun. Aged 120, Moses then dies, his long labours and struggles unrewarded by a peevish God, but the Almighty at least condescends to bury Moses personally in a secret place — probably so no-one would say "Holy Moses — guess who I found?" when they dug the body up.

As Moses' story ends, Joshua's begins. God didn't seem to mind that Joshua, now around 85, should have been told to stay behind with the rest of the old guys and doesn't see this anomaly worthy of explanation either. Joshua leads the Israelites through another parting of the waters, this time the River Jordan and, now himself in personal communication with God, embarks on a Blitzkrieg campaign against the Canaanite cities on his behalf. His genocidal mission is to free the 'Promised Land' of idolatry, by slaughtering the population in its entirety. The nearby city of Jericho had to be taken, in order to establish a safe bridgehead and we've all probably heard the story immortalised in song, of Joshua ordering the Ark of the Covenant to be marched around the city walls and on the seventh day, following a blast on the war trumpets, the walls miraculously came tumbling down.

Joshua next took the strategic city of Ai, this time by the use of cunning tactics to lure the army out and into an ambush. Four Gibeonite cities surrendered and their inhabitants were spared because they claimed, though falsely, that they were not natives of the land. Joshua then set about the defeat of a combined army of Canaanites. There seemed to be too many soldiers to kill over the course of the day, so Joshua called upon God to halt the passage of the sun, so he could end the fight in daylight. God obliged and Joshua completed the mass slaughter. The cities of the south were next to fall to the Israelites and then finally those of the north. Following another great battle against a combined army of Canaanites, Hazor, the most important city in Canaan, was destroyed. This meant Joshua and the Israelites had conquered their 'Promised Land': the Israelites divided up the land between their twelve tribes and settled down. It would have been nice if God had decided they would all live happily ever after, but as history tells us, it's been downhill for his chosen people ever since.

We have seen that the story of the Exodus has no archaeological evidence to support it, so is there any to confirm Joshua's dramatic conquest story? We could well start by considering the physical state of numerous Israelites emerging from forty years of wandering in a desert. Had they spent a long period living in a harsh barren land, with little or no food and virtually no grazing for any animals they might have brought out of Egypt, they would have been in a very poor state of health and large numbers of them would have died of starvation, thirst and disease. If one considers the needs of modern–day refugees, in the Sudan for example, they could only survive with UN aid and by the time it reached them or they it, they were unable to resist the aggression of their persecutors. The Bible states that the Israelites were vulnerable to attacks from Canaanites and when they finally decided to head up to the 'Promised Land', they were refused passage by the Edomites and had to take another route. Yet we are expected to believe that the Israelites, who felt unable to tackle the inferior Edomites, were soon to defeat the powerful Canaanites armies. The *facts* are incompatible.

The next question we might ask is how did the Israelites arm themselves when they had been living in the desert in a destitute state for forty years, every day a struggle for survival. Seemingly out of nowhere, they conjured up enough weapons to equip a very large body of men. In those times, metal weapons and armour were highly prized, very expensive and very difficult to get hold of. If they had the weapons, then surely God had performed another miracle, but one the Bible story tellers forgot to boast about.

If an even *greater* miracle had been performed and the Israelites had been in the desert and somehow concealed all trace of their existence from modern day archaeologists, they would still have emerged as a ragbag stream of migrant refugees. That being so, allowing that some of the men under forty — the others weren't allowed in don't forget — were fortunate enough to be in strong physical shape and armed, they would have been burdened by a far greater number of women, children, cripples and the sick, together with all their baggage and animals. Unless, of course, they left the vulnerable behind with those who had come out of Egypt and the Bible scribes forgot to tell us. Nevertheless, such a miserable human train would not have passed on their way unnoticed and they would have been easy pickings for raiding bandits and extremely vulnerable to any hostile force, who would have found a sitting target.

History shows us that any fighting force which aims to succeed, needs to be well organised, well armed, well trained and led by people who have some experience of warfare and a good knowledge of military tactics. There have been odd examples, throughout history, of a rabble force overcoming a well–trained professional one, but in these cases, the victory tends to be a fluke, often caused by carelessness, and always, these unexpected battle victories are soon reversed and the wars comprehensively lost.

In the Bible account, things are suddenly transformed. The struggle of refugees who cross the Jordan, are instantly transformed into a formidable fighting force. They immediately find the strongly–fortified Canaanite cities, with their heavily–armed and armoured professional troops and even chariot corps, easy to defeat. Rational consideration, of the Judean scribes' Biblical claims, makes us conclude that the Israelites unstoppable, all–conquering army is yet another of their fantasies.

Archaeology has shown that at this period, Canaan was relatively weak. Canaan had no strongly–fortified cities ruled by powerful kings and princes. The cities were, in reality, little more than residences of the nobility with modest palaces, a temple, administrative buildings, a few houses for high officials and bureaucrats to live in, a few inns and storehouses; the sites were often unwalled compounds and there were no large powerful armies. The rest of the Canaanites lived out in the countryside on farms, working the land.[10] Unlike the earlier period, of the Middle Bronze Age, by the time of the supposed Exodus in the Late Bronze Age, the large cites had gone, or had dramatically reduced in size.[11]

Archaeology has shown the Canaanites to be weak and this would have made it easy for the Israelites to invade, but there was a very good reason why they couldn't do so. The Canaanite rulers were militarily impotent, but that was because of the Egyptians. By the Late Bronze Age and particularly during the thirteenth century, the Egyptians were at the peak of their power and influence. They controlled the whole Palestine region, right up through Syria to the Euphrates. Canaan was an Egyptian province and totally under Egyptian control, with Egyptian garrison troops stationed at several key sites. At Beth–shean, south of the Sea of Galilee, the Egyptians had a fortress, which according to inscriptions found there, showed it occupied during the time of Ramesses II, the supposed Pharaoh of Exodus. Nearby, just to the west, is Meggido, which the Bible claims Joshua took. That could not and did not happen, because there was a strong Egyptian garrison

---

[10] Coote, R B & Whitelam, K W. *The Emergence of Early Israel in Historical Perspective*
[11] op. cit. Finkelstein

there. It is implausible for the Egyptians to have allowed themselves to be cut off in northern Canaan by Israelite invaders, let alone allow a garrison city to fall. One might argue that if Joshua took the city, then it must have occurred in an earlier period, but then the city was in the hands of either the Egyptians or the Hittites. No matter how you shift the time to make it more convenient, it still does not work. So the evidence shows that there was absolutely no need for defensive cities and armies, since the Canaanites' security was the responsibility of the Egyptians. Successful conquest would have been impossible, for had the Israelites had such an intent, it would have incited the full wrath of Egypt, whose forces would eliminate every one of the invaders.

Were one to suppose that, at this unspecified time, the Egyptians had not been there, Canaan still could not have fallen to the Israelites, for in northern Syria the powerful Hittite empire was straining to expand and had the Egyptians not been there to hold back the Israelites, then the Hittites would have swept southwards to annex Canaan. The Egyptians, as we know, kept very detailed records and a great number of diplomatic letters were sent from Canaan to Egypt, however there is absolutely nothing about an invasion. It simply did not happen.

The final flaw in the authenticity of the Exodus Canaan Invasion story concerns the Israelites' leader, Joshua. He was, allegedly, born in Egypt and given his name before Moses had his conversation with God — the conversation where God informed Moses that he no longer wished to be called *El*, as he was by the Patriarchs, but would from then on be called YHWH, or Yahweh — the Christians' Jehovah.

Unintentionally, the Jewish scribes slipped up on two major counts. They give away the fact that the original Israelites were already from Canaan, as *El* was the name of the Canaanite god. They then caused a problem with Joshua's authenticity as the name they chose and he was supposedly given at his birth translates as 'Yahweh is Salvation'. But of course according to the Moses story, the name Yahweh did not exist until after Joshua was born. This error leads one to conclude that Joshua had to be a fictional character created after the time in which the events in the story were set.

For many years, right up into the 1950s, archaeology, motivated by the prime need to prove the truth of the Bible accounts, claimed to have unearthed finds in Canaan which proved the Israelite invasion had occurred[12] — but in reality this was totally incorrect, as some of the more open minded knew[13]. Modern–day archaeologists have been able to prove

---

[12] Albright, W F. *The Biblical Period from Abraham to Ezra*
[13] Kenyon, K. *Digging Up Jericho*

that if Joshua had seen the fortified walls of Jericho come tumbling down to the sound of trumpets, it was in someone's imagination as Jericho was completely unoccupied during the thirteenth century BCE, the supposed time of Exodus and the invasion of Canaan. In the previous century, the inhabitants were poor and the place was sparsely occupied and there had been no walls. It had walls once, but they had fallen during an earthquake. There was no evidence of any violent destruction having taken place, it simply withered away and died from abandonment, long before the time of the Israelites.

The city of Ai, where Joshua concocted his clever ruse to draw out and defeat its occupants, was a large powerful city, but 1,000 years before the time of Exodus. Excavations revealed that during the Exodus period, the site had long been deserted. The same thing is to be found in the other places mentioned in the Exodus story, such as the Gibeonite cities, which though occupied in the Middle Bronze Age and the much later Iron Age, were totally unoccupied during the Late Bronze Age, when the Israelite invasion supposedly took place.[14] The Bible's story is totally contradicted by hard archaeological evidence — at the supposed time of Exodus, many of these cities that fell to the Israelites, simply did not exist. But what of some other cities, such as Meggido, Lachish and Hazor, which seemed to show a sudden and sometimes violent demise.[15] Firstly, the troubles that afflicted these particular places were actually much later than the conquest timeframe allows. These cities did not fall together in just a short period of some seven years, but they fell independently over a period of 100 years. By the time of the early twelfth century BCE, Egypt's power was beginning to wane and the general economic situation throughout the middle–east was in sharp decline. In Canaan, the slow economic collapse led to civil strife and to the piecemeal abandonment of cities over a period of about a century. Coincident with this and aided by this turmoil, there were ethnic movements taking place. The main movement was of a group known as the Sea Peoples, whose piratical raiding expanded into more concerted incursions.

One of the main tribes of these Sea Peoples was the Philistines, who following their initial raids on the coast, forcefully moved in and settled into the power void. The violent demise inflicted upon a few of the existing Canaan cities, may have been either self–induced or as a result of the gradual Philistine incursion in the twelfth century BCE, but it definitely was not caused by a sudden Israelite invasion one hundreds years earlier in the thirteenth. It is of course quite possible that a few Israelite raiding parties,

---

[14] Pritchard, J B & Hyatt, J P ed. Culture and History, *The Bible in Modern Scholarship*
[15] Bright, J *A History of Israel*

from their highland villages, may have sought to take whatever advantage they could of the general chaotic times.

When recounting the aftermath of the conquest, the Bible stories contradict themselves once more. Firstly, we are informed that Joshua wiped out all the people who dwelt in the 'Promised Land' and then the Israelites had a rest from war and turned to farming the land. Later on, the Bible tells us that the Canaanites hadn't been wiped out at all, they were still there, now posing some sort of *challenge* for the Israelites, as were many of the rulers whom Joshua had supposedly defeated already. We also learn that far from being at rest from war, the Israelites were constantly beleaguered.[16] It transpires that the Bible actually admits that Canaanites and Philistines, as well as other tribes, live in close proximity to the Israelites. Indeed, far from being totally exclusive, intermarriage was quite common,[17] which suggests that the tribes of Israel were far from deadly enemies with those original inhabitants of their 'Promised Land'. It was only in the more remote hill country to the south, which was the land of the tribes of Judah and Simeon, that the Canaanites were eventually expelled, whereas in the larger and more prosperous northern lands, the Canaanites remained.

However, in truth, the inhabitants of both Judea and Israel were originally Canaanites. Indeed, the people of Israel should, more correctly, be called Samaritans, because there is no real evidence, other than what was written in the Bible, for the existence of Israel at all. There was however a Samaria, which developed after the decline of the ancient Canaanite city–states and Samaria appears to have occupied just about the same area as Israel.[18] There are indications that Israel might actually have been an invention of second–century scribes to legitimise the expansionist ambitions of the Hasmodean rulers of Judea. Academics generally agree that this was when the 'Old Testament' was put into its final form and that much inventive propaganda took place, so the scribes' political tampering with their already dubious historical accounts, may well be the source for the insertion of Israel into stories attributed to earlier centuries.

It is difficult to separate the truth from amongst the invention and it may never be found, but myth usually stands out starkly, because of its fantastical deeds. Memories of these unstable times were woven into local tales which exaggerated and invented great deeds for local tribal heroes and these can clearly be seen in the superman–style military feats described in the Book of Judges, which follows the post–conquest period: Shamgar, single–handedly

---

[16] Joshua 13:2
[17] Judges 3
[18] Tappy, R E. *The Archaeology of Israelite Samaria, Volume 1*

slays 600 Philistines, using an ox goad;[19] Othniel single-handedly defeats an army;[20] Samson performed similar feats using the jaw of an ass and then went on to pull down a whole stone temple.[21] Strange how we dismiss the Greek tales of the superhuman deeds of Hercules, yet we are supposed to believe the same stories because they are recounted in the Bible — though these days only fundamentalists believe them to be true. But if the Bible has been recounting fantasies, can one accept that any of it is true, for after all, we are told everything in the Bible is absolutely true and written at God's personal direction. Little wonder that the priesthood constantly demanded that their followers refrained from questioning and gave themselves over to total belief. What is clear from the Jewish writings relating to this period is that a fantasy was written with a political purpose and reflected political and military aspirations. The geographical areas, places names and underlying politics, all very much relate to what was taking place in the seventh century BCE.

Finally, we must look at Moses himself. As a baby he is hidden in a basket floating on the Nile and later on he is raised as a prince. The story of a baby being hidden in a basket on a river has a plot that is common throughout the middle-eastern lands and is certainly not unique to the Hebrews. The same story is attributed to King Sargon the Great of Akkad and Judean scribes could well have appropriated this tale during their exile as captives of the Babylonians. The story is also ascribed to the Greek god Dionysus, who was also set adrift on the Nile. These and other similar stories were based on the Egyptian story of Osiris.

Moses is raised as a prince, supposedly because a princess found him. For a member of Egyptian royalty to rear the baby Moses as her own would be impossible. Egyptian royalty considered themselves to be related to the gods so it would be unthinkable for one to foster a mortal commoner. Even if Moses had been brought up as an Egyptian prince, how could he know his real people were Hebrews and even if he did, why as a prince, would he choose to give up his position and align himself with supposed slaves. As a prince, he would have been educated and thoroughly immersed in the Egyptian culture, religion and mindset, and anything non-Egyptian would be both totally alien and abhorrent. Finally we have the story of Prince Moses killing a work overseer to protect his old kinfolk and needing to flee: a prince would be free to kill any commoner without concern of retribution and he certainly would have no cause to 'escape into exile'.

---

[19] Judges 3:31
[20] Judges 1:12
[21] Judges 15:15

The whole story of Moses and the Exodus is filled with Egyptian symbolism and reveals none that is associated with a group of Semitic people. If the Biblical Exodus story had any kernel of truth to it, it may link to a small exodus, led by Egyptian priests and nobility and the book investigates this in some detail later on.

THE GREATEST LIE EVER TOLD

Chapter 5

David and Solomon — Superheroes

"Religion is the frozen thought of men out of which they build temples."
Jiddu Krishnamorti

After the Exodus story, the Bible gives us a lot of self–righteous ranting against the ungodly neighbours of the Israelites and we are treated to more fantasy with the Herculean adventures of heroes, like Samson. At the command of a psychopathic God, the Israelites kill hundreds of thousands, sometimes with a donkey's jaw or more simply stone a few babies. With the nod from God, they even enjoy a spot of cannibalism and prove beyond any doubt that the Israelites really were a 'special' people.

Fortunately for those of us too squeamish to find Judges a good read, the Bible moves away from fantasy heroics, to a period of Israelite history with heroics that are more realistic — though with no better morality — and thereby are the Christian academics greatly comforted.

The Book of Samuel, known also as the first Book of Kings, recounts the tale of David and Solomon. It is now that the story becomes less like myth and more mundane, real history that is based upon sound facts.

But will the facts fit the story here, any more than they did in the fantasy phase, many of us will have our doubts. The truth is, that this part of the Bible gets off to a bad start. Just when we think that the Israelites have finally shown their enemies the door, we discover them lurking by the window. The story of the Israelite invasion was one of total conquest and ruthless extermination of their foes. Yet we now find that the Israelites are under severe pressure from their annihilated enemies. They clearly could not have been exterminated or they wouldn't be there to cause the problem, so the Judean scribes have lied to us, once again!

At a time of intertribal rivalry and political tension, things are so bad for the diverse tribes that make up the Israelites, that they ask God for a king. Saul, from the lowest family, in the lowest tribe, of Benjamin, is revealed as their leader.[1] Through Saul, we encounter more of the inexplicable contradictions with which Israelite history is fraught. For some unfathomable reason, one of Saul's first tasks is to avenge the Israelites on tribes who harassed them on their journey through the wilderness, 300 years before. Saul makes a partial attempt at this and has to be reminded by God to go back and finish the task. He has some success at establishing his rule over Israel, but its defences are weakened by fear and a diminished population, as their old enemies the Philistines soon have them struggling desperately for their survival.

This simply does not make sense, according to the stories recounted in Joshua and Judges. The Israelites should have grown in numbers, strength and resources since they crossed the Jordan and escaped the ravages of their wilderness wandering. However, if one looks at the alternative offered by modern archaeology, then it does all make sense, because the small tribes of indigenous hill people — which now saw themselves as Israelites rather than Canaanites — would indeed be weak and vulnerable to attack from their more powerful neighbours inhabiting the coastal plain and in particular the Philistines: these invaders had established themselves and become the dominant power in Canaan.

Though the Bible story reveals how, in the Israelites' moment of great peril and need, the prophet Samuel is advised by God that he should elevate the goodly Saul into Israel's first king, to unify the disparate beleaguered tribes, it takes a shepherd boy from the tribe of Judah, to fulfil the task. David comes to our attention when he defeats the Philistine champion warrior, an improbable giant named Goliath, whose demise supposedly caused the whole vast Philistine army to flee.

After this, we start, once again to see the flaws in God's judgement: Saul neglects his duty to Israel, in pursuit of his obsession to kill David, whom he recognises as God's choice of successor. Naturally Saul dies and David goes on to assume leadership of the Israelites and became their great king. David soundly defeats his powerful enemies the Philistines, to secure the Kingdom of Israel; he then goes on to defeat the Ammonites, the Moabites, the Edomites and the Arammeans, and in doing so, carves out a glorious empire, stretching from Egypt to the Euphrates.

After David, his son, Solomon, consolidated his father's achievements and dramatically overtook them in scale. Before we know it, Solomon built the fabled Temple in Jerusalem to house the Ark of the Covenant and constructed a fabulous palace and erected great fortified walls for his capital as he did at Megiddo, Hazor and Gezer. He raised a huge army, which required the construction of a massive stable to house 40,000 horses for his

---

[1] 1 Samuel 9:20

cavalry and chariot forces. Solomon also gained recognition as a wise and fabulously wealthy king who was lauded all around the ancient world.

In 1 Kings, the Bible informs us explicitly:

> 'Thus Solomon excelled all kings of the earth in riches and in wisdom. And the whole earth sought the presence of Solomon to hear his wisdom, which God had put into his mind'

and

> '… silver as common in Jerusalem as stone'.

These and similar claims, led to the period being described as Israel's great 'Golden Age'.[2]

This remarkable success was achieved in an astonishingly short time. Like something out of a *Boy's Own* comic, 'in one mighty bound' the Israelites move from being defeated underdogs to rulers of a fabulously rich and militarily mighty empire. Again, this sounds like yet more fantasy and indeed, what archaeology reveals about the great kings, David and Solomon and their glorious city of Jerusalem, comes as something of a shock to the gullible traditionalists.

If as the Bible states, the whole world was in awe of Israel, we can look at the powerful neighbours of this new Israelite kingdom, for confirmation. From both Egypt and from Mesopotamia, there is not one single line recorded, that mentions either David or Solomon, or a great empire that stretched from the very border of Egypt to that of northern Mesopotamia.

The Greeks were great travellers and like the historian Herodotus, they gathered stories about people from every region, to feed their fascination with their differences and oddities. Herodotus wrote in detail about Egypt, but it wasn't until 100 years later, when Alexander the Great invaded the region, that the Greeks first heard of Israel. So how could they possibly have missed such a supposedly unique race, why had they not heard of the 'special' country, why had they not heard anything of the great King David and his 'world famous' son King Solomon, why had they not heard of the great golden empire of Israel? Why — because it was all a lie.

This omission cannot simply be dismissed as *bizarre*, nor can one merely call it *suspicious*, it is clearly an unarguable indication that this Israelite kingdom of David and Solomon and their empire never existed. If it had, the records at the time would have shown it.

If the great empire never existed, then what of the great building programme undertaken by Solomon, surely this would support the Biblical claims. The problem is, that modern archaeology has failed to find any great

---

[2] Maxwell Miller, J. "Old Testament History and Archaeology"

structures that might have been built by Solomon. In the past, the opposite was the case: early archaeologists hoping to prove the Bible to be true looked for anything that would confirm it, even if they were fairly liberal with the actual dating. The destructive fires that consumed cities like Megiddo for example, were quickly attributed to David's victory over the Philistines; above the burnt ruins, were the remains of later structures, which were immediately attributed to Solomon. For a long time, excavations appeared to prove the Biblical stories — the pillared remains found at Megiddo were pronounced as being 'royal stables' built by Solomon.

In the 1960s, new archaeological research discovered that above the burnt ruins and beneath the 'stables', lay the remains of a palace, which was then attributed to Solomon — but that meant the so called 'stables' were much later and not of Solomon's time and were attributed to King Ahab.[3]

Further excavations unearthed very distinctive six-chambered gates at Megiddo, Hazor and Gezer; and these were interpreted as 'fortified palace gatehouses', all incorporating a common design plan. It was decided that these structures, which had some Phoenician elements, must have been built by craftsmen belonging to Hiram, the king of Tyre, whom Solomon supposedly hired from his ally. Eventually however, the dating was also found to be badly flawed and wrong.

The latest refinements to carbon 14 dating, left no doubt that the dating at Megiddo was misplaced.[4] The results of dating the burnt timbers, originally attributed to David's assault, showed them to be 100 years after David's time. As a consequence, this also proved that the palace built two layers above the burnt ruins, could not have been constructed by Solomon, but was of a far later time. Furthermore, archaeologists finally began to question how Solomon's builders produced this distinctive architectural model. Even if Solomon's builders were the creators of this style, it would have been quickly imitated by others, but there is no sign of this having been done anywhere in the whole of the middle-east around this period.

Another question that needs addressing, is how would Solomon suddenly acquire such highly-skilled architects, ones whom no-one else seemed to have employed. This indicates that they could not have been foreigners, such as the craftsmen hired from the Phoenician king of Tyre, otherwise the distinctive style would have been reproduced elsewhere; but nor could they have been Israelites, for they would have had absolutely no skills nor experience in this kind of grand construction work. The simple truth is that these impressive constructions are most certainly not of Solomon's time, but

---

3 Kenyon, K M *Archaeology in the Holy Land*

4 Finkelstein, I & Piasetzky, E. Comments on "14C Dates from Tel Rehov: Iron Age Chronology, Pharaohs and Hebrew Kings"

matched the style which was to appear much later in the region. They were designed and erected in the ninth century — over 100 years after Solomon's time.[5]

So these constructions have to be dismissed as examples that prove Solomon's empire building, but they are an excellent example of how academics can be led astray by their desire to verify a belief, rather than investigate with a detached open mind.

Now we have the problem of Jerusalem itself — the capital of the great Solomonic empire. We are given the image of Jerusalem as a place of impressive grandeur, having a magnificent Temple and a great gleaming palace to house Solomon's 700 wives and 300 concubines, all protected behind huge stone fortress walls — a glorious fabled city which reflected the glory of God. Alas, it is all romantic nonsense. Despite extensive excavations, archæologists have failed to locate any signs at all that there was ever a Solomon Temple, or palace, or great fortifications. Christian scholars and some biased archæologists, still continue to argue that the remains of the Temple and palace were totally obliterated by Herod's large-scale reconstruction. This may sound plausible, but on every archaeological site, demolition and rebuilding never completely eradicates every trace of earlier structures — as even those biased academics know full well.

In Jerusalem, not a single trace of the Solomon Temple has been unearthed.[6] In the 1970s and 80s, intensive research revealed that beneath the remains of the later Temple building by Herod, there were no remains of Solomon's supposed structure, indeed, no evidence for any kind of monumental building, only a few broken pottery shards dated to the tenth century BCE were found. This indicated a small population at that time; beneath the sparse bits of pottery, at a lower level, there were plentiful traces of late Iron-Age and Middle Bronze-Age artefacts. This was clear indication that at the time of David and Solomon, Jerusalem had actually diminished, rather than escalated in splendour. Since it had been very modest before this decline, it must then have been exceedingly poor indeed.

Had Solomon constructed fortifications, they would have been added to, as was common practice. It would have been totally illogical to dismantle them and make a completely clean start — which is the desperate excuse of some scholars. If you needed defences, what sense would it make, to leave the site completely defenceless for a long period while you rebuild them anew, and why would you want the extra massive building work and the huge extra costs. Besides which, if Solomon had constructed fabulous fortified walls, why would some later king think them worthless enough to dismantle the whole

---

5 Wightman, G J "The Myth of Solomon"

6 op cit Finkelstein, I & Silberman, N A *The Bible Unearthed*

lot — wouldn't it have been considered sacrilegious to destroy the work of the iconic Solomon.

The real facts reveal a very different Jerusalem from the one of legend and the truth is that during the time of David and Solomon, Jerusalem had diminished from its modest state of earlier periods, so that at that particular time, it was barely occupied and nothing more than a typical Judean hilltop village.

So what does this mean — realistically, this backward settlement was not developed enough to indicate a society which was either large enough, or literate enough, to be the site of an important kingdom, let alone a large empire. To carve out an empire and then to maintain it, takes a great deal of wealth and a large amount of manpower.

At that time there would have been no more than 50,000 people inhabiting the whole land that might be defined as belonging to all the tribes that made up the Israelites. In Judah, the power base of David and Solomon, the terrain was steep and rugged, and was not really suitable for agriculture, only pastoral husbandry and as a consequence, only about ten per cent of the total Israelite population lived there, something like 5,000 men, women and children. If one discounts the old and infirm males, it is likely that the Judahite fighting force which Solomon had at his disposal — to not only conquer and control his empire, but to keep the disaffected northern Israelites from rebelling — would be well under 1,000 men. In any battle, a sizeable percentage of men would be lost, but because of the small manforce within Judea, very few could be replaced, resulting in the Judeans having a rapidly diminishing army, bringing about a spiral of certain defeat.

There are more reasons that make it impossible. Had Solomon ever built a formidable army, it would have been deemed a threat to Israel's powerful neighbours and provoked attacks from Egypt and Assyria. To supply any army with weapons and armour, takes quite a bit of wealth; to equip and pay a large standing army to control and defend an empire, takes enormous wealth. The territory of the tribe of Judah was an extremely poor, wild and arid land, and not one which generated even a small amount of income for its inhabitants and whilst the northern hill country of the other tribes was more fertile, it was still far from a land of milk and honey. It is said, that Solomon had a well organised society and government; he also raised taxes — which means keeping accounts and written records — but again it takes money to pay the administrators and bureaucrats, not to mention the professional soldiers, who would be needed to run and police both a *bona fide* kingdom and an empire.

The other problem that makes the whole matter questionable is that at that time the Israelites and especially the Judeans, were basically a pastoralist society. They did not possess the literate men who would be needed to undertake the specialised work of record keeping and accounts. They would have needed a bountiful food supply for the large numbers of bureaucrats and soldiers, not to mention the 700 wives and 300 concubines idling their time away in the royal harem. All these Judean men who were employed full-time by the king, would no longer be working the land. As the male agricultural workforce was severely depleted, who would grow the food; but then the land itself would have been unable to yield sufficient crops necessary to maintain an excess to be commandeered into a State food supply. Solomon might have employed mercenaries, but though it would increase the strength of his army, it would weaken his purse, for mercenaries did not come cheap — but as the scholars have shown, there was no great wealth, Jerusalem was a poor village on an isolated hilltop.

So what of the great wealth attributed to Solomon? Wealth could have been obtained by looting conquered city-states in Canaan, but as we have already seen, the archaeological evidence disproves any invasion of Canaan from a Judean base, by either David or Solomon. Solomon supposedly was a great trader in goods, but Judea was an out-of-the-way inhospitable backwater, well away from any established trade routes. Traders did not go there at Solomon's time, nor did they have much reason to go there later in history. After the fall of northern Israelite lands to Assyria, Judea began to grow vines and olives, which then attracted merchants, but at the time of Solomon, the Judeans had nothing to trade. The final possibility concerns the myth that Solomon had fabulous mines in Africa, but this is a nonsensical fantasy. Such a thing would never have been allowed by Egypt and its army would soon put a stop to any impertinent attempts at exporting from within territory under its control.

The next issue is unification of the disparate hill-country tribes, which became known as the Israelites, though this is a question that cannot, and probably will not, ever be proven one way or another. A coalition of some sorts is a possibility, but whether it included every tribe and whether it was truly united under a single leader, is questionable. There certainly is no factual evidence to support this belief and the only mention of these Davidic episodes comes from one source and that is the Bible, which as we have already seen, is biased and unreliable. From what the Bible says, there were supposedly serious rivalries from the beginning, even before Saul was made king, and after Solomon, there was an extremely bitter north-south strife, which allegedly degenerated into open warfare.

It is possible that Saul and then David were elected as war chiefs to lead a coalition of tribes, but then again, there is no evidence to prove that there was any coalition, or that there was any enemy threatening them. Even if they were being attacked, the northern tribes might, with some reluctance, have agreed a pragmatic solution, temporarily accepting a Judean as an overall war leader, but they would have been totally against continuing with such an arrangement after hostilities had ceased and they would most certainly not have been willing to accept David the Judean as their king. Would David have had the power to establish himself as king over all the tribes and then to enforce his authority — possibly, but very unlikely against the vastly superior manpower available to an amalgam of northern tribes.

Was Solomon the king over a united Israelite state? Well, the Biblical sources say "Yes," but then as scholars know the earliest Bible histories were written by the Judeans after the joyous fall of their old enemy, the alleged northern state of Israel to the Assyrians, so the account is likely to be at best biased and at worst, a total fabrication. The likelihood is that if there were a Solomon, he was not king of a united Israelite people, but only of Judea and possibly not even that. The harsh truth is, that both David and Solomon — if indeed they actually existed, which we must doubt since there is no contemporary evidence to support that they did — would have been little more than tribal chiefs. Considering the poverty of the region and its historical reputation for banditry, both David and Solomon nestling in their remote hilltop village, could well have been bandit chieftains.

There is no real evidence to confirm that either of these two kings actually existed, but what we do have is legend, which came about following the story's vigorous promotion by the later Judean state. More than 300 years after the alleged reign of Solomon, in a major propaganda coup, the scribes enhanced their rulers' lowly status into that of descendants of great Judean kings, who ruled over a magnificent united Israelite kingdom and empire; this empire not only equalled, but excelled any other in the history of mankind. To explain the contemporary absence of this great joint kingdom, they invented a convenient civil war and when Assyria invaded the north and exiled its people, there were no records to contradict the claims.

An excellent insight into the composition of Jerusalem and its rulers in these times can be had by studying the Amarna Letters,[7] written during the reign of the Egyptian pharaoh, Akhenaten. Tell Amarna is the present day name for Akhenaten's capital city and in the ruins, discarded inscribed clay tablets were found. These were correspondence sent to the pharaoh from around the Egyptian empire. Though they were written in the fourteenth century BCE, nearly 400 years before the time of David, from the information contained within the letters, archaeologists discovered that very little altered in this area until around the very end of the eighth century BCE, well after the David/Solomon era.

From these letters, it is known that there was a ruler, called Abdi–Heba of the southern hill country of Palestine, which corresponded to what became

---

7 Moran, W L *The Armana Letters*

Judea. His hilltop stronghold was called Urusalim — the original Bronze Age name for Jerusalem — and it was basically a village that occupied the plateau ridge site of what eventually became known as the City of David. Though his place of residence was small, Abdi–Heba's kingdom covered some 900 square miles, but the landscape was harsh and arid, and as a consequence, was largely devoid of people; there were very few villages, possibly less than a dozen and the total population, including that of Urusalim was under 2,000, though that number would be slightly swelled by nomadic pastoralists. In the letters, the writer mentioned that there were troublesome renegades and outlaws, known as the Apiru. It is probable that these outlaws were living in the remoter areas, which was most likely under their control; over the following centuries, little changed. It is a strong possibility, judging by the description given in the Bible, that if David was indeed real, that he and his armed followers could well have been some of these Apiru outlaws and at some stage in time, they took control of the village of Urusalim.

Another early name is used for Jerusalem, Shalem, which is a name attributed to one of the Canaanite gods. Though such a thing might seem puzzling, it would nevertheless be quite expected, since the place would have been Canaanite originally. However, what is strange, if Shalem had once been its name, is that the Judeans never thought it necessary to change it, especially as they were supposedly seeking to eradicate all other deities. The conclusion one is forced into believing, is that Jerusalem's people, who continued to have shrines to other gods, were not especially concerned about, nor was the population exclusively dedicated to Yahweh.

Whatever the truth of the area, there was no sudden miracle where a vast horde of gold fell from Heaven into David's lap. There was no large population from which he could recruit a great army with which to conquer and then hold not only a country, but also an empire. His ridge–top stronghold at Jerusalem remained at best, pretty much as it had always been — a modestly–sized village with a probable population of less than 1,000 people. The changes and development which occurred were very slow and gradual — there was no wealth, no great buildings, no monuments, no strong fortified walls, no palace, no Temple. Archaeology has revealed that there were no trappings of a royal court, no bureaucratic office with its records, seals, weights and measures; there was little if any literacy and certainly no centre of poetry and the arts. There appeared to be no production sites, such as those for making pottery and metal work, which would be necessary for the making of armaments.

Furthermore, there is no evidence that Jerusalem was the centre of religious worship and indeed, all the evidence indicates that there were many holy sites scattered about the whole of the lands inhabited by the Israelite tribes and most likely the priesthood operated independently of any centralised authority. Indeed, the Israelites, like their Canaanite cousins, worshipped regional gods as we see from the Biblical stories. They were also venerating mountains and high places and the stars. What is clear, is that there was a schism which existed: the majority of people, stayed with their old traditional gods whilst adopting Adonay, as well as accommodating any new ones from neighbouring lands; the small minority dedicated themselves exclusively to their monotheistic god.

By the time of the seventh–century BCE writing of the Bible stories, Jerusalem had grown into what was called a small city. This was in fact no more than a modest town, whose wealth had increased through trade. It became a city with a centralised religion and a single temple to their God, and it had a king, administrators and a small army, to run a small compact kingdom. With no one to dispute its authenticity, it was this contemporary image of their society, which Judean scribes transposed onto the story of David and Solomon, then embellished it even further, into the glorious golden age of which we have heard so much.

Chapter 6

The Seventh–Century Propagandists

"If you tell a lie big enough and keep repeating it, people will eventually come to believe it. The lie can be maintained only for such time as the State can shield the people from the political, economic and/or military consequences of the lie. It thus becomes vitally important for the State to use all of its powers to repress dissent, for the truth is the mortal enemy of the lie, and thus by extension, the truth is the greatest enemy of the State."

Joseph Goebbels

Propaganda has long been the tool of those who seek power and control. Once they attain their goals, they usually record their path to success with no mention of their contriving or manipulation, and leave us once more with a history written by the victors. The Judean scribes of the seventh century BCE repeated themselves over and over and the accounts were so outlandish they just had to be true! In more modern times, Goebbels was prepared to promote his methods openly so we could all understand that a lie, if audacious enough and repeated enough times, will be believed by the masses. It may have surprised Goebbels and his Jewish victims to know, that this principle that is so well understood, yet still works every time, owed its 2,600 years of successful application to the Judean priests and kings.

The purpose behind the propaganda employed by the Judean and Nazi regimes was primarily to maintain and tighten political control, then secondarily, to alter the beliefs, thinking and behaviour of the people. Nazi Germany's aim was to convince its people that they were racially superior, the master race. To achieve this, Goebbels invented an idealised, romantic, fantasy history, and in addition, forwarded the notion that the German people had always been hard done by, been betrayed, and were surrounded by racially inferior neighbours, ever ready to strike at and destroy them.

It is perhaps perversely ironic, that the greatest ever, as well as the earliest piece of monumental myth–making propaganda, was concocted in ancient Judea. It set out to create a glorious history, which showed that the Judeans were singled out by God and as his *chosen* people, were racially superior to all others who inhabit the earth. Unpalatable lowly ethnic beginnings, a history fraught with bleak times and defeats, constant pressure from more powerful neighbours, all were transformed into an ego–boosting glorious supernatural history — all were invented by a king and his priests. It was a history fashioned to be inexorably linked and utterly dependent upon its religion. It was written so that the stories would endure as solid foundations, would forever regale people and would serve as an awesome reminder of the dreadful consequences that befall those who fail to obey the 'Laws' from God absolutely.

With brilliant cunning, the king and priests created a god, an exclusive religion and a history, which would totally and passionately bind the people to the state. If times became tough, it would not be the king's fault, but would be a punishment from God, inflicted upon the people for failing to adhere to the 'Laws' in every detail.

It might sound harsh to liken Nazi philosophy to that of seventh and sixth–century Judea, but the Nazis were a pale shadow of the Judeans when the propaganda machine became extreme enough to justify ethnic cleansing on a massive scale in the second century BCE. Though in fairness, we must remember that we know the Nazi atrocities were real, such a charge only applies to the Judeans, if one believes that the Bible stories are actually true.

In our time of hypersensitivity to belief systems and cultures and awareness of what may or may not be politically correct, it might seem superficially offensive to point out such similarities, however historical use of propaganda is full of similarities and to shirk from the truth because of concern about offending sensibilities would be a weak and immoral excuse.

The underlying intent of propaganda is always the same and that is to control, but to have an unquestionable justification makes it easier for those seeking power to succeed. The propaganda does not need to be extreme or even malicious: do we not see that the United States is given to believe that it is superior to all other nations and that it too enjoys the special protection and favour of God; are not God and America constantly linked together in political statements and speeches?

The later Roman emperors, from the time of Constantine, also recognised that a rigid, centrally–controlled religion, founded upon supposed real history, could be a valuable political tool. It was far more effective to maintain tight control over the empire's subjects, by binding them together under a commonly shared religion — military force was always expensive, sometimes weak and often unpredictable. The rigidly–controlled fundamentalist religion practised by the Rome–based sect of 'literalist' Christians, ideally suited the Emperors' purpose. These Roman Christians, long separated from the esoteric knowledge of their religion, now believed that the Bible stories, Jewish and Christian, were actually true. The fact that this sect's 'literalist' beliefs were mocked and derided by bemused members of the sects who still had access to the esoteric teachers, was irrelevant to an emperor set on a political mission.

Over time the Roman leaders of the reinterpreted Christianity, pulled off the greatest propaganda coup of all time, not only by concocting a supposedly 'new and exclusively unique' religion, but also by inventing a history to give it credibility. It is the same old theme employed over again — but on this occasion, the consequences were to have a devastating effect upon the world, spanning nearly two thousand years of fraud and deception, from which thousands upon thousands died and millions are still suffering.

To understand how a religion and a history came to be created, we must first look at what supposedly transpired in the aftermath of Solomon's rule. At this stage, it is also important to point out, that the Jewish religion did not spring out of nowhere, neither was it a clean-sheet invention by the seventh-century priests of Jerusalem; it did owe much to the Moses' connection, but it was not as recorded in the Bible — but we shall look at this in due course.

As we already know, the stories concerning David and Solomon were not as written in the Torah. That does not mean that every aspect of the story was false, though clearly it was wildly exaggerated until it flew off into the unrestrained realm of fantasy. This period of history does correspond with the Israelites struggling to exert their *differences* over their neighbours, to become independent from the political and economic control of the Canaanite city-states. When independence calls, quarrelling tribes will temporarily bury their rivalries and fight together in a common cause — and in dire times, probably elect an overall ruler. This could well have been the background to the tribes' reluctant acceptance of Saul as their battle king in the Biblical account. Saul was suitable because he was from the tribe of Benjamin. As this was the smallest tribe and the least influential, Saul's appointment would be more acceptable to the larger factions than having a rival for a leader. Nevertheless, it is worth noting that the southern tribe of Benjamin was closely allied to the Judeans and David was a Judean, so one must wonder, despite Saul's late life 'bad press', if this part too, was just another invention of the Judean scribes.

But old rivalries rarely lie dormant for long and often, new ones are created. According to Biblical accounts, strife amongst the tribes seemed inherent and after Saul, the trouble continued brewing during David's reign. His son, Absalom killed his older brother, and then instigated a revolt; the younger son, Solomon was propelled forward, upon David's death to become the new king. According to the Bible, Solomon's son, Rehoboam became king, but the northern tribes, angered at his harshness and high taxes, decided to break away and appoint their own king. In the next two hundred years, various royal dynasties came and went in the north, but the Israelites' bitter rivalry with the Judean southerners continued largely unabated — once again, provided one accepts that what the Bible records say, is true.

Regardless of the veracity of the Biblical history, what is absolutely clear is that the northerners and southerners were always divided, even going as far back as the Middle Bronze Age. The two did share things in common, such as the regional language and a god called Adonay, though they both worshipped other regional gods as well, and they probably had some shared legends, but otherwise, there were many things that separated them. Their cultures and life-styles were different from each other. The north was a larger and more fertile land with economic prospects. This encouraged a more sedentary and agriculturally-based existence for its people, who maintained close links with their surrounding neighbours and had a more open, *cosmopolitan,* attitude, so that intermarriage was accepted.

The harsh highlands of the south meant the smaller population was obliged to live as semi-nomadic pastoralists and as happens with such remote and vulnerable people, the lifestyle engendered a policy of aloofness, defensive aggression, isolationism and segregation, shunning all neighbouring peoples and culminating in the elevation of their status to rank far above their supposed brethren in the north.

Inevitably, a clash of interests would surface. It seemed to have been there from the beginning and escalated as time went by. Although these two groups of loose-knit tribes shared certain things in common, it is questionable whether it is right to clump the two together as an ethnic group, since they were both merely former Canaanite outlanders, who developed certain individual characteristics in common. This may have had more to do with regional factors, than religio-ethnic ones. These people were not a united ethnic group of tribes that fled out of Egypt, but they were Canaanite villagers who formed locally *into* tribes. The reality is that the northern peoples had no real link with those of the south, other than being joint members of a regional movement, which had broken away from the lowland Canaanite city kingdoms. It is a perplexing problem, which has caused much heated debate amongst scholars, whether there ever really was a united kingdom of Israelites.[1] We only have the Bible that says so, but as has been shown many times over, the Bible is a totally unreliable historical source — there simply is no alternative or independent record, so there is no hard evidence to substantiate or refute the claims. This said, there might

---

[1] Na'aman, N. "The Contribution of the Amarna Letters to the Debate on Jerusalem's Political Position in the Tenth Century B.C.E."

[2] Lemche, N P. *The Old Testament: Between Theology and History*

have been some kind of temporary military unification in a time of war, but whether this possibility continued is obviously unknown. Certainly, it would be very strange if the more numerous and far wealthier northerners, once the fighting against aggressors from the coastal plain had stopped, should continue to accept as their high king, a southerner, an ex-shepherd, possible part-time bandit, from the far-off *badlands* of lowly Judea.

There are good reasons to believe that the David/Solomon kingship did not extend outside of their Judean realm. It is very possible that the larger and more powerful northern tribes, within the land of Israel, had always been independent and that the Judean rule had been just another piece of fantasy and propaganda concocted in later times by jealous and politically ambitious Judeans. However, there is another factor that could have fuelled a feud, a matter about which the Judean leaders would be unable to compromise. This point of disagreement has its roots in their religious beliefs, inherited from Egypt long ago; beliefs which, by this time, had become confused, misunderstood and reinterpreted into a new fundamentalist hybrid. This religious mongrel became exclusive and intolerant, and when mated with the Judeans' inferior and defensive mindset, its offspring grew up into an aggressive beast with notions of superiority, leading the Judeans to believe that they needed to eradicate all rivals.

The actual historical event which changed this ongoing feud between the two separate lands, came in the form of an invasion out of northern Mesopotamia by the ferocious Assyrians in the second half of the eighth century BCE. Initially, the Assyrians were bought off by the payment of a sizeable tribute and the Judeans swearing fealty. But this did not put a stop to the local warfare and the final act was played out when the kingdoms of Israel and Aram attacked Judea. The Judean king, Ahaz pleaded for the Assyrians to intervene on their behalf. This the Assyrians did with devastating effect, though not out of any affection for Judea, but for a desire for stability within their new empire and an opportunity of acquiring slaves. The supposed kingdom of Israel was invaded and totally destroyed.

A greater part of the population was enslaved and removed to Assyria and in their place, the Assyrians brought in new settlers to occupy the now largely-vacated land, though it appears that Israelite farmers in the remoter areas were allowed to stay, since the Assyrians would see no sense in disrupting the production of valuable agricultural produce. Those Israelites who managed to flee, were forced to seek sanctuary in Judea; and for the Judean authorities, a swelling of their population and an increase in their pool of fighting manpower was a much-needed bonus in those extremely dangerous times. Nevertheless, no sympathy was offered to what were supposed to be their brethren in the north and according to the gloating

Biblical tirade, the sinful Israelites got what they deserved — it was, of course, God's punishment. I suspect that the real truth was that Israel had been attacked because it had joined a northern alliance against Assyria and as a consequence suffered a retaliatory invasion. It is also highly likely, if only because of Judea's close proximity, that it too suffered a partial invasion, but bought off the invader with what wealth it could muster.

After a period of uneasy respite, the Assyrians suffered from internal problems following the death of their king, Sargon in 705 BCE. Judea and other states saw his death as an opportunity to throw off the Assyrian shackles and so entered into a regional alliance headed by Egypt. In 701 BCE, the Assyrians with their new king, Sennacherib, returned with a large formidable army. The new Judean king, Hezekiah paid what tribute he could — according to the Bible account — but then the Assyrians demanded total surrender. Hezekiah appealed to God for help and it came in the form of an angel who slew 185,000 of the besiegers, which then encouraged the rest to leave and return to Assyria — a very impressive account from the Judeans. Predictably, the Assyrian account written on Sennacherib's Prism — a clay hexagonal prism, engraved with the deeds of Sennacherib — says that it was the Assyrians who won and needless to say, there was absolutely nothing recorded about a rampaging angel.[3]

The real truth is that after having their country sacked and totally looted, the Judeans holed up within Jerusalem were forced to buy off the Assyrian invasion by paying a huge tribute. What is certain is that in the real world, rather than the fantasy world of the Bible, the small number of inhabitants of Jerusalem, could not have withstood the Assyrian army's onslaught, even if they were behind new solid walls. The heavily-armoured professional Assyrian soldiers with their array of siege towers, battering rams, scaling ladders and mining sappers, were well experienced at patiently working to overcome defensive fortifications. The only way they would have withdrawn is if they had been bought off and had been assured of future fealty.

Whatever the details were, the end result was that the kingdom of Israel was no more and that the Israelite refugees flooded southward. Within a single generation, the population of Jerusalem exploded from around one thousand inhabitants to some fifteen thousand and the size of the area increased from around ten acres to 150 acres, tightly packed with houses, inns and workshops. Out in the countryside, small insignificant villages grew in size, with some growing as big as towns. The demise of Israel and the protection that Judea bought from Assyria, had the effect of transferring the lucrative Arabian trade southwards to Jerusalem and Judea's wealth began a rapid growth. With a large population influx and rapid growth in wealth,

---

3 Luckenbill, D D. *The Annals Of Sennacherib*

came the true beginnings of Judean statehood, with the first signs of an administrative bureaucracy, public buildings, large building projects and manufacturing workshops. Hezekiah's rebellion was a disastrous hiccup, but one from which the Judeans quickly recovered.

Hezekiah died within three years of the siege and his successor, Manasseh, began his long reign by relaxing the strict religious reforms of his predecessor; this encouraged a rural economic revival and ensured wholehearted loyalty to the state. These were crucial times and the survival of Judea depended wholly upon what action Manasseh undertook. He made the right decisions and soon reversed the decline of Judea. The Assyrians were happy to restore Judea's status as 'favoured state,' especially since Judea's geographical position made it a strategic buffer zone against the Egyptians.

Despite all of his success in saving Judea and reviving their economic wealth, the Bible account of Manasseh has damned him as a sinful king. His successors chose to be offended by the fact that he had reversed Hezekiah's decision and allowed free worship in the country. The Biblical scribes were clever writers, but their masters were nothing if not petulant in their insistence that certain characters be portrayed as either pious or wicked. There are indications of some sort of coup-attempt, in which the perpetrators were slain, hence the Biblical reference to blood-letting, which also suggests that it was the survivors who blackened Manasseh's name.

Regardless of the political and religious undercurrents, the turnaround in Judea's state of affairs, gave rise to political ambitions of Judean expansion, particularly laying claim to the lands of the old defunct Israel. When Josiah became king, it rose to the top of his agenda, but to make his claim, he needed to justify his ambition and it is partly through this objective, that a new history came to be written, a history where the Judeans invented an ancestor who could lay unarguable claim to the northern lands — and this man they named Abraham.

So the seventh-century Judean scribes invented an appropriate ancestry. It was also necessary to include a source of their religion, which was alien to the region and was a secret religion that had once been the preserve of royalty and a select priesthood. From Abraham, 'the Father of his people', the epic drama rambled on, going from father to son, cleverly linking generation to generation, whilst throwing in astonishing tales of superhuman heroics, all leading deliberately onward to the glory time, when Judean David saved the northerners from the terrible Philistines and created a fabulous kingdom centred upon Jerusalem. This was then made even more fabulous by Solomon — the most glorious kingdom that ever existed — but was torn asunder by ungrateful idolatrous Israelites. Throughout these stories, a clear emphasis on the importance and seniority of Judea was cunningly intertwined — every important character had Judean links. To give this assertion credibility they make the unsubstantiated claim that the Patriarchs were buried in the cave of Machpelah in Hebron — in Judean territory.

Judea was portrayed as ever striving to live purely, whilst honouring their God and waging wars on idolatrous neighbours. The Israelites were constantly having their character blackened by accusations that they did not keep the 'Laws' and were condemned for worshipping foreign idols and intermarrying with unclean foreigners. Judea was God's kingdom, whilst Israel was a land plagued by idolatry, greed, wanton lust and murder. However, the truth is that Israel was an enlightened cosmopolitan country, a country that had possessed the economic and military clout to wield some political influence amongst its neighbours and to undertake limited military actions. Judea, by contrast, was a small insignificant backwater, with extremely limited manpower and wealth, but that is not the picture which has been passed down through history — for a very good reason, it was Judea that recorded its version of how things had been.

To give unchallengeable authenticity to all of this contrived history, Judea devised holy men singled out by God — the Prophets. Given at appropriate times, their prophecies appear to predict very accurately what was to come, and according to Biblical writings, the authenticity of the prophecies was eventually confirmed by the events of history — as written in the Bible! The words of the Prophets came from a direct line with God, so whatever took place was justified from above. In 1 Kings 13:1–2 an unnamed prophet rants against King Jeroboam who was officiating at a shrine at Bethel: "Behold, a son shall be born to the house of David. Josiah by name; and he shall sacrifice upon you the priests of the high places who burn incense upon you, and men's bones shall be burned upon you."

One must realise that these predictions were written down, after the events they referred to and that almost certainly, the predictions were a later invention contrived to match the earlier invented 'history'. In the case of the example above, this 'prophecy' was inserted to glorify King Josiah as God's choice, and thus justify his murderous ambitions and ethnic cleansing. It was all clever, but ultimately unsubtle propaganda, written by Judean priests, ensuring that Judeans were the good guys and Israelites were, at best, their black sheep brothers. The Judeans were shrewd enough not to make themselves whiter than white; through their crocodile tears, they lamented when certain of their kings strayed a little from God and their angry God punished them, justly, of course. By this clever contrivance, they were able to explain away their problems and military reverses, which of course they kept to a minimum, to ensure that their nation was always honoured and beloved by God.

So let us look at what allegedly occurred following King Solomon's death. This is where some semblance of real history begins, after the 'glorious empire' fantasies have been left behind and the Judean scribes had to contend with the reality of their own times where in that real world, they could no longer keep up the lie. First of all, to explain, or excuse the collapse of the golden empire, it was attributed to God's displeasure at Solomon's 'human weaknesses' and suitable prophecies were inserted with warnings of what would take place. Because Jerusalem was far from being the magnificent city the scribes described, with its majestic Temple and palace, this strongly suggests that this Biblical description must have been inserted after the city's destruction by the Babylonians and the people's long exile. Any earlier date and the people would have been witness to the fact that their city had none of the supposed wondrous buildings. Fortunately for these later scribes, the Babylonians had destroyed all the evidence, which would have exposed the sham; when the first of the Judeans returned home, the city was totally in ruins. It is worth reminding ourselves at this point, that in the records of the surrounding civilisations of Egypt, Phoenicia, Canaan and those within Mesopotamia, there was never a single mention of a powerful Israelite kingdom and empire, nor of Jerusalem being a wondrous city, which is a clear indication that these things were never there to be mentioned.

The 'history', that the Bible hands down to us, tells us that an official of Solomon's court, Jeroboam, usurped the leadership of the ten northern tribes which were to make up the kingdom of Israel, whilst Solomon's son, Rehoboam became rightful king of the two southern tribes of Judea and Benjamin, which made up the kingdom of Judea. To explain away this demise in Judean hegemony, the scribes attributed it to God's anger against both Solomon and his son for straying from the path of righteousness. In the fifth year of Rehoboam's reign, the scribes tell us that the Egyptian pharaoh, Shishak attacked Jerusalem and left with a tribute in treasure — this makes clear that it was God's punishment.[4] [5] Egyptian records authenticate this historical event, however, they do differ in some crucially important ways and give a true insight into what occurred and the true state of affairs in Judea.

The Egyptian records tell of their invasion into Canaan and of their victories against various peoples and at least 154 cities and villages.[6] The Canaanite cities were clearly the main target on the hit list and the Israelites

---

[4] 1 Kings 14:25

[5] 2 Chronicles 12:2

[6] Wilson, K A. *The Campaign of Pharaoh Shoshenq I into Palestine*

and Jerusalem, were deemed quite minor. These records deny the claim that there could have been a powerful kingdom and empire in Solomon's time, for not only had the Egyptians not heard of it, it clearly did not exist in any form when Shishak invaded just five years after Solomon's supposed demise, in 926 BCE. Even allowing for a kingdom that was split into two independent states, each would still be in possession of a share of their partitioned empire, and each would have a portion of the large army which held together and defended the conquered lands within that empire, but there had not been anything resembling that great powerful army, which Solomon supposedly had gathered into his service. It is unlikely that his son would have decided to dismantle such a necessary force, especially as he now had a new enemy in Israel.

One is forced to conclude, from the invasion, that during this period, both the Israelites and Judeans were militarily weak and had little wealth, and the 'great golden city of Jerusalem' was definitely not the golden capital of a great empire — certainly the Egyptians never found one. Modern-day historians know all this, so why are the facts ignored — the answer must be to maintain the lie, to preserve religious belief.

An interesting result of the Egyptian devastation of the Canaanite cities was that it left behind a power and economic vacuum and it was into this vacuum that the Israelite hill tribes of the north, expanded unheeded. There can be no doubt that it was the era following the Egyptian invasion, which saw the true growth of the northern tribes and their obtaining a modest degree of power and economic wealth within the region, while the arid southern kingdom of Judea continued to struggle in a state of impoverishment.

The Bible lists kings for both Israelite and Judean sides, descending from Solomon, but the fact is that there is no evidence to authenticate the existence of these early kings, though there is some secondary evidence to suggest that the later lineage, after Josiah's time, might be reasonably accurate — these kings, of course, being more or less contemporary with the first written accounts, which eventually became the Bible. Lists of kings might be true, but that does not mean that the events associated with them are truthful. Whether there had been any kind of 'united' kingdom under David and Solomon is highly questionable and not just logic, but hard evidence, would suggest that this scenario was extremely unlikely. Even if there had been a temporary military alliance and leadership of it given to a Judean warlord, the northern tribes would not have allowed this state of affairs to continue any longer than absolutely necessary. For the larger and more powerful northern tribes to be forced to stay under Judean rule, by a tribe that the northerners would consider to be their weaker, poorer and backward southern neighbours, would have been both unlikely and unenforceable. However, the Bible gives a picture of the northern tribes being kept under subjugation, with Solomon putting high taxes upon the Israelites and using them as forced labour. In reality, we must remember that there is absolutely no evidence for Solomon, nor his great buildings and wealth, so one must also be sceptical about any subjugation. For the numerically smaller and weaker tribe of Judeans to hold dominion, is so far fetched as to be preposterous.

But whatever the truth, the Bible goes on to describe a worsening relationship between the two kingdoms, which it claims came to a head when the Israelite king, Jeroboam, died and his son, Nadab, was overthrown in a military coup which supposedly annihilated the Jeroboam family. The new Israelite king Baasha declared war on Judea, thus escalating the hostility and finalising the bitter split. Baasha's son very briefly inherited the crown before being ousted in another military coup but then that leader was overthrown by yet another coup seven days later. The tone was set: Israel was portrayed as a place of instability, avaricious ambition and bloody murder. While we may not have the evidence to the contrary, it cannot be dismissed as just malicious propaganda, but it certainly gives one reason to doubt its veracity!

Omri was the next new Israelite king, but it was the son who succeeded him, who drew the greatest vilification and damnation from the south — this was the infamous Ahab and his wife Jezebel. In shocking and scandalous tales, the couple were portrayed as being the epitome of all that was sinful and evil. We have to be highly sceptical about these stories since there is absolutely no evidence to back up the Judean charges. We cannot know what really went on in Israel at that time, as the only record comes from the Judeans, who portrayed their enemy to the north as monsters. Yet in reality, even if *some* were bad, it is extremely unlikely that every one of them was morally degenerate, whilst the Judean kings were of high moral character. What we do know is that Israel grew in economic wealth and political standing with all its neighbouring kingdoms, which suggests good kingship, whilst Judea remained a poor backward country. Prophets such as Amos and Hosea make raging denunciations in the Bible, accompanied by accusations of corruption and idolatry that indicate a bitter jealousy on the part of Judea towards its wealthy northern neighbour.

As we have read, the eventual outcome of hostilities was when the Judeans, with supposed Assyrian military aid, happily saw the destruction of Israel. The majority of the Israelites were either killed or exiled as slaves and the Assyrians brought in other people to repopulate the captured country, under their rule. The largest part of the enslaved population was of those living in the cities and towns, as it appears that the Israelite or perhaps more correctly, Samaritan farmers in the remoter areas were allowed to continue working the land; the Assyrians wanted to keep the profitable rural economy, particularly around the hill country of Samaria.

The hapless majority of Israelites, those who were enslaved, were absorbed into the far-away lands of the Assyrian empire and in time, no doubt following an initial attempt to *preserve* all aspects of their ethnic culture and customs, would eventually weaken and change, so finally they became completely absorbed into the customs of their new lands and thus, if there ever were 'Israelites', they became lost to the world and became mere memories in ancient history.

As a result, there was an extremely important, but often ignored, tragic loss — a literary and historical loss. If the northern tribes had survived as a nation, then critical alternatives would also have survived — an alternative history and also an alternative religion, with its own priests and prophets. These, I don't doubt, would have offered a very different account of all aspects of Jewish and Christian religion and history, from that which is generally accepted today. The victors write history, which in this case is basically true, except that the Judean scribes were more the fortunate survivors, than the victors. Following the destruction of 'Israel' and its people, there was in reality, no-one left to challenge the Judean version of things. The 'Israelite' refugees, who escaped to seek refuge in Judea, would have been humbly grateful at being allowed shelter, so they would have had neither the inclination, nor the ability to challenge any views held by their hosts.

This now was the world which affected the thinking and needs of the seventh-century Judeans. Their cousins in the neighbouring northern lands were largely gone, their rivals were no more, their own existence — though having gained new trade and wealth — was precarious and dependent upon the whims of a ferociously aggressive empire of conquerors. A change of attitude was called for, a redefining of purpose, a need to unite the people, a need to bolster their self-confidence and self-belief. Like any country which is threatened, its people unite, draw inwards, consolidate; they reassure themselves how strong and resilient they are. Old myths and legends are revived which recount great heroic tales of victories fought against the odds and what better way to reassure a people than to tell them how they have the special protection of the one and only God — who was their own and shared by no-one else. It was necessary also to be selectively inclusive of the refugees, now amongst them. The story had to show that the northerners shared a common ancestry with the Judeans, that they were family, but the story had to show in quite certain terms that the Judeans were superior and that the 'Israelites' had destroyed the glorious united kingdom, had strayed — misled by wicked kings — into sinful ways and thus had brought about their own downfall by provoking the terrible wrath of Adonay. So now the

Israelite refugees were being given a chance to reject their past, to be 'born again' and become 'God-fearing' Judeans and subjects of the Judean king.

Besides justifying political ambitions of expansionism and forming a united Judean–Israelite kingdom, religious ambitions came to the fore. In this new state with its new-found wealth and influence, having a disparate number of religions would have been seen as a threat to stability and centralised control. Throughout Israel and Judea, other gods had been worshipped alongside Adonay, but it was really only during the reign of the Judean king Hezekiah, that action was taken to adopt a stricter faith. Hezekiah made it his task to put a halt to the alternative religions. The traditional places of worship were altars, set up at what were called 'high places' and in groves, and these, together with idols, were outlawed. The Bible also states that Hezekiah broke the brazen serpent made by Moses, whilst demanding that the Laws of Moses be strictly adhered to; this peculiar action seems contradictory, even sacrilegious, however, if Hezekiah understood that Moses was merely a fictional character, breaking a fabricated idolatrous treasure was of no importance, or real loss and made a point that idols were not to be tolerated — in this course of action, we will see later on, he was merely following the example set long ago in Egypt by an Egyptian king. To Hezekiah and his Judahite priesthood, it was formulating religious laws, that was of primary importance, for these would control the minds and actions of the people, who would be subjected to their exclusive God's protection and also implacable wrath, if they transgressed.

In reality, Hezekiah fell well short of his ambition to outlaw the other religions and their gods. The sudden attempt to put a stop to the traditional religious practices, engendered strong and bitter resentment, especially in the rural villages, where, as with all rural dwellers, the traditional ways and religious practices are deeply ingrained and fiercely adhered to.

For some inexplicable reason, Hezekiah did not heed the fate of Israel at the hands of the Assyrians. It makes one wonder whether this is a repeat scenario, or perhaps Israel and Judea did fall to them at the same time. Whatever the case, Hezekiah's folly of seeking to overthrow Assyrian control by joining an alliance with other neighbouring kings, provoked a savage reprisal. The Assyrians laid waste to most of Judea and took control of most of the land, and Hezekiah was forced to pay a heavy tribute to save himself and Jerusalem. This disaster brought down the wrath of the rural priests, who laid the blame for this reckless debacle at the king's feet, accusing him of angering the old gods by destroying the altars at the venerated high places. The king's position was now extremely tenuous, he could not afford any possibility of insurgence within the fragile remains of his decimated kingdom and this led to a pragmatic unofficial relaxation of his edict banning alternative beliefs, in order to *buy back* the support of the people.

Within three years of this disaster, Hezekiah died and his twelve-year-old son, Manasseh took the throne. During this period, the old traditional shrines, including some in Jerusalem itself, were re-established. This picture shows that the somewhat loose-knit confederation of tribal villages which composed the Judean people, was far from being united in following the one God, Adonay. In the Bible, Manasseh is condemned as being a sinful monarch, but the reality was that he was a pragmatist and that he understood what needed to be done to salvage the fortunes of Judea and to save her people from further military onslaughts. Manasseh aligned himself closer to the Assyrians and busied himself with the task of rebuilding the devastated economy. To do this, he needed the full support of all the people, so he set aside the strict reforms of his father and ran a relaxed regime, which allowed his people to worship as they pleased. Naturally, this moderation did not sit well with the strict Judean priesthood, who, after Manasseh's death, took revenge by blackening his character.[7]

Whatever his detractors thought of him, despite the loss of rich farmlands by his father to the Assyrians, Manasseh worked miracles by reviving the economy; vine and olive orchards expanded and the population increased. But to the priests his relaxed religious policy was all that mattered and it was an anathema, so Manasseh was forever to be known as an abomination, whereas his father's disastrous folly of going to war, the terrible defeat and loss of lives, the great loss of land and collapse of the economy, were ignored. Instead, he was lauded as a great and heroic king, who had saved Jerusalem with the aid of Adonay. Right from the start of literacy arriving in Judea, it was the scribes who defined what the history should be and truth was dispensed with, in preference to political and religious propaganda.

Following on from Manasseh's long and bountiful fifty-six-year reign, his son, Amon, had a short rule of under two years before he was assassinated in an attempted *coup d'état*. The conspirators were slain and Amon's eight-year-old son, Josiah, was put on the throne. Things continued for a while, much as they did under Manasseh's rule and the young king, whatever his ambitions, had to wait for adulthood and ensured security, before setting off in pursuit of any changes. According to the Biblical account, it was not until the eighteenth year of his rule that Josiah was able to surmount the difficulties experienced by his predecessors and bring about a transformation in religious practice.

---

7   2 Kings 21: 3-7

After eighteen years of kingship, Josiah would probably have surrounded himself by loyal followers within the court, military and priesthood and he would have built up the strength of his army, thereby giving himself a stronger position to counter any risks of insurgency from inside the palace, as well as out in the countryside. It was in this nineteenth year, during the renovations of the Temple, which Josiah had ordered, that supposedly, a long–lost religious text was rediscovered. This convenient find revealed that the religious practices of the Adonay cult had been flawed and that the commandments contained within the 'rediscovered' text, demanded a strict absolute adherence to the Laws and that all idolatrous religious practices must cease. This text, so scholars believe, is what we now know as original writings which made up the book of Deuteronomy, giving the basis for a centrally–based monotheism and outlining the religious festivals and observances, the moral and judicial laws.[8] This is probably when the Laws of Moses were formulated, including his story of the Ten Commandments. Typical of Biblical texts, there is confusion and contradiction over the tale of how this occurred: Exodus tells us that Moses received the Commandments on Mount Sinai, but then Deuteronomy states that it was at Mount Horeb; Exodus first claims that the stone tablets were engraved by God, but three chapters on, says that it was done by Moses. Nevertheless, the consequence of this profound discovery of these divine revelations given in this supposed long–lost text, gave Josiah the moral authority and excuse to undertake the religious and political reforms first instigated by Hezekiah: to make an effective purge of all 'pagan' cults and their shrines.

By Josiah's period, Assyrian power had gone into serious decline and pressure in their homelands caused them to withdraw control over their western empire; in contrast, the Egyptians were experiencing a power revival and had taken control of the Canaan coastal plain to the west of Judea. With the political climate being so unrestricted and fluid, eventually, Josiah felt confident enough to pursue a long–held Judean ambition. With his army, he marched into the old Israelite lands. Finding himself largely unhindered, he extended his land grabbing northwards, whilst, according to the Bible, carrying out a destructive purge, by obliterating the old Israelite shrine at their sacred place of Bethel and slaughtering all the priests he could find. Whether this actually happened we cannot know, for we don't know if the now–departed Assyrians left any shrines untouched when they invaded Israel or whether they left any priests behind, instead of deporting them as slaves, when they went. The story could simply have been another

---

[8] Wright, C. *Deuteronomy New International Bible Commentary*

contrivance to make the point that the old religions were dead and now there was only one God, one religion.

Whether truth or invention, the story was meant to convey the final eradication of every vestige of possible opposition from those left in the old land of Israel and from within Judea itself. The alternative religious centre at Bethel, which had rivalled Jerusalem for so long, was no more and those refugee Israelites dwelling in Judea, had now only the Judean religion of the Jerusalem Temple. In a later chapter, we look at how this story may well have been an invention, or at least a gross exaggeration by much later scribes, who needed to re-adapt the fictional history to give a precedent which would justify the actions of the Hasmonean rulers of Judea in the late second century. Whether Josiah's destructive invasion actually took place, has a serious question mark hanging over it.

There was still work to be done to secure Josiah's achievements, as well as justifying his actions and ambitions, for Josiah knew that the people under his rule were still feeling fragmented and that their loyalties still were to their traditional tribes and village communities rather than to the Judean king. Experience would have taught him that their traditional religious faiths were not to be simply changed overnight. To achieve a lasting and permanent transformation, it was necessary to create a common heritage. To this end, Josiah, having understood that this one thing more than any other would draw together a disparate people, encouraged his priestly scribes to compose a history suitable for all his people, to strengthen their resolve and commitment and to justify any territorial expansionist dreams. Josiah would give his people a history that was to be an account of how they came into being and how they came to have a religion that honoured just one god. In a region where the majority of the population had followed a myriad of traditional regional gods and goddesses, it appears that Josiah succeeded where Hezekiah had failed, in converting the largely rural people to this one-god religion.

The religion had long been exclusive to a particular priestly sect and to the ruling elite. It was a religion which had long been preserved, it was an imported alien religion, it was one which had gradually disguised its true origins and meanings and yet now in subtle ways, it became transformed to suit a new nation with its own particular needs. How successful Josiah actually was, we don't know, for the continuity that might have given historians the answer, was to be broken by the Babylonian invasion. Unfortunately, it also remains unknown whether the northern Israelites had followed the same religious practices; the fact that the Judean priesthood were so intent upon totally destroying the Israelite priesthood, suggests that they had some important religious knowledge which the politically motivated Judeans needed to hide. An alternative, more open version of their religion would have totally undermined the Judean political ambitions.

What is beyond any doubt is that this was the time when literacy first appeared in Judea and that it was the period in which what was to become the Hebrew Bible, first began to be formed.[9] Perhaps some of it first began to be formulated during Hezekiah's reign, but scholars' investigations into literary styles of Deuteronomy indicate that the period of its writing was in Josiah's time.[10] After the Assyrian invasion of Israel, when Judea was merely a puppet state, a new hybrid language arose, one which is known as Mishnaic Hebrew and which revealed to linguists, that the Bible was first written between the Assyrian invasion and the Babylonian captivity. It is believed that Genesis was written post–exile. What is less clear, is exactly when, and to what degree, the priestly scribes gathered together the many disparate tribal myths and legends, cherry–picked those which would be of particular use and cut and pasted them into a linear 'historical' story, into which the preserved religion of the Judahite priesthood was woven in its new form. It is likely that it began in the Hezekiah–Josiah period and was then heavily revised and extended during the exile, while further additions and re–editing took place in the final two centuries of the millennium; in other words, it was a continuous process over some four hundred years.

A critical flaw that the scribes made in the writing of Biblical history was to set the stories into their own contemporary world. It was the only world they knew; they were not historians, nor geographers, they were not well travelled, so their knowledge and understanding of former times was extremely limited. There were no historical records prior to this time, so they would not have realised that things had changed, that in the past much had been very different. This accounts for the inaccuracies and flaws, which expose the Bible to be largely a fictional historical record, not a true one. It is also very clear that the writings glorified Josiah and endorsed his reign as the religious high–point in his people's history, the culmination of everything which had gone before and an event no less important than God's covenant with Abraham, Moses' leading the Exodus and God's promise to David. Clearly, one can detect the hand of sycophantic scribes. The evidence for this can be seen in the Biblical narratives found in 2 Kings 23. They contain all the great characters from Judean and Israelite history and compare them to Josiah, then the reforms instigated by Josiah are pronounced to be a holy purge to wash away the sins of their nations past and allow a new pure relationship with God.

---

9 Levine, E., "How the Bible Became a Book: Textualization in Ancient Israel"

10 Weinfeld, M. "Deuteronomy, Book of,"

It was in fact a new beginning; it was a new united nation, with new strict laws dictating the social, moral and religious life, which had to be adhered to by its entire people, and to protect itself, it excluded all outsiders. The years of propaganda had worked.

Chapter 7

Holy Book of Horrors

"The best political weapon is the weapon of terror. Cruelty commands respect. Men may hate us. But, we don't ask for their love; only for their fear."
Heinrich Himmler

Josiah had brought about a new beginning, new religion, new laws, new united nation, but Josiah had fallen into an old trap: he became greedy. Josiah's thirty-year reign came to a dramatic end when he was slain at Megiddo, by Egyptian hands. The shocked scribes glossed over Josiah's demise, but he had probably paid the ultimate price for his political and territorial ambitions.

It appears that Josiah's social and religious reform movement stalled on his death. Certainly times became extremely unsettled and in fairly rapid succession, four monarchs came and went, within just a decade. Three of the kings were Josiah's sons and the fourth was his grandson. With the collapse of the Assyrian empire, the Babylonians became the new ambitious power-brokers. In the twelfth year after Josiah's death, during the reign of his grandson, Jehoiakim, the Babylonian army besieged Jerusalem. The king surrendered and he and the Judean aristocracy and priests, with numerous artisans and warriors, were taken back to Babylon.

This was the first step in the dismantling of the Judean kingdom. The Babylonian king, Nebuchadnezzar put Jehoiakim's uncle Zedekiah on the throne to rule his vassal state. In the end, Zedekiah proved to be anything but a docile puppet king and after ten years, he joined an alliance that sought to overthrow the Babylonian rule. The Bible records that the Babylonian army returned to Judea. They sacked all the Judean towns and then finally Jerusalem fell. Judea was totally laid to waste and Jerusalem and its Temple to Adonay, were destroyed. Most of its people were taken as slaves into Babylonia, but some, including numerous priests and amongst them the prophet Jeremiah, escaped and of all the places they could have fled to, chose their traditional enemy, Egypt as their protector. For the priests to choose the 'enemy' Egypt is not as strange as it may appear, for Egypt was their spiritual home, the homeland of the ancestors of the priests of Adonay.

Was the Bible telling the truth about this great exile into slavery — well, no it was not, for archaeology has shown a very different picture. Although Jerusalem had indeed been completely destroyed and left deserted, other towns such as Bethel, Gibeon and Mizpah continued to be important settlements, which survived without disruption. At Mizpah, evidence was found to show that here, just eight miles north of Jerusalem, was the new political centre from which the remaining Judeans enjoyed a degree of self-government.[1] The fact is that Judea was not totally devastated and empty and that much of Judea carried on as it had always done, but now under Babylonian rule. There is no knowing exactly how many Judeans went into enforced exile, but the latest research indicates that at the very most, only some twenty thousand would have been deported as slaves, whilst at least three quarters of the population remained in place.[2]

Unlike the Assyrian destruction of Israel, with its consequent deportation of most of the population and their replacement with foreigners, the Babylonian invasion had been far less devastating. What seems to have happened was that only the Judeans who had any kind of political power were taken away: this meant royalty, priests and court officials. The Babylonians would also have taken those of some practical use such as scribes, artisans and toolmakers and their families, whilst any captured warriors would be enlisted into the Babylonian army. The great tragic exile and an empty ruined Judea, was yet another myth, or at least a colossal exaggeration

Academics know that much of the Bible, that we call the Old Testament, was written, revised and added to, during this captivity. There is plenty of evidence which definitely links much of the Biblical compositions to this precise period, continuing the work begun in the days of King Josiah; though ultimately the final compiling, editing and additions and the its tone of merciless brutality, came even later, in the second and first centuries BCE.[3] Since the Judean religion did not appear to offer any threat, the Babylonians allowed the Judahites the freedom to worship as they wished. As might be expected when people are exiled and enslaved, many will draw closer together for comfort and they hold on more tightly to their traditions and religious practices, though some choose the alternative and believe the best and easiest course is to assimilate themselves fully into the culture of

---

[1] Coogan, M D. ed. *The Oxford History of the Biblical World*
[2] Finkelstein, I & Silberman, N A. *The Bible Unearthed*
[3] Eskenazi, T C. *In an Age of Prose: A Literary Approach to Ezra-Nehemiah*

their new homeland. For those determined to hold on to their beliefs and culture, the enforced exile turned their religion back to fundamentalism.

There was, however, an extremely serious problem, which the priests had to address immediately, to make their religion acceptable to their captors, and that was the very obvious Egyptian connection. The Babylonians and Egyptians were bitter enemies and the Judeans' lives would have been in jeopardy, had the Babylonians realised the true source of their captives' religion. So it came about, that the Judahite scribes must make a hasty rewrite of their books and eradicate the Egyptian roots of their religion, or at the very least disguise them beyond recognition.

During the exile, the name for their Lord God was altered to hide its Egyptian source. Though Adonay continued to be used as the spoken name, in its written form, which would be open to public scrutiny, they decided to use the form of four letters, YHWH. Although this name was never meant to be spoken aloud, the individual letters would be spoken as Yod–Heh–Vau–Heh, nowadays more generally combined and pronounced as Yahweh. The Dead Sea Scrolls make it evident that to begin with, this new name was neither widely nor readily accepted by the Judahite priesthood. This clearly reveals that Yahweh was not the original name given to God but a later insertion, indicating that where the name appears in the Bible prior to the Babylonian exile, it was because it gave an Egyptian link but didn't *sound* Egyptian.

It would perhaps be pertinent at this point, to consider the matter of the Hebrew language and its written alphabet. Though scholars insist that the Hebrew alphabet was derived from the Phoenician/Canaanite alphabet, especially as they both have twenty–two letters, this belief has never been more than an unproved theory. The flaws in the belief are shown up when one studies the individual characters of both alphabets, for their forms reveal them to be very different. In fact only four characters in the two alphabets show the slightest similarity. However, when one compares the Hebrew letters against the appropriate Egyptian hieroglyphs, there is an astonishing match, which can leave little doubt, other than stubborn prejudice, that one is derived from the other.[4]

If that is indeed so, we should be able to see it in the sacred Hebrew name for God, YHWH, so let us compare the two against each other. The Hebrew Y, or Yod character has a match with the Egyptian hieroglyph called Yod — which represents the Great God, creative energy of the universe and in its hieroglyph form, is that of the Reed, which is the image of the king of Upper and Lower Egypt. The Hebrew Heh has a matching

---

[4] Massey, G A. *Book of The Beginnings*

hieroglyph, which represents the Divine Breath. The Hebrew Vau or Vav again has a matching hieroglyph, which represents the horned viper and the fiery door of the temple. Because Vau or Vav, is read as 'U' and Heh is mute, so in the pronouncing of Yahweh, it should really sound like Yahu

Significantly, this name Yahu, is first found in an Aten temple built at Soleb by Amenhotep III and the particular inscription reads, 'The House of Yahu in Shasu land.'[5] The Shasu, a Semitic people, were brought as prisoners by Thutmosis II, from the land that was later to become Edom, and were resettled in Egypt at Soleb. It is probable that Yahu was their local deity, but now as Egyptians, their god would be the pharaoh. The likelihood is that they gave the name Yahu to Amenhotep — who was also titled, 'Radiant Aten' — so the Sashu would have referred to the Temple of Aten, as the House of Yahu. This piece of evidence, though slender, is the first recording of the name and because of the Atenist link and the close proximity of Edom to Judea, it is not too unsafe to surmise that the name YHWH and thus Yahweh came from this source.

That Babylon and Egypt were sworn enemies is absolutely crucial to how the Bible came to be written in the form passed on to all the subsequent generations of not only Jews, but also Christians and Muslims. It is quite intriguing that the Bible paints the Egyptians as the great idolatrous enemy and has the exiled prophet, Jeremiah, ranting continually against his protecting hosts. Yet, if one considers the matter from a different standpoint, this Egyptian sanctuary appears far from strange. What the enslaved Judahite scribes were certainly not going to do, since Babylon and Egypt were sworn enemies, was explain why so many of their people felt at home in Egypt, for to do so, would enrage their captors. Likewise, the probability is that Jeremiah's contradictory tirades against his hosts were most likely not his words, but ones that were later ascribed to him, with the purpose of hiding the actual truth. That Jeremiah was advising the exiled Judeans how they should live in Babylonia[6] should alert one to the dubious authenticity of these words. The prophet was then living far away, by the Nile and had no contact with his enslaved people residing forcibly along the Euphrates. Neither would the scribes in Babylon know what Jeremiah might have said in far away Egypt, but they could *imagine* what his words might have been.

This is possibly another example of character invention, for outside of Biblical accounts, there is no evidence of Jeremiah's existence. Whether he was real or not, it was certain that those of the Judahite priesthood who had evaded capture by the Babylonians had returned to their spiritual homeland

---

[5] Sabbah, M & Sabbah, R. *Secrets of the Exodus*
[6] Jeremiah 29:5-6

of Egypt.[7] The Egyptian authorities would never allow enemy priests to settle in their country and of course they did not. The true situation would almost certainly have been that the priests of Ra at Heliopolis gave sanctuary to the Judean descendants of their exiled priestly brotherhood, unbeknown to the rival Amun priesthood in Thebes. These earlier exiles from Egypt had, long before, been relocated to the remote north–eastern boundaries of the Egyptian empire, to the lands along the river Jordan; they had been the exiled priests of the monotheistic Atenists.[8]

Little is actually known about what occurred during the period of the Babylonian exile, since the Judean scribes chose to omit any details of this time. After about fifty years, the Babylonians' grip on imperial power came to an end when, following internal troubles, the Persians invaded in 539 BCE. The Persian king, Cyrus, then allowed some of the captives of the Babylonians, people from many lands, to return home.

Initially, those who returned to Judea, now called Yehud by the Persians, were small in number and were largely 'trustee' Judahite priests who were totally loyal to their new masters. The Persian's release of the Judeans was not motivated by a kind heart, but rather by an astute policy that traded cultic religious freedoms for political loyalty. Though the first to return were insignificant in number, the status bestowed on them, by their Persian overlords, afforded them immense authority. For their old countrymen, who had remained in Judea, the Judahite priesthood — the priests of Moses — had returned.

The royal family were no longer the rulers, they remained captive 'guests', so Judea was given a Persian–appointed governor to oversee political affairs. But in every other aspect of life in the new satellite state of Yehud it was the priesthood who exerted absolute control and they had the Persians to enforce that 'their will be done'. Finally and crucially, the priests were able to banish all religions other than their own from their land; no more would the rural villagers be able to exert pressure upon Jerusalem and retain their old traditional deities.

If one were to judge the loyalty of these returnee priests to their original religion and to their former king and country, one could not call them anything other than traitors. These returning priests, whom the Persians paid to enforce *their* laws, vehemently condemned the life styles and practices of their countrymen who had remained in Judea. They enforced harsh, newly revised religious and moral practices and laws upon them. These were not motivated by any spiritual insights gained in Babylon, but a

---

[7] op cit Sabbah, R

[8] Collins, A. & Ogilvie-Herald, C. *Tutankhamun – The Exodus Conspiracy Mystery*

means to do the job the Persians had given them. In Ezra 4:3, we see the Judahite priesthood now promoting a hard–line policy, meant to exclude every foreigner. When the Samaritans offered to aid the rebuilding of the Temple, they were sent packing with the rebuke 'you have nothing to do with us in building a house to our God'. And again in Ezra 10:16, Ezra demanded that the men of Judah and Benjamin separate themselves from foreigners and even from their foreign wives. We again see the Judahites making themselves an exclusive race with an exclusive God and an exclusive religion. At this point, it is necessary to inject a degree of caution; as has been shown, in any Biblical text there is a question of authenticity. In the above story, there are very strong elements again of religious extremism and it is an indication that though the event may have had some historical basis, there very likely had been some further hard–line doctrines inserted into the account by fanatical Judaean scribes sometime during the second century BCE.

The returning priesthood had another problem to face when they got home, they had the awkward task of having to explain to their people, why Jerusalem fell to the Babylonians and why their God had allowed it to happen. This they solved by shifting the blame onto the people, saying that it had been God's punishment for past misdemeanours and for failing to live up to the Laws. The solution had been so simple, no need for complex excuses, but most of all it also acted as a dire warning that the people had to toe the line in future.

Another thing that the priests promoted, which they had invented whilst in exile, was that their return out of Babylon was a glorious mirror of the Moses Exodus story. When they wrote down the story of the original priesthood's exile out of Egypt, it was necessary for them to disguise and encode the real facts and to cast Egypt as the villain — a vilification that would please their new Babylonian masters. During the exile amongst the Babylonians, the Abraham story was contrived into yet another exodus story, with the hero, their nation's invented father portrayed as a citizen of Chaldean Ur. The ambiguity of which city of Ur it was supposed to be did not really matter. Indeed the duality suited the plan perfectly: the famous southern Ur of the Sumerians gave a shared ancestry with their Babylonian overlords and also afforded them the prestige of originating in that centre of civilisation, whilst the northern Ur, near Harran, retained the Judahite priesthood's secret connection with the Egyptian star religion.

The truth of the exiles' return to Judea was different from the story they told. It was not a second mass exodus of the 'Chosen People', joyously returning to the 'Promised Land', whilst giving grateful thanks to their God who had freed them. The exiles did not flood back *en masse* at all, but rather a small number trickled back over a very long period of some one hundred and fifty years. The reason for this was two-fold, I suspect. Firstly, the release had not been altruistic, but a tactical political ploy. The Persians had not released all the Babylonian slaves captured from all over the Middle East, but rather they allowed a limited and controlled return to their homelands. It would not be economically sensible to deny yourself such a large work force. The second reason was, that the captives had settled into their new bountiful homeland and had established roots; some would be second generation and married to other captive workers from various lands; most had no urgent desire to return to their old homeland with its harsh environment and even harsher laws and restrictions on personal freedoms, imposed by religious zealots; they would be returning to lost homes and possessions, and confiscated land — life was better where they were.

It is certain that a great many never returned at all and most definitely not the artisans and soldiers — skilled people that the Persians would not wish to lose. Only those who would not be of any use to the Persians would be free to leave and they would be few in number. Those belonging to the exclusive Adonay sect could go, for their religious zeal allied to assurances of loyalty, meant they would be of great service by returning to Judea to control those of their old countrymen, who had avoided slavery and exile. So the true facts were covered up, for it would be quite an embarrassment if it were known that the majority of the *Chosen People of God* had *chosen* to stay behind in Babylon and thus forsaken both their *land of milk and honey* and the god who gifted it to them.

And so the era for the Yehud — the Jews — had begun. Their country was now a small province within the large Persian empire. They had a king no more, only a foreign governor who dictated political life; every other aspect of their daily lives was ruled by a priesthood who demanded absolute obedience to the Book of the Laws and absolute allegiance to their one god, Adonay/Yahweh and failure to obey would provoke that god's psychopathic wrath. Old myths now started to become history, whilst real history was hidden, a loving god was distorted into a vengeful god — truth became what the priesthood wished it to be.

Mainly due to political necessities, sheer survival and zealous ambition, the Judahite priests had corrupted their religion and disguised its true origins. However, the sacred inventions had not quite finished and another final round of creative writing at the instigation of political necessity and ambition, was yet to occur a couple of centuries later on, near to the end of the millennium.

Under the Persians and during a long period of peace, Jerusalem prospered, at least compared to previous times, but by the mid-fourth century, the storm clouds were gathering again. Alexander the Great and his Greek army swept into the near east and sent the Persians reeling in defeat. Once the Persian Empire had collapsed and had been replaced by that of the Greeks, the middle-eastern world changed in character. The new world which Alexander had envisaged, sought to break down national and ethnic barriers, there was to be freedom of movement, freedom of trade, freedom of religious and philosophical beliefs, a commonwealth of man; men were to be the cosmopolitans — promoted by the Pythagorean philosophers and the initiates of the Eleusian Mystery religion.

To the frustration of the Jerusalem priesthood, it lost not only political power, but also its authority to exclude outside religions from returning to Judea. The world had changed, it became Hellenised — affected by all spheres of Greek influence. It was like a breath of fresh air sweeping into the world, it offered new things, it was 'modern', it became fashionable to copy the Greeks. In northern Palestine, the lands that had once been Israel, including such places as Bethlehem, Capernaum and Galilee, became heavily Hellenised — Galilee was actually known as the 'land of the Gentiles'. It was not only Greek culture and often the Greek language that was adopted, but also their religion — the region of Galilee became a centre for Mystery cults.[9]

Over time, regional variations, 'localised' adaptations of the Eleusian Mysteries, were formulated. For the better educated and wealthier Jews, the Mysteries offered a more intelligent understanding of God; for Jewish women, the Mysteries offered something else, freedom and equality, it allowed them to throw off the shackles of subordination which male-dominated Judaism demanded. In the new Greek city of Alexandria in Egypt, many from the very large immigrant Jewish community, converted to the Mysteries; amongst them numerous women, who eagerly grasped this new-found freedom and sought education at the Greek academies, with some rising to become respected philosophers, mathematicians, scientists and doctors.

An interesting and revealing event, which occurred in 270 BCE, throws a new light on life in the 'holy' city of Jerusalem. Hezekiah, the High Priest, together with many of his friends and associates, abandoned Jerusalem and emigrated to Alexandria. This splendid cosmopolitan city with its reputation of being the world's centre of learning, was made more attractive to the Jews because it afforded them favourable status, in gratitude for the help given to Alexander by Jewish exiles. The city was attractive to anyone seeking a better life. In stark contrast, Jerusalem, by then a small city, was no place of splendour; it was an isolated, bleak, claustrophobically cramped parochial backwater. It was also an unstable place filled with rival groups of

---

9 Mack, BL. *The Lost Gospel*

bigoted religious zealots, who were intolerant towards other religions and despised all foreigners; who also fought viciously amongst themselves. It says much when the High Priest felt disposed to desert the 'sacred city of God'. Hezekiah's move to Alexandria is indication that the more learned amongst the Judean priesthood, did not see their people as *special*, but rather that they understood that they were a part of cosmopolitan mankind. It also indicates that Hezekiah knew that his religion and god were not exclusive to his people and as High Priest, he was also fully aware of his religion's Egyptian roots.

Despite the unhelpful threatening undercurrent posed by the zealots, Judea prospered under Greek control far more than it had ever done in the past and Jerusalem flourished and for the first time, grew into a genuine city, albeit a modestly-sized one. The Greeks introduced the backward world of Palestine to the many benefits of Hellenisation — just like British imperialists introduced the modern world of the 19th Century to eastern kingdoms still living in oppressed middle-age societies. Agriculture flourished, modernised through the introduction of not only the plough and better farming tools, but also waterwheels, waterscrews, irrigation channels and the addition of Greek know-how to grow vines and olives. In the city, the Greeks introduced better techniques for pottery and metalworking and they also dragged the Judeans into the modern world, dispensing with trading through barter and introducing coins as currency. Perhaps the greatest gift, and curse, that the Greeks brought to Jerusalem, was the gymnasium — their name for a university. Many Judeans, including many of the priesthood, grabbed at this free opportunity enthusiastically and dedicated themselves to study. Whilst learning about the philosophy of Socrates, Plato and Aristotle, the poetic stories of Homer and the histories as compiled by such men as Herodotus, could only bring benefits to everyone, learning to read and write was also a double-edged sword. Discovering how stories, both mythical and historical, could have a big impact upon the minds of people did not always have a positive effect. Too soon, the negative potential was starting to surface.

A small number of Judeans began to make fantastic claims at the expense of their benefactors, almost certainly because of the ingrained religious propaganda that made the Judeans superior to all other races because they were God's special people. Clearly peeved at being educated by the 'inferior' Greeks, they redressed this disagreeable situation, by writing a new history. Judean writers, despite their Greek names like Aristobulus and Hermippus claimed that their Judean ancestors had actually taught the Greeks. Hermippus asserted that Pythagoras had received his wisdom from the Jews and Aristobulus reinforced the ridiculous proposition by stating that Plato and Aristotle had plagiarised Moses. They also extravagantly asserted that Moses had created all the inventions attributed to the Greeks, that the Greeks had read Judean books and even claimed that Moses had taught the Egyptians how to write in hieroglyphs.[10] The fact that the Egyptians could write at least two thousand years before the alleged time of Moses, or that the Hebrews did not have any books of any kind, let alone ones in a language the Greeks could read, seems to have been overlooked. Perhaps these Judean fantasists skipped the classes in logic when it was taught at the Jerusalem Gymnasium.

Once the ball was rolling, the extravagant inventions continued unchecked and truth was confidently cast aside like an unnecessary encumbrance. Having usurped the position of honour afforded to the Greek sages, the great Alexander was next to be put in his place. Alexander never personally went into Judea, let alone Jerusalem, but the fantasists had it that he had been there. In their version of history, when Alexander set eyes upon the magnificent Judeans in their splendid shining white robes, overwhelmed by the glory of God which emanated from them, he fell to his knees before the High Priest of the Temple. Turning to his companions, Alexander then revealed that in a dream, he had seen this priest and that he had told him to conquer Persia. The priest then revealed to Alexander, that it had been God's communication to him and then he showed Alexander the Book of Daniel, which contained the prediction that a Greek would overthrow Persia. The Book of Daniel, experts date to the second century BCE, well after Alexander's lifetime. This kind of Biblical *hindsight* prophecy is not uncommon — many and most probably all were written well after the events had occurred.

The facts show that the Greeks had a very different view of the Judeans who supported their Persian masters: rather than exalting the Judeans, the Greeks enslaved 30,000 of them.[11]

Unperturbed by the truth, the astonishing garbage continued unabated. In their insane religious zeal, the Judean scribes felt no shame; their words were pronounced to be the words of God. As for their uneducated followers, they would blindly believe their leaders' pronouncements and kill any who dared to say them false. It is sad to say, but there are many modern–day historians who have also been duped into believing this nonsense, usually because they want believe it must be true, as it reinforces their preconceived notions and for some, their faith.

For the hard–line members of the Judean priesthood, the coming of the Greeks and all the other foreigners that the new Hellenic empire

---

[10] Hengel, M. *Jews, Greeks and Barbarians*
[11] Mathews, S *A. History of New Testament Times in Palestine, 175 B.C.–70 A.D.*

encouraged to move around freely, was bad enough, however to have to give its people access to the Mystery religion with all its variants, would destroy the progress they had made to be rid of the old traditional deities inherited from their Canaanite past. Despite the opposition from the zealots, the enlightened free-thinking Hellenic influences had a profound effect upon the ordinary Judean people and few would have deliberately tried to distance themselves from it. Not only was the laity affected, but there were also complaints that even the Temple priests were avoiding their duties by hurrying off to study at the gymnasium. Many people would have effectively become 'Greek' and would, to various degrees, have happily abandoned their old life controlled by strict Mosaic laws. But as always happens when a religious sect feels under severe threat, the hard core zealot element will draw closer, they defend themselves and their beliefs by distancing themselves from outsiders, they become more extreme, they concentrate on promoting the less tolerant and more violent aspects of their religion. They were forced to suffer the influences of the 'unclean' foreigners and their 'traitorous' converts and to bide their time, brooding upon how they and their god will one day exact revenge when the day of 'cleansing' arrives.

Though Alexander created a huge empire, in 325 BCE, he died before fulfilling all his ambitions. The empire was divided up amongst Alexander's generals. Alexander's close friend Ptolemy took possession of Egypt and ruled from the new city of Alexandria on the Nile delta; he also ruled Palestine. For about a century and a half the new Hellenised world flourished in peace. Perhaps inevitably, control waned after Alexander's generals died, their separate mini-empires increasingly became prone to infighting over who should assume power and this allowed political fragmentation to begin. In Italy, the city-state of Rome was beginning to exert its influence internationally and to flex its military muscle, with the intention of picking up Alexander's reins. In Palestine, this weakening of control and the increasing fragmentation into smaller kingdoms, saw Antiochus Epiphanes, the king of Syria, take control of Judea.

This unpopular ruler inflamed fundamentalist Jews and they began to have ambitions to free themselves of all foreign influences, which encouraged them to riot and undertake terrorist attacks. In 161 BCE, one of these factions, led by a man known as Judas Maccabeus, made an alliance with Rome to help them gain independence from Syria. The revolt succeeded, however, the Judeans failed to appreciate that such an alliance was short-sighted, for it should have been obvious what Rome's long term ambitions would be. Nevertheless, short term, Judas Maccabeus got what he wanted: a Judea free from foreign control and over which he made himself ruler, establishing the Hasmonean dynasty. This dynasty managed to survive for the next hundred years, though as time went on, the inevitable power struggle emerged, with family infighting as brother fought brother. The fanatical element within the priesthood, who had been active during the revolt, took full advantage of their newly-regained power and once again set about recreating a strict fundamentalist religious state and zealously resorted to blood shedding to enforce their doctrine and decrees.[12]

How religiously motivated Judas Maccabeus and his family were is questionable, for their lust for political power and the riches and luxury trappings that go with it, seemed to take precedence. Judas was not just satisfied with ruling Judea, but sought to expand his domain and so began to build up his army. With Judas, we have a parallel with the alleged ambitions and actions of King Josiah. To legitimise his claims to the lands he wished to annexe, he announced that he was a descendent of David and Solomon and that their kingdom was his birthright. To further legitimise his expansionist ambitions, he had his scribes turn their attentions to their religious and 'historical' texts. How much was new invention and how much was reworking, is not clear, except that during this era, academics are certain that what we now call the Old Testament, reached its final form. Alas, by this stage, the Egyptian origins of the religion brought by the Atenist priests, had long been forgotten, so were now lost to all but a select few. Certainly much was misunderstood; the writing of ancient local myths into an invented history had only helped to confuse the situation. All that was left were some truths which had been encoded, but were sadly, no longer understood; some condemnation of a range of foreign customs and practices; a fictional history, that was now believed entirely and a God whom Jews would please by destroying everything that was contrary to his rules and whose protection they received in return.

With these new 'historically-based' scriptures to justify his annexing of lands, Judas and his heirs could cite their divine right by use of the precedents set in the scriptures: had not Joshua been given divine authority to take the lands of Canaan, then had he not been authorised to slaughter the idolatrous Canaanites; had not David and Solomon expanded these lands into a great empire; had not Josiah re-conquered the lands which had once been Israel and slaughtered the idolatrous Israelites and their ungodly priests.

When one looks at these blatant parallels, one can only be suspicious. As we know, the invasion by Joshua was a fantasy that never occurred historically just as the empire of David and Solomon never existed. So the stories concerning King Josiah, were they true, or were they just another

---

[12] Schäfer, P. *The History of the Jews in the Greco-Roman World*

invention — or at least a gross exaggeration — meant to serve a political purpose? The scriptures telling of how Yahweh approved of the invasions and slaughtering of the sitting populations, by Joshua and Josiah, were written during the time of the Hasmoneans, with the single intention of justifying the otherwise inexcusable actions of the Hasmonean rulers.

In 100 BCE, the Judeans invaded Galilee, Samaria and the lands across the river Jordan. But it was no normal invasion, where acquiring land and extending political control was the aim; their lust was to denude these lands of all the hated Gentiles. They slaughtered men, women and children on a massive scale. A few men were given the choice of being circumcised and converting to Judaism or being butchered. Some people managed to escape before the holocaust hit them: Samaritans, Greek settlers, Hellenised Jews, even Judaic Jews, fled to escape the bloodthirsty ethnic cleansing. Amongst those taking flight, were Jewish intellectuals who had been initiated into the Mysteries. Many of then sought sanctuary in Rome and because of their much-respected academic abilities, a number of them became advisors and even friends to influential Romans, even those at the highest levels, like the exalted Pompey and Mark Anthony.

The belief that the Hasmonean dynasty merely cast out the pagans and their ungodly religions and idols, whilst returning Judea to the sacred Laws of Moses and the worship of merciful Yahweh, is not only a fallacy, but a sick joke. The law that states, 'thou shall not kill', had no place in this land run by crazed megalomaniacs and fanatical priests. The frustrations suffered by these fundamentalist priests over the long years of foreign rule, were released and they seized their new freedom and power by pursuing their vision of pure Judaism. Anything other than total adherence to their extreme demands of not only worship, but how to conduct one's day-to-day life, was severely punished. An example of this extreme brutality occurred during the rule of Alexander Jannaeus, one of the Hasmonean rulers, who had not even bothered to take a Jewish name: whilst he lay toying with his concubines, he spectated at the crucifixion of some 800 Pharisees, who were considered too liberal. To make their suffering even more excruciating, as they hung there in their agony, they were forced to watch their wives and children being slaughtered.[13] If there were ever Hell upon Earth, then it would have been found in and around Judea during the time of 'pure' Judaism. It even makes the more recent mad fundamentalist oppression by the Taliban in Afghanistan seem moderate by comparison.

Judea was not as Hollywood tends to portray it, a land of pious dignified peace-loving people, led by benign sagely priests; there were no faces

---

[13] Hadas-lebel, M. *Flavius Josephus Eyewitness to Rome's first-century conquest of Jude*

shining with saintly light, no heavenly choirs. Rather it had more in common with the Hollywood blood and gore horror movies depicting a land ruined by rampaging bands of psychopathic zealots. The only evidence of nobility and dignity was found amongst the thousands who had chosen to desert the Satanic maelstrom that was Judea and relocated themselves mainly in the civilized world of Ptolemaic Egypt.

The Old Testament is full of large-scale slaughter, sanctified by the bloodythirsty, psychopathic Yahweh. That both the Jews and then the Christians could ever call this book holy is beyond belief. The Biblical passages seem to repeatedly condone extreme barbarity and manifest extreme contradictions. Whilst passing over the continual failure to adhere to the Laws of Moses, in order to justify atrocities that the Jews commit, the Bible portrays the ancient Jews as the innocent suffering victims. Yet in the next breath, it blames these innocent people for their own misfortune, as they didn't live according to the harsh laws, which would have prevented their distress. The lack of compassion, morality and ethics, in a supposed religious document, is beyond belief and logic. Even their enemies never acted against the Jews with such callous barbarism. That said, reality seems to indicate that those stories of sanctified slaughter, are, excluding Judean actions under the Hasmoneans, mostly fictional and inventions of the insane psychopathic priests, to give holy justification and precedent to their own murderous undertakings.

Extremism encourages dissent and factionalism, which in turn encourages strife; and that strife became wide-spread and political anarchy became the norm. As time passed by, things actually got even worse; feuding families were at each other's throats: brother killing brother, father killing sons, sons killing fathers. And wherever this occurs the trouble invariably overflows borders. Towards the middle of the first century BCE, Rome had moved into Syria and was attempting to exert its influence in Ptolemaic Egypt, so the overflowing turmoil in the Hasmonean lands was becoming a problem that could not be overlooked. Finally, Rome decided to take action — in 67 BCE Pompey led an army into Judea and sacked Jerusalem.

After a brief lull, once more instigated by the fanatical zeal of the fundamentalists, serious trouble flared again and this provoked Mark Anthony into leading a second campaign to restore order. But as fundamentalist provocateurs tend to do, they melt away from the battle and then return after the mess is cleared up, to stir up further strife. This time it continued unchecked because Rome became distracted by its own civil war between Julius Caesar and Pompey. The victor, Julius Caesar then turned his army eastwards to sort out the Palestine problem once and for all. The fractious Hasmoneans were all dispatched and a local puppet government was installed, with Antipater made the procurator. Antipater made his son, Herod, the governor of Galilee. Herod's successes in dealing with local insurgents and bandits raised his profile with Rome and in time, he was made governor of Palestine. This caused renewed strife, especially in and around Jerusalem, since Herod was seen as both a puppet of Rome and a liberal by the hard–liners. Eventually Herod's vigorous efforts against the fundamentalists were rewarded when Rome made him King of Judea in 39 BCE.

During the latter part of Herod's reign, around 20 BCE, when he had finally restored the country to a reasonable semblance of peace, in an attempt to elevate his low popularity, he undertook the rebuilding of the Temple. Money to fund the building flowed in from the exiled Jews who had never returned to their homeland, nor ever planned to. Despite the relative peace and new prosperity following the Hasmonean chaos, Herod's own family intrigues and strife ensured that the stability was fragile. The fundamentalists were still active and out there. There were even small groups of zealots causing trouble, each with their own leader claiming to be the Messiah who would once more free Judea from the unclean foreign imperialists. Messiahs became commonplace and though a minor destabilising irritation, were not generally afforded any great attention: the claimants would provoke little more than an uninterested yawn, a sigh, or a weary shake of the head.

THE GREATEST LIE EVER TOLD

Part Two

And in the Beginning — Egyptian Monotheism

Chapter 8

The Egyptian God of Creation

"Denial ain't just a river in Egypt."

Mark Twain

The first part of this book has considered the rationale behind the writing of the Torah and the Old Testament of the Bible. We know that the Judean scribes had their priests' political message to impart, but they didn't just write a bogus history, they used it to convey an encoded religion and keep it hidden. So where did the Judahite priests' monotheistic religion originate, if not with Abraham and Moses? We find the answer when we look behind the fictional Moses story, at the reality of what happened in Egypt. As we have already seen so often, there is always an Egyptian connection. Egypt cropping up with such regularity, suggests far more than a recurrent coincidence. Whereas we have found the Biblical stories full of ambiguity, contradiction, false history, a great deal of wishful thinking, fantasy and politically motivated propaganda, Egyptian history has been factually recorded in great detail and usually during the period of the events described in the Bible, not retrospectively, as we have seen with the Bible itself. Though occasionally patchy, the prolific Egyptian writings of the time are largely an accurate record of contemporary events, with some obvious degree of exaggeration when a war campaign could be used to exalt a victorious pharaoh.

Christian scholars have studiously ignored the sequence of events in Egypt, which gave rise to what is widely accepted amongst historians as the world's first monotheistic religion. When peddling a dodgy commodity, with a high-powered sales team, the company management is not going to confess that it has pirated the original, given it a tacky paint job, cobbled together a revised instruction manual and is selling shoddy counterfeit goods under its own brand label. Yet this happened twice, the first time it was traded as the core of the Old Testament and for most people, even more disagreeably, the sequel became the New Testament.

This book's intention is to expose the falsehood of the Bible, but more importantly, to expose the truth that it brutally disguised. I have shown in Part One that the Bible and Egypt are linked and in Part Two I reveal how the Bible reworks Egyptian religion. I start by looking at Egypt, its religion, its mythology and some of its history and certain classical Egyptian structures that are linked to its religion.

Both theologians and historians, either deliberately or unintentionally, have continued to misrepresent the Biblical truths. Through sloppy research, Egyptologists concocted a shameful deceit about the origins of certain structures that have an important bearing not only upon Egyptian religion, but also upon its possible origins. I do not wish to divert into another complex subject in this book, but neither can I leave a total void after my demolition of the pseudology of the Judaic/Christian religion, so I need to touch briefly upon matters that seem to have a bearing upon the possible source of the Egyptian religion.

It is common to think of the religious beliefs of the Egyptians as a naïve, bizarre hotchpotch of gods, many with animal heads. Sir Wallis Budge, the great Egyptologist and former Keeper of Egyptian and Assyrian Antiquities in the British Museum, highlighted this problem when he stated that Egyptian ideas and beliefs were sadly misrepresented and ridiculed by some writers. He wrote:

> "A study of ancient Egyptian texts will convince the reader that the Egyptians believed in One God, who is self–existent, immortal, invisible, eternal, omniscient, almighty and inscrutable; the maker of the heavens, earth and underworld; the creator of the sky and the sea, men and women, animals and birds, fish and creeping things, trees and plants, and corporeal beings who were the messengers that fulfilled His wish and word...."

Budge went on to say that this definition is the very basis for the whole theology and religious ideas held by the Egyptians.[1] The reality is that the stories of the gods contain a wealth of complex information presented in the form of allegorical tales that allowed them to be read on two levels of understanding — this Egyptian art of ambiguity, often causes frustrating dilemmas for academics to resolve. The problem is compounded by limited knowledge about the Egyptians' language. The meaning of many words still remains a total mystery and this shortcoming is further frustrated by the fact

---

[1] Budge, E A W. *Egyptian Religion*

the Egyptian scribes liberally employed ambiguity, because many words had more than one meaning. Neither do we know how the language was pronounced. In Egyptian hieroglyphs, there are no vowels, so academics have to guess at how the word or name might sound.

The god Amun, for instance, is also variously written as Amen, Amon but it could also even begin with the letter E, I, O or U — we do not know and can only guess. Our understanding of Egyptian religious beliefs is also hindered by the fact that the Egyptian priesthood operated largely in secret — they possessed knowledge which they felt should never be shared with anyone who was not a member of the elite initiates — so much can never be known.

This religious secrecy is not unique. At the Druidic colleges, for example, where students studied for up to twenty years, knowledge was not recorded in books deliberately, but passed on orally and had to be committed to memory in full by the students. The Druids believed that to make profound knowledge easy to acquire and open to all would lead to it being devalued and even to it being held in contempt and ridiculed.

What is clear is that the multitude of gods was merely different facets of the One God, the Creator of the Cosmos. That the Egyptians had so many different 'gods' has led to the misunderstanding that they must have been naïve, superstitious, polytheistic idolaters, but nothing could be further from the truth. As Budge explains 'gods' are only forms, manifestations and phases of Ra, the Sun God, who was himself the type and symbol of God.[2] The educated Egyptians never placed these manifestations on the same level as God, nor did they imagine that people would ever think they did. The pantheon, whose list would fill a large book, allowed the people to commune with God without the impertinence of addressing him personally, but rather they addressed a particular manifestation that was appropriate to their need. It was easier for uneducated people, to focus upon different deities, each of which had its own specialised field to help with everyday human problems. The people felt that their particular needs would be listened to more sympathetically through an entity with a particular interest in their problem, just as the later Roman Christians assigned these various duties to their saints. There is no difference in the belief of uneducated folk now than there was in prehistoric times.

Unfortunately, the Egyptians' one Creator God gets forgotten and the optional and local 'deities' with the varying stories attributed to them leave non-academics totally confused. Add to this, the problem of regional cult diversities, further widened by rivalries, jealousies and politics, and Egyptian

---

[2] ibid

religion and mythology become inextricably intertwined. In reality, all these things are just thin veils and the underlying core of belief is easily revealed.

It is useful here to look at the dates given in most texts relating to Egyptian history, though they are far from absolute being the best guess of a group of academics. Historians have had to work backwards from more recent times, working through the long line of pharaohs and calculating the years of their individual reigns to try to give them a date. However this method is flawed, because not only are the lengths of reign rather vague in some cases, but the further back in time one goes, the more unreliable are the lists of kings. In fact, there are only three surviving lists and not all are intact. These lists too, compiled some two thousand years after the first dynastic period in the late period of Egyptian history, are unreliable. The earlier dates are too distant to be considered accurate, the later contemporary ones are hopefully more so. The problem is compounded by the fact that the lists we have do not even agree and then there are the problems of omissions, leaving us with not only missing dates but also missing kings, deliberately erased from the lists. Nevertheless, historians still use these lists to establish working dates, which is quite reasonable as long as one admits they aren't definitive. Dates relating to the second millennium are tentative, dates going into the third millennium could be out by as much as several centuries, though many Egyptologists lead the public to believe the dates are accurate: to don the mantle of certainty, flatters the speaker with the illusion of authority.

The current time given to the start of a united Egypt under the rule of a single pharaoh is 3,100 BCE. Earlier Egyptologists, said it was 3,800 BCE, a massive difference of seven hundred years, almost a millennium. I do not favour either date, but accept that all dates are a best guess — we must also remember that modern scientific methods of dating certain artefacts have often been seriously flawed. Nevertheless, I will use the present day standard dating recognised by orthodox Egyptology.

From early times, before the country was united, there was a north/south divide defined as Lower and Upper Egypt, and rivalries often lead to warfare. Around 3100 BCE, Hor–aha or Menes — the more familiar name given to him by the Greeks — united the two countries, though this event is assumed and not yet proven. The rivalries continued, despite the unification. It was not only about political control, but differing religious beliefs divided the countries too; each had its own, slightly different, version of the creation and the Creator.

From very ancient times, certainly well before the beginning of the Dynastic period, the most important personification of the Creator was the Sun God, known as Ra or Re. The sun was chosen because it gave life to everything upon earth but the Egyptians never believed that the sun was

THE EGYPTIAN GOD OF CREATION

actually God in person. The Egyptians were also well aware that the sun was not always benevolent; it was also dangerous, even deadly.

It sounds complicated but the Egyptians liked to sub-divide not only the Creator, but his other manifestations and even these again into lesser gods — it is easier to imagine the Creator as a multi-faceted crystal from which the one light passes out from its many faces, but all the faces are in fact part of the whole. In this manner, Ra had various names depending on the time of day Ra-Horakhty the falcon-headed god at sunrise; Khepri the scarab beetle as the sun climbs in the morning sky; Ra from noon; Atum-Ra at sunset; Khnum, the ram-headed god, as he passes the night hours travelling through the netherworld of the Duat upon his solar barque. Osiris and Horus were aspects of Ra with particular tasks, as were the goddesses Isis and Nepthys. Sekhmet, Ra's earth scorching, lion-headed daughter and goddess of destruction and the cat-headed Bast, who represented the gentle benign heat of the sun represented two further facets. It might seem unnecessarily complex to modern thinking, but to the Egyptians, it was perfectly clear and comprehensible and was helpful to the people. If modern man finds it difficult to understand, then perhaps it is because the ancient Egyptians' intellectual capabilities were superior to our own.

There were regional variations too, of the manifestation of the Creator. In the north was Lower Egypt, so called because it was the lower course of the River Nile where it spread into the delta before emptying into the Mediterranean. Memphis was the ancient capital of the combined kingdom and inside the city's great necropolis just a little way further up the Nile to the south, lay the great pyramids at Giza or Rostau, the Greek interpretation of the name Ra-stau, which was the original name of the place. Just across the river, now lying beneath the suburbs of modern Cairo, stood the very ancient city called Annu, more commonly known by its later Greek name Heliopolis, meaning 'Sun City'. This was the centre for Egypt's oldest religion, dedicated to the god Ra. The original chief deity of the city was a version of the Creator known as both Temu and Atum, god of the setting sun then at some extremely early date which is unknown, Atum was fused with Ra to become Atum-Ra, the name used at that time of day when the sun was setting.

Atum created the world and created himself standing on the Primeval Mound at Heliopolis. The seniority of Heliopolis is unquestioned; its true age is lost in the mists of time, but it is absolutely linked to Giza and since geological research has dated some important structures there to possibly beyond 10,000 BCE, it is not unreasonable to conclude that there would have been also been a site very nearby, inhabited by a priesthood, almost certainly at Heliopolis.

In the south, at Thebes, we find the 'Mysterious Invisible God' Amun, or Amen, or Amon, as there are no vowels in Egyptian hieroglyphs. Until relatively late in Egyptian history, Thebes was a fairly unimportant place and even in Thebes itself, the Amunian cult was thought to follow a minor, local god, but as Thebes grew in power, so did its god. In their creation legend, it was at Thebes that the Primeval Mound arose from out of the cosmic ocean at the beginning of time.

Memphis too had its own creator, named Ptah and the city touted itself as another creation mound site; though over the course of time, this version was sidelined by the other two more powerful followings. The priests of Heliopolis redefined Ptah as a manifestation of Ra; Ptah was also fused together with the Memphite god of the necropolis, Sokar, who himself became identified with Osiris. At first, this plethora of gods seems confusing in the extreme, but remember that they were all just manifestations of the one creator god, with each manifestation merely taking on a specific role or task according to local needs.

On the island of Elephantine, at Egypt's southern border, another creator called Khnum fashioned all things on his potter's wheel, whereas further north, Ptah had 'thought' things into life. With the ascendancy of Amun, Khnum maintained the role of the 'craftsman' creator, but was designated secondary to Amun. The Elephantine priesthood did not accept this inferior status willingly and chose a subtle ruse to indicate that their god was more ancient; they portrayed Khnum as a ram–headed god, as Amun too was portrayed. Khnum, however, had corkscrew horns, just like the oldest domesticated rams in Egypt, whereas Amun had smooth horns like the later rams. When Ra is shown riding the solar barque, he is depicted as Khnum; possibly this was the Heliopolis attempt to give Khnum prominence over Amun.

All along the Nile, the creation myth was reinterpreted regionally and the local god took the lead role. The Atum–Ra version from Heliopolis appears, however, to be the oldest. The importance of the Ra religion and its great antiquity will be examined a little further on in this book.

The cult of Amun, did not rise to significance until circa 1985 BCE when the new 12th Dynasty rulers of Upper Egypt promoted it. They also elevated Thebes from a provincial town to a city. Prior to that the prominent Theban god was Montu, a falcon–headed god of war, usually shown wearing a headdress of a sun disk with two plumes, clearly indicating a connection with Ra and the two were later fused into Montu–Ra. Though Amun was considered to be the invisible god, he was depicted as a man with a ram's head as the new astronomical/astrological age of Aries the ram began.

THE EGYPTIAN GOD OF CREATION

Amongst the older Ra cult, certain goddesses were depicted wearing headdresses of horns containing the sun. This was not so much to identify them with the sacred cow that suckles the world, but rather to indicate the preceding age of Taurus the bull. At Giza, the heartland of the Ra cult, the lion–bodied Great Sphinx suggests an even more ancient age, that of Leo.

As Thebes grew into a great city, its new rulers became increasingly powerful and promoted the local god Amun, to whom they built a great temple. As the political power swung in favour of the Theban pharaohs, so the influence of the Amunian priesthood grew. From that time onwards, the cults of Amun and Ra became rivals and though they each remained largely confined to their own south and north regions, their priesthoods struggled to gain political supremacy. Eventually during the Eighteenth Dynasty at the beginning of the New Kingdom era, when the Hyksos had been expelled from northern Egypt, the two camps reluctantly agreed a pragmatic compromise and put a superficial end to the rivalry for religious predominance, by combining their creator gods into the single Amun–Ra.

So this was the situation in Egypt, when the ancient religious capital of Heliopolis vied for supremacy with its upstart southern rival Thebes. There were numerous other gods beneath the creator god Amun–Ra, divided by hierarchical rank and duties, but above the ranks of lesser gods were those designated as the offspring of Ra, the first born, known as the Ennead. The most significant of the Ennead were Osiris, Isis, Horus and Set: the divine family of the Father, Mother, Son and Satan. Tales were attached to them, which superficially seem to be purely mythical but were actually important allegorical teachings and these formed the basis for what became Christianity.

Amongst all of them, the most important god was Osiris. It is thought that his cult was centred upon the city of Abydos, but there is evidence that strongly links him to Giza. Osiris was seen as an aspect of the Creator, entitled the Son of God and he was seen as the god who came to live on earth as a mortal man. The Egyptian temple records state that many thousands of years before the records were written down, Osiris ruled as the first king of Egypt. This sounds like an unbelievable claim, but when one considers the age of certain Egyptian structures, it becomes a little more possible. Certainly the extraordinary, mysterious structure known as the Osireion Temple at Abydos, shares the same monolithic style as the Valley and Sphinx temples at Giza and their extraordinary weathering indicates a vast age. How far back in time the worship of Osiris goes is not known, but it is certainly into pre–dynastic times; the earliest surviving mention of Osiris has been found on a IVth dynasty coffin of King Men–Kau–Ra, which carries an inscription dedicated to Osiris. Osiris was given the aspect

'God, the Son of God', which to Christians, might sound disturbingly familiar.

Even more discomforting is the fact that Osiris was deemed to be the son of Ra, the son of God, who came to earth as a mortal man, suffered a cruel death and then with the aid of his female half, Isis, was resurrected back to life. He then went to rule his new kingdom of the dead, whose subjects stood before him to be judged before their spirits could ascend to the heavens and reunite with their Creator.

It seems to be little known that there were two falcon–headed gods called Horus. The one commonly known is the son of Osiris and Isis who battled against the evil god Set. However, though obscure, there is another whom Budge defines as Horus the 'Elder', whom he thinks was another aspect of Ra.[3] The Heliopolian god, Ra–Horakhty, sometimes written as Horemakhet both basically meaning Ra–Horus of the Horizon, is the embodiment of the dual aspects of the double horizon, representing the sun's solar disc in the east at sunrise and in the west at sunset. The talismanic 'Eye of Horus' was not that of the son of Osiris, but of the elder Horus and this 'eye' was actually another version of the 'Eye of Ra'.

Below these higher deities were numerous minor gods, whom the populace prayed to for 'specialised' assistance with particular everyday problems, problems which were deemed far too trivial to trouble the higher aspects of God with.

Unlike other societies, in Egypt there was an absence of human sacrifice. This is an indication that the Egyptians were not a society in fear of their deity, or of a blood–lusting priesthood. Society, which was centrally controlled, merely carried out its daily life and work as best it could and in a calm certain manner. The people believed in Ma'at, the goddess of order and balance, harmony and justice, which meant they did not have to be unduly concerned with the placation of God or gods; though of course, assistance in certain daily matters would be sought through application to the appropriate demigods.

Having said that, religion was absolutely central to their lives, but it was not so much a concern for their present earthly incarnation, but their life after death. Religion and God, via the gods, were manifest in every aspect of life and yet, life itself was of secondary importance to death. Uniquely, it was a society obsessed with death, with much time, energy, wealth and thought, dedicated to the afterlife, for death was the doorway to a better existence — the return to the stars, the spirit rejoining the cosmos, taking on an eternal existence back with the All One Creator.

---

3 Budge, EAW. *The Gods of the Egyptians Vol 2*

THE EGYPTIAN GOD OF CREATION

Dr H Brugsch collected epithets[4] that are applied to the gods from texts taken from all periods of Egyptian history and Budge recounts them in his book *Egyptian Religion*.[5] As Budge points out, "… from these we may see that the ideas and beliefs of the Egyptians concerning God, were almost identical with those of the Hebrews and Mohammedans at later periods."

'God is One and alone and none existeth with Him; God is the One Who hath made all things.'

'God is from the beginning and He hath been from the beginning; He hath existed from old and was when nothing else had being. He existed when nothing else existed, and what existeth He created after He had come into being. He is father of beginnings.'

'God is the hidden Being, and no man hath known His form. No man hath been able to seek out his likeness; He is hidden from gods and men, and He is a mystery unto His creatures.'

'No man knoweth how to know Him. His name remaineth hidden; His name is a mystery unto His children. His names are innumerable, they are manifold and none knoweth their number.'

'God is truth, and He liveth by truth, and He feedeth thereon. He is the King of truth, He resteth upon truth, He fashioneth truth, and He executeth truth throughout the world.'

'God is life, and through Him only man liveth. He giveth life to man, and He breatheth the breath of life into his nostrils.'

'God Himself is existence, He liveth in all things, and liveth upon all things. He endureth without increase or diminuation, He multiplieth Himself millions of times, and He possesseth multitudes of forms and multitudes of members.'

'God hath made the universe and He hath created all that therein is; He is the Creator of what is in this world, of what was, of what is, and of what shall be.'

'God is the father of the gods, and the father of the father of all deities; He made His voice to sound, and deities came into being, and the gods sprang into existence after He had spoken with His mouth. He formed mankind and fashioned the gods.'

'God is merciful unto those who reverence Him, and He heareth him that calleth upon Him. He protecteth the weak against the strong. And He heareth the cry of him that is bound in fetters; He judgeth between the mighty and the weak.'

'God knoweth him that knoweth Him. He rewardeth him that serveth Him, and He protecteth him that followeth Him'.

---

4 Brugsch, H K. *Religion und mythologie der alten Aegypter*
5 op cit

These epithets were hardly written by primitives, whose only concern was with fertility gods, and clearly they were not polytheistic idolaters. Their thinking was intellectually sophisticated and they believed that there was but one Creator God, a being that created itself before creating a cosmos to fill an empty universe. It is also evident that they were also very advanced in their scientific concepts, having an understanding of the universe, they understood the concept of God being everything and everything being a part of God — in other words, they knew that they and everything else in creation, were all actually God. So this was the religion of the Egyptians, albeit a somewhat complex one.

At one point in Egyptian history, a period just before the supposed time of Moses, a pharaoh turned the world of the Egyptians upside down by deciding to rationalise religion. It was a back–to–basics leap, where all gods and images of gods were banned and there was only to be the One God, the invisible formless Creator, whose visible manifestation was the disc of the sun, which gave out its life–giving light.

Before we look at this historical event, which was to have such world–changing consequences, the event that gave birth to Judaism and laid the foundations for Christianity and Islam, it is important to look a little further back in time and also to have some knowledge of the foundation mythology of the Egyptian religion. Though their creation story appears strange and even naïve, there are elements within the secondary post–creation phase, which are closely echoed by similar stories from other civilisations and ethnic groups from all around the world.

The second phase tells the stories of the coming from the stars of the 'immortal man–gods', the great civilisers and teachers of mankind. In Egypt in particular, these demigods were given individual responsibilities in the religion and became associated with facets of the One God, the Creator. Though these strange stories seem ridiculous, there are elements within them that are crucial to the forming of the first monotheistic religion.

There are many variations of the Amun creation–story as the story would have been simplified with the usage of imagery so that uneducated people could understand; it would not have been understood if the priesthood had employed complex theological and scientific concepts. Amun is the creator 'First One Who Gave Birth to the First Ones' after emitting a mighty honk like a goose, which burst the stillness of the universe causing a cosmic reaction — scholars recognise this account as equivalent to the 'Big Bang Theory.' From out of the cosmic ocean, arose a Primeval Mound and upon this was a cosmic egg, which produced the Ennead, the 'First Gods'. Amun was the 'Hidden God', concealed from even the other gods. As one text records, 'The Ennead is combined in your body; your

THE EGYPTIAN GOD OF CREATION

image is every god, joined in your person.' Amun was inaccessible, beyond knowing, too great to comprehend. From this description, Amun is far more the distant mysterious creator, than is the Biblical God, who is depicted with distinctly human foibles.

The other version, which is far older, is that from Heliopolis. It states that out of the chaotic cosmic ocean, a Primeval Mound appeared. At some point, going further back than the first Dynasty, this representation of the primeval mound was somehow crystallised into an object known as the Benben stone. One theory is that the Benben was a solidified drop of Atum's semen. Though the original stone disappeared, a replica stone was mounted on top of a tall pillar at Heliopolis outside the Mansion of the Benben, which was supposedly the place of Sep Tepi or the 'First Time,' the point of creation. The first being to materialise on the mound was Atum-Ra, 'He who came into being of himself' and then by masturbating, his seed created eight other gods the Netjeru. The first of these were the twins, Shu and Tefnut, who represented air and moisture, thus forming the Earth's atmosphere. The twins them coupled to produce Geb and Nut who were earth and sky. Next Geb and Nut begat four children who were Osiris and Seth — the gods of order and disorder — and their consorts, Isis and Nephthys. Next came nine gods, the Lesser Ennead, followed by nine more. All these gods were merely manifestations, or facets of the One Creator God.

Thoth and Ma'at were two extremely important deities. Thoth was the teacher who would come to instruct mankind in all the arts, crafts and sciences. Thoth is often depicted with the dead before Osiris, as Thoth had given his knowledge and morality to mankind, enabling them to ascend spiritually. The goddess Ma'at was the embodiment of cosmic balance, harmony, justice and truth; her ostrich feather was the counter-weight to balance the heart when the dead were to be judged before Osiris — today she is commonly represented by the astrological sign of balance Libra, and as the female justice depicted outside law courts holding the sword and scales.

Another divine group warrant a special mention, these were known as the Urshu, or 'Watchers'. Intriguingly, the 'Watchers' are mentioned in the legends of other widespread cultures around the world — which provokes some interesting questions. The Urshu were intermediaries between the Netjeru gods and mankind, which is certainly the origin of Judaic/Christian angels. In the Book of Enoch, they play a controversial part, which has always deeply disturbed the Christian hierarchy, so much so that they attempted to destroy every copy, as its whereabouts became known.

The final group of interest are the Shemsu-hor, or the 'Followers of Horus,' who were also known as the 'Divine Souls.' Horus was the son of

Osiris, who became ruler over the Earth. The Shemsu–hor were said to have ruled for thousands of years before the First Dynasty. The priests of Heliopolis claimed that these demigods created the oldest structures in Egypt; they were the founders of Heliopolis and its temple, which was called the Mansion of the Lords and later became the Mansion of the Benben. The priests also claimed that the same demigods built the Sphinx and the Great Pyramids; they did not boast that they themselves were the builders. This is a most important assertion, for there is no evidence of a denial of responsibility for a structure of any kind elsewhere. The unbeatable opportunity to declare your superiority over rival priesthoods, does not make any sense, it is out of character for the priests and kings to deny themselves the glory of erecting such stupendous magnificent monuments. It is imperative to apply logic when considering such situations, whilst suspending preconceived and sometimes, illogical ideas. In this single matter, Egyptologists have deliberately chosen to ignore the statements of the priests completely. The traditional age and usage attributed to the building of the Giza monuments, as given by orthodox Egyptology, is not supported with hard evidence —I consider this further on in this chapter.

At some early stage, it is not clear when, it was Atum's aspect of the sun, the giver of life–creating light, known as Ra, which took on importance and the principal godhead became known as Atum–Ra, which again, with the passage of time, became just Ra. The sun god also had another, lesser–known aspect and this was personified as Aten, the sun's disc. It sounds confusing, but the Egyptians liked to be ambiguous with most things they recorded and in the case of the gods, they are usually to be found grouped in triads, as in this case with Atum, Ra and Aten.

Because the Egyptians closely guarded the inner secrets of their religion and particularly, their claimed 'knowledge of God,' they avoided being explicit and as a consequence, life is made particularly difficult for scholars, because the few sacred texts which remain, contain many words and concepts which are still defying translation and understanding. The situation is worsened by the fact that the ancient Egyptians had three types of writing: the every day demotic style, hieroglyphics and a symbolic or coded cipher called hieratic. The three types would cause confusion, with many texts being interpreted literally, owing to a lack of awareness of their different purpose.

It is worth remembering, that the Egyptian religion had a single creator of the universe, the One God, and that their other gods were not simply nature gods as other primitive religions, but aspects of the One God. It is also important to bear in mind that the Egyptian religion was not Earthbound, it had little concern with mankind's physical life, but was wholly rooted in the stars and the cosmos, and with the transfiguration of

THE EGYPTIAN GOD OF CREATION

the dead person's spirit, so that it became one with the Light — the Creator.

It is easy to dismiss the philosophical importance of the Egyptian religion on the grounds of the unbelievable mythological stories; to do so would be a major error. We accept that the Egyptian elite was astonishingly knowledgeable in mathematics, geometry, sciences, building and astronomy; it therefore makes no sense to then think them to be naïve fools in their religious beliefs. When one studies their religious writings and their complex concepts, it becomes clear that their spiritual beliefs are extremely sophisticated and that their mythology is merely a superficial veneer. To modern-day scholars, much of the Egyptians' religion still remains a mystery, because the Egyptian priesthood kept secret most of its true knowledge, both religious and scientific and quite deliberately never recorded it in hieroglyphics.

What is clear is that they invented stories concerning the creation, which was stripped of any scientific cosmological complexities and was delivered in a form that the uneducated peasants could comprehend. Likewise, the stories of the gods were both symbolic and allegorical and set into tales of a family, with nurturing gods who would address every aspect and problem of daily life. The religion was presented in a way that could easily be understood by those without extensive education.

The Jewish Bible stories were written in a similar fashion, but instead of discussing God and cosmic matters, they contrived a special history for the Jewish people and recounted their dealings with a parochial god, whose only concern was the earthly affairs of one small group of wayward humans.

Before examining how the monotheistic aspect of the religion gained prominence in Egypt, we need to consider some extremely contentious matters concerning the age of Egyptian civilisation and of some of its monuments. These matters have great relevance to the myths described above, to the religious cleansing and to the return to the One God.

One major problem plagues research into ancient Egypt: so much remains unknown. Much that is promoted as fact is no more than theory devoid of supporting evidence. The academic world prefers to maintain the *status quo*. It wishes that history remain as we know it — safe, easy to understand, non-controversial. It raises fewer illogical questions if we accept that mankind dragged itself up from ape–man to cave–man and hunter–gatherer and finally through the numerous stages of civilisation that we can classify, to where we are today.

Egyptologists are perhaps the most conservative of any academics. They have their 'history' of Egypt plotted out and it is now set in concrete. If for no other reason, conservatism is retained because the truth would be costly.

To change every historical text-book would cost millions. Minor adjustments are acceptable, though not without much debate, but major paradigm shifts are treated as abominable heresy. Sadly, the high historical ideal of seeking the truth, no matter what it is, is not paramount if it affects reputations and careers. The academic world is savagely self-policed and anyone holding radical beliefs is likely to find permanent unemployment.

In Egypt, this rampant suppression is not hidden away in the dark corridors of universities, but basks openly in the harsh desert sunlight. To suppress any great shifts in belief, the Egyptian Council of Antiquities controls all excavations in Egypt rigidly. The Council is aware of alternative proposals for Egypt's most ancient history, but it has no desire to accept evidence which might indicate that any of the great monumental structures are outside its accepted historical time-frame.

National pride is also an influence as the Egyptian historians contemplate the frightening prospect that the original builders were not native Egyptians. I also suspect another reason for their discomfort is that they are well aware that things might be uncovered which could undermine their Islamic religion. A covert 'acceptability' code defines what archaeologists must believe, if they wish to get permits to conduct any research work in Egypt. The Egyptian authorities strictly police all research projects to enforce the *status quo*. On a number of occasions, research teams who make embarrassing finds have been told to leave and never granted permits to return.

Such was the fate of Dr. Robert Schoch and his team of geologists from Boston University, who in 1991 undertook scientific investigations of the Great Sphinx's erosion patterns.[6] Schoch's team discovered things which as geologists, they considered to be very obvious and wondered why no-one had spotted them before — in actual fact the anomalies had been noted as early as the 1920s,[7] but deliberately ignored by Egyptologists.

Schoch's team observed that the rock had been weathered not horizontally by the dry desert wind, as had always been claimed, but rather vertically, indicating extremely prolonged torrential rainfall. The geologists knew that the period when Egypt was last affected by heavy rainfall ended around 4,500 BCE. This implied that the Sphinx and the surrounding quarried walls of its enclosure, had to be even older to account for the heavy rain scouring. They found this same rain scouring on the nearby structures of the Valley Temple, the now virtually non-existent Sphinx Temple next to it and the Upper or Mortuary Temple, indicating that they were contemporaneous with the Great Sphinx. These structures were all built

---

[6] Schoch, R. *Voices of the Rocks*
[7] Schwaller de Lubicz, R A. *Le Temple de l'Homme*

during or before Egypt's age of heavy rainfall, so they could not possibly belong to the traditionally accepted date of 2,500 BCE. Further evidence for this can be seen in the mud–brick royal tombs at Saqqara. Supposed to predate the Sphinx, these structures, despite being made of fragile material, show absolutely no signs of rain weathering.

These Giza temples, like parts of the Great Pyramids and the mysterious cyclopean structure known as the Osireion at Abydos are 'different'. Their construction incorporated stones of a colossal magnitude weighing between 100 to 400 tonnes. The Giza temples' colossal and weather–worn limestone blocks were, at a much later date, covered with a granite facing. This indicates that Khafre probably undertook the protective work, making him a renovator rather than the builder. He may have done the same with the Sphinx, which is believed to have been renovated around his time.

The Osireion is sited next to the thirteenth–century BCE, temple of Seti I. The Osireion has no decoration apart from two discreet cartouches to Seti. Outside the walls, there are two adjoining chambers not contemporary with the Osireion and decorated with astronomical inscriptions. Seti built these chambers, yet the adamant opinion of most Egyptologists has been that Seti built the Osireion too. Such a ridiculous conclusion exceeds the bounds of normal scepticism; isolated cartouches are not normally considered evidence of origin. Pharaohs routinely laid claim to structures that already existed. What is revealing is one other inscription found upon a pottery shard, which pronounces, 'Seti is serviceable to Osiris', indicating that Seti uncovered and renovated this temple to Osiris. The type of construction of the two temples differs enormously; the Osireion's plain cyclopean blocks are in sharp contrast to the typical thirteenth–century style of architecture and decoration of Seti's temple. Geologists, also point out that the Osireion's floor level was fifty feet down below the level of Seti's temple, which suggests that it had been buried by the desert sands for an enormous length of time.[8]

Rational thinkers would be deeply sceptical about a scenario that suggests for a hundred years around 2,500 BCE, the Egyptians suddenly ceased using manageable small stone blocks and mud bricks and decided to use unbelievably massive stone blocks weighing hundreds of tonnes, at the end of which period, they resort back to the mud–brick. The Egyptologists, however, accept this preposterous idea without question.

There are constructions elsewhere in the world, made of massive unwieldy slabs, though their builders are deemed even more primitive than the Egyptians. Archaeologists never give due consideration to why or how these buildings, from megalithic materials, were made. They excuse the

---

[8] Naville, E. *The Times*

'why' as the whim of man's vanity and brush off the 'how' with ropes, logs and sledges powered by teams of men. Their explanations of the curious mystery of megalithic construction are crassly simplistic, engendered by ignorance that they try to hide and closed minds that they fear to open. Certainly when asked to account for how the massive 2,000 tonne stones at Ba'albek in the Lebanon were transported uphill from the quarry, their glib explanation becomes laughable. In 1996, when asked how the feat would be achieved now, Baldwin's Industrial Services attempted to provide a solution. Though it was theoretically possible — there was a crane that could lift 2,000 tonnes — it was a static crane, so to transport the block would require not just a set of vehicles, but also a suitable mile–long road to be laid. It was still a vast engineering project requiring the best of 20th century CE technology and expertise.[9] According to our archaeologists, the earliest civilised men could do it with bits of rope, logs and muscle power. This kind of explanation exceeds logic — to put it bluntly, it is nothing short of cretinous.[10] Yet the nonsensical has become part of the orthodox belief system, archaeologists even model it with 10 tonne blocks and try to extrapolate, and no–one is allowed to challenge the belief without incurring the unmerciful and savage wrath of the academic establishment!

Nonetheless, the embarrassing questions will not go away — how did those ancient engineers suddenly acquire the technology to achieve the seemingly impossible task. There was no technological advance that preceded it, it just suddenly happened overnight — a freak moment in history. Egyptologists insist that the Great Pyramids were the result of centuries of experimentation, the honing of technical skills and long experience of working with stone. This is utter rubbish; there is no evidence to support their view and they know it. Nothing of this experimental, trial and error learning process happened prior to the building of the Great Pyramids. Earlier structures were crude and technically inferior in every aspect and nearly always made of simple mud bricks. Just a few were made of small stone blocks of an easily manageable size. No large stone blocks, let alone massive ones were used in any tomb construction prior to the Great Pyramids.

All the preceding structures were crude block–style mastabas and simple step pyramids; the step pyramids are actually a series of mastabas built on top of each other. Indeed, the famous Saqqara step pyramid of Zoser, acclaimed as the first pyramid, actually had at least ten preceding it. It shows clear evidence of this form of construction where the pyramid was built up gradually and added to on several occasions. It was Flinders Petrie's

---

9   Alford, A F. "The Baldwins Challenge"
10 Sader, H. ed. *Baalbek 1898-1998: Rediscovery of the Ruins*

opinion that the Saqqara and Meidum pyramids showed clear evidence of having been finished then later extended. Different forms of style and construction indicated that they were the work of several kings, undertaken over an extended period. To support his conclusion, beneath the Zoser step pyramid, Petrie found around 35,000 shards of pottery inscribed with the names of earlier kings. This, he thought, indicated that the structure was not a tomb for Zoser and that the earliest structure had been continually used, probably as some kind of temple.[11] This probability is further supported by the fact that Zoser's contemporary name was Tosothros and he was also called Netjerikhet, thus implying that Zoser, meaning 'holy one', was a title which was given to a number of kings, not the given name of just one of them.

No pyramid has ever been found with evidence that suggests that a body had once been buried in it. No evidence has even been found that would authenticate a pyramid as a tomb. Pyramids were not tombs, this is absolutely certain. The hypothesis was confirmed by the discovery of two completely undisturbed pyramids of Hetepheres and Sekhemket; the intact sarcophagi within them were empty.[12] Yet because the experts will not allow themselves to consider any other possibilities, they continue to promote an obvious falsehood.

This tunnel vision has blinded Egyptologists to another serious problem in their orderly world. How was it all accomplished? Someone quarried millions of huge blocks, together weighing many millions of tonnes, and shipped them hundreds of miles — a monumental feat in itself. Why would anyone go to this incredible trouble? Certainly not to construct tombs to flatter the egos of vainglorious pharaohs, who couldn't even be bothered to put their names on them, let alone use them. There is also the practical feasibility of constructing the Great Pyramids. It has been estimated by Egyptologists that Khufu's pyramid took twenty years to build. Engineers thus estimated that the stone blocks would needed to be placed in position at an incredible rate of one every two minutes.

Clearly such a thing is impossible. This two minutes included the slow and laborious work of quarrying, dressing the stone to size and smoothness, transportation down the Nile, hauling up the alleged ramp and the final manoeuvring into position, in a precariously confined space. Then there is the thorny problem, which has caused much heated debate, of the alleged building ramp. Construction engineers dismiss out of hand the suggestion that a massive sand and rubble ramp could have been used. They say it would have collapsed quickly. A ramp would need to be built of stone

---

[11] Petrie, W M F. *The Pyramids and Temples of Gizeh*

[12] Goneim, Z. *The Buried Pyramid*

blocks and climb at a workable gradient of 1:10; to reach the higher elevations, it would need to stretch back nearly a mile. The biggest problem that such a an enormous ramp would present, is that it would have taken an enormous amount of stone to build — more stone than is contained in the pyramid itself.[13] Then there is the question of the amount of time it would take to construct such a ramp. It would need continual extending and rebuilding in order to adjust its height and elevation to accommodate the increasing height of the growing pyramid. The construction requirements for the ramp would mean that the estimated construction time for the pyramid would double to forty years, and over twice as many stone blocks would need to be quarried and shipped in. Within such a time-span it is impossible for one pharaoh to build his own tomb; indeed, even the accepted twenty years would be too long for an adult to complete the crucial task, when life-spans were routinely short. The orthodox construction theory is banal nonsense — but then Egyptologists are not construction engineers, just as they are not geologists and they are not interested in logic; they are interested only in promoting obsessive delusions of how things were.

The structures supposedly built immediately following the Great Pyramids, were not built with the same engineering skill and were not built with large stone blocks. By contrast, they were completely ramshackle and had a short life-span as their mud bricks quickly disintegrated. Egyptologists attempt to justify this by blaming a shortage of funds, but this desperate excuse does not explain why the technical skills disappeared overnight.

The Pharaohs Khufu, Khafre and Menkhaure, it is claimed, constructed the three Great Pyramids. Egyptologists also claim that between building the first and the third pyramid, two others were built, but of these, at Abu Roash, Khufu's son Djedefre's pyramid is a virtually flat ruin. The Egyptologists claim that initially the Romans plundered the stones, including the internal core. Their only evidence for this ridiculous assertion is the finding of a single Roman mallet. Unbiased experts have declared that the substructure has the design and foundations of a step pyramid and that it was built of small stones and mud bricks.[14] The unfinished pyramid of Bicheris, allegedly built after Khafre's and before Menkaure's, again has step pyramid foundations and was poorly built. Once again, we find Egyptologists refusing to apply logic, adhering to dubious theories and ignoring evidence that does not support their orthodox beliefs.

---

[13] Brier, B. "How to Build a Pyramid"

[14] Mathieu, B. "Chantiers archéologiques et programmes de recherche. Etudes égyptologiques et papyrologiques. 1. Abou Rawash."

To any rational intelligent person, the orthodox Egyptologists just don't make any sense. The only realistic, unbiased conclusion is that these structures were not built in the period that the archaeologists claim. We know they weren't built later, so we are left to deduce, no matter how preposterous, that they came from a much earlier age. In every way, they bear no resemblance to anything that came before or after. Only the so-called Red and Bent Pyramids at Dashur give sufficient indication that they should be attributed to the same builders as the three Great Pyramids of Giza.

The number and size of stone blocks, the hi-tech tools, the design geometry and mathematics — including the use of Pi — the building techniques for colossal structures are all strong indicators of a construction date which does not match the limited abilities of the 2,500 BCE builders and points to advanced technological know-how. The thorny problem of weathering on the stones is not readily dismissed and throws open what are deemed unacceptable possibilities. The insistence that the Giza constructions were designed and built by primitives using muscle power, sledges and ramps, is only supported by illustrations from far later periods, which depict large statues moved into position, pulled on sledges by gangs of workers. There is no evidence to show that these methods were employed to build the Great Pyramids, the Giza temples and the Osireion. Any method other than the use of primitive muscle power is totally unacceptable to Egyptologists, so they refuse to consider alternatives.

Occasionally the Egyptologists attempt to demonstrate how the building work was done. Mark Lehner's television documentary had him successfully constructing a tiny pyramid in three weeks. However this was just a demonstration of hauling stone and an 18ft pyramid didn't approach any of the real problems of vast scale. It certainly did not address the daunting complexities of the Great Pyramid's internal design surveying and construction.[15] The whole exercise was a pathetic contrivance, a deliberate piece of propaganda, which made no attempt to make a true replica, but rather to say, 'there, see how easy it is.' It was like making a model boat to sail on a pond, then saying 'this proves no great skill was required to build a liner like the QE II.'

Modern Egyptologists tend to hold a unified view of how things were, including a king list and time-frame. Though the academics rely on them, the king lists are largely worthless. The dating system derived from the lists of kings is fragile because it has no verifiable dates and is based purely on a hypothetical average length of reign. Anything that predates the New Kingdom period, circa 1,550 BCE, is confused and uncertain. That most

---

[15] Lehner, M & Hopkins, R. "Pyramid"

important king, Khufu, the alleged builder of the Great Pyramid, is not even on these lists. This has led some to question whether Khufu was merely one of numerous titles afforded to the kings. The time–frame has been contrived, with no significant evidence to support the academics' dogma. There are only three tablets listing names of kings, but none agrees with another. Academics use the list compiled in the last days of the Egyptian kingdom by Manetho, however this only survives in two later rewritten versions, which alas also disagree with each other. One list has 560 kings over 5,520 years and the other has 360 kings and spans 4,480 years. Too much that is presented as fact, is little more than an article of faith. Theory and speculation has become the 'gospel' truth and Egyptologists are happy with things to remain as they are.

When Professor Schoch and his team's report was published,[16] it shook the Egyptologists out of their comfort zone and they did not like it — in fact they were livid. Schoch and his team came under a great deal of virulent criticism, but he was unbowed, knowing that his scientific conclusion was absolutely correct, and this received strong support from the geological community. In response to the Egyptologists' vitriol, Schoch stated

> "As a geologist, the current evidence taken as a whole, suggests to me that the Great Sphinx of Giza is considerably older than its traditional attribution of circa 2500 BC. Indeed, I am currently estimating — based on evidence at hand — that the origin of the colossal sculpture can be traced to at least 7000 to 5000 BC, (the end of the rainy epoch) and perhaps even earlier."

When Schoch's findings were eventually made public, all hell broke loose. Later research had pushed back the dating even further, to somewhere around 10,000 BCE. As the period of heavy rains ceased around 5,000 BCE the severe weathering on the Sphinx and temples must have happened over a long time period prior to the fifth millennium BCE. The consequence of this bombshell was that the Egyptians banished Dr Schoch and his team from the site and since that time, no other geological research has been allowed there. But the cat was now out of the bag and these geological findings had given real credibility to the research and astrological calculations of those investigators who have linked the edifice to the age of Leo with a date around 10,500 BCE.

Schoch's conclusion ran contrary to the standard opinion of Egyptologists; to their minds it was impossibly early, as the Egyptians had neither the technology nor the social organisation to build such structures in

---

[16] op. cit.

THE EGYPTIAN GOD OF CREATION

pre-dynastic times. Such findings ruined their neat picture of how history was and were totally unacceptable, so the scientific evidence was ignored.

Dr. Hawass, Secretary General of the Supreme Council of Antiquities in Egypt protested
"There is absolutely no scientific base for any of this."
This statement, besides being untrue, clearly reflected the prejudice and desperation of the Egyptian archaeologists. Professor Schoch's response was rightly dismissive

> "I don't see it as being my problem as a geologist ... it's really up to the Egyptologists ... to figure out who carved it [Sphinx]. If my findings are in conflict with their theory about the rise of civilization, then maybe it's time for them to re-evaluate that theory."

Schoch makes an extremely important point relevant to many things attributed to Egypt's Old Kingdom: the Great Sphinx, the Great Pyramids and certain temples. Egyptologists' conclusions are not facts but conventional theory, with no more and often less validity than the theories offered by the scientists and mathematicians, whose research offers an alternative approach. At least the experts in other disciplines can usually back their theories with some hard facts.

Dr. Schoch's geological evidence was not all that fell foul of the wrath of Dr Hawass and his Supreme Council. In 1991, seismic readings were taken by geophysicist Dr Dobecki, of what appeared to be a regularly-shaped man-made chamber, beneath the paws of the Sphinx.[17] The authorities used a weak excuse to end the work, claiming that vibration, caused by drilling bore holes into the ground — essential for their tests — was endangering the structure, a structure which had managed to survive numerous earthquakes over thousands of years without coming to harm. A second team, from the University of Florida and the Schor Foundation, carried out further tests, which discovered at least nine more chambers or tunnels, all housing metal contents.[18] This team also has not been allowed to continue the research.

The authorities said that the ban was because of 'irregularities'. They then explained that the reason for the seismic scans, was not to look for the legendary Hall of Records beneath the Sphinx, as had been supposed, but to find out whether the ground was safe for tourists to walk on. The excuse sounds barely plausible and arouses speculation that the Supreme Council

---

[17] Dobecki, T & Schoch, R. "Seismic Investigation in the Vicinity of the Great Sphinx of Giza, Egypt"
[18] Hancock, G & Bauval, R. *The Message of the Sphinx*

of Antiquities wants to take advantage of the technology and skills of foreign investigators to find out if there is something under the Sphinx, but doesn't want anyone foreign to know what it is that they found.

If one accepts the findings of these reputable researchers, this subterranean discovery is especially significant to the story of the Egyptian religious revolution. Other underground chambers have been found some 200 metres from the Sphinx. Dr Hawass states that an upper chamber, 10 metres below the surface, contained the remains of several aristocrats and that it is dated to around 500 BCE; the lower chamber is flooded, with a raised central stone island, which is reminiscent of the Osireion temple at Abydos, a structure which some believe to be, possibly, the oldest structure in Egypt. In this lower water–filled chamber is a shaft, which seems to travel in the direction of the nearby Sphinx. This shaft is unusual as it narrows to a tiny bore, requiring a fibre–optic camera to probe it. So far no public announcement has been made about whether this work has been done, or what might have been found.

Egyptologists insist that Khafre built the Sphinx, mainly because the Upper Temple, which stands next to the Khafre Pyramid, is connected to the Valley Temple by a causeway, which runs alongside the Sphinx. Egyptologists also insist that the face of the sphinx is the same as that on the Khafre statues, however to just about everyone else, they look completely different. This has been confirmed by two separate studies undertaken, one by the New York Police forensic identikit artists and more recently, German forensic experts who use computers to reconstruct faces; both have definitely dismissed the belief that it might have been the face of Khafre and also they rejected the alternative that it might be Khufu.[19] Besides it is absolutely evident, when one looks at the Sphinx that the head is completely out of scale with the body. It is clear that the original head — possibly that of a lion — has been drastically re–sculptured at some unknown date.

At one time Egyptologists believed the Sphinx to be far older than the time of Khafre, but modern Egyptologists simply cannot bring themselves to accept that at some pre–dynastic time, people had the technical skill to build such a structure. In a discreet report, Dr Hawass admitted that the facing stones, which protect the Sphinx, were added in the Old Kingdom period, 2,700–2,160 BCE.[20] If this restoration work was completed at the end of this period, it would be about 340 years after Khafre's reign. There is no possibility that the original limestone blocks underneath could have suffered such severe erosion in just a few hundred years. Dr Hawass knows this, but will not say so.

---

[19] ibid
[20] Hawass, Z. *The Pyramids of Ancient Egypt*

THE EGYPTIAN GOD OF CREATION

So what evidence do the modern–day establishment academics use to conclude that Khafre was the builder of the Sphinx.

    i   The name Khafre was mentioned on a line of the now heavily-worn and fragmented Sphinx Stele erected by Thutmosis IV, when he rescued the buried Sphinx out of the sand. The syllable 'khaf' occurs on line13, this was assumed to signify Khafre. The text either side of the syllable has flaked away.

    ii   A few badly smashed statues and one almost intact one, found at the bottom of a well, which supposedly depict Khafre, have been found in the area of the Valley Temple.

    iii   To modern Egyptologists, the face of the Sphinx looks like Khafre.

    iv   The Upper Temple, which stands near to Khafre's pyramid, is linked to the Valley Temple standing near to the Sphinx by a causeway clearly linking Khafre to the Sphinx.

That is the sum of the experts' evidence. So how does it stand up to scrutiny?

    i   Professor E A Budge pointed out that there was no cartouche (the oblong frame which always surrounds the royal name) around the inscribed word on the Sphinx stele. It is therefore, not Khafre but khaf, which translates as 'he rises'.[21] Old Egyptologists such as Budge, Petrie, Maspero and Mariette were of the opinion that Khafre undertook some early rescue work. Present–day Egyptologists have unbelievably cast aside any requirement to be meticulous and instead mule–headedly taken this isolated syllable, with gaps either side, to mean 'Khafre built the Sphinx.'

    ii   The walls of the Valley Temple have no inscriptions of any kind. Khafre would certainly have ordered them, had he been its builder. On any other archaeological site the finding of objects such as the statues would be considered inconclusive. They could be what are designated as 'intrusive artefacts' put there at a later time. There is also strong reason to believe that Khafre decided to install statues of himself into the 'gods' house' and this act was later viewed as sacrilegious, so his statues were smashed, thrown down the well and 'cast out of the holy place.'

    iii   Forensic investigation has repudiated the possibility that the face on the Sphinx is Khafre's.

    iv   The Upper Temple contains a gigantic stone block estimated to be around 470 tonnes and the temple is constructed in the same

---

[21] op. cit.

way as the rain-scarred Valley and Sphinx temples and the Osirean temple at Abydos. This certainly groups these unique structures together, but according to the independent geologists, their time predates that of Khafre. The huge limestone blocks show evidence of surface 'smoothing' before the granite facings were attached. This indicates that renovating and preservation work was undertaken much later, which probably accounts for Khafre's link to the site. This same outer casing was put on the badly-worn Sphinx.

One has to say that the supposed evidence for Khafre's building the Sphinx is so flimsy, that it is embarrassing and totally unworthy of any academic whom one assumes to be intelligent.

Controversy also hangs over the Sphinx's intimately close neighbours on the Giza plateau. The dating of the three Great Pyramids is especially contentious and far too complex to deal with in much detail in this book. It is important to mention though, that there is an enormous weight of evidence that causes us to question who the architects were and how and when the structures were built. Establishment Egyptologists always ridicule anything that opposes their own opinion; they never confess that they are often only theorising; and they never explain the serious questions that remain, concerning the building and dating of the pyramids. The so-called evidence used by Egyptologists is tenuous and even dubious; the more honest amongst them, admit that they are baffled by the supreme precision and technology and by the baffling interior designs. The explanations that the Egyptologists give us for these constructions appear at first to be down to earth and plausible, but when subjected to close analysis, they are banal and unscientific and lack any serious evidence to support them. At the same time the Egyptologists condescendingly dismiss the far more weighty evidence that opposes their views. Serious questions continue to go unanswered.

The use of Pi and Pythagorean triangle geometry, were intrinsic to the construction of the Pyramids, apparently thousands of years before Pythagoras 'discovered' them. The Great Pyramid also incorporated within in its dimensions, exact scaled down measurements of the size of the Earth, besides numerous other mathematical anomalies. Egyptologists dismiss all these as coincidences, but Egyptologists are not mathematicians, astronomers or engineers, so their objections carry little validity and lots of prejudice. The banality of continued accusations of 'coincidence' beggars belief and puts into serious question the professional integrity of any scholar who prefers orthodoxy over veracity.

THE EGYPTIAN GOD OF CREATION

Even when the ancient Egyptians themselves have recorded information about the Pyramids, the Sphinx and the two temples, Egyptologists selectively choose to ignore what they said, simply because they don't want to believe it. The 'Inventory Stele' states that the structures were already standing in the time of Khafre's predecessor, Khufu and that they were constructed by the gods in a far distant age during Sep Tepi, the 'First Time'.[22]

The deliberately plain construction, lacking any decoration or inscriptions, of the Pyramids and in the remains of the nearby temples, is totally unique in Egypt. Elsewhere every inch of every wall was covered in decoration, engravings and inscriptions; one only needs to look at the extravagantly decorated tombs of the Valley of the Kings for confirmation.

The other structures surrounding the three Pyramids, three temples and the Sphinx, such as the little crumbling mastabas, are intrusions from a later time.

The workers' village at Giza is sited about a mile away from the great Pyramids. Egyptologists claim that it belonged to those who built these vast structures, however they are just as likely to have been employed in the constant building work that took place all over the necropolis during the whole period of Egyptian Civilisation. Giza would have needed a vast complex to accommodate and feed the large numbers of pilgrims, known to visit the necropolis and particularly the Great Pyramids.

Modern Egyptologists ignore other aspects altogether, such as the artefacts first queried by the great Egyptologist, Flinders Petrie. His conclusion was that the Egyptians had used tubular drills, lathes and saws and drills both tipped with ruby or sapphire, particularly on the coffer in the King's Chamber of the Khufu Pyramid. Modern Egyptologists laugh and insist that no such tools were then known and the primitive builders only used stone and copper tools, aided by abrasive sand slurry to wear down ultra–hard surfaces. However, Petrie had found drill cores made by tubular drills and suggested that the perfectly symmetrical grooves in the granite could only have been made by diamond–tipped drills.[23]

American technologist and toolmaker, Christopher Dunn, more recently studied this problem and his research conclusively proved that the tools which were used on numerous building blocks and artefacts which were attributed to the Old Kingdom, could only have been diamond–tipped ultrasonic drills which were rotating at between 19,000 to 25,000 cycles per second — yes, per second, not per minute! Even more astonishingly, the calculation done on the measurements of the rotational penetration

---

[22] Budge, E A W. *The Gods of the Egyptians*
[23] op. cit. *The Pyramids and Temples of Gizeh*

indicated that the downward force applied was 500 times more powerful than any drill available today.[24]

Very thin and delicate pots and vases, attributed to the Archaic Period, 1st and 2nd Dynasty, pose a puzzle about how they were made. Their slender necks and wide bodies were carved by tools that reached down the narrow necks, hollowing out and shaping the objects from the inside — a seemingly impossible feat. Yet even more puzzling, these vases and pots were made from immensely hard stone such as quartz, diorite and basalt, materials, which even today are immensely difficult to work with. Modern Egyptologists, of course, will have us believe, that primitive peasants using simple stone or copper tools, which were softer than the materials they were working with, achieved the impossible with such ease that they manufactured thousands of the products. The true experts haven't the slightest idea how the manufacture was achieved, but the so-called experts maintain their ridiculous claim, that it was definitely achieved by using stone tools.

Egyptologists peer aloofly from the pedestal they have hauled themselves on to and treat earlier Egyptologists or modern-day engineers and scientists beneath them as simpletons. Backed by qualifications obtained by maintaining a *status quo*, they yet again issue a definitive answer of how things were done, whilst laughing off any possibility of an advanced culture and machinery. Even if the evidence points to it, it can't be true, simply because they say it is impossible. When pressed on the subject, they become angry, ignore the questioner and fall silent. They employ no logic, no open-mindedness in seeking the truth, just banal theories masquerading as fact. Their maxim is at all costs lie cover up the fact that we don't know, particularly if the evidence indicates the workings of highly intelligent people using highly sophisticated tools and machinery. As researcher John Anthony West observed, 'Egyptologists are the last people in the world to address any anomaly'[25]

Discounting the unacceptable 'high tech' nightmare, the question of the Egyptians' advanced culture is an ongoing thorn in the side of Egyptologists, who begrudgingly acknowledge that the Egyptians skills, even 'low tech' ones, had to originate somewhere, but fail to pursue the matter any further. Historians like to insist that the cradle of civilisation lies in the region around the mountains of the upper Euphrates, but things were starting to happen in Egypt around 13,000 BCE. They and Egyptologists are loath to admit this as it disrupts the fixed ground plan of orthodox history.

---

[24] Dunn, C *The Giza Power Plant: Technologies of Ancient Egypt*
[25] West, J A. private correspondence

THE EGYPTIAN GOD OF CREATION

Palaeontologists have discovered that there was a society in Upper Egypt, which abandoned fishing and began farming. These people suddenly began using an advanced micro–blade technology which produced sickle blades for harvesting cereal crops, grind stones for extracting grain and were employing animal husbandry — as if there had suddenly been a local need for greater food production.[26] Interestingly, skeletons found in this region included those of tall northern Europeans. If advanced outsiders had settled there, they would naturally aid the local farmers to produce extra food more efficiently, in order to meet their own requirements.

Between 13,000 and 9,000 BCE Egypt was savannah and filled with animals, the climate was mild but suffered torrential rainfall. The following two thousand years were arid and saw the land turn to desert. Another rainy period then lasted until around 4,000 BCE, which saw the desert bloom and new settlement occurred in the millennium prior to the generally accepted date for the Old Kingdom, but then the arid climate returned again.

Somewhere around 10,000 BCE, the unique agricultural advancement which had arisen along the Nile, disappeared and hunting and fishing resumed; but then it suddenly reappeared in the Upper Euphrates around 9,000 BCE. The indications are that whoever introduced this farming technology into Egypt, was then compelled to move. This exodus would coincide with the devastating floods that assailed the region as the arctic ice sheets rapidly melted; the indications are that the catastrophic weather compelled a northward exodus to the safety of the Anatolian mountains. The implications are, though this cannot yet be proved, that an advanced culture had introduced the natives to a more efficient means of farming to boost production, so that they could take the surplus. But who they were and what they were doing for those missing 1,000 years, remains a mystery. Egyptologists have dismissed that there could have been an advanced civilisation in northern Egypt about 12,000 years ago because no real evidence has been found to substantiate such a claim. However this dismissal is actually unrealistic for the reason that in those ancient times, any cities by the coast would have been submerged beneath the rising Mediterranean and the River Nile was miles away from its present course, so if cities or other signs of civilization were there to be found, no one has yet looked in the right places.

Researcher Ralph Ellis accidentally spotted another oversight when his attention was brought to the weathering on the base blocks of the Great Pyramid. He saw that there was a dividing line between the erosion of the base, which had always been exposed and the inner section, which had once

---

[26] Hoffman, M A, *Egypt Before the Pharaohs*

been covered by the angled facing stones. Knowing when the blocks had been pillaged, he thought the inner section should have shown just less than half the weathering erosion of the outside, but it did not. Weathering on the outside, which had been exposed from the time it was built, was far greater. Using his measurements of this wear and the length of time the inner surface had weathered, he calculated that the outside had been exposed for around 13,000 years. This put the date around 11,000 BCE — a date which fell into the era when the Sphinx may have been built. There is other research based on astronomical alignments, which also indicate this period.[27] Whether one wishes to accept such sensational dating is up to the individual reader, but it is pertinent to air the possibilities, for it is with these colossal structures at Giza, that the attempted reformation of Egyptian religion began, and from that came the Hebrew religion and eventually Christianity, then Islam.

Though I do not wish to go any deeper into the fascinating subject of Egyptology in this book, the sole purpose of which is to expose the falsehood of the Bible and reveal the truth, it nevertheless is important to consider the wider background to the origins of the Bible stories, and to remind the reader that there were extremely intelligent minds at work in very early Egypt. Whoever they were, they not only influenced building, engineering, geometry, mathematics, astronomy and the arts, they must have also had a profound influence upon philosophical religious thinking.

It is extremely easy to be seduced by the down-to-earth answers supplied by figures of authority representing a respected establishment, but how often are we assured that authority figures are telling the truth, only later to find we have been blatantly lied to. Politicians seem to have it as a 'stock-in-trade'; medical research is 'shelved' by university departments when pharmaceutical companies threaten to withdraw funding if they see their profits threatened; petroleum and motor companies used to buy up technology that might give us alternative cheap fuel. "Trust us... we are the experts, we have your best interests at heart... you are merely simple people who need to believe and follow the doctrines and dictates of the learned men, who are here to advise you what to think and believe. Follow us, we are here to lead you." — and so the ignorant and common herd is hoodwinked time and time again. For so long, theologians and the better-educated priests have been promoting a truth called the Bible and damning those who do not believe, whilst all the time, knowing it was all a great lie.

Academics operate in much the same way, they should be above such shameful behaviour, but sadly they are not. One of the worst examples of their manipulation of the truth comes in the depressing tale of

---

[27] Ellis, R. *Thoth, Architect of the Universe*

anthropologist Thomas E Lee from the National Museum of Canada who found artefacts of the first post–ice–age immigrants into North America at a site on the Great Lakes. He had unearthed tools that greatly disturbed him because they predated the standard views of when the New World was peopled. Worried by the reaction his discoveries would have because they were so sensational, he had his excavation levels confirmed by highly regarded geologists from four different universities. Instead of finding artefacts belonging to the accepted period of around 10,000 to 12,000 BCE, the strata levels indicated an age of 125,000 BCE.

When Lee's findings were revealed, the wrath of academia crashed down upon his head — all attempts at publication were blocked. Lee resigned and suffered eight years of blacklisting and unemployment. The Director of the National Museum, Dr Jacques Rousseau was fired and sent into academic exile for refusing to sack Lee. His finds were boxed up and 'lost' in the museum vaults and the excavation site declared a 'nonsite'.[28] This is the tip of a huge iceberg. Many similar cover–ups are recorded in the 900 pages of *Forbidden Archaeology* by Cremo and Thompson.[29]

Depressingly, many academics are simply lazy and accept the history as it has been taught to them. Some are frightened for their career prospects and so refuse to undertake any radical nonconformist research and then there are those who have reached the top, the pillars of the establishment. They seek to protect their reputations, which they have been firmly nailed to the mast of orthodox history, so they brutally attack anything that threatens to undermine them. Alas, there are occasions when the truth is ignored, or even worse, deliberately hidden. So often we hear the 'tap–tap–tapping' of archaeologists hammers, urgently banging square pegs into round holes, then declaring with supercilious smugness — 'There... you see... it fits perfectly!'

For readers who wish to know more about the research into the likely beginnings of ancient Egypt, the Pyramids, the Sphinx and their builders, I would recommend the books of Andrew Collins, Ralph Ellis, Christopher Dunn, Graham Hancock, Robert Bauval, Adrian Gilbert and John Anthony West. Although there is some small divergence between them concerning background detail and some dating, the findings of their independent research and of many other researchers, are too consistent to be ignored.

There is a great deal of both old and new evidence which Egyptologists refuse even to consider and there is a whole catalogue of serious questions which they either shrug off with banal answers, or simply ignore altogether.

---

[28] Lee, T E. "Canada's National Disgrace"
[29] Cremo, M A & Thompson, R L. *Forbidden Archeology*

The virulent derisive mocking of these historical researchers and their findings is unworthy, unintelligent and unacademic, and it is a defensive reaction — and one is only defensive when one has something significant to hide.

Archaeologist, George Carter defines the double standards that plague research; he says

> "When a new idea is advanced, it necessarily challenges the previous idea. This disturbs the holders of the previous idea and threatens their security. The normal reaction is anger. The new idea is then attacked, and support of it is required to be of a high order of certainty. The greater the departure from the previous idea, the greater the degree of certainty required, so it is said. I have never been able to accept this. It assumes that the old order was established on high orders of proof, and on examination this is seldom found to be true."[30]

Michael Cremo and Richard Thompson expand further on this same subject by stating

> "What happens in practice is that is that evidence agreeing with a prevailing theory tends to be treated very leniently. Even if it has grave defects, these tend to be overlooked. In contrast, evidence that goes against an accepted theory tends to be subjected to intense critical scrutiny, and it is expected to meet very high standards of proof." [31]

Cremo and Thompson point out that there are some observations that contradict accepted theories so violently, they are never accepted by any scientists and that these then end up being reported by non-scientists in popular books and magazines. The process of rejecting a new theory does not usually involve careful scrutiny of the evidence by those who reject it; the reason for this is that academics devote their time to their own work, rather than spending time scrutinizing unpopular claims. Cremo and Thompson also point out that when the scientific/academic community hears about certain theories or evidence being dismissed as allegedly bogus, they will avoid reading the evidence for themselves. Indeed, some actually administer a rancorous attack without ever having read the theory they are attempting to destroy — an action that brings nothing but shame upon these supposedly learned and intelligent scholars.

---

[30] Carter, G F. *Earlier Than You Think*
[31] op. cit.

THE EGYPTIAN GOD OF CREATION

The academic world is notoriously racked by jealousy, resentment and bitter rivalry, and that is just amongst its establishment peers with whom they broadly share the same beliefs and theories. When the orthodox view comes under threat, they unite and turn their venom upon the heretical challengers. Academics, for the sake of their reputations and careers, will strenuously avoid associating themselves with unpopular theories, especially if they contradict the current trends. When evidence does exist, the norm is to bury it, sometimes literally and if new research scholars come along, they are likely to be unaware that alternative theories and evidence once existed. It is fortunate that organisations like the Bhaktivedanta Institute, who publish *Forbidden Archeology*, exist to dig it up.

Whilst one cannot go so far as to say there is a deliberate organised conspiracy, it is still a conspiracy, an unorganised conspiracy, which results from the consequence of academics attempting to protect their careers by defending their mainstream theories and by destroying the dangerous *newcomers*. These virulent acts of *demolition* merely draw attention to the fact that the Egyptologists, like the Christian Church are embarrassed and worried; they know that it is only a matter of time before the lid blows off the bubbling cauldron, but they all hope that the lid stays on in their own lifetime.

The true fact about ancient history is that the true facts are often tenuous. Theories are drawn up from the fragmentary pieces of evidence available to archaeologists and historians but they are only theories and not irrefutable fact, as the historians so often like to make out. Much that we read in books on ancient and pre–history, we accept as hard facts — the absolute truth of how it was and the academics like us to believe that. The truth is that in our more recent past, some scholars have theorised and their followers — usually to secure their own careers — have promoted those theories into fact. Just as in so many court cases when the jury has been convinced by the evidence proffered by our 'learned friend' the barrister, they are convinced of the absolute correctness of the verdict; then after appeal — sometimes numerous appeals — the verdict is overturned and they are shocked to find that the evidence was faulty or even totally false.

Though much of this seems to be straying from the subject we are here to discuss, the thinking and workings of so many academics, whom we unthinkingly trust as being both right and truthful in their pronouncements, needs to be carefully reviewed. It needs to be understood that false timber has been used to shore up a mock facade of history whilst the unpalatable real face of the edifice remains hidden away. Looking behind this facade will enable the reader to understand what instigated the dramatic revolution in Egypt that led to the world's first monotheistic religion, later redeveloped into the better known 'first' monotheistic, pseudo religion called Judaism.

THE GREATEST LIE EVER TOLD

Chapter 9

Uncovering the One God

"Fear has many eyes and can see things underground."
                                              Miguel de Cervantes

The origins and purpose of such monumental edifices as the Sphinx lie back in the times of unrecorded history. Once history is recorded it is patchy, but significant events in the development of Egypt's monotheistic religion took place at the time of the Hyksos rule over Lower Egypt. The name Hyksos is a Greek rendering of the Egyptian 'heka khaswt,' meaning 'foreign rulers.' After arguing over the meaning for years, academics have now dismissed the traditional meaning of 'shepherd kings.' They have also largely rejected the theory that the Hyksos might have been invaders. Though lacking in conclusive evidence, the current popular belief, is that the Hyksos were peaceful migrants who drifted south, out of the Syria/Palestine region, during one or more periods of drought and famine. They took up residence in the Nile delta region of Egypt, probably some time just before 1700 BCE. These immigrant settlers are thought to have grown significantly in numbers because of the length of time they resided in Egypt.

At first, relations between the Egyptians and the incomers seemed amicable — they adopted Egyptian customs and even became followers of the Ra cult of Heliopolis — but with population increase comes increasing influence and ambition. In the century and a half before the Hyksos arrived, during the thirteenth dynasty, there had been some 60 pharaohs in just 150 years, indicating that political rivalries had made this a time of instability and internal conflict. A new dynasty of Theban rulers took over, who continued their rule from the traditional capital of Memphis. Egypt had by that time been weakened by long–term internal strife and lost the southern land of Nubia. These problems had allowed the foreign immigrants to exert their influence on the delta region. They consolidated their authority and gradually, without force of arms, took political control of northern Egypt.

At first, having realised that his forces lacked strength to retake control, the pharaoh accepted the humiliating loss of the more productive half of his kingdom. He withdrew back to Thebes and awaited the time when he would be strong enough to retake what he had lost: he never did, the situation didn't change for 150 years. The Egyptians studied how the foreigners were armed and particularly their use of chariots. They followed the Hyksos examples and re-equipped and retrained their army in the use of the new weaponry. Around 1560 BCE, with their strengthened forces, the Egyptians began to assault the Hyksos. Finally, the Hyksos saw defeat and the pharaoh Kamose expelled them from Egypt circa 1555–50 BCE.

During the Hyksos period, the Theban priesthood of Amun was in Egyptian territory, whilst the Ra priesthood in Heliopolis was outside of Egypt's now reduced, but ethnically clean, border. The Ra priests could no longer exert any political influence. In their absence the Amun priests consolidated their power behind the throne. Although the temples and libraries of Heliopolis remained a renowned place of learning, the influence and finances of the temples of the sun god went into a painful, but unbowed decline — though it was not to be a permanent one.

The expulsion of the Hyksos heralded a great revival in Egyptian fortunes and a new golden period saw imperial expansion under the rule of powerful Theban pharaohs. During this time, the Amun priesthood began to exert ever-greater political power. It reached its climax when Thutmosis II died in 1479 BCE. His principal queen, Hatshepsut had not produced a male heir, the throne was passed on to his son by a minor queen, the future Thutmosis III. When a pharaoh was too young to rule, the principal queen would usually become the regent.

An event took place that became the catalyst for the religious revolution to come. The politically ambitious Amun priests elevated Hatshepsut to the position of pharaoh, effectively usurping the position of the boy pharaoh. Women were forbidden to hold this position, as the pharaoh was the living embodiment of Horus. Hatshepsut, however, was declared the divine child of Amun and presented herself in male royal costume and even wore the traditional pharaoh's false beard. She ruled for fifteen prosperous and peaceful years, whilst the young Thutmosis III, found himself politically sidelined.

On Hatshepsut's death, Thutmosis re-exerted the masculine power of the pharaohs. He immediately undertook brilliant military campaigns, consolidating and expanding the Egyptian empire. Though he took care not to alienate the Amun priesthood, he did not forget their meddling in his affairs and their promotion of his hated step-mother. To prevent a repetition, Thutmosis refused to appoint a principal queen. He ensured his succession by making his son, Amenhotep II, who was born and raised in Memphis in the north, his co-regent In the final year of his 54-year-long kingship, Thutmosis III took his revenge upon Hatshepsut. He had her name erased from all monuments and records: names had great spiritual importance to the Egyptians and the removal of a person's name was a declaration that they never existed. The memory of Hatshepsut's usurpation and the Amunian priests' ambitious connivance was neither forgotten nor forgiven by the descendents of Thutmosis.

Amenhotep II died without appointing a successor and because of his father's decision that there should no longer be a principal queen; none of his sons had any claim to seniority. The subsequent transfer of power was less than smooth and some disaccord was likely, though the records are far from clear. It was Thutmosis IV, son of a minor wife, a queen of northern origin, who took the throne. The northern origins proved to be very significant, for the family's religious allegiance was to Ra. It is likely that any efforts to promote a Theban candidate as Pharaoh had been hampered by Thutmosis IV's father and grandfather's continual erosion of the power of the Amun priests.

A huge stone slab, known as the Dream Stele, which lies between the paws of the Great Sphinx tells how Thutmosis was destined to become pharaoh. The text, dictated by Thutmosis, describes how he fell asleep in the shade of the long-neglected Sphinx, which at that time was largely buried in the enveloping desert sand. While Thutmosis dreamt, the Sphinx spoke to him. Part of the long text, recounts its words:

> "Look at me, observe me, my son Thutmosis. I am your father Harmachis-Khepri-Ra-Atum. I shall give to you the kingship upon the land before the living. You shall wear its white crown and its red crown upon the throne of Geb, the heir. The land in its length and breath will be yours and everything which the eye of the Lord of All illuminates. Good provisions will be for you from within the Two Lands and the great produce of every country and a lifetime great in years. My face belongs to you; my heart belongs to you and you belong to me. But behold my condition is like one in illness, all my limbs being ruined. The sand of the desert, upon which I used to be, faces me aggressively; and it is in order to make you do what is in my heart that I have waited. For I know that you are my son and my protector ..."

Whether the account is true or fictitious is not important, but what Thutmosis makes absolutely clear on the stele, is his allegiance to Atum-Ra. The name 'Harmachis in the horizon,' is that of 'Horus on the horizon,' a god who was assimilated with Ra–Horakhty. He was one of the Ra aspects of the Heliopolis Temple. There can be little doubt that at some point, Thutmosis had the political support of the Ra priesthood, who forcefully ensured that he gained the throne. The inscription on the stele clearly shows their influence. This is the first occasion during this period that there is no reference to the god Amun.

Thutmosis acceded to the request of the Sphinx, clearing its buried body from the desert sand and restoring it. If the story were simply an invention, there would surely be nothing for Thutmosis to gain by undertaking the arduous task of excavating an old redundant monument. Rather than renovate, the common practice was to build some new and better structure. There would seem to be no advantage even to the Ra priests. In this very odd excavation, lay the answer to the phenomenon that was soon to hit not only Egypt but eventually, the whole world.

As might be expected, Thutmosis, installed northerners in positions of power. He reduced the importance of the military, since Egypt was now secure and concentrated on civil matters. He revived the fortunes of the Ra cult of Heliopolis and even went so far as to erect a monument to Ra in the Amunian centre of Thebes. But something with great long–term significance occurred; Thutmosis commenced the subtle promotion of a new solar manifestation of Ra, that of the Aten. The Aten was Ra's living embodiment as the sun's light and its life–giving cosmic energy was represented by the sun's disc. Aten means 'Giver of Life', the same name as the hieroglyph by which it is represented; it was not the name of the Creator, whom the Atenists knew to be without name.

Archaeologists have found references to Aten, some centuries earlier than the time of Thutmosis IV, but how and why this aspect of Ra began to be promoted at this time, is something that has puzzled scholars. They have found no apparent reason why the traditional Ra could not have continued, just evidence that makes it appear that the older aspect of Ra no longer seemed to be acceptable to the Egyptians from the time of Thutmosis IV.

Something had clearly happened and it seemed to be an unsolvable puzzle. There is an answer though, one which lies between — or rather underneath — the paws of the Sphinx. The recent seismic soundings of the ground in front of the Sphinx[1] showed what appeared to be underground chambers whose regularity indicated that they could well be man–made. Since underground chambers are common in Egypt we cannot dismiss the possibility that there is one under the Sphinx, as the Council of Antiquities prefers to do. They are being extremely selective with what they allow the public to know.

---

[1] Dobecki, T & Schoch, R. "Seismic Investigation in the Vicinity of the Great Sphinx of Giza, Egypt"

Far back in ancient times, there has been a legend of a 'Hall of Records' supposedly lying somewhere beneath the Giza plateau and traditionally said to be under the Sphinx. This hidden place was reputed to be a repository of knowledge, left by the old ones — the Followers of Horus. The Egyptian priests passed the things that they knew down from generation to generation, from father to son within the closed world of the Atum–Ra Temple. We cannot know what they knew unless the Council of Antiquities decides to excavate. Unfortunately, this exciting prospect is most unlikely: the Council of Antiquities has far too much to lose if it finds a repository. The more worrying prospect is that it may undertake secret excavations with the intention of destroying what is there. The Council risks not only the loss of the hugely–inflated Egyptian pride if it were shown that the early civilisers and builders of the great monuments were not Egyptians, but also the potential trauma of having the Islamic religion completely undermined. It cannot afford for the truth to be known.

If this repository did and still does exist, then the Ra priests would have known of it. It is possible that they knew of its existence, but had never dared open up what they believed to be a sanctuary closed by the divine ones, making its opening taboo. Perhaps because of their reduced circumstances, they became desperate and decided that opening up this hidden place might forever restore the exclusive position of Ra — we cannot know, but can only speculate on what their motives were. Rather than a response to a dream, Thutmosis' uncovering of the Sphinx was more likely to have been at the instigation of the Ra priesthood, who felt that the time was right to open up the underground vaults. If they were opened up, it is likely that what the priests and the pharaoh found, made them revise their religious beliefs and it is almost certainly due to this event, that Tuthmosis decided to promote the Aten as the living embodiment of the Creator God.

Tuthmosis wisely felt it necessary to act with discretion and to avoid the shock waves and disruption that a sudden change would cause. Egyptian society was very conservative and balance and harmony were paramount; carrying out a religious revolution, a turning over of established religious cults, would likely provoke great discord. At the moment, this theory cannot be proven, but no other reason has been proposed for the sudden appearance and elevation of the Aten. Though it was not promoted immediately, it was clear that the followers of the Aten, the Ra priests, believed that there was only one God and that there really was no need for any other gods, which were only aspects of the creator.

The son of Thutmosis IV was Amenhotep III. He raised Atenism to another level. Though he continued the latter–day tradition of ruling from Thebes, he built himself a new palace at Malkata. The palace was deliberately sited across the river, at the furthest point away from the great Temple of Amun — it was a discreet but clear statement, distancing himself from Amun. Though the composite Amun–Ra was the king of gods and the official state divinity, it was only a token fusing and the rivalry between the two priesthoods remained. Though Amenhotep did the conventional honouring of Amun, he now gave only lip-service that and it was done merely to ensure continued harmony within the two lands of Egypt. The pharaoh was now clearly dedicated to the solar entity and particularly interested, not only in the cult centre of Heliopolis, but also, significantly with the necropolis at Giza, the great Pyramids and the Sphinx.

A strange anomaly, is that within the Amun Temple at Thebes, is a depiction of Amenhotep III, but what makes it particularly special, is that it depicts a fictitious sacred story where Amenhotep is born to a virgin and shows the annunciation, conception, birth and adoration. Yes it sounds familiar and it is. It is the story of the birth of Jesus, the son of God, but the depiction on the wall of the Amun Temple, predates the story recounted in the Gospel of Luke by over a millennium. This is not an astonishing fluke, a chance foretelling of the story of Jesus, but it is the original version of the story of the dying-resurrected son of god. This story was to be exported and refashioned into the Greek Mystery religion of Dionysus and then spread around the eastern Mediterranean to spawn numerous regional variations each with their own *local* leading character. On the wall of the Amun Temple, it transposes the Pharaoh Amenhotep into the role of the god Osiris, the original god made mortal, the dying-resurrected son of the One God, Ra.

There is absolutely no question that Amenhotep was totally dedicated to the new Aten aspect of Ra; he assumed the title of Aten–Tjehen — 'Dazzling Sun Disc'. Further evidence can be found in the dramatic elevation of importance of Atenism when Amenhotep appointed Aper–el, his vizier of northern Egypt, as High Priest of his newly-built Aten temple at Heliopolis. At the same time, in Thebes, Ramose, the southern vizier was made 'Steward in the Mansion of Aten.' Amenhotep's palace at Malkata was called, 'Splendour of the Aten,' whilst his royal barge was named the 'Dazzling Aten'. Amenhotep also started to be depicted wearing a magnificent collar made up of large gold beads, which signified his solar divinity — this was a clear statement of the pharaoh's religious belief. In the final decade of his life around 1367 BCE, Amenhotep crowned one of his sons as pharaoh and co-regent to become Amenhotep IV; this son was to elevate the religion to a position of total supremacy.

Chapter 10

Akhenaten
The Man Who Gave Us God

"If one does not understand a person, one tends to regard him as a fool."
Carl Jung

From the early days of his boyhood, Amenhotep IV was educated by the priests of Heliopolis, where he was immersed in the solar cult of Ra and all its secrets — including those of the Aten. The boy was not the eldest son, yet it seems he had been singled out, for some reason, by the Ra priesthood. In the inner sanctum of the Temple, the holy of holies, known as the Star Chamber, he was primed to be not only Pharaoh, but also the man who was to revolutionise religion.

When the teenage Amenhotep took on the co-regency with his ailing father, all the traditional symbols and elements of the traditional Ra religion sat complementary with the Aten, since the Aten was an aspect of Ra. A question, which few scholars have considered, is why should the priests of Ra decide to promote the Aten above any other aspect of Ra. The only answer to this conundrum has to be that something had changed the way they felt about how to preach their religion.

Some scholars think that the influx of foreigners and the increasing numbers of slaves had brought about a more cosmopolitan society within Egypt, to whom a new godhead would be more appealing. This is unlikely, however, because Egyptian society was very conservative and traditionalist and would not seek to appease foreigners. Certainly the priesthood, deeply immersed in its beliefs, would be fiercely loyal and dedicated and thus never contemplate a fundamental change to their religion. Nevertheless, something did inspire them, not just to change, but also to instigate a revolution.

Something of great significance had occurred and as we speculate, the only conclusion that makes any sense is the deliberate uncovering of the Great Sphinx at Giza with the discovery or rediscovery of the hidden underground chambers. There would be no good purpose for a major excavation unless there were some specific prize to achieve, so it makes sense that the priests knew or suspected that there was a repository left by the builders of the Sphinx. They would not have sought anything so mundane as gold, they had plenty of that, but rather they expected to find gnosis: the knowledge of spiritual mysteries.

Gnosis will reappear in later chapters, when I discuss the development of Christianity. The religious movement of Gnosticism, which derives directly from the Egyptian Mystery religion, unwittingly gave birth to this simple-minded offspring.

Since Amenhotep had been initiated into the secrets of the Ra Temple, if a repository had been unearthed, he would have been enlightened to the knowledge it contained. Although Amenhotep effected a complete ban on idols and animalistic imagery, he allowed one exception when he depicted himself as a sphinx and there can be little doubt that this depiction was deliberately chosen to represent the Great Sphinx of Giza. This blatant exemption must have been to communicate something of great significance. There can be little doubt that Amenhotep was highlighting a connection between the Sphinx and the Aten.

Whatever he had learnt as a boy, had a most profound effect on Amenhotep IV and his whole life became an obsession to promote the Aten as the visible personification of the One God, the Creator. Strangely though, in the early years of his reign during the co-regency, he had Ra-Horakhty as the godhead. An appropriate veil for the Aten perhaps, due to restrictions imposed by his father, or more likely, the caution of the Ra priesthood awaiting the right time to reveal the Aten. The falcon-headed Ra-Horakhty with the solar disk on its head, was the aspect of Ra that embodied the dual horizon. The Aten was later to become associated with the sun's appearance over the eastern horizon.

This traditional god was merely a mask, to be used until Amenhotep felt secure and strong enough to bring about his monotheistic religious revolution. It remains a mystery to scholars, how and why the young Amenhotep was chosen to be the new pharaoh. Why the elder son was not chosen, is not known, neither is it known what happened to him. One thing that is certain is that the young Amenhotep must have had the firm backing of the Ra priesthood and it is likely that he was made their prized acolyte. If this was the case and the Ra priests were themselves on a mission, they would want the next pharaoh to share the passion of their quest.

The records of this period are not complete, so the fate of the elder son is not known, he might have been sickly in some way, he may have died, he might have fallen from grace because of some misdemeanour, or he could have been demoted due to pressure exerted upon the compliant father by the priests of Heliopolis, who were also embroiled in their plan to promote the Aten as the one and only god. Whatever happened, the eldest son's fate went unrecorded and he simply disappeared from historical record without a trace.

Unlike his father, who disliked the Amunians but pragmatically chose not to abrogate their already reduced authority, the new co-regent Pharaoh took a decidedly confrontational approach to promoting Atenism. His first great building project was the construction of a temple dedicated to Aten in Amunian Thebes, and he deliberately sited it with intrusive closeness, across the entrance to the great sanctuary of Amun. Like the temples of Ra and the other temples to the Aten, with their open-air solar courts which offered no barrier to the light of the sun's rays, this new temple was at the opposite extreme from the totally enclosed and dark secret temples of Amun. The new pharaoh would no longer consider the sensibilities of the Amunian priests, nor indeed any other cult.

His next step was to commence construction of a new holy city, one dedicated to the Aten. As the young pharaoh became more open about his plans to elevate Atenism, his relationship with the Amun priests became potentially explosive. It is possible that the old pharaoh began to see that his over-eager son needed to be restrained, to maintain the peace and this may have meant the young pharaoh agreeing to banishment within the boundaries of his newly-built city. Whether this was what actually happened, we will probably never know, but what is known is that the young pharaoh stayed there willingly and never wished to step outside of its boundaries for the rest of his life. Within his city, he had free rein to follow his religious vocation.

Amenhotep IV was on a divine mission, to dispense with the over-complicated family of gods and to revive the secret elements of the Ra cult through a new figurehead deity, the Aten aspect of Ra. He was not only the prophet, but also the living embodiment of the Aten, and it was through his personal teachings to the people that the cosmic light of the Creator would be revealed — he was to be the 'Lightbringer'. It seems that the young pharaoh was not only intent on streamlining the traditional solar religion through a 'back to basics' approach, but making it appeal to both Egyptians and non-Egyptians. He was promoting what he knew to be a universal God, the one and only God of creation.

In Egypt, names were of extreme importance — take away a name and that thing is destroyed, it no longer exists. Within five years of becoming pharaoh, Amenhotep IV took a monumental step, he dispensed with his own name which meant, 'Amun is Satisfied': a politically-chosen given name that must have tortured him. He changed his name to Akhenaten, which means 'Spirit of Aten'. The die was now cast and there was no going back, no more compromise, the mission had to be realised.

After the death of his father, Akhenaten's power was without restriction and he discharged it to promote his dream. The single greatest and most provocative act undertaken by Akhenaten was to ban all religious images and statues. If this weren't sufficient to provoke the Amun priests and those who followed other religions or cults, he then imposed a ban on the worship of all gods other than the Aten; setting a precedent for the Judahites in another five hundred years. Needless to say, the Amun priesthood did not appreciate these enforcements. They would have riled at their power being curtailed, but to banish their religion altogether would have them seething with thoughts of assassination. The army and Akhenaten's paramilitary police ensured that dissention did not escalate into open rebellion. The ban would have upset many of the common people, with their plethora of deities to suit every purpose or person. They would have had no understanding or explanation of why they must renounce their old gods, leaving them bewildered and confused.

There was just one exemption: the sacred Mnevis bull of Heliopolis. The bull was regarded as the incarnation of Ur–mer, the 'life of Ra', and this is another indication of the intimate kinship of the Ra and Atenist cults. It is not, therefore, so strange that there was no uproar and resistance amongst the followers of Ra and Osiris, because the Ra priesthood were fellow promoters of Atenism, along with the pharaoh.

The full name for the Aten, 'Ra lives, ruler of the horizons returned as Aten' also indicates that Ra and the Aten were indisputably linked. Clearly, there is no thought of discarding Ra, but of promoting a different aspect, that of the *visible* face of the god, which was the sun. Understandably priests are the most conservative of any profession, for to allow any change in a religious belief would destroy the very foundations of that belief, yet here we have the Ra priests discreetly undertaking a radical transformation, apparently for no real purpose. So perhaps there was a purpose, caused by an enforced revision of beliefs, provoked by what had been found in the opened underground chambers at Giza.

Although we had one God and now one religion in Egypt, things were far from simple. There appeared to be a flourishing second religion, contemporary with Atenism. Curiously, it complemented the worship of the Creator, Atum–Ra. Atenism was the religion of the priests, this religious cult was a religion for the common man; a religion that was meant to teach morality and spirituality, in the way Christianity is supposed to do. The religion, based in the ancient cities of Heliopolis, Memphis and Abydos, was known as the Egyptian Mysteries. They told of the son of Ra, Osiris, his consort Isis and their son, Horus. Osiris was a godman who came to help mankind, he suffered an unjust death, but was resurrected and then became the ruler of the underworld, assisting the spirits of the dead to return to the stars and reunite with the Creator God. The following afforded to Osiris appeared to rival that of his father, Ra — but this has an exact parallel in the Christian worship of Jesus that seems to equal that given to his father, Jehovah.

The 'everyman' Osiris cult was clearly connected to the secret and exclusive inner cult of Ra. It used a handful of gods, in a very human story, to communicate its allegorical teachings, aimed at the uneducated common man. Akhenaten felt that another set of teachings was unnecessary. He feared that its allegorical stories might be believed literally and in addition, it complicated and detracted from the truth. Akhenaten deemed it unnecessary and wished to hone religion to its original, purest and simplest form. Later in this book, when I consider the New Testament, I will show that the Osiris Mystery religion was actually the true source of what became Christianity.

The second major undertaking that the new pharaoh felt compelled to devote himself to, was, as we have seen, the building of a new city, which he named Akhet–Aten. This new city dedicated to the Aten, was constructed on virgin ground, a place with no past associations, a place untainted: it was to be the City of God. The site chosen, at first appears to be bizarre, since it was in the unpopulated centre of Egypt, next to the Nile on a treeless narrow plain of arid desert, closely hemmed in by an encircling ridge of steep hills. Some scholars attribute this choice to the need for Akhenaten to put himself beyond the murderous clutches of the Amun priesthood, but this explanation is rather weak, for if this were Akhenaten's sole purpose, he could have sited himself even further north, in one of the cities in the Ra heartland. There are some who think that Akhenaten's city came about because his father thought it a good compromise, which confined the co-regent's extremism to one isolated area, leaving each with his own kingdom. Indeed, one of the new city's boundary stelae seem to confirm this theory:

"… Concerning the southern stela which is on the eastern mountain of Akhetaten.
it is the stela of Akhetaten, the one that I had erected to the end. Nevermore shall I go beyond it to the south.…"[1]

Whilst it appears that Amenhotep III wanted to distance his son, one should remember that he was also a devoted Atenist — his two viziers for Upper and Lower Egypt were made 'Steward' of the Mansion of Aten and 'High

---

[1] Hari, R. *New Kingdom Amarna Period: the Great Hymn to Aten*

Priest' of the new Temple of Aten at Heliopolis — unequivocally indicating his politico/religious inclinations. Though Amenhotep might have made efforts not to alienate the Amun priests, it is difficult to accept that he felt obliged to build a city–kingdom especially for the purpose of exiling his over–enthusiastic son. It is, after all, quite clear that the building had been solely Akhenaten's idea. Whilst there was a probable concern over internal strife and Akhenaten was possibly agreeable to confining his powers to within his new city, in actual fact, he had no desire ever to step outside the sprawling boundaries of what he considered to be God's City. This theory is given credibility by the fact that when Akhenaten became sole ruler, he still did not leave the city's boundaries. He was residing in a new paradise, with no reason to leave; indeed, were he to do so, he would be deserting his God.

Akhenaten claimed that the site was chosen for him by God. At this place he witnessed the sun rising out of a natural U–shaped indentation in the ridge of eastern hills, which mimicked the hieroglyph used for the word for 'akhet,' meaning 'horizon' and so the city was called Akhet–Aten, 'Aten on the Horizon.' This was where his city of God needed to be; he was fiercely adamant about it and made a declaration that he would never be moved from it by anyone.

From his tent, where he set up an altar to the Aten, he surveyed the construction and controlled the planning and architecture of the city personally. It was a city centred on two open–air temples, one of them immense. A large palace was linked to his private residence by a bridge, which spanned the wide ceremonial Royal Road. His police barracks and administrative buildings were located in this 'central city.' Within the wide boundaries, Akhenaten built five royal palaces, for like other pharaohs, he had numerous queens, despite his elevation of Queen Nefertiti to be almost his equal. In the northern suburbs, he built a royal palace with a large zoo, to observe the animals and contemplate their part in God's creation. In the cliffs of the eastern hills, he excavated tombs, for, even in death, Akhenaten had no intention of leaving the boundaries of his holy city

It is extremely unlikely that this middle–of–nowhere site was chosen by a pharaoh who just happened to be passing and saw a sunrise that provoked an association. The saddle–back shape in the hills, which cupped the sunrise at certain times of the year, was probably a useful coincidence, but the geographic location of this city made it unique. The site was exactly halfway between Heliopolis and Thebes, a distance of 172 miles, or 275 km from each — it was set on a latitude which placed it precisely between the farthest northern point of Egypt, Behdet in the Nile Delta and the southern most point, at Elephantine, Aswan as it is now known, both 269 miles or 417 km away. The city's longitude was exactly one minute east of the axis of Egypt.

The city boundaries were marked out with 14 stelae and their purpose has baffled scholars. Professor Livio Stecchini, a mathematician, metrologist and amateur Egyptologist found the answer; though it's one that academics prefer to ignore. Stecchini realised that using ancient pre-dynastic measurements, the distance between the northern and southernmost stelae, were in exact proportion to the distance of 106 *atur* between Behdet and Elephantine — exactly 1/12 of the distance from the Equator to the Pole. Stecchini says that Akenaten wanted to prove that Thebes was not the geodesic centre of Egypt and that he had chosen the geodesic centre at Akhet–Aten. The boundary stelae marked the dimensions of the city according to a geodesic system that predated even Pharaonic Egypt. Stecchini also found that within the dimensions of the great Pyramid, the geodesic measurements related to the size of our planet Earth.[2] There has been much measurement and calculation of the Great Pyramid and all confirm that the structure's geodesic form is an exact microcosmic representation of the dimensions of the northern hemisphere.

Egyptologists, whilst accepting the very precise scale measurements, dismiss the results as a catalogue of coincidences. But how large a catalogue of coincidences is required before the evidence is accepted as fact — five coincidences ten, twenty, fifty, … — the answer is that they will never accept the evidence because it is simply incompatible with their views. Egyptologists have their grand plan of how things were and stubbornly refuse to consider that anything could be different from how they have decided it was. Even world renowned philosopher and mathematician Professor Stecchini couldn't make historians take the implications of his incredible mathematical findings seriously:

> "The study of Greek temples much later led me to the study of ancient geography and geodesy. But I was gradually forced to accept the fact that scholars of ancient history do not read numbers, neither in ancient texts nor in research papers. I noticed a number of times, when I submitted a paper for judgement to a specialist of a particular area, that he would quickly turn a page if he saw numbers on it. In many different guises I was told that "numbers do not constitute evidence in ancient studies". Finally, I learned that I had no choice but to pursue my interests in splendid isolation."

Egyptologists tell us that Ancient Egyptians were primitives who employed primitive building methods, albeit that the results were often outstanding.

---

[2] Stecchini, L C A. *History of Measures*

They dismiss sophisticated construction techniques and knowledge of measurement, mathematics, geometry, astronomy, mechanics, architecture, building and the use of lathes and diamond–tipped sonic drills are completely out of the question. The wealth of facts and evidence is substantial, but academics show no interest in trying to make sense of the great many anomalies

If the Egyptians were indeed primitives, who had dragged themselves up from farming and hunting onto the first step of civilisation, it is absolutely astonishing that in this most ancient time, the Egyptians suddenly had construction engineers of supreme ability. How did the primitive priests suddenly know how to carry out intricate surveying over great distances and how did they suddenly have the knowledge to carry out extraordinarily complex measurements and calculations with such precision. Indeed, one cannot escape the notion that the ancient Egyptians possessed some kind of geographic overview. The skills of surveying and measuring, which Akhenaten employed had not been used since the Great Pyramids were built, sadly the engineering skills of their builders had mysteriously disappeared. Akhenaten created a city of God, a new earthly paradise, by employing precise measurements to establish the exact geodesic centre, a point of balance, a microcosm of Egypt, from which he would live in the harmony, the embodiment of the perfect cosmic order of *Ma'at* in the period immediately following the Creation.

Akhenaten was attempting to recreate the harmony of the golden age, Sep–Tepi, 'the First Time', of the Netjeru gods after the creation. He was creating his own beginning, with his holy city as the new embodiment of the primeval mound. He confirmed this by setting up his own Benben stone — that early representation of the primeval mound — despite his ban upon religious statues and clearly he not only saw himself as the living embodiment of *Ma'at*, Akhenaten also saw himself as the embodiment of the Bennu bird, or phoenix, the mythical bird which was an aspect of Atum–Ra, that landed on the creation mound at the moment of the very first sunrise. Within Akhet–Aten he built the Great House of Aten and within this vast open–air temple, on the eastern side, stood the Mansion of the Benben, housing a sacred pillar to support a conical stone which was a representation of the Benben; and upon this stone the first brilliant rays of the rising sun would alight every day.

The relevance of this might seem obscure, not to mention naïvely archaic and hardly complementary with a new monotheistic religion. Akhenaten and the priests of Ra considered the distant past to be crucially important, so retained the ancient symbolism and what it represented. These symbolic stories carried within them elements of the truth that they wished to remember and preserve. This link with the past is highlighted by

Akhenaten's choice of an ancient system of measurement, one which was pre–dynastic, old before the time of the first pharaohs, perhaps going back to the age of the Netjeru gods and the Shemsu–hor. Akhenaten was obsessed by a religious belief unlike any other pharaoh — how much his father and grandfather were similarly obsessed is not clear, as they had felt more constrained politically. Although at the time, it appeared that Akhenaten was promoting a new god and a unique monotheistic religion, it was in fact a recreation of the original religion that had once existed.

Egyptologists these days believe, with no real evidence, that the Egyptians built the Great Pyramids and the Sphinx around 2500 BCE and choose to ignore what the Egyptians actually said about their constructions. In ancient texts, of which some have survived the passing millennia, it tells that the priests of Ra believed that the Netjeru built the Great Pyramids, the Sphinx and certain temples and monuments, many millennia before the time of the Horus kings. Most of these edifices were sited around Rostau/Giza and Annu/Heliopolis. Akhenaten's grandfather, Tuthmosis had written "Rostau... the horizon west of Annu... the splendid place of the First Time." The priests also claimed that they preserved some of the knowledge and wisdom of these ancient gods. Until Tuthmosis unearthed the Sphinx from the desert sands, there had been no significant religious changes, then suddenly three pharaohs decided to promote a new aspect of the One God, and the priests of Ra, who were the core of the Aten priesthood, decided to revise their religion.

Once more, we must ask why this happened; the answer must be there to be discerned. Perhaps our solution lies, yet again, with the Sphinx Stele, which has a stylised picture of Tuthmosis standing before the Sphinx, inscribed upon it. The reclining Sphinx is drawn on top of what appears to be a structure containing an enormous doorway. Since the Sphinx monument is *on* the ground, one is left to infer that the stylised structure must be *beneath* it. Could the stele be informing us that underground lies the fabled 'Hall of Records'? Yes it may seem fantastic, but as we know, seismic investigation has confirmed underground chambers beneath the Sphinx.

At present, we cannot be certain what caused three pharaohs and the Ra priesthood to promote a new monotheistic form of religion; a religion so intrinsically linked to a belief in ancient beings, who are fabled to have created the first monolithic structures and who brought knowledge and civilisation to primitive man. Hopefully, one day, we will know — perhaps when the Egyptian authorities have the courage to place truth and knowledge above their national vanity and religious belief and openly excavate and show all that is discovered to the world.

It is not the purpose of this book to give the full story of Akhenaten and his monotheistic religion, nor is there the space; there are many books that the reader can turn to find out more. However, it is worth pointing out that some biographers feel obliged not only to criticise and demean, but some even demonise Akhenaten to the ridiculous extent of comparing him to Hitler and Stalin, simply because he banned the Amun cult and the worship of images of gods. Akhenaten, unlike Hitler and Stalin, did not perpetrate mass murder and ethnic cleansing; there is no evidence to show that he killed off any of his opponents. One thinks of life being cheap in ancient times, but Egyptian society had no off-hand attitude to killing, let alone a thirst for blood letting. The religion promoted by Akhenaten discouraged killing, so he is unlikely to have enforced its belief by doing something that it opposed. Perhaps these harsh portraits are the biographers' desperate attempts to sully and discredit Atenism, in order to maintain the Judaic claim to be the first monotheistic religion and as a consequence, also uphold the claims of the Christian Church.

Alas, too often historical biographers write their books with deliberate prejudice, hoping that their harsh critical stance will gain them plaudits amongst their academic peers. Too often writers fail to grasp the wider picture, or bother to consider the events before them with an open mind. Instead they restrict themselves within the narrow confines of unshakable orthodoxy. It is also important to understand that though some scholars like to write with arrogant authority, the truth is, that too little is known about this period and certainly not sufficient to claim absolute knowledge and understanding of every nuance of what occurred, for in fact the sum of what we know is all too little. I will attempt to summarise what took place... as far as we know!

Within the holy city of Akhet–Aten, Akhenaten was now not only the divine ruler — as were all pharaohs — but the sole intermediary between God and mankind; he was the high priest, prophet and spiritual teacher. Some academics see this as being dictatorial and megalomaniac, but that is opinion, not fact. To accomplish the religious revolution, he needed a firm hand, for a tolerant attitude would have seen the old traditional practices continue as they had done through his father and grandfather's time. The charge of megalomaniac is weak, he was pharaoh and thus the acknowledged mortal personification of God, so he, like all pharaohs, was expected to be a strong leader whose word was sacred and must be obeyed without question. This is how it was and had always been in Egypt, this is the way he was expected to be, so the fact that he promoted himself as the earthly intermediary between God and the people, was, in fact, completely normal and expected. This is far from being an act of a megalomaniac, unless Egypt had always been ruled by one. Only the pharaoh could call for religious change. As a 'god,' the pharaoh was the highest priest, but generally left mundane duties, such as preaching, to the temple priests.

Akhenaten however, felt his earthly mission was to lead by example and to preach the message personally, so like any good prophet, this is what he did.

To a degree, it would have been necessary for Akhenaten to employ certain actions, which to ignorant people might appear to be high handed: old temples had to be closed down, graven images had to be destroyed if they had not been cast aside willingly. But weaklings waiting for public consensus will not achieve great works. If Akhenaten had shown anything less than total commitment and been anything other than absolute in his endeavours, he would have had little success. The Amun priests would have put a stop to his efforts and would have arranged his assassination quite quickly.

Akhenaten fully understood the dangers; what was needed to fulfil his aims, and how to stay alive. The establishment of a remote holy city was crucial to his aims. The population of the new city was filled not only with the elite of Egyptian society — those nobles who converted to Atenism — but unusually, many foreigners. To cement friendships and alliances, Akhenaten received gifts of foreign princesses; each wife brought her large entourage. In the Atenist religion, all men, regardless of creed and colour of skin, were equal under God therefore Akhenaten strove to cast aside the traditional Egyptian distaste of foreigners. Some of the foreign workers were also in the lower levels of the social strata: administrators, scribes, craftsmen and their families. Akhet–Aten became a truly multi–cultural, multi–ethnic city as its new unilateral religion was intended to embrace not only Egyptians, but also all of mankind. Some scholars question how much Akhenaten cared about foreigners, for he seemed to show no interest at all in the empire or anything outside of Egypt. Up to a point, this is probably true, but then neither did he show any real interest in Egypt itself. The only world that mattered to him was that which existed within Akhet–Aten: that holy city was meant as the earthly representation of Heaven. Akhenaten is certainly guilty of neglecting both empire and kingdom, but they were of no importance to him, he was not concerned with earthly matters, only spiritual ones — what mattered was living a natural family life, appreciating and contemplating God's gifts of nature and praising the glories of God, the Creator of the Cosmos.

The philosophy that is at the core of Akhenaten's religion is illustrated in this extract taken from *The Great Hymn to Aten*,[3] which he composed. It is clear that this is also the foundation of the monotheistic religion promoted in the Bible:

---

3 op. cit. Hari, R

> "One God without equal, Thou didst create the universe according to the consciousness of Thy heart, so that Thou art One alone. Thou extractest eternally thousands of forms originating from Thyself. Thou dwellest in Thy unity. No being engendered by Thee exists for any reason other than to contemplate Thyself alone."

This is but one example, one extract, but there is much more. In all the Atenist hymns, the same theme is repeated over and over, praising the glory of the One God, the sole Creator of the universe and all living things. There can be no doubting that the Bible is promoting the same God, and using modestly-revised hymns and psalms taken directly out of Egypt.

Chapter 11

The Pharaoh In Gods' Image

"It doesn't matter how long my hair is or what colour my skin is or whether I'm a woman or a man."

John Lennon

Akhenaten broke with many traditions, but not least he transformed the way in which the pharaoh was portrayed. Traditionally, artistic depictions of the pharaohs, though imposing and beautiful, were perhaps slightly naïve in style, as well as employing stiff posture and formal situations. Akhenaten introduced a new artistic style that was more fluid and natural, both in form and subject.

Almost all pictorial depictions of Akhenaten and his family show informal circumstances, where he appears as a family man enjoying life with his wife and children. Often the family members were portrayed naked, relaxed and unashamed, rather like Adam and Eve in Eden before the fall. It is highly likely that this was encoded as the source of the Biblical creation story.

There was to be no shame, no moral repression, just the restraint imposed by one's conscience, or higher self. These ideas are very much those of the later Greek philosophers and hierophants of the Eleusinian Mysteries, which developed later from the Osiris Mystery. Besides contemplating God, Akhenaten set the example that everyone should live a natural family life and enjoy the natural world that the Creator had gifted to them, unconstrained by religious dogma and ritual.

Akhenaten instructed his artists to portray him and his family in rather peculiar stylised and elongated images; this insistence has long caused much debate amongst academics. Besides the thin elongated form, he was represented with certain female characteristics. Even more strangely, rather than emulating the slender form which typified Egyptian women, he chose an age-old depiction which everyone could readily recognise, one with swelling belly, broad hips and heavy thighs.

Inevitably, some scholars took the depictions literally, rather than recognise that they were symbolic and deliberately chosen to transmit esoteric information. The literal choice has caused speculation about various rare hereditary diseases that Akhenaten might have suffered from. These have been discounted largely on the grounds that scientists found nothing within the body of Tutankhamun, probably his son by a minor queen, to indicate a genetic defect that might have contributed to such deformity. Akhenaten's wife was also portrayed in the same manner and she would not have inherited any problems attributed to in–breeding within the Egyptian royal family as she was definitely of foreign birth, from Mesopotamia.

The final proof came from the mysterious tomb 55, located opposite that of Tutankhamun in the Valley of the Kings, near Thebes. It is believed that Akhenaten and his mother were moved from Akhet–Aten and re–entombed here. Tomb 55 was in bad condition when discovered, having suffered from water damage and it also revealed evidence that it had been opened, looted and then hastily resealed.[1] Initially, it appears that the re–internments had been done respectfully, as befits a burial supervised by Tutankhamun.

The desecration took place 200 years later, during the quarrying, higher up the hill, for the tomb for Rameses IX. Someone had hurriedly looted the tomb and subjected the coffin to deliberate damage. The coffin had its names removed to leave the occupant anonymous, the face had also been largely destroyed with the intention of denying the spirit its needs for air, sight and sustenance. Clearly the dead king in the coffin was deemed an evil heretic — it could only be Akhenaten. At some stage his mother's mummy had been relocated a second time, to remove her from the evil presence and is probably one of those discovered in the tomb of Amenhotep II. Though the coffin and canopic jars in Tomb 55 had been made for Akhenaten's secondary wife, Kiya, the body was that of a male. Anatomical examinations have revealed that the male was over 35 years old, closely related to Tutankhamun and without any of the physical deformities in the depictions of Akhenaten.[2]

These depictions which exaggerated, even deformed the king's body are deliberately stylised. This is also confirmed by the early images of Akhenaten and those from shortly before his death, which show him possessing a totally normal form, as the yellow limestone statuette, which is now in the Louvre does. Scholars have long known that the face mask, from the second of the three coffins containing the mummy of Tutankhamun, was not that of the boy king; though they have remained mute about whose

---

[1] Ayrton, E R. "The Tomb of Thy"

[2] Hussein, F and Harris, J E, "Abstract Papers"

THE PHARAOH IN GODS' IMAGE

it was. Along with many of the other treasures found in Tutankhamun's tomb, it belonged to his father. That glorious golden face, renowned throughout the world, is that of Akhenaten.

So if Akhenaten was actually good looking, why this extraordinary, asexual and distinctly unearthly portrayal of himself, especially as he considered himself to be the earthly embodiment of God? To many people, particularly when gods and pharaohs were depicted as magnificent specimens of manhood, such grotesque depiction might appear to be blasphemous. The decision had not been a mental aberration, but rather like everything Akhenaten did, the intent was to *portray* something. What it was, is likely to be linked once more to the priests of Ra and probably to something they had discovered in the repository at Giza — the Hall of Records. One can only guess, but perhaps Akhenaten was attempting to replicate the appearance of the founders and builders of Heliopolis and Giza — the Netjeru.

When scholars speculate over the rather bizarre human form that Akhenaten chose in depictions of himself and his family, they seem to ignore the possibility that he was actually imitating some representation that he had seen. Some scholars think that he was decadent and wished to portray himself and his family as different from the rest of his subjects. This may have been true, but does not explain the bizarre choice. For anyone, let alone a pharaoh who is supposed to be the earthly embodiment of God, to portray himself in such an unflattering, even ugly way, makes no sense. To do so would surely undermine his royal dignity and damage his credibility, by inviting ridicule from his subjects. Akhenaten was not a fool, he was a highly intelligent man who carefully devised and designed everything he ever did. These depictions were extremely important to his plan.

Despite examination of Akhenaten's remains disproving it, the most popular reason still aired by many scholars, is that he suffered from Frœhlich's Syndrome; certainly the depictions of the pharaoh might suggest it, but sufferers are impotent and mentally retarded. Clearly Akhenaten was neither of these. Marfan's disease has also been proposed and whilst the list of deformities seem to fit the stranger pictures of Akhenaten, if he did suffer from this in some way, he did not have every symptom and the anatomical study of his remains does not indicate he had any of them.

If Akhenaten had been suffering from a genetic deformity, this would not explain why he chose to draw attention to his weakness and physical impairment. To do so would be extremely unwise for any ruler — rulers were normally portrayed in an imposing heroic form, even if they had few of the attributes. The other question that we need to ask is why exaggerate everything and include bodily defects which he did not have — it just does not make any sense. Abraham Lincoln is said to have suffered from

Marfan's disease, but the president's long lean face and frame are nothing like the unworldly depictions of Akhenaten.

The narrow face and bizarrely elongated cranium shown in the pictures are definitely not true–life depictions. They are also not unique to Akhenaten and his family. The oldest such depictions of very elongated craniums, go back to around 6750 BCE, when baked–clay heads distinctly displayed this extraordinary abnormality. These heads were found in Kurdistan, in the region described as the cradle of mankind and of civilisation and the area associated with Abraham and the Egyptian star–god cult. The later Ubaid culture, which existed between 4500 and 4000 BCE in this region, before moving south into Mesopotamia, also had strange figurines displaying a more stylised version of the same long heads.

Some human remains were discovered belonging to the early Ubaid period and out of the thirteen skulls that were examined, it was discovered that eight of them had been artificially deformed. This had been effected by wrapping pieces of wood tightly, with bandages, around the skulls of young infants, resulting in a sloping forehead and extended rear cranium. The skulls of both Akhenaten and his son Tutankhamun had slightly more than normal protrusion at the rear, though no sign of artificial influence.

This strange desire to develop a freakish head shape was not just confined to the middle east, but was found to have occurred in South America also, in early Andean cultures, amongst certain members of the priesthood of the Mayan culture of Central America, and it was also practiced in North America, amongst the Chinook tribes.[3] The Americas is a long way from the middle east, however there are certain archaeological finds which suggest that the Egyptians might have landed there and this argument gains further weight by post–mortems carried out on some Egyptian mummies, which have revealed traces of substances that could only have come from the American continent. Despite a possible limited Egyptian presence in the Americas, this elongated head fetish would not have been copied from there, as no evidence has been found in Egypt of this artificial reconstruction of the skull shape.

Graves dated to pre–dynastic times, discovered at Abydos, contained the remains of members of an unusual non–native Egyptian race. The remains revealed a skeletal frame of a larger size than common in Egypt and a most unusual skull, which was of a great size and what is technically described as dolichocephalic shaped, meaning long and narrow.[4] Egyptologist Walter Emery considered that these remains belonged to a distinct aristocratic race, which over a long period, 'fused' with the common natives and originally

---

3 Favazza, A R. *Bodies Under Siege*
4 Emery, W B. *Archaic Egypt*

The pharaoh in gods' image

had markedly different social and burial customs. Other long skulls have been found at deep levels at the Sumerian city of Kish, which suggests that perhaps these people were the ones who came to Sumer as civilisers. Scholars have always puzzled about where the Sumerians came from, but what is more intriguing is the origins of those who taught them the skills of civilisation.

So we have some definite evidence that shows that there was not only a prevalent wide-spread culture of elongated skulls, one which seemed to be largely exclusive to royalty and the priesthood, but that there was actually an unknown 'alien' race who came as civilisers, who, Walter Emery suggested, could be identified with the Shemsu–Hor. This surely is a more realistic reason for religiously obsessed Akhenaten's strange choice of royal depictions. There are good reasons to believe that this desire for elongated skulls was not merely an extreme desire to look different, but rather it was to copy the natural appearance of a group of extremely influential and celebrated people, who may have been known to numerous societies around the world.

Besides the cranial oddity, there is also the curious question of why Akhenaten chose to be depicted as a non-sexual being. Once more, we must consider if his choice was influenced by the teachings of the Ra priesthood at Giza. The answer is surely yes. What he might have learnt, we cannot know, but we might find a clue from a different source. It will take a lengthy diversion to give the idea some consideration, but hopefully, the reader will consider it worthwhile in what is learnt.

Akhenaten's depiction, as a being of neither sex makes sense when one reads an account of the true form of the 'gods' which is given in the rather enigmatic *Book of Enoch*.[5] It is an intriguing and complex jigsaw puzzle, which is worthy of serious consideration. Whilst we must be very cautious of accepting things written in any books connected with Judea, this particular work does relate some intriguing information that is not given anywhere else. Some recent research seems to authenticate important information given in this esoteric book.[6]

The original source of this work is totally unknown, but it is highly unlikely that the early part of the Enoch story would have originated in Palestine. It is probable that the story was passed down orally and then eventually written down and added to further at later dates. Fortunately, the Essenes at Qumran hid the scrolls with their Enochian texts, in caves, when they realised that their community was under threat of destruction from the Romans. This secretion also assured the Book's long-term survival, for when the Church of Rome carried out a purge against 'heretical' works, it

---

5 Black. M & VanderKam J C. *The Book of Enoch; or, 1 Enoch*
6 Knight, C & Lomas, R. *Uriel's Machine*

particularly targeted this extremely alarming work. As a consequence, it seemed that the Book of Enoch had been lost forever.

There is little information given about Enoch in the Bible itself, with the first reference appearing in Genesis 4:16–23, where the genealogy has him as the son of Adam's son Cain and the great, great, great grandfather of Noah, builder of the Flood Ark. The biblical scribes obviously had second thoughts about Enoch being fathered by the murderer Cain, so in Genesis 5:21–29 Enoch's father is changed to Seth, Adam's third son. Typically, the scribes failed to remove the earlier conflicting genealogical lineage. Strangely, these are the only references to Enoch in the Old Testament. The real flesh of Enoch and his unique adventures, is found in the book of his name, which in Hebrew means Initiate.

Both the Essenes and the Enochian element amongst the Judaic priesthood, who appear to have distanced themselves somewhat from the proponents of Moses, held the Book of Enoch as an essential work. Many scholars of the Dead Sea Scrolls believe that the texts indicate that there had actually been two distinct sects amongst the priesthood, the Enochians and the Zadok priesthood who followed the doctrine of Moses.[7] It appears that these two groups came together with a compromise, following the Maccabean Revolt. However, a group of Enochian hard–liners, followers of someone entitled the Teacher of Righteousness, attempted to take control, but their failure to do so caused them to break away and led them to found the Qumran community.

Following their virtual extinction during the Jewish war against Rome in 68 CE, what distinct influence this faction once had was lost. As a consequence, the Book of Enoch was not incorporated into the mainstream Judaic scriptures, as the surviving rabbinical priesthood was now solely immersed in the books and laws attributed to Moses. There was much more to gain politically from the stories of Moses than from the esoteric and apocalyptic Enochian texts. Despite this, the Book of Enoch survived, if only in fragmented form, but nevertheless it was popular amongst early Christians, though later it was dismissed as *pagan*.

The more learned members of the Christian Church would comprehend some of what the Book of Enoch contained and recognise its potential to undermine not just the very foundations of the Bible's Genesis story, but the religion itself. The Church authorities attempted to destroy all copies, but fortunately, separate fragments survived in obscurity.

In the early 17th century, a Flemish scholar, J J Scaliger, toured European libraries looking at old manuscripts; by accident, he stumbled across some tracts written in Greek by a ninth–century monk called

---

7 ibid.

Syncellus. In this long undisturbed work, Scaliger found that the monk was quoting liberally from the Book of Enoch, which meant that he must have had access to a long-hidden copy. When Scaliger published the shocking extracts, they provoked great interest around Europe and rekindled the search for this lost *forbidden* work. In the 18th century, a member of the Scottish Freemasons, James Bruce, a descendent of Robert the Bruce and from a family with Knights Templar links, found three copies in Ethiopia.

The books' return to Europe provoked some startling responses at very influential levels. One copy was given to the King of France, who installed it in the National Library of Paris; the second copy was intended for the Bodleian Library at Oxford and the third Bruce would retain for himself. But before Bruce left France for Britain, an expert on Egyptian Coptic studies was rushing to Paris with letters from the Secretary of State to the British Ambassador in France, to secure immediate access to the copy in the Paris library, so that it could be translated. Strangely, this translation was never made public, so to whom did the translation go and what had been the unseemly hurry? Why could they not even wait until the Bodleian received its copy?

Once Bruce was back in Britain, he was elected a Fellow of the Royal Society. This esteemed scientific institution has a history steeped in covert activities. It had strong links with Freemasonry, members like Newton and Boyle conducted secret alchemy experiments and the society had an active interest in Megalithic and Egyptian weights and measures.

It was not until 1821, nearly fifty years later, that a translation of the Bodleian copy was made public and when it was, it caused a great sensation all around Europe. We then had to wait until the 20th century, to find a new light shining on the Book of Enoch, when nine further fragments were found at Qumran, amongst the Dead Sea Scrolls.

The Book of Enoch is not generally given any credence by scholars who dismiss it as a confusion of narrative and discourse, but there are some who recognise that this enigmatic work is like an intricately devised puzzle that defies all attempts to understand its full and true meaning. Part of the book's content, in a section called *The Book of the Heavenly Luminaries,* has been dismissed as nonsensical. It includes an account of the sun seen to rise and set when viewed through different 'gates' or 'portals' and uses this to obtain the 'co-ordinates' of the location to which an angel takes Enoch, to visit the gods. Enoch records very carefully all that he is told and describes what he sees as best as he can understand, however it comes across clearly that he is an uneducated man, certainly a man with no scientific knowledge who is struggling to find suitable words to describe what he is shown.

After a deal of careful study and a lot of lateral thinking, two academics, Christopher Knight and Robert Lomas revealed that the co-ordinates were astronomical ones, based upon the sun's movement throughout a year through different positions, or 'gates'.⁸ Enoch gives lengths of daylight as fractions of the full day. This is quite a significant piece of information as altering lengths of daylight were unknown in the Mediterranean region until the Romans moved northwards into Britain, but even then, they did not understand that the length of daylight varied with latitude.

The book's calendarical movement of the sun has long baffled experts and seemed to defy interpretation it has therefore been commonly dismissed as nonsense, but not by all scholars. Professor Otto Neugebauer, of the Institute of Advanced Studies at Princeton, managed to draw some conclusions: he stated that the astronomical elements in the Book of Enoch do not relate to old Semitic calendaric units, nor are the linear schemes for daylight to be found in the Old Testament. Though he attempted to find links to Babylonian and Egyptian calendars, but with no real success, Neugebauer concluded that Enoch's calendar was unique.⁹ It was clear that Enoch was not a mathematician or astronomer, but merely attempting to record what he had been told by his angel guide, and no doubt any precision in the original account would have been watered down with countless retelling and translation.

It is interesting to find that scholars, who have worked on the Dead Sea Scrolls, have found that every fragment was linked to the Essenes solar calendar. This indicates their obsession with the calculation of time. The Essenes were called the 'Sons of Light' and the 'Sons of Dawn,' which, though sounding Druidic, may indicate a link with Atenism, but certainly confirms their interest in the sun. Whilst the writing is not Judaic, it implies an Egyptian connection and that might explain why the Essenes were so fascinated by the content of the Book of Enoch.

Knight and Lomas discovered that the movements of the sun and the length of daylight recorded in the *Book of Enoch* offered a rough means to calculate latitude on the planet. However, due to the crude units for fractions of day length used in place of hours, the latitude is lacking in exact precision. Because of this, Knight and Lomas's calculations needed to allow a margin of five percent latitude either way. This inexact placing gave a location bounded by the latitudes of 51 and 59 degrees north, a distance of 320 miles on the ground. A complex rationale and numerous calculations enabled them to deduce the place that Enoch was taken to. The resulting latitudes and what seems to be a description of astronomical observatories, led Knight and Lomas to conclude that the only realistic location was what

---

8   ibid.

9   op. cit. Black & VanderKam

is now Britain.[10] Their conclusion is further supported by Enoch's reference to the weather: violent winds, cold, rain, hail, frost and snow — elements which do not belong in the middle east, but certainly to wintry northern lands and a place with weather that no native of Palestine could ever have imagined. We can attribute some significance to this inference, because of a link between the ancient Egyptians and the early Druids and because of certain stories contained within Celtic legends.

The first section of the *Book of Enoch,* tells of a meteorite strike, deliberately targeted at Earth and the subsequent great deluge that will engulf the planet. The next chapters of the book focus on the regularity and harmony of nature and how their study can bring about an understanding of the Creator. They are followed by the story of Enoch's involvement with mysterious entities named as both the Watchers and angels. The book then recounts a collection of parables and Enoch's interpretation of the Final Judgement.

After this, the book deals with the movements of the sun, the planets and the stars, followed by a section which reveals Enoch's visionary dreams, but since they include the second century BCE Maccabean Revolt and the future visions of New Jerusalem, it is clearly a late addition by Essene authors and has no connection with the original work. The final part tells of Enoch's advice to his great grandson, Methuselah and his family and mentions the miraculous birth of Noah, a new beginning and a tirade against sinners, which once more indicates the authorship of the Essenes. When scholars dismiss the book because it appears to be composed by numerous authors, they are failing to separate the final part of the book, which is clearly a first century BCE addition, from the undatable original.

On first reading, the story does sound rather like a religious fantasy with its tale of gods — good and bad — angels, meteorites and world-wide flooding. It also seems that directing a meteorite to induce a flood, is a rather extreme way to destroy the illegally-bred offspring of rebellious angels — the giants, genetically engineered creatures and subverted humans — in such an unselective manner, for in practice this draconian execution would affect all life forms. Fanciful, the Book of Enoch may seem, nevertheless this detailed explanation seems to fill in the background details of not only the Biblical Flood story, but also all the many others meteorite/flood legends from every region of the planet. Most of these describe the falling fire from the sky, the ferocious blast of freezing wind, the burning debris raining down on the survivors, the tsunami floods and then the years of dark skies hiding the sun and moon and the resulting desperate food shortage. It does sound brutally callous to use such a method for elimination, but if the need were to kill off large numbers of undesirable

---

[10] op. cit. Knight & Lomas

beings, scattered around the world, some in hiding, a meteorite would be the perfect weapon to use. It would certainly explain the sudden ultra-rapid meltdown of the ice sheets, which has baffled scientists. It would also explain the huge tsunami flood and the instant violent destruction and even extinction of animals in North America and Siberia.

But it seemed the 'gods' were not totally heartless. Though the Bible's version only has Noah and his family being saved and other legends from around the globe recount individuals being spared in a similar way, there are other stories that describe many innocent people being helped to find safety and in various places around the world there are many deep underground tunnels and dwellings, capable of housing vast numbers of people. In the Anatolian highlands, there are apparently, 35 known underground cities. They are built in numerous descending levels, with deep ventilation shafts and some cities interconnected by long 'road' tunnels, one of which runs for five miles. One of the cities — now a tourist attraction at a place called Derinkuyu — is estimated to have held some 20,000 people. This conservative number is much debated — other estimates push the number up to over 50,000, which would mean that these 35 known cities would have the capability of sheltering between half and one and a half million people. These are extraordinarily large numbers, even if one wishes to take the lower figures. An estimate of the fourth-century CE population of the Eastern and Western Roman Empires, at the time of Constantine and Theodosius, is given by Josiah Cox Russell as 56,000,000.[11] The further back in time you go, the larger the percentage of the world you could fit in these underground cities.

The cautious historians attribute these subterranean cities to groups of fleeing Christians hiding from Muslim persecution, but there is no evidence for this ridiculous belief. If ever Christians were hiding there, they could have been only very small in number and certainly not in the colossal numbers that the cities were built to house. There is no evidence to suggest that they built these underground shelters; the insurmountable stumbling block is that the huge complex would have taken a long time to excavate, so could not have been constructed by people fleeing for their lives from Muslim invaders and they certainly would not have built on such a excessive scale.

There are no signs of excavated debris, earth or rock and in an urgent situation, there would have been no time to disperse such vast amounts — a natural dispersion and flattening could have taken place, but would need many thousands of years. The cities would have taken a long time to stock with necessary food supplies and these subterranean cities could never be

---

[11] Russell, J C *Late Ancient and Medieval Population*

The pharaoh in gods' image

realistically defended. If refugees had somehow remained hidden, eventually they would have to resurface and face their persecutors. There is no record that this ever happened. Nor could the fugitives have remained down there, for no mass skeletal remains have been found. There is nothing to date these tunnels, so determining the purpose for which they had been constructed is made more complex. There is a possible hypothesis that does make some sense.

Some historians have concluded that the people who sailed from Anatolia to settle on the Greek islands, were not emigrating, but were returning to their old homes, from which their ancestors were forced to flee at a time of catastrophic sea flooding. Sited on the high Anatolian plateau, could these subterranean cities, capable of holding such unusually huge and concentrated populations, be long–term shelters, excavated to offer protection from some extraordinary surface catastrophe. Could they be shelters from a calamity such as described in the Book of Enoch: the meteorite strike, the tsunami waves, the fall-out and subsequent rising sea levels due to cataclysmic ice–pack meltdown? Many will dispute this scenario, but there is a great deal of varying evidence to support it, whilst there is virtually nothing to oppose it, except prejudice.

Whoever planned, organised and engineered these marvels, in such a supposedly primitive age, must have been extremely skilled. Who was it, with the influence and power to persuade far flung races to abandon their homes, travel great distances and live underground for many years? If this were the situation, then how did these 'saviours' know in advance that there was a great catastrophe on its way? They could not, unless they had sophisticated science and technology, enough to know that something out in distant space would one day collide with the earth.

Could all these catastrophe stories from around the world be mere coincidences, as the 'experts' like to claim? Well the sensible answer is no, astonishingly, the stories are all too similar. They also describe extremely accurately what would occur if a meteorite struck the sea and the short and long–term aftermath. These descriptions could not possibly be invented, they must have been known. Each individual must decide what to make of this story attributed to Enoch. My view is that if one removes from the story the terms 'gods' and 'angels' and what clearly appear to be later Biblical–style additions, written by the Essenes, and if one takes into account that the storyteller, Enoch, is a simple bemused man attempting to recount fantastic wondrous things beyond his comprehension, then the story takes on a different and more realistic slant.

Genesis claiming Enoch as the grandson of Adam, the alleged 'first man', puts him into an extremely early time frame and setting. The supposedly autobiographical account of Enoch professes to give an account of the background to the great flood. In his version it is caused by seven meteorites

— directed by his gods — which are meant to destroy the handiwork of recalcitrant angels who disobeyed the rule of non–interference on the planet; the resulting impact caused massive flooding and destruction. This story matches scientific research which suggests that such an impact did take place, with a meteorite descending from the northwest across North America, hitting the Atlantic Ocean somewhere off Florida. This would have caused a colossal tsunami and the after effects would have caused subsequent rapid global warming.

Astonished scientists researching the ice in Greenland have discovered evidence that suggests that the Ice Age meltdown happened in just an unbelievably short time of possibly only two years![12] This would have resulted in huge areas of coastal land being drowned by the released water, but the massive tsunamis, particularly from meteorite impact, would also have swamped the land for hundreds of miles in from the coast. Many legends, especially from central America — the nearest point to the claimed impact — speak of a blast of searing heat and the sky turning to fire before the flood came, and then the sky turned black for a great many days and the air became thick and poisonous. Perhaps these are just legends, but then they also give an authentic account of how such a catastrophe would unfold. The first reaction is to think that it all sounds fanciful, yet there is no evidence to disprove it, whilst on the other hand there is scientific evidence that gives some support to its authenticity. There are many vague jigsaw pieces, but when we put them together, a picture begins to form.

What is especially interesting is that in the Enoch story, which involves the Elohim or gods, as well as the angels and fallen angels, there is a group of angels described as the Watchers. This echoes the Egyptian Watchers, the Urshu. This could be dismissed as a coincidence until we consider a class of beings described in Assyrian inscriptions named Rayi, which is translated as Observers, or Watchers. In even older Sumerian scripts there is frequent mention of The Watchers, very tall, striking–looking godmen, who lived amongst the Sumerians and gifted them new skills and learning. Though not called by the same name, beings with the same role are recorded in ancient Celtic legends, in legends from south and north America and even amongst the Australian Aboriginals. In the fragments of Enoch in the Dead Sea Scrolls, not only does the same descriptive name appear, but the writing also reiterates that their role was as civilisers:

> "For in those days the angels of the Lord descended upon earth — those who are named the Watchers — that they should instruct the

---

[12] Alley, R B et. al. "Abrupt Increase in Greenland Snow Accumulation at the End of the Younger Dryas Event"

The Pharaoh in Gods' Image

children of men that they should do judgement and uprightness upon earth."

In the story of Noah's birth, his father, Lamech worried over the child's unworldy appearance, his beauty, his white hair and shining eyes. This led Lamech to wonder if a Watcher had impregnated his wife. Enoch assures Lamech that she had been faithful to him — but was this assurance a later addition, added by concerned scribes, so that Noah, the new father of the human race that survived the flood, would be seen as totally human. Whichever is true, the description of Noah's physical appearance does match that given by other sources for the gods who brought civilisation.

The descriptions are always the same, be they from Britain, Egypt, Mesopotamia or the Americas: they were beautiful in countenance, very tall, blue-eyed, with white, blond or red hair. Certainly, if Enoch was ever a real person, the age in which his story is set, as well as the other non-semitic elements, disqualify him from being proto-Hebrew. Intriguingly, the 'cursed' offspring of the mating between the rebellious 'angels' and human women were called the Nephilim in the Bible, usually translated as 'giants'. However the root of the Aramaic word *nephila*, is the name for the constellation of Orion, so the true meaning is far more likely to mean, "people of' or 'people from' Orion'. Once again, we encounter an Orion connection.

Some scholars believe the origins of the *Book of Enoch* can be traced back to Persian influences picked up during the Judeans' exile. This may be partially correct, however these scholars appear ignorant of the Egyptian connections, which are far older than those of Persia. The core of the Enochian story appears to be very ancient, far older than Persia and seems to have more to do with the ancient ones who constructed the earliest pre-dynastic Egyptian edifices. It does appear, however, that these ancient civilisers had operated in both lands.

The purpose of my highlighting the *Book of Enoch* was in relation to Akhenaten, and in particular the asexual appearance with which he was portrayed. In this extract from the book of Enoch, which recounts Enoch's meeting with the Elohim we find the link with the imagery that Akhenaten demanded for himself. It is useful to point out that the name Elohim, used for God, derives from the plural Canaanite word meaning 'gods' but El gives it a singular form. The *Book of Enoch* tells us:

> 'On the seat of power, sat two radiant Beings, whose robes were brighter than the sun, and whiter than anything in creation. Surrounding them were the sanctified, who had been saved out of all the creations of the Elohim. These continually praised them who sat on the seat of power, centering in their radiant Light, but they did not give

counsel to the Beings who sat on the seat of Light, for they needed none. I stood in their presence, trembling at their majesty, but one of them spoke to me. "Approach us, Enoch," he instructed, "and hear our holy word." Then I was lifted up, and approached their seat of power, but I hardly dared look at them. One of them spoke to me again. "Look at us, Enoch," she said, "for we are the Elohim, male and female, even as we have begotten mankind in our own likeness. But this is the great secret, Enoch. We are not different from each other, but different manifestations of the same reality. The Elohim are Elohim; they may appear to you to be male or female, but if they were either, they would be halves, not whole, and wholeness is the attribute of Deity. The Elohim are not male or female, but Elohim. The sanctified are not male or female, but sanctified. All of mankind are incomplete, as long as they view themselves as male or female, for half of their reality is veiled from them. You must see beyond the illusion of separateness to the essential oneness of Being, in order to perceive Truth. Until then, you cannot relate in a proper manner, with the rest of creation. Look at us, Enoch, and perceive Truth." Then they opened up to me a great mystery, and I saw the meaning of what I had heard.'

Can there be any doubt that Akhenaten had been privy to this same information? His decision to portray himself as a being which had the attributes of both sexes had been made in an attempt to supply his subjects with an image upon which to meditate, so they might understand that they were living a life of illusion and that they were truly neither male nor female and that they needed to return to a oneness. So here was the asexual being combining the slender entities with the long skulls and the male with the swollen belly and heavy thighs.

Another extremely important point concerning this revelation is that the principle of becoming asexual and returning to the oneness of the Creator was the central theme of the Osiris Mystery religion of Heliopolis. Though this was a pre-eminent teaching and the Osiris Mystery was conducted by the Ra Temple priests, Akhenaten clearly felt if he were to promote Atenism, he could not allow any alternatives. We know how the Aten was defined and we know that religious ceremonies took place daily to honour the Creator, but beyond that, we do not know what religious philosophy was taught though something obviously was. Because of the intimate Ra/Osiris roots to Atenism, it would be logical to conclude that the Atenist teachings would have paralleled that of the Osiris Mystery.

The same asexual oneness was also the central part of the later Eleusinian Mysteries of Dionysus, the exported version of the Osiris Mystery in Greece, and this would once again be reinterpreted into other forms, including the Jesus Mysteries, more commonly known as Christianity.

Tantalisingly, these Elohim clearly tell Enoch that they are the creators of mankind, whom it made in their own likeness — it was not the work of a cosmic creator God — so is this a clue that humans were the result of these entities' genetic engineering. So much from early human history throws up not only parallel legends, but hard evidence to suggest that some kind of aid was given, especially regarding man's unexplainable quantum leap forward from the apes: the sudden ability to walk upright, the ability to speak, the acquisition of a large brain and then the sudden explosion of skills in animal breeding, crop farming, metal smelting, monumental building, architecture, mathematics and astronomy, which all seemed to happen overnight. In the last line of the extract from Enoch, there appears a probably unnoticed, but key word 'Mystery'. In the final part of this book, when we look at the true story of Christianity, we find its roots in the Mystery Religion cults which originated in Egypt, where the inner initiates experienced the great mystery and discovered the knowledge and truth of God the Cosmic Creator.

THE GREATEST LIE EVER TOLD

Chapter 12

From Egypt to Exile

"There is a time for departure even when there's no certain place to go."
Tennessee Williams

Alas, Akhenaten's 'new beginning', a revival of the fabled Golden Age was deeply flawed, not in its spiritual concepts, but simply in its disregard for the down-to-earth needs of a realm. Akhenaten lived his 'new beginning' from his new holy city; he dedicated himself to his religion, but he neglected his worldly duties. He neglected his armies, he ignored the calls for help from his vassal states, he neglected the need to maintain the empire, he used his nation's wealth in his capital, he alienated most of his subjects by denying them their traditional religion, he made redundant the many artisans required to build and maintain temples and manufacture religious idols, he took no interest in the day to day running of his country and he ignored the worsening plight of his people. Nothing outside of the holy city of Akhet-Aten had any importance. Allegedly, towards the end of his reign, the plight of Egypt was dire. It is impossible to ascertain exactly how bad things were because of the considerable amount of political bias against him after his death. Akhenaten had been a mystic prophet rather than a king; he had been too religious, too unworldly to make a good political ruler.

Upon his death, in the seventeenth year of his reign, a pharaoh succeeded him called Smenkhkare. Virtually nothing is known about this mysterious figure; some scholars have said he might have been a younger brother, others say he was a son by a minor queen, but there is also a theory suggesting that it might have been his wife Nefertiti, who for a brief period attempted to rule by taking on the role of a male pharaoh, in the way that Hatshepsut had done. Whoever it was, Smenkhkare continued to promote the Aten religion, but Akhenaten's death gave the Amunian priesthood an opportunity to reinstate itself. Taking advantage of the perilous state of Egypt, they revived their own cult and re-exerted their dormant power.

Smenkhkare lasted only about eighteen months. The pharaoh's fate is unknown, but assassination is a possibility, since he or she, stood in the way of an Amunian politico-religious reformation.

A boy king was next in line — most probably Akhenaten's son by a minor queen — his name was Tutankhaten. Being too young to rule by himself, a regent was appointed. The regent's name was Ay; he had been Akhenaten's Grand Vizier and as such had been burdened with the onerous task of having to run the country as best he could on behalf of his uninterested king. Ay was also the High Priest of the Aten Temple at Akhet-Aten and he was the bearer of the title 'Divine Father'. As we see what took place during Ay's rule, we will become aware that his actions were to have a profound effect on the Biblical stories and his legacy is still having a profound effect today.

Though an Atenist, unlike Akhenaten Ay was a pragmatist who realised that ruin was threatening the land, that the Aten religion could no longer be sustained in the manner promoted by Akhenaten and that things needed to return to how they had been for the country to survive. One of the first steps he took was to remove the boy pharaoh from Akhet-Aten and transfer the seat of government back to the ancient capital of Memphis. Some academics say it was Thebes, but being a northerner, a follower of Ra and then Aten, Ay would have no desire to hand back power to the priesthood at Thebes. He would have also been aware that the young pharaoh's life would have been at risk in Thebes; the boy king had been raised as an Atenist and the Amunian priests would have feared a possible revival, so assassination was a real possibility.

In a move to appease the Amunian priesthood, Ay's next step was to change the boy's name to Tutankhamun. What is clear however, gleaned from various pieces of historical evidence, is that the boy king remained true to the Aten despite his name change and the fall of the religion. Indeed, Ay himself, who despite being the architect of the revival of Amun-Ra as the state religion, had been the High Priest of the Aten Temple and there are indications that he probably continued to be an Atenist. This would explain why Ay's successors destroyed all references to him, along with those to the three Atenist rulers who had preceded him.

It appears that the city of Akhet-Aten was abandoned suddenly, probably within the first year of Tutankhamun's reign. The Amunian priests would have considered the city's large and expanding cosmopolitan population, led by its powerful Atenist priests, to be a serious and continuous threat, both to themselves and to the well being of Egypt as a whole. It was clear that the presence of Atenists was intolerable and a rapid solution had to be found, which led to the forceful expulsion from Akhet-Aten. The order could only have been issued, albeit reluctantly, by Ay, in his position as regent. Many of the Egyptians in the expelled population, relocated to other cities, especially to Memphis, the reinstated ancient capital. Large numbers of foreigners, probably several thousand were ejected from the country *en masse*. These foreign exiles included Akhenaten's renowned negro–African police force, known as the Meses–ay. In their book, *Secrets of the Exodus,* Sabbah and Sabbah give strong evidence to suggest these Africans, who were expelled southward, are the present day Massai people. [1]

This might appear to be straying from the subject of the Bible stories, but has a real relevance, for the Massai exodus closely matches that of the supposed Hebrew story. Indeed, the origins of the 'Lost Tribe of Israel' can be sourced to the Massai being separated from the other Atenists and due to the fact that they were never seen again, they became the 'lost tribe'. Massai oral tradition, which has been passed down through the generations and still is, tells that they were expelled from paradise, in the north, in the land of the white bird, probably the Egyptian ibis, because they ate the forbidden fruit. Their compassionate Divine Father, promised them a new holy land, a land of endless grass which would feed their cattle, a land of milk and honey, this probably sounds familiar, but it's the staple diet of the Massai. After a very long and arduous trek, starting along the Nile valley, they wandered through the desert lands of Nubia, then down the Rift Valley into east Africa.

The Massai links with Egypt are numerous:

- the Massai are monotheists whose god, the great creator, is called Enkay — probably derived from either the Egyptian Ankh–Ay, which means Life giving Breath of the Divine Father, or Anok–Ay, which translates as 'I am the Divine Father';
- an alternative name the Massai use is Motoni, which is 'the god who is male and female,' clearly relating to the male–female depictions of Akhenaten.
- the Massai, who are divided into twelve tribes, call themselves the 'Elect of God', which corresponds with the 'Chosen People' and the twelve tribes of Israel;
- the name Massai is close to the name of Akhenaten's police, the Meses–ay and probably derives from Mess-Ay, meaning 'Sons of the Divine Father';
- the Massai sacred colour is red, which corresponds with the red sacred cloth of Upper Egypt and the red crown of Lower Egypt and

---

[1] Sabbah, M & Sabbah, R *Secrets of the Exodus*

- the Massai also consider the red cow to be sacred, as did the Egyptians;
- the ornaments of the Massai nearly always contain the pierced circle, which is the symbol of Ra; as a protection, warriors wear what looks like two cartouches over their kidneys; they wear their hair in a fashion which mimics the striped shawled headdress of the pharaoh;
- like the Egyptians, who appear to have originated the practice, the Massai practise circumcision of boys;
- after seven years of being warriors, the men shave their heads — like Egyptian priests — and are consecrated into a contemplative religious life;
- the Massai high priests carry a rod and whisk, like the rod and flail of the pharaoh, who was also the supreme high priest;
- like the Egyptians, the Massai have a taboo on mixing meat and milk, whilst they also share an aversion to consuming fish;
- the Massai have a moral code which is virtually the same as the Ten Commandments;
- the Massai conduct morning and evening prayers, which follow the theme of the Atenist hymns of thanking God for all the benefits received and paying homage to the beauty of nature. Whilst the priests deliver the prayer the congregation listen in silence and after each blessing they respond with the cry 'Heh' — which is the sound of the Egyptian and later the Hebrew symbol for the Divine Breath.

The large number of links to Atenism and Judaism are surely far too many to be brushed aside and dismissed as mere coincidence.

Those Atenist priests who would not abandon their monotheistic religion were unquestionably foremost amongst the residents of Akhet–Aten who had to be exiled. Killing them was against Egyptian religious beliefs, besides which, Ay had been their High Priest in the Aten Temple and probably remained an Atenist, he could never have contemplated such a heinous action, and so exile was the only course for them. A major exodus of priests is confirmed by the knowledge that when the old cults were revived in the old temples, there were not enough priests. In Egypt, positions within the priesthood were passed down through families, from father to son, but suddenly the old bottomless well had virtually dried up. The situation was desperate and the temples were forced to recruit from a number of sources such as the sons of soldiers and civil servants. The only explanation for this extraordinary predicament is a large disappearance of not only priests, but also their sons, indicating that the Atenist priests refused to return to their old religious cults and went into exile with their families.

In other words, a unique exodus from Egypt took place, with the priests carrying with them a new monotheistic religion. This was not an exodus of Hebrews, directed by a leader who had given them a new 'One God,' it was an exile of the multi-ethnic population of the city of God, led by the priests of Aten. This was not a dramatic escape from a vengeful un-named pharaoh, as the Bible tells us, but the real exodus was a controlled exile and re-settling into the Egyptian empire's frontier lands in Canaan, ordered by a sympathetic co-regent, the Divine Father, the Lord Ay or as it was then pronounced, Adon-Ay. The exiles were both Egyptians and loyal foreigners, who still offered total fealty to both the pharaoh and to the divine Father, so they were relocated in Canaan — the 'promised land'. There they were far enough away from Egypt, but might still do Egypt service, as an Egyptian presence on the frontier with their enemy, the Hittites.

Aten priests would have led the exiles and it is likely that the Tribe of Levi, who became the Hebrew priestly sect, was actually these same Atenist priests. As I mentioned in an earlier chapter, the only difference that archaeologists had found which distinguished the early Hebrews from their Canaanite brothers, was that they had no pigs. This peculiarity, which set the Hebrews apart from all their neighbours, was not unique to them however. The Egyptians had long before held a taboo on the hippopotamus and the pig, considering them both to be 'unclean' animals. Strangely, scholars seem to have ignored this very obvious connection, despite the fact that only Egyptian priests could have introduced such an alien practice into the hill villages of the Canaanites. That such a taboo should suddenly come about on an eccentric whim and then become widely accepted by the Canaanite hill tribes, is extremely unlikely. It would make no sense to deny yourself a valuable source of food in a land of limited agricultural resources unless there was a deep-rooted tradition behind it.

The Egyptians would not wish to see the Atenist priests settled into Canaanite cities in case they might convert their populations to Atenism. So Ay would have little option but to settle the exiles where they would do least harm, away from the fertile and populated plain of Canaan and into the remote villages of the hill country west of the River Jordan; in exactly the place where a new monotheistic religion suddenly appeared. Ay would have ordered them to dispense with the name Aten, to avoid alarming the Amunians back in Egypt and to protect those who had once been the stewards of his flock from the anger of Egyptians in the Canaanite cities. Since Ay was, after Tutankhamun's death and his own enthronement, accepted to be God's representative upon earth, the title Adonay — 'Lord Ay' — would seem quite appropriate and fitting as a new title for the Aten. Almost certainly, the exiles' settling-in would have been fostered not only by Ay and Tutankhamun but, as we shall see, they were probably discreetly protected by the *closet* Atenist pharaohs whose reign immediately followed Tutankhamun.

Following Tutankhamun's short reign, which had ended suddenly, possibly with his murder on the orders of Amunian priests, Ay took sole control of the throne. He could have dismantled the Aten cult by letting it fade away, though no doubt the Amunians would have applied increasing pressure to speed up the process. Once the holy city was abandoned and the Atenist priests had gone, the memory of the Aten religion had to be eradicated. This meant not only destroying the temples, but also removing every inscription to the Aten, since the Egyptians believed that without a name, a thing or person did not exist. Virtually all references to Aten and the royal family were chiselled out, but, fortunately for historians, some escaped. Stone blocks taken from Akhet–Aten were reused to build new temples to Amun and the reversed blocks still had the original inscriptions, now hidden away on the back.

Ay's successor, Horemheb, finished the task of publicly eradicating Atenism, by totally dismantling Akhet–Aten and carrying the stones away to build new temples in Thebes. Though the Amunian temples were reinstated, the pharaohs that followed after Ay — Horemheb and Rameses I, two northern generals, and Seti, the son of Rameses — were followers of the Ra cult, though they appeased the Amunians by reinstating and building temples for the pre–Atenist godhead of Amun–Ra. At Heliopolis, the priests, although they were forced to abandon their Aten experiment, would without doubt, have reinstated Ra and carried on as before. It is likely that the Ra priests *buried* Atenism with the intention of *resurrecting* it again at some appropriate time in the future. That new opportunity was never to present itself.

It is certain that the enforced name change did not alter Tutankhamun's religious belief and that he remained an Atenist. The same was probably true for Ay, since his anti–Atenist actions were merely the political actions of a pragmatist who wished to save his country from total ruin and civil war. Horemheb did not act like an Atenist, since his actions were to try and destroy every trace of Atenism, but perhaps his actions too were driven by ambition not belief. What makes us reassess Horemheb is that his military colleague Rameses, who late in his life became pharaoh, appears to have espoused Atenism.

If Horemheb had really been anti–Aten Rameses would have had nothing to base his belief on. Atenism was supposedly banned after the death of Smenkhkare; forty years later, by Rameses' reign, it should have been long dead and buried, however a startling chance find in 1904 by

Flinders Petrie put this into question.[2] Petrie unearthed a stone stele near a mountain in the Sinai Peninsula; Rameses was depicted on it in the pictorial style favoured by Akhenaten. The surprising inscription on the stele proclaims — 'Prince of every circuit of the Aten'. So long after the death of Akhenaten, it appears there were still followers of Atenism. Whatever these pharaohs' religious inclinations were, for the sake of the ruined country's revival and stability, it was expedient to take an anti–Atenist stance — at least publicly — in order to avert civil war with the Thebans, to revive the economy and to reinstate the integrity of the empire.

Fortunately for posterity, the valuable building stones from dismantled Aket–Aten were reused; reversed, so that the still–intact inscriptions could not be seen on the new building projects, but when discovered by archaeologists, the story of Akhenaten and his holy city made its way back into history. The discovery at Tell el–Amarna, the modern name for the site of Akhet–Aten, of many inscribed clay tablets, known as the 'Amarna Letters,' has enhanced our knowledge of this period. This diplomatic correspondence, written to Akhenaten, gave detailed information of contemporary events.[3] It is fortunate that the tablets were thrown away, rather than smashed, by Horemheb's men when they dismantled the city.

Space does not allow me to go into all the detailed evidence which shows that Ay, along with Akhenaten, were the two pivotal figures in the story which came to be retold as Moses and the Exodus out of Egypt, I can attempt a brief outline, but to read a more detailed account the reader should look at the work of Talmud and Torah students, Messod and Roger Sabbah, *Secrets of the Exodus*.[4]

To any honest historian, there should be no doubt that the story of this Atenist exodus was the one remembered by the ancestors of those who took part, in their new Canaanite home. To begin with, this story was retold orally over generations and then with the passage of time, the story was revised and adapted to suit the constantly changing politico–religious requirements which held sway at different times in the history of the Middle East. The largest revision took place during the Babylonian captivity, which saw the Egyptian roots removed from the story, to avoid antagonising the captors. Nevertheless, the evidence is still there which unequivocally points to the truth, that the Hebrew religion is an adaptation of the banned Atenism and that aided by time, confusion and heavy political tampering,

---

[2] Petrie, W M F. *Researches in Sinai*
[3] Petrie, W M F. *Tell el–Amarna*
[4] op. cit. Sabbah

Adon–Ay, the Divine Father, was fused with the Aten to become the Hebrew God Adonay.

Revealingly, there is another name given to God in the Genesis and Exodus accounts and that is El. El means god and this name is Canaanite, belonging to a Canaanite deity. Since the Hebrews were supposedly virulently against Canaanite gods and everything Canaanite, to use this name appears both astonishing and blasphemous. However its usage reveals two things — firstly, it is further proof that the Hebrews were themselves Canaanites and that they would naturally have used their own language, before it later evolved into Aramaic; secondly, that the continued use of this name indicated that these stories were written down in a piece–meal fashion, and that it was done long after the alleged events, in a time when the authors clearly did not appreciate the connection of the name El with that of a Canaanite god.

The pieces of evidence are all there and just need assembling to give the full picture. In the next chapter more pieces of the jigsaw, Biblical stories, which in isolation appear to make no real sense or at least have no significance or relevance, become transformed into lucid records of events passed down from the exiled Aten priests.

Chapter 13

Akhet–Aten to Eden

"A belief which leaves no place for doubt is not a belief; it is a superstition."
Jose Bergamin

The Bible appears to be a linear history, but as the earlier chapters show us, the Judean scribes wove together a history for their people using old legends, pure invention and some genuine, but often disguised pieces of history. Bits of remodelled history were slotted into various Biblical stories where it seemed appropriate, without any concern for truth. The truth was irrelevant, as long as someone knew what history the story hid.

Often we can read of incidents or the use of numbers, which seem to have no real significance to the story being told and too often theologians point to these puzzling pieces of trivia as proof of authenticity. When one realises that the stories are remodelled accounts of the original tales that the Aten priests brought with them from Egypt, they actually reveal something very different.

Some of the links refer to mundane pieces of history and are easy to spot; others are far more esoteric and would have needed an Aten priest, or his descendent, to explain. Akhenaten separated his city of Akhet–Aten from his father's kingdom with boundary markers. This is an easy event to find in the Bible. In the Biblical story in Genesis 31:51, boundary stones were set up between Jacob and his father–in–law Laban to accommodate the political and religious differences between them.

Amenhotep III elevated Akhenaten above his eldest son, as we know. In another story, Jacob's father, Isaac, elevates him above the eldest son, Esau. This transforming and encoding of events is then repeated in the Biblical tale of Joseph, when he is given the coat of many colours by his father Jacob; once more a father favouring the youngest son over his older brothers. This repeating of incidents in the Bible is quite common and was probably meant to highlight a theme and thereby give prominence to the real hidden story.

Another link between Akhenaten and Jacob can be found in the length of the pharaoh's reign. Akhenaten reigned for seventeen years and seventeen years was the length of Jacob's stay in Egypt. Abraham's life span was given as an unlikely 175 years, however this is doubtless another encoding which retained the seventeen. To use this number for his age, the scribes merely tagged on the number five and the rather long lifespan, which resulted, afforded the patriarch the same special gravitas as the Bible's other early *heavyweights*. Thus two goals were achieved: the length of Akhenaten's reign is recorded and the status of Abraham is reinforced.

If we look further at the Abraham story, we see how it encodes more themes from the story of Akhenaten. God instructed Abraham to leave the paternal home and to settle in a new land chosen for him. The Aramaic Bible says this place was an open plain, called the Valley of the Kings, which was free of trees and other obstacles and that it contained a race track used for the amusement of the king, it was the place where 'all nations united in common accord, chose Abraham as king.' When Abraham first arrived there, he built an altar then he left again, eventually returning and pitching his tent at the altar. Akhenaten visited the plain chosen by God then returned to build his city and personally supervise its construction; he lived in a great tent that contained an altar to the Aten. Akhet–Aten had a long curving highway, along which Akhenaten and Nefertiti raced their chariots.

Abraham, like Akhenaten broke the idols of his father. Abraham sacrificed a ram, which encodes the story of Akhenaten sacrificing the ram–headed god Amun to the Aten.

In the Bible, there is that strange and seemingly inexplicable tale of Abraham entering Egypt, pretending that his wife Sarah was his sister, but still losing her when she was taken as the pharaoh's queen; then regaining her when God threatened to curse the pharaoh. The source of this macabre story can once more be traced to Akhenaten. It appears that Akhenaten desired the Mitanni princess, Nefertiti, but she became the wife of Amenhotep III and one of his minor queens. The elderly pharaoh was sick and infirm, there is no knowing if the marriage was consummated, but there was no child. It is possible that Amenhotep saw his illness as some kind of curse, since he had erected an extraordinarily large number of statues of the goddess of destruction, Sekmet, whom he presumably was attempting to pacify or ask to heal his affliction. Somehow, though it is unrecorded how, Akhenaten gained Nefertiti for his own wife; perhaps the old pharaoh knew that Nefertiti was being 'visited' by his son and decided that it would be more seemly if he passed her on to him. In the Aramaic Bible, Genesis 16:1, there is a clue in the story, where it recounts that an Egyptian maid of his wife Sarah, was given to Abraham as a wife, to produce a boy child; the Egyptian father of the maid resigned himself to the situation when he says, "It would be better for my daughter to be a servant in such a house, than his mistress in another house."

The other thing linking the two stories is the use of the term 'sister.' Taken at face value, the Bible story of Abraham protecting *himself* by pretending that his wife was his sister is outrageously shameful and makes no sense. However, in Egypt, besides the fact that the pharaohs often married their sisters, the word 'sister' was commonly used as a term of endearment; not only for family members such as cousins, but also for mistresses and concubines. This Egyptian use of the word would explain its inappropriate transplant into the Bible story; it seems as though it should have been edited out, however I believe that it was deliberately left in, to draw attention to the real story encoded within the story of Abraham.

The extraordinary similarities continue, the Bible claims that Abraham is childless and laments that he had no son and heir — female children had no value and could not inherit. Akhenaten had daughters, but had no son to inherit the throne. Eventually, Akhenaten got his son from a lesser queen, called Kiya; the jealous Queen Nefertiti, then had Kiya and her son sent away. In the Biblical version, Abraham has a son from the Egyptian maid supplied by his thoughtful wife, but then Sarah becomes jealous and sends the woman and her son away.

In a totally different Biblical story, the expulsion of Adam and Eve from Eden, we can see the coded story of the expulsion from the earthly paradise of Akhet–Aten. Adam and Eve were told by the serpent, that if they consumed the forbidden fruit they would experience immortality on a par with God. Within the Aten temple grounds stood the Tree of Immortality, an apple tree whose fruit was carefully engraved with the royal cartouche and meant only for the pharaoh to consume — that pharaoh who was the earthly embodiment of the immortal God. However, after Akhenaten's death, as things began to fall apart, the priests were tempted into eating the fruit for themselves; allegedly egged on by the ambitious foreign princesses, to whom they were married. The priests thought the consequences of their crime would bestow on them the sacred gifts received by the earthly incarnation of god and thereby make them equal to the pharaoh–god. This sacrilegious act would have enraged the Divine Father, Ay and perhaps stiffened his resolve to banish the priests and their wives from the paradise of Akhet–Aten..

The Biblical serpent also has its origins in Egypt, where the evil serpent, Apophis is often depicted beneath the sacred tree. In this story, we see one of the story 'reversals' which took place, when the Biblical scribes were confronted by a clash of ideology. The Egyptian myth has the gods Seth and Isis combine to destroy the serpent Apophis. In the Biblical Adam and Eve story, the Judean scribes portray the man and woman as too weak to overcome the evil serpent. This is probably due to the thinking of their much later time, which could not allow a mere man, let alone assisted by a woman, enough power to take on and defeat a great supernatural entity. Another reversal occurs in the Biblical account of the shame of Adam and Eve's nakedness, for this also has its roots in Akhet–Aten. In the holy city, nakedness before God was deemed natural and became the norm: Akhenaten and his wife and children were often depicted as totally naked and with pride. Probably the original mention of sense of shame about *nakedness,* was meant to link with the shame of *expulsion* out of the paradise of Akhet–Aten, when the priests' sin had been discovered by the Divine Father. This part of the story being retold as Adam and Eve becoming ashamed of their nakedness, when the consequence of their sin made them aware of their nudity. In itself, this Judahite version makes little sense, since the veil may have been lifted from their eyes through the acquisition of knowledge, but there is no reason why natural God–given nakedness should suddenly be seen as wrong and shameful.

There are many other links between Egyptian history and the tales contained within the Bible, but they are so numerous that it would be too burdensome to trawl through them here. However, there are some well-known Bible stories with their origins in Egypt that are worthy of a mention.

The Ten Commandments were inscribed by the Hebrew god, onto two stone tablets, then given to Moses and he had somehow to carry these hefty weights down a mountain. In Egypt, these heavy stone tablets are called stelae, but in Egyptian language the word *stele* derives from the verb to command. So a stele is a 'commandment' given by god incarnate — that is, the pharaoh. And Moses brought ten 'commandments' down the mountain, a much more feasible task and an unlikely coincidence, I believe.

The story of the Burning Bush has its roots in Egyptian religious mythology and was retold in the Bible in a simple form stripped of its complexities. Its origins require some detailed description, but the connection should become clear. The Desert Palm *Balanites aegyptica* is a spiny tree, which was known to the Egyptians as the Ished tree. The Hebrew word for the Burning Bush is *cenah,* derived from the word 'to prick,' so it is usually described as a 'thorn bush.' In Egyptian religion, the gods are often associated with sacred trees. There are two gods linked with the Desert Palm, Thoth and Khepri, the facet of Ra represented as a scarab dung beetle, which carries the morning rising sun. In the tomb of Rameses II, there is a depiction of the Ished tree, which is claimed to be the tree of the eastern horizon out of which the sun rises. In the scene we see Osiris, in his capacity of 'the opener of the ished tree,' thus allowing Ra, the sun, its passage out of the underworld, in the form of a winged scarab beetle. So the bush of fire is a representation of the sunrise and the part that the gods play in this.

Theologians have been puzzled about whether it was an angel or God in the bush. In Exodus 3:2 and 3:4, it says:

> "There the angel of the Lord appeared to him in a flame of fire out of a bush" and "when the Lord saw that he had turned aside to see, God called to him out of the bush."

The Hebrew word for angel means messenger. The names that the two gods linked with the Desert Palm are known by, gives us an understanding of the puzzle that the theologians have tried to resolve. Thoth carries the epithet messenger and the name Khepri derives from the word meaning 'come into being.' Yahweh the Hebrew name for God, also means 'he who comes into being.' Clearly the two deities associated with the ished tree, Khepri and Thoth — both representations of Ra, caused confusion for the Judean scribes who were trying to reinterpret Egyptian religious myth in order to incorporate it into their new Exodus story; leaving us with the subsequent ambiguity of the 'messenger' and Yahweh, simultaneously appearing in the bush.

In the Exodus story, Moses flees into the Sinai desert, after killing an overseer, and later, during the Exodus, he travels through the Sinai desert again to the Mount of the same name and here receives the Laws from God. When the Judean scribes invented the story of Moses, they set their character on a journey to the temple of Sopdu on the easternmost edge of their realm.

The Hebrew name Sinai comes from the Proto–Semitic 'sinn', in Western Chadic, which means 'tooth' or 'sharp point'. In Egyptian the word for sharp generates the name Sopdu, the hawk–god and personification of the eastern frontier of Egypt, where Sinai is located. In the Sinai Peninsula at Serabit el–Khadim, there is a temple dedicated to Sopdu. So it appears that Sinai actually means 'Land of Sopdu' and the Sopdu temple on the mountain of Serabit el–Khadim surely indicates that this is the Mount Sinai to which Moses was sent.[1]

By the end of the Exodus story Yahweh is denying Moses access to the 'Promised Land' yet he personally undertakes Moses' burial in a secret location. In Deuteronomy 34:6, we are informed:

---

[1] Harnam, D. *The Real Moses and His God*

"in a valley in the land of Moab opposite Beth–Peor, but no one knows the burial place to this day".

The place must be left vague, so that no-one would discover that there was no grave and no Moses. It also allows those who understand the significance to know of the importance of the Egyptian Duat at Rostau/Giza, the site of the Great Sphinx and the Great Pyramids. Mount Peor was the abode of the Moabite god Baal–Peor, who can be identified with Sokar, the Egyptian god of the Duat of Rostau/Giza. Rostau means 'mouth of the passage' that leads down to the Duat or underworld. The Moabite Peor derives from pa'ar, meaning to open wide (the mouth), or to gape. Again this duplication can be no coincidence: behind the contortions of the Biblical scribe's account, they were keeping alive their history, for those with the 'eyes to see.'

When Akhenaten was constructing Akhet–Aten, his tent contained the altar to God. This is clearly the forerunner of the tent in Exodus, the 'Tabernacle' containing the Ark of the Covenant. The mobile temple was in fact a tented copy of an Egyptian temple, which in turn became the design for the Jerusalem Temple, whose inner sanctum, the Holy of Holies, was copied from the Star Chamber of the Ra Temple.

The Ark itself, which was supposed to have contained the Laws of Moses, was a gold–lined coffer carried on long poles; this was a common piece of equipment in Egypt, used to carry around 'gods.' The Ark's winged cherubs were nothing other than Egyptian winged goddesses and since they were normally depicted guarding Osiris, these two 'cherubs' would almost certainly have been Isis and Nephthys. The so called Mercy Seat, between the two winged guardians does not actually indicate that it was the dwelling place, or throne for Yahweh; this error is due to a mistranslation of the Hebrew word 'Kapporeth' which simply means 'cover.' Though not recorded in the Bible, traditional oral accounts of the Ark described it in more detail.[2] There were three inner containers that sat inside of the outer casing of the Ark, two made of gold and one out of wood. It is interesting that archaeologists were drawn to the similarity, when Tutankhamun's tomb was discovered. Inside the Pharaoh's funerary chamber, was something resembling a tabernacle–like tent, but it was actually a large linen cloth which covered the coffer beneath. This coffer held three inner containers; the first two were made out of wood, covered in gold and the third one was pure gold. The fourth coffer was the red granite sarcophagus, which itself contained the three coffins, one within another. The third and fourth coffers were engraved with the double goddesses with their

---

[2] Lévy, S & O. *The Pentateuch According to Rashi, Exodus*

outstretched wings, which met in the middle, exactly like the winged cherubs of Biblical fame. The similarity is too striking to be dismissed as another one of those convenient coincidences.

Such an intricately-crafted object as the Ark, could not have been built by a people on the run, trying to survive in a harsh desert, as the Biblical account claims. They would have lacked the skilled craftsmen, the right tools, the materials required and most of all, the time on an enforced march. If they had such an object at all, it must have been taken from Egypt — but then why burden themselves with such a bulky object if they are fleeing for their lives; and how did they acquire it, by theft? In the Moses story, it does not make sense, but then, in reality, there was no Hebrew Exodus, only an orderly exile of people from Akhet–Aten, who would have possessed such objects and had the time and the means to transport all the goods they required with them.

Did the Ark of the Covenant ever exist? Well firstly there is absolutely no evidence at all that it did. The Bible states that eventually, David took the Ark to Jerusalem and then when Solomon built the temple, it was deposited there. The problem with this account is that intense archaeological searching has revealed absolutely no trace of Solomon's Temple. So the Ark could hardly have been installed there — but if the Temple had existed, where had the Ark been kept for all that time before the Temple was built.

We need to consider the story of the Ark in relation to Hebrew history and particularly what effect their political masters would have on Hebrew allegiances. In the period when the Exodus story was set, the Egyptians dominated the Palestine region, so the promotion of things Egyptian, including an Ark and its winged guardians, would not displease their masters. From the time of the fall of Jerusalem and the Judeans' exile to Babylon, the Ark is never mentioned again. This might seem extremely peculiar and of course various stories arose to say that the Ark had been hidden or spirited away. All are nothing but speculation, without historical foundation or fact and certainly do not account for why the scriptures never mention the Ark again. If we look at who took over Palestine when the Babylonians had gone, the answer is blatantly clear. The Hebrews' new masters, the Persians, considered 'graven' images to be blasphemous, so naturally the story of the Ark was better forgotten.

Since the Ark had never actually existed, this was no great problem for the Judean priesthood; had it existed, they would have found a way of preserving the story and would have resurrected the Ark after the fall of the Persians — but they did not and their Temple remained empty. Had the Ark truly been the abode of Yahweh/Jehovah, they would have been extremely concerned by its absence, they would have been despondent and demoralised and would have made every effort to relocate the Ark to the

Temple. The Ark belonged only to the Exodus story and since the Moses Exodus was fiction, there was no need to keep the Ark myth alive in later stories.

In the Bible, people and stories were deliberately reborn in parallel narratives, some on several occasions and the purpose was to reinforce the message they contained. The Ark is an example of this, both its name and its symbolic use parallel that of its Biblical predecessor, Noah's Ark, which was itself a version of the Egyptian arks, the solar barques. The story of the Great Flood probably derived from the Mesopotamian flood legend that the Judeans heard about during their Babylonian captivity. It all sounds rather like a pick and mix selection, but that is exactly what the Bible is, the writers added whatever was deemed politically prudent at the time and extracted anything which was too dangerous to keep.

The political revamping can be seen again in the Biblical account of Moses issuing instructions on the building of the Temple — that it should not be identical to the Egyptian temples and that it should not have obelisks.[3] These are the instructions recorded in the Bible, yet they do not appear to have been followed. There can be little doubt that this warning by Moses was to appease the Babylonians during the Judeans' enslavement. From what has been written about the design, the later Temple was, in fact, similar to Egyptian temples. The fact that it was roofed like the Amun temples is probably a practical decision because of the more inclement winter weather in Judea. The time of its building reflected the time of Egyptian power in Palestine, when the Amunian priesthood were once more exerting their influence. By this period, half a millennium had passed since the resettling of the exiled Atenists and much of the religion had been watered down and even lost. What was left had been so disguised and encoded, that few would have been aware of the complete facts. The two pillar–like obelisks, erected either side of the entrance porch to the Temple show further Egyptian influence. The original two pillars, one in Upper and the other in Lower Egypt, represented the Djed–pillar or 'backbone of the world', which stood on the primeval mound as a perch for the Creator God.

Though no trace of Solomon's Temple has been found, a red cow was supposed to have been sacrificed there and this act can again be traced to Egypt, where the Great Temple of Amun in Thebes, saw sacrifices of red oxen. The thought does come to mind, that if Solomon were a 'revised' Atenist, he should not have been following an Amunian practice, but the Bible records that Solomon allowed other gods, so perhaps at the period in history when the Bible story was first created, it would have been a pragmatic move to adopt a religious practice that served as a sop to the

---

3 Deuteronomy 16:21

'Amunian' Egyptians, who were the region's overlords. By the time it was finally written into Judean history, its meaning was lost.

Another clue to the true source of the Jewish religion comes from the traditional articles of clothing worn at prayer. They compare with the attire worn by the pharaohs at the time of the Atenist exile. The golden mask of Tutankhamun is well known; he is wearing the azure blue and gold striped shawl–like headdress. Unseen, beneath this headdress is a skullcap — in this case, adorned with engraved golden seals of the Aten, confirming that unto death, Tutankhamun remained an Atenist. The pharaoh also wore a golden headband with the serpent and vulture insignia of the two lands of Egypt. At the back of this headband, falling down the back of the neck, hung the ends as two straps. On the left arm of the pharaoh, there was a bracelet around the biceps and further bracelets on the forearm, whilst the right forearm had seven bracelets. On the left hand he wore two rings, on the middle and the ring finger. The parallels with Jewish attire are easy to recognise: the Tallith, or striped shawl, which originally had an azure blue band and fringes and the Kippa, or skull cap form the same pharaonic head gear.

The Tefillin, with its headband that falls behind the neck in two straps, has a small container holding the divine name of God on the front. A second Tefillin is worn around the left arm beginning at the biceps. It is a long strap, wound in seven loops around the left forearm, passing across the palm and ending by being wound around the middle and ring fingers. It has particular significance in the context of the Aten priests' exodus as *The Torah* commands that it should be worn to serve as a sign and remembrance that God brought the children of Israel out of Egypt. This seems a very curious thing for exiled Jews to do, those Jews who left Germany to avoid the persecution of the Nazis, do not wear stormtrooper leather overcoats and swastikas in memory of God's getting them to safety.

In Egypt, the colour blue, which signified the spiritual plane, was the colour of Isis and this is copied again by the Christians, who clothe the Virgin Mary in blue. Isis is actually the Greek interpretation of her name, but in Egyptian it had been Est and Est gives us the name Easter. The colour blue also represented the goddess, Ma'at, who was the personification of harmony, balance, justice and truth. Egyptian priests and priestesses wore blue sapphire amulets engraved with the symbol of Ma'at on their breasts; the High Priest of the Hebrews also wore a similar blue sapphire amulet engraved with the word 'Thimin', meaning 'truth and justice.' This replication of attire and accoutrements are too exact to be coincidence, but the duplications extended much further, to ritual and practice as well.

The confessional originated with the Egyptians, though their form was more reflective — considering one's spiritual struggles and shortcomings — there was no guilt attached to it and no resulting chastisement or penance to be suffered. Though the Jewish faith, had no confessional between man and priest, they practised a confessional between man and God, which suggests that it was, like that of the Egyptians, more reflective in nature. By contrast, the Christian confessional concentrated not upon the spiritual, but upon the moral Laws of Moses, which the Church sought to impose vigorously, through fear and the ultimate sanction of excommunication and its consequent eternal damnation. The Christian Church wanted its members to believe that they were ever straying and sinful. The priesthood was not there as spiritual teachers and guides, but as the enforcers, there to both police and punish all offenders.

The ritual of the washing of hands, which is part of Jewish, Christian and Islamic religious practice, originated in Egypt. Akhenaten is pictured having water ceremoniously poured over his hands. The washing of feet, so common in the Bible, has its precedent in Egypt. In Akhet–Aten, the homes of priests and nobles had an inclined slab upon which water was poured to wash the feet of those entering.

The uncommon practice of considering pigs to be unclean, had to have been introduced into the villages which were later to become Hebrew, by the exiled Egyptian Atenist priests. Egypt was previously, the only land where this occurred.

Circumcision, so everyone believes, is a Jewish religious practice, which originated from God's instruction to Abraham, to remove the foreskin from his son and for all his people to do the same thereafter as an act of covenant. The truth is that the circumcision originated in Egypt and probably derives from their almost paranoid obsession with cleanliness, which also often included shaving off head and body hair. I have wondered if this Egyptian obsession with cleanliness might originate with their monument–building civilisers coming from a far distant place into a disease–prone environment and taking extreme measures to guard their health — but this is only a personal observation.

That this strange practice of circumcision appeared amongst the Hebrews exclusively, rather than any Egyptian neighbours, and just like 'pigs being unclean', indicates that the ritual could only have been introduced by Aten priests, who not only brought their religion with them, but also other traditional Egyptian practices. As we already know, the Massai too practice circumcision, originating from their time in 'Paradise' before the expulsion by Enkay 'Adon–Ay'.

Messod and Roger Sabbah provide further convincing links between the religions of ancient Egypt and modern Judaism, highlighting amongst other things, the links between Egyptian hieroglyphics and the Hebrew alphabet and words.[4]

Some will argue, out of sheer prejudice, against the inescapable conclusion that the core of Judaism emanated from Egypt. However, when one considers the numerous connections, the question once again is, 'Can all these matches be dismissed as coincidences?' If so, then how many coincidences does it take before one finally accepts that they are *not* coincidences. One or two matches may be coincidence; three or four perhaps, then one begins to speculate. When one is faced with a whole catalogue of matches, yet still calls them coincidences, then that is the time to ask if one just might be blinding oneself to the truth.

The facts to consider are these:
- archæological evidence confirms that the first known monotheistic religion occurred in Egypt;
- it shared many things with Judaism, which it predates by, at the very least, six hundred years;
- there was no large population of Hebrews in Egypt;
- the only historical religious exodus out of Egypt, was that of the Atenists;
- the Aten was the visible aspect of the Cosmic Creator, a god who was there for all mankind, not just Egyptians, it is a Universal God.

But the reader could choose to still believe that the Judaic religion is based on true historical events. One could ignore the fact that this religion, which really began with Moses and the Exodus, has no archaeological credibility and ignore that it has none of the traditional 'historical authenticity' with which it was once falsely accredited. One can continue to ignore that historically, it is deeply flawed and indeed, false, and that it has been discredited by the most recent excavations and research, carried out, not by atheists, but by Jewish university archaeologists.

In the Judaic/Christian religion, one is expected to believe in a whole catalogue of supernatural 'miracles,' delivered by a deity who delights in a repertoire of theatrical tricks — wonders which he has not deigned to repeat since ancient Biblical times. Since that time, this deity, for no discernible reason, seems to have withdrawn totally and disappeared completely, not only from his small Middle Eastern theatre of operation, but from the entire world. Of course some 'believers' will say, 'one cannot know the workings of God', but this is purely an easy evasion of the truth. There never was a nonsensical deity who selected an exclusive people; nor was there a god who

---

4 Sabbah, M & Sabbah, R *Secrets of the Exodus*

suddenly appeared, performed supernatural feats and behaved in a generally bizarre, eccentric and thoroughly un-godlike manner.

Though *believers* may think of their God as a *universal* god, he never was that, rather he was the god of the Hebrews. Selecting a tiny unimportant tribe to be his special people is small minded and parochial and not the action of a universal god at all. Indeed, this god's conduct and actions reveal him as not only compassionless, vindictive and sadistic, but as a bloodthirsty psychopath. All the characteristics of this deity fit the requirements of the ambitious leaders of a small insignificant people perfectly. A people who wished to be special and to warn off aggressors by claiming they were protected by their personal fearsome god, whilst simultaneously warning any independent thinking Jews, that a failure to adhere to the laws of Yahweh would result in extreme punishment.

There are many who would approve of this god and his punishments — deeply devout Jews and Christians — and yet they disapprove of impassioned Muslims citing the same excuses for their bullying threats and large-scale murder in the name of Allah.

I have placed the facts here for the reader's consideration, but it is for him or her to make their own decision based upon them. The choice will depend on whether the reader wishes to be objective, rational and open-minded, or to be closed-minded and prejudiced. Truth and Wisdom and the Knowledge of God will come only from the unrestricted pursuit of knowledge; the finding and understanding of facts and the result of true personal experience. Belief and Faith reject the pursuit of knowledge, they promote non-thinking, they are static, they demand unquestioning blind obedience, they promote prejudice and engender anger, fear and defensive aggression.

This restriction upon knowledge of the truth, this ongoing ignorance of one's own subjugation, is vividly highlighted near the beginning of the Bible. The story of what transpires in Eden is very revealing, though unintentionally so. It tells of God putting a restriction upon the first man and woman, Adam and Eve: they may not eat the fruit from a particular tree, the Tree of Knowledge. The two failed to obey the command and so were banished from Eden. We are told that Satan, in the form of a serpent, tempted Eve into disobedience. Satan was slotted into the tale to diminish mankind's culpability in the crime, whilst also affording the Jews an excuse to demean women because of Eve's original sin: disobeying God and then using her wiles to tempt man into a foolish action.

It is curious to note that around the world, the serpent, sometimes depicted in the form of the dragon, is generally seen as a benevolent entity. In China the dragon was a heavenly creature; in the Americas the 'Feathered Serpent' was a godman who came as a civiliser and educator.

Yet amongst Christians, St Michael *slays* the *evil* serpent, which is bizarre when one considers that Michael was identified with the Celtic godman and 'lightbringer,' Lugh. The Christians twisted the tale so that the 'lightbringer' Lugh/Michael slays the 'lightbringing' serpent. Of course the orthodox Christians had no desire for people to be free thinkers in search of 'dangerous' knowledge and truth. The Eden story provided a perfect warning to those who contemplated tasting the forbidden fruit of knowledge; and if they did, Jehovah need not trouble to dish out the punishment, the Holy Inquisition would do it in his name.

Gnostics too offered a different view of the serpent, one that was totally opposed to that of Jews and the later orthodox Christians. To the Gnostics, the serpent was the benefactor of mankind, the 'lightbringer,' the 'enlightener,' who not only raised mankind from savagery to a state of understanding the need for civilised behaviour, but also gave knowledge and revealed the truth. To the Gnostics, and the Apostle Paul, Yahweh/Jehovah was not the Creator God, but an evil demiurge.

Certainly this god's behaviour throughout the Biblical Eden story is bizarre, for not only is he petty and full of jealousy, but he acts in a distinctly un–godlike manner. This 'all-seeing' god was unable to find Adam and Eve when they were hiding in the undergrowth; he had an evil entity, Satan, running free in his realm; this god felt threatened by Adam's acquisition of knowledge; this god was unaware of things that were occurring in his close presence. Even if one persists in the belief that some entity was involved, these were not the actions of an all–powerful, all–seeing God of Creation, but of a charlatan pretender to the role.

Throughout the Old Testament, Yahweh's interceding appears haphazard, sluggish and so often his 'thunderbolt' punishments seem to desert him, leaving humans to complete his dirty work for him. In the New Testament and later, when he should have been protecting both Jews and Christians, he fails to make any appearance at all.

It is fascinating to read the Gnostic version of the Biblical Eden story; part of the Gnostic library found at Nag Hammadi. It certainly delivers a very different picture from the Garden of Eden plot and gives us some exceedingly enlightening revelations:

> 'What did god say to you?' the Serpent asked Eve. 'Was it "Do not eat from the Tree of Knowledge?"'
> Eve replied, 'He said, "Not only do you not eat from it, but do not touch it lest you die!"'
> The Serpent reassured her by saying. 'Do not be afraid. With death you shall not die, for it was out of jealousy that he said this to you. Rather

your eyes shall open and shall come to be like god's, recognising good and evil.'

Further on, in this Gnostic version, after Adam partakes of the fruit from the Tree of Knowledge, Yahweh/Jehovah, feeling jealous and angry, regales his demon followers, bewailing that Adam is now knowledgeable like them and fearing that having acquired gnosis/knowledge, Adam would next seek to eat from the Tree of Life and become an immortal as they were. Adam was therefore ejected quickly before he could gain immortality and banished to Earth, to the physical world, to lose his memory of the higher plane, to live his life in ignorance of good and evil, ignorant of his true immortality, ignorant as to the real aspect of Yahweh/Jehovah and in ignorance of the fact that there is a higher god, the true unknowable God of Creation.

The wise Serpent had been attempting to alert Eve to her higher-self, the immortal part of her and to inform her that it was her right to acquire knowledge — rather than exist in blind ignorance — so that she could return to the cosmic soul. When Adam had acquired knowledge and was thereby in possession of the truth, he would know that he needed to fill himself next on the fruit of another tree, the Tree of Immortality, in order to claim that immortality which was rightfully his. Only an evil entity would seek to deny man his divine right, so therefore, by endeavouring to deny mankind, Yahweh/Jehovah reveals himself as an evil entity.

Of course, the Gnostic version of the Eden story is a parable, like all Gnostic Biblical stories, which endeavours to highlight the need to seek knowledge and not be denied the right to do so, and by attaining knowledge one is eventually initiated to the truth — the truth that man's soul is immortal.

The goal for the original Christians was Gnosis and Sophia — Knowledge and Wisdom — thus their religion had no place for Belief and Faith. But perversely, as happened with the corruption of Atenism into Judaism, original Gnostic Christianity and their fictional parables became corrupted into Roman Catholic Christianity; and tragically, both Judaism and Christianity ended up far removed from the truth. Like the Biblical Adam, most of mankind still languishes in the darkness of ignorance.

Part Three

New Testament — The Jesus Myth Corruption

Chapter 14

Out of Egypt Once More

"History is a gallery of pictures in which there are few originals and many copies."
Alexis de Tocqueville

Within his Gospel, Mark reports the baptism of Jesus, where God announces:

'This is my beloved son with whom I am well pleased.'[1]

The words below were taken from the Egyptian Pyramid Texts. They were written around 3000 years before Mark's gospel and attributed to God celebrating the coronation of the pharaoh.

'The king is my eldest son who split open my womb, he is my beloved son with whom I am well pleased.'[2]

What makes Christianity so special, what exactly sets it poles apart from the debased Pagan religions? The answer, or at least the answer given by theologians, is Christianity's uniqueness. It is a unique story of God manifesting through a virgin birth as a human baby, then as a man, preaching and performing miracles, unjustly being killed, but then being resurrected back to life before ascending to heaven. However, if one asks the crucial question, 'Is it a unique story?' the answer is an unequivocal, No! If one asks, 'Is it a true historical account?' the answer is again No! In the same manner as the Old Testament, the New Testament stories were adopted, adapted and much later, perverted. As a historical document, it is yet another blatant and deliberate lie!

---

[1] Mark 1:11
[2] Faulkner, R O *The Ancient Egyptian Pyramid Texts*

Christians will naturally, protest and with quite rightful indignation. This cannot be true; …it is a very special and unique story; …a story recording the life of a real historical person, the Son of God himself; …it is a million miles apart from the childish mythological fantasies of gods and goddesses! But there lies part of the problem; people's ignorance of the subject. Christians do not know what they are talking about. When most people think of pagan gods their thoughts inevitably turn to the Greek gods and it becomes easy to dismiss these gods immediately, with their almost human weaknesses and rivalries and constant meddling in earthly affairs. That is fair enough to a point, but what these critics have not understood is that these stories were not about people who were *real*, they were meant as *allegories* of human behaviour, from which people were supposed to learn.

It has been convenient to disguise this truth and it helps to promote the idea that before the coming of Christ, people worshipped these kinds of gods. Once, long ago in more primitive times, the early Greeks did follow their own local deities. By the time of Classical Greece however, philosophers like Plato dismissed such naïve beliefs. Around 400 BCE, we find the Greeks following new allegorical stories, part of a two–tier religious cult with mythological allegories used as a teaching aid for the majority of citizens and a teaching and knowledge that was kept secret for those who chose to advance to a higher spiritual level.

The complicated two–tier system, with its true knowledge kept exclusive, had quite a simple purpose, to preserve its purity from abuse. The philosopher Sallustius explained:[3]

> 'To wish to teach all men the truth of the gods causes the foolish to despise, because they cannot learn and the good to be slothful, whereas to conceal the truth by myths prevents the former from despising philosophy and compels the latter to study it.'

This Greek concern to protect the truth from distortion, abuse and mockery was common to the Druids and the Egyptian priesthood also. All three groups forced students to memorise every detail of the knowledge that they were taught in order to enhance their understanding, whilst avoiding reliance on written texts that can suffer from careless mistakes and misinterpretation. It was too easy for written texts to fall into the wrong hands, or to be destroyed and lost. The unwritten word could be disseminated and preserved in its purest form.

This new 'pagan' religious philosophy which gained rapid popularity in the Greek world, became commonly known as the 'Mysteries.' The

---

3 Sallustius *Concerning the Gods and the Universe*

Mysteries was not a nationalistic religion, but one open to all mankind — a truly cosmopolitan religion. Its content immediately found wide appeal and rapidly expanded throughout southern Europe and the middle-east. Because the stories were allegorical, they were malleable, and different regions adapted the religion to suit their own ethnic tastes, usually inserting one of their local mythological gods into the lead role, whilst still retaining the same central core of the religious story. As a Scandinavian native looks different from an African, if one ignores superficial appearance, in reality, they are identical, so the Greek Mysteries was identical to the Mystery religion found in Syria. The Mystery religion was a religion for everyone, with no ethnic or national barriers; a Greek could attend, take part in and understand a Mystery service in Syria and vice-versa.

The basic allegorical story that manifested through so many interchangeable ethnic gods, who took the starring role in this cosmopolitan Mystery Religion, was a dramatic chronicle of the appearance upon Earth of God the Creator, incarnating in human form as his own son. No doubt this theme sounds familiar, however the original story-line belonged to the Mysteries and it began circulating around the Mediterranean region, some four centuries before the alleged birth of Jesus Christ. Many readers may be tempted to think that this is a freak coincidence. If this were the only coincidence, it might well be so, but these Mystery stories have further elements in common. As the Pagan Mysteries chronicle the life of the Son of God they tell us that:

- God, manifests into physical human form;
- He comes as the Son of God, the saviour of mankind;
- His birth is prophesied by the appearance of a star;
- He is born of a virgin;
- He is born on the 25th December;
- He is born in a humble cave or cowshed;
- He offers his followers baptism, so they can be 'born again;'
- He has twelve disciples;
- He turns water into wine at a wedding;
- He performs miracles;
- He rides in triumph on a donkey; crowds wave palms in honour;
- His disciples take Communion with bread and wine;
- He is unjustly accused of heresy;
- He dies at Easter time;
- He sacrifices himself to redeem the sins of the world;
- His body is wrapped in linen and is anointed with myrrh;
- His cave tomb is visited by three women disciples;
- He descends to the Underworld and resurrects on the third day;

- He ascends to Heaven, where he becomes the judge of the dead.

Yes, this is the story of Jesus Christ, but long before his story, it was the story of Dionysus in Greece, Mithras in Persia, Attis in Asia Minor, Adonis in Syria, Bacchus in Italy, Serapis in the Alexandria of Ptolemaic Egypt and amongst the Jewish initiates residing in that same city, Joshua ben Nun. All these named were the Mystery Religion's Son of God, represented in his local form. The Jewish version of the Mysteries elevated a heroic character out of Exodus, Joshua ben Nun, to be their own Son of God. From the translation of Joshua or 'Yah(weh) is salvation,' from the Hebrew form of the Aramaic name, through Greek into Latin, comes Jesus.

By chance, the Jewish/Christian version of the Mysteries was born not in Palestine, but amongst Jewish intellectuals residing in Egypt. From there it was exported to their old homeland. The Mysteries started its circulation around the Mediterranean region from Greece, but its true origins lay elsewhere, and it will hardly surprise the reader to find that the original form of the Mysteries came from Egypt. Its beginnings stretch way back in time to an unknown era, but this sacred drama was recorded in the Pyramid Texts dated at around 2700 BCE. Budge wrote:

> "However far back we trace religious ideas in Egypt, we never approach a time when it can be said that there did not exist a belief in the Resurrection, for everywhere it is assumed that Osiris rose from the dead."[4]

The fundamentals of the Osiris religious story and teaching, are virtually identical to Christianity, but preceded it by over 3000 years.

Originally, it was known as the Mystery of Osiris and centred on each of the three ancient cities in northern Egypt — Heliopolis, Memphis and Abydos. It is essential to point out that the religious philosophy contained within the Osiris Mystery goes beyond the rather basic Osiris story, for above the simple allegorical mythology lay a secret higher level of teaching and knowledge. One of the very few foreign initiates privileged to have been inducted into the Ra Temple at Heliopolis, was a brilliant scholar from Samos and it was he who exported the Osiris Mystery to Greece. Eventually, after undergoing modification to suit Greek tastes, it became the renowned Eleusinian Mysteries of the godman Dionysus. This Samos scholar is one that everyone knows — his name was Pythagoras.

Following the expulsion of the foreign residents of Akhet–Aten, Egypt became something of a closed land to foreigners. Much later, in 671 BCE

---

4 Budge, E A W. *Egyptian Religion*

and 663 BCE, when Israel was destroyed and Judea fell under the control of Assyria, Egypt too suffered attack. Just after the first attack, the pharaoh allowed the Greeks a trading port in the Nile delta, probably having recognised the importance of gaining foreign allies. This coincided with a relaxation on the entry of foreigners into Egypt and a number of Greeks seeking knowledge and wisdom were allowed in to study at the renowned Ra Temple at Heliopolis.

For twenty-two years, Pythagoras studied there and allegedly became a priest of the Ra Temple. There can be little doubt that as a consequence, he would have been initiated into the Osiris Mysteries. We know that Pythagoras learnt a great deal about science, mathematics and astronomy from the ancient store of knowledge held in the temple libraries. The higher mathematical teachings were only given to the inner initiates and the priests would have relayed the more *sensitive* spiritual knowledge to him too. There is absolutely no doubting that discoveries attributed to Pythagoras, such as the value *Pi*, originated in Egypt. As we know, *Pi* was used in the construction of the Great Pyramid and whatever dating one might care to use, its construction was at least two millennia before the time of Pythagoras, so clearly he had been the pupil and not the originator. If Pythagoras had been taught such advanced mathematics, this meant he was an initiate of the Ra priesthood and would also have been inducted into the banned cult of Atenism, as the priests would almost certainly have continued with its teachings in some covert manner.

Pythagoras is generally remembered as a mathematician, but as was common in ancient times, educated men were inducted into all the sciences and arts and were multi-talented. That certainly applied to Pythagoras, who was a scientist, astronomer, musician, philosopher, socialist, educationalist and a priest. After leaving Egypt, around 530 BCE, he returned to Greece and settled in Magna Græcia, a Greek colony in southern Italy, at a town called Crotona. There he founded a moral and religious school. The Greek authorities were strict to enforce allegiance to the traditional pantheon of gods of their state religion and they were not tolerant of Pythagoras and his imported heresies. Eventually, he was forced to flee from persecution and settled a short distance away at Megapontum in Lucania.

His school was rather like a commune for mystics. It welcomed both men and women, who, if they became higher-level students, gave up all their possessions and shared everything equally within the community. However it was far from a *hippy* lifestyle, for moral abstinence was expected — love without sex. As well as being expected to live pure lives, the members practised non-violence to all living creatures. They were strict vegetarians and they rejected the traditional Olympian temples that offered animal sacrifices. It was the latter that initially caused trouble for Pythagoras and his followers. The authorities disliked non-conformists and viewed them as subversives.

For new initiates to the colony, life was especially arduous, they were not allowed to speak in lessons for the first few years, but must listen, reflect and learn. Besides teaching science, mathematics, geometry, music and philosophy, the school also taught a new form of religion, the one Pythagoras had learnt about in Egypt, a religion that included the transmigration of souls between successive bodies. There was also another specific link with Egypt and the cult of Ra and the Aten: every day the community welcomed the dawn arising of the sun over the horizon.[5]

If one reads Robert Graves' book on Greek Myths,[6] one is likely to conclude that any rites which were held at Eleusis, were primitive even orgiastic ceremonies fuelled by the intake of intoxicating mushrooms. Graves implies that the ceremonies celebrated the more base elements of the gods and provided acolytes with hallucinatory visions. It is not known if there was a very early temple at Eleusis, which was dedicated either to Dionysus or Demeter before the arrival of the Pythagorean mystics. Whatever the case, the wild excesses and banal belief in the ancient Olympian gods, not to mention drug-induced hallucinations, are totally opposed to the philosophy and moral restraint practised by the puritanical Pythagoreans and their later disciples, the Athenian philosophers. Clearly the rites of the Eleusinian Mysteries, whose initiates included the likes of Socrates, Plato and Aristotle, bore no resemblance to anything suggested by Graves.

Pythagoras held the title 'Hierophant of the Mysteries of Demeter and Dionysus,' which indicates that he and not his later disciples adapted the Osiris Mystery to the Greek culture. Demeter replaced Isis and Dionysus, Osiris in the Greek version of the Egyptian stories. Pythagoras allegedly performed many miracles; this ability was later attributed to other 'pagan' sages and then hundreds of years later, Christian scribes attributed the ability to their prophets and saints. I suspect that in the case of the early pagans, these miracles may have been the result of scientific arts that originated in Egypt. Another feat attributed to Pythagoras, was bilocation, the ability to appear in two places at the same time. Whilst this may seem totally unbelievable and I don't wish to suggest that it did happen, it is in theory possible, according to quantum physics. Photons can be caused to

---

5 Strohmeier, J & Westbrook, P. *Divine Harmony: The Life and Teachings of Pythagoras*
6 Graves, R *The Greek Myths: Complete Edition*

bilocate and recent work has found ways to intensify this effect.[7] It may be highly unlikely, but that does not mean it isn't possible.

The appearance of the goddess Demeter, in Pythagoras' title of Hierophant or High Priest, might seem unusual, but the goddess is a crucial part of the Mysteries. Quite simply, it is the feminine aspect of God. In most religions, the mother goddess figure was extremely important, especially in ancient shamanic worship, where she was deemed – dubiously in my opinion — to have been supreme. My scepticism has been substantiated by recent archaeological finds of male figurines, which have suddenly cast doubts in the minds of academics about the traditional view of the mother goddess, which had been based on tentative evidence and theory yet promoted as fact.[8][9][10] If ancient civilisations were taught by 'unknown' civilisers, then surely these teachers would have told the primitive peoples about the equality of the sexes, or at least that a 'goddess' cannot give birth without the crucial male facet of the godhead.

Though scholars, like Robert Graves in his book *The White Goddess* and JG Frazer with the *Golden Bough,* like to promote the idea of all primitive and early civilised religions having mother goddesses, before being ousted in favour of a male–dominated society and the installation of male gods, this format cannot be applied to the oldest of them. Egypt, as we have seen did not have this supposed common belief. When Enoch was taken to the entities called the Elohim, he was greeted by a male and female god, who then informed him that they were merely 'appearing' as two aspects of the one being that they really were. In the Egyptian Aten religion, Akhenaten and Nefertiti enacted the roles of the male and female aspects of God upon Earth, whilst their portraits indicated the sexless androgynous nature of God.

Within the Mystery temples was a holy inner sanctum, known as the 'bridal chamber,' in which an initiation marriage took place. People like Graves, have suggested that it was a sort of fertility celebration, in the form of a symbolic marriage to honour the goddess Demeter; with or without a sexual enactment by acolytes inflamed by magic mushrooms. This assumption is totally wide of the mark and is not a mistake that would be made by someone with a thorough knowledge of the Mysteries, rather than just Greek mythology and ancient religious/fertility customs. The sacred marriage was an important part of the Mysteries, it was a symbolic spiritual

---

7 Hogan, J. " Quantum trick may multiply CD capacity," *Nature*
8 Ucko, P J. *Anthropomorphic Figurines of Predynastic Egypt and Neolithic Crete*
9 Fleming, A. "The Myth of the Mother Goddess"
10 Hutton, R. *The Pagan Religions of the Ancient British Isles*

reunion between the godman and the redeemed goddess — Dionysus and Demeter — but the marriage had no sexual element, this was no physical consummation, but related to a spiritual union of the soul. There is some indication that in the initiation rites the veiled initiate — be they male or female — took the role of the 'bride,' to be married spiritually to Dionysus, who represented the state of complete Consciousness. This 'marriage' was not some kinky rite, but an intellectualisation of a divine comprehension, through a formal sacred role enactment. The god represented the disincarnate Self, whilst the 'bride' (initiate), represented the incarnate (fallen) Self; so it was a spiritual uniting of the opposing elements of the initiate, a coming together to remake the whole.

The married god and goddess theme is common throughout all the variant forms of the Mysteries. In the original Egyptian myth, the crucially important figure in the Osiris story is Isis, his sister–wife, the mother of all living things. These two, together with their son Horus, formed the Egyptian Divine Trinity. Each regional Mystery cult had its own ethnic goddess to partner its god figurehead. In Asia Minor, Attis had Cybele; in Syria, Adonis had Aphrodite; in Mesopotamia, Tammuz had Ishtar; in Persia, Mithras had Magna Mater; in Phoenicia and Canaan, Baal had Astarte.

Without wishing to complicate things, it is necessary to explain that these mother goddesses were usually portrayed in both the form of dual aspects and also as a triad. The purpose was to teach by means of the allegorical myths. It required some intellectual effort to understand the *meaning* of these symbolic combinations, but the inner initiates who understood them had committed the time and thought to do so. Alas, later on these mythical mystical intellectual concepts were dumbed–down by Christianity, resulting in an over–simplified, misunderstood myth, which it corrupted into historical fact.

The feminine duality was used to highlight not only the virgin and the mother aspects, but also the foolish and the wise; the innocent and the blemished; the fallen woman and the redeemed woman. So Isis is paired with her twin sister Nephthys, the wife of the evil god Set. Another representation was Isis as the mother of life, whilst another aspect was that of Sekhmet the destroyer. In the Greek Eleusinian Mysteries, Demeter, the Earth and corn/harvest goddess, is paired with her daughter Core or Persephone, who was forced to live and rule as queen of the dead in the Underworld for three months every year — both of them were cited as the wife of Dionysus. Later, in the Christian myth Mary was both virgin and mother, who had her alter–ego in Mary Magdalene, the fallen–redeemed woman.

OUT OF EGYPT ONCE MORE

Grouping gods into threes was common in pagan religions, these triads complicated matters a little more. In the Christian myth, there is a symbolic insertion of three Marys at the cross.[11] In later Christianity, the female was deemed unworthy and downgraded, so the Holy Trinity, that had originally included a Mother, was changed to include the Holy Spirit instead. The early Celtic Christian Church, which was deeply connected to the Druids and at odds with the Church of Rome, did not diminish the position of women, who like the fabled St Brigid, not only held the position of priestess, but also headed mixed–sex monasteries and regularly conducted baptisms. It is not without significance that both dualities and triads are common in the Celtic myths and there is some evidence that suggests that the original Druids and Egyptians were closely connected.[12]

Although it is diverting somewhat from the investigation into the Bible truths and lies, it is worth a brief look at the subject of the Druids. Their link to both the Egyptians and Greeks shows the claims of Hebrew exclusivity in a new light. Intriguingly, there are accounts that connect Pythagoras with the Druids, some of these reports insist that much of his philosophical knowledge came from them, rather than from the Egyptians and that he spent some time in southern Gaul, presumably at a Druidic college, though academics hold differing opinions on this. Allegedly, Pythagoras stated that 'the Druids were the wisest men in the world.' Pythagoras' successors also made mention of the Druids; Aristotle said. 'philosophy began with the Druids'; whilst Herodotus said that, 'the Druids had a knowledge of the heavens which was proof of the depth of their scientific thinking.' [13][14]

When one mentions the Druids, a modern stereotypical image springs to mind: bearded, long–haired men in floor–length robes, standing amidst the vast pillars of Stonehenge, one raising a dagger over a terrified sacrificial virgin lying on a altar slab, awaiting her hideous fate, or perhaps even the extreme thoughts of a burning giant wicker–man filled with its screaming victims. The dreadful portrait painted of the Druids is totally unjust and without foundation. The Druids were anything but the bloodthirsty savage priests, commonly portrayed by lazy *comic–book* historians, who bizarrely continue to adhere to the discredited propagandist depictions given by Julius Cæsar. Scholars accept that Julius Cæsar undertook a campaign to paint his political opponents in the worst possible light, to gain support for

---

[11] John 20:25
[12] Massey, G. *Book of the Beginnings, Part I*
[13] Diogenes Laertius. *The Lives and Opinions of Eminent Philosophers*
[14] Herodotus *Herodotus: The Histories*

his own ambitions. In truth, he really only knew them as opponents of his brutal empire building, but had no real knowledge or interest in what they were or did. Despite all of this, his acknowledged lies and distortions are still what many people think defined the Druids.

It is a sad fact that there are far too many unimaginative, frightened historians who cannot break free from the traditionalist dogma. Too often, their tunnel vision does not permit them to consider real evidence because it would upset the status quo. This lack of thinking can be seen when historians, without any factual proof, link almost everything in the ancient world to religious worship of the sun/nature spirits/mother goddess and wherever possible, animal or human sacrifice. This seems to stem from a desire, even fear, that causes modern man to dismiss and demean his ancient predecessors as foolishly superstitious and primitive. The possibility that they were our equal, or worse, that they were superior in some ways, is viewed with abhorrence, as such an elevation would be a slur upon our achievements and ascent.

In the same manner, the careless automatic assumption that every priest, cult practice and ritual sacrifice within the Celtic world, is a Druidic one, indicates their ignorance. There is no single piece of conclusive evidence to link the Druids to bloodshed. That there were other religious cults about appears not to trouble the thoughts of most historians, who jump to unsubstantiated conclusions whenever the remains of a 'ritual killing' are is unearthed. To call the Druids priests is not correct, but rather one should think of them as sages, in the manner of the Greek sages. They would have taught about the One God, but probably only to their students. They would have officiated at certain ceremonies because of their position as lawgivers and judges. Blood sacrifices would not have been part of any Druid ceremony. If priests had been involved in sacrifices, they would not have been Druids, since Druidic philosophy was opposed to blood–letting and violence.[15]

It is interesting that the civilisers, or 'gods' — recorded by the various south and central American early civilisations — vigorously promoted peace and non–violence and were totally opposed to all forms of blood sacrifice.[16] These civilisers delivered instructions for building, tool making and farming, but the physical descriptions given were the same as those attributed to the Druids: white men, bearded, blond hair, belted tunics, carrying a long staff. The Druids were not only philosophers, but on a more practical level they were internationally praised as highly–skilled scientists, astronomers,

---

[15] Ellis, PB. *A Brief History of The Druids*
[16] Spence, L. *The Myths of Mexico and Peru*

doctors, surgeons, musicians, poets, historians, law makers and teachers. The many Druidic 'Colleges' — forerunners of our universities — were renowned for their excellence of learning and they attracted students from all over Europe. When asked how they acquired all their skills and learning, the Druids did not seek to flatter themselves by claiming credit for what they knew, but stated that the 'gods' themselves had taught their Druidic ancestors. Since the Druids believed in a One God, then clearly these other 'gods' who instructed them, would not have been thought of as gods in the literal sense. As to who they might have been, I can only suggest that they were the same people or entities who brought 'light' to the early Egyptians and the pre-civilisation peoples of the Americas.

The Druids are sometimes dismissed as illiterate, but this is far from the truth. They could and did write, but generally only wrote mundane things such as accounts.[17] Having had long associations with the Mediterranean civilisations, it would be illogical for them to scorn literacy: such scholars as the Druids would have been literate long before they made their southern contacts. There were actually very strong reasons for not documenting their important works: the Druids were wise enough to know that written knowledge was prone to censorship and corruption.

In a world of fluid immigration, of invasions and ensuing destruction, documents of whatever kind are in danger of being cast aside as worthless or deliberately destroyed. There is also the problem of students reading documents in isolation. Without a teacher misinterpretation and false conclusions can so easily result, this leads to loss of meaning and is exacerbated by careless scribes who copy documents incorrectly.

Like the Ra priests at the Heliopolis Temple, the Druids chose to commit their knowledge to memory and every new student had to undergo a rigorous education where everything learnt had to be memorised and recounted over and over again until word perfect, thus ensuring the longevity and purity of the information. This method also ensured that the student was dedicated and worthy enough to be given the knowledge, since easy access to scrolls containing the same information would produce lazy minds that had not been fully immersed in the subject. Keeping the knowledge restricted and secret, also had the benefit of protecting it from abuse and scorn from ignorant detractors.

Unfortunately, very little detail of the Druids is known and, dismissing most of the Roman propaganda used to demonise the Druids, the only other information is derived from later Celtic tales and snippets passed on by the Greeks. However the Druids promoted certain revealing things and the following were amongst them:

---

[17] Julius Caesar. *Gallic Wars*

- there was but one God, of which everything in the cosmos was a part;
- everything in the universe was made up of atoms;
- matter could not be destroyed but only transformed;
- there were many other planets which contained life forms;
- men and women had equal status;
- a belief in non–violence;
- the promotion of legal courts of justice, fines and community service for crimes and the opposition of capital punishment;
- the encouragement of communities to look after their orphans, the old, the sick and mentally handicapped;
- encouragement to learn the arts, sciences and medicine.[18]

These things are hardly consistent with a group of fanatical primitive heathens, lusting after blood sacrifices.

Britain was both a great exporter of mined metals and of manufactured tools and weapons.[19] Phoenician ships traded with Britain and it is believed that Egyptian ships did also. Trade links have always led to an exchange of ideas and beliefs between cultures. Though it is still disputed by the ultra–conservative Egyptologists, many scholars now accept that the Great Pyramids mirror the stars of Orion's Belt. Researcher Ralph Ellis has discovered that the Red and Bent pyramids are also part of the ground plan, but he also discovered that in Britain, the sites of Stonehenge, Avebury, Silbury and Uffington repeat the very same layout.[20] From the celestial alignments of both sites, by measuring the Earthly celestial pole positions, he believes he has discovered the dates of construction of both sites —and these are very ancient and almost coincident.

Researchers Christopher Knight and Alan Butler undertook a study of the unit of measurement, known as the Megalithic Yard, discovered by Emeritus Professor Alexander Thom. This unit of measure was used to construct all the megalithic sites that Thom studied in Britain and western France. Knight and Butler discovered that this extraordinarily accurate stone–age measure was the foundation for not only other ancient systems, such as the Minoan and Sumerian, but also for the more modern Imperial and Metric systems. The Megalithic Yard provided a standard for not only

---

[18] op. cit. Ellis, P B
[19] op. cit. Herodotus
[20] op. cit. Ellis, R

linear measure, but weight and capacity too.[21] Included in this group are the Egyptian measures. Together with the principal unit the 'royal cubit', the 'remen' is the diagonal across a square that has sides of one cubit. The Great Pyramid of Khufu, has the strange and intriguing dimensions of a height of 279 royal cubits, a corner–to–corner diagonal measurement of 279 remens and a base length on each side of 279 Megalithic Yards. The Megalithic measure again appears on Menkaure's pyramid, its perimeter is an exact 500 Megalithic Yards. The Egyptians also had a unit of area called a 'setat', though the quarter–setat unit was most commonly used. The setat corresponds to exactly 4,000 Megalithic Square Yards and the quarter–setat is 1,000 Megalithic Square Yards. At Stonehenge; the inner edge of the Sarsen ring encloses an area of 1,000 Megalithic Square Yards, identical to an Egyptian quarter–setat.

Clearly a link exists, the mathematics do not permit dismissal as coincidence. There is a wealth of evidence to validate the authenticity of these linked ancient systems and I would strongly recommend *Civilization One* by Knight and Butler to anyone who wishes to learn more about the developments of Professor Thom's work. Orthodox archaeology rejects links between Britain and Egypt because no artefacts have been found, but since any interchange would have involved only a small number of scientist–priests, they would not have left identifiable artefacts carelessly lying around. There may be no evidence to suggest that there was an exchange of knowledge between the two groups, but there is equally no evidence to prove that there was none.

The symbolic representation of the sun god provides another important link between the Druids and Egypt. The image of the Sun with emanating rays that end in hands reaching down to the Earth is a well–known depiction of the Aten and this symbolic depiction was also used for Ra. The Celts too had a sun god, one who was called the 'Lightbringer', the godman who brought civilisation and the sciences to mankind. This god was known as Lugh Lamfada: Lugh meaning 'light' and Lamfada meaning 'long arm.' In Gaelic Lamfada could mean either long hand or long arm, or may even imply both. The designation has long puzzled scholars and caused some ridiculous theories to be proposed, such as the name indicating that Lugh was good at throwing a spear! As I looked at an engraving of Ra depicted as the solar disc with his long ray arms reaching down to Earth, the explanation became obvious: here was the true meaning of Lugh's long arms. Lugh, Ra and the Aten are identical, whilst Lugh the civiliser also corresponds to Osiris and Thoth.

---

[21] Knight, C and Butler, A. *Civilization One*

This is not the place to delve into the fascinating and labyrinthine subject of the roles and personifications of Lugh, Osiris and Thoth, but it is useful to be aware that a link was almost certainly there and that there was a sharing of philosophical and scientific thought.

Having diverged briefly to visit the Druids, we should now return to consider how the Egyptian Mysteries were *exported* and then blossomed into their no longer recognisable form. Despite the initial problems and hostility from the Greek authorities, the Pythagorean school survived. The major factor in this survival was the realisation that to make their teaching acceptable to the hostile authorities and the conservative nature of the Greek people, it was pointless to promote the *Egyptian* Osiris Mystery, so it was astutely remodelled to reset the story into traditional Greek mythology. This new format proved to be a great success and its appeal spread right across the social divide to every level of society. The Pythagoreans' reputation spread very quickly and they established more communities.

In some ways their appeal seemed strange and unlikely, certain aspects would have appeared rather esoteric, such as Gematria, the relationship between names and numbers. This sacred mathematics was to become a part of the Gnostic Christian Gospels, though the story of feeding the five thousand with five loaves and two fishes is nowadays seen as a 'miracle' not an encoding of spiritual information. But despite the intellectual concepts, it was the fairness of the Pythagorean philosophy, which had the greatest effect upon people. This philosophy was also to have a profound influence upon all future Greek philosophers. Parmenides, an Italian from the Pythagorean school, went to Athens where he tutored the young Socrates and that set an unstoppable ball rolling. Nonetheless, its early motion was somewhat precarious. The Athenian rulers did not care for Socrates' teaching of Pythagorean philosophy; nor were they indifferent to his condemning their lack of morality. The Athenian rulers did not practise religious tolerance and they charged Socrates with heresy against the state and its religion, put him on trial and found him guilty; leaving the sage to execute himself with a dose of poison. In true philosophical fashion and no doubt strengthened by his religious belief in immortality of the soul, he contentedly faced his end whilst encouraging his devotees and pupils to be of good cheer and to celebrate his life and passing over to his next one.

Plato, as a friend and associate of Socrates, was forced to flee Athens with other philosophers and spent some time at the Pythagorean school in Italy. Virtually all Plato's work has its foundation in Pythagorean teaching and the Mysteries. Eventually, when the authorities became more tolerant, Plato returned to Athens. He created an academy inspired by the Pythagorean school, but concentrated on philosophy and the sciences rather than attempting to run an impractical whole-life commune. Plato's academy became the breeding ground for philosophers, scientists and poets, whose influence and work rapidly propelled Athens into a golden age. One of the illustrious pupils of the academy, who later became a teacher there, was Aristotle.

Aristotle privately tutored the young Alexander the Great; though some scholars believe that the master's influence upon the head-strong boy was minimal. Though Alexander was clearly not of an academic inclination, during his war with the Persian Empire, he did a very strange thing, which suggests that certain things learnt from Aristotle had had a profound effect upon him. Following a great victory over the Persians, Alexander uncharacteristically ignored the sound military practice of seriously disabling the enemy when the opportunity presented itself. Instead of pursuing the fleeing army eastwards to stop them from regrouping, or bothering to protect his western flank by denying the Persian fleet from landing forces in Phoenicia, he sped south to claim Egypt from the Persian occupiers. This move was not really necessary as, had he waited until he had overthrown the Persian king, Egypt would have been his anyway, without a fight.

Once in Egypt, Alexander did another bizarre thing, he travelled across the desert with just a small escort, with the intention of visiting a remote oasis temple of Ra. It proved to be a long and arduous journey, on which he got lost and almost died. The only conclusion that I can draw from this eccentric episode, is that the temple was the reason why Alexander chose to go to Egypt at the first opportunity he had. Clearly information that someone had given him influenced this childhood plan. Accompanied by the Egyptian priests alone, Alexander went into the temple. What took place inside is not known to anyone except his mother; he never divulged the secret to anyone else and it died with him.[22]

Some scholars make the banal suggestion that it was simply an egotistical quest to have his fortune read, or to have confirmation that he was a god, but these explanations are irrationally nonsensical; his fortune could have been told anywhere, why risk his life for flattery by such a dangerous journey when flattery abounded from everywhere and why such a rush and at the risk of jeopardising not only his war campaign, but also his great ambition of unifying the civilised world. Clearly he had a very special motive for going to that particular remote place. It was strange behaviour and whatever lay behind it, it appeared to have a profound affect upon him.

---

[22] Plutarch

The rashness continued, together with an unexplained sense of urgency. Displaying incautious military tactics, Alexander rather carelessly rushed to conclude the Persian campaign. However with his victory, he did not then stop, rest and count his rich spoils, but undertook a hurried march up into the desolate Himalayas. If he merely wished to invade northern India, why take this route, the coastal plain offered an easier and quicker passage. The Himalayan route was a wildly eccentric and inexplicable route into nowhere. Was Alexander looking for something in particular in that mountain wilderness, had he learnt of something that had set him off on a secret quest? I do not know, but the question is not an unreasonable one and worthy of consideration. If the reader is interested, *K2 Quest of the Gods* by Ralph Ellis may supply a plausible answer to the conundrum. Personally, I haven't yet decided.

What is clear, is that whatever Alexander's motives, his obsessive interest in some special aspect of Egypt had to have been learnt from Aristotle: something which had been communicated from Pythagoras to his immediate disciples, then down to Socrates and Plato and on to Aristotle.

The consequences of what had been learnt by Pythagoras at the Ra Temple and libraries of Heliopolis, then later exported to Greece, had a profound effect upon the world. The greatest philosophers, scientists, mathematicians, playwrights, poets and sculptors of the western world were initiates of the Mysteries, an impressive list of people which included Pythagoras, Socrates, Plato, Aristotle, Plotinus, Heraclitus, Euripides, Diogenes, Archimedes, Anaxagoras, Sophocles, Aristophanes, Apuleius, Hippocrates, Herodotus, Pindar, Virgil, Seneca, Cicero, Celus and Lucian.

One has to conclude that these philosophers and scientists, who had rejected religious nonsense such as the Olympian mythology, would not be fooled into another fictional fantasy. Clearly the Mystery religion was profound enough to not only convince these brilliant thinkers to become initiates, but also to change and direct their lives. And these geniuses of the classical world were not just great academics but many of the philosophers were also great mystics; sometimes their demeanour might have been considered unworldly and even eccentric, as they withdrew into long contemplative silences, or even sought to abandon the materialistic life altogether.

Without taking anything away from the Greeks' great achievements, particularly in the scientific and mathematical realms, it is now considered certain that much information originated from Heliopolis.[23] Geometric theorems and the practical applications of Pi had long been used in Egypt

---

[23] Diodorus Siculus *The Library of History*

and it was there that Pythagoras and a few other Greek scholars learned of them. There is little doubt that the water-screw, attributed to Archimedes, came from things learnt during his studies in Egypt. Hippocrates, 'the father of medicine,' would have collected medical knowledge and practice from Egyptian physicians. Plato's treatise, concerning the form and function of the cosmos, comes from Egypt, via Socrates and Solon: though exactly how the Egyptians learned about atomic particles and the composition and movement of stars and planets, is a mystery. They do not claim that they worked it all out themselves, but insist that the 'gods' passed the information onto them. Whether those Greek scholars had full access to the 'cache' of knowledge held by the priests, we cannot know, but I strongly suspect that the Egyptian priests had not opened all their doors to the foreigners.

Greeks who may have studied at the libraries of Heliopolis, or later at Alexandria, may not have been allowed to copy texts directly and therefore had to memorise what they discovered, leading to a less than complete transfer of knowledge. Though the Greeks were allowed to study, it is also likely that the Ra priests would not transmit all of their secrets, but offered mere *tasters* in what they knew. Though a vast amount of knowledge was eventually documented and deposited in the Great Library at Alexandria, there is reason to wonder whether what was there was less than fully explicit. Considering the tradition of the Ra priests for guarding their secrets stringently, I cannot believe that they would suddenly hand them all over to public scrutiny. Some things would most certainly have remained *sub rosa*; to be revealed only to the highest initiates. Nevertheless, the effects of the Pythagorean teachings were colossal and it is widely accepted that it is this input that transformed scientific, philosophical and cultural thinking, directly giving rise to Classical Greece and elevating Athens to the centre of the civilised world in this 'golden age.'

But the item which had the biggest effect upon the civilised world, was a new religion, though in truth, it is not possible to separate Greek philosophy from this new religion, for they were deeply intertwined. This new religion owed nothing to the traditional formats of religious practice, which had generally been used as a political tool to bond individuals together into a social and nationalistic group. The Mysteries was a religious philosophy, which promoted a spiritual teaching that encouraged individual pathways to enlightenment by undergoing various mystical visions and experiences, which would lead to higher states of consciousness.

The Egyptian Mystery of Osiris was transformed by Pythagoras and his disciples, retailoring it to accommodate Greek tastes. Osiris, the dying–resurrected god, was replaced by a little known minor deity on the sidelines of the Greek pantheon, the god of wine and regeneration, called Dionysus. Dionysus was probably chosen because he shared certain attributes with

Osiris. Dionysus was the vine god, the god of corn, of growth and of harvest, he was the equivalent of Osiris, who was always depicted as green reflecting his status as the god of vegetation, growth and regeneration. Even today, the great cathedrals and churches of Europe have the sculptured head emblem of the pagan 'Green Man' everywhere and in great profusion. Such pagan imagery should have been heretical, but is still there nevertheless. The Knights Templar built most of these edifices; the deliberate insertion of such blatant pagan iconography, is just one piece of evidence which indicates that this enigmatic order was neither orthodox Christian, nor 'devil' worshipping, but comprised initiates of a revived Mystery cult.

The centre of the Pythagorean religion was transferred from the Greek colonies in southern Italy to just outside of Athens, at a place called Eleusis, which had long been associated with Dionysus. As a consequence, the Mysteries of Dionysus became known as the Eleusinean Mysteries. The evidence to show that the Osiris Mystery and the Dionysian Mystery, were essentially the same and one was not copied from the other, is given in a report by the Greek traveller and historian, Herodotus.[24] In the fifth century BCE, Herodotus visited Egypt. Whilst he was there around Easter time he witnessed an annual sacred festival, attended by thousands of people. He saw the Passion of Osiris dramatised to celebrate the death and resurrection of the god after his killing. As an initiate of the Dionysus Mystery, Herodotus clearly recognised the same Passion Play that was celebrated at Eleusis. Herodotus, like all other initiates, had sworn a sacred oath, which forbade the revelation of the Mystery's rite, so had little to say about the content of the ritual that he saw, other than that he witnessed the familiar one that he knew.

This unfortunate secrecy has left historians in the dark concerning the detail of any ritual and knowledge given to initiates, so the full details will never be known. After 1,100 years of existence, Eleusis was destroyed by Alaric the Goth, with the enthusiastic aid of fanatical Christian monks. The fearful zealots of the Church of Rome banned the Mysteries, demolished its temples and murdered its priests and teachers. Because the followers had not been permitted to write down anything that would directly reveal the rites and knowledge of the Mysteries, we have only a variety of indirect sources, such as philosophical treatises, plays, poetry, pottery, sculpture and post–initiation comments by ecstatic initiates, to give us some hints of the form it took. The best source of information is the fictional initiation story entitled the 'Golden Ass' though its author Apuleius was severely

---

[24] op. cit.

reprimanded for revealing too much. Plato also offered a clue when he related

> "We beheld the beatific visions and were initiated into the Mystery which may be truly called blessed, celebrated by us in a state of innocence.
> "We beheld calm, happy, simple, eternal visions, resplendent in pure light."

It seems that initiations into the higher realms of the religion, which were allowed after periods of study, took the form of an introduction into a drama, played out in the blacked–out inner sanctum of the temple, which incorporated some kind of brilliant light display.

Whatever occurred, those initiated into the highest level, came out in a state of euphoria, through having 'experienced' God. The evidence is strongly against initiates 'tripping out' on hallucinogenic substances. In modern day shamanic or meditative rituals, altered states of consciousness are easily achieved without them. Though the initiates would have been introduced to secret truths and knowledge, things which the Egyptian priests had probably passed down through vast generations of priests, it seems that it was not simply a case of finally being told what God was, but through their experience 'becoming' part of God, through realisation that that is what they were. Indeed everything was God. It seems that the initiates came to understand that if they harmed someone or something, they harmed themselves, for everything was one, separateness was an illusion. As one initiate, named Sopatros, confided "I came out of the Mystery Hall feeling like a stranger to myself."[25]

What we know about the Mysteries has been pieced together from small shreds of evidence, leaving us to fill in some large gaps, for everyone who belonged to the Mysteries swore an oath never to divulge its secrets. If anyone did break the oath, that record of the secrets has not survived. Considering the large number of followers of the Mystery religions, this might seem surprising and even highly unlikely, however this is not quite the case. Though indeed there were eventually huge numbers of followers of the various Mystery cults, which spread right around the Mediterranean and the Middle–East — over the centuries the total numbers would run into millions — the vast majority of those followers would have been the 'outer initiates.' These people would have been inducted into the simple allegorical stories, in much the same manner that modern Christians are told Bible parables in order to guide the conduct of their lives, so they had no real secrets to divulge. Those who had studied and were deemed worthy were

---

[25] Burkert, W *The Orientalising Revolution*

selected for higher initiations. Those worthy select few — wealth, rank and even kingship, were no key to entry — had undergone so many trials before gaining enlightenment that they could not be tempted into the folly of disclosure.

The Mysteries' celebration was not uniform, as the many and varied cults were imbued with traditional ethnic tastes and practices. Whilst many would be meditative and sombre, some might take the form of more exuberant ceremonies, which could possibly even permit animal sacrifice. The Mithras cult supposedly sacrificed a sacred bull, though this is surmised rather than proven. Nevertheless, at the heart of the varied Mystery cults, lay the core of the dying–resurrected godman. The wide expansion of the Mystery teaching, was aided greatly by Alexander's conquests, for within his empire and its aftermath, the world from Spain across to India was largely stable, at peace and in harmony, with much cultural interchange. The sanctuary at Eleusis became the heart of the Mysteries and the great centre for pilgrimage. Over its thousand–year existence, it attracted devotees which included the full diversity of mankind, from Roman emperors to humble slaves, for the Mysteries had no social barriers — men and women, rich and poor — all mankind was deemed equal. Neither were there any ethnic barriers, with pilgrims coming from all over the then known world. The mutual understanding of what was being taught by the Mysteries is emphasised by visits of Brahmins from India. The Mysteries, through their many and varied cults open to all, transcended national identities and barriers. This open 'brotherhood' inspired Socrates and other initiates to declare themselves 'citizens of the cosmos': cosmopolitans. Followers of the Mysteries shared a common belief, regardless of the particular name of their god, for as Celsus explained:

> "It does not matter at all what one calls the supreme God — or whether one uses Greek names or Indian names or the names used formerly by the Egyptians."[26]

According to Herodotus, at the annual autumn religious festival of the Mystery of Dionysus, some 30,000 people made the barefoot pilgrimage from Athens to Eleusis. After undergoing several days of purification and fasting, those amongst the throng about to be initiated into the inner esoteric Mysteries, would be ritually insulted and abused and even beaten with reeds and branches — as Jesus was on the way to Calvary — as they made their way along the sacred road. At the doors of the Telesterion, the huge purpose–built initiation hall, following ritual purification, the masses

---

[26] Hoffman, R J *Celsus on the True Doctrine*

stayed outside and only those already initiated to the inner secret Mysteries and those about to undergo initiation, were allowed to enter. Those people left outside were the ones who had undergone the first, exoteric introduction to the Mysteries and been inducted into the superficial allegorical religious myth stories.

What occurred inside we can only surmise: a divine drama was performed which depicted the struggle and hardships suffered in life's journey, the betrayal of the godman, his sacrifice and death and ultimate triumph, through resurrection to eternal life with the cosmos and the Creator. The drama appeared to have been very much a theatrical performance with the a darkened hall lit by a huge fire and the experience was intended to stimulate the senses in order to heighten states of awareness with the use of flashing lights and strident sounds, in contrast with moments of soft music and stillness.[27]

The inner initiates were not mere spectators at a theatrical performance, but the whole drama was intended to involve fully all those present at the proceedings. Each person was not only to witness the godman's suffering, death and resurrection, but also to share in it, to understand it totally, to experience it and thereby undergo a spiritual purification and redemption themselves. Those selected as worthy of initiation had already undergone lengthy study, the dramatic ceremony was designed to allow them not only to intellectualise what they had learnt, but also to experience it emotionally, with each doing so in their own individual way, to leave behind the 'self' and to commune with God, to experience the divine possession of being the Oneness.

In *one-to-one* sessions, the priests would have revealed to the inner initiates that the stories they had heard as outer initiates, were no more than spiritual allegories. They would be taught the real secret meanings and the truth which lay behind these stories. From this first inner initiation, the initiate progressed, on future occasions, through a number of further initiations — the number varying from cult to cult — with each leading to ever more deepening levels of comprehension, until the initiate finally 'communicated' directly with God.[28]

Unlike other religions, the Mysteries was not there to convey a dogma, there were no strict rules, no formal set of religious teaching; it was rather a shared journey for individuals to return to the Oneness of God. Also, unlike other religions, the role of the priests was different. They were there not there to control and regulate, but to conduct ceremonies and to act as

---

[27] Otto, W F. *Dionysos Myth and Cult*
[28] Kingsley, P. *Ancient Philosophy, Mystery and Magic*

guides to explain the truth that lies encoded within the Mystery story. This task was not designated just to temple priests, but to philosophers, which indicates clearly that the Mysteries was not a primitive religion, but a science–based philosophy. Initiates were given guidance but also freedom to think for themselves and to formulate their own idea of the Truth, that would be revealed through their own individual experiences. Heliodorus, a Mystery priest, sums up his role:

> "Philosophers and theologians do not disclose the meanings embedded in these stories to laymen, but simply give them preliminary instruction in the form of a myth. But those who have reached the higher grades of the Mysteries, they initiate into clear knowledge in the privacy of the holy shrine, in the light cast by the blazing torch of truth."[29]

There is no doubt that the Mysteries coaxed people away from the old primitive religions with their sky and nature gods, whilst retaining a pair of their local ethnics gods in the roles of the godman and his consort. It enabled simple people to understand that there was just one shared God, the Creator, the Great Oneness. This truth also encouraged people to wean themselves off their self–destructive reliance on identity through ethnic nationality: the cause of so much conflict between nations. The way that the Mysteries had taken root in the ancient world of the Mediterranean and Middle–East meant, had things taken their natural course, that eventually, all the varying godman deities would have merged into just the one, probably Dionysus or possibly even reverted to Osiris, but this was not allowed to happen. By political contrivance just one godman from the plethora of Mystery cults did end up standing alone and supreme, though this did not come about through willing consent of his followers. Alas, a chance misunderstanding unexpectedly escalated a deviant off–shoot out of one of the many Mystery cults. The truth, which lay within the Mysteries became lost, as the new cult falsely promoted its own myth as a true historical story. The Jewish Mystery cult of Jesus was perverted and its new uninitiated followers, the descendants of exiled Jewish slaves in Rome, transformed it into Christianity. Through ignorance and a greed for power, the greatest lie ever told was born.

---

[29] Fidler, D. *Jesus Christ, Sun of God*

Chapter 15

From Mystery to Mayhem

"Pride goeth before destruction, and an haughty spirit before a fall."
Proverbs 16:18

After the annexation of Egypt by Alexander the Great, the country was never again ruled by an Egyptian pharaoh; Queen Cleopatra, we need to remember, wasn't Egyptian, she was a descendent of the Greek Ptolemy dynasty. When Alexander died in Babylon in 323 BCE, his body was brought to Egypt to be buried in his new city of Alexandria. He had intended that Alexandria become the capital of his new empire, a genuinely multi–racial city that would set an example for men of all nations to live in peace as brothers. With this noble aspiration, he and his generals had married Persian women as a clear statement that there would be neither enemies nor old animosities; that the new world would be truly cosmopolitan, not one divided by race and nationality.

Numerous historians have sought to dismiss Alexander as an egotistical megalomaniac, but though this is understandable his overall actions tell a different story and he is certainly very different in his expressed ambition and deeds when compared with other great conquerors. Indeed his ambition for a cosmopolitan world and a brotherhood of man, though easily dismissed and mocked as disingenuous, actually fits perfectly with the image of a ruler brought up as an initiate of the Mysteries.

It may appear strange that Alexander had chosen to rule from Egypt when his Macedonian homeland seemed a likelier choice. Whilst political motivation might have caused him to seek a site external to Greece, it was his mysterious fascination with Egypt that made him put his capital where he did. After all, Egypt was the centre of the Earth's landmass, the land where the ancients thought that the balance and harmony of Ma'at could be found.

After Alexander's death, his empire was split amongst his generals and it was his friend Ptolemy who became ruler of Egypt. At the end of his long reign, Ptolemy abdicated in favour of his son, following the Egyptian custom where an ageing pharaoh elevated the crown prince to co–regent in order to ensure a smooth transition of power. Alexander would have approved of Ptolemy II as a successor, though in this time of peace he had no need to gain a reputation as a great soldier, he proved himself to be a great statesman and scholar who knew how to promote his multi–cultural state.

Perhaps the greatest achievement of Ptolemy II was the founding of the great library and museum in Alexandria. Ancient Egyptian papyrus manuscripts were deposited and translated into Greek and Ptolemy purchased manuscripts of Greek literature to add to the collection. When ships arrived carrying philosophical, historical and scientific documents, these documents were taken to be copied; the originals left at the great library and the copies given back to the owners. The library grew quickly and manuscripts from around the known world were collected and deposited there; eventually the library housed millions of documents. Ptolemy II enticed many Greek intellectuals to come and live in Alexandria, which, with its vast library and priceless store of knowledge, especially scientific, became a honey–pot for academics from every nation. Alexandria quickly superseded Athens as the centre of the world for learning.

Alexandria also became a magnet for Jews looking for a better life. Exiled Jews who had aided Alexander were granted an area within the new city and it is believed that they may have contributed up to half the city's original occupants. This sizeable enclave in a prosperous and fertile area appeared attractive to many Jews. Doubtless they were tired of grubbing a mean living in the harsh backwater that was their homeland, at the time sorely afflicted by violent fundamentalist zealots. There was a large influx of Jews who saw no benefit from staying in their 'land of milk and honey' that 'promised' nothing to the thinking mind.

Outside of Egypt, the post–Alexander empire had been divided up amongst his loyal generals. A decision that was to bring an end to Alexander's hopes and ideas. On their deaths the squabbling heirs ensured a quick disintegration. The ensuing turmoil offered Judea the opportunity to seize independence, but fanatical Judaism transformed the country into 'Hell on Earth'.

Inside Egypt, things changed; the outside world finally intruded into the timeless land. With the demise of Egyptian rule and power, so the old cities of Heliopolis, Memphis, Abydos and Thebes diminished in importance and the Egyptian religion waned. Not only the temples of Ra and Amun fell into disuse, but so too did the Mystery of Osiris, though Mystery cults elsewhere continued to grow and flourish.

In Alexandria, Ptolemy II wanted a new version of the Mystery religion that would appeal to both Egyptians and Greeks, so he invited a priest from Eleusis, a charismatic sage called Timotheus, to create a suitable hybrid by combining Osiris and Dionysus into the Mystery of Serapis.[1] It was to this religion, that most of the Jews of Alexandria turned, abandoning traditional Judaism. The Jewish settlers became known as Hellenic Jews, as they willingly adopted not only Greek ways and lifestyle, but also the Greek language in order to allow complete integration into the multi–ethnic community of which they were such a large part. This integration had the result of relegating Aramaic and Hebrew to their second or third language. Not only was Greek used in their everyday conversation, it was even used in synagogue services.[2]

The strong intellectual body of the Hellenic Jews was largely educated as Pythagoreans and Platonists. They would naturally have spent a great deal of time studying in the Great Library and would have been deeply immersed in Egyptian history and religion, and because of what they learnt, Hellenic Jews of Alexandria would have recognised the true history of the Jews. Understanding the truth, they would have been aware that the Biblical stories were allegorical and have refuted the historical authenticity of the traditional Jewish scriptures. So Alexandria became not only the new centre of civilisation and learning, it became the centre for the leading religious Jewish scholars and the Alexandrian rabbis became known as the 'Lights of Israel'.

Amongst these Hellenic Jewish intellectuals, were a group of religious scholars who though still strongly attached to their Judaic roots were passionate Pythagoreans and Platonists and as a consequence they were also initiates of the Mysteries. From the surviving writings of someone who was possibly their hierophant, a Jewish philosopher called Philo, we are told they were known as the Therapeutae. Amongst the things that Philo wrote about them, he stated that they dressed in white robes, men and women were equals, all possessions were shared commonly, and they led a 'contemplative life' within a monastic community. These were also attributes of a Pythagorean community.[3]

Philo also clearly states that though they adhered to certain Jewish observances, such as the Sabbath and Pentecost, they also practised rites that were the same as the Dionysian Mysteries. Their community was based at Lake Marenotis, just south of Alexandria; this was the lake of the sacred

---

[1] Beard, M et al. *Religions of Rome: Volume I*
[2] Fraser, P M. *Ptolemaic Alexandria. Volume I of III*
[3] Philo Judeaus *De vita contemplativa*

site where Herodotus witnessed the great annual Egyptian Mystery Passion of Osiris, thus underlining the fact that the Therapeutae were Jewish initiates of the Mysteries. The progeny of the Therapeutae, the Alexandrian Gnostics, were actually cited as participating in the Mysteries of Osiris in its later remodelled form of the Mysteries of Serapis.

As initiates of the Mysteries the Therapeutae understood the allegorical nature of the Books of Moses, so they felt no concern over blending it into their Jewish version of the Mysteries, which Philo referred to as the Mysteries of Moses. Though Philo was committed to the Dionysian–Serapis Mysteries, he encouraged the Jews of Alexandria to be initiated into the new Jewish version, understanding that they would still be part of the cosmopolitan brotherhood of Mystery initiates. As we have seen, it was common practice for differing ethnic groups to adapt the Mysteries to their culture, so for the Jews to do likewise was unremarkable. The early fathers of the Christian Church criticised the followers of the Mysteries, because they were always reinventing new versions — but they were encouraged to do so by their teachers, who insisted that initiates demonstrate their understanding by reinterpreting the allegorical stories in a form that was more suited to them as individuals.

It is by an ironic quirk of fate that we know what we do about what took place at that time, since virtually every Pagan literary work, including the priceless Great Library of Alexandria, was destroyed in the 4th Century CE by the rampaging mobs of Christians encouraged by the Church of Rome. This fortunate quirk of fate came about due to an ignorant misinterpretation by Bishop Eusebius, the Church's propagandist and inventor of historical Christianity: he was to the Pope, what Joseph Goerbbels was to Hitler. Bishop Eusebius allowed Philo's works to escape burning by his thuggish henchmen. Seeking evidence of early Christians for his new *History of Christianity*, Eusebius stumbled across Philo's description of the Therapeutae celebrating an Easter religious festival and wrongly attributed it as evidence of the earliest orthodox Christian Church in Alexandria. Philo's work had been written some twenty years prior to the crucifixion of the fictitious Jesus, so the Therapeutae were clearly not Christians. It is possible that Eusebius was in ignorance of this, but it is more likely that he knew that the Therapeutae had been initiates of the Mysteries and that he simply did not care about the truth. Eusebius invented much of Christianity's so-called history and we explore his work in more detail in a later chapter.[4]

So the Jewish Mysteries, yet another version of the dying–resurrected godman allegory, was created by Pythagorean Jews in Alexandria to make it

---

4 Eusebius, *History of the Church*

more acceptable to new Jewish converts, just as the Pythagoreans were forced to set the Osiris Mystery into traditional Greek mythology to make it acceptable to the conservative Greeks who would not otherwise tolerate a foreign religion. The Theraputae held the important character of Moses in very high esteem and they appeared to have elevated him to the godman role.[5] Naturally, the Jewish Mysteries did not remain localised to Alexandria and it was taken into Judea, possibly by missionaries but more likely by visiting Hellenic Jews who shared the new story when they returned home. Somewhere the traditional story underwent yet another transformation: one that would eventually lead to unforeseen and devastating consequences.

Judea fell to the Babylonians and after their vanquish, it became a vassal state of the Persian Empire until the time of Alexander. The Jews no longer had their own king, the nationalists amongst them always hoped for an upturn in their fortunes that would establish the golden time of David and Solomon once more and they longed for a king, someone from the line of David, who would lead them into this new golden future. The years rolled by frustratingly; the Greeks incorporated Judea into their new–age empire and much of Judea willingly adopted Hellenic ways, but for the fundamentalists the frustration lay grumbling beneath the surface of Hellenic tolerance.

Matters worsened after a couple of hundred years as the now divided Greek Empire started to fall apart. The Judeans took advantage of the dissent and staged a revolt, which gave power to the Hasmodean dynasty. The 'chosen people' soon found that regaining their fantasy was an illusion; their 'land of milk and honey' was one whose fruits they could not harvest. They had no time to reap the benefits of their independence as they found themselves on a roller coaster ride down the road to hell. With independence they gained internal chaos and violence, which spilled over the borders to threaten the stability of the region. The new superpower Rome stepped in to reduce the infighting — by invading.

In Judea, nationalists and religious fundamentalists longed for a political Messiah to step forward and lead them from the control of foreigners. They wished to re–establish strict adherence to Judaism, in much the same way that we encounter a few fanatical Islamic fundamentalists whom 'God has chosen to rid the people of infidel foreign influence,' whilst the true Muslims agree that Allah wants us all to get along.

At this stage, those fundamentalist Jews who longed for freedom, had gone through a number of self–proclaimed 'Messiahs' who had failed to win freedom through a force of arms. The word Messiah means Anointed and was originally used for kings and high priests, who were ritually anointed

---

5 Willoughby, HR. *Pagan Regeneration*

with oil. In the Old Testament, the word was often assigned to the reigning monarch. Through the Greek translation of Messiah, we get the word Christ, which means Anointed also, not Son of God, as many believe. The failure of a successful leader to emerge brought about a realisation that to rid themselves of the omnipotent Romans would require not just a normal man to free them, even one descended from the legendary David, this man would need to have godly powers, would be someone sent by Jehovah. In this state of failure and increasing desperation, the word Messiah, took on more supernatural proportions and it became linked to the new dying–resurrected godman of the Jewish Mystery.

So whilst recording the background mood of dissatisfaction and seething rebellion within Judea, a new local version of the Jewish Mysteries was formulated. It reflected the times, but kept its connections to Egypt and all the other Mysteries. The first thing that the new story needed was a suitable godman. Their only god was Jehovah and they did not want to use Moses, as the Alexandrian Therapeutae had, for he already had a distinct role in their religious history, so they looked to the other great hero of the Exodus story Joshua ben Nun. Joshua son of Nun couldn't be better suited to the role; Nun was the Egyptian god of the sky or 'cosmic waters,' as they were otherwise known and Joshua was the fictional character who led the tribes of Israel to freedom and victory in claiming their 'Promised Land'.

The name Joshua eventually became transformed into Jesus through a deliberate Greek translation of Joshua into Iesous. This later contrivance by the Gnostic Christian Greeks gave the name a specific mathematical value of 888. Amongst the Pythagoreans and initiates of the Mysteries, numerology was of great importance. The Pythagoreans knew that mathematics underlies everything within nature, the world and the cosmos; so the use of numbers in their writings conveyed a secret sacred teaching. In Greek, every letter of the alphabet had a numerical value, so that words could convey mathematical information.

The initiates of the Jewish Mysteries and those Greek or Gentile initiates of the subsequent Jesus Mysteries continued using Gematria, the art of secret mathematics and this became incorporated into many words used in the Christian Gospels. Hence we have the very sacred number 888 for the godman Iesous/Jesus: 888 is the sum of all the numerical values of each Greek alphabet letter. The famous *number of the beast* 666 is another example, though this is always misinterpreted, as are many things in the enigmatic Book of Revelation of St John. The full wording: 'Here is wisdom. He who has understanding, let him count the number of the beast; for it is the number of man and its number is 666.' The word *beast* has been wrongly interpreted for it does not refer to a *demon*, but to 'those with eyes to see'. To Pythagoreans, 666 is the important harmonic string ratio of the fifth tone and 888 is the perfect string ratio of the whole tone. 666 is no more than the number of man, before he becomes whole and 888.

The use of encoded numbers is numerous within the Gospels, for example in the seemingly baffling number of 153 fishes which Jesus helped his twelve disciples to catch.[6] Pythagoras, too estimated a catch of 153 fishes according to the story by Iamblychus, though the significance lies in the number 153's link to the ratios apparent in the vesica pisces, the 'sign of the fish', obtained when two circles intersect so that the edge of one passes through the centre of the other.[7] The feeding of the four thousand is reported by Mark[8] and John reports that Christ fed five thousand.[9] If these events were so remarkable, they were important enough to be remembered by the other disciples, who make no mention of them. Of course it was not a historical event, just an invented story that was meant to convey a secret teaching of a sacred mathematical coding; the importance of encoding this information is highlighted in Mark's gospel story, when Jesus becomes frustrated at his disciples' inability to comprehend and he is given to exclaim:

> "Though you have eyes, you do not see, and though you have ears, you do not hear. Do you not remember when I broke the five loaves for the five thousand, how many basketfuls of scraps you cleared away?"
> They said unto him, "Twelve."
> "And when I broke the seven loaves for four thousand, how many basketfuls of scraps did you clear away?"
> And they said, "Seven."
> And Jesus said to them, "And you still do not understand."

The incident is meant to relate particular mathematical information but the disciples, like dim–witted pupils or would–be initiates who have not reached a high enough level, are baffled by its meaning. This meaning also baffles modern minds, for the significance of these carefully chosen numbers and allegories has been lost through the meticulous eradication of the Mysteries by a fearful Christian Church.

The inventors of the Judean Jewish Mystery now had their own *local* dying–resurrected godman whom they named Joshua/Jesus. He was to be the king

---

[6] John 2:1-11

[7] Taylor, T trans. *Iamblichus: Life of Pythagoras*

[8] Mark 8:1-9

[9] John 6:4-15

of the Jews, so he needed a lineage back to David. In creating the new story of Jesus, the Mystery writers chose Bethlehem, where David had been born, as his birthplace. Though David wasn't real, Bethlehem does hold some real historical status, given to it by the Mysteries. Bethlehem had long been the site of an important sanctuary dedicated to another of those dying–resurrected godmen, Adonis.

Adonis had been remodelled into the Syrian Mystery godman, whilst in even earlier times the Syrians and Canaanites, had a fish god who was also variously known as Nun and Dagon. The name Nun is the Egyptian's name for the god of the cosmic waters of the sky, so the Syrians adopting this name for their 'aquatic' god is hardly surprising and we already know that the leader of the Exodus Hebrews into Canaan, was Joshua ben Nun.

Bethlehem was close to Syria and the region going up through Galilee, was subjected to ethnic, political and religious influences from there. Following the Greek annexation, this region was strongly populated with Hellenic Jews, many of whom would have adopted the local Mystery cult of Adonis. This may well be an indication that the final version of the Judean Jewish Mystery was composed in this area to create an acceptable localised Mystery for the conservative Jews steeped in the traditional belief of David, who hoped for a 'coming Messiah' and had been reluctant to embrace the Mysteries up to that time because the local version wasn't Jewish enough.

The geographic placing of Jesus in Galilee was not included in the original gospel texts. Studies show that the mention of Galilee in Mark's gospel was a later insertion, because of the word's ungrammatical usage in the Greek syntax.[10] The purpose of the subsequent insertion was clearly to give the Jesus story a more realistic and definite setting in the non–Jewish Gentile lands above Jerusalem. According to Mack, the name Galilee or *Gelil ha goim* means 'the land of *goim*' or the Gentiles[11] and this Hellenised land provided the perfect setting for the new version of the Mysteries written for the occupants of formerly Jewish land.

The New Testament gives two versions of the lineage from David to Jesus and there has been much debate because the genealogies do not match each other. The fact that there were two conflicting lineages given in the New Testament, by two different Gospel authors, should have been unimportant because everyone who heard of them would understand that they were not recording historical fact, but telling an allegorical story that illustrated the importance of the hero.

Much more confusing might have been the suggestion that the Son of God was related to David through Joseph at all, as Joseph, according to the

---

[10] Wells, G A. *Did Jesus Exist?*
[11] Mack, B L. *The Lost Gospel*

From Mystery to Mayhem

story became Jesus' mother's wife and God himself was Jesus' father. God's divine intervention did not invalidate the claim to succession made by the original authors, but was the whole focus of the new Jewish Mystery story.

The rest of the story was straightforward, the writers simply placed the original Osiris/Dionysian Mystery story into a Judean setting: the story would have their godman's birth announced by the appearance of a star in the East; he would be born of a virgin; he would be born in a humble cave or stable; his birth needed to be witnessed by shepherds. When he grew up he would be baptised, perform thirty–three miracles, gather twelve disciples, preach, ride on a donkey into a city in triumph, be betrayed, be falsely accused, die and resurrect. The Jewish initiates took all the common elements from the stories of dozens of pagan gods and created a story that was appropriate to their land and their ethnic customs.

The story line for the final version of the Jewish Mystery, its setting into their own time and world of Roman–occupied Judea — not some dateless ancient mythological time and place — the merging of the godman with the by–now superhuman Messiah, all this had an unintentional, unforeseen and detrimental long–term effect. What should have been unmistakably fictional characters and events, took on a potentially confusing aspect with the use of down–to–earth characters living in contemporary times. We see the complications that arise today when simple–minded folk believe characters in soap opera are real, sending money when a character has financial difficulties, or applying for vacancies at fictional workplaces. The discrimination of fact from fiction is dependent on the truth being taught correctly and passed on meticulously to new initiates. Without this safeguard, when recounted just a generation on, let alone a century later or more, fiction could seem real and myth could be believed as fact. If the people lose their teachers, who would tell them that the story was only an allegorical teaching tool?

A century on, in a foreign land, exiled Jews began to believe that the inspirational Jesus story had really happened, that it had been real history, that Jesus had really lived, had died and been physically resurrected to Heaven, they believed that he was the Son of God.

So how did it all go wrong, how did the fictional story of a Pagan God come to be believed as fact? The answer is pathetically simple, it all happened just by chance. The catalyst was the large–scale displacement of the Jews from Judea. Just as today we have Muslim extremists who disrupt life under the pretext of opposing an occupying power, a serious rebellion eventually erupted in Judea in 70 CE, provoked by a hard core of fanatical Jewish zealots. Many Romans were killed and the remainder forced to abandon Jerusalem. This violent revolt against the authority of Imperial Rome left the enraged Emperor Nero with no choice but to react with brutal severity to restore order. As well as redeeming dented pride, the Romans needed to make a severe example of the Jews and an explicit statement to others who might harbour similar ambitions. The Roman Legions returned with a vengeance and the areas of sedition were brutally devastated. A great many Jews were killed and an even greater number were enslaved and deported. Jerusalem and its Temple — the focus for Jewish nationalist dreams — were totally destroyed and the site barred to all Jews. The Sanhedrin and the Jews loyal to Rome were moved out to Jamina, 45 km north west of Jerusalem, whilst members of any sect which was considered subversive were eradicated. It has been claimed that early 'literalist' Christians escaped north to Pella, 40 km south of Galilee, however archaeology has failed to find any evidence of this. Indeed, the only evidence, in such places as Jerusalem and Capernicum, was of Gnostic initiates of the Jesus Mysteries.[12]

Inevitably, a large proportion of Jews ended up as slaves in Rome. It was here in Rome, amongst a fairly-sizeable Jewish population, that the Jesus Mystery story became distorted and where myth was transformed into history. Deprived of the higher initiates who understood the true esoteric meaning and history of the Mysteries, and who would have been their teachers, the offspring of the initiated slaves learned the exoteric dying–resurrected godman story from parents who were not privy to the full meaning of the Mysteries. Over very little time, the awareness that the already blurred contemporary story of the godman Jesus was allegorical, was lost and just as quickly, a small proportion of the inhabitants of Rome came to believe that it was fact. Like all vulnerable, abused people, the Jewish slaves turned to their religion to bind them together against the world which was abusing them, it was all they had left, it was 'them and us', 'our religion against theirs', 'we may be slaves, but our religion is the true religion and is greater than theirs'.

The lack of Jewish teachers and the 'real and recent' history of their godman were undoubtedly major factors that stopped these enslaved Jews from listening to their Roman masters who recognised another Mystery allegory The ignorant slaves also denied the truth, when the initiates of other Mystery sects attempted to help and correct their mistake by telling them that their godman was merely a fictitious character and that the Christian doctrine was absolutely no different from that of any other Mystery cult. The Jews had lost everything and were hopeless slaves, but they could elevate themselves by believing that their religion was better than that of their masters, that theirs was unique, that they were the blessed

---

[12] Lüdemann, G quoted in Sanders, E P ed. *The Shaping of Christianity in the Second and Third Century*

followers of the living Son of God and they found comfort and solace in that 'come the next life', they alone would be elevated into Paradise to be with their God.

These Literal Christians, who came to believe that the Jesus myth was real history, were a new minority sect based initially in Rome. The educated Christians, who had become true inner initiates, continued to understand that the Jesus story was just fiction and that it was merely another variant on the shared Mystery theme and these initiates, though Christian by designation, fully accepted that they were part of the cosmic brotherhood and were far closer in every way to the other cults of Dionysus, Mithras and Serapis than they were to those misguided Christians who took the myth as true history.

Because these literalists were obstinate and would not listen, they became mocked for their naïvety and foolishness, but this merely made them cling tighter to their mistaken belief. They stubbornly maintained that they were right and that everyone else was wrong and beguiled by Satan. They became increasingly more aggressive in defence of their fundamentalist stance. From out of this simmering hotbed of vulnerability and discontent, arose the fundamentalist preachers demanding unquestioning adherence to the holy scriptures. In such an environment, the lowly and despondent were easy pickings as new converts, beguiled with promises of a better life to come, whilst their rich masters would be denied entry to Heaven. Later on the early preachers invented Hell as a punishment for their oppressors. The threat of eternal damnation in a terrible Hell, frightened many into becoming converts: there was nothing to lose by conversion, so why risk damnation.

Inevitably, when religious passions are aroused amongst uneducated people, unreasoning fanatics are made and from out of those, pathetic individuals emerge seeking heavenly reward by deliberately sacrificing their own lives for the 'cause'. Fortunately, there were very few of them, far fewer than Hollywood accounts make us believe, but those unjustly glorified as innocent Christian Martyrs were nothing other than demented and brainwashed religious fanatics.

The greatest lie ever told

Chapter 16

The Gospel Truth

"How often have I said to you that when you have eliminated the impossible, whatever remains, however improbable, must be the truth?"

Arthur Conan Doyle *as Sherlock Holmes*

Whilst the perverted Jesus religion slowly seeded itself amongst the Jews in Rome, the *bone fide* Jesus Mysteries spread amongst the Jews scattered widely through Roman–controlled Hellenised Asia–Minor. As had happened for five hundred years, variations of the Jesus Mysteries' stories appeared to suit local need and the new initiates made up their own personal version of the central story so that gospel interpretations abounded.

Though seemingly baffling discrepancies reveal themselves within the four Christian gospels chosen for the New Testament, they are perfectly normal when viewed as personal interpretations from different authors. The early *Gnostic* members of the Jesus Mystery sects knew that the Jesus story was allegorical, so the variations were not historical contradictions as the members were recounting significant events in a story, not real historical ones. The Bible writers selected these four gospels from over thirty that are known to have existed, however there can be little doubt that many more had been destroyed during the Literalist Christian purge.[1] Thirty different gospels may seem a large number, but none of the gospels were historical accounts by eye–witnesses, they were just variants of the Mystery story, meant to show that the initiates who wrote them, had an insight into the teachings. No one gospel was any more important or valid or real than any other: in the late Roman times, the Gospel of Thomas and the Gospel of the Hebrews were the most frequently read and quoted.[2]

---

[1] Macmullen, R. *Enemies of Roman Order*
[2] Pagels, E. *The Gnostic Gospels*

As the Literalist Christian sect expanded slowly from Rome into other parts of the Empire, different versions of literalism emerged too, as the various groups of literalists began to diverge in their teachings. A number of factors had a bearing on this including the original local religious beliefs, culture and politics; a wish to be independent from Rome; egotism of the individual leaders and in particular local Gnostic influences. This growing divergence threatened to cause a disintegration of the Rome Christian cult and eventually forced the early Church Fathers to look at ways to bind their followers to a hard core of belief. They recognised the need for strict definitions of the foundation of their belief and the need to document it so that there were no variations within their church and therefore no disputes over what had happened historically.

These early church leaders of the second century CE were not scholars themselves and had no religious texts of their own, so they were forced to use the gospels of the original Jewish followers of the Jesus Mysteries, whom they knew as the Gnostics — meaning the Knowers. Using Gnostic gospels for their own purpose was far from straightforward since many gospel versions differed alarmingly and could be blatantly identified with the Mysteries. When they decided to collate gospels to form the New Testament, they chose to include the four that seemed most closely matched and innocuous. In future years, when suddenly the literalists' sect was elevated from relative obscurity to pre–eminence, they declared the rest of the gospels heretical and systematically destroyed them. Fortunately many were hidden away and in 1945 a cache was dug up at Nag Hammadi in Egypt, at the site of a Gnostic monastery. The dry desert conditions ensured that the gospels had survived.[3]

In 1980, a farmer in Egypt unearthed yet another version, which is entitled the Gospel of Judas. It remained locked away in a bank vault until recent years, when experts examined it and confirmed that it was a genuine second–century document from the time that the New Testament gospels were written. This particular gospel had not been written by Judas the disciple, but by a Gnostic initiate who wished to give a new and different insight — from the traitor's point of view — into the teachings of the Mystery's dying–resurrected Son of God.

When the Gospel of Judas was presented to the public in 2006, it came as a shock for most people and caused great controversy amongst theologians and despondent alarm amongst the clergy. A Literalist Christian viewing this gospel will read it as a challenge to traditional orthodox beliefs: Judas the traitor is trying to say that he was the good guy, that he was the closest to Jesus, that Jesus understood and approved of his role which ensured that

---

3 ibid.

his master took the final difficult steps in order to accomplish his divine mission.[4]

At the time when the gospel was written, it would have been read in its true context and not as a historical document, composed by a historical character. The readers would know it to be an alternative version of the dying–resurrecting godman story. They would have viewed it as nothing exceptional and certainly nothing disturbing or shocking. Its purpose was to recount the mythical story in a different and personal way. The reason for so many different versions was to enable the initiate telling the story to demonstrate that they understood every aspect fully, with the additional benefit that new initiates had a thought–provoking and enlightening read. In the case of the Judas Gospel, the writer regarded the apparent *betrayal* as a *helping hand* to the godman to assist him to cast off, to let die his earthly self, within which his spirit was imprisoned, and thus enable its return to the higher spiritual self. By carrying out this act of sacrifice, Judas showed that he alone amongst the disciples understood the meaning of the Mysteries and thus was far closer to Jesus than any of the others.

Academics, theologians and clerics discussed, argued and agonised over this gospel in 2006; as though it had some historical importance, when in fact they know, or should know if they have truly studied and researched the historical documents, that like every single Christian scripture, it is merely allegorical. Yet they carried on with the shameful charade to protect their public face, to preserve the order of things — to preserve Christianity.[5]

It is still commonly believed by most contemporary Christians, that the gospels are the eye–witness accounts of the disciples of Jesus and therefore they are true historical documents. This is simply not true and if they have studied their subject, all Biblical scholars must know this. Though many also admit the fictitious nature of the stories, the message is not actively promoted to the general public. Even the Archbishop of Canterbury, Dr Rowan Williams has managed to dodge the issue quite deftly in his 2006 Easter Address. You can almost read, "It's just another story, why are they making a fuss?" between the lines of his cynical second paragraph.

> "One of the ways in which we now celebrate the great Christian festivals in our society is by a little flurry of newspaper articles and television programmes raking over the coals of controversies about the historical basis of faith.

---

4 Kasser, R et al. eds. *The Gospel of Judas*
5 Williams, R. 2006 *Conspiracy Theories Don't Match Up to the Truth of the Gospel*

> "So it was no huge surprise to see a fair bit of coverage given a couple of weeks ago to the discovery of a "Gospel of Judas", which was (naturally) going to shake the foundations of traditional belief by giving an alternative version of the story of the passion and resurrection.
>
> "Never mind that this is a demonstrably late text which simply parallels a large number of quite well-known works from the more eccentric fringes of the early century Church; this is a scoop, the real, 'now it can be told' version of the origins of Christian faith. ..." [6]

Mark's Gospel is regarded as the earliest of the four in the New Testament, but it is obviously not an eyewitness account, since Mark does not claim to have ever known Jesus. Indeed because of this, many in the early Church of Rome were very much against the adoption of Mark's gospel and much argument ensued between the various literalist sects as to which texts ought to be adopted.[7]

Dating these old documents is not accurate, but researchers suggest that this first gospel, copied from earlier fragments, could not have been written until at least 70 CE, but it could also be as late as the first quarter of the second century. The other three gospels were written up to seventy years later. The authors were of course, not disciples who, even if they did exist, from their descriptions in the New Testament were illiterate.

In the New Testament, the Gospels and the Acts of the Apostles come first and thus precede the Letters of Paul. This chronology implies that Paul follows the Gospel writers in time, but this is a false conclusion for the Gospels were written between twenty and a hundred years *after* the life of Paul. The Gospels were an attempt to make a historical record of the life of Jesus and they needed to be given prominence because Paul never mentioned a living Jesus in his letters. Paul promoted the spirituality of the Mysteries and the mystical rites of a mythical resurrected Christ/godman, so his work needed to be demoted and some of his letters doctored and even forged; we look at this in more detail in a later chapter.

It is unlikely that the story of Jesus could have been written at a later date and still be an authentic and accurate account of what took place historically. Even if the events had been historical rather than fictitious, such a long time after the event any record of what took place would be deeply flawed. There would have been no eye-witnesses, so the writers would have had to rely upon a pot-pourri of hearsay, rumour, invention, exaggeration and propaganda. The suggestion that Christians clung on to the holy words

---

[6] ibid

[7] Metzger, BM. *The Canon of the New Testament*

of Jesus is ludicrous in the extreme, since the writers weren't alive to hear his alleged words. As we know all too well, conversations that are not written down as they are spoken, are both quickly distorted and soon forgotten. Literal Christians expect us to believe these words were those that Jesus spoke, even when they were written over a hundred years after he supposedly delivered them. Logic alone dictates that what is written in the gospels is most certainly not the actual words spoken by a historical character.

The four New Testament gospels are too full of mistakes and contradictions to be *bone fide* historical documents. The Gospel of Mark offers no witness to events and it appears that the writer or writers of the Gospel of Mark, were not even from Palestine as their geographical knowledge is weak. They state that Jesus left Tyre and passed through Sidon on the road to the Sea of Galilee, but Sidon was in the opposite direction and in the first century there was no road between there and Galilee. Gerasa, the town on the south–eastern border of the lake, is wrongly located thirty miles to its north.[8] They make another glaring mistake by saying that Jesus was raised in Nazareth and even call him 'Jesus of Nazareth'. At that period there was no town of Nazareth; even the most thorough investigation by Roman Catholic theologians has been unable to find any archaeological proof.[9] Ancient Jewish sources make no mention of Nazareth prior to the third century CE.[10] If a fundamental fact such as this is completely wrong, it has to bring the rest of the gospel into question.

One clear indicator of the Gospel's true source comes in a story of Jesus pronouncing upon a Jewish woman divorcing her husband. Divorce was not allowed in Jewish culture so there were no divorced Jewish women, but divorce was allowed in Greece. This ignorance of Jewish law indicates the author or authors, the Mark or Marks, were from a Hellenic rather than Jewish background. Whoever wrote the Gospel of Mark was or were Hellenic, probably living outside of Palestine in a Greek city under Roman occupation, at a time long after the alleged events attributed to Jesus.

Compiled in the early part of the second century, the gospels of Luke and Matthew are considered to be largely reworked and independent copies of Mark's gospel.[11] This is a further example of Gnostic initiates undertaking personal reinterpretation of the allegorical storyline, the Outer Mysteries' stories written for new initiates. The Gnostic gospels focused not on the life

---

8 Wilson, I. *Jesus, The Evidence*
9 Bagatti, B. *Excavations in Nazareth*
10 Strange, J. *Anchor Bible Dictionary*
11 op. cit. Wilson, I.

of Jesus, but upon the secret teachings of the resurrected Christ. A most relevant detail in this respect is that the very first historical mention of Matthew's gospel, describes it as merely a collection of oracles.[12] It must, therefore, have been very different from what it later became, so it follows that it was tampered with and transformed substantially by later scribes. Scholars consider that the Gospel of John was the last to be created, at least one hundred years after the supposed events of the early first century, so the author was not a *disciple* named John.[13] This gospel is particularly Gnostic in content thus disproving irrefutably the claim of authentic eye–witness testimonies.

These gospels were not attributed to anybody originally. They were anonymous fragmental works, written in Greek not Aramaic by various authors, each of whom came from a different sect. This confirms them as allegorical stories recomposed to suit the individual whims of an individual Mystery sect. The early texts were difficult to read since there were no capital letters, virtually no punctuation, no spaces between words, there were no headings and no chapter or verse division. The early Church Fathers scathingly attacked this practice of writing so many varied gospels, believing that it was an indication of their worthlessness. The reality could not have been further from the truth. If the Mystery followers wanted to be initiated into the higher levels, they had to show their understanding of the myth through personal experience of Gnosis. To demonstrate this awareness, they were encouraged to formulate their own versions of the Mystery story.

The attribution of named authors to the four gospels came much later and indicates that these authors were fictitious rather than historical. The possibility is that the four names given to the Christian Gospels derive from names mentioned in the letters of Paul. Paul was not naming any disciples of Jesus in his letter, as Paul well knew that there had been no disciples, because there had been no Jesus. The cherry-picking of unrelated names mentioned by Paul is an indication of the scribes' desperation to validate their gospel stories.

Anyone who declares that the gospels are authentic historical documents is indulging in wishful thinking, lacking in common sense and has a total disregard for historical knowledge and truth. We have seen the flaws in Mark's story which would not be there if the tale were told by a resident of Judea, let alone a disciple. If we take a look at the four versions, they not only contradict each other, but also are quite different in the story they relate. That the Christian scribes, who later re-edited and added to the

---

[12] Mead, GRS. *Fragments of a Faith Forgotten*
[13] op. cit. Wilson, I.

gospels, failed to correct these glaring differences is strange. Perhaps the fault can be attributed to the lack of learning of both clergy and scribes and a naïve failure to co-ordinate the jealously-promoted gospels of the vying factions.

The four gospels fail to deliver a consistent story about the birth of Jesus. The birth is clearly an extremely important part of the story, since it tells us that the Son of God was not fathered by a mortal man but was born of a virgin, impregnated by the Holy Spirit. Mark's gospel, the earliest to be written, does not give this crucial event the slightest mention, neither does it tell us about Jesus' birth in Bethlehem, nor his lineage to King David. By its very omission its critical importance is conveyed. It indicates that the whole birth story and the David link were of no interest to the author or authors. It had no relevance at all, to what they wished to relate in their gospel. If Mark's gospel were recounting the greatest true story in the history of mankind, then this part of the account would not have been omitted — it was ignored because it was of no importance, because it was not a real event. Similarly, John's gospel ignores the birth story and like Mark's gospel, begins the account with the baptism of the adult Jesus.

Matthew and Luke, tell the full familiar story that we all know concerning the birth, but their versions fail to agree. They are also historically flawed. If as many people propose, they were disciples, such unbelievable discrepancies indicate that they were not there at the time of the alleged events. The gospels are supposed to be both sacred and historically accurate, but right from the very start they are at odds — Matthew states that the birth took place during the reign of Herod *the Great*, the king who died in 4 BCE; but Luke states that the birth occurred during the Roman census undertaken by Quirinius in 6 CE. Though Luke mentions the conception in the time of the reign of Herod, at the time of the census this was Herod *Antipas,* from whom Augustus Caesar withheld the title of king. Hence Luke uses the word *reign* rather than giving Herod an incorrect designation of *king*. This contradiction in the two gospels covers a notable span of ten years and two different rulers.

The next disparity between Luke and Matthew concerns their lineage from King David to Jesus. The only point of agreement in the patrilineage is Joseph, Jesus' stepfather; every other name listed is different. In addition, Luke lists 26 generations between Jesus and David, whilst Matthew has 41 and fails to acknowledge Solomon. Clearly, these lists indicate a lack of real knowledge and are obviously pure invention. But they raise an interesting question: why put in a link from Joseph to David at all? Jesus was not born of Joseph, but fathered by the Holy Spirit. He doesn't need to prove his lineage; he is the Son of God. Surely this indicates that these clumsy links to

David are careless later insertions, an unsubtle attempt to afford Jesus the right to earthly kingship.

The disagreements continue with each gospel having its own version of the geographical region where Jesus allegedly preached. Surely if the disciples wrote the gospels and took part in the events described, they would be able to agree on where they and Jesus had been and how long they had been there. In John's gospel, Jesus does not meet Simon Peter and his brother Andrew as they fished at Galilee, as he does in the other three accounts, but instead Andrew met Jesus at the River Jordan with John the Baptist, and then went to find Simon Peter and introduced him to Jesus. From there, they went to Galilee to find Philip. Although the other three gospels agree on location, only Luke tells us of the miracle of catching the fishes, Mark and Matthew presumably thought the miracle was not worth mentioning. Such an embarrassing variation does not make authentic history.

The conflicting *historical* accounts blunder on, seemingly unnoticed. The two occasions of feeding the multitudes are inconsistent and muddled in their telling, with only Matthew and Mark recounting both events. If one ignores the silly *miraculous* element of the stories and concentrates instead on the purpose behind them, all versions indicate that the authors do not comprehend the coded meanings; whereas to a Gnostic initiate the numerical implication would have been quite explicit. Only John recounts the turning of water into wine at the wedding, perhaps the other three weren't invited. John ploughs his own furrow again, when he has Jesus cleansing the Temple near the beginning of his story, but Matthew puts the event at the end, just before the Last Supper.

The shambolic incongruities continue into the crucial crucifixion and resurrection story. The accounts of the Last Supper — what was said, the interplay with the disciples and especially Judas — are not the same. The trial and pronouncements are recounted in three different versions. What Pontius Pilate said and did, is different in each story. Although they recount facts and describe events, none of the disciples was actually present. We might have a tale of Peter denying he knew Jesus, but anyone found in his company would have been arrested too. Had his disciples been at the scene, they would have been put in jail with him and tried for sedition. So there would be no-one left alive to tell precisely what took place and what was said and by whom. The only other source would be Roman records of the trial and though many have looked, it seems the Romans forgot to write anything down about the whole incident.

Jesus, we are told, was crucified; the common form of Roman execution, but the crucifixion is not mentioned in Acts. Peter's account states that Jesus was "hung on a tree". In the Mystery story, Jesus was not to suffer the execution of a common criminal: as the godman Attis was popular in Rome, the writer chose to replicate his end, so Jesus was "bound to a tree". Paul too gives no mention of a crucifixion but says the godman Christ was "hung on a gibbet". There are no early depictions of the crucifixion amongst the iconography in the Roman catacombs, quite simply because it was not a real event.

Not surprisingly, the accounts of who witnessed the crucifixion vary too. Matthew and Mark say that Mary Magdalene, with Mary mother of James and other women viewed from afar. Luke gives no prominence to anyone, merely mentioning that followers viewed from a distance. John states that Mary, the mother of Jesus, Mary's sister who is also called Mary and Mary Magdalene are at the foot of the cross. This seemingly strange coincidence of three Marys is another example of the Gnostic writing in John's gospel. The author was making use of the triad mother–goddess, which was commonly employed in the Mysteries. If the mother of Jesus had been present and the other three gospel writers were there, it is bizarre that they had not spotted her. All three clearly differ in where everyone was standing too, but then none of the disciple authors mentioned that they were there either, just the beloved John, who was obviously written into the event in a late gospel version that was given his name.

As might now be expected, the description of what took place at the climax of the crucifixion differs and on some points, markedly so. Only Matthew mentions an earthquake as Jesus dies: how could the others not notice the tumultuous disturbance. They even fail to report the final words of Jesus with any consensus; this is surely one thing that they should have got right! Mark and Matthew tell us that Jesus said, "My God. My God, why hath thou forsaken me." Luke hears Jesus uttering, 'Father, into thy hands I commend my spirit," before he dies. John has Jesus slipping away with the words "It is finished."

After Jesus' death, Joseph of Arimathea claims the body for internment; in Mark's account, he asks Pilate's permission and the governor is very surprised that Jesus has died so quickly upon the cross. John contradicts this; he claims that Pilate had given permission to hurry along the death by breaking the legs and then finally using the spear to check that death had occurred.

The gospels insistently tell us that the resurrection would take place *after* three days, but when the time came, this didn't happen and things were speeded up. As the death fell on Friday afternoon and the tomb was opened on Sunday morning, revealing the absence of Jesus' body, the resurrection took place just one and a half days after his death.

The events at the tomb are also not recorded with any historical accuracy. Matthew tells us that amidst another earthquake, Mary

Magdalene goes to the tomb alone, finds the stone rolled back with an angel sitting on top of it; the angel tells her that Jesus has arisen and everyone should go to Galilee to meet him.

Mark dispenses with the earthquake and reports Mary Magdalene and Mary mother of James, and Salome, arriving at the tomb. Seeing the stone has been removed, they find a young man sitting inside the tomb and he tells them to tell the other disciples to meet Jesus at Galilee.

Luke initially seems more vague about who exactly was at the tomb. He says there were women from Galilee, later mentioning that the women were Mary Magdalene and Mary mother of James, and Joanna. The inclusion of the names in a different part of the text indicates that this section is a later addition to the account. The women find two men sitting inside, who say that Jesus has arisen but offer no directions about meeting in Galilee. When Jesus does meet his disciples, it is not in Galilee, but in a village on the edge of Jerusalem.

John has a completely different story: Mary Magdalene goes to the tomb alone and finds it completely empty, so she runs off and when she finds Simon Peter and John, they run back with her and confirm what she has said. After they leave, Mary lingers behind weeping, she turns and sees what she initially thinks to be a gardener but then recognises Jesus and he tells her to inform the disciples that he has arisen. Later that day, Jesus meets them in Jerusalem and then Jesus meets them again when they at fishing at the Sea of Tiberius.

There is little agreement about what happened at this climax to the gospel story, which clearly indicates that the authors were not *present* at the events but were merely writing their own versions of a traditional myth. The events did not matter, only the allegorical meaning was important.

A final point to consider, when investigating the gospels' authenticity and accuracy, is how the infallible Son of God, who knows all things, got his predictions so badly wrong. In more than one version, Jesus predicts an apocalypse that would occur before the people living in his time had passed away. His warning is absolutely explicit, yet it did not happen in his time and still has not happened up to ours. I suspect that the apocalyptic predictions did not belong to the original Gnostic gospels, but were added later by Literalist Christians. Why they inserted a prediction of something that had not occurred is somewhat baffling, though their clumsy insertions are numerous. Perhaps the mistake was one of grammar or syntax, but left in to act as a frightening warning to keep the flock from straying from the fold, for when the worst did happen, true Christians alone would be saved.

The Gospel stories are all quite similar, but vary in far too many things: more than I have highlighted here. There are too many contradictions for the accounts to be considered as genuinely historical. They were clearly not eye-witness accounts by disciples of the same name. Scholars confirm, from the dates of the earliest fragments of the gospel, that the others were based on the story designated the Gospel of Mark. Thus any intelligent person must conclude that none of the authors was there, be they disciples or anyone else. The truth authorship belongs to Gnostic initiates writing their own individual versions of a mythical story, which had been recounted all around the Middle East for centuries.

The Church suggests that the gospels are the 'words of God', though it has no evidence for its assertion; indeed if they were sacred, then why have they undergone countless additions and alterations and shown a vast number of differences in the story compared with the early manuscripts.

The early Christians centred in Rome, had not only to repel the criticisms of the visiting Gnostic masters and the Roman initiates of the Mysteries, but had to meet the challenge of the many Gnostic gospels in circulation, because they themselves had only these few as their sacred texts. By the time of Justin Martyr circa 150 CE, there had been no mention of a New Testament. Justin Martyr was a fervent Literal Christian propagandist and he certainly would have promoted the Christian Gospels had they existed. Yet within a couple of decades, suddenly there they were. Around 170 CE, Justin Martyr's protégé, Tatian, was making efforts to produce a single compilation from the numerous Gnostic gospels and by doing so, he hoped to rid them of the troublesome contradictions of the Jesus story contained within these Gnostic works.[14]

This proved to be more difficult than he could have envisaged, his efforts weren't welcomed within the Christian community. The early Literalist Christian Church lacked cohesion, indeed it was as loose-knit in nature as the Gnostic communities were, with many differing notions of what the Jesus story should contain and this was exacerbated even further by regional groups jockeying for pre-eminence. Following on from Tatian's efforts, Irenaeus canonised four gospels claiming they were authentic accounts each written by a disciple of Jesus. However the bitter squabbling over which texts should be included in constructing the New Testament, raged on from the second century into the fifth. Not only did the scribes continually reject each other's proposed gospel texts, but they also dismissed them as forgeries or condemned them as heretical.[15]

Eventually, despite the wrangling and rivalries, matters were resolved and a compromise saw four gospels included in the canon. This decision to use four gospels, which had gradually evolved over time into their final form, was not simply to reinforce the story. Each gospel was proposed and

---

[14] Lüdemann, G. *Heretics*

[15] op. cit. Metzger, BM

favoured by different factions, who wanted something close to encapsulating their own particular version of the story and what was deemed important within it. This explains why they differ in some important aspects and why there are puzzling omissions instead of a consistent story.

Having finally forced a compromise on what should be included in their holy book, Literal Christians took another strange step. Probably because of their need to feel superior to the other pagan religions, they felt compelled to make use of the Hebrew Bible as a foundation for their newly-fledged New Testament. According to Tertullian, their religion gained credibility if they could say it 'rests on the very ancient books of the Jews.'[16] The Hebrew Bible was renamed and became the Old Testament with the claim that it was the true history of the Hebrews and the one God. By manipulating the final part of the Old Testament with its prophetic mentions of the *expected Messiah*, they had an introduction of sorts to take the reader into the New Testament story of Jesus.

This pragmatic merger with a sacred book of the Jews is a gross misrepresentation, as well as being an unseemly perversion and outrageous hypocrisy. Paul and the Gnostics, had striven to rid the Jesus story of any associations with Judaic law and religion; and over time, the followers of the Jesus Mystery had changed from being almost entirely Jews, albeit Hellenised ones, into being mainly Gentile. In Rome the misguided literalist Christian sect, into which the Roman working classes were inducted, became completely Gentile. With the Jewish influence being absent, it allowed anti-Jewish sentiments to rise. Influential figures within the early church, such as Justin Martyr, Tertullian, Eusebius and St John Crysostom, wrote protracted and abusive dissertations attacking the Jews.[17]

Literalist Christians wanted the kudos of an old Jewish history, without the constraints of Jewish dogma. Much of this was due to nothing more than their living in Rome and having a largely Roman laity. Because the Literalist Christians actually believed in the Jesus story as a real historical event, someone had to be blamed for the death of Jesus. This meant it had to be either Rome's representative, Pontius Pilate, or the Jews; pragmatism decided there was no contest. Pilate was transformed into a good man and a good Christian. It was reasoned that since the Jews had rejected Jesus, they had thereby rejected God by killing his son, so the Old Testament scriptures now wholly belonged to the Christian Church.

The shameful juggling of religious texts to construct a literalist Christian canon, was not done covertly, but was common knowledge. Commentators and critics, such as Celsus, complained that the Christians had altered the

---

[16] Brandon, S G F. *Religion in Ancient History*

[17] op. cit. Lüdemann, G.

original gospels many times, with the intent of overcoming the arguments of their detractors.[18] Origen, a Gnostic Christian philosopher complained that in his day there was much diversity amongst manuscripts, which he attributed to either careless scribes, people who audaciously corrected texts, or people who deliberately set out to add and delete as they pleased.[19]

As I have mentioned in earlier chapters, the Old Testament is fictitious and far from authentic history. Likewise, all of the New Testament must be dismissed as a book that documents historical events. In fact the New Testament is a greater lie than the Old Testament, which at least contains some elements of encoded truth. Those who claim the gospels are authentic accounts of events that actually took place, should not just say it is fact but attempt to prove it, which of course they cannot. Instead, they criticise, bluster and find endless excuses that enable them to continue promoting the same monumental lie. The Christian Church has dug such a deep hole for itself that it cannot climb out.

---

[18] op. cit. Wilson, I.
[19] Stanton, G. *Gospel Truth*

THE GREATEST LIE EVER TOLD

Chapter 17

The Man Who Never Was

"A wise man proportions his belief to the evidence."

David Hume

Even now, there will be those amongst you who still believe that Jesus had actually lived and who will perhaps be attempting desperately to formulate a theory which will explain away the fact that the Alexandrian Jews rewrote the Osiris–Dionysian Mysteries to create an acceptable form for their nationalistic brethren that became known as the Jesus Mystery. If it is your wish to claim that the Jesus story has any basis in true history, then you must find some evidence other than the dubious inaccurate gospels. Since the Roman Christian Church was first founded, a vast number of people have searched for this evidence, over a vast number of years and so far none have succeeded. At the end of his search Albert Schweitzer concludes:

> "The Jesus of Nazareth who came forward publicly as the Messiah ... never had any existence. This image has not been destroyed from without, it has fallen to pieces, cleft and disintegrated by concrete historical problems which came to the surface one after another."[1]

This is a view shared by a great number of scholars, researchers, historians and archaeologists. Though some scholars, like Hermann Samuel Reimarus, did not share his work *On the Intention of Jesus and His Teaching* until he was dying;[2] others lost their jobs because they spoke the truth that they had found. David Friedrich Strauss of Tübingen University published

---

[1] Schweitzer, A. *The Quest of the Historical Jesus*
[2] ibid.

The Life of Jesus in 1835 and caused such a furore that he was dismissed from his post. Needless to say, their opinions are not shared by academics who are dedicated Christians and who continue their desperate search for any crumb of evidence.

Though 2000 years ago is a long time in the past, the world of that period in human history was a particularly literate one. Going back further in time, the Egyptians, Assyrians and Babylonians, kept written records, initially inscribed in stone and clay, later written on papyrus. The Greeks were renowned for their literacy, and their influence encouraged its spread within the cities of the greater Hellenised world created by Alexander. Later, the Romans helped spread literacy throughout their own empire. As did the Greeks, the Romans wrote plays, poetry, philosophy, science and history, but as a very organised state and later an empire, they made and kept detailed accounts and records, official decrees and reports and both official and personal letters. This has enabled historians to develop a very clear picture of Roman life from what they documented. It is only after Roman times that things are more fragmented and this later age of Christianity gave us what have been justly termed the Dark Ages!

In and around the period in which Jesus allegedly lived, there is a wealth of writers including Pliny the Elder, Plutarch, Juvenal, Seneca, Martial, Pausanias, and Ptolemy. None of these writers have mentioned a single word about Jesus, his followers led by Peter, or of any of their alleged activities. Official Roman records of that period also fail to make a single mention of them. The Prefect of Judea, Pontius Pilate was based in Jerusalem. He would have been legally bound to keep meticulous records of what took place in his province, yet he makes no mention or Jesus nor his trial. Considering the serious subversive background to this claimed event, with the great public unrest and the official involvement of the Sanhedrin, to have no official report is beyond belief. In the vast literature, official records and letters, there is not one single mention of supposedly the most important man who ever lived, a man who was renowned for performing incredible miracles authenticated by large numbers of witnesses, a man whose teaching drew thousands of people over the three years of his work.

A Roman historian named Suetonius, CE 69–140, made references which theologians enthusiastically cite, however since these do not actually mention Jesus, they are worthless as evidence.[3] The first of these refers to the Emperor Claudius who banished all the Jews from Rome, because they were continually making disturbances at the instigation of someone called Chrestus. The second reference occurs about ten years later in 64 CE, during the time of Nero. Suetonius, when discussing various legislative

---

3 C. Suetonius Tranquillus *The Lives Of The Twelve Caesars*

changes wrote "...interdictum ne quid in popinis cocti praeter legumina aut holera veniret, cum antea nullum non obsonii genus proponeretur; *afflicti suppliciis Christiani, genus hominum superstitionis novae ac maleficae;* vetiti quadrigariorum lusus, quibus inveterata licentia passim vagantibus fallere ac furari per iocum ius erat; ..." Roughly translated this tells us that cooked meat could no longer be sold in taverns, just vegetables and pulses, whereas previously anything could be sold, followed by the significant piece of information that Nero *inflicted punishments on Christians, a race of man who held a new and harmful superstition*; before going on to tell us, in the same sentence, that Nero put an end to the antisocial behaviour of racing charioteers who gained amusement from fraud and mugging.

Predictably, theologians' excitement hangs on the names Chrestus and Christians, however in real terms this does not offer them anything. Chrestus was a popular name at that the time, so it could well be the name of a man who was the ringleader of a riotous gang of Jews; there are frequent reports of the Jews being subversive and troublesome. Theologians wrongly assume that Chrestus is a misspelling of Christos, the Greek translation of Messiah, but such a literary error is highly unlikely as we can see that Suetonius knows and uses the word *Christiani* correctly. Over quite a long period, the Jews were plagued by a plethora of freedom fighters/terrorists, all claiming to be the expected leader and in this account from Suetonius, the *leader* appears to have been very much alive and leading the troublemakers through the streets of Rome, prior to their expulsion.

The Roman historian, Tacitus gives an account of Nero and the burning of Rome in 64 CE which at first sight appears more promising. "... ergo abolendo rumori Nero subdidit reos et quaesitissimis poenis adfecit, quos per flagitia *invisos vulgus Chrestianos appellabat.* auctor nominis eius Christus Tibero imperitante per procuratorem Pontium Pilatum supplicio adfectus erat;..."[4] He tells us that Nero, who had been accused of starting the fire himself, puts the blame onto those "infamous common people called Christians." Tacitus then mentioned that the person to whom they are responsible, Christ, was humbled by Pontius Pilate, the procurator of the Emperor Tiberius.

The problem with this account is that Tacitus may have been an eyewitness to the burning of Rome, but he was only seven or eight. He wrote this down forty years later, in the early second century, so this was well after the time of Jesus. He had no first-hand accounts and obviously used hearsay, not the actual records, as he gives Pilate an incorrect title of procurator. Procurators were civil governors and the title wasn't used prior to Agrippa the first, governor from CE 41–44. At the time of Pilate, the

---

4 Tacitus. *Annals Book 15*

governor had a military role with the title of prefect. That he held this title we know from excavations in Caesarea Maritima, where a stone says: "[...]STIBERIEVM [PON]TIVSPILATVS [PRAEF]ECTVSIVD[EA]E [...]E[...]".[5] There have been various proposals for the missing letters, but all archaeologists are agreed on the rank and name of Pontius Pilate Prefect of Judea.

Pontius Pilate does not mention Jesus nor any incidents such as those recorded in the New Testament. By the time of Tacitus, both the mythological Gnostic story of Jesus, as well as the Literalist Christian version, would have been in common circulation. His version doesn't mention an execution but that 'this Christ' was subjugated by Pilate in some way: "...supplicio adfectus erat...."

The only other reference to Jesus comes from the Jewish historian Josephus. During the Jewish revolt in 68–70 CE, Josephus changed sides and transformed himself into a pro–Roman; he fled to Rome and became a historian under the patronage of two emperors. His two books *The Jewish Wars* and *Antiquities of the Jews* have been an invaluable reference for historians into Jewish affairs. His own opinion of the Messiah was that his ex–countrymen were misunderstanding the prediction in the scriptures, which alluded to one who would come to free them from oppression. Josephus himself believed that it actually predicted that it would be Vespasian, who was proclaimed Roman emperor whilst leading the army in Judea. From this is seems clear that Josephus would not then proclaim Jesus as the true Messiah and yet remarkably, in just one small section his work speaks of Jesus being the expected Messiah and recounts the events of his death and resurrection.[6]

This was long used by Christians as conclusive proof of the authenticity of the Jesus story. However, modern literary experts studied the writing style and discovered that this section, which anyway seemed a strange interruption in the narrative, was in fact a later forged addition.[7] This forgery has been traced to the fourth-century work of Bishop Eusebius, who is regarded as the Church's propagandist and inventive writer. To give the assertion of forgery further weight, prior to Eusebius *finding* it, earlier Christians never mentioned that Josephus wrote anything about Christ. Eusebius made a disgraceful and dishonest insertion into an existing historical work, but it was not the only forgery that was undertaken to make

---

5 Charlesworth, J H. *Jesus and Archaeology*
6 Josephus, *Antiquities* 18.3.3
7 Gauvin, M J. *Did Jesus Christ Really Live?*

the great lie appear true, for the practice was widespread and common.[8] Yet there are still some theologians and committed Christians who continue to cite the writings of Josephus as the proof that Jesus lived.

Perhaps even more destructive to the Christian cause are the works of a prolific Jewish writer named Philo. He was a philosopher and historian, who lived during the period when Jesus was supposed to have been causing a great stir in Judea. Philo wrote extensively — fifty books survive — on both religious and historical matters in Judea, including much about Pontius Pilate, however, there is not one single reference to Jesus.[9] If Jesus had done any of the things attributed to him, it is inconceivable that Philo had not known and written about it. That there is no account of Jesus would be beyond belief, had Jesus existed.

Another Jewish writer who lived at the same time, was a man called Justus of Tiberias. He wrote a history of the Jews covering the period from Moses to his own time. He too did not mention Jesus. Justus lived at Capernaum, a place where Jesus was said to have spent much time. Is it possible that Justus could not have heard of this teacher who had a large following of disciples, the preacher who attracted crowds of thousands to hear him speak, the miracle worker who cured the sick, a man reputed to have been born of a virgin, a descendent of King David, the expected Messiah. Could a historian have really lived in the same little backwater town and been totally unaware about the great phenomena on his very doorstep? Most certainly not, it would have been impossible.

The Jewish Talmud written about 200 CE, even later than the gospels, has been cited by theologians as offering some significant evidence. There are a few mentions of the name Yeshu, or Joshua from which the name Jesus derives through its translations. Yeshu is an extremely common name as John, Michael, William and Paul are today. The references are vague; one mentions a Yeshu who had five disciples named Buni, Mattai, Nakkia, Netzer and Todah. There were many individuals at that time who attracted followers and in this case, the Talmud clearly was not referring to Jesus and his twelve named disciples. There is also a mention of a disciple of *Yeshu the Nazarene* but, as we know Nazareth did not exist in the time of Jesus and Nazarene was the name of a religious sect of Gnostic Christians, who also accepted all aspects of all the varying Mystery cults and commonly employed the names Osiris, Attis, Adonis those of the other Mystery Godmen. It is important to keep remembering that Yeshu/Joshua/Jesus was an extremely common Jewish name; that the middle east was full of preachers, healers and miracle workers, both genuine and charlatans; that

---

[8] Wheless, J. *Forgery in Christianity*
[9] Kingsland, W. *The Gnosis*

Judea, up to the mid first century CE, had a bountiful number of rebel-rousers all claiming that they were the expected Messiah, who would lead the people to throw out the Roman imperialists. There is no reason to consider that these passing remarks in the Talmud are a reference to the Christian Jesus.[10]

The fact is that there is not one single piece of evidence to suggest, let alone prove, that Jesus, the Messiah, the living Son of God, was ever a real human being. For nearly two millennia countless people have been on a desperate search which has remained fruitless. There is a wealth of contrary evidence, however, to confirm that Jesus was nothing more than a mythological figure, an invention by the Jewish initiates of the Mysteries; Jesus was simply the Jewish version of Osiris/Dionysus.

---

[10] op. cit. Wells, GA.

Chapter 18

Isis — The Real Mary

"True wisdom is less presuming than folly. The wise man doubteth often, and changeth his mind; the fool is obstinate, and doubteth not; he knoweth all things but his own ignorance."

Akhenaten

Dan Brown's novel *The Da Vinci Code* has caused speculation amongst the media, denials by the clergy, arguments amid the theologians and fury from the historians. The public have read the novel and have seen the film and have no doubt that there's been a cover up. The book's plot reveals a search to find the bloodline from Jesus and his secret wife Mary Magdalene to their contemporary descendants and reveals the deadly secret kept by the Christian Church for 2000 years.

The novel's central premise coincides largely with Baigent, Leigh and Lincoln's historical theory work *The Holy Blood and the Holy Grail*. This book attained a certain cult success through its controversial theory that Mary Magdalene married Jesus, but Dan Brown's novel got the message to far more people because novels can sell in millions where an academic work may just sell thousands.

Baigent, Leigh and Lincoln's seemingly plausible theory was that, after her husband's death Mary Magdalene fled to France with their child. This child then married into the aristocracy and the descendants' holy bloodline continued on through the French royal family. Baigent, Leigh and Lincoln's work was poorly researched, involved far too many giant leaps of wishful thinking and had one major flaw, because Jesus and Mary Magdalene never existed. They were fictitious characters and a little basic historical research would have made this apparent, with the resultant abandonment of their fantasy theory.

The Vatican appointed a Cardinal to try to debunk the conspiracy theories at the heart of the plot and he held a series of public debates.[1]

---

[1] Owen, R. *Times*

Cardinal Bertone's task was "to unmask the lies" so that readers could see how "shameful and unfounded" *The Da Vinci Code* was, particularly in suggesting that Jesus was not celibate. However, the truth is that the Vatican is not really worried about what it knows is a false theory, but what does concern it is the doors that may open to reveal the real truth, the real conspiracy, the truth which once exposed, will bring down the Christian Church: that the Church has always lied and that Jesus Christ never existed.

The character of Mary Magdalene is naturally of great importance to Brown and Baigent *et al*. Their flights of fancy pronounce that she was the closest disciple to Jesus, that Peter hated her, that she became Christianity's greatest missionary and many more unsubstantiated assertions. Mary's supposed historical background as an equal partner to Jesus, her demeaning by the sexist Peter, her strength of character, all appeal to those wanting to promote the status of women, especially within the church. Just like Jesus though, there is absolutely no evidence that a person who might have been Mary Magdalene ever lived.

In southern France, stories abound that Mary Magdalene landed and lived there. There is even a church at the site of her supposed debarkation. Local legends point to a cave, which is now a shrine, where she spent her last years as a recluse. The truth is that there is no historical evidence for any of this but that the legends, churches, shrines and the collections of holy bones were all created nearly a thousand years after she could have been there.

The south of France had been a Greek colony from 600 BCE and then later a Roman province, so for over a thousand years there had been a strong cult of the 'Queen of Heaven' or *Regina Coelis* in its Latin epithet. This designation was a title which the Egyptians gave to the goddess Isis, who was also called 'Star of the Sea' or *Stella Maris*. In the Christian era, this designation was given to the Virgin Mary, as the devotion to Isis diminished with the spread of Christianity. The last temple to Isis, at Philae in Egypt, was handed over to the Christian Bishop Theodore, on the orders of Emperor Justinian in 550 CE and became the church of St Stephen.[2]

In the eastern Mediterranean, it had been common practice for sailors, about to undertake a voyage, to make a sacrifice of some kind to Isis, the Queen of Heaven. The dark waters of the ocean were often combined with the watery heavens and the barque was not only a sea-going vessel, but a solar ship in which to traverse the stars. The ship in which Mary sailed across to France has been described as being without oars and sails. As a historical practical feat, it makes impossible nonsense and the claim that it is a miracle is moronic; quite clearly the intelligent assumption is that the

---

[2] Evans, J A S *The age of Justinian*

unpropelled vessel indicates a reworked version of the tale of the solar barque of Isis. Sites dedicated to Isis and her other Greek and Roman personifications as Demeter, Artemis and Cybele later became linked to both the Black Virgins or Madonnas and to Mary Magdalene.[3] The name was merely changed from Isis, Demeter, Artemis or Cybele to suit the requirements of the new popular local religion, so a later change to suit a later religion was to be expected.

Isis was in France so long before Christianity that Paris was named after her. Some historians say that the city was named after the Parisii tribe who dwelt in the locality, however that name is not Gallic and is one which the Romans gave to the tribe, following their conquest. Paris has a long association with Isis, whom Napoleon incorporated on her barque into the Paris coat of arms. Suggestions range from the ship–like shape of the island in the Seine on which Notre Dame now stands leading to the name *Par Isis* meaning 'barque of Isis,' to it deriving from the Egyptian words for 'temple to Isis' *Per Isis*, as one once stood on the left bank.[4] We might not be sure which phrase gave Paris its name, but what is indisputable is that for over two thousand years Isis has been connected with the city.

The legend long associated with the south of France and given ridiculous prominence in both *The Holy Blood and the Holy Grail* and *The Da Vinci Code* tells that the three women who found the empty tomb of Christ, Mary Magdalene, Mary Salomé and Mary Jacobé went into exile there. The unlikely tale is that they fled Judea to find safety in Egypt. After some years, they took a ship from Alexandria, which landed them on the mouth of the River Rhone, at a place known as Oppidum–Râ. Since 1838 'the town of Râ' has been called *Les–Saintes–Maries–de–la–Mer,* 'The–Saint–Marys–of–the–Sea.'

Though the *triad of goddesses* is venerated in a gypsy pilgrimage each year, Mary Magdalene has been usurped by the black *Sara la Kali,* thought to be a representation of Asherah, the goddess of the Phoenicians, and Kali brought from India by the gypsies. Curiously the church in Saintes Maries dedicated to Saint Sara is called *Notre Dame de la Barque* and is traditionally a place of pilgrimage for Catholics seeking help with their fertility!

The tradition of the region also has Mary Magdalene preaching the message of Jesus for a while and then retiring as a recluse to a grotto in the mountains at La Sainte Baume; after thirty years she died. Some stories say that Sarah was the daughter of Mary and Jesus, others that she was a

---

3 Begg, E. *The Cult of the Black Virgin*
4 Hancock, G & Bauval, R. *Talisman*

servant from Egypt, it is the former that figures in *The Da Vinci Code* and *The Holy Blood and the Holy Grail*.

Moving from legend to logic, let us suppose that Mary had existed and see how it would have affected history. Judea had a vast number of *Messiahs* over two thousand years ago, so Jesus would have just been one amongst the multitude. There would, therefore, be no reason to fear his wife. Women had no standing in Judean society, though in the Hellenic Jewish Mysteries, women were amongst the priesthood.

That the authorities would have been frightened by an unborn child who might cause problems twenty or thirty years in the future, because his or in this case, her father was an executed rabble–rouser is a completely ridiculous supposition. If one followed the unsubstantiated theory that Mary Magdalene went to Alexandria in Egypt, with its large Jewish community and particularly Gnostic Jews, she would have been perfectly safe and at home there and under no threat from Judean authorities. There would be no reason to leave and nothing to take a small child to France for. Southern France had a small Jewish community at the time, but one can think of no reason, why after a number of years, Mary Magdalene would suddenly decide to settle in an alien land, when she was under no pressure to uproot herself. There is no known historical reason, nor any logical one, why Mary Magdalene would take her child and her family to a new land, to start a new life. Though for some unscrupulous cleric, it could become a nice little earner.

When Christianity was attempting to establish itself in the first few hundred years, and wean indigenous peoples away from their old deities, it built churches on the old pagan temple sites. To give them an additional attraction, from the second century, sacred relics of 'saints' were added to rituals and beliefs. Where relics were housed, pilgrims travelled, money was spent and donated and the local community thrived. This early trade in pseudo–spiritual tourism led to competition from individual Christian churches desirous to elevate their own importance. Countless skulls and bones of saints suddenly arrived from the Levant to be housed and displayed. John Calvin made an inventory of all known relics in 1543. He wrote about the *True Cross:*

> "There is no abbey so poor as not to have a specimen. In some places there are larger fragments, as in the Holy Chapel in Paris, at Poitiers and at Rome, where a good–sized crucifix is said to have been made of it. If all the pieces that could be found were collected together,

they would make a large shipload. Yet the Gospel testifies that a single man was able to carry it."[5]

It became an obscene circus with churches arguing with each other about who had the genuine remains and three heads of John the Baptist existed simultaneously. The site with the most prestigious relic had the most pilgrims, the most revenue and the most influence on politico-religious matters.[6]

On December 12, 1279, some ambitious priests came into the possession of bones belonging to Mary Magdalene and the others of her travelling party. A handy cave became the place Mary Magdalene had chosen to retire to. This grotto in the St Baume mountain was transformed into a holy pilgrimage shrine, ensuring a good living for the astute locals. The Church soon earned enough to build a grand Basilica from the legend it had created, based loosely on the mythological figure of Isis, the Queen of Heaven and her solar barque.

The story of Mary's secret marriage to Jesus and her flight with his unborn child ending in France, where the child, or some say children, married into the Merovingian royal family, whose descendants live on to this day, is a new idea and a ridiculous one. It has been suggested that the Knights Templar knew of the bloodline and were its protectors until the true descendants of Jesus were established on the throne.[7] These theorists claim that the Templars went to Jerusalem to find evidence: a marriage certificate perhaps? Twelve hundred years after a marriage took place, some ambitious men go in search of documented proof! They choose to look in the Jerusalem Temple, which had been totally destroyed 70 years after the death of the male party to the marriage and with which he had had no connection during his life! I hardly think they would expect to find much. A search for the lost Ark is equally nonsensical. These suppositions are the result of faulty research and leaps of faith, but mainly they are due to a naïve misunderstanding of Gnostic teachings by modern day researchers who, because of their Christian upbringing, misguidedly make myth into fact.

Had the Templars found anything, it would have been the many Gnostic gospels that had been hidden safe from the Literalist Christian purges. If the Templars suddenly came into great wealth and power and gained the patronage of the Pope, the most likely reason would be that they extorted

---

5 Calvin, J. *Traité Des Reliques*
6 Brooke. R & C. *Popular Religion in the Middle Ages*
7 Baigent et al. *The Holy Blood and the Holy Grail*

their gains, using the newly acquired Gnostic gospels to threaten that they would expose the false religion of the Church. In Provence, there are simply no legends, let alone any historical evidence, of Mary Magdalene having had a child by Jesus.

Another aspect relevant to a married Christ, which is usually overlooked though it puzzles many historical or theological experts, is the other Mary, Mary of Bethany. In the gospel story, before Jesus goes to Jerusalem and his death, he and his disciples visit the house of Mary of Bethany. This Mary washes the feet of Jesus, dries them with her loose hair and then anoints him with oil. It is a particularly intimate scene with an extremely significant symbolism, not understood by Christians. It appears strange that Mary of Bethany seems to disappear out of the story as Mary Magdalene becomes the important player, however there is a simple Gnostic explanation.

In Jewish society, a woman did not let down her hair in public, or in front of men and neither would she wash a man's feet. A woman would only perform the act described in the gospel story under one circumstance, if she were his wife. So the implication in the Bible story is that Mary of Bethany was married to Jesus, not Mary Magdalene.

In Judaism, women were not permitted any religious office, so Mary certainly could not ritually anoint anyone. Yet according to the gospel story, she did something that was not permitted in Judaism; but it was permitted in the Mysteries, where women were members of the priesthood and could anoint others. The details show that this story was not about an act performed by anyone of the Jewish faith; nor was it written by anyone of the orthodox Christian faith, which did not allow female priests; whoever wrote the story must have been a Gnostic.

The writer Mark even mentions the ritual oil, which Mary used, it is said to be spikenard.[8] Spikenard is an oil from India, where it was applied in the manner described in Tantric sexual rites, thus indicating that the anointing preceded a sexual act. The account of the marriage where Jesus turned water into wine, gives every indication that the marriage he attended was his own. Wine has great significance in Jewish culture and is considered symbolic of life beginning as pure grape juice, then going through the sour stages of fermentation, and emerging as a pure and delightful divine blessing. The wine is used for the Seven Blessings which link the bride and groom to each other reuniting their souls into their original state of being as one.[9] Who else but the mother of a Jewish bridegroom, whose responsibility it was to provide the wine, would tell him that it was running low and he must dispatch himself to the kitchen immediately, to sort things out.

---

[8] Mark 14:3
[9] Latner, H. *The Everything Jewish Wedding Book*

Allegorical marriage stories form a significant part of Gnostic teaching; hence this incident begins John's Gospel and is the first of the seven miracles that John recounts to assert Jesus' divine status. He puts the anointing by Mary of Bethany and the consummation at the end, before the arrest, crucifixion and resurrection.

The story was explicit and familiar enough for any initiate of the Mysteries to understand, but for orthodox Christians, not taught to recognise the symbolism and unable to draw comparisons with the same enactment recounted in other versions of the Mystery stories, its meaning was indiscernible. The encounter with Mary Bethany was not explicit enough to offend the sensibilities of the New Testament compilers and therefore their censors failed to edit out this most significant spiritual story.

Because the characters involved were fictitious, as all the New Testament stories were allegorical, obviously no real marriage took place. However, like the other stories written by Gnostics, its inclusion indicated that the message it was relating was important. Obviously, to orthodox Christians, this marriage of Mary to the Son of God would be blasphemous, however to initiates of the Mysteries, this story tells one they are familiar with, from their own initiation. It does not describe a physical marriage between two real people, but is the same story that originated in the Egyptian Mysteries of Osiris and Isis. It was part of a ritual sacred marriage, where the pharaoh/king–high priest would be ritually anointed by the queen–high priestess in ceremonial preparation for their marriage, which was not a physical union, but a spiritual one. It signified the conjunction of the male and female higher aspects — the God and Goddess — returning back out of separateness and becoming One once more with the Godhead.

The *sub rosa* Bible story line has Mary of Bethany as the wife of Jesus, then she seems to disappear, whereas Mary Magdalene is cleansed of seven demons in Luke and then reappears to minister to Jesus at his crucifixion. These two Marys are in fact portraying the same person. The concept is complex, but recurs frequently in the Mysteries, where the godman marrying a *fallen woman* is a common theme.

Simon Magus appears early in the first century CE in Samaria. In their Gnostic stories he takes a similar role to Jesus. There has been much debate as to whether he was a historical character or not, but he had a female spiritual partner Helen, who was a *fallen woman* whom he took out of a brothel in Tyrehis. Simon's title *Magus* was given to the wise men of the eastern Mysteries. If he existed, he was one of the two great heretics declared by the Church of Rome — Paul the Apostle was the other — because he called himself a *Christ:* a Gnostic designation similar to 'becoming a Buddha' attributed to followers of Buddhism who attain this elevated state of enlightenment. Another teacher of the Mysteries,

Dositheus, who allegedly taught alongside Simon, had a female companion also called Helen, when he succeeded Simon. Meander, another of Simon's disciples, announced that he also was a *Christ* come to rescue the Goddess lost in the world. Being a *Christ* was a claim to have achieved a spiritual state and not an attempt to usurp the title of Jesus. The recurrent use of the name Helen for the fallen females seems to have been a deliberate re-use of the name of Helen of Troy, the fallen woman of Classical Greece.

The story of Helen of Troy as related in Homer's *Iliad* and *Odyssey* is well known: the woman was kidnapped and taken to Troy, then the vengeful Greeks turned up to rescue her. The Pythagoreans interpreted the story as an allegory that told of spiritual concepts. To them, Helen was seen as Sophia and represented the psyche; her abduction was the psyche's fall into mortal incarnation.

Sophia is the personification of wisdom. Sophia is a complex concept, which without Gnostic teaching, it seems impossible to explain or understand. She combines all the aspects of the Mother Goddess and all else beyond her. She is a spiritual archetype, who is living, infinite and divine. She is the consummation of the union of spirit and flesh. Hence by relinquishing and accepting earthly life and accepting union, physical and spiritual with Christ, she is of the earth and heavens. She is the initiate's ultimate goal, to become what Sophia is, to become God.

Euripides further interprets the spiritual story by announcing that it had only been Helen's image, known as the *eidolon,* which was abducted and taken to Troy; it represented the physical world, whilst the higher psyche of Helen continued to dwell in perfect safety in Egypt. Egypt symbolised the primordial home of the gods for the Gnostic Christians and they saw the mythical Helen as an important allegory which taught the concept of the split psyche, with its *lower* aspect falling into incarnation. The same *fallen woman* is portrayed in other pagan stories. In Eros and Psyche, Psyche's older sister is Helen, but her oldest sister is Sophia. Demeter too loses her daughter Persephone to an incarnate life and a marriage of sorts, but Persephone finds a way to free her spirit to make the most of the union between spiritual and physical existence: all the stories teach the same message in different forms.

In the story of the goddess Demeter and her other aspect of her own *fallen* daughter Persephone, *lost* down in the Underworld, the two aspects of the goddess were reunited at the end of the Eleusian myth. In the Jesus myth, the two aspects of the goddess, the mother, the Virgin Mary and the *fallen* Mary Magdalene, stand before the cross. Jesus commends them to each other, by saying, "Mother, behold your child," then he tells Mary Magdalene, "Child behold your mother." If this version sounds a little different from the one you may have heard,[10] we have to remember that the New Testament compilers give a different version of the original Gnostic story. They thought John was writing about what he saw, they didn't realise he wasn't there, but just telling a story, so in most translations we find child changed to son, as if the fictitious Jesus were talking to the author of the story. Thus the two Marys are brought together, the two aspects of the goddess are reunited immediately before the mystical marriage with Consciousness, which is represented by Jesus' ritual death and return to the Godhead, thus is the earthly mission fulfilled.

The Biblical imagery makes this explicit, where it announces at the death of Jesus, that the Temple veil is rent; the veil symbolises the goddess's hymen, which is torn upon the mystical marriage's consummation. In Judaic traditions, the Jerusalem Temple's inner sanctum, the Holy of Holies, was alluded to as a bridal chamber. This may seem somewhat incongruous for the puritanical Jews until one recalls that their traditions originated in the temples of the Egyptians. In the Mysteries of Dionysus and Demeter, the Eleusian Temple contained a sacred inner sanctum, which was known as the bridal chamber; it was here that initiates, be they male or female, were designated *brides* and were ritually married to the goddess Demeter to attain Gnosis. The bridal chamber can also be interpreted as the womb, which will give the initiate a rebirth back into the Higher Self.

There are three Marys in the gospels because of the mystical number three, so too the Father, Son and Holy Spirit and the traditional triad of goddesses. However, they were really only two personifications, one of which was the Virgin Mary, the other two named, Mary of Bethany the priestess and Mary Magdalene the fallen woman, were actually one and the same. This apparently impossible conundrum of virgin mother, priestess and fallen woman/whore, is just another thing that requires some understanding of Gnostic teaching. In the ancient middle eastern world, amongst certain religious sects, temple priestesses would *prostitute* themselves in place of the goddess, in order to consummate the ritual marriages of those sect members giving themselves to the goddess for the first time. Though this probably offends modern moral thinking, it would be wrong to consider this religious prostitution as a person selling sex for money. There is no reason or evidence for this taking place, it was, most likely a reference to a symbolic act. Similarly, the use of the word whore in the gospels indicates the *fallen woman,* but not one who sells sex for monetary gain, but simply the symbolic rendition of the lost incarnate soul trapped in a mortal shell.

---

[10] John 19: 25-7

The mystical Gnostic allegorical teachings are very different from the literal teaching of supposed Christian history, they employ the same story line, but the understanding is at opposite poles: there are those who *know* at one end, with those who have *faith* at the other and there are those *with eyes to see* or their opposites *who are blind*. To make it easier to understand how the mortal being needed to reunite with God, the Gnostics used a simple allegorical story. This same story also contained a high level of teaching for initiates. Jesus represented the inner self, the Consciousness. The female — the Greek Sophia, or the Gnostic Christian Mary — symbolically represented the mortal body, be it male or female. The physical world had two aspects; the lower represented the corruptible mortal. The psyche or soul, which has fallen into the physical body, is at first lost and identifies with the body. The higher aspect represents the incorruptible part of the psyche, which is in contact with the inner Consciousness. The story relates how the lost corruptible psyche falls from its original goodness to recognise its true self. These two now eventually return to the oneness. The teaching is quite simple and tells us that each of us must do the same: recognise the illusion of our lower self and reunite with our higher self so that we become a *Christ* and thereby return to the Oneness of God.

Put into the simple teaching form used in the Gnostic Mysteries, the two aspects of Mary, the virgin and the fallen woman, are each sought out and saved by Jesus. He brings the two opposite poles together into Mary of Bethany and through symbolic marriage and sexual intercourse there is a spiritual rebirth that reunites Mary to the Christ. Some researchers who have read this symbolic allegory, which appears in some non-canonical scriptures, have allowed themselves to do what the Church did: take things literally. They thought that they had come across forbidden texts which the Church had tried to destroy — as indeed they had — but alas the heretical gospel stories which spoke of Mary being Jesus' beloved, of the passionate kisses, sexual intercourse and marriage did not imply a hidden bloodline, they were merely allegorical teaching aids and purely symbolic.

Those who wish to know more about this complex esoteric subject and indeed about the true meanings encoded into the real Christianity which is so confusingly delivered in the many gospels might find that *Jesus and the Goddess*[11] by Timothy Freke and Peter Gandy answers most of their questions.

---

[11] Freke, T & Gandy, P. *Jesus and the Goddess*

Chapter 19

He Who Points The Finger To Orion

"Obstacles cannot crush me. Every obstacle yields to stern resolve. He who is fixed to a star does not change his mind."
Leonardo da Vinci

In Chapter Three, Orion and the Patriarchs, I spoke briefly of the link between John the Baptist and the constellation of Orion, usually represented as the Hunter. There was a recorded link between Mary Magdalene and the Knights Templar, but they also had an apparent great interest in John the Baptist too. Hence theories have been spawned, as strange as Jesus having a jealous rivalry with John that even led to his involvement in John's arrest and murder. Though researchers have brought forward evidence, which may sound convincing or at least plausible for these ideas, the basic flaw still lies in the fact that there is no evidence to show that the characters themselves ever lived and far too much that shows instead, what their stories represented. In this chapter, I hope to show a little of what is really known about the Knights Templar and Priory of Sion and how John the Baptist in his Orion personification helps make some sense of that.

The mysterious Priory of Sion figures strongly as a covert society in both *The Da Vinci Code* and some theoretical books on the Templars, though it has been ridiculed as a fictitious organisation by most academics. Rejection of the Priory's existence stems largely from the debunking of the claims of some Frenchmen in the 1960s that they were members of it. Their rather odd claims — odd from the point of view of members of a highly secret society courting publicity — were later discredited and remain without any authentication.[1] The order's supposed Grand Master, Pierre Plantard's behaviour has long indicated that he was an egotist and the claims made with his collaborators, allowed them to revel in the notoriety of a brief

---

[1] Pinot, N. "An Interview with Pierre Plantard de Saint-Clair"

celebrity. I was, however, intrigued to learn of the hoaxers' insistence, that the Queen of Heaven whom they honoured above all, was Isis. Though it would have taken Plantard and his associates just a little research to become aware of the connection between Isis and the title, it makes it all the more strange that Templar writers rarely go back to her and still focus on Mary Magdalene.

There are many occurrences in French history of *Notre Dame de Sion*. The first recorded Catholic use is the dedication of a church on a hill above the Moselle river, at Sion–Vaudémont in the 10th century. From the Gallic period, people climbed to the *'Plateau de Sino'* to honour *Rosmertha*. The Romans later built a temple to Mercury there. Rosmerta was the Gallic name for the companion of the Celtic god Lugh, who translated to the Romans as Mercury. Of course the original representations of the gods by many later names were Osiris and Isis. As Isis was linked with two snakes, so Rosmerta carried a stick of two snakes intertwined.

What we see from this chronology is that the use of *Notre Dame de Sion* goes back to pre–Roman times and even its use by the Catholic Church predated the Knights Templar, so the name was in use, before any connection with Mount Zion. The full name of the Priory is the *Prieuré de Notre Dame de Sion;* the rarely used *Notre Dame* in the name would indicate its dedication to Isis the Queen of Heaven. The group first appear in records some time in the 12th century and is linked with the Templars. The Priory Of Sion had coexisted happily with the Templars for a hundred years and they are said to have separated at the felling of the Elm at Gisors that divided Henry II and the Plantagenets from King Phillip II of France.

The discrediting of a group of 1960s self–glorifying attention seekers is unimportant. Whether these claimants were charlatans or not is no proof that there never was, nor even that there is not still, a Priory of Sion. Although we can't find evidence that it does still exist, neither have we evidence that it doesn't. There is some documentation that provides evidence that it did exist; perhaps they were exclusive founder members of the Templars. It appears however, that there came a point when the two orders split acrimoniously over some contentious matter. It may be speculation, but possibly the enlarged Templar organisation saw its leaders become too concerned with acquiring secular wealth and power at the expense of spiritual development. It is also possible that the Templar expansion across Europe was a long–term plan to eventually undertake a political revolution that would reinstate the Gnostic Mysteries.

As an extremely secretive society, exactly what the purpose and agenda of the Priory were remains unknown, though I believe there is a powerful clue in their original connection with the Templars. Some people, like the authors of *The Holy Blood and the Holy Grail,* like to believe that the Priory of

Sion was concerned with promoting the claims to power of the descendants of the royal Merovingian family, who they claim are of the bloodline of Jesus and Mary Magdalene. There really is no certain evidence for any of this, just a vague ragbag of tenuous links and circumstantial proof: the Merovingians allegedly did not cut their beards, apparently this hardly unusual practice intimately linked them with Nazarenes, who supposedly did not cut their hair. We cannot give such assertions credibility as one thing they make very clear is that the authors are oblivious to the fact that the pivotal characters, Jesus and Mary Magdalene, existed only in a story. They are also completely ignorant of the teachings and beliefs of the Gnostics, which are fundamental to understanding the stories that they quote.

It is assumed that Sion, in the Priory of Sion name, refers to Mount Zion in Jerusalem and indeed that sounds very plausible. However, when one studies what the Templars and by implication, the Priory of Sion were secretly about, it makes no sense to have a Judeo–Christian name. Available evidence points to the fact that their religious beliefs were Gnostic Christian, but when you study them carefully and in detail, you start to find clear evidence which suggests that they were actually a hybrid mixture of Egyptian, Druidic and Gnostic. The Templars understood that Jesus was a myth and like the Gnostics, made use of the Christian characters and symbolism as a teaching tool and a protective veil. By using the familiar names and symbols, it gave the impression that the Templars were orthodox Christians, thus protecting them from the charge of heresy. The things that puzzle Christian scholars about the Templars are fairly easy for a Gnostic to understand. For example, in France, the Templar's battle standard showed two knights riding one horse. This depiction which many decide is indicative of their early poverty, is much more obvious when one considers the Gnostic concept of the higher and lower psyche or soul journeying in one body. Thinking scholars could hardly consider that the Templars were poor and had to share a horse, when the Templar's Charter states that on joining each Knight received three horses and a squire![2]

The Templars were connected with a Gnostic sect in southern France, known as the Cathars. It was a dangerous association because of the Cathars' heretical status and their affording Cathars discreet protection strongly indicates that they shared similar spiritual beliefs. Even though the Vatican admitted that the Cathars were innocents and morally pure in their lifestyle, it saw their teachings as a great threat to the orthodox Christian doctrine. When they refused to recant their beliefs, the Pope declared them heretics.

---

[2] Ralls, K. *The Templars & the Grail: Knights of the Quest*

Pope Innocenti III came to power in 1198 and determined to deal with the Cathar problem. Over ten years he sent various people to convert the Cathars with little success, just as had happened with Bernard of Clairvaux fifty years before, so the Pope asked the French King, Philip Augustus to intervene. When the king dragged his feet, the Pope went ahead with a *Holy Crusade* against the Cathars. In one dreadful assault against them in Béziers in 1209, the Catholics were allowed to leave the city, but chose to stay to fight alongside their Cathar friends. When the crusaders asked Arnaud, the Cistercian Abbot–commander how they would tell Catholic from Cathar, his reply, recorded by Caesar of Heisterbach, a fellow Cistercian was "Caedite eos. Novit enim Dominus qui sunt eius," — "Slay those [there]. The Lord will know who are his." In a letter to the Pope in August 1209, he says that 20,000 people were put to the sword, irrespective of rank, sex or age. If ever a man, let alone a pope, was inaptly named, it was Innocenti III whose onslaught continued for a further twenty years until, in November 1229 the Inquisition was established in Toulouse, to take this *holy mission* to its barbaric conclusion. They burned the last known Cathar 'monk' in 1321.[3]

The Templars had no official part in this crusade, though individual Templar members gave protection and shelter to escaped Cathars and buried their dead on Templar land. By the end of the 13th century the Templars were the target of much jealousy. They owned property, wealth, power and through their banking system, the vast debts of some very influential people. In 1307, one of those debtors, whose wars they had financed, Philip IV, secretly ordered the arrest of every Templar Knight, on Friday, October 13th. The captives were charged with heresy and their organisation declared illegal; not because of their alleged beliefs, but because of the envious greed and ambition of the French king. The even more secretive and influential Priory of Sion escaped attention and seemed to vanish completely. Some have speculated that it had a hand in plotting the Templars' downfall following their private dispute and separation, but this seems highly unlikely. The architect of the Templars' downfall was the greedy Philip IV, the King of France and his weak puppet Pope Clement V.

The Templars, offered protection to the Cathars and here we see our first link with John the Baptist. The Cathars reputedly associated Elijah with John the Baptist[4] and, as mentioned in Chapter Three, Biblical characters like Nimrod, Samson and Elijah portraying the wild strongman and the story of St Christopher taking on the same role in a newer updated version in the time of Jesus, all represent the same original character of Orion the

---

3 Le Roy Ladurie, E. ed. *Autour de Montaillou*
4 Barber, M. *The Cathars*

Hunter. Matthew tells us that John the Baptist too is Orion when Jesus declares that John is Elijah.[5]

I suspect there were two reasons why the Templars made St John the Baptist their figurehead — firstly, by elevating John, they encoded the significant fact that *Jesus* was not of importance to them; secondly, by giving prominence to John they reaffirmed his older link as a representation of Orion/Osiris. One of the four things that all Templar prisoners throughout Europe confessed, independently to the Inquisition, was the odd fact that at their initiation as a Knight Templar, they received a cord that had been bound around a severed bearded head.[6] Surely, this head represented Orion through John the Baptist and the cord, which they wore around their waists, represented Orion's Belt. Bauval and Gilbert's work tells us that Orion's Belt was mirrored in the plan of the Giza pyramids at the vernal equinox in 10,450 BCE. At dawn that day, the Sphinx was staring directly at Leo in the east. I have mentioned previously, that the Milky Way had been important symbolically to the ancient Egyptians, as it represented the route of the soul's journey back through the stars to the All One God. The Nile represented the Milky Way and the pyramids and Sphinx, Orion's belt, as it would relate to it.

The Templars protected the pilgrim routes to the Holy Land and in the 12th century, pilgrims who wanted to visit the holy places of Jerusalem but could not afford the expense or speak the languages that they needed en route, looked for alternative places to receive miraculous blessings instead. One route that grew in popularity and where hospitality was provided by Templars or their associates was *O Camiño de Santiago,* literally meaning the Santiago road, but much more curiously, it was the Galician phrase for the Milky Way. Along the way, the pilgrims stopped to pay homage at shrines; shrines that all held Black Madonna statues. This route to what is now a Spanish town grew in popularity from the 10th to 12th century and consequently caused an economic boom in parts of France as the pilgrim routes converged on the Pyrenees. The road was dotted with Black Madonna shrines and Templar, Cistercian and Benedictine hostelries, before reaching *Santiago Compostela,* the place where the beheaded St James was buried in the *Compostela,* Field of the Star.

The Cistercians had influenced the formation of the Templars through Bernard of Clairvaux. When he headed the floundering Cistercians, he steered them back to the strict rule of St Benedict early in the twelfth century and through his political connections, elevated the order right across Europe. Bernard founded his monastery at Clairvaux in 1115. In

---

5 Matthew 11:10-15

6 Pinkham, M A. *Guardians Of The Holy Grail*

1128, he assisted his uncle at the Council of Troyes to draw up the Charter for the Knights Templar.

As a student he had written several treatises on the *Queen of Heaven,* the name given to Isis thousands of years before. Bernard began to teach a new faith where prayers were offered to the Virgin Mary, leading to his rather odd assertion that "No one can enter Heaven unless by Mary, as though through a door."[7] He is considered to have taken the objective Christian faith of the Early Middle Ages into a more subjective faith where Jesus is presented as a role model and Mary is the key to mediation with the supreme deity.[8]

Norman Cantor tells us:

> "Bernard played the leading role in the development of the Virgin cult, which is one of the most important manifestations of the popular piety of the twelfth century."

Besides his obsession with the Virgin Mary/Isis, he was known for two things, his eloquence and his mysticism. His Templar connections in Jerusalem gave him access to Sufism, Pythagorean and Platonism and the Sacred Geometry that is so evident in the Cistercian buildings still standing on ancient Druidic sites.[9] His interest in Islam's Sufism must have strengthened his connections with the Gnostic Cathars. Like the Cathars and Pythagoreans before them, he was a vegetarian and made this part of Cistercian life. I cannot believe that the use of the name *Milky Way* for the pilgrimage route to *Santiago Compostela* had been a coincidence. Any adherents to the Mysteries and Isis would be aware that to the Egyptians, the Milky Way was the heavenly road to immortality and the soul's reunification with God.

I am certain that it is extremely significant, that in art work that has Templar or Priory of Sion connections, whether it be paintings in churches and monasteries or works commissioned privately by politically influential people; people who were allegedly connected right through to the 18th century with the Templars, a symbol of their beliefs was presented for those *who had the eyes to see.* This encoded symbol became the contemporary *logo* for John the Baptist. Wherever we find a Templar connection to the artist or person commissioning the picture, we see the secret of John's message, given by the symbolic uplifted hand with the index finger or sometimes he holds a staff, both pointing up to Orion and the stars.

---

7 Liguori, A. *The Glories of Mary*

8 Cantor, N. *The Civilization of the Middle Ages*

9 Devereux, P. *Places of Power*

The subject of the Templars is complex and cannot be debated fully in this book, but it is important to mention the various pieces of evidence which indicate that the Templars inherited some far older Celtic Christian traditions. The major cathedrals built by the Cistercians are on earlier Druidic sites. The Pelagians, Celtic Christians who were active in Britain during the 5th and 6th centuries, culminating with the infamous Pope Joan/John VIII in the 9th century incorporated more ancient Celtic traditions, such as the symbolic honouring of the severed head. This connection with the ancient tradition is strongly reinforced by the day chosen to commemorate St John the Baptist. June 24th is also the day that the Celts celebrated their Queen of Heaven, Danu the Celtic Isis.

One final intriguing thought: in the Celtic language of Brythonic, the name for John, our Orion personification, is Siôn. It is quite compelling to believe that the Priory of Sion is really a very ancient Priory of Orion.

The greatest lie ever told

Chapter 20

Some of Our Apostles Are Missing

"Jesus was all right, but his disciples were thick and ordinary. It's them twisting it that ruins it for me."

John Lennon

There is an even greater mystery attached to the real lives and works of the Apostles than there is to Jesus, for nothing is really known about these crucial characters, these supposed first missionaries of Christianity. The Acts of the Apostles, through the letters of Peter, James, John, Jude and Paul, plus the Revelation of John are supposed to recount the works of the Disciples following the resurrection of Jesus. Alas, like the gospels, these are not reliable historical documents.

Exactly who the Disciples were is something of a mystery, and what the gospels say is less than convincing. The first three gospels have Peter, James and John as those closest to Jesus, yet in John's gospel, James and John are never mentioned and Peter has a bit part. John then mentions two others, Matthew and Luke, whom Mark, in his gospel, ignores completely.

The lists of disciples in Mark Chapter 3 and Matthew Chapter 10, verses 2—4 seem to have been late additions, afterthoughts, perhaps someone thinking it better to give names to the twelve people who were mentioned in the stories, though it then becomes clear that only John, of the Gospel writers was a chosen Apostle. The use of *twelve followers* is what is really significant in the stories, not the people themselves. The number twelve had a mathematical and astronomical significance in the Mysteries. In Gnostic teaching, the godman was represented the sun and the twelve disciples depicted the constellations it passed through.

Like any teacher or prophet, the master needed an entourage. He has to be accompanied by a circle of close followers, not only to make himself appear important and charismatic, but also so that in the dialogue reported between them, the master can pass on his words of wisdom. In this scenario, you need someone, usually willing but dim, who appears unable to understand the meaning of all that is being said, there needs to be someone to ask naïve questions so the master can give a full and explicit answer. Jesus picks up the disciples rather like jetsam from the shore. The manner is as unlikely as the people whom he collects. If Jesus, as a teacher, needed to groom an elite following to carry and spread their master's teaching, he could hardly have chosen a worse bunch. He mostly picked simple parochial fishermen and the odd publican, men who were uneducated and, men who would find it difficult to grasp philosophical concepts, men who had no training in the delivery of oral tutelage or effective argument in a debate: their shortcomings were a recipe for certain failure.

These unpromising characters were slotted into the story to make it appear that those closest to the Son of God were not the great and the mighty, but ordinary simple men. The story was intended to appeal to all people, to indicate that anyone could become close to the Son of God. The story was not based upon reality, it was fiction and so the authors could introduce any number of unlikely characters and events without concern, in order to get their important messages to the masses.

The Church likes to imply that Acts records how the Apostles spread the word of Jesus following the resurrection and how they played a major part in laying the foundations of the Christian Church. This is a little odd as virtually nothing is said about nine of these important men, other than their names. Only three of them appear to have done anything worth mentioning. The reason that we never read about what the missing nine did is because they did nothing; they could only do *nothing* because they never existed. The New Testament compilers' attention was focussed on creating a tale about Peter, they did not need to complicate things with a set of sub-plots for the rest of the phantom players. The style in which Acts is written puts it squarely into the realm of a poorly-written fantasy adventure with a wealth of contradictions and nonsense; the opinion is not just mine, but that of many New Testament scholars.[1] The historian Randel McCram Helms makes a particularly interesting observation, that Acts used phrases and plots from Euripedes' work[3] implying a very Gnostic approach to writing.

The narration changes suddenly from first person to third as the late Christian writers attempted to fill in some of the holes in Christian history and cobbled this hot-potch of individual pieces together into one clumsy document to become Acts. Since the Tübingen School in the mid-19th

---

[1] Gaus, A. *The Unvarnished New Testament*
[2] Freke, T & Gandy, P. *The Jesus Mysteries*
[3] Helms, R M. *Who Wrote The Gospels*

century,[4] scholars have been certain that Acts is not written by the disciples of Jesus and they surmise that it was written just after 150 CE. In the stories of Acts, as in the Gospels, we once again find evidence of a lack of knowledge about Jewish law and customs and ignorance of the Aramaic language, strongly suggesting that the authors did not originate from Judea. Christians of the mid-second century including Justin Martyr, a writer and virulent defender of Christianity, knew nothing of the Acts, but then sometime around 180 CE, it suddenly appears on the scene and is regarded as holy scripture. In fact by that time a wealth of texts that recounted the lives and deeds of the disciples was in circulation, in much the same way that there were many gospels. Eventually, the Church took action to weed out all those scriptures that it disapproved of and designated them as heretical. They kept the few that seemed closest to the Church's doctrine and called this exclusive set *Holy*. As the heretical gospels were burnt, so too were the unwanted accounts of the Apostles.

The so-called letters of the Apostles Peter, James and John were long proposed as proof of authenticity: to have written letters, their writers must have been real living people proclaims the Church's faulty logic. The disciples of Jesus were supposedly simple uneducated men who would not have been literate. It is highly unlikely that they felt compelled to learn to read and write so late on in their lives. As modern research has proven these letters of the Apostles are desperate attempts by the Literalist Christians of the second and third centuries to combat the *heresies* of the Gnostics by writing clumsy forgeries. Quite simply they wanted to prove that the people were real, but as there was no proof, they created some. Bishop Eusebius was the zealous propagandist of the orthodox Christians, yet was honest enough to dismiss the letters of Peter, James, John and Jude as being of dubious authenticity and completely dismissed Revelation.[5] Manufacturing forgeries of the scriptures was not the only thing that these early writers did, many letters written supposedly by early Christian Church leaders such Clement, Justin Martyr, Ignatius — letters that supported the apostle myth whilst attacking Gnostics — were not even genuine.[6] Scholars have revealed that these forgeries were still being produced as late as the 5th century CE. This shows how long the Church of Rome was still struggling against the Gnostic critics. It also shows that despite the Church knowing all these letters are forgeries, they still promote them as genuine. If this is not a heinous lie with the sole intention of misleading people, then what is?

---

4 Cross, F L ed. *The Oxford Dictionary of the Christian Church*

5 Eusebius, *History of the Christian Church*

6 op. cit. Cross, F L ed.

There is no evidence to show that the disciples were any more real than Jesus. We must assume that if Jesus were a fictitious character, then the Apostles must be too. Some stories claim that Peter went to Rome, preached and was crucified there, but then other stories say that he never left Judea and preached there until his death. The character of Peter related through the Bible, shows him to be an illiterate, uneducated fisherman with a feisty temper; a bigoted oaf who disliked women; a coward of questionable loyalty and faith and a yokel who displayed a dull-witted lack of understanding of much that Jesus taught. This parochial dullard is hardly the kind of person to up sticks and decamp to any foreign parts. In sophisticated Rome he would be totally out of place.

Neither would an astute Jesus promote the class dunce and worse still the bully to be the top man to pass on his teachings — even more odd, when Peter himself seemed bemused by most of them. By sleight of hand, the Church transformed this intellectually and socially challenged peasant into a brave and charismatic sage. Historically, there is no evidence for Peter's existence, let alone his travels to Rome. The list in which the Vatican cites Peter as the true first bishop of Rome is a fanciful concoction aimed to give credibility to the ultimate authority of popes, who ridiculously claim descent from St Peter and thereby from Jesus.

There is no evidence for the reality of any of the disciples, but there is one person whom Acts calls an Apostle, who historians think actually lived. Even though he was not a disciple, nor had he ever met Jesus, apart from the rulers and officials like Augustus Caesar, Quirinius, Pilate and Herod, Paul of Tarsus is the sole central living character within the New Testament. Yet nevertheless, Paul is regarded as a great enigma and a great problem for theologians and New Testament scholars and this is because Paul can be proved to exist, yet gives no account of the life of Jesus. This distressing omission has caused deep concern to those who believe in the historical authenticity of Jesus as a living man. Paul's strange teaching, with its apparent side-lining of Jesus, had prompted some theologians to charge Paul with *hijacking* Christianity, whilst others have labelled him an anti-feminist, a hard-liner and intolerant — but these views are the result of accepting the Bible's version of Paul, whilst being oblivious, or indifferent, to the truth. I write more about Paul in the next chapter because he does not belong here with the fictitious Christian apostles. Paul was an enemy of what was to become the orthodox Christian Church.

Chapter 21

Paul — Dangerous Heretic

"I was bold in the pursuit of knowledge, never fearing to follow truth and reason to whatever results they led, and bearding every authority which stood in their way."

Thomas Jefferson

According to the Christian Church, Simon Magus and Paul of Tarsus were two great heretics. Paul's divisive teachings were inspired by the Devil; he was a dangerous lying serpent who needed to be cast out.[1] This shocking statement reflects the virulent opinion of early Literalist Christians, who considered Paul as their great enemy. If it doesn't make sense because the Paul you know of was the greatest Christian, the great missionary — that was indeed true and that was also the problem. Paul was a powerful and influential missionary who brought Christ to the Gentiles, but the early Christians didn't like it at all. The teaching that Paul was spreading was not of a historical Jesus Christ, but of the *Christ* that was the *Consciousness*, the soul reunited with God, where man becomes God. This was not the Christ of the *literalist* Christian Church.

Before trying to understand the problem, it is important to understand Paul's background and particularly the place where he was born, raised and educated, for this is crucial to what occurred. Paul was born in Tarsus the capital of Cilicia, a province of what is now southern Turkey. For three hundred years Tarsus was a Greek city until Pompey the Great added it to the Roman Empire in 66 BCE. Like many Greek cities Tarsus had an intellectual tradition and by the first-century CE time of Paul, it had become a great centre of philosophy and learning; according to Strabo:

"The people at Tarsus have devoted themselves so eagerly, not only to philosophy, but also to the whole round of education in general, that

---

[1] Lüdemann, G. *Heretics*
[2] Pagels, E. *The Gnostic Paul*

they have surpassed Athens, Alexandria, or any other place that can be named where there have been schools and lectures of philosophers."[3]

Tarsus also had its share of great men; the stoics Antipater, Archedamus and Nestor were born there. The most dominant intellectual figure in the first century BCE was Posidonius. Considered the greatest polymath of the age — as a great astronomer he discovered, supposedly from the Druids during one of his trips to Britain, that the moon controls the tides — he was thought to be the leading influence amongst the Stoics in Tarsus.[4] Posidonius also had strong connections with the power brokers within the Roman Republic including Pompey and Cicero; his disciple Athenodorus, became tutor to Julius Caesar's nephew, the future emperor Augustus.

Tarsus was no backwater but a great centre of learning and as an important trading port, it became a honey–pot for scholars and students from many lands. Tarsus was cosmopolitan in make–up, though with the highly esteemed Greek culture and language predominating, ethnic groups including the Jews, would have adopted Hellenic ways. It is important to understand that the Jews of Tarsus were very different from the Jews of Judea: they would feel more Greek than Jewish and be relatively contented citizens of the Roman Empire.

The Dionysian Mysteries were long established in Tarsus by the time of Paul, as was the slightly later regional variant of the Mysteries, that of the godman Attis. Around 67 BCE, the Mystery of Mithras suddenly appeared in Tarsus, Posidonius, undoubtedly introducing the powerful astronomical elements within the story.[5] Because of the cosmopolitan nature of Tarsus, other Mystery religions, such as those of Serapis, Adonis and Bacchus also had temples sited there. The city's community of Hellenised Jews ensured that the new Jewish variant of the Mysteries would join all the older ethnic versions.

The Mysteries, in all its various forms, was the predominant religion of the city and the city's academics would have been initiates into the higher inner Mysteries. Initiates had inclusive access to any variant of the Mysteries and would often be active members of more than one sect. Almost one hundred years after the time of Paul, in 134 CE the Emperor Hadrian wrote that this practice was common in Alexandria:

---

[3] Jones, H L *The Geography of Strabo*
[4] Ulansey, D *The Origins of the Mithraic Mysteries*
[5] ibid.

"From Hadrian Augustus to Servianus the consul, greeting. The land of Egypt, the praises of which you have been recounting to me, my dear Servianus, I have found to be wholly light–minded, unstable, and blown about by every breath of rumour. There those who worship Serapis are, in fact, Christians, and those who call themselves bishops of Christ are, in fact, devotees of Serapis. There is no chief of the Jewish synagogue, no Samaritan, no Christian presbyter, who is not an astrologer, a soothsayer, or an anointer. Even the Patriarch himself, when he comes to Egypt, is forced by some to worship Serapis, by others to worship Christ."[6]

We cannot doubt that Paul was initiated into the Mysteries, for in Corinthians he describes himself as a 'Steward of the Mysteries of God' — *steward* was the term used to refer to the priests of the Mysteries of Serapis. In multi–ethnic Alexandria, the hybrid Greek/Egyptian godman Serapis had taken over in popularity from the specifically–Egyptian Osiris, though Isis continued to be the female consort. The cult of Serapis was widespread throughout the græco–Roman world, so as well as being the centre for Mithraism and the Dionysian Mysteries, Tarsus would certainly have had a Serapis temple too. Perhaps Alexandria's strong Jewish connection influenced Paul to choose their version of the Mysteries, though it is likely that he would have been associated with other sects as well, and clearly at some stage, as its popularity spread he decided to use the Jesus Mystery as a channel for his preaching. Even in the second century CE the critic Celsus stated that Mithraism and Christianity were teaching the same doctrine.[7]

More proof of Paul's initiation into the Mysteries is found in his writings in the original Greek; the later Latin contains profuse misinterpretation. Paul frequently makes use of terms that belong to the Mysteries, but have no meaning to *literalist* Christians:

Gnosis — meaning *knowledge* of the divine
Sophia — meaning *wisdom*
Pneuma — meaning *spirit*
Eidolon — meaning *image* or *ego*
Logos — the guide on the path to attaining *Sophia* and *Gnosis*
Teleioi — meaning the *initiated*
Hylic — one who identifies with the material body, the *outer–self*

---

[6] Giles, J A. *Hebrew and Christian Records*
[7] Origen, *Origen Against Celsus*

> *Psychic* — the first-stage *soul* initiation from being a *hylic; psychics* were the first-stage initiates who received the outer exoteric teachings, they identify with the soul or psyche
>
> *Pneumatic* — the second-stage *spirit* initiation from being a *psychic; pneumatics* were the second stage initiates who were taught the inner esoteric teachings, they identify with spirit or Consciousness.

In the Gnostic Mysteries the beginners, the lower initiates, are referred to as *psychics,* whilst the higher inner initiates are *pneumatics.* Without this basic Gnostic understanding, the terms are incomprehensible when you read this extract from Paul's letter in 1 Corinthians 2:14:

> "The *Psychic* does not receive the things of the spirit of God; they are foolishness to him; he cannot recognise them because they are *Pneumatically* discerned, but the *Pneumatic* discerns all things."

To the uninitiated, to orthodox Christians, this statement of Paul's is unintelligible. If Paul were an orthodox Christian and anti-Gnostic, then he definitely would not have used Gnostic terminology, nor sent it in a letter to Christians who would not be able to *understand* it.

Paul's statement, that he had "ascended to the third heaven", makes absolutely no sense to Christians, but it does to Gnostic initiates. Modern empirical research into the Afterlife claims that there are different levels or spheres of different vibrations. On death we go to the sphere that can accommodate the vibrations that we accumulated through life on earth. Higher vibrations take us to higher spheres. Most people it seems are likely to go to the third sphere.[8] This research also confirms the Jewish Mystic view. The Talmud relates the tale of the Rabbis whose eloquent discussion of Ezekiel's mysterious vision of the heavenly chariot, prompted a voice from the Heavens to say: "A place is prepared to you, and a table is set for you — you and your students are admitted to the third level."[9]

In the Mysteries, the *seven heavens,* linked to the sun moon and planets, were promoted as levels of spiritual ascendancy, though Paul himself spoke of ten heavens — seven lower and three higher level heavens. We still use the idiom, when things exceed our expectations: 'I'm in seventh Heaven!' and incorporate the concept of the multiple spheres surrounding our own each time we make reference to 'Heavens above!'

---

[8] Zammit, VJ. *A Lawyer Presents the Case for the Afterlife*

[9] Scholem, G. *Jewish Gnosticism, Merkabah Mysticism, and Talmudic Tradition*

Strangely... or perhaps not... depending on your viewpoint, theologians seem to ignore the idiosyncratic words that Paul often uses, though in Christian terms they make absolutely no sense. Christians also employ some of their ignorant misinterpretations in an attempt to show Paul as anti-Gnostic. Saint Augustine uses '*Gnosis* puffs up' in 1 Corinthians to disparage Gnostic belief by implying that it gives one ideas above one's station: "... it exalts man to arrogance which is nothing but a kind of windy emptiness."[10] In Gnostic terminology, this seemingly odd sentence has a very specific meaning: Gnosis — knowledge — was the Pneumatic intake of the divine breath or spirit, hence 'puffs up.' Paul follows the statement with a sentence that relates to the Psychics " Gnosis phusioi, agape oikodomei." literally 'Gnosis inflates, loves builds [a house].' Christians can make neither head nor tail of it and still construct the most complex argument to explain it,[11] yet Gnostics know exactly what it means.

Many problems of interpretation also arise from the fact that Paul's letters were clever teachings delivered on two distinct levels, as Gnostic Theodotus informs us "each one knows the Lord in his own way: and not all know him alike."[12] Paul taught in two ways at once. The first was the superficial level — the one normally read by orthodox Christians — aimed at the outer initiates of the Mysteries, the Psychics; then there was the higher encoded level, which would be understood by Pneumatics who had been initiated into the secret esoteric levels of the Mysteries.

This two-tier system applies to Paul's letters and all the gospels; creating the same problems for both. Elaine Pagels points out in *The Gnostic Paul* that the Gnostic followers of the Alexandrian poet Valentinus, stated that the Christians make the mistake of reading the scriptures literally, whilst they — the Gnostics — read both the scriptures and the letters of Paul on the symbolic level, as Paul intended. Paul even mentions the problems himself. In his first letter to the Corinthians he expresses his disappointment and frustration because his student followers had still failed to rise above the allegorical teachings to attain the higher level, so that they themselves could become teachers.

Paul's teachings contain frequent reiterations of Mystery doctrines, his use of 'reaping and sowing', rather than the expected order of 'sowing and reaping' was a common Mystery imagery to symbolise an initiate's mystical death and resurrection This teaching is further underlined by his revelation that 'the seed you sow does not come into life until it has first died'. In other

---

[10] Bettenson, H tr. *City of God*

[11] Benson, BE. *Journal of Philosophy and Scripture*

[12] op. cit. Pagels, E

words the initiate had to experience the rite of his mystical death before his spiritual resurrection. On another occasion Paul advises, 'If someone thinks he knows something, he still does not know the way he ought to know,' which is a simple reworking of Plato's 'He is the wisest who, like Socrates, knows that his wisdom is worth nothing.' Again quoting Plato, in 1 Corinthians 8:2. Paul wrote, 'For now we see through a glass, darkly; but then face to face.' Plato's original version was that we only see reality 'through a glass dimly.'

This subject usually inspires strong reactions, even from religious people, who accept life after death in theory and Faith, but then, generally through fear, refute the possibility of making contact with the living spirits of the dead. There is not one shred of proof that there is no after-life, whilst there is a body of evidence to strongly suggest that there is.[13] Now whilst this sounds to some like nonsense, or to others the practice of charlatans, modern research has shown that a particular procedure of dark mirrors does indeed provide astonishing results in making contact with those who have died. Raymond Moody, MD taught philosophy at East Carolina University before taking up residency at the University of Virginia Medical School. He researched human consciousness and developed a procedure for apparitional encounters that has been successful with hundreds of individuals wishing to contact deceased relatives and friends.[14]

Moody selected his guinea-pig group for his initial experiments most carefully. He deliberately chose psychologists, medical doctors, counsellors, graduates and other professional people — people with no occult leanings, who were emotionally stable, articulate and interested in human consciousness. Moody's success has led to his mirror-gazing method being employed by other physicians, psychologists and psychotherapists, and at the Californian Institute of Transpersonal Psychology, Professor A Hastings has incorporated the procedure and apparatus into the curriculum and it is taught to trainee psychotherapists.

The use of mirror-gazing has been condemned by the Catholic Church, but this is understandable since religious establishments always seek to control and lead their followers, so they clearly could not condone people seeking to conduct their own spiritual experiences, especially if they were far more profound than anything the church could offer.

It is only in December 1996 that the Vatican announced it had changed its stance on mediumship; one of its foremost theologians Father Gino Concetti wrote:

---

[13] op. cit. Zammit, V J

[14] Moody, R & Perry, P *Reunions: Visionary Encounters With Departed Loved Ones*

"According to the modern catechism the Church has decided not to forbid anymore dialogue with the deceased ... this is as a sequel of new discoveries within the domain of the paranormal."[15]

This Vatican U-turn apparently came about following successful results obtained from its own mediums. Though mainstream science shies away from everything spiritual, there is a significant minority, including some big-hitters, who are becoming interested in some of the things which had previously been dismissed as unscientific mumbo-jumbo. Moody and Perry have written a book *Reunited* that explains the background and procedures to mirror-gazing and the psychomanteum, a mirrored room in which contact with the apparition takes place.[16] The progress of the Vatican with Moody's methods may be greater than we think. In 1998, Pope John Paul II replied to the question "What actually happens to us at the moment of death?"

"Quite special conditions prevail after natural death. It concerns a transitional phase in which the body dissolves and where the life of a mirror-image entity (the soul) begins."[17]

It may only be a matter of time, before we see a more open and honest theological view of Paul's 'looking through a glass darkly'.

A little incident in the life of Paul, which is recounted in the New Testament and generally passes unnoticed, holds the key to whether we can refute the idea of his being an orthodox Christian. The event occurred when he was in the seaport of Cenchreae near Corinth waiting to board a ship to Ephesus. In Acts 18:18 we are told that Paul 'cut his hair, for he had made a vow'. This account has long baffled and troubled theologians and the best they can do is guess that Paul had taken a Nazarite vow, as one of the Nazarite requirements is to let the hair grow, even though theologians have nothing to suggest that Paul was a Nazarite. The curious incident is only baffling if one looks no further than the end of one's nose. Research a little wider and the answer is there.

This simple act of hair-cutting takes on a very different meaning if one dismisses the notion that Paul was an 'orthodox' Christian-Jew. In Cenchreae there stood a temple dedicated to Isis and it was here, to the personification of Isis as Stella Maris, that sailors cut off their hair and

---

[15] Concetti, G. *Osservatore Romano*

[16] Moody, R & Perry, P *Reunited: How to Meet Loved Ones Again Who Seem Lost to Death*

[17] Pope John Paul II 'Das Leben nach dem Tod'

dedicated it in offering, in order to gain the blessing of the goddess to ensure a safe voyage. This is what Paul did and had he followed the Judaic or orthodox Christian faith, he would never have done so, it would have been an unthinkable heresy. However, when one accepts that Paul was not only an initiate of the Gnostic Jesus–Christian Mysteries, but appeared also to be a Steward of the Mysteries of Serapis and Isis, his actions would be quite legitimate, they would make perfect sense and the act itself would be entirely acceptable.

Paul is said to be anti–Gnostic, but as we have seen, the evidence shows that the opposite is true. Beyond the eccentric claims in the forged Letters, there is no indication that Paul battled against the Gnostic Mysteries. The Gnostics certainly never gave a single indication that Paul was an enemy, though as has been shown, the early Christian fathers cited Paul as the great anti–Christian heretic. If Paul had been anti–Gnostic, then why would Gnostics acclaim him as the 'the Great Apostle'. The only group to acclaim Paul as the 'great enemy' was the Literalist Christians. Valentinus — an Alexandrian Gnostic who wrote *The Gospel of Truth* rediscovered at Nag Hammadi, and founder of a school in Rome around 140 CE — claimed that his teacher and initiator, Theudas, had been one of those who had been initiated by Paul himself, into the deeper Mysteries which revealed the secret doctrine of God. I would suggest that this statement alone is explicit enough to show that Paul was teaching the Mysteries.

Paul's introduction into the New Testament is under the name Saul, allegedly his Jewish birth name. His mission is portrayed as that of a sort of witchfinder general whose appointed task was to forcibly weed out all Christians, particularly in Jerusalem and then Damascus. Historically and archaeologically there is no evidence of Christians — other than Gnostic Ebionites who held strongly to Jewish traditions — being in Jerusalem at that time.[18] Paul makes scathing verbal attacks on the Ebionites for their insistence that only Jews, or those who effectively convert to Judaism, can become Gnostic Christians, whereas Paul wants an inclusive Christianity for everyone.[19][20] There has certainly been no evidence of a Christian Church that was headed by anyone called James in Jerusalem as the Catholic Church alleges was the case at the time of Paul.

Even more untenable, is the idea that there were orthodox literalist Christians already established in distant Damascus. If there had been, they would have been incredibly few in number and there would have been absolutely no reason for the Jewish authorities to persecute them. Jerusalem would have had no authority over what went on in Damascus, which was a

---

[18] Colossians 4: 10–12
[19] Corinthians 11:4
[20] Galatians 5:12

Roman province. Neither does Acts really explain why Saul/Paul, should be so far from home, nor for whom he was supposedly working.

Some theologians claim that Paul went to Jerusalem to study Jewish law,[21] because it says so in Acts 22:3 but this makes no sense, since Hellenised Jews had no time for traditional orthodox Judaism and Paul was very much against the Jewish religious practices which were also central to their laws. In the scriptures, it also says that he was a tent maker in Jerusalem,[22] but it seems very unlikely that someone so well educated would move to a backwater like Jerusalem to pursue such a menial career. Intellectual Jews had long abandoned Jerusalem and decamped to such places as Alexandria. Athens, Rome, Rhodes, Salamis, Ephesus and Tarsus. Neither does it make any logical sense for a Hellenised Jew, to be given the job of hit–man for the Sanhedrin. For an initiate of the Mysteries, such action would have been impossible in every way.

At this point, it is worth considering whether Paul in any way adhered to the traditional Jewish beliefs, customs and laws. The character of Jesus portrayed in the gospels certainly presents him as a traditional Jew who had Yahweh as his God. The things that Paul wrote reveal that he was virulently against everything to do with Judaic teaching, custom and practice; this makes it impossible for him to have been a follower of a Messiah steeped in Judaic ways. Of course, Paul never was a follower of Jesus, not least because there never was a living Jesus. Paul never recommended any of the Jewish aspects of Jesus, because Jesus was never Jewish, he was a mystical mythical figure, employed as a human character so that lower initiates of the Jewish Mysteries had someone to relate to.

Writing to the Galatians, Ephesians and the Philippians, Paul blatantly states that he considers the old traditional Law of Yahweh/Jehovah to be decayed and rotten, needing to be cast away and replaced by a new covenant, one given by Jesus of the Mysteries. In Philippians 3, Paul criticises the Law of Jehovah that is practised by the Jews to such an extent that by verse 8 he considers it to be rubbish in some Bible versions and dung in others; Luther quite clearly prefers 'excrement.'[23] For someone who was supposed to be both a Jew and an orthodox Christian, is it not bizarre that Paul had no fear of blaspheming and railing against Jehovah, if he believed this god existed? Paul considered Jehovah to be an invention of Judea; he was a tribal god.

To Gnostics, religious laws, rituals and traditional customs were an anathema. Paul rails against Jehovah's Laws, stating that the

---

21 Acts 22:3
22 Acts 18.3
23 Luther, *Bibel*

commandments given by Jehovah to Moses and translated into draconian Judaic Laws, had no place in a world where mankind should be seeking spiritual freedom.[24] [25] Paul wrote that those who depended upon the law were under a curse and that Christ redeemed people from the curse of the Law that subjugated them.[26] [27]

The Commandments given to Moses, which Judaism and Christianity promote as if they were unique, are no more than simplistic imitations of more ancient and far more profound moral laws. As the reader can probably guess, one source is Egyptian — *Negative Confession* [28] — while another is the *Codex Hammurabi* [29] written by the Amorite king of 18th–century BCE Babylonia.

The Code of Hammurabi was a list of conditional statements carved into various large stones situated in a number of towns, giving penalties that would be incurred by someone performing the specified action: 'If any one open his ditches to water his crop, but is careless, and the water flood the field of his neighbour, then he shall pay his neighbour corn for his loss.' The *Negative Confession* contains a monologue to be learned and used when the deceased Egyptian met Osiris. The deceased would greet the Lord, then list those of the thirty–eight sins that he had not committed: 'I have caused no man to suffer.'

The Ten Commandments, in contrast, begin with rampant egotism: 'Thou shalt have no other God but me.' This arrogant god then unashamedly breaks one of his later laws by confessing that he is a jealous god, but of whom he is jealous we cannot be sure. The Creator, the One God, would surely have no competition, unless he had created an exact replica of himself. Then whilst Jehovah declares 'Thou shalt not kill', with unashamed hypocrisy, he ignores his own law and slaughters at whim. Following his example, his leading prophets happily indulge in mass murder too. It seems that genocide was of lesser importance to Jehovah than coveting the ox or wife of a neighbour.

Jehovah must have driven Moses distracted with the avalanche of laws he demanded he enforce. They controlled every aspect of life, with a particular obsession for hygiene. Jewish Law prescribes numerous lists of things being clean and unclean, from animals to sexual behaviour. In effect

---

[24] Ephesians 2:15
[25] Colossians 2:14
[26] Romans 7:4,6
[27] Galatians 5:1,4
[28] Massey, G. *Ancient Egypt - The Light of the World*
[29] Harper, RF. *The Code of Hammurabi*

these were not laws passed down by the great Creator, but by a priesthood intent on domination, which could be achieved by controlling every action and detail of an individual's life.

Whereas the Code of Hammurabi was based on presumed innocence and the onus of proof for an accuser to show you had disadvantaged a neighbour and the Negative Confession was a guide to what you were expected to do to live an honest life — which on death you must affirm that you had not transgressed — the Laws of Moses were a set of ludicrous irrational demands, that gave a group of power-obsessed men the right to despise or admonish you.

During his life, Paul's biggest battleground was Jerusalem, where his opponents, the Jewish Gnostic Christians known as the Ebionites were based. Though they claimed to be Gnostic, these Jewish Christians insisted on retaining their links with the traditional Jewish religion. Paul's anger was inflamed by their arrogant self-regard that they were superior because of their Jewishness, and their refusal to relinquish their adherence to the traditional Jewish Laws. The practice of circumcision and their insistence that all non-Jewish Christian men must be circumcised, brought Paul into open conflict with them. His contempt for them was highlighted by his warning to the Philippians, cautioning them to be wary of those "axe-wielding circumcisionaries," whom he calls, "those dogs, those evil workers." The ritual act of circumcision signified the battle which raged between the Jerusalem-based Jewish faction which sought to impose the traditional Judaic Laws upon Gentiles wishing to join the Gnostic Christian Mysteries and Paul who regarded the idea as totally opposed to the very fundamental concepts of the Mysteries which promoted unrestricted cosmopolitanism and acceptance of the outward physical person in whatever form the individual had chosen.

These opponents of Paul were Jewish-Gnostic Christians, not the Literalist or Orthodox Christians who followed a historical Jesus. There was no legendary Christian Church of Jerusalem, only a Gnostic group. In Paul's time, there could be no literalist Christians to battle against, because the literalist belief did not develop until after Paul's death and the fall of Jerusalem.

Paul's campaign was clearly to free Jews from the Laws which were not only the foundation of their religion, but dictated their everyday lives and deprived them of free choice. He wrote, "All who depend upon works of the Law are under a curse," he could hardly be more condemning than that.[30] To Paul and the Gnostics, Jehovah was a parochial god, the Jewish tribal god, a mythical demi-god who mediates between Jews and the All One

---

[30] Galatians 3:10

Creator God. Paul despised everything to do with traditional Judaism, its rituals, its laws and the accompanying restrictions. Had Literal Christianity actually existed in his lifetime, which it did not, he would have despised it with equal vehemence because it too has its base in the all-controlling Judaic Laws.

Paul failed to convert the traditional Jews to Gnostism and was met with hostility, however he found converts amongst the Hellenised Jews and the Gentiles, both fascinated by this new and what seemed exotic variant of the Mysteries, which Paul had cleansed of any unsavoury Judaic aspects. The effect of this ethnic transference was that the Jesus Mysteries' godman was no longer seen as the saviour of the Jews but was now portrayed as the saviour of humanity. Paul's influence saw the Jewish Jesus Mystery sever the Judaic links and return the Jesus dying-resurrected god/man back to its original cosmopolitan form.

The miraculous conversion on the road to Damascus depicted in the New Testament is unlikely to be an actual event and if Paul himself used the story, it would have been as a teaching allegory amongst initiates of the Mysteries. Paul refers to experiencing Christ not Jesus, which means he achieved his enlightenment. Being sent to Damascus with letters of authority from the high priest in Jerusalem to persecute followers of the Way — supposedly Christians — cannot be true because Damascus was in the Roman province of Syria, over which the Jerusalem high priest had no authority whatsoever at any time.

Damascus was an alternative designation for the Essene community at Qumran, just to the east of Jerusalem. The Essenes, like Paul, hated the Jerusalem Laws. Philo described the Essenes as a Jewish wing of the Therapeutae and Josephus called them Pythagoreans. *The Dead Sea Scrolls*, written by the Essenes, mention the Mystery that has long been hidden, which clearly indicates their philosophical and spiritual affiliations. Some scholars, who believe in the authenticity of a living Jesus, believe he and his parents were Essenes. Had he been real and an Essene, he could not have been the character described in the Christian Gospels with his concern for Judaic law. No kind of record anywhere points to an Essene Jesus.

An assessment of Paul's teachings and his usage of passages taken from Greek philosophers, make it extremely likely that as a young man, Paul had been considered both intelligent and worthy enough to have been inducted into one of the academies which gave instruction in the teachings of the Greeks sages like Pythagoras, Socrates and Plato. Remembering that besides being philosophers and men of science, these sages were Hierophants of the Mysteries whose teaching would promote love and peace, non-violence and tolerance, for Paul to then have left behind all of this profound philosophical and religious experience and for no known reason, to have suddenly gone off to a distant land to undertake a fanatical purge of a tiny insignificant religious sect on behalf of Judaic authorities is nonsensical in the extreme. But then the authors who cobbled together Acts did not understand the story, were not interested in truth and had found the chance to produce a dramatic piece of Christian propaganda.

What is generally known of Paul and his teaching comes to us from his letters. But here we immediately have a problem. Whilst Paul's early writings have been attributed to him, modern expert analysis has declared that his supposed later works, including the Pastorals, were actually forgeries.[31] This fact is fairly transparent since the contents of the forgeries contradict what Paul was promoting in the earlier letters. But even that is not so clear cut, for the experts also conclude that even Paul's genuine letters have later insertions, alterations and cuts with the purpose of making them more acceptable to the Literalists.

All Paul's letters are preceded by prologues. Modern research has determined that seven of these prologues were of common origin, corresponding to the seven genuine letters, whereas the later forged letters were clumsily put together with prologues written in the fourth and fifth centuries CE. All the genuine letters were addressed to places that later become Marcionite–Gnostic centres. Marcion, the founder of this Gnostic sect, claimed to be the true heir to Paul and by the end of the second century, his was claimed to be the predominant church in Asia Minor.

Even the translations of his actual words have been made to disguise Paul's true allegiance and teachings. In the first letter to Corinthians "We speak wisdom amongst the perfected," does not sound quite right, nor does it really make sense. The true translation should have been "We speak Sophia among the initiated" which not only makes sense, but also belongs quite evidently to the Mysteries and to Gnostic Christianity. Paul's letters are littered with Gnostic terms, some obvious like "the Gnosis of God's Mystery" in Colossians 2:3. Many Greek words are wrongly translated, sometimes through ignorance of the true meaning of the words, sometimes intentionally to mislead.

Whole passages of teaching have taken on completely unintentional meanings and the result proffers a very different, very alien, religious teaching, one which misrepresents the Gnostic Christianity taught by Paul, in order to match the Literal Christianity taught by the Church of Rome. Paul never taught that people would be resurrected after death, with corpses revived with the Second Coming to be transcended to Heaven. This bizarre belief is still adhered to by large groups of intellectually-stunted Christians, who either lack imagination or wish to feed a ghoulish fantasy. Imagine the

---

[31] Lüdemann, G. *Heretics*

scene, thousands of millions of skeletons rising simultaneously from their graves; some still with dried or barely rotten flesh dropping off their bones, somehow digging themselves out of the ground and then what... shambling about all over the land, or perhaps standing to attention to await their heavenly transport? If these macabre deceased sect members were conscious of their resurrection, they would find themselves in a state of utter bewilderment, abject horror and self–loathing; their longed–for resurrection has the makings of a nightmare to disgust even Satan. Of course the whole notion is utter garbage. What Paul taught, was that resurrection was achieved amongst the living; the resurrection of the second coming would be spiritual.

Though expert analysis has exposed the truth about Paul's works, theologians and clergy ignore the factual evidence. They have absolutely no desire to consider what Paul had really been teaching, but prefer instead to propagate the great lie. When one analyses what Paul wrote about, the main thing which strikes the discerning eye, is that he gives absolutely no indication that Jesus had been a living historical man. What is obvious is that all the references indicate that he is referring to a mystical personification, the godman of the Mysteries. Paul was quite explicit about the scripture being myths; in 1 Corinthians 10:6, he states that the events are 'symbolic'; in Galatians 4:24, he describes the scripture stories as 'allegories'.

Paul's life supposedly overlapped that of Jesus and he was teaching at around the same time as the Apostles, so he would have been contemporary with all the alleged events and would have had some second–hand knowledge of them; Paul was supposedly converted by the spirit of Jesus and from that moment, he undertook to promote the teachings of his holy master. However, Paul gives no indication that he believes that Jesus had been a real man, he does not meet nor team up with any of the disciples, but goes it alone, which is a strange thing to do at any time, not least in a time of great difficulty for the fledgling religion when followers would be binding together. What Paul teaches never mentions the important events, people and places that were recounted in the gospels, all the significant alleged historical events are ignored. Paul's genuine writings and all his teachings, were done well before the gospels were written — he was in fact the first, the original — so since he does not mention anything of what the gospels recount, the conclusion to be drawn from this is that it never actually happened. This conclusion concurs with all the evidence that proves that the gospels are merely late variants on the godman Mystery story and not based upon historical events at all.

If Paul were teaching the Mysteries, having decided to promote the Jesus Mystery, as it was created by the Hellenised Jewish Gnostics, little wonder that the early Christians in Rome saw him as their great enemy who threatened their 'literalist' version of Christianity. There is only one passage in Paul's writings that gave any allusion to Jesus being a real person and this appeared in the Letter to Timothy, but this letter is one of the forged works. Theologians are forever deeply troubled by the fact that Paul seems to make no reference to the living Jesus, or to the stories recounted in the gospels and they wonder why, but they never allow themselves to progress to the obvious and inevitable conclusion — that there never was a Jesus.

But what of Paul's constant references to Christ? The Christ he was referring to was not Jesus, but the word 'Christ' represented the Consciousness. Paul says in his letter to the Colossians, that God gave him the mission of delivering the secret that has been hidden through long ages and many generations. The secret message he gives is 'Christ in you'. In other words, he was delivering the secret of the Mysteries, that within every one of us abides the Universal Soul, the Mind of the Creator. We are all part of the one and when a person inflicts harm upon another person, they are actually harming themselves; in Ephesians 4:25, Paul reveals — 'Let each of you speak the truth with your neighbour because we are parts of each other.'

Paul was relaying the eternal truth of the Mysteries, which taught that we needed to stop seeing ourselves as male or female, or as individuals ruled by the ego, as being separate, but that we were a combination of everything, because we were everything, because we are God.

THE GREATEST LIE EVER TOLD

Chapter 22

Pearls Before Swine

"Give not that which is holy unto the dogs, neither cast ye your pearls before swine, lest they trample them under their feet."

Matthew 7:6

When we read the Gospels we find them festooned with profound utterances from a man who is named as Jesus. We also know that the stories are fictitious and Jesus didn't exist, so if not from the mouth of Jesus from where did the pearls of wisdom come?

The words we read in a work of fiction are usually those of the author, but just as the narrator starts a children's story with *'Once Upon A Time ...'* then tells the familiar tale in their very own words, so the authors of the Gospels were retelling the Mystery story in their own words too. The initiates, from the time of Philo and the Therapeutæ early in the first century CE, were immersed in the Hellenised Dionysian version of the Mysteries, the Egyptian Osiris stories having been long-since abandoned. These contemporary Mystery stories were enriched with the moral and spiritual teachings of Greek philosophers who had been initiates of the Mystery religions. It had been a long-held premise of the Mystery schools that knowledge was useless when imparted to those incapable of understanding it. Matthew was giving a familiar Gnostic warning when he had Jesus speak the fate of pearls cast before swine.

Originally the Literalist Christians acknowledged that the New Testament had taken much from the Greek philosophers, but later, as they became more defensive and belligerent, their leaders, the so-called Church Fathers began to claim exclusive rights to all the teachings, no matter what their origins. These shameless men brazenly claimed, just like the Jewish scribes of the post Maccabean war had done, that the Greeks had plagiarised their philosophies from Moses. The words of Jesus, the Christians claimed, were the originals, they were unique, but this was far from the truth and virtually everything attributed to Jesus was stolen from Egypt then revised and expanded by the Greek philosophers. The New Testament had a little from Mesopotamia and India, the Greek philosophers, the Mysteries and the Gnostics too. Nothing in the New Testament was original.

In the previous chapter, we saw that the Ten Commandments were a simplified version of far more sophisticated Laws already in existence in both Egypt and Mesopotamia. The Psalms too were appropriated from Egyptian poetry and other religious texts.

Although in a different order, *Psalm 104* is similar to the *Hymn to Aten* found on the tomb of Queen Ty and attributed to Akhenaten[1]:

Hymn to Aten	Psalm 104
How manifold it is, what thou hast made!	*O LORD, how manifold are thy works! in wisdom hast thou made them all: the earth is full of thy riches.*
They are hidden from the face (of man). O sole god, like whom there is no other!	*Thou hidest thy face, they are troubled: thou takest away their breath, they die, and return to their dust.*
Thou didst create the world according to thy desire,	*Who laid the foundations of the earth, that it should not be removed for ever.*
	Thou coveredst it with the deep as with a garment: the waters stood above the mountains.
Whilst thou wert alone: All men, cattle, and wild beasts,	*He sendeth the springs into the valleys, which run among the hills.*
Whatever is on earth, going upon (its) feet,	*They give drink to every beast of the field: the wild asses quench their thirst.*
And what is on high, flying with its wings.	*By them shall the fowls of the heaven have their habitation, which sing among the branches.*

Most of us have heard or even sung Psalm 23. It begins 'The Lord is my shepherd' and later says 'Yea though I walk through the valley of the shadow of death, I will fear no evil; for thou art with me; thy rod and thy staff they comfort me'.

---

[1] Teeter, E & Brewer, D J. *Egypt and the Egyptians*

When we start to think about the words, the inclusion of the rod and the staff may seem a little curious; why should God need two staffs and this second staff that is designated as a rod, what is that for? It does not seem to make sense, until that is, one looks at Egyptian pictorial engravings and paintings, where both Osiris and the divine pharaohs are often depicted carrying two staffs. One is in the shape of the royal sceptre with an extra appendage of the life–giving ankh, but Osiris always carried the 'protecting' or 'comforting' shepherd's crook, hence giving us the source of *the Lord who is my shepherd.*[2]

In the Egyptian spiritual symbolic doctrine we also find the meaning of *the valley of the shadow of death*. The soul of the deceased is required to pass through lakes of fire in the *Duat*, or underworld, on its way to reuniting with God. If the deceased has been evil, he is burned in the lakes of fire and then buried in *Ått–Kek*, which Budge tells us translates as "Valley of the shadow".[3] In the Egyptian *Book of the Dead* it says: "Let the deceased who is united with Osiris, advance into the valley of the shadow".[4]

Psalm 23 is relaying the same information that we find in the Book of the Dead, but it is an abbreviated set of information:

> *The Lord's my shepherd, I'll not want.*
> *He makes me down to lie in pastures green; he leadeth me, the quiet waters by.*
> *My soul he doth restore again; and me to walk doth make within the paths of righteousness e'en for his own name's sake.*
> *Yea, though I walk in death's dark vale, yet will I fear no ill; for thou art with me; and thy rod and staff my comfort still.*
> *My table thou hast furnished in presence of my foes; my head thou dost with oil anoint, and my cup overflows.*
> *Goodness and mercy all my life shall surely follow me; and in God's house for ever more my dwelling place shall be.*[5]

When we consider the Festivals of Ancient Egypt, there is one that Psalm 23 describes very well.[6] The Beautiful Feast of the Desert Valleys celebrated the reunion between the living and the dead. It took place in the harvest season before the Nile flood. The worshippers followed in procession from Thebes to the Valley of the Kings. The procession was headed by the

---

[2] Newberry, PE. *The Journal of Egyptian Archaeology*
[3] Budge, EAW. *An Egyptian Hieroglyphic Dictionary Vol I*
[4] Budge, EAW. *The Book of the Dead*
[5] Rowe, F. *The Lord's My Shepherd, I'll Not Want*
[6] Seidel, M & Seidel AG. *Das Grab der Nacht: Kunst und Geschichte eines Beamtengrabes der 18. Dynastie in Theben-West*

Pharaoh who took the role of Osiris, the Good Shepherd with his shepherd's crook and flail, leading the participants as they followed the statue of Amen.

The people could rest in the green fields near the quiet waters of the Nile until they reached the place where they would reunite with their ancestors. They laid a great feast that lasted through the night and were anointed by their priests as they crossed the thin veil between the living and the dead where they would dwell forever in the house of the lord Amen.

Proverbs too was taken from Egypt, based on the Wisdom text known as the *Instructions of Amenemipet son of Kanakht*.[7] Budge documented parallels between these instructions and Proverbs, Psalms and Deuteronomy.[8]

> "The testimonies, directions for behaviour, and commandments mentioned in the above lines [the *Instructions of Amenemipet son of Kanakht*] are the equivalents of the testimonies, precepts, and righteous judgements spoken of by David in Psalm cxix, and the "instruction of wisdom, justice and judgement and equity," referred to by Solomon in *Proverbs*, Chap. I."

Many of the Biblical miracles are found in Egyptian texts and these were also attributed to the Greek sages. Jesus' first miracle of turning water into wine was also recorded at the wedding of Ariadne and Dionysus.[9] Asclepius, the teacher of Hippocrates, supposedly cured the sick and raised the dead. Celsus and Origen vied, in their writings, to promote their respective Pagan and Christian opinion about which of Asclepius or Jesus were the greater, though it now seems apparent that the name of Asclepius was changed to Jesus to create many New Testament stories.[10]

Jesus, the dying–resurrected son of God was nothing other than an ethnic version of the Egyptian–Osiris Mystery hero. There are hard historical facts to support this view, which explain why the events recounted in the Bible are *claimed* to be true and unique, then found in earlier texts from other countries and in particular from Egypt. Why did the Biblical scribes plagiarise on such a vast scale? The answer by now should be glaringly obvious.

The reason for myth becoming imagined history has its roots in the turmoil in Judea after the second–century BCE Maccabean revolt. The social unrest agitated by religious fanatics and nationalistic opportunists

---

7   Nicholson, P & Shaw, I. *The British Museum Dictionary of Ancient Egypt*
8   Budge, EAW. *Teaching of Amen-Em-Apt, Son of Kanekh*
9   Lietzmann, H. *The History of the Early Church Vol 3*
10 Angus, S *Mystery Religions*

continued well into the period when Judea was annexed by Rome in the vain hope of halting the civil unrest between orthodox and reformist Jews and restoring peace and sanity to the region. The unrest continued, now further provoked by the rebels' riling against the imperialist invaders.

The Maccabeans' ruthless refusal to tolerate alternative religious views made them opposed to most people who, as in present day Afghanistan and Iraq, would be happy just to have a safe and peaceful life. A minority was determined to set the country ablaze in order to maintain its power over and subjugation of the many. Away from the cities was *bandit country* where hoards of brigands attacked robbed and killed anybody and everybody and doubtless — as the few mindless Muslims do today — proclaiming that they were doing God's work! There were many psuedo–political bandits as well as genuine political agitators who claimed to be Messiahs and many used the name Joshua or Jesus to authenticate their pretence by association with the Exodus Joshua.

The contemporary Judean historian Josephus recorded the happenings of those awful times, complaining that Judea was full of brigands and miracle workers promising deliverance from Rome.[11] Great numbers of Jews who lived in the worst affected areas, especially in and around Jerusalem, fled the country, fearing that the fanatics would inflict a terrible apocalypse upon Judea. Large numbers went to Alexandria in Egypt; the Gnostic Jews living there generously gave financial assistance to resettle these refugees.

The unrest eventually erupted into open revolt against Rome in 66 CE, during the Judean governorship of Gessius Florus. After ineffective intervention by Cestius Gallus, the governor of Syria, the Emperor Nero decided to send General Vespasian to put an end to the problem. During the summers of 67 and 68 CE Vespasian quashed the revolt and captured all the Judean towns except Jerusalem.

In 68 CE, political strife broke out in Rome following the death of Nero. Various candidates struggled to gain power, which finally resulted in Galba's victory. Galba lasted just a year and the continuing chaos caused Vespasian to ignore the problems of Jerusalem and return home. Vespasian's popularity elevated him onto the vacant throne. Once the dust had settled in Rome, Vespasian passed the leadership of the army in Judea to his son Titus who then resumed the campaign against the Jerusalem rebels.

Quelling the revolt had caused all the hard core orthodox Jews to flee to Jerusalem, where they were determined, both men and women, to defend the city unto death. Estimates assume to 600,000 people, including refugee rebels from all over Judea, crammed inside the city walls. During the reign

---

[11] Josephus, F tr Whiston, W et al. *The Works of Flavius Josephus*

of Emperor Claudius, Jerusalem had *bought* permission to fortify the city. The lessons learnt from the fall of Jerusalem to Pompey highlighted the deficiencies in the city's defences and so this time Herod the Great hoped it would better withstand any future siege warfare. The resulting fortified Jerusalem had a complex of massive walls surrounding its hill top position, though insufficient to have daunted the Roman war-machine.

The besieged Jews were far from a *noble people defending themselves against the evil empire outside*. Inside, the city was defended by three independent rebel armies; each commanded by a religious zealot and each hating and killing each other's supporters. The outer perimeter walls were defended by forces led by a man called Simon; the inner city was defended by forces under the command of John; the smallest force, which held the Temple complex was under the control of Eleazar.

The three factions were bitter rivals and their behaviour and ambitions echoed that which ravaged the country during the Maccabean revolt and the subsequent Hasmonean dynasty. Whilst the Roman army stood off awaiting events in Rome, in Jerusalem the three sides fought and ambushed each other; and one of the first consequences of this lunacy was that great stocks of vital corn were destroyed. John then thought up a ruse to eliminate Eleazar. John sent some of his men to the Temple under the pretence of offering sacrifice, but instead they caught Eleazar unaware and he and his followers were slaughtered, gaining John control of the Temple Mount. It was only when Titus resumed the Roman offensive that the two remaining factions reluctantly ceased their own hostilities.

Eventually the Romans broke into the city. The defendants continued to fight in every street, alley and building with the inevitable consequence that both combatants and non-combatants were slaughtered in the mayhem. In the chaotic tumult, it would have been extremely difficult for Roman soldiers to distinguish bystanders from foes. Much of Jerusalem was destroyed, including the Temple and palace. Afterwards, orders came from Rome to empty the ruined city of its population and a prohibition prevented all Jews from entering the city's confines again.

During the campaign, many thousands of people were imprisoned and enslaved; the historian Josephus claimed that out of the Judean population of three million, one million were killed and some hundred thousand were taken as slaves.[12] Though these numbers cannot be assumed to be completely accurate, they at least indicate the scale of the tragedy. Of the slaves, some would have been insurgents or people with sympathetic affiliation to the rebels' cause, but there would have been many people who were simply unfortunate enough to have been in the wrong place at the

---

[12] ibid

wrong time. Rome was the final destination for most of the slaves, with a great many becoming servants in Roman families.

Amongst this mixed bag of unfortunate Jewish slaves, there would have inevitably been some — unlucky to have been caught up in the chaos — who followed the Jesus Mystery religion. Any of the higher initiates or masters of the inner Mysteries, would have been far removed from Jerusalem and the towns that had been strongholds of the fanatical Judaic fundamentalists, so it is highly unlikely they would have been enslaved. Indeed, contrary to romantic belief, not all Judea took part in this forlorn uprising; the Hellenised regions, such as Galilee, which had little to do with the Judaic–Temple cult of Jerusalem, had refused to come to Jerusalem's aid. Rome subsequently rewarded the Hellenised Galilean town of Sepphoris, by making it the political capital and financial centre of Judea. Of all the traditional Jewish sects, only the moderate and pro–Roman Pharisees were allowed to remain active; the rest, the anti–social zealots were outlawed.

To many Jews, the consequence of around two centuries of turmoil engendered by rival fanatical sects was disillusionment in the Judaic religion. Probably some of this was the harvest of seeds set long before. Their religion insisted that the Jewish race was special, it had an exclusive covenant with God... and yet it had been enslaved into exile by the Babylonians and ruled as vassals of the Persians. Its country then fell under the control of Greece and finally God had allowed its subjugation by Rome, with the subsequent destruction of the Temple and holy city.

The majority of Jews had never returned to their homeland, either because they had died as slaves, or because upon their release, they opted to remain in exile in the belief they were better off staying where they were than returning to the harsh and unstable life that Judea offered them. Many Jews had chosen to leave Judea voluntarily, in order to escape the chaos and the harsh impositions of the fundamentalists, and in a hope that they could continue practising a more moderate form of Judaism far away from the *land* that had failed to yield what once had been *promised*.

Many of those who had settled in eastern Mediterranean countries converted to the Gnostic Christian version of the Mysteries. Yahweh's time ran out when the Judean revolt resulted in disaster on a terrible scale. The Jews questioned how Yahweh could abandon his people yet again and allow the infidels to destroy his Holy of Holies. People felt betrayed and became understandably bitter. Jewish literature of the time reflected this bitterness — the prophet Baruch told the Judean priests to fling the keys of the sanctuary at the heavens and he angrily commanded Yahweh to guard his own house.[13]

> *"And ye priests, take ye the keys of the sanctuary,*
> *And cast them into the height of heaven,*
> *And give them to the Lord and say:*
> *'Guard Thine own house; for lo we are found unfaithful stewards.'"*

With these painful feelings of loss, abandonment and betrayal by Judaism and the Jewish god, the Jesus Mysteries would be an obvious sanctuary for the disconsolate Jew. Paul's esoteric mystical Jesus would have perhaps seemed too vague for those used to the rigid structure of Judean religious ritual and dogma. These sentiments probably incited some of the unenlightened and impatient new converts who had only been *outer* initiates of the Jesus Mysteries, to transform Jesus into something more. They made him into a Messiah who had not come merely to save their souls, but who had also come as physical saviour, a living prophet, a son of God, telling of better times to come — where Heaven would descend upon the earth.

The Christianity that we know today was born not in Judea, but in Rome, amongst those slaves who worked as servants to Roman families. These slaves had some semblance of their own family life, living within the families of wealthy Romans. They did not suffer the inhuman life style of the criminals who were galley and quarry slaves. Though deprived of their freedom, these slaves were still able to live a fairly normal life: they formed their own expatriate community and their own religious groups. As many Jews had felt betrayed by the their religion and Yahweh, so they turned their backs upon Judaism and looked to the Jesus Mysteries, which those unfortunate initiates who were enslaved along with the Judaic insurgents promoted.

These initiates had a problem, they were members of the *outer* Mysteries, the lower strata of followers who had been given the allegorical stories to reflect upon. They would not have been initiated into the higher level *inner* Mysteries, where they would have been told that the stories were no more than allegories and that to progress, they must abandon the Jesus myth in order to attain Gnosis of God. No-one was there to tell them that the Jesus story was fictitious, all the inner initiates, the teachers, the masters were out of reach, still resident in the eastern lands.

So the promoters of the new religion, out of a necessity imposed by their deprived circumstances, became the new teachers, even though they had little comprehension of the religion they followed. The understanding that Jesus was a mythological character quickly became lost, and suddenly the

---

[13] Charles, R. *Apocalypse of Baruch*

Messiah who had come to save all oppressed peoples was transformed into a real historical man.

The Jewish slaves in Rome had lost their freedom, their families, their homes, their possessions and their old religion because Yahweh had deserted them. They felt alienated and angry, but now at least they were given a new religion and a new hope ... their only hope ..., the salvation offered by Jesus. The allegorical stories of the mythical Jesus were now taken as the literal truth. When Gnostic teachers finally arrived from the east and realised the mistake being made by the Roman Christians, it was too late. The Jewish slaves did not want to hear the *truth* being promoted by these strangers, these freemen, they did not wish to be told that Jesus was not real, Jesus was all they had and they would not abandon their real living godman for some intellectual mystical concept.

What was even worse, the Gnostic teachers' proposal was neither unique nor Jewish. Their Mysteries appeared to be identical to the Mysteries followed by the Jews' Roman masters. As people will when they feel alienated and oppressed, they band tightly together and become hardened in their customs and beliefs. The Jewish slaves closed ranks and roughly rebuffed the strangers from the east who claimed to be Hierophants of the Jesus Mysteries.

As one might expect, these Jewish slaves became immersed in Roman life and customs. They and especially their off-spring, took on Roman ways and within a short time, effectively became Romans. The Roman notion of a structured organisation with centralisation and control influenced how these new Christians controlled their new church. They elected leaders whom they soon designated bishops.

These new leaders of the new church were not going to permit Gnostics missionaries intruding from the east to demote and belittle them. They reacted angrily against these missionaries, whom they considered to be perverting the truth of Jesus Christ and defended their new Faith by denouncing the Gnostic teachers *truths* to be not only heretical, but Satanically inspired.

It was not just the eastern Gnostic Christians who tried to enlighten these misguided Literalists to the truth. Initiates of the other Mystery sects — Dionysus, Bacchus, Mithras — all tried to persuade the Literalist Christians of the truth, but all found that their words fell on deaf ears. Tacitus and Pliny first recorded the Christian fanaticism and fifty years later around 170 CE, Celsus criticised their irrational beliefs.[14] By 270 CE the philosopher Porphyry was so disturbed by the absurdity and immorality of the doctrines

---

[14] Hoffmann, RJ. *Celsus on the True Doctrine*

that he wrote fifteen volumes of criticism.[15] The new *literalist* Christians of Rome would not listen to the truth from anyone. And so the madness was born; a madness that was to ravage the world for the next two thousand years.

---

[15] Wallis, RT. *Neoplatonism and Gnosticism*

Chapter 23

Tall Tales of Mystery Martyrs

"Religious persecution may shield itself under the guise of a mistaken and over-zealous piety."

Edmund Burke

Ever since the time of Socrates, philosophy and subversion have travelled hand in hand. During the late twentieth century in countries like China, Cambodia and Vietnam, intellectuals were persecuted. Wherever philosophy is seen as a threat to a dictator's power, or to the political stability of the state, ways are found to suppress the thinker. Rome was particularly sensitive to the threat that philosophy posed to its stability, so for almost two hundred years before the time of Jesus, there had been a love–hate relationship between the State of Rome and the Mystery teachings.[1] The Roman people felt excited by the originality of different cults, but the authorities felt nervous because the teaching promoted free thinking and liberalism — attributes which no state authority ever feels comfortable with.

The Christian Church has long promoted the notion that the early Christians were so passionately enamoured of their belief in Jesus, that if asked to renounce their Faith they would stoically go to their deaths instead. It tells us that Rome was the evil empire, intolerant of worship of gods other than those of its own pantheon: Jupiter, Saturn, Venus and Mars. It tells us that the Roman authorities outlawed Christianity and forced the poor beleaguered Christians to worship in secret in the catacombs beneath the city. It tells of the many thousands of Christian martyrs thrown to the lions and of whole cities of Christians being slaughtered.

Second-rate historians perpetuated this nonsense, passed it on to Hollywood and now it must be true because it's what the world believes.

---

[1] Gibbon, E. *The History of the Decline and Fall of the Roman Empire*

Many *credible* historians must also be held to account, for they did know the truth but chose various excuses to keep it hidden amongst themselves.

Just as the early Church concocted a New Testament from perverted Gnostic gospels — forging and altering letters by not only Paul, but its own bishops too — it also invented a glowing history for itself. Truth was irrelevant and the Church created a glorious beginning, telling of Peter's coming to Rome to found and lead the new religion and giving him a heroic death which suitably mimicked that of Jesus.

This Roman Catholic propaganda was cobbled onto the rest of the inventions in a much later age, when the Roman Empire was no more. It portrayed the first Christians as peaceful pacifists filled with the light of God, innocents who stood up for their Faith against the brutal state and went heroically to their noble martyrdoms.

Roman society was at times brutal — as were societies all around the world — and political prisoners and criminals did go to their deaths in the arenas. But there is no evidence that the Romans habitually rounded up every dissident and slaughtered him or her for fun and entertainment. This is another ill-informed myth.

Prior to the establishment of the Roman Empire, individual tribes — the Jews amongst them — fought and argued over whose god was the right one, and forced others to conform to their beliefs. The Romans by contrast, allowed religious tolerance, so that the Greek and Roman Pagan religions, Gnostic Mystery religions, Christianity and Judaism all had equal protection from the State of Rome. As long as the religion posed no threat to the state, had no intention of undermining it or being subversive in any way, then its followers were free to have their individual temples and conduct themselves as they pleased. Rome's only concern was to ensure the *loyalty* of all its citizens, throughout the empire. There may have been occasional demands to accept an emperor as divine, or offer sacrifice to a roman god, but this was the only religious expectation from a citizen of Rome and its Empire. There was no requirement to give up persuasions or practices or take up any alternative belief-system instead.

The authoritarian Roman regime did purge itself of those considered to be political dissidents, dangerous liberals and sometimes philosophers who were deemed subversive. Contrary to popular belief, the Mystery cults suffered from state persecution far more than Christianity ever did and this had happened in the early days of Rome, some two centuries before Christianity. By the start of the first century CE, the Romans had no reason to single out Christians for persecution, for the Mystery religions were commonplace in Rome and the Literalist Christians were regarded as just another sect, albeit a rather naïvely foolish and misguided one.[2]

The fear of imported religions was far greater in the pre–imperial days of the Republic. It had been perceived as a particular problem in 186 BCE, when the Rome authorities prohibited the cult of Dionysus, perhaps with reasonable concern and justification. The Mystery religions had often been introduced and were largely followed by slaves, who far outnumbered Roman citizens. There was a logical fear that these potentially–subversive religions might bring about the fall of Rome — given the rebellion of the slaves led by Spartacus in 73 BCE, this fear was not unfounded. Nevertheless, there were still many Romans who remained dedicated to the cult. The Mysteries owed much of its popularity to its promotion by Cicero, one of the Republic's great politicians and orators, who had been initiated at Eleusis in 80 BCE.[3]

It was not until the end of the Roman Republic, when Julius Caesar lifted the ban on the Mysteries, that these religious practices became accepted openly. No doubt this decision was made in order to curry political favour with the populace, who were enthusiastic followers of the Mysteries of Bacchus despite its illegality. At this time, many high-ranking Romans had also become followers: Mark Anthony was an initiate of Dionysus and Caesar's nephew, Octavian, who later became the Emperor Augustus and founded the Imperial Roman Empire after his uncle's assassination, was initiated at Eleusis.[4]

During the time of the Republic, when the Mysteries were deemed subversive and likely to cause an overthrow of the state, the authorities response was harsh — shrines were destroyed, followers of the cults were hounded and many thousands, who refused to give up their religion, were executed. A text known as *The Acts of the Pagan Martyrs,* recounted the integrity and stoic courage of the initiates of the Mysteries, who went unbowed to their deaths.[5]

There was a distinct difference between the attitude of pagan martyrs and those later Christians who actually *sought* martyrdom. To initiates of the Mysteries, if one had to meet one's death because of a refusal to abandon one's beliefs, one should accept one's fate whatever it be. The pagan initiates, however, considered that to *seek* martyrdom was not only foolish and futile, but an obscenity, especially if that person was deluded and

---

[2] Tacitus *The Annals of Imperial Rome*
[3] Rawson, E. *Cicero: A Portrait*
[4] Freke, T & Gandy, P. *The Jesus Mysteries*
[5] MacMullen, R. *Enemies of the Roman Order*

thought that martyrdom ensured his place in heaven. This reasoned attitude is in antithetical contrast to the early Literalist Christians, who had amongst their number, fringe groups of death-seeking fanatics who parallel the Islamic extremists of today. The Christian leaders provoked their members into believing that they were God's warriors and guaranteed that heaven would give them a special welcome. Bishop Cyprian illustrates this insane thinking in the third century CE in his glorification of these simple-minded psychoneurotics. He announced that the Lord would be "delighted at the spectacle of flowing blood which quenches the flames and fires of hell by its glorious gore."[6]

As with modern-day Muslim fanatics, the Christian leaders who urged martyrdom, usually avoided the fate themselves. Cyprian had stayed hidden during the persecutions under Emperor Decius, but later, during the reign of Valerian, was arrested, tried and beheaded, so he did eventually suffer a martyr's fate himself. Yet still there were but a few Christian martyrs. For the first two hundred years, there was no oppression or persecution of Christians, and any Christians who faced execution were individuals found guilty of specific capital crimes, just like any other Roman citizen. The crime perpetrated most frequently by Christians was a refusal to participate in the obligatory rituals that showed a citizen's loyalty to the Empire. Their punishment had nothing to do with eradicating Christianity.

That Christians were not 'persecuted' by the state, is indicated in correspondence between Pliny, as Governor of Bithynia-Pontus and the Emperor Trajan. During the very early years of Christianity, around 100 CE, the Jewish followers were causing a great deal of trouble with their violent riots. As a result, Trajan had outlawed the perverse and troublesome cult. Any Christian guilty of a seditious or violent offence was brought to trial, any peaceful Christian was left alone and the Emperor specifically instructs that this should be so. Pliny writes,

> "... I have never participated in trials of Christians. I therefore do not know what offences it is the practice to punish or investigate, and to what extent...."

to which Trajan replies,

> "... They are not to be sought out; if they are denounced and proved guilty, they are to be punished, with this reservation, that whoever denies that he is a Christian and really proves it — that is, by worshiping our gods— even though he was under suspicion in the past, shall obtain pardon through repentance. But anonymously posted accusations ought to have no place in any prosecution. For

---

[6] Lane-Fox, R. *Pagans and Christians*

this is both a dangerous kind of precedent and out of keeping with the spirit of our age."

As well as telling Pliny that Christians were not to be sought out and that he must reject anonymous accusations, Trajan later wrote to Pliny to instruct him that anyone making an accusation against a Christian must pay the prosecution costs and the accused Christian must be afforded a proper trial.[7]

This benign tolerance and adherence to the law is further evidenced by the edicts of the Emperors Hadrian and Antoninus Pius who, as Edward Gibbon wrote, "expressly declared that the voice of the multitude should never be admitted as legal evidence to convict or punish those unfortunate persons who had embraced the enthusiasm of Christianity."[8]

This hardly equates to the popular view of the cruel injustice meted out by the Romans. The reality was that the Romans merely thought that most Christians were deluded simpletons. Gibbon also concludes that the fourth and fifth-century church historians based the tales of persecution and martyrdom on their own mindless zeal, assuming that the Romans must have had the same barbaric lust that they themselves were keen to demonstrate to religious dissenters.

Most Christians complied with the modest requirement of the law, however there were some hard-line Christians who refused to undertake the ritual of making a sacrifice to pledge loyalty, but even then Gibbon tells us, the authorities sought to find loopholes that gave a way around the problem.

If a prosecution did take place, punishment was not an inevitable consequence of conviction. Christians were given a choice of keeping their life or choosing death as an enemy of the state. Magistrates even suggesting that if the religion forbade the eating of sacrificial meat, then instead they could offer a few grains of incense upon the altar. Amongst the Romans, it was deemed the duty of a humane judge to endeavour to reclaim, rather than to punish any deluded Christian. Lane–Fox mentions several provincial governors' attempts to reduce the demand for martyrdom. One governor is recorded as pleading with a group of Christians who seemed determined on death, to take a few days to think it over; reminding them of the beauty of life and entreating them to show compassion to themselves, their families and friends.[9]

---

[7] ibid.
[8] Gibbon, E. *The History of the Decline and Fall of the Roman Empire*
[9] op. cit. Freke, T & Gandy, P.

The law was enacted with a civilised decency rarely seen today — if a charge was brought against a Christian, the prosecutor informed the accused party of the charge and he was allowed a convenient amount of time to settle his domestic affairs before presenting himself to the magistrates to answer the charge. This also allowed a good amount of time for the accused to flee should they so choose. These actions clearly showed that those in charge were not too concerned about the religion. There was no law that demanded the arrest or slaughter of a Christian. Christians could evade making a sacrifice of meat, by offering incense but in some provinces governors went so far as to sell under the counter the certificate that showed that the accused had complied with the law and given an appropriate sacrifice of allegiance.

There were three periods when Christians were actively punished if they refused to make sacrifices: under Emperor Decius from 250–1 CE, from 257–9 under Valerian and the so-called *Great Persecution of Diocletian* which lasted from 303–5. The total time was five years.[10] Most Christians made the required sacrifice of incense rather than face a pointless punishment. After these brief periods of oppression were over, the Christians returned to their reinstated churches. Origen who himself was tortured under the Diocletian persecution, wrote about the small number of Christians who died. The numbers recorded in the vast city of Alexandria were ten men and seven women.[11]

Hard-line Christian leaders had wanted martyrs and Tertullian, at the end of the second century CE wrote a fanatical treatise against the *slackers*, ranting that they were criminals who were in denial of God, by fleeing from execution; the more martyrs there are, the more the church will flourish *"Semen est sanguis Christianorum"* — the blood of the Christians [martyrs] is seed — he wrote.[12] Ten years later Tertullian had changed his mind; he left the Roman Church and became a Gnostic.

None of the recorded facts fit the stereotypical picture of cruel Romans soldiers brutally rounding up every Christian that they could find to cast them into filthy cells before throwing them to the lions. Though the Roman populace did have a perverse enjoyment of blood games, the intellectuals and the higher classes of Roman society in general, strongly disapproved of it; Roman law was on the whole just and often compassionate. The death penalty was not common even for convicted Christian dissidents and most were exiled, imprisoned or put to work in the mines. During the *persecutions*, magistrates often gave a sentence that could later be rescinded and the

---

[10] ibid.
[11] op. cit. Gibbon, E.
[12] Tertullian *Apologeticum, 50*

convicted person pardoned, because the judges trusted that the current regime would soon change and that the sentences would consequently be overturned.

Though Emperor Domitian, who ruled from 81 CE, was described as a despot and persecutor of Jews and Christians, by Eusebius in the fourth century, Brian Jones, Reader in Classics and Ancient History at Queensland University has studied all the surviving sources and believes that evidence for his reputation is none existent.[13] The likelihood of his finding any Christians to persecute eleven years after the fall of Jerusalem is quite remote, there were too few for any Roman writer at the time to mention, but there were some Jewish troublemakers, who were severely dealt with.

Gibbon too wrote of Domitian, that "his persecution — if it deserves that epithet — was of no long duration" and that after Domitian's death, the emperor was condemned by the senate, who rescinded all the acts he had introduced relating to alleged *religious persecution*; recalled exiles; restored rank and lost fortunes to innocent people and pardoned, or at least did not punish the guilty. So again we find more evidence that to the Romans justice was deemed important and when there was a blip and justice had not been done, it was soon afterwards restored.

The martyrdom of Cyprian, Bishop of Cathage, two hundred years on, throws a revealing light on how Christians were treated. Having survived the persecutions under Decius, in the time of Valerian, Cyprian refused to honour the official Roman deity. He was arrested and taken into custody, but his jail was not a prison cell, he was taken to the home of one of his arresting Roman officers, who dined and entertained the bishop and allowed him visitors from his church. Following Cyprian's continued refusal to make sacrifice, the authorities felt duty-bound to make an example of this leader of the volatile dissidents, who at that time were disrupting the city and endangering imperial security. The magistrates decided to subject him to beheading, the quickest and most humane execution rather than opting for one of the more painful or demeaning methods available to them. After his death, they allowed the Christians to give their bishop an appropriate and respectful public funeral.

Death sentences were rare and only pronounced on the most influential and truculent zealots. Groups of extreme fanatics arose from time to time and these madmen actively sought an imagined glory from martyrdom. Antoninus was a popular governor of Asia, known for his compassion and integrity, he was highly thought of in the Senate in Rome too. As pro-consul, he was confronted by a group of fanatical Christians, who pleaded that he should put them to death. Disgusted by their suggestion, Antoninus

---

[13] Jones, BW. *The Emperor Domitian*

refused and told them "Unhappy men! Unhappy men! if you are thus weary of your lives, is it so difficult for you to find ropes and precipices?"[14]

The popular picture we are given is of the Christians being persecuted and killed from shortly after the death of Jesus. Tradition states that Peter was crucified in Rome and some even give the same fate to Paul. Both are utter nonsense. As we have seen, Peter was a fictional character and it was impossible for Christians who believed in the literal story of Jesus to have been in Rome at such an early date. The Jews were not enslaved until after 70 CE and their arrival in Rome was forty years after the 'death of Christ,' when Peter, had he ever been alive, would have been over seventy.

It is sometimes said that the Emperor Nero blamed the burning of Rome upon the Christians and then took reprisals against them. During Nero's reign, there were no religious persecutions and the notion that there were persecuted *Christians,* comes from Tacitus' historical works. Tacitus wrote well after the alleged events and relied entirely on second or third-hand accounts, which were unreliable. The people whom Nero chose to blame — either justly or unjustly, for we can never know — were the Jews. There is certainly evidence for some justification of this allegation, since during that particular period, there was a great deal of violent disturbance caused by Jewish troublemakers who were emulating the rebellious behaviour of their zealot brethren in Judea. The idea that it was Christians derives from a mistaken assumption. During the time when Tacitus was writing, the majority of the Jews in Rome were exiled slaves from Judea and many of these, feeling disillusioned with Judaism, had become converts to the Jesus cult.

It was not until 250 CE, as a consequence of a plague that swept through the Mediterranean world and almost caused the collapse of the Empire, that the so-called *persecutions* started. The irascible Christians were certainly not liked, though they were pitied as misguided fools and sometimes also reviled. They had never been persecuted for their religious *beliefs,* despite the fact that groups of Christian zealots, occasionally given to troublemaking, sometimes caused violent disturbances. With a plague ravaging the Empire, the Emperor Decius ordered sacrifices to be made to ensure its safety. Those who complied received a certificate of confirmation; those who refused suffered the official punishment for not obeying the law.

A few prominent Christians refused to comply and were killed, including Pope Fabian, but it was far from *a majority* who stood against this decree.[15] To call this a persecution however, is ludicrous. A law was passed, which all the people within the empire must obey. Just as today, even if one disagrees,

---

[14] op. cit. Gibbon, E.

[15] Scarre, C. *Chronicle of the Roman Emperors*

one must obey all laws passed by our government or suffer penalties. Sikhs, asked to put their Kirpan in their luggage for airline safety, do not say that they are being persecuted. No-one is allowed to wear a dagger on a plane, the law applies to everyone. Decius' decree applied to all people of all religious persuasions; the Christians were not singled out or specifically targeted. His successor Valerian reintroduced the edicts when plague threatened the empire again a few years later, leading to the death of Cyprian as we have read.

The third and final occasion developed into a more direct confrontation with Christianity. Emperor Diocletian's reign saw the empire ravaged by another plague, so he called upon his army to give a sacrifice to appease the gods. Within the army there was a sizable minority of Christian soldiers and many of them refused to comply. This infuriated the desperate emperor and he demanded that disobedient troops be executed. The opposition posed by some Christian leaders provoked further reprisals, which included the closing down of churches. Imperial rage then went further, though remaining within the law it gave no compassion and Christians refusing to give sacrifice were arrested and executed. Because the early Church had nurtured numerous single-minded zealots amongst their number, many of these were delighted to seek the special position in Heaven they had been promised; no doubt realising the error of their ways when they made the posthumous discovery that they had missed their destination and disembarked the earthly plane before the heavenly stop.

The Christian myth implies that there was a single on-going, long-term persecution, in which thousands of innocent Christians were put to death. The truth is very different. In summary: the first officially sanctioned so-called *persecution* of Decius in 250 CE, lasted for just one year; the second *persecution* ordered by Emperor Valerian in 257 CE lasted two years; the third and final *persecution* occurred in 303 CE, under Emperor Diocletian and also lasted two years.

There is a discrepancy between the historical fact and the wild historical fantasy propagated by the Church. Some Christians were prosecuted by the Roman authorities over their refusal to adhere to the law, mainly in 303–305 CE, some died, but not in their thousands. The relevant edicts that required sacrifice to the Divine Emperor were effected on three separate occasions and the combined length of time they were part of Roman Law was five years.

When Gibbon discusses the allegations of Emperor Domitian's persecutions he states that the problems attributed to the emperor did not even deserve to be called persecution. I totally agree with Gibbon's assessment — the word persecution is not only inappropriate because it is subjective, but it is also inappropriate because it is particularly emotive. The word is systematically employed when attempting to take the moral high ground and so it has to be regarded with some suspicion in exactly the same way as one judges the choice of the words *terrorist* and *freedom fighter*. The winners always get to write the history and in the case of the Christians, they cunningly chose the most moving and powerful language to describe their deceitful fabrications.

Rome had no problem with Christianity in itself, even in the *persecution* years, the only problem was with followers who refused to give their allegiance to the state; since everyone had the choice, those who refused courted punishment. To the Gnostics, these zealous Christians were misguided fools as they said they were dying for Christ, whilst remaining in total ignorance of what Christ actually was. Worse still, these ignorant Christians could not go to heaven, for they had not received Gnosis to know the secret of God.

So how many Christians were killed during these *persecutions*? Well the number can never be known, but considering that they only lasted for five years out of a period of 250, and that only the more hard-headed fanatics would have refused to make a token sacrifice, the numbers could not have been great. The Church propagandists make out that the tally was huge — many tens of thousands — but Gibbon gives a more realistic number of two thousand, however even this is likely to be an over-estimate. I suspect that many of those prosecuted would have been sentenced to work in the quarries and others places: to the practical and commercially minded Romans, labourers had greater value than corpses. Even Eusebius, the early Church propagandist, can only find nine bishops who were executed. Eusebius records ninety-two Christians who were martyred in Palestine during the whole period of *persecution*.[16] This is not quite what we have been led to believe. We have been duped by the Church's propaganda into believing the kind of nonsense attributed to the ninth century scholar Anastasius Bibliothecarius, who claimed that ten thousand Christians were crucified on Mount Ararat.

The widely-held pagan opinion of the time was that the martyrs were just small groups of extreme fanatics seeking to imitate death in honour of their religion's leader Jesus. In contrast, Tertullian's typically-exaggerated account of the pro-consul Antoninus' visit to an assize court in 185 CE, in which he claims that the whole town came forward demanding the privilege of death, is another example of his wicked perversion, which the Church held up in glorious tribute to its members. Christian historical accounts simply cannot be trusted. Gibbon reveals that Eusebius himself indirectly

---

[16] Eusebius *History of the Church*

confesses that he has related whatever might rebound to the glory of Christianity and suppressed all that could disgrace it.

The facts remain, and indicate that there were a few genuine Christian martyrs whose numbers were swelled by lunatic zealots deliberately seeking a glorious death. The aggregate of what the Christian Church promotes is a self–glorying fiction. Perversely, many of their stories of martyrs were rewritten accounts of actual Dionysian martyrs who suffered persecution and death during the early years of the Roman Republic, or even worse, later Gnostics murdered by Christian fanatics.

Besides the fabricated numbers of those who died, so too the manner of their deaths was an invention. The type of tortures that the martyrs supposedly endured were not Roman, but the ones later devised by inventive Christian psychopaths of early Mediæval times. As Gibbon observed:

> "Monks of succeeding ages, in their peaceful solitudes, entertained themselves with diversifying the deaths and sufferings of the early martyrs, have frequently invented torments of a much more refined and ingenious nature."

One of the favourite themes of these perverted fantasists was of comely virtuous Christian virgins, who having refused to give up their faith, were then encouraged to change their minds by repeated rape by virile young Romans until they relented — which of course they never did — instead, the nubile young women chose to endure the torment until they expired. Such obscene sexual fantasies are recorded in *Acta Sincera Martyrum*.[17]

In Jerome's *Legend of Paul the Hermit,* he writes

> "Another [martyr] who was in the bloom of youth was taken by his command to some delightful pleasure gardens, and there amid white lilies and blushing roses, close by a gently murmuring stream, while overhead the soft whisper of the wind played among the leaves of the trees, was laid upon a deep luxurious feather–bed, bound with fetters of sweet garlands to prevent his escape. When all had withdrawn from him a harlot of great beauty drew near and began with voluptuous embrace to throw her arms around his neck…" [18]

The youth, it transpires bit off his tongue to avoid the attentions of the harlot. Clearly, these are the fantasies of sexually deprived males, but

---

[17] op. cit. Gibbon, E.
[18] Schaff, P *Nicene and Post-Nicene Fathers... Jerome...*

unfortunately many of them plummet into the deepest pits of depravity when their sick minds gloriously wallow in diabolically inventive tortures and bloody gore.

Even had there been a prolonged and intensive persecution, the numbers of Christians who were actually killed could only have been small because the numbers of early Christians was small. Of course Christian propaganda tells a different story. The typical picture is of Christianity spreading at a very rapid rate across the civilised world, but this is a lie for up to 250 CE, there were virtually no references to Christians in writings. Gibbon tells us that Tertullian remarkably made the claim that by the end of the second century "nearly all the citizens in all the cities are Christians," and that "Christianity had penetrated into parts of Britain inaccessible to the Roman arms." Such statements are just more outrageous lies and the religion that became wide spread throughout the Roman Empire was Mithraism, not Christianity.

About a hundred years before Tertullian, Justin Martyr had proclaimed:

> "There exists not a people, whether Greek or barbarian, or any other race of man, among whom prayers are not offered up in the name of a crucified Jesus to the Father and Creator of all things."

Gibbon wryly observes, that according to the primitive Christian fathers, Christianity had, within a century of the death of Jesus, already spread to every part of the globe. Clearly, the claim was ridiculous, but what is lamentable is that in the modern Church, many theologians and some pathetically awful historians still give credence to the accounts given by these wild fantasists and liars. On the other hand, reputable scholars have estimated that around the mid–third century CE, about two percent of the Empire's population might have been Christian, but at that time the majority would still have been Gnostic Christians, not the Literalist Christians of the Church of Rome.[19]

The growth of Literalist Christianity during the first three–hundred years of the first millennium would not have been particularly notable, for at that time all the Mystery religions were experiencing a surge in popularity, but especially those of Dionysus and Mithras. Once Julius Caesar had lifted the restrictions placed upon the Mysteries in Rome, they became socially acceptable and attracted all classes, including the ruling one. The popularity of the Mysteries is reflected in the religious inclinations of the emperors: Augustus was an initiate of Dionysus; Claudius of Attis; Vespasian of Serapis; Domitian of Osiris; Commodus turned to Mithras and the

---

[19] op. cit. Lane-Fox, R.

emperors that followed attempted to make Mithraism the official imperial religion and it did indeed become so in 304 CE — just seventeen years before it was replaced by Christianity.

Even Christian scholars accept that during the early centuries, the cult of Mithras seriously rivalled that of Christianity. In truth, across the whole empire, Mithraism was far more popular than Christianity, which was an extremely minor and very idiosyncratic Mystery cult, in danger of withering away. To disguise the true facts concerning its unremarkable beginnings, the Church Fathers undertook the construction of an utterly outrageous and totally false history for Christianity and the Church of Rome — its unstoppable widespread popularity, its persecutions by pagan Roman emperors, its multitude of saintly martyrs were all shameless fabrications. A tall tale told by those who created a history many years after its time.

THE GREATEST LIE EVER TOLD

Chapter 24

Buy Me a Bishop

> "All religion, my friend, is simply evolved out of fraud, fear, greed, imagination, and poetry."
>
> Edgar Allan Poe

The term *orthodox* Christianity did not come into use until after the Literalist schism, when Christianity became the official religion of Imperial Rome three hundred years after its invention. Christianity, this small and insignificant sect was thrust into a position of power to serve the purpose of a shrewd Roman emperor. The Church then used its newly-acquired position and authority to designate its peculiar beliefs as orthodox. In reality, the true *orthodox* Christians were the much older and more widely accepted Gnostics, not the Literalist upstarts who preached a misguided perversion and remained largely isolated in Rome.

A parting of the ways between the two factions of Christianity was inevitable since the Literalist Christians *believed* that their myth recounted true history and the Gnostic Christians *knew* that it didn't; not only that but the latter knew what the Jesus myth was meant to convey. They were named the Gnostic Christians because *gnostic* means *knower*. Gnostics knew the truth. The Literalist Christians refused to accept it. For them, Faith was at the core of their belief — not faith in God, but faith in the Church. The Church leaders decreed that their followers must have blind absolute Faith and never question what they were told. To Gnostics, this was anathema; this was the doctrine of control and enslavement. Faith to the Gnostics was only the *first step* along the path to finding Truth and achieving Gnosis.

Gnostic initiates were encouraged to question in order to acquire knowledge and to seek truth. Those who did not question would remain outer initiates of the Mysteries and those who questioned well would encounter the inner teachings and ultimately know the Truth of God through their experience. Opposing this *gnostic* teaching were *literalist* Christians whom we still find today, choosing to believe in every word of their dying–resurrecting godman story. The Literalist Christian sect could not allow open discussion and questioning since this would inevitably reveal the structural weaknesses of its Church, so the leaders demanded blind unquestioning obedience and belief from their followers and dealt severely with those who stepped out of line.

The sad truth is that the literalists purged themselves of liberals, intellectuals and philosophers: the type of thinking people who might undermine their doctrine and their leaders' absolute authority. In effect, bishops became demi–dictators ruling their flocks, not with a shepherd's crook but with a rod of iron. Their behaviour equalled that of those modern–day Muslim Mullahs who brutally enforce absolute allegiance to their own Faith. 'We say how it is and shall be and inquisitive questioning minds are not tolerated, for they do the devil's work.' Thus the Roman Church Leaders achieved absolute control and of course in Rome, where the skills of controlling a large population were constantly honed, it was not long before the political advantage of having such command over people was spotted by another astute dictator — the leader of the failing Roman Empire.

Their shared origin enabled the two Christian factions to maintain a fragile link for quite some time, but their fundamental difference in belief provoked ongoing bitter disputes. The Literalists despised the Gnostics for sharing so much with the pagan Mystery cults. Because they did not understand, nor wish to understand, they sought to demonise the Gnostics, insisting that they had fallen under Satan's beguiling influence. Gibbon observed that Christians considered Pagans to be demon worshippers and they would therefore not deserve, nor could they expect, any pardon from an angry God. He goes on to reflect

> "These rigid sentiments, which had been unknown to the ancient world, appear to have infused a spirit of bitterness into a system of love and harmony. The ties of blood and friendship were frequently torn asunder by the difference of religious faith…"

and furthermore, that the Christians were

> "seduced by resentment and spiritual pride to delight in the prospect of their future triumph."[1]

In the ancient world, though there were political and economic wars, there was no religious conflict. The world, prior to the coming of the Literalist

---

[1] Gibbon, E. *The History of the Decline and Fall of the Roman Empire*

Christians, was an age of religious *laissez–faire*. Provided that their followers did not promote political sedition, there was a general, tolerant, relaxed acceptance of other religions and practices. There was no *them* and *us*, no *demonising* of alternative deities — until the Literalist Christians arrived on the scene and the world changed for the worse.

The attacks launched by Christians were not just against pagans, but were also aimed at other Christian sects. Because their religious beliefs held only half–baked notions of what Christianity was, each Christian sect had its own ideas and none of them exactly matched any of the others. Additionally, the leaders of each group were in a constant struggle to convince others of their superiority, thus meriting overall leadership. Celsus observed

> "Christians utterly detest each other. They slander each other constantly with violent forms of abuse and cannot come to any sort of agreement in their teaching."[2]

Unwisely, and ultimately unfortunately, the Gnostics shrugged their collective shoulders and dismissed the literalist sects as a small disparate group of misguided children who would one day see the error of their ways, see sense and return to the truth. Over time, the Gnostic masters gradually woke up to the problem of the wayward sect in Rome as it slowly gathered converts with its misguided teaching. The Literalists had no–one who had greater spiritual knowledge than anyone else. None of them had studied for long enough or widely enough to become an inner initiate and all that they had been taught and all they could teach, were the basic outlines of the Jesus story. The self–appointed leaders of this schismatic sect arose from the ranks of the egotists, the ambitious and those naturally inclined to be zealots. They gave themselves the title of bishop and taught that everyone who believed would be saved and receive eternal salvation. That was basically all their religion could offer… believe and have faith; there was no philosophical teaching, no sacred revelations, no ecstatic experience of the spirit of God… and there was no questioning, no gaining knowledge, no self–discovery. In far later times, when Bibles had been written and circulated, this prohibition on questioning was tightened by the Roman Catholic Church, who forbade all but the clergy from owning, let alone reading the Bible. On pain of death, the Bible's inconsistencies and nonsense had to remain concealed.

By the time the Gnostics had woken up to the problem and sent their masters to Rome to rectify the situation, the literalist sects had become so

---

[2] Hoffmann, RJ. *Celsus on the True Doctrine*

self–protective and antagonistic as to rebuff most aggressively those sent to help. The self–appointed bishops took offence at the Gnostic teachers. The Gnostics tried to explain to the Literalists that they were uninitiated *psychics,* those who *understood* nothing of the Mysteries and desperately needed teaching how to gain enlightenment so that they could then become *pneumatics* and find Gnosis of the secret inner Mystery of God.

In retaliation, the Literalists accused the Gnostic masters of perverting the sacred scriptures by pretending to be in possession of the real knowledge of God and accused them of heresy.[3] The rebuff also became violent, so fearing for their safety, the Gnostic masters abandoned their mission to end the nonsense and returned home.

Having effectively cut itself off from its roots, the *literalist* sect was free to pursue whatever course it wished to follow. This allowed the loudmouthed fanatical preachers to gain the ear of the lowly, disaffected, uneducated and gullible, and gradually they built up a small, but dedicated, even zealous following. But the process was slow and certainly not the dramatic unstoppable surge recounted in the Church's version of history. In 250 CE, this isolated little sect of *cranks* was so small that Christianity of both Literal and Gnostic versions, was rarely mentioned in contemporary writings.[4]

The Christian communities would have been tiny and the title bishop referred merely to an overseer, so the bishop may have been leading a church of just a few dozen followers. Christians had not spread throughout the world awaiting rightful recognition by their Imperial masters any more than today the Plymouth Brethren could claim to be the most populous Christian sect world–wide, or that they represent Christian orthodoxy, or that they deserve the right to become predominant. Christianity finally flourished due to sheer chance — and the world still suffers from that fluke of fate.

Exasperation is probably the best word to describe how the initiates of the Mystery cults felt about the *literalists*. The literalist Christians claimed exclusive rights to God, alleging God despised all other religions. They asserted that their religion was inimitable, that uniquely their Son–of–God was born of a virgin, performed miracles, was unjustly killed, but resurrected back to life.... They laid claim to all philosophical teachings, and whilst being forced to admit that the Greek philosophers long ago said the same things, they countered the accusation by accusing the Greeks in turn — of retrospective plagiarism, with the Devil's cunning connivance. Satan, knowing what Jesus was going to do and preach, shared out all this information amongst the wicked pagans centuries before the advent of his

---

3   Pagels, E. *The Gnostic Gospels*
4   Lane-Fox, R. *Pagans and Christians*

rival. Every charge the critics brought against the *literalists* was countered by angry excuses whose banality knew no bounds. No matter how ridiculous, or blatantly untruthful, anything that the *literalists* said came to be accepted amongst them as the *gospel truth*. Naturally, this mindless acceptance within their own ranks merely encouraged further lies and deceits as time went on.[5]

As the Christian Church gained more followers amongst the uneducated classes, it became more vocal and more people began to take notice of this quirky sect. Self control was deemed a desirable attribute amongst Romans, so many of them found the Christian fanatics, with their loudmouthed enthusiasm, emotional public outbursts and haranguing of non–Christians whilst simultaneously talking nonsense, deeply upsetting. Whenever they were challenged to account for their beliefs, they would merely answer by repeating the well–worn mantra that it was wrong to question and that one should just have total faith. Needless to say, their moronic responses only fostered further derision and vilification. Celsus complained

> "Taking its roots in the lower classes, the religion continues to spread among the vulgar; nay one can even say it spreads because of its vulgarity, and the illiteracy of its adherents."[6]

The distaste for Christianity was heightened by its being riddled with corruption. Many Christian leaders had attained their positions by self–promotion and bribery. In 260 CE a wealthy woman bought the position of Bishop of Cathage (then a Roman city, now in present day Tunis) for one of her servants. Clearly, a good position within the Church was considered not only lucrative, but it granted one an opportunity to be heard. The woman, frustrated by Rome's political prohibitions on her sex, saw a way to wield influence and at the same time increase her wealth.[7]

Within every society, there are those who see ways to turn a profit from any situation. The Christians' enthusiastic evangelism amongst the illiterate masses and their inveigling of unquestioning fools, gave their church the perfect opportunity to exploit the vulnerable. Milking a gullible flock, which knew never to question its leaders and was in fear of eternal damnation if it transgressed, enabled the confidence tricksters to create their own very comfortable paradise on earth. They always found reasons for raising money — new churches and their upkeep, ritual ornaments and vestments

---

5   Justin Martyr *First Apology* in Bullock KO.
6   op. cit. Hoffmann, RJ.
7   op. cit. Gibbon, E.

to give dignity to both the church and their priests and of course, ultimately just to glorify God.

From the middle of the second century CE rival *literalist* groups competed with one another and with the existing temples of the older Mystery cults. *Grandeur*, both to elevate their standing and impress new converts, was imperative, whilst spirituality was never considered. Drawing rich converts — gullible *nouveau–riche* merchants with little education — into the flock was naturally a priority. Such converts could frequently be persuaded to donate generously to the church, thus ensuring the donor an easy passage into Heaven on their death.

Many converts played a tactical game, making a donation to preserve their souls from damnation whilst continuing their association with some other religion — it was quite common for people to play safe and have a foot in both camps. The pursuit of money quickly became the main interest of many church leaders and this kind of shameful irreligious practice was widespread. In time, this practice of attaining wealth would eventually make Christian bishops amongst the richest people in Europe and the Catholic Church became the owner of vast wealth and huge tracts of land. Even the more intelligent Christians — as few as they were — had to admit that their religion was polluted by corruption. People saw Christianity as an easy way of making money, and this is sad in itself, but what is unpalatable, is that these early Christian leaders are lauded as being especially pious, even saintly people. The satirist, Lucian, mocked the Christian Church for swindling money from its gullible followers:

> "If a professional sharper who knows how to capitalise on a situation gets amongst them, he makes himself a millionaire overnight, laughing up his sleeve at the simpletons."[8]

By their actions as well as their foolish belief that the godman had been real, the Christians made themselves pariahs amongst thinking people. That ever–vigilant commentator Celsus described the Christians as

> "A people who had cut themselves off from civilisation."[9]

During these early centuries, a significant number of notable *literalist* Christians, people who had gained a reputation as Gnostic critics, actually turned to Gnosticism. Tertullian, who became a *literalist* Christian in 195 CE, was both a zealous heretic–hunter and writer of anti–Gnostic tracts but

---

[8] Freke, T & Gandy, P. *The Jesus Mysteries*
[9] op. cit. Hoffmann, RJ.

in 207 CE he converted to Gnosticism. Then and even now, the Church cites him as one of its own, but fails to mention that he eventually saw the light and deserted its cause. Many other important early *orthodox* Christians were actually Gnostics, but the Church deceitfully made out that they were committed to its cause.

Saint Anthony, the ascetic recluse and visionary, who is famed for setting up the very first Christian monastery, sited in Upper Egypt, in 305 CE was a Pythagorean. This almost certainly means he was a Gnostic and thus damned as a heretic, since the literalist Christians damned all Greek philosophers as such.[10]

The Catholic Church beatified Clement of Alexandria as a great orthodox Christian. He was born in Athens and educated in Alexandria, which alone suggests he might have been Gnostic and his written works are distinctly Gnostic in content.

Pachomius was supposedly an orthodox Christian but in the fourth century CE he had founded the monastery at Nag Hammadi in Upper Egypt. His monastery was the site where the Gnostic gospels were hidden from Christian heretic–hunters, which should be sufficient to indicate that Pachomius and his monks were Gnostics. Further indication of Pachomius' Gnosticism can be inferred from the knowledge that he had to submit to investigation for heresy.

Origen is considered to be another orthodox Christian. In Alexandria, he studied Pagan and Greek philosophy then later studied under Clement. His works have been claimed to be Christian, though in the fifth century the Catholic Church posthumously declared him a heretic. His works are distinctly Gnostic in tone.

These examples give some idea of the distortions perpetrated by the Church propagandists. On the superficial level of the Jesus story, there is little to differentiate between the literalist Church and the Gnostics. The differences in doctrine would be difficult for those with only the outer initiates' teaching to discern. Literalist Christians did not have educated men amongst their numbers, whereas anyone who had a good education would have attended one of the academies that taught Greek philosophy and sciences and would therefore have been immersed in the Mysteries. Once enlightened, it is extremely unlikely that an intelligent person would abandon all that they have learnt and take the illogical and retrograde step of converting to the nonsense of literalist Christianity. To do so would negate the spiritual teachings they had absorbed.

However, despite that, there is always the one exception that can be found. Bishop Eusebius was educated at the academy founded by Origen in

---

[10] Lietzmann, H. *The History of the Early Church*

Caesaria, then made bishop of that city. Eusebius was a follower of the heretical Arian doctrine and as its delegate, attended the Council of Nicæa in 325 CE to argue its cause. Though the argument was lost and its leader, Arius banished, the heretic Eusebius somehow emerged as the Emperor Constantine's biographer. Clearly to have accomplished such a feat, Eusebius owned a silvery tongue and obsequious nature. Ditching his former beliefs, he transformed himself into the Church of Rome's historian and head propagandist. Needless to say, we must consider the work of such an unprincipled man, at best seriously unreliable and at worst, shameful invention. Gibbon as we know, cites Eusebius as recounting what benefits and ignoring what discredits Christianity. Obviously, here was a man whose overriding ambition trampled his sense of integrity into the ground and turned his theological commitment into dust. He nevertheless is deemed worthy enough to be hailed a great Christian... it seems an ecclesiastical oversight that he was never made a saint.

Chapter 25

For Mine Is the Kingdom, the Power and the Glory

"This agglomeration which was called and which still calls itself the Holy Roman Empire, was neither Holy, nor Roman, nor an Empire."

Voltaire

At the start of the fourth century CE, the Roman Empire was approaching anarchy. Gradually, over the previous couple of centuries, the foundations of a once–great Rome had started to disintegrate. A lack of active war–service forced a decline in the effectiveness of the army; the populace lost vigour and became indolent and greedy; its politicians became even more ambitious and corrupt; too many emperors had been seduced by luxury, avarice and perversion and the traditional attributes of a once *noble* Rome were rarely evidenced.

By this period in its history, constant strife over who should wear the imperial purple had effectively split the Roman Empire into East and West. The Roman emperors took the title *Cæsar*, from Julius Cæsar, whose family name it was. An especially worthy emperor or one of the highest rank was called *August*, after Julius's nephew Octavian, who changed his name to Augustus when he established himself as the first Imperial Emperor. Three hundred years on, as the third century CE turned into the fourth, there were two Augusti, each with two Cæsars politically aligned to him. This effectively left the Empire with six Cæsars vying for supreme control. Inevitably, this volatile situation was untenable and civil war erupted. Constantine — the Cæsar in Rome — emerged the victor; even regaining the eastern empire after a successful assault on Byzantium.

Though there had been a decline in many aspects of Roman life it is important to remember that the ambition, greed, lasciviousness and violence often attributed to Rome had not always been there. From 44 BCE to 14 CE the first Imperial Emperor Augustus strove to rule justly during his

THE GREATEST LIE EVER TOLD

long reign and the period raised Roman civilisation to new heights that were later exceeded. As Gibbon says[1]

> "If a man were called to fix the period in the history of the world, during which the condition of the human race was most happy and prosperous, he would, without hesitation, name that which elapsed from the death of Domitian to the accession of Commodus. The vast extent of the Roman Empire was governed by absolute power, under the guidance of virtue and wisdom. The armies were restrained by the firm but gentle hand of four successive emperors whose character and authority commanded involuntary respect. The forms of civil administration were carefully preserved by Nerva, Trajan, Hadrian and the Antonines, who delighted in the image of liberty, and were pleased with considering themselves as the accountable ministers of the laws. Such princes deserved the honour of restoring the republic, had the Romans of their days been capable of enjoying a rational freedom."

Gibbon clearly wants us to know that all of these emperors wished to restore the republic of Rome, but wisely recognised that the citizens were incapable of acting responsibly in their use of the accompanying freedom. Actually Gibbon's *four* emperors should have been five, as he mentions *the Antonines*. Wishing to ensure the long-term stability of the Empire, Hadrian did not seek to pass the throne down through his family but sought an outstanding senator to succeed him. He found one in the elderly statesman Titus Antoninus Pius and appointed him and a seventeen-year-old orphan, Marcus Aurelius, as joint rulers at his death. Titus adopted Marcus Aurelius and married his daughter to him, so the boy became part of the Antoninus family. Instead of naming a biological son as his successor, Titus ensured that Marcus would continue to reign on his death, as Hadrian had wished. The rule of these two unlikely partners pushed the civilisation of Rome to its greatest peak. Gibbon elaborates:

> "Their united reigns are possibly the only period of history in which the happiness of a great people was the sole object of government."

Can we even find a modern government that has come close to fulfilling such an ambition? What leaders have there been who have not risen and ruled by falling prey to personal ambition, political deceit and the employment of varying degrees of corruption?

---

[1] Gibbon, E. *The History of the Decline and Fall of the Roman Empire*

For Mine Is the Kingdom, the Power and the Glory

Rome and the Romans were not all corrupt, they were not all bloodthirsty pagans and their emperors were not all depraved evil tyrants, yet this is how they are all too often portrayed. Many Romans displayed the very highest morality and academic proficiency. Emperor Marcus Aurelius is an outstanding example of a model emperor. He was far from an idle-minded libertine embracing a life of pleasure and luxury — he was a stoic philosopher who lived a severely simple life. As an initiate of the Mysteries educated in the philosophy of Socrates, Plato and Aristotle as well as the arts and sciences like his father Titus, Marcus Aurelius was of refined and intellectual inclinations. Alas, following his death in 180 CE, Rome's golden age came to an end.

Men of unbridled political ambition began squabbling over the vacant throne. All too often their characters were readily tarnished by the corruption which power afflicts upon the overly ambitious. If an absolute leader is not morally strong and imbued with wisdom and a keen sense of justice, he quickly descends into egotistical despotism. The Emperor Constantine — the fourth-century promoter of Literalist Christianity — somehow contrived to fall between the two descriptions.

From the beginning Constantine proved to be an emperor with a deeply ambiguous character. He could be severe, cruel and even murderous, but paradoxically his humanity moved him to introduce numerous laws with which he hoped to improve society. One of them was an attempt to stop the common practice of putting unwanted babies out to die of exposure. Instead, if the family could show the magistrates that they suffered poverty, the state would care for the child's education and welfare. Unfortunately this well-meaning law made limited practical difference because its interpretation was still rather vague. Another was the law against rape and not just violent rape, but ones described as 'the gentle seduction which might take an unmarried woman under the age of twenty-five from her parents house'.[2] Regrettably the prescribed punishment of death could be excessively severe as it included the young woman if she consented to the seduction and any slaves who assisted it.

Power supposedly corrupts and extreme power does so even more markedly. Whilst this is generally the case, there are always notable exceptions, unfortunately Constantine was not amongst them. Though well meaning at the outset, during his eventual decline he managed to murder both his wife and son.

Nonetheless, Constantine was an astute politician and was all too aware of the precarious state of the empire. Rome had for a long time been racked

---

[2] ibid.

with strife and civil wars. The consequence was not just a rapid turnover of *emperors* but also a weakening of the binding fabric of *empire* that assured not only the loyalty of its widely dispersed subjects, but also their interest in maintaining the commercial and political life of the empire in which they lived.

In an empire that stretched from Mesopotamia in the east, to Britain in the west and right across northern Africa, the ethnic and religious diversity couldn't have been greater. During its early years, a strong military presence ensured peace, if not wholehearted loyalty to Rome. As time went on, in many places, the military presence was deemed necessary only at vulnerable frontiers and over generations many people benefited from imperial peace and prosperity and were reasonably happy to be subjects of Rome. But as the centuries passed and as central government weakened through constant upheaval, there were factions who started to show dissatisfaction, with some harbouring hopes of a return to independence.

On a more intellectual political level, the empire had many influential critics, constantly speaking out against the abuse of power and the limitations imposed upon people's lives. These critics were mostly initiates of the Mysteries, whose philosophies encouraged freethinking and liberalism and opposed dictatorial central control.

Constantine realised that Rome could no longer rely on its diminished army with its paucity of experienced battle–hardened troops to hold the empire together. He turned his mind to an alternative, as several previous emperors had done with no success. Instead of employing a physical force to ensure the continuing loyalty of all the empire's subjects, it would be far easier to bind the huge diversity of peoples together by making them all adherents of one state religion, with the emperor in his traditional post of *Pontifex Maximus* — the chief high priest — at its head. State and religion would become one.

Until the time of Constantine, there had never been a religion that would in any way fulfil this overtly political role. The advantage of Constantine's scheme was that it recognised the transience and unreliability of the people's political loyalty, but at the same time recognised that people very rarely changed their religious beliefs. If Constantine had all citizens of the Roman Empire committed and faithful to a centralised Roman religion, he could ensure their full subservience and loyalty. Constantine's official biographer and historian Eusebius explained to his flock that just as God's Word guides and governs the Heavens, so the Roman Emperor expresses the will of God in the government of the civilised world. According to Constantine's wish, Eusebius proclaimed the Emperor as the voice of God.[3]

---

3 Eusebius *History of the Church*

Constantine had the right plan, his problem now was to find the right religion: one that he could manipulate and mould quite easily to meet his needs. The many Mystery cults, one of which he belonged to, were unsuitable: they were widely spread and very popular — the cult of Mithraism had been adopted as the state religion under an earlier Emperor — but they were hotbeds of liberalism and dissension. These cults were diverse and mutable in their format and beliefs and left far too much to individual choice.

Constantine's advisers would have made him aware of the one small deviant cult that held some of the widely popular Mystery teachings but which was quite different from the rest. Its difference lay not only in that it taught the literal reality of the godman myth, but also in the aspect that was of crucial importance to the Roman leader: it exerted rigid control over its members. It would not tolerate dangerous dissenting intellectuals in search of spiritual enlightenment, but initiated followers into a rigid belief system with an aspirant central authority that used fear of damnation to ensure unquestioning control.

Constantine would have known of this cult's overriding ambition. It pursued exclusivity and the eradication of all religious rivals because, having failed to understand the fundamental gnostic concept, the members imagined all Gnostic groups as antagonists. Its wayward status and ongoing incessant conflicts caused the sect to feel vulnerable and paranoiac, making it ripe for imperial patronage and protection. Constantine's vast intelligence network would have informed him of the greed and corruption rife within the hierarchy of the Literalist Christian church. A religious hierarchy already established through bribery would ensure that no moral objections obstructed the path of Constantine's political control and direction.

The ambitious emperor knew that the Christian Church was small, disunited and unstable, but nevertheless it suited his plans perfectly. Constantine took a gamble by making use of Christianity but considered that alienating the rest of the empire should he fail to be worth the risk; he had so much to gain were he to succeed. It was a perverse irony for Constantine to make use of a Mystery religion with distinctly Judaic roots and its accompanying Jewish trappings that would never have existed had Rome not destroyed Jerusalem and its Temple and killed and enslaved great numbers of the ever-troublesome Judeans.

As a follower of the Helios Mysteries, Constantine would have known of the malformed nonsense fundamental to the Christian belief that Jesus had actually been a real living person, but he did not allow any concern over truth to impede the fulfilment of his political quest. His only real concern would have been the successful completion of his strategy.

THE GREATEST LIE EVER TOLD

There is a story that prior to the battle of the Milvian Bridge, against his rival Maxentius in 312 CE, Constantine had a vision that led to his conversion to Christianity. On the eve of the battle he and his army saw a cross in the sky, inscribed with greek words, given in Latin as *in hoc signo vinces* — 'in this sign, you conquer'. Puzzled by what he had seen, Constantine found the answer that night when Jesus, bearing the same symbol, appeared to him in a dream and instructed the emperor to use its likeness in the battle. The following morning, Constantine ordered that the symbol be painted on the shields of his soldiers. Constantine was victorious: he killed his rival and entered Rome.

The story sounds fictitious and gains little credence when it appears that it was first told by Constantine many years after the supposed event.[4] The tale is even less believable when it tries to portray Jesus, the *Lamb of God*, the *Prince of Peace* as condoning bloody warfare and taking sides between two egotistical, ambitious and brutal tyrants. This blasphemous ploy of receiving a vision to justify a fight became a common and degrading excuse for Christians, and later Muslims, to commit atrocities with divine approval. It appears that no one else saw this battle-eve vision in the sky, for not one account is given by any of the many thousands of soldiers who were present. It is only Constantine who made the story known... but even that is questionable. Allegedly Constantine related this account in conversation many years after the event, with no mention of why he had never before thought to tell anyone about this stupendous miracle; and the person he recounted this story to was Bishop Eusebius — the Church's notorious propagandist.

In reality this story is nothing other than a politically-inspired nonsense, there is clear evidence that Constantine had no sudden religious conversion. Following the battle, as was the practice commonly employed by a new emperor seeking to glorify himself, he constructed a triumphal arch in the Forum in Rome. The arch depicts military scenes with the battling Roman soldiers receiving holy assistance from above, however it was not Jesus who intervened divinely, but the usual Roman deities; there was not a single trace of anything Christian on the arch. Further evidence is provided from Constantine's huge statue dedicated to the sun god Helios; there is no doubt that Constantine wasn't a Christian because he had the image of his own face on the sculpted head of the sun god. Constantine was known to be especially devoted to the sun god Apollo. His coinage gives us further confirmation. Constantine had coins minted for a further twelve years, which bore images of the sun god and he had medals made depicting Jupiter, Apollo and Mars. As if that evidence weren't enough, Constantine

---

4   Lane-Fox, R. *Pagans and Christians*

restored numerous pagan temples. These verifiable events certainly do not paint a picture of a man suddenly converted to Christianity by a miracle in the sky and a visit from Jesus in a dream.

The holy symbol that Constantine saw and sought victory through, was not the traditional simple Christian cross, it was the *Chi–Rho* — a circle containing an X with a vertical shepherd's crook through the centre looking a bit like a curly topped letter P. This symbol, though not common today, will still be familiar to many Christians. However this is not really a Christian symbol. Pagan scribes used it as a margin note to mark prophetic passages; the *Chi–Rho* stood for the Greek *chreston* meaning auspicious. So Constantine cunningly employed a pagan symbol and turned it into a Christian one. He thought it would appeal to both pagans and Christians, though as it lacked much significance to either group it was not particularly popular. The symbol still appears on liturgical vestments today, but apparently only because of its link to Constantine.

Constantine was an exceedingly clever politician, not least because he somehow managed to remain on the throne for thirty years. This in itself was quite an achievement considering that some of his predecessors had barely dressed themselves in the purple before they were laid out in a shroud. He was a pragmatist and a man without binding affiliations. He manipulated by the carrot and the stick; and when he wielded the stick, it dealt a heavy blow for he was ever a ruthless and vicious despot. During his life he was only a *Christian* when it suited a particular political purpose and he remained a pagan throughout. What he gave to Christianity during his lifetime, was equal status with the other religions, which he did not outlaw for two reasons, first he was still a pagan himself and second he had no intention of alienating steadfast non–Christians, who still formed a large majority of his citizens. If proof of this were needed, Constantine retained the position of the high priest of all the *pagan* religions, because he continued as *Pontifex Maximus,* High Priest of the Empire.

Despite keeping a foot in both camps he was accepted by the Christians because he had elevated their religion from obscurity to a status that they had only dreamt of, though his dark reputation caused some concerns. In 325 CE, four years after becoming the first Christian emperor, Constantine presided over the Council of Nicæa. If he were to bind his citizens with a state religion, he needed its leaders to agree on what they taught. He called a gathering of clergy to hammer out the problems that were tearing the Christian Church apart. Finally all were required to sign the Nicene Creed, the statement of common belief still used in Christian churches today, those bishops who refused were exiled.[5]

---

5 ibid.

At its conclusion, the emperor set to resolving some problems closer to home. The murders of his son and his wife were followed by many others, both of those who thought they were his friends and those who knew they were his enemies. The Christian Church, though uneasy with these acts, was not inclined to challenge the emperor about this unholy manifestation of his *Christian* credentials. It waited to show its abhorrence of its first patron's deeds until after his death. His mother Helena's 'holiness' was acknowledged by sainthood, her son just got a name change to Constantine the Great.

Constantine's pragmatic nature allegedly made him take baptism eventually, just in case the Christian's warning of sinners suffering eternal damnation was correct. He supposedly postponed his baptism until he was on his deathbed, when all his sins would be forgiven. However, as Eusebius writes, "The bishops performed the sacred ceremonies according to custom,"[6] the veracity of the Church's claim that Constantine was baptised has to be treated with a certain amount of suspicion just because of the person who wrote the story.

The Christians promised every sinner forgiveness for all sins previously committed and offered eternal salvation. This practice of baptism and forgiveness enraged the followers of other religions, who saw it as a licence to sin. Porphyry, a pagan philosopher, wrote a devastating critique in 270 CE that exposed all the literalist absurdities, the falsehoods and impossibilities of Christianity. The work condemned the promise to criminals that they would be absolved from their crimes and would enter paradise, as long as they were baptised before death; Porphyry lamented that this practice undermined the very foundations of a civilised society of decent people.

> "They introduce into the world a form of society which is without law, and teach men to have no fear of ungodliness; when a man sets aside a pile of countless wrongdoings simply by being baptised. Such then is the boastful fiction of the saying."[7]

One of the fundamental differences between Christianity and the other Mystery cults was the Christians' insistence that they possessed the only way to God — the 'narrow straight path' — an exclusive private path of the Christian Church's own making. The Gnostics took a wider, more universal view, insisting that there was not just *one* way back to God but an infinite number. The Mysteries taught that each person must follow their own

---

[6] op. cit. Eusebius
[7] Porphyry *Against the Christians*

individual path back to God. They also refrained from telling people how to live their lives; they taught that there was no right and wrong way, but that one's true path would be guided by one's conscience. For instance, initiates were free to be celibate or promiscuous — the only proviso being that they should not cause harm to anyone. Whatever the Gnostics chose to do, they knew that after mortal death, they would have to account for their actions to their Higher–Self, before they could ever experience God.

Prior to considering how Constantine affected the development of Christianity, it is worth a brief look at the contribution made by his mother Helena. Unlike her son, she was a real Christian — a committed, unreasoning Literalist. Because she was implicated in the murder of Constantine's family members, she was forced into exile. To show her Christian commitment, she made good use of her time away by journeying to Palestine, wishing to see the places where Jesus had been. I rather doubt that she was there to do penance, but more likely to gather up any old objects which she could claim as genuine holy relics on her return to Rome, in order to free herself of the stigma of the old charges against her.

Some three hundred years after the fictitious events were set, she miraculously found the very crosses that had been used to execute Jesus and the two criminals alongside him. No–one raises the question of just how she found the *genuine* pieces of wood in a place that had seen thousands of executions over the intervening three centuries. In reality any and all crosses would have been recycled as building material — timber being in short supply in Judea — and any surplus used as firewood. These relics did not come with certificates of authenticity or letters of provenance. Not only did Helena find the *true* cross on which Jesus was crucified, but she also discovered the very tomb where Jesus had been interred and went on to score the hat trick and found the very cave where he was born! She chose a cave not a stable as the birthplace — the cave was the most common site amongst the Mystery cults for the birthplace of the various characters who personified their Son–of–God incarnate.

One can imagine the Jerusalem locals rubbing their hands with glee at the arrival of a mad, but extremely rich, elderly Roman noblewoman seeking holy sites and relics. She must have found it hard to decide which of the multitude to believe; but obviously this exiled murderess would choose the real pieces of wood and the right location, because Jesus guided her. Constantine authenticated her holy sites by building churches on top of them.

Fragments of the holy timber were shipped around the empire and installed in sacred shrines. In gratitude for her efforts, this mother of a tyrant and complicit murderess was honoured with sainthood and designated *St Helena Discoverer of the True Cross*. The early Catholic Church never displayed shame, had an abundance of ambition and always an eye for the main chance. Helena's *evidence* to authenticate its religious claims would have seemed like all its Christmases in one go, except it hadn't heard of Christmas way back then.

St Helena inspired other relic-seekers to follow her example and suddenly all manner of articles, including remains of apparently multi-limbed and multi-headed apostles, appeared from nowhere. These sacred articles dramatically enhanced the status of any church they were deposited in; and of course, they brought in huge profits from the thousands of pilgrims who came to ogle the holy junk and be cured miraculously of their ills if allowed to touch it. The original residence of the early popes, across the city from modern day St Peter's, at the Palace of St John Lateran, supposedly contained Christianity's most sacred relics including not only the heads of Peter and Paul but even the very marble steps, up which Jesus had trudged in Pilate's judgement hall. Seemingly nothing was sacred and being truthful certainly wasn't.

Just as scavenging from the sacred scrap-yard went unchecked, so too the invention of historical truths flew off into the realms of total farce. When over-zealous scribes rewrote the latter days of Pontius Pilate, they chased the ball that Tertullian had set rolling when he claimed that Pilate had intuitively known that Jesus was divine and confided this to the Emperor Tiberius.[8] Tertullian's tale has an inspired Tiberius attempt to place Jesus amongst the gods of Rome, but apparently the emperor was forbidden from doing so by the senate, so instead he turned his efforts to protecting beleaguered Christians from his own oppressive laws. Well, it was a good story, but clearly our author Tertullian did not know that there *were* no oppressive laws against Christians for the obvious reason that at the time of Pontius Pilate there were no *Christians*. Another fact that he was unaware of was that the mighty Tiberius never listened to his toadying senators and the emperor despised all forms of religion.

The eager post-Tertullian fantasists even went as far as writing a text called the *Acts of Pilate* and then elevated this fictitious work into the ridiculous *Gospel of Nicodemus*.[9] In this new tale, Pilate is brought in chains to face the enraged emperor, who berates him for his crime of executing Jesus; as the emperor utters Jesus' name, all the statues of the gods collapse to dust. Pilate defends himself by blaming the Jews, which inspires the emperor to issue an order to destroy Judea and disperse its evil population into slavery. Pilate is then executed and as he expires, is received by an angel of the Lord; seeing this wonder, Pilate's wife, Procla, collapses and dies of joy.

---

[8] op. cit. Gibbon, E.

[9] ibid.

For Mine Is the Kingdom, the Power and the Glory

The Coptic Church made Pilate a saint and the Eastern Church did the same for his wife. Whilst this ludicrous story is obvious invention, such rubbish was readily believed and Christians dutifully honoured these unlikely blessed heroes. In modern times, theologians are a little more selective and reject the story, but yet they still adhere to other things written by these very same authors and insist that their *history* is true.

With Helena digging up Judea like an early Indiana Jones, back in Rome Constantine had not been partying his time away, he had been overseeing some serious construction work. On a hill outside the city walls stood the Circus of Nero and next to it was an old cemetery; this, by oral tradition, was the place of Peter's execution and burial. A simple monument had supposedly marked Peter's grave and it was over this that Constantine built a huge basilica. By the mid–fifteenth century this was to become St Peter's Church and its surrounding area the Vatican.

The building, which was to stand for some 1200 years, was hurriedly constructed. Constantine cannibalised various monuments including the Pantheon and made use of Nero's old arena. He also demolished a Temple of Mithras that was standing on the spot where the new basilica was erected — Constantine was not a man to let sentiment or loyalty to an old god stand in his way. He announced that this was the actual spot where St Peter was buried, obviously with total disregard for the existing story of the *grave marked by a simple monument* because the site of a Mithraic temple and any cemetery beneath it would have pre–dated the time of Peter.

Oddly, it never seemed to occur to anyone to question why or how an executed malefactor, a mean–born Jewish troublemaker came to be buried beneath the hallowed marble foundations of a Mithraic Temple. Of course Constantine knew full well that Peter had not been buried there, as he knew that Peter had never been to Rome because he knew that the apostle had never existed. To have the alleged disciple who had been given leadership of the Christian Church, buried on the site of his new headquarters, suited Constantine's plan to centre Christianity in Rome, the capital of the empire and to divert all religious focus away from Judea.

Things had moved rapidly, as was the Roman way, but the Christians had not got quite everything they desired. The pagan Mysteries and the heretic Gnostics were still permitted, but at least the Literalist Christians now felt that they held the high *moral* ground, though to most citizens they were still the derided pariahs. Equal status was not good enough for the Christians, there could be no harmonious coexistence with other cults and they had to work towards the total eradication of their rivals. Neither was there peace and harmony within the Christian ranks; the various groups were still at each other's throats, resulting in frequent unseemly violent clashes. Christians failed to agree on almost all matters of their faith, from the trivial to the fundamental.

In 319 CE, a Christian presbyter in Alexandria named Arius had argued that the Son being *equal* to the Father in the Trinity was wrong. Arius considered that Jesus was not co-equal or co-eternal with the Father because the Father had created him, he was therefore only the first and highest of beings created by God. He won some support, but his argument caused him to be deposed and excommunicated in 321 CE. However the bitter debate continued, so the Synod of Nicæa was called to sort out this and other problems. There it was decided that the three members of the Trinity were equal and Arius was banished as a heretic, though recalled in 334 CE. He died two years later in Constantinople and the Arian sect and its belief that the Trinity were not equal continued in dispute. Constantine developed an interest in Arianism and this interest continued through his successors until Theodosius was crowned emperor, except for one dissenter, the pagan Julian.

The Council of Nicæa was a defining moment in the history of the Christian Church; the thorny issues and fundamental disagreements were addressed, though they were not all resolved immediately and many of the disputes continued to rage. Some bishops dug their heels in and vigorously held their views, some partially relented, whilst others completely bowed to pressure and changed their theological stance. Amongst the latter was Bishop Eusebius of Caesarea, the moderate heretic for, typical of the man, his position fluctuated between Arius and *orthodox* Athanasius. It was Eusebius' sudden leap into hard-line literalist *orthodoxy*, which probably had the greatest effect upon Christianity. Eusebius' affection for honesty and integrity was shallow, so he was never likely to have wrestled with his conscience in order to become an obsequious sycophant and court favourite with Constantine.

Constantine was probably unconcerned that Eusebius was a tarnished ex-Arian heretic; no doubt the emperor could readily recognise an ambitious scoundrel when he saw one. In fact an accomplished ingratiator was exactly the type of person most suited for the job that Constantine had in mind for Eusebius. He wrote Constantine's biography with all the fawning flattery that the job required, whilst sensitively glossing over the emperor's many misdemeanours. It is probably from Eusebius that Constantine developed his interest in Arianism; though any discourse would have been in private, since Eusebius was supposedly an *ex*-Arian at that time.

The job of writing the glowing biography behind him, his reputation enhanced and his position in the imperial circle and the Church secured, Eusebius next turned his dubious talents towards organising and collating

Christian works — of which there were very few. His task was broadened to the creation of a suitable Christian history; one that would hide the real truth and give it a much-needed makeover and an illustrious window-dressing to attract new converts. Nowadays Eusebius is recognised for what he truly was and modern scholars deride him as a thoroughly dishonest historian who falsified most of what he claimed had historical authenticity. Eusebius's audacity extended to the forgery of a letter that he ridiculously alleged was written by Jesus to the Prince of Edessa.

The many deceits and forgeries did not just stem from Eusebius. The mood prevalent at the time amongst Christians was that anything that furthered the glory of their religion whilst castigating all others was perfectly acceptable. No fantasy was too extreme, nor was it ever deemed too late to tack some new myth onto an old one. At Ephesus, there was a famed temple dedicated to Diana/Venus that suddenly became one of several places where the Virgin Mary died and was buried. Strangely, the Christians living there prior to the fifth century CE were in total ignorance of this significant event. This was clearly just another late-Christian attempt to claim a pagan cult centre for its own.

Constantine had kicked off for the Christian Church and from then on the game began to gain momentum with successive emperors wooing the fan-base and binding the empire's populace to one national team. Christianity did nothing to temper the actions and morals of the emperors, but then considering the appalling behaviour of the church leaders, one would hardly expect an improvement. With perverse irony, there was just one emperor who stood head and shoulders above the rest — another benign leader in the mould of Marcus Aurelius — the Emperor Julian. Greece was the country of his birth and Greek was his first language. He was a virtuous scholarly man who became a humane and pious emperor. Julian was unexpectedly plucked out of his life as a scholar and forced to take the purple as deputy to Emperor Constantius II. Though not trained as a soldier, he reluctantly accepted his duty to the empire and served with such great distinction on the Rhine that when in 360 CE a new emperor was needed, this unlikely intellectual was proclaimed as such by his adoring troops.

Julian's desire was to attain peace and happiness for all the people and having publicly proclaimed himself a pagan, he initiated a vigorous policy of promoting and reviving the old pagan Mystery cults and the teachings of Plato and Aristotle. Though he hoped to put a brake upon Christianity with its violent confrontational policies and corrupt conduct, he magnanimously did not seek to persecute its followers. Unfortunately his altruistic and humane endeavour was frustrated by his short reign, when he died fighting the Persians in 363. Perhaps had he lived longer, the history of the west might have taken a very different course and we would live in a world with more liberal–philosophical and spiritual–religious beliefs and one that had never known religious wars.

Julian's pagan revival was too short–lived and so it failed to check the Christians' insidious expansion. This said, the Christians were still far from a majority and their internal squabbles, as well as their struggles to overcome the pagan Mysteries and the Gnostics, were to stutter on for a long time. Despite the empire being Christian, Constantine's long–term plan failed to slow Rome's continuing decline. With its power rapidly waning and its empire shrinking, what remained became more decrepit and a pale shadow of what it once had been. Retreating from the growing threat of the so–called *barbarian invaders* from the north, the empire was ruled from its eastern capital of Constantinople. It was from here that the second major boost for the Christian cause came in 379 CE.

Theodosius I, known as *the Great,* became emperor, typically due to his military abilities. He solved the threat from the migrating hordes of Goths by converting them into his allies. His title of *Great* came from his robust championing of orthodox Christianity and unlike his predecessors he was overtly anti–Arian. Theodosius elevated the Christians above their position of equal status with other religions, by banning the rest. His edict made Christianity the only religion permitted to all the people. He was a dedicated dictator and that meant there was no place in his empire for religions that encouraged liberal thinking — what he desired was a church which condemned thinking and encouraged blind faith and subservient loyalty.

So the Christian Church finally achieved its highest ambition, it became the one and only religion of the Roman Empire, though its victory was a shallow one. Fifteen years later in 410 CE, the Visigoths sacked Rome. Various Germanic tribes such as the Franks and the Burgundians had moved into Gaul; the Anglo–Saxons had migrated into Britain; the Vandals had crossed the Straits of Gibraltar into the north–African coastal provinces; the Lombards had settled into north–western Italy whilst the Visigoths had also invaded Spain. Although originally pagan, these Germanic tribes had largely converted to the so–called heretical form of Christianity known as Arianism.

In a relatively short space of time, the western Roman Empire contracted to virtually nothing. In the east, the empire still held in the most part, with Constantinople growing into its largest and most powerful city. Cut adrift from the west, this somewhat isolated city was to become the hub of the Byzantium Empire.

In 468 CE, the eastern Emperor Leo I attempted to rescue the old western empire and the northern African provinces from the barbarians but his campaign was a disaster. In 533, Emperor Justinian repeated the campaign, this time with rather more success. His forces defeated the Vandals in North Africa then in 540 CE they finally overcame the Ostrogoths in Italy and captured their capital of Ravenna. Sadly, after a conflict that lasted twelve years, Italy was left devastated and much of the glory that had been Rome lay largely in ruins. Justinian did not restore power to either Rome or to Ravenna but ruled his new Roman Empire from the safety of Constantinople. This partially–united empire was not to last much beyond his lifetime and its remnants began to draw away from Rome back to eastern Constantinople. This new contracted empire lost its *Romanity* and became much more of a *Greek* melting–pot incorporating much from middle–eastern culture.

Despite the political turmoil afflicting Europe, the bitter theological haggling still raged, especially between eastern and western churches — increasingly the two held ridiculous arguments over the finer points of Christian theology, usually over Jesus Christ's divine and human natures and how they related to each other. Alexandria had held its own ideas since Christianity first started with Philo, but in five hundred years Rome had moved in a different direction and formed its own identity, this difference inevitably led to theological battles, both for doctrinal dominance and the right to leadership. The Christianity which developed in Constantinople, fell somewhere between the two and promoted itself as a conciliator and ecclesiastical unifier.

Justinian's personal lifestyle is intriguing, he appears to have been a pious man who was dedicated to his faith and seemed to have been very much an orthodox Christian, however, his personal habits included drinking only water, eating only vegetables and herbs, enjoying the company of monks and discussing theology; all very much traits of the Pythagoreans and Gnostics. The type of religion that developed in Byzantium was centred upon monasticism, which was also the way of the Gnostics and the Celtic Christians, whereas the Church of Rome, though it too had monasteries, was governed and influenced by the churches and their controlling bishops.

Deprived firstly of effective emperors in Rome and then of any emperors at all, its people looked to the Bishop of Rome for both religious and political leadership; dramatically handing enormous power to the Popes who were to follow. Only the eastern–empire, which became known as Byzantium, successfully held on to its autonomy and indeed, it flourished into a great, but somewhat isolated civilisation. Even this would not be for long as the sudden appearance of Islam in the early seventh century and its rapid military expansion, wrestled away the Byzantines' control over Egypt and the middle–eastern provinces. Somehow Byzantium held out against the Muslim expansion and managed to retain Anatolia, but it was now an empire centred entirely on Constantinople. Byzantium and Rome ended up being very different and divided entities, each with its own struggle to survive.

After 800 CE, with the rise to power of the Frankish kingdom and the Carolingian rulers, once Charlemagne had been crowned Holy Roman *Emperor*, the newly-formed Holy Roman *Empire* became a schizophrenic body. Charlemagne's political capital was at Aachen in Germany, whilst the religious centre and the seat of the Pope were in Rome. John I, the Bishop of Rome in 523 CE, had appropriated the title of Pope formerly used by the Archbishop of Alexandria, and assumed the rôle as Head of the Church. This division of politics controlled by Germans and religion by Latins, caused an uncomfortable divide between State and Religion. In Byzantium, emperor and patriarch worked *cheek by jowl*, which created a greater stability and harmony. The Popes' lack of real political power led to *sub–rosa* intrigues, which were, by necessity, supported by threats of excommunication and damnation as the only effective means to enforce their own *secular* requirements.

Byzantium and the Holy Roman Empire were divided in many other ways. In the west, much of the civilisation created by the Roman Empire had been destroyed. Education was crucial to rebuilding civilisation, but the Roman Catholic Church viewed education with great suspicion and did nothing to promote it. Only the clergy and a few of the nobility were educated and literate. In Byzantium, education was valued and most people had the benefit of some learning, for which Constantinople was a centre.

Rome had been largely destroyed and lost its grandeur, and its wealthier citizens moved to Constantinople. This, combined with Greek culture and further influences from the Middle–East, stimulated Constantinople's growth and it developed into a thriving vigorous hybrid. The language of Byzantium became Greek, with Latin demoted to a second language spoken by few of its subjects. The elite members of society developed an interest in Greek culture — Constantinople had plenty of classical statues adorning its squares — they also reputedly had an interest in pagan teachings. Classical Greek and even Gnostic texts were accessible and this promoted a certain free–thinking which led intellectuals to take a private interest in the Mysteries and philosophy.

The inhabitants of Constantinople saw themselves as the chosen–people of the New Testament and their city as the new Jerusalem, though this view was very much one from their own perspective. The new Rome was not included in this vision, for the people of Constantinople became contemptuous of Latin Christianity, with its papal claim to authority over all Christians through its succession from St Peter.

For Mine Is the Kingdom, the Power and the Glory

The Roman Empire had dramatically gone into free fall: a great civilisation with its countless achievements had stood for a thousand years, but within just a few years of Christian ascendancy, it plummeted headlong into the dark ages. The truth is that the superstitious, anti-science, anti-thinking, compassionless, brutally-inhumane Christians encouraged this descent and actively worked to ensure that humanity remained in its soulless pit. The Church struggled hard to keep the *light* concealed, for it knew then, and knows now, that once light exposes the truth, the church will be finished and reviled. Somehow, with a little good fortune and a lot of force and terror, the Church suppressed, repressed and struggled on.

The rules of engagement were established when Theodosius banned all religions other than that of the Church of Rome. The Roman Church and State had licence to kill off all opposition, be they so-called pagans, original Gnostic Christians or members of the non-orthodox Christian churches. They plunged the civilised world into a lawless insanity of suppression and slaughter by a ruthless religion that was to last 1,000 years.

THE GREATEST LIE EVER TOLD

Chapter 26

The Prince of Peace and His Reign of Terror

"The gods aid the stronger"

Tacitus

Julius Firmicus Maternus was a Christian writer contemporary with Constantine and his sons. Instead of preaching Christ's message of peace and love as one could justifiably expect a follower of Jesus Christ to do, in 346 CE, he entitles Chapter 29 of *De errore profanarum religionum*[1] 'Let the Emperors Stamp Out Paganism and Be Rewarded by God'.

In this profound spiritual treatise, he implores the sons of Constantine to eradicate the old religions with the utmost brutality and earn God's reward!

> "But on you also, Most Holy Emperors, devolves the imperative necessity to castigate and punish this evil, and the law of the Supreme Deity enjoins on you that your severity should be visited in every way on the crime of idolatry."

If the Emperors are in any doubt how to proceed, Julius Firmicus Maternus tells them what God requires,

> "He bids spare neither son nor brother, and thrust the avenging sword through the body of a beloved wife. A friend too He persecutes with lofty severity, and the whole populace takes up arms to rend the bodies of sacrilegious men. Even for whole cities, if they are caught in this crime, destruction is decreed, and that your providence may more plainly learn this, I shall quote the sentence of the established law."

---

[1] Julius Firmicus Maternus, *The Error of Pagan Religions*

God wanted the emperors to slaughter all pagans, every man, woman and child, and this slaughter was even to include the friends of pagans. In case the Emperors doubt the validity of these imperatives, Firmicus Maternus quotes the actual words of God as he wrote them in the Holy Bible! God had made his desire known through the holy book and his self-appointed agent Firmicus Maternus made sure that the Emperors knew that God wished to see the entire population of all pagan cities wiped out. He was promoting a holocaust — a total religious cleansing.

In the reign of Constantine, Christianity had been granted equal status with the older pagan religions in the Empire. Within thirty years of Constantine's death, pagans were suffering unspeakable persecutions. By the end of the fourth century Emperor Theodosius had closed all the pagan temples and declared that Christianity was the only religion permitted within the Empire.

In all their activities Christians rarely displayed any form of humanity let alone any attempt to uphold their own sacred moral Commandments. They lied, they forged and worse, they tortured and murdered — all too often in an especially barbaric manner, seemingly rejoicing in the agonising suffering of their victims. Historians have documented their atrocities [2] [3] but the Church has never acknowledged them; instead it has always managed to project itself as the innocent victim of persecution.

The early Church fathers constantly regaled pagans and Gnostics with their violent fantasies of the gruesome tortures awaiting them in Hell; all invented by the perverted fanatical minds of underdogs who dreamed of being king. They filled the heads of their flock with this silly nonsense too; then goaded the zealot elements, inciting them to destroy their enemies at any cost. Once it had gained ascendancy, by the fourth century, the new Roman Catholic Church began a brutal and bloody campaign of terror against its old rivals. The evidence shows that it was not the Christians who suffered the true religious persecution and awful deaths, but the pagans.

In 384 CE, a desperate pagan Roman senator Quintus Aurelius Symmachus pleaded with the Emperor Valentinian II for religious tolerance,

> "Does it matter by what method each man seeks the truth, for one cannot arrive at so great a secret by only one road." [4]

---

2   Croke, B & Harries, J. eds. *Religious Conflict in Fourth-Century Rome*
3   Gibbon, E. *The History of the Decline and Fall of the Roman Empire*
4   Matthews, JF. *The Letters of Symmachus*

An obvious fact, but the emperor refused to listen. In those times, the emperors were feeble and allowed the Catholic Church to direct their thinking. It was a world suddenly gone mad, with the lunatics now in charge.

Christian leaders who had for so long suffered theological insecurity, who had been mocked as sad uneducated fools, who believed that an old myth was history, suddenly found the sword of power in their hands and they lusted for vengeance. Even during the years when the pagans were lawfully allowed to practise their religions, legal protection was too often ineffectual; the violent intimidation and destruction that were running rife throughout the empire were simply ignored by those whose duty it was to uphold the law.

Frenzied mobs of fanatical Christian monks, too often drunk on wine, were allowed to run amok attacking whomever and whatever their madness found in its path — they destroyed and looted, used violence and murdered. The writer Eunapius, a 4th-century Greek Sophist and historian, says of these so-called men of God:

> "In these 'sacred' places 'monks' were installed, those creatures who resemble men but live like pigs.... In that period anyone who wore a black robe had despotic power! In the abode and in place of the gods, henceforward worship was rendered to the skeletons of a few wretched ex-convicts, slaves who deserved the whip: the 'martyrs'"[5]

The early Christian monks had never heard that cleanliness was next to godliness, in response to the nakedness, luxuries and 'the monstrous sensualities' in the public baths, Christian Church leaders disapproved of washing.[6] We see too the early veneration of bones of saints, which as Gibbon points our became big business for the church:

> "In the long period of twelve hundred years, which elapsed between the reign of Constantine and the reformation of Luther, the worship of saints and relics corrupted the pure and perfect simplicity of the Christian model: and some symptoms of degeneracy may be observed even in the first generations which adopted and cherished this pernicious innovation."[7]

---

5 Turcan, R. *Cults of the Roman Empire*

6 Stuller, J. "Cleanliness has only recently become a virtue"

7 op. cit. Gibbon, E.

In truth, these early unwashed monks who worshipped bones of so-called martyrs, were not men seeking spiritual tranquillity as in later times, but were unintelligent, unthinking, thuggish religious fanatics, who spent their time drinking or rampageously attacking pagans, trashing and looting shrines, temples and public buildings and raping pagan priestesses when the opportunity occurred.

This is yet another desperate appeal to the Emperor Theodosius I in 386 CE by a Greek-speaking teacher of rhetoric named Libanius, whom though a pagan, the Emperor had made an honorary prætorian prefect:

> "You have not ordered either that the temples be closed or that no-one should enter them. You have not driven out from the temples and altars, fire or incense, or the offering of other perfumes. But this black-garbed mob, who eat more than elephants and drain huge amounts from the cup — these people, O King, although the law remains in force, run against the temples carrying cudgels and stones and bars of iron, while some, without these, use their hands and feet. Then there is complete destruction as roofs are pulled down, walls demolished, statues are dragged down, altars pulled up and the priests must be silent or die. When the first is destroyed, there is a rush to a second and a third, and contrary to law, trophy is heaped upon trophy. Most take place in the countryside, but some even in the cities. The attacking forces in each case are numerous, but after countless abuses these separate groups come together and demand an account from each other of what they have done, and it is shameful not to have done the greatest damage."[8]

The rule of law had ceased to exist, except when selectively employed by the Emperor and his cronies. From 381 to 392 CE Theodosius issued fifteen edicts that forbade a range of activities from visiting temples to discussing religion. He even banned looking at the broken remains of pagan idols and he made divining from the entrails of chickens high treason.

Just as the Nazis used invention to discredit the Jews, the Christians made all kinds of ludicrous charges against the pagans: sacrificing babies and pouring their blood upon the altars was a favourite. No-one cared about truth, let alone justice — the mad zealots made their own justice and punishments. Shrines and temples were destroyed or requisitioned as Christian churches; if the congregations defended their property, the Christians fought and killed them. In Alexandria in 389 CE, a decree annexed the ancient temple of Bacchus as a Christian church. When the

---

[8] Norman, AF. trans. *Libanius: Selected Works*

The Prince of Peace and His Reign of Terror

mob arrived to claim their prize, the pagan congregation was forced to flee. The followers of Bacchus sought sanctuary in the temple of Serapis, but the Christian mob followed them and after another violent confrontation that building was destroyed.

When pagan temples were taken, their priests were either driven out or were beaten then chained inside their temples and left to starve. When pagan prophets and sages fell into the hands of these rampaging mobs, they were subjected to the most hideous tortures: tortures that demented minds sought to make ever more varied and extreme.[9]

On November 8, 392 CE, Emperor Theodosius stirred himself out of the indifferent stupor that had inflicted the previous emperors when it came to protecting pagans' lawful rights; Theodosius decreed that heresy was to be a crime against the state. Since the official religion was already Christianity, this meant that all other religions were now finally outlawed. The Gnostic Christian sects did not escape the purge; Theodosius brought out some hundred laws against the Gnostics.

The very foundation of Gnostic beliefs was denied by the edict which announced that there shall be no opportunity for any man to publicly argue about religion, to discuss it, or give any counselling. For Gnostics, the only path to Truth came through rational argument and discussion and now, by law, all Roman subjects were denied access to God.

Another edict made sure that all heretical books were burnt. On May 10, 1933 the German Students' Association started its campaign against the 'un–German spirit' with a massive book bonfire in Berlin. Emperor Valens had set the precedent in 370 CE, but the edict of Theodosius on May 2, 381 saw libraries looted and their contents thrown on the fire. The Christian mob led by savage monks, seized all the pagan books they could find — works of philosophy, spirituality, poetry, history and science — and heaped them onto huge bonfires. The mob was illiterate and did not discriminate, so any book was tossed onto the pyres; the literate instigators understood the dangers of the written word, words that would undermine their Church, and they needed the words of truth and wisdom to be obliterated.

Eyewitness accounts lament how whole libraries were consigned to the flames and how a great terror gripped the people. Knowledge acquired over some three thousand years of mankind's civilisation, was gleefully destroyed. Fortunately some books were hidden and preserved, but far more were lost forever. This manic destruction and murder was not undertaken by ravaging barbarian hordes, but by so–called pious, peace–loving, gentle Christians in the name of Jesus the Prince of Peace; causing Gibbon to comment on the sad irony:

---

9 Deschner, KH. *Kriminalgeschichte des Christentums*

> "Such was the persecuting spirit of the laws of Theodosius, which were repeatedly enforced by his sons and grandsons, with the loud and unanimous applause of the Christian world."[10]

Even in Alexandria, the city that was built as the 'open-to-all' cosmopolitan city, the city of learning, science, philosophy and spiritual religions, the dark shadow of Christianity fell heavily. Despite the edicts against them, the Gnostics continued to survive in Alexandria for a few years after Theodosius' death. Early in the fifth century the Patriarch of Alexandria was an ambitious zealot called Cyril. As was common practice, Archbishop Cyril did what he could to persecute pagans and Gnostic Christians. The Christian Prefect of Egypt, Orestes complained to the emperor that Cyril was illegally expelling Jews from Alexandria. Cyril reacted angrily to what he saw as inexcusable interference in his pursuit of heretics and hired a mob of fanatical monks to attack the Prefect.

This mob of monks from surrounding monasteries were known as the *Parabolani* — those who disregarded their own lives — and made themselves available whenever strong action was needed. Originally founded as a charitable organisation to visit the sick and bury the dead during the plague of Gallienus, they were gradually enlarged and at the same time began to abuse their position by selling privileges. They were employed by successive archbishops to act as bodyguards and as bullying enforcers used to persecute Jews, pagans and Gnostic heretics.

When Cyril came to power, one of his first acts had been to use this force to expel the wealthy Jews from the city — some 40,000 people — and to pillage what was left behind to fill his coffers. The behaviour of these monks was extremely savage, brutal and compassionless, and their appalling behaviour during the time of Cyril eventually provoked the emperor to impose sanctions on them, which included limiting their numbers.

Despite the large force of *Parabolani* attacking Orestes and his small escort deserting him, good fortune was with him. Seeing his plight, he was rescued by the enraged citizens of Alexandria, who had no tolerance of these hated Christian thugs. The leader of the *Parabolani*, a monk called Ammonius, was taken prisoner and punished by flogging; the monk later died from his punishment. Cyril then ordered that the deceased be carried in solemn procession to the cathedral, where his tomb was decorated in a manner fit for a martyr. The patriarch climbed the pulpit to give praise to the would-be assassin and incited the congregation to follow the monk's example. With unrepentant audacity, Cyril then had Ammonius accorded

---

[10] op. cit. Gibbon, E.

the status of a Christian martyr and changed the thug's name to *Thaumasius* 'the wonderful'. The clear Christian message was that being a brute was a wondrous thing.

Archbishop Cyril though ambitious was enough of a pragmatist to realise that he could not safely take on Orestes, so he sought to wheedle his way back into the Prefect's good books. Cyril knew that there was just one obstacle in Alexandria to this reconciliation — a young woman called Hypatia. She had been formally tutored in both Athens and Alexandria in the philosophy of Plato and Aristotle, and in mathematics and geometry. Despite her young age, Hypatia was described as having both beauty and maturity of wisdom. Not only did Hypatia teach, but people from all walks of life also sought out her wise counsel. Cyril felt sidelined — jealous of the fact that the rich and influential people of Alexandria, as well as other places within the empire, went to Hypatia for advice — but it was not only professional and political envy, he was also jealous of her wealth.

Orestes was one of Hypatia's powerful friends; as long as he remained friends with this pagan woman, any overtures to Orestes were bound to fail. Cyril only had to tell his fanatical friends that Hypatia stood in the path of the Church and State's harmonious co-existence in Alexandria and the zealots devised a plan to solve their master's problem. A mob of the *Parabolani,* led by a man with the spurious name of Peter the Reader, ambushed Hypatia as she travelled through the city. They pulled her from her chariot, stripped her clothes off and dragged her to a church where, with frenzied relish, they inflicted an unbelievably gruesome and excruciatingly slow death on her, before casting her remains on a fire. The outrage was widespread and long-lived — a shocking event that left a black stain upon history and which, unlike many pagan persecutions, has been remembered and recounted since its time.

Horrifyingly, though perhaps not unexpectedly, Archbishop Cyril was honoured with sainthood, in recognition for this and other 'great Christian deeds'. We need to remember that different societies at different times, had different ways of dealing with mindless mobs and murderers — the early Christian Church chose to assign the highest honour to them. Yet the modern-day Christian Church feels no need to atone, by acknowledging Cyril's guilt and withdrawing his sainthood. It seems that the search for abundant Christian morality is still a pointless task!

Following the draconian decree of Emperor Theodosius, which required all citizens to be Christians, many Gnostics were forced to change and at least superficially join the state-controlled religion, though some were, inevitably, determined to keep promoting Gnostic teachings. Synesius of Cyrene was a Gnostic who had studied Neo-Platonism with Hypatia at Alexandria; he married a Christian and later became the Bishop of Cyrene in 410 CE. He still taught that the only true religion was philosophy and attempted to convey the thinking behind the Mysteries. Of course he could not be allowed to continue, but rather than being dismissed or imprisoned, he was simply forced to promise that he would desist from conducting such heretical discourse in public and that he should *philosophise* in private if he must.

Despite the law, the authorities sometimes felt wary of eliminating popular figures, for Christianity's imposition had no endorsement by the majority of the populace and the fear of angry uprisings sometimes tempered official action. According to some scholars, Synesius doubtless knew this and so did not give up entirely.[11] Though Jay Bregman suggests that Synesius's insistence that philosophy was independent of pagan mysteries or Christianity and therefore could be used to interpret both the Christian myths as well as the pagan ones, gave him the originality and flexibility to exist purposefully with both of them.[12]

Alas, so much was lost in the outlawing and persecution of everything that was not orthodox Christianity. The edicts of Theodosius encouraged the frenzied hordes of monks to set out on a crusade which saw almost every temple destroyed, just those that were transformed into Christian churches surviving. Tragically, the world-renowned Temple of the Dionysian Mysteries at Eleusis and the Library of Alexandria were included in this orgy of destruction.

Thousands of years of thought, effort, inspiration and wisdom were lost forever. The great libraries were burnt down; great literature was destroyed; scientific, philosophical and religious works, all were cast into the flames of the bonfires. In 529 CE, the Emperor Justinian abolished the Platonic Academy in Athens. Thinking was decreed a danger that would harm the Church and State. The Emperor deemed that people should be kept in total ignorance and subservience. In its zealous madness, the Christian Church plunged the western world into 1,000 years of deliberate ignorance — the period of history so appropriately named the *Dark Ages*.

Despite the numerous purges, Gnosticism continued: the Arians, the Marcionites, the Paulicians, the Valentinians and the Novatians survived, to the fury of the Roman Catholic Church. In large cities like Rome, Constantinople and Alexandria, prohibition was easy to enforce. In Asia Minor and the Middle-East, where the land was vast and wild and little populated, the Empire's officials were thin on the ground and in the remoter outposts the Gnostic sects remained. The political rulers thought that these out-of-the-way liberal-minded cults posed no threat to imperial

---

[11] Marrou, H-I. "Synesius of Cyrene and Alexandrian Neoplatonism"
[12] Bregman, AJ. *Synesius of Cyrene*

stability, so it mattered not if they refused to follow the imperial religion. The Church knew the threat was most terrible: if Gnostics were allowed to exist the truth could spread and truth was a poison that would one day kill Christianity.

THE GREATEST LIE EVER TOLD

Chapter 27

The Mystery to Misery Millennium

"The infliction of cruelty with a good conscience is a delight to moralists. That is why they invented Hell."

Bertrand Russell

Despite everything the Catholic Church could do to kill off Gnosticism, it managed to survive the outright onslaughts and sporadic sniping. From time to time, throughout the subsequent centuries, Gnosticism pushed its head above the parapet and came up fighting. One is left with the strong impression that there must have been an underground organisation that actively preserved the Gnostic teachings and knew of the ancient Mysteries too. Whenever a brave group of individuals arose to pursue their beliefs openly, they were prompted and encouraged by this clandestine organisation. James M Robinson edited *The Nag Hammadi Library*.[1] He claims that the Nag Hammadi writings hint that there was a covert group called the 'Organization' and that their long-term aim — for they realised it would be a long haul — was to overthrow the false Christianity of Rome and reinstate the Gnostic teachings.

There has been much debate about the secret organisation mentioned briefly in Chapter 19, which became known as the Priory of Sion and which may have been the instigator of the Knights Templar. Some observers believe that the Priory of Sion was a myth invented by some egotistical twentieth-century con-men, whilst others firmly believe that it did and may still exist — absolute proof to settle the argument is so far elusive. I believe that there is reasonable evidence, which increases the probability that an organisation did exist and though unfortunately it cannot yet be proved, I think, based on what is known, it is also probable that the Priory of Sion might have been part of the 'Organization' that Robinson mentions.

---

[1] Robinson, J M. *The Nag Hammadi Library*

The Mystery religion in all its varying cults was widespread throughout the Roman Empire and Gnostic Christianity would have been one version of it. As the Empire gradually collapsed and the central control from Rome disintegrated, religious edicts, issued from the time of Constantine to Theodosius would have been unenforceable in most of the west and effectively been ignored.

In western Gaul and the British Isles — the old lands of the Celts and Druids — a form of Christianity developed which was unacceptable to the Church of Rome. The religion became known as Celtic Christianity but its format had far more in common with Gnosticism. How it became established in Britain is unclear, but the likelihood is that once Rome started its forceful promotion of Christianity, the Druids chose to support the intellectual Gnostic version, whose spirituality they could readily accept. Roman Christianity, with its inability to develop spiritually, would have been abhorrent to the educated Celts.

Celtic Christianity certainly did not evolve from Joseph of Arimathea — the myth was invented by the monks of Glastonbury with an eye to profiting from the fame it brought — his bringing Christianity can be dismissed as fiction. William of Malmesbury wrote a history of Glastonbury in the early 12th century and made no mention of Joseph, nor of any of the Arthurian legends associated with the place.[2] Glastonbury acquired its legend at the end of the 12th century when the monks sought to raise funds to rebuild the burnt–down abbey: attracting pilgrims meant making money. Another obvious indication of the myth is that in the time when Jesus was supposed to have lived, there was no place known as Arimathea and none has been found since.[3]

The Vulgate and Didcot versions of Grail stories say Christ instructs Joseph of Arimathea in "the secret words of Jesus"[4] — this is clearly a Gnostic phrase. It is of course possible that Joseph might have been used in the later Grail stories to portray St Paul, the first promoter of the Christian faith. The Grail romances clearly imply that an alternative apostolic line existed in Britain, and that there was secret knowledge unknown to the Roman Catholics. The secret knowledge again indicates that these were the secrets of the Mysteries, which the orthodox Christians had never learned. The only person who could be considered the true *leader* of the real Christianity — Gnostic Christianity — is the Gnostic Paul not Rome's fictitious Peter. It was Gnostic Christianity that was first introduced into Gaul and Britain, not the Roman Catholic version of it.

---

[2] Scott, J. *An Early History of Glastonbury*
[3] Hoover, R. *Jesus' Resurrection: Fact of Figment?*
[4] Phillips, G. *The Search for the Grail*

What happened to Paul is unknown historically; we can dismiss the nonsense of his suffering crucifixion in Rome. It appears that Paul was meant to go to Rome to answer some charges, but whether this is fact is not certain. One story says Paul drowned *en-route* when his ship sank; another suggests he travelled to Gaul. So there is a possibility that if Paul had been seeking to avoid the Roman authorities for any reason, one of the few places of refuge, where Rome's control was still tenuous would have been Britain. Paul would probably also have been aware that the Greeks had linked Pythagorean spiritual philosophy to that of the Druids.[5] Whatever the truth, the fact is that Paul's fate remains unknown and unfortunately we are only able to speculate and unlikely to ever find conclusive proof.

History books generally give the impression that Druidic knowledge was wiped out when the Romans invaded the island of Anglesey off the northwest coast of Wales, but this is not the truth. The Druids survived, even in places under control of Rome, but there were many parts of Britain where Rome's authority was either tentative, or did not exist at all, particularly northern Scotland, the Scottish Isles and Ireland. Anglesey was certainly not the last stronghold of the Druids; the Druids were not a centralised body, if anything they operated largely independently. They were men interested in philosophy, medicine and science, not warriors, so they would not seek a fight, rather would they have dispersed intelligently before the troops arrived. One must always be aware that Roman history regarding the Druids is not only extremely sparse, but was written as propaganda intent on discrediting the Druids whilst simultaneously enhancing Roman success. The truth was that at that time the constant resurgent rebellions of the Britons left the Romans hanging on by their finger-nails in their attempts to keep control.

Within Celtic Christianity, we find the footprints of the Druids. What seems almost certain, is that the ancient Druidic centres of learning, the colleges, were transformed almost overnight into Christian monasteries.[6] The Church of Rome made a point of complaining that British monks had their heads shaved in the manner of the tonsure of the Druids. They also found the role of women in the Celtic Christian Church unacceptable: St Brigit was leader of a Christian community in Ireland and her monastery was mixed, with both sexes having equal rôles. Within the Druidic world, this was quite normal and these practices were transposed into the new Celtic Christianity. Unlike the rest of the Christian world, in Britain females were practising priests who conducted the mass and gave baptism — much to the wrath of Rome. Celtic Christianity had a humanistic doctrine that

---

5 Ellis, P B. *The Druids*
6 Rolleston, T W. *Myths And Legends Of The Celtic Race*

was in opposition to that of Rome; it retained many elements of Druidism and this was because Druids shared the same fundamental philosophical beliefs as the Gnostics.

In the fourth and fifth centuries, Celtic Christianity became known as Pelagianism, taking its name from a British priest called Pelagius. Pelagianism openly opposed the fundamentalist Catholic doctrine of 'original sin'. Pelagius argued against the belief that man was born 'sinful', a notion that probably started pre–Constantine, when Christians still believed in reincarnation. Pelagius stated that it was man's duty to accept responsibility for his actions in order to achieve salvation. There were certainly other profound matters over which the two churches clashed, but I suspect that these were omitted from the later histories. Foremost amongst these was the disagreement over the Apostolic Succession. The Celts basically rejected the right to leadership of the Roman Popes who claimed their authority through a direct line to Peter. The British and Gaulish Celts seemed to consider that there was an alternative line of succession. Unfortunately, there is no documented record, so it is not known with whom this alternative line starts, but common sense tells us that it must refer to Paul, as the eastern Gnostics believed that he was the only true apostle.

In 380 CE Pelagius set out for Rome to put forward his case but, not surprisingly, he was unsuccessful. Despite arguing over dangerous theological differences, Pelagius seemed to have been treated with great respect, yet later, in 416 CE, the Church proclaimed Pelagius's teaching to be a heresy. This declaration had little effect in Britain and Gaul where the Church continued to ignore the papal decree. In 425 CE the Pope persuaded Emperor Honorius to order the Pelagian bishops of Gaul to renounce their heresy within twenty days or face severe consequences; this finally forced their capitulation.[7] However, since the imperial withdrawal, Rome had no authority in Britain and the British leader Vortigern, was not going to give any heed to its decrees. In the same year Pope Celestine sent Germanus, Bishop of Auxerre, to put pressure on the Britons, but he too had little effect.

There was some support for the Catholic faith, but this was from the minority who wished Britain to return to Imperial rule and it was mainly found in the old Roman cities of London, York and Colchester. The stories of Germanus mix myth with fact and little evidence. Once they start to tell of a *victory* achieved by deafening the enemy with the sound of "Alleluia" issued by the troops, we must recognise the fantasy propaganda concocted by Rome to cover up its failure to disband Celtic Christian belief.[8]

---

[7] Gibbon, E. *The History of the Decline and Fall of the Roman Empire*

[8] Thompson, E A. *Saint Germanus of Auxerre and the End of Roman Britain*

Germanus returned twenty-two years later and obtained a little more success. Success that was possibly due to British fears of the increasing Anglo-Saxon incursions. Those who hoped Rome would help to suppress invasion gave more sympathy to its religious views, though Germanus was far from making any kind of major breakthrough. Indeed, in the region that was the power-house of Britain's resistance against the foreign raiders, where the kings such as Vortigern, Ambrosius and Owain Ddantgwyn claimed lineage from the British-based general Emperor Magnus Maximus, the interest was not in Rome's church but in regaining their line's rightful claim to the Imperial purple.

The Celtic Church shared a major problem with the Gnostics; its structure was almost entirely monastic. Though the Gnostics had their base within the monastic system, the Celtic Church inherited its base from the Druidic colleges. So without the large churches and the worldly, ambitious, power-seeking bishops and priests that infested them, the isolated and self-contained monastic system suffered from a lack of the centralisation necessary to mount an effective defence against the Church of Rome's continuing pressure. The former Druids were, after all, interested in *spiritual* development not *political* progress.

Once the empire had been conquered and secured, the need for a vast standing army diminished. Romans wanted to enjoy their wealth and live the comfortable life and so the formidable Imperial Legions virtually ceased to exist and they relied increasingly upon foreign mercenaries to guard the frontiers. Rome had become soft and dissolute and paid little heed to the warning signs that its borders were under pressure from barbarian tribes on the move. In 406 CE, Stilicho, a Vandal who had been made commander of the eastern Danube frontier as part of a political intrigue, was charged with inviting barbarians into the Empire; the Vandals were amongst them and having crossed the Rhine into Gaul, they moved on and settled in Iberia. What control Rome still held onto in the west largely collapsed in 410 CE, when the Visigoths under their leader Alaric, sacked Rome, before moving on westward into Iberia and driving out the Vandals into north Africa. The Vandals helped themselves to the large coastal estates owned by Romans; they adopted Roman ways and lived alongside the Roman colonials, but when they encountered resistance from those of the Roman Catholic faith, they responded with fines and confiscation of property, for the Vandals were Arian Christians, willing to reciprocate the earlier Catholic persecutions of the Gnostics.

In 452, Attila and his army of Huns and Germanic vassals fell upon Rome; the city was saved by Pope Leo I, who paid a tribute after the jealous Emperor Valentinian refused to accept help from Ætius, a Roman nobleman and military leader, who had defeated Attila the previous year in

Gaul. Effectively, these events saw the end of the western empire; the huge Imperial army under the command of Ætius had some Gallo-Romans but was comprised in the main of Visigoths, Franks, Burgundians, Alans, Sarmatæ, Saxons, Angles and a number of Celtic Britons. On removing the Hunnish threat, these tribes realised that Rome could defend itself no more and that they were free to do as they pleased. The Franks and Burgundians carved out kingdoms for themselves in northern and eastern Gaul, whilst the Visigoths had southern Gaul and Iberia.

Somehow, Rome — now confined within the Italian peninsula — still managed to stumble on, but by this time Germanic foreigners were in many positions of power, particularly within the military, for Rome's legendary armies were no more; long since allowed to wither. The Romans now relied upon hired German forces to defend the sad rump of the empire. Ironically, most of these barbarians were Arians, but as with the Visigoths in Iberia who became tentative allies of Rome, they appropriated certain aspects of the Roman culture and by marrying into Roman nobility, they adopted the Catholic form of Christianity.

Yet another sacking of Rome, this time by the Vandal naval expedition from Africa in 455 CE, eventually provoked the eastern emperor Leo the Thracian, to put an end in 468 CE, to both the Germanic threat and their affiliation to the heretic Gnostic sect of Arianism. Despite putting an eastern sympathiser Anthemis on the throne of Rome, Leo's attack on the Vandals in northern Africa ended in disaster. Let down by the retreat of his arrogant brother-in-law Basiliscus who commanded his troops, bankrupt and licking his wounds, Leo effectively gave up any aspirations for the west.

The Germans' allies and mercenaries within Rome, aware of how feeble and dissolute the Roman regime had become, inevitably took advantage. In 476 CE, Ordoacer, king of the Heruli and commander in chief of the Roman armies, overthrew the ineffective Romulus Augustus, the last native Roman emperor. The title Augustus no longer holding any value, Ordoacer made himself *King* of Italy. Though officially a barbarian employed to fight Rome's wars, he was well mannered, prudent and a humanitarian who was sensitive to Roman traditions. Like many of the Germanic barbarians he was a follower of the Arian heresy. His tolerance allowed a relieved Catholic Church to remain in place, though obviously he lifted the draconian restrictions placed on the Gnostic sects. Needless to say, the Catholic bishops and priests were less than happy at *Germans* with *Arian* beliefs settling on *Italian* land and thereby undermining and diminishing the authority of the Catholic Church.

For fourteen years Ordoacer ruled, before Theodoric, king of the Ostrogoths overthrew him. Theodoric, who had been in the employ of the eastern emperor in Constantinople, was under orders to capture Italy; this

The Mystery to Misery Millennium

he did, but for himself not Byzantium. Like Ordoacer, Theodoric was a heretic Arian and had little appetite to remain subservient to any Catholic pope. Once again, Theodoric was no uncouth barbarian; Gibbon writes of him:

> "... a hero of war and government, who restored an age of peace and prosperity and whose name still excites and deserves the attention of mankind."[9]

In the early 6th century, the eastern emperor, Justinian I, briefly regained control of the west again, but the Ostrogoths revolted and Italy, ravaged by a long and bloody civil war was left broken and without power — except for the Catholic Church, which though left weak, sought a revival through the Apostolic Succession: the lie that the Pope in Rome was given his office directly from Peter, who himself was appointed by Jesus. However in the new imperial capital of Constantinople — a city of magnificence thanks to Justinian's ambitious building programme — the long-lived emperor was taking his Christianity away from the overpowering authoritarian Church of Rome to carve out a distinctive theology which often clashed with what rapidly became its rival.

Over the next three centuries, up to around 800 CE, western Europe was broken into small kingdoms ruled over mainly by Celts and the widely resettled Germanic and Scandinavian tribes. By this time, the greatness and glory that had once graced Rome had long gone and Rome was now decrepit: a place poor in culture and refinement, but rich in duplicity and corruption. It was a city in decline; it had shrunk in size; its buildings had decayed; its wealth had gone. The Roman upper classes, the administrators and the educated were no more; the Church sought to fill the void, but did so poorly. The absolute religious pre-eminence of the Catholic Church had also withered dramatically. The power, influence and intellectual theology was with the eastern Byzantine Church in Constantinople, that brilliant city of art, culture and learning, whose Greek emperors considered themselves to be the leaders of the new Greco-Roman Empire and their church to be the true leader of Christendom. These were desperate times for the Church of Rome, but this was not as much attributable to the barbarian threat as to the Church's own weakness and lack of intellectuals within their ranks. With no imperial throne to shore them up, their edifice was in danger of collapse.

To add to the Church's woes, the Germanic tribes with their *heretical* Arian version of Christianity left the Catholic Church of Rome feeling vulnerable to complete demolition. Of especial discomfort was the close

---

9 Gibbon, E. *The Decline and Fall of the Roman Empire*

proximity of the Lombards, originally from Northern Europe, they had lived along the Danube and now settled into northern Italy alongside the Ostrogoths. The Germanic barbarians cared nothing for the laws made by previous Roman emperors which had made the Catholic Church the sole religion of the empire and outlawed all others, whether pagan or alternative Christian. An unlikely saviour arrived to repair the foundations that these Arian barbarians had begun to undermine.

In the early 6th century, the pagan Franks led by Clovis had settled in the Rhineland and northern Gaul. To win favour with the Gallo–Roman people of Gaul, Clovis took the political decision to adopt the Roman Catholic faith. Over a number of generations, the Franks emerged as the dominant power within western Europe and they gradually consolidated their position by forcefully bringing onside their *cousins* the Burgundians, Saxons, Thuringians, Alemanni, Bavarians, Visigoths, Ostrogoths and Lombards. It was to the Franks that the Catholic Church had called for help whenever it felt under severe pressure, which first happened just after the death of Clovis, during the time of Justinian. The threat of the Arian heresy supplanting Catholicism presented the greatest fear. The Frankish king, Pepin, was asked to intercede to restrain the Lombards from expanding southwards towards Rome. Later the Church made a repeat call to Pepin's son Charles, asking him once more to check the Lombards. His forceful incursion into northern Italy in 773 CE resulted in the incorporation of the Lombard kingdom into the empire of the Franks and put an end to the Arian threat. Charles was afforded the title *Carolus Magnus*, to become better known in later times by the French version of this name, Charlemagne.

Pope Leo III looked to Charlemagne to rejuvenate papal fortunes and hegemony. The Arian heresy which had been resurrected by the Germanic and Scandinavian tribes had been checked, but the threat of subjugation by the Byzantine Church still loomed large. The problem was that Charlemagne had no intention of becoming another Roman Emperor and residing in Rome — he was a Frank and proud to be so. Charlemagne had his own ideas; his plan was to construct the town of Aix and make a new centre of empire; a new Rome and move the papacy there. Leo saw that a transfer by the Frankish king into Frankish territory, would render the papacy subservient and that the Pope would become no more than head-bishop within the Frankish Empire. The Empire would no longer be Roman and neither would the church be Roman Catholic, it would be a religion vulnerable to the whims of a German king. The papacy knew it needed to remain within its own territory if it were to retain its independence.

In 800 CE, Charlemagne was invited to Rome to attend the Christmas Mass. As he knelt at his prayers, Pope Leo surprised him by placing a gold circlet upon his head to represent the imperial crown and proclaimed him "*Imperator Augustus*", Emperor of the Romans. The stage-managed chorus of approval and confirmation from the compliant congregation gave the crowning its support and thus its legality. The Frankish entourage was furious at the rigged coronation; it had been deliberately deceived and physically sidelined, incapable of intervention. Charlemagne, concerned that what the Pope had conveyed, the Pope could take away, determined that hence-forward the king of the Franks would set the crown upon his head himself — *Deo Gratias* — cutting out the middle-man and leaving the king with no obligation to any church.

Pope Leo had also had a plan to reunite the eastern and western parts of the empire but that never came to fruition. This second scheme involved the betrothal of Charlemagne to the widowed Empress Irene of Byzantium; it was abandoned when she was suddenly deposed because of her unpopularity in Constantinople. Whilst Charlemagne might have enjoyed being sovereign of the reunited empire, the loss was of no real concern to him; for Pope Leo, however, it ruined his ambition for pre-eminence over all Christendom.

As the ninth century dawned, Charlemagne sat, like a new Solomon, on his throne in Aix, while the Pope remained in Rome. For Charlemagne, Rome held no attraction, nor did a claim over the Byzantine Empire. Charlemagne was far from Romanised, nor was he the ideal orthodox Christian. Despite the Franks long legacy of immersion in the faith of the Roman Church, the traditional pagan ways of Charlemagne's ancestors were still strong within him. Though interested in the promotion of culture, the arts and learning, he could read a little but could not write; he clothed himself in the simple manner of his Germanic people, enjoyed hunting and eating, though he did not drink. If he were truly committed to the Catholic faith, it seems strange that he did not embrace the Christian belief of monogamous marriage, for besides the wives he married through the Christian ceremony, he took other wives in traditional Germanic-pagan ceremonies, giving a final unholy count of nine wives and four concubines.

Charlemagne's dynasty did not manage to last for long. Charlemagne unwisely decided to divide his empire up amongst his four sons. Increasing family rivalries ensured that there would be no return to a single kingdom and so the prospect of a state that would have encompassed all of modern France and Germany was shattered forever. The Carolingian dynasty was to last for less than seventy years before falling to the invading Norsemen — who took their French name into the history books instead. Nevertheless, the foundations laid by Charlemagne had been set and the shrewd

Normans saw how to build on them. Employing astute political acumen in order to further their ambition for power, the Normans embraced both the Christian religion and the Frankish culture. The Holy Roman Empire continued; not always carrying with it great political or military power, but it enhanced the political power of the Roman Church most successfully.

In Britain, events were to cause the Church there even greater set-backs. During the mid 5th century, the pagan Anglo-Saxons slowly pushed deeper and deeper into Britain. Some of the Celtic Britons opposed them and were killed, some retreated westwards, but many stayed and lived alongside the newcomers. Eventually many Germans took British wives, which sometimes led to their adoption of Celtic Christianity. The Celtic language of Britain below the Forth river in Scotland was Brythonic. Intermarrying often resulted in offspring with Brythonic names and so we find a strong Celtic influence amongst the people's leaders. Cerdic, the name of the founder of the Saxon ruling dynasty of Wessex, derives from the Brythonic Ceretic; the same Brythonic element appears in the names of Caedwalla the king of Wessex and Caesbeth the king of Lindsey. Celtic craftsmanship was valued by the newcomers, particularly the work of the potters and the smiths, who were skilled at intricate ironwork and decoration and this ensured that the Celts and Celtic Christianity stayed where it always had been.[10]

Well into this period, there were still sizeable Celtic enclaves in eastern England. We can see this in the names of rivers, streams and *topographical features* where the use of *Brythonic* increases in density moving westwards across England, whereas the original *settlement* areas of the south east show a high density of *Germanic* names. Across England, a look at settlement names shows that the great majority is Germanic and later Norse. The settlement name is more an indication of dominant political influence than proof of racial occupation; who lived there is more often shown by the names of the natural features of the land. Archaeological evidence indicates that many areas under Anglo-Saxon occupation were not devoid of a Celtic-British population. Additionally we find a number of historical references, for example in the *Life of St Guthlac,* who encountered Brythonic speaking Britons living in the Fens of East Anglia around 700 CE. In southern England records show that towns had their independent Celtic-Briton communities; in Exeter there was a quarter known as Britayne until the 13th century.[11]

The first westwards wave of Anglo-Saxon incursion had been one of land grabbing by Germanic farmers; the second wave was mainly political. In

---

[10] Frere, S S. *Brittannia A History of Roman Britain*
[11] Fisher, D J V. *The Anglo-Saxon Age*

places like western Wessex — roughly covering the area of modern-day Gloucestershire and Wiltshire — the Celts retained much of the land. Intermarriage amongst the ruling classes assisted harmonious integration and induced the bridegrooms to adopt the Christian religion of their brides. As a result, from western Wessex to the borders of London, the Celtic Church was granted land. In many other areas, the first wave of Anglo-Saxon pagan invaders had pushed Celtic Christianity westwards but then Roman Catholic missionaries arrived from across the Channel and made some progress in converting the Saxon ruling classes, particularly in the southeast of Britain. By the middle of the sixth century, the Celtic Church with its Pelagian influences was squeezed right across into Cornwall and Wales, and remained particularly strong in the kingdoms of Powys and Gwynedd.

Pope Gregory the Great had little knowledge of what was occurring in Rome's lost western province and entertained the notion that the people would be desperate to be converted. As a consequence he sent Augustine — later Saint — to 'save' the inhabitants of Britain. In 597 CE, Augustine landed at Thanet with forty fellow monks, including Frankish interpreters. The Saxon king of Kent, Æthelberht, gave permission for the missionaries to preach and lodged them in an old church in Canterbury. The popular myth is that Æthelberht and 10,000 of his people converted and were baptised within the year.[12] Some scholars argue over the date and insist that it was more likely to have happened in 601 CE,[13] however the application of rational thought to the magnitude of the number of converts makes one doubt the likelihood that the event took place at all. Had Æthelberht accepted conversion, it was unlikely to be a spiritual one, but a sensible political act. One must certainly question the king's commitment, for his second marriage was to a pagan princess and his son Eadbald remained a pagan. Æthelberht's nephew ruled the London area and he too was a pagan, who rejected the missionaries.[14]

Augustine's report back to Pope Gregory must have inflated whatever slight success he really achieved, for as a result of the 'wonderful news', the deceived Pope proposed that London and York would each hold Archbishoprics of the Catholic Church and that twelve bishops would be ordained to attend to his new flock in the north. In reality Britain proved a hard nut to crack, its people, both the Germanic newcomers and the rural Celts, clung onto their traditional religious practices. They were obstinate and too ready to resort to violence to repel outsiders trying to enforce

---

[12] ibid.

[13] ibid.

[14] ibid.

changes so it took many years for Gregory to achieve his aims. Once Pope Gregory was advised of the true state of British Christianity, he wrote to Bishop Mellitus, his London representative, to tell him that the Church should avoid open confrontation with the British or any attempts to force change. Gregory knew that the Celtic Church operated from their largely remote monasteries and he realised the advantage of operating from churches in centres of population. As the Catholic Church had done elsewhere in Europe, he decided to co-opt the old pagan temples as Catholic Churches.

From far-off Rome, Pope Gregory did not understand that the *pagan temples* of Britain were not great stone classical structures like those of Athens, Rome and other cities, but sacred groves and springs in remote locations. He wrote that the idols should be broken up, but the 'well-built temples' retained and purified from Devil worship by the sprinkling of Holy Water. In some cases attempts were made to dismantle a henge and re-use the stone to build a church, but these were infrequent, impossible or achieved much later.[15] Bishop Mellitus realised the miscomprehension, but nevertheless saw the advantage of utilising the traditional pagan sites. Thus the building of the traditional Saxon village-church began. Though Christianity was not adopted readily and little was achieved during Mellitus' lifetime, eventually almost all old churches in Britain were constructed on ancient pagan holy places.

My opinion, shared with others from scientist and astronomer Sir Norman Lockyer to members of the British Association of Dowsers, is that the structures were placed over the energy vortices in the groves. Whatever one chooses to believe about energy healing, the fact remains that the Church attempted to requisition the pagan healing traditions in the hope of gaining great esteem from the miracles it would perform. Once the churches were built, the altars acted as cap-stones which blocked the natural energy forces used for the healing cures these sites were once renowned for. Those who knew how to use the energies to heal had already left or been removed. The Roman Christians made use of the 'healing wells' to perform their baptisms and when the cures stopped, they told the people that it was because they were not worthy enough. The churches obviously could not be seen as failures so miracles would still happen from time to time, but only to *pious* Christians.

Pope Gregory died in 604 CE and Augustine shortly after. Archbishop Laurence was consecrated as Augustine's successor at Canterbury but he found that the reality of his missionary work was bleak. He failed to persuade the British and Irish clergy to adopt Roman Catholic practices

---

15 Knight, P. *Ancient Stones of Dorset*

and the Celtic Church was not averse to demonstrating its hostility, Laurence reported that a visiting Irish bishop not only refused to eat with his community at Canterbury, but also even refused to eat in the same house.[16] Things got worse when Æthelberht died in 616 CE and his pagan son Eadbald succeeded to the throne. In Essex, when King Saeberht died, he too left a pagan heir. Following this turnaround in Roman Christian fortune, Bishop Mellitus of London and Bishop Justus of Rochester fled to Gaul. Before Laurence could flee, Eadbald changed his mind and allowed him to stay in Canterbury. Justus was allowed to return, but in London and Essex, the rulers refused to allow the Christians back.

In the north, the Angle ruler of the newly created kingdom of Northumbria was Æthelfrith. When in 616 CE he was killed in a battle, his son Edwin became king and in 625 CE married Eadbald's sister, Æthelberg. She had become a Catholic and had journeyed north with Paulinius, who was ordained as the first Bishop of York prior to the journey. Edwin eventually agreed to convert, together with his court. In 632 CE Edwin died in battle against the coalition of the pagan King Penda of Mercia and Cadwallon the Celtic Christian king of Powys. Edwin's brother, Oswald, who had been in exile in Ireland, returned to claim the throne after Cadwallon had finished devastating Northumbria.

Whilst away, Oswald had spent some time at the Celtic Christian community on Iona and been baptised there. When Oswald decided to return home, he brought with him a monk named Aidan and had him consecrated bishop, making him Bishop of Northumbria and Abbot of Lindisfarne. Aidan's influence was great and he was well liked, even by Bede, who was a severe critic of the Celtic Church. Bede even went so far as to suggest that the slothful Catholic clergy would do well to follow Aidan's example. The acceptance from the Catholics was aided by Oswald's relaxed attitude. Instead of opposing them, he stood as sponsor to Cynegils, his subject king of Wessex at his baptism by Bishop Birinus from Rome and allowed him to set up an Episcopal See in Wessex. Aidan was on friendly terms with the Catholic clergy and his example created a thawing between the two Churches, but his altruism and Christian spirituality were soon to prove misguided and contribute to the Celtic Church's demise.

After Oswald's defeat and death at the hands of Penda, the tables were then turned. Oswald's son King Oswy defeated and killed Penda. Penda's sons, Paeda and Wulfhere, under pressure from the victors, accepted conversion into the Celtic Church. This now meant that the influence of Lindisfarne stretched right down into the Midlands of England, whereas

---

[16] ibid.

Rome's influence — badly stalled after King Æthelberth's death — was contained in Kent and parts of East Anglia.

In Ireland, the Catholic Church made some inroads, but only in the very south of the island; in the northern parts the Celtic Church held sway. In Scotland, on the isle of Iona around 563 CE, St Columba set up a base for Irish missionaries who would convert the pagan Picts of the north. Iona was a noted Druidic centre, so the early Celtic Christians could only establish themselves there with the blessing of the powerful Druids, confirming the close link between the two. Columba and his followers were not Catholics; they belonged to the Celtic Church and had fled Ireland because they were at odds with the Church of Rome. This struggle continued for over a century.

The fact that the pagan Anglo–Saxons were gradually converted to Christianity did not please Rome, for they were being converted to the Celtic Church. However, as the Celtic Church relocated in Wales, it had no desire to return and convert the Anglo–Saxon invaders who had moved them out of the southeast and its truculent and short-sighted policy was to prove its undoing. Had the Celtic monks thought to *convert* the Saxons in southern Britain, they could have stopped the Catholic missionaries from returning, thereby assuring the supremacy of the Celtic Church. Though the Vatican was preoccupied by threats to its survival within Italy, there was still concern about the Christians in Britain. It was not simply a concern that a Christian Church was operating outside of Vatican control, but a greater concern, that in many ways this church was radically different. The Church in Rome saw a potentially dangerous fusion of Druidism and Gnostic Christianity and even worse, one that questioned and denied papal authority. The Celtic monks were unworldly creatures with no interest in such things as wealth or status, nor of following strict religious doctrines. They were, like the Druids, given to living in remote retreats away from the cares of life and even worse, they were footloose and given to wandering without plan to wherever the mood took them. This was coupled with the Celtic disposition to being wilful and no great respecter of authority. That Irish missionaries were sailing eastwards into Europe and founding their own monastic centres would have been of particular concern to Rome, fearing that from these new outposts, the Irish might spread their own version of Christianity.

Columbanus (543–615 CE) provides a good example of how the Irish monks expanded their influence into Europe and why they persisted in the defence of their beliefs. He set up monasteries at Anegray and Luxeuil in France, at Bregenz in Switzerland and at Bobbio in northern Italy — the last two were in Lombard territories where the heretical Arian Christianity was being practised, so it appears that Columbanus felt at home and unthreatened amongst Arian Christians. In letters attribute to Columbanus, the author refers often to philosophy and the need to avoid confrontation. He uses quotes from Paul's Epistles and even explains to Pope Gregory that he could come to Rome to discuss his differences of opinion with him, but would not do so in case it led to disagreement. In all of his letters he refers frequently to Christ, but rarely to Jesus. His polite and tactful letter sets out his argument with the Pope, which is not theological, but philosophical. His first two letters mysteriously did not reach Gregory, but in the third he states,

> "... through the various clashes of this age and the turbulent treasons of the tribes that lie between, as though I were shut in upon a vessel of the sea, I have not been able to satisfy my wishes, opposed by the really un–gentle and un–crossable swell, which you best know, of a sea that is not so much material as intellectual."

Columbanus makes an interesting point before he concludes the letter:

> "... grant to us pilgrims in our travail the godly consolation of your judgement, thus confirming, if it is not contrary to the faith, the tradition of our predecessors, so that by your approval we may in our pilgrimage maintain the rite of Easter as we have received it from generations gone before."

Columbanus insists that the Celtic Church's calculation of Easter, which he argued from a philosophical and astronomical view in the previous letters, derives from generations of previous teaching. As this was not the Roman teaching, in order to go back a long way, it could only have come from the Druids.

What really shows that he is following an older yet parallel and compatible teaching is written as he concludes the letter by reinforcing his decision to follow the Celtic path. He reminds Pope Gregory of a decision made at the first synod called by Emperor Theodosius in 381 CE.

> "Farewell, Pope most dear in Christ, mindful of us both in your holy prayers beside the ashes of the saints, and in your most godly decisions following the hundred and fifty authorities of the Council of Constantinople, who decreed that churches of God planted in pagan nations should live by their own laws as they had been instructed by their fathers."[17]

---

[17] Walker, G S M. *Letters of Columbanus*

The scientific teachings transmitted by these Irishmen posed another major concern to the Roman Church. Some of the knowledge they possessed could only have been learnt from the Druids — the Druidic colleges had been renowned as centres of great learning.

An Irish missionary named Fergal, who from his Latin name Virgilius became known as Virgil, arrived in Salzburg, now in Austria, then part of Bavaria, around 746 CE on the death of the local bishop. He became Abbot of St Peter's monastery and Bishop three years later. Virgil was well educated, interested in the arts and had a strong knowledge of geometry, mathematics and astronomy. He apparently knew so much geography that the monks at his abbey in Ireland had named him 'The Geometer.'

For the Church of Rome, Virgil's knowledge and personality formed a dangerous combination. Outspoken and in a position to influence, before he arrived in Salzburg he had frequently crossed intellectual swords with the papal legate of Bavaria. Many Saxon missionaries had sailed over the channel to convert and preach to the Franks, one of them, a Wessex man named Wynfrith, was the legate. He took the name of Boniface and was later sainted. Boniface brought the Pope into an argument that Virgil must re-baptise a lot of converts as a poorly-educated priest had been overheard baptising them with incorrect Latin: "*Baptiso te in nomine patria et filia et spiritu sancta.*" Virgil argued that God would know that the priest did not really mean, 'I baptise you in the name of the fatherland and daughter and Holy Spirit' and therefore the baptisms were valid. When Boniface complained to the Pope, the Pope sided with Virgil.

Some time later Boniface found a more outrageous reason to report the conduct of Virgil. He was shocked to overhear Virgil teaching of 'other men' who lived in 'other lands, under the earth.' The charge he made to Pope Zachary was one of heresy as these 'men' were not descended from Adam. He also charged Virgil with teaching a heresy that the Earth was a globe that circled round the sun. Virgil was duly summoned to Rome to answer the charges, which Zachary duly discounted; he sent him back to Salzburg, later awarding him the rank of bishop.[18]

Virgil continued to flourish, opening schools for priests throughout Bavaria and sending missionaries out into the surrounding lands. He built Salzburg's first cathedral, a large domed structure that was considered a wonder by those who saw it. After his death in 784 a new bishop was appointed and a new wave of *Catholicism* replaced his.

Virgil's words about the men from the 'other lands beneath the earth' will strike a familiar chord to those familiar with Celtic religion, for the

---

[18] op cit Rolleston, T W.

residents of the Otherworld are the Fair–Folk, as Celtic legend tells: the angels who were known as the Nephilim.[19]

Virgil's story shows us that the Celtic Church still continued to spread its teaching far and wide. The final battle for supremacy was already lost, almost a hundred years before, shortly after the time of Columbanus. It took place in 664 CE, at the Synod of Whitby in Yorkshire, where the clergy of Britain met supposedly to agree on the dating of Easter, yet in reality to fight to retain its independence from Rome. The truth was that the matter had little to do with religion at all. The most powerful ruler in Britain, Oswy, King of Northumbria, had called the synod. Oswy saw that he could exert his political hegemony over the other smaller autonomous kingdoms with their independent Celtic monasteries, by subordinating them to his church, which was the Church of Rome. Oswy came to favour the Catholic Church over the Celtic Church for pragmatic not spiritual reasons. He married Edwin's daughter, who had been brought up in Kent and had adopted the Catholic Faith as did his own son, Alchfrith. Oswy saw that the different observances in his own family, if spread further within his own kingdom, might at some future time lead to conflict. To have one official religion supported by the king would eliminate the differences and prevent the discord — Rome's dogmatic teaching better suited a strong king than a religion based on intellect or philosophy.

The synod's debate was bitter, but the Roman faction led by Bishop Wilfred won the day against the Pelagians and followers of Columba, led by Bishop Colman of Lindisfarne. The theological debate was settled in favour of Rome, when Wilfred allegedly suggested that Oswy, who chaired the debate, might not be let through the gates of Heaven if he ruled against Rome. It is unlikely that Oswy would have given any heed to such a warning, having already decided what the outcome was to be. Despite finding in favour of the Catholic Church, Oswy had no intention of giving Rome any *political* power though they could make all the *religious* rules from then on and he would support them.

To the Celts, the matter was far from done and dusted; Colman resigned his position at Lindisfarne and retired to Iona, as Columba had done from Ireland and there the influential monks continued to ignore Rome. Another of the delegates arguing against unification was Cadwaladr, the king of Gwynedd, who upon the death of his wife had become a monk. Infuriated by the decision, he left for Rome, to continue the protest. His objection was against the claimed authority of Roman Popes. He died mysteriously on arrival, no doubt murdered on the orders of Pope Vitalian. Cadwaladr was not to be the last king from Britain who was to meet his end in Rome.

---

[19] Evans-Wentz, W Y. *The Fairy-Faith in Celtic Countries*

Some two hundred years later, King Cyngen of Powys undertook a mission to Rome. Cyngen considered himself to be a direct descendant of Magnus Maximus, Emperor of the western Roman empire, who had left Britain for Rome in 383 CE. Magnus Maximus had the ambitious intention to take the eastern throne as well; he was defeated and killed in the battle with Theodosius of Constantinople. Back in Britain, the family of Maximus had not given up their claim to the throne of Rome.

It was around 854 CE, when King Cyngen and his entourage, which may have included a daughter, went to Rome to dispute the right of Charlemagne's successors to the Imperial throne. To validate his claim, he took with him the Imperial sceptre of Maximus described in the fifth-century *Visentium*. Cyngen failed and was executed by the Holy Roman Emperor, Louis II and the imperial sceptre of Maximus disappeared.[20]

Linked to Cyngen's mission to Rome, is the story of Pope Joan. There are numerous accounts of this and there is some discrepancy over dates. It seems that Joan was Pope John VIII, who reigned from around 872 CE but the exact dating of Popes around this period is uncertain. There is an account by Marianus Scotus, a Benedictine monk who when writing about the year 854 CE says

> "Pope Leo died, on the Kalends of August. He was succeeded by Joanna, a woman, who reigned for two years, five months and four days."

There is much dispute about its authenticity and the date is far too early for the papal coronation, but coincides with Cyngen's arrival, so it might be the date when Joan arrived in Rome. The dates of Popes in the lists vary and at times there are two at once, so we can't say there was never a Pope Joan and need to consider who she might have been and how she might have been elected to the role. Only males were allowed to be priests and thus Pope in the Roman Catholic tradition, though females had equal roles in the Celtic Church. Naturally Vatican records will not show a female Pope, but the few stories that survive, do tend to be consistent.

We do not know her real name, so we shall refer to her as Joan. In the Brythonic, later Welsh language, there is no letter J, instead there are the letters Si which sound "Sh" and were corrupted by english scribes to change the name Siôn — pronounced "Shone" — to John and Siôn's into the sound familiar in the common welsh surname Jones. Joan's current Welsh equivalent is Siân or Sioned, so her name might have been the female form of Siôn.

---

20 op. cit. Phillips, G.

The story of Joan says that she left Britain accompanied by her father. Joan arrives in Rome, though her father is no longer given a mention. The common thread in the tales, tells that she had strong religious inclinations, but being frustrated by the restrictions imposed against females, she disguised herself as a monk. Once in Rome, she set up a school and acquired such a great reputation that she was elected Pope. Allegedly, she became pregnant and the inopportune birth led to her discovery. It seems that shortly afterwards, she died under *mysterious* circumstances, so is assumed murdered.[21]

The Catholic Church naturally denies that the events ever occurred, however after the death of Pope John VIII, the papal electoral process was reformed. It is not known when the specific procedure started, but up to the death of Pope Leo X in 1521, the elected pope had his genitals examined to ensure he was male. The chair on which he sat until the inspecting Cardinal declared, "*Testiculos habet et bene pendentes*," was donated to King Louis XVIII by Pope Pius VII and is now in the Louvre Museum.[22] This leaves many people to deduce that the practice was introduced in response to such an extreme incident that it must never be repeated. Clearly this specific rule change was to ensure that a female passing herself off as a man could never be elected as Pope, but why would you think it was something you needed to monitor, unless it had happened once before!

Though this is not *proof*, it would be an exceedingly strange coincidence that King Cyngen and his daughter *and* Joan and her father all left Britain and arrived in Rome in the same year. One pair to claim the throne and the other the papacy. These two recorded sets of a father and daughter arriving from Britain at the same time have surely to be the same two family members who believed themselves the true claimants of both the Imperial and Apostolic lines.

Although the Catholics deny there was ever a female Pope, Pope Joan was much mentioned around the time of the crusade against the Cathars in the 13th century. The founder of the Dominican order, Dominic Guzman attacked the Cathars' female priests and specifically mentions that they claimed their spiritual ancestor to be the female pope, whom Guzman calls *Joanna Aquila* or Joan the Eagle. This symbol appears in Tarot Cards, which the Cathars invented to help them avoid persecution, because they could claim they were playing a card game, not teaching their beliefs. The cards each held a coded pictorial representation. One of the Trump cards is the Female Pope.

---

[21] ibid.
[22] Pirie, V. *The Triple Crown*

During their persecution, the Templars secretly aided the Cathars, and the Templars were also strongly associated with the Priory of Sion. Is it then a coincidence that Pope Joan/John's name derived from Siôn? I strongly suspect that Pope Joan indicates close Celtic links to the Priory of Sion, but my notion is based on speculation not evidence, until some honest soul reveals a lost document long–hidden in the Vatican archives!

While Celtic Christianity in mainland Britain was subject to frequent harassment from Rome, in Ireland things generally took a different course. Ireland lacked the fairly–centralised political control that was common in the area that later became England. There were no large towns or cities, but rather a tribal village society. Ireland, like Britain in Celtic times, had no churches, just isolated monasteries and none of these were under any kind of centralised ecclesiastical control, so this independent system was ripe for picking off, bit by bit, by the missionaries of the Church of Rome.

The monasteries were almost certainly communities with a mixture of ecclesiastical and secular academic interests. There had only been one local body of people who offered scientific insight, philosophy, arts and spiritual learning, so we must infer that these religious sites were former Druidic colleges.[23] As in Britain, there is compelling evidence to indicate that here too there had been a form of Gnostic Christianity which had a strong link with the Druids. Druids were men and women of learning, not the primitive shamanic priests that ancient Druids are sometimes portrayed as in modern accounts.

Stories abound about the life of St Brigid but they consistently provide a good insight into the religious communities of the time. Brigid, as priestess and abbess, was in charge and under her administration the monastery had both male and female members, with the females having equal standing with males and the right to preach and baptise. She chose an oak tree under which to build her 'cell,' thus giving the name to the town Kildare — Church of the Oak — a druidic oak under which she healed. In one tale Brigid is made a Bishop, an odd fact for a historian to record unless her status was high and she was regarded with great respect. Such things were alien to the Catholic Church, but common–place amongst the Druids. Brigid should have been reviled as an evil heretic by the Catholic Church yet such was her undying popularity, it dared not blacken her name and so the stories report great miracles and resorting to the Roman Church's usual practice, the pagan priestess was made a saint. Whether Brigid's stories are

---

[23] op. cit. Rolleston, T W.

true perhaps doesn't matter, in the words of the Cill Dara Historical Society:[24]

> "So, was the Christian Saint Brigid a real historical person, or the mythical Celtic pagan goddess in another form? The truth is that we don't know. Somebody established a Christian foundation on the hill of Kildare. That foundation prospered and became the great and unique Celtic Christian monastery of monks and nuns."

Likewise, St Patrick's true roots may have been misrepresented. Authenticating virtually everything about his life is no more than tenuous, so one must be wary of claims from the Catholic Church that declare Patrick as one of their own. *Confessions* is allegedly written by Patrick, but this work too must be viewed with suspicion. When one reads the *Confessions*, the first page sounds like an expansion of the Nicene Creed, it does not sound like the writings of a great Celtic Christian philosopher and spiritual leader.[25] There are too many reminders of the wrath of God and little of the spiritual teaching that Patrick, at that time in Ireland or Britain, would have known. As we have seen, from earliest times, the Church was not averse to unauthorised additions, censorial extractions, or even complete forgery. Fortunately this adulteration was often conducted in a careless and disjointed fashion, which afforded scholars the means by which to detect the falsehoods.

The dates for Patrick are vague, but he began preaching probably around the mid fifth century. Little is known about his early years other than that he was born and raised somewhere in western Britain. The religion that had total dominance in Britain and was especially strong in the west was that of the Celtic Church. It must also be remembered that Pelagius was not only attacking the false *doctrine* of the Church of Rome, but also disputing their claim to an authentic and authoritative apostolic line. All the contemporary circumstances support the likelihood that Patrick would have been raised as a follower of the Celtic Church. When he was kidnapped and taken to Ireland, he would have encountered similar or Druidic pagan beliefs there. If, when he escaped, he went back to Britain, why would he go all the way to Auxerre to study theology under St Germanus. If we look to Germanus himself for evidence, we have already seen that he lacks any credibility at all.[26] Rational consideration of what is

---

[24] Connelly, J *Saint Brigid*
[25] Skinner, J. *The Confession of Saint Patrick and Letter to Coroticus*
[26] op. cit. Thompson, E A

known casts grave doubts upon the claims made about Patrick by the Catholic Church and there is nothing to support it in the *Confessions*, where he mentions just one brief visit to Gaul.

A clue to Patrick's real affiliations can be found in his nickname of *Talcend*, meaning 'Adze–head'. An adze being a form of axe whose blade was set at right–angles to the conventional axe, this strange nickname was descriptive of his monastic appearance and derives from his hair being shaven into the triangular shape of tonsure. The conventional Christian monks tonsure has the top of the head shaven, however Patrick's tonsure had the front of the head shaven leaving the hair in a Delta pattern, which resembled the shape of an adze–head. Many Druids wore this style of tonsure, though not all of them, and those Druids continued to wear it when they became the monks of the Celtic Church.[27] When the Catholic Church gained ascendancy at the Synod of Whitby, they forbade the continuance of the Druidic tonsure.

It appears that Patrick had a curiosity about the stories of the Celtic gods and one in particular, Lugh Lámhfadha. Such an unsanctioned interest would have provoked the wrath of the Church of Rome... had Patrick been a Catholic, but if he belonged to the Celtic Church with its strong Druidic connections, such an interest would be totally understandable and acceptable. I have always been conscious of the seeming conflict between Patrick's interest in the gods and fairy–folk and his alleged condemnations, but this contradiction is easily explained if one sees that these were not Patrick's condemnations, but ones concocted by the Catholic Church at some later date.

Many modern–day Catholics undertake an annual pilgrimage to the summit of a mountain in the west of Ireland, which is today known as Croagh Patrick. Allegedly, Patrick climbed this mountain and spent forty days — the ubiquitous sacred number 40 — on this exposed bleak summit in contemplation. There were more practical yet still suitably austere locations that would lend themselves to solitary contemplation, so the choice of this summit swept by the fierce Atlantic winds seems bizarre on first consideration. In Patrick's time this mountain was supposedly sacred to the solar deity Lugh. According to Gaelic mythology, a race of semi–immortal beings, whom they called the *Tuatha de Danaan*, landed on a mountain in the west of what is now Ireland, though at that time the whole land looked very different — perhaps the end of the ice–age, before the rising sea made it an island. There is a legend that says that the Danaans descended from the sky and the whole mountain was shrouded from sight by a thick pall of smoke for several days whilst they secured their base. These *gods* were described as

---

[27] Mc Carthy, D P. "On the shape of the Insular tonsure"

beautiful, blond–haired, with very tall slender bodies and piercing pale eyes — rather like the elven Fairy–Folk of mythical tradition and as described in the stories of JRR Tolkien. The description also matches that given by the Egyptian priests of their gods who they claimed, came from the west.

There is a further connection between the Danaans and the Egyptian gods, Lugh was the Celtic and scholars think also the neolithic, solar god.[28] The name Lugh means light and he is known as the 'Lightbringer'. As the bringer of light, Lugh brought morality and knowledge to mankind and was the teacher of science and the arts. Amongst the Egyptians, these gifts were dispensed by those facets of Ra represented by the gods Thoth and Osiris; in Greece by the sun god Apollo.

Lugh's second descriptive name was *Lámhfadha* meaning long–armed, or long–handed as the old Gaelic name for arm and hand was the same. This name has puzzled scholars, with the most popular explanation being that it was in praise of Lugh's ability to throw a spear a long way.[29] This theory is at best down–to–earth and practical but it is clearly derived for lack of any better idea and thus at worst banal. If these scholars had looked outside of the *Celtic box* and in particular towards Egypt, they would have easily found their answer. Both the sun god Ra and his solar disc personification as the Aten, are depicted as a sun from which emanates rays of light in the form of long arms at the end of which are hands which reach down to offer life–giving light to the Earth. For this singular image to have no connection to the Lámhfadha description of the Celtic sun god is highly unlikely and cannot be dismissed as a coincidence.

In the Irish tales, Lugh was also given the surname *Ildanach* or *Samildanach* meaning The All–Craftsman[30] in honour of all the skills that he possessed: carpenter, metal–smith, warrior, poet, musician, scientist, physician amongst them. One of his skills was as a shoemaker and this epithet with his name persists in places ranging from Sweden, through Brittany to Spain.[31]

Though, largely thanks to the Catholic Church, Lugh is virtually unknown today, yet in the Celtic and possibly the pre–Celtic world, his name was revered. Many modern towns and cities have their names derived from fortified settlements dedicated to Lugh. The original Lugdunum, meaning 'fortress of Lugh' gave its name to London and Luguvallum, a town near Hadrian's Wall. Carlisle was also originally called Lugdunum. In France we find Lyon, Loudan, Leon and Laon and in Holland Leyden; in

---

[28] op. cit. Rolleston, T W.
[29] Macalister, R A S. *Lebor Gabála Érenn: Book of the Taking of Ireland*
[30] op. cit. Rolleston, T W.
[31] op. cit. Ellis, P B.

Switzerland there is Lugano and Lucerne; in Spain Lugo and Lugones; in Italy Lugo; in Germany Liegnitz and Lugde. Lugh was also known by a third name 'Find', meaning Fair One and in this form was honoured throughout Europe, commonly as Vindonous and its localised derivatives like Vienna the capital of Austria and Vienne a town in northern Provence, which was home to the Gallic tribe who later founded Lyon when the Romans moved them on.

Not just towns, but an exceedingly large number of the old Christian sites that are dedicated to that fictional Archangel, St Michael, were originally sites dedicated to Lugh and the sun god. Those now consecrated to St Mary were originally devoted to the Danaan mother goddess Danu or Isis, and the moon.

The early Catholic Church in Europe had to compete with the Celtic Christians and the veneration of Lugh. It made some progress in the larger towns where it was able to exert the authority decreed to it by the emperor, elsewhere the people resisted. The Church was up against a mightily revered opponent and its crude and dishonourable course of action was to demonise Lugh the Bringer of Light.

The Roman name for Lugh was Lugus. The Latin translation of light is *lux lucis* and from *lucis,* which also means clear and bright, came the name Lucifer. Why Lucifer the Light Bringer should be another name for the devil, the Church fails to explain; he is not mentioned in the Bible though there is a Babylonian king given the same name in Isaiah 14:12. This in itself is odd, to find a Latin name in a Hebrew document. The original Hebrew names the Babylonian king as "Heylyl ben Shachar" which translates as Day Star, Son of the Dawn. When we know that the Roman name for Venus, the Morning Star, is Lucifer, we may assume that some biblical translator, probably Jerome, had innocently called the king by the Hebrew name 'Day Star, Son of the Dawn' Lucifer in the Latin translation, with no fourth-century intention to demonise him. Indeed Jesus too is Lucifer in the Greek texts of Peter 1:19 and Revelation 22:16, he is *phosphoro* 'the bringer of Light.' As Elaine Pagels clearly shows, the early Bible writers had no concept of Satan, but the political use to which such a character could be put has evolved over the years.[32]

Pope Leo I first declared there was a Devil in 447 CE at the Council of Toledo. The Council even issued a description

---

[32] Pagels, E. *The Origin of Satan*

> "... a large black monstrous apparition with horns on his head, cloven hoofs, asses' ears, glittering eyes and gnashing teeth, endowed with an immense phallus and sulphurous smell."[33]

The similarity to the Greek god Pan was of course entirely intentional but a precedent had been set, wherever a pagan god proved troublesome, demonisation was the way to go.

So why did Patrick climb that mountain assigned to one of those pagan deities Lugh Lámhfadha, why did he spend so much time on the summit in contemplation — if we are to believe the account. If he had been a Catholic, climbing a mountain would not have impressed the local pagans, nor converted them. More likely the volatile Irish would take offence at his confrontational showboating and speedily dispatch him to meet his god. On the other hand, if Patrick belonged to the Druidic–Celtic Church with their Gnostic affiliations, it would explain his interest in the place and he would have had free access to it. The Catholics' Patrick mythology was added much later, when he was no longer around to contradict them.

After the Synod of Whitby, most of Britain accepted the rule of the Catholic Church, though this was done neither happily, nor quickly, and outposts, particularly in Celtic kingdoms, discreetly clung on to their old ways for quite some time. In Ireland, this resistance to and defiance of the Roman Catholic Church stubbornly continued and various events testify to it. In 1172 the Council of Cashel brought the Celtic Church of Ireland under the Roman Catholic control of Henry II of England: Ireland was a gift from the Vatican! The Bull from Pope Adrian IV, giving Ireland to the King starts

> "Adrian, bishop, servant of the servants of God, to our well beloved son in Christ, the illustrious King of the English, greeting and Apostolic Benediction. Laudably and profitably does your Majesty contemplate spreading the glory of your name on earth and laying up for yourself the reward of eternal happiness in heaven, in that as becomes a Catholic Prince, you propose to enlarge the boundaries of the Church, to proclaim the truths of the Christian religion to a rude and ignorant people, [the Irish] to root out the growth of vice from the field of the Lord; and the better to accomplish this purpose, you seek the counsel and goodwill of the Apostolic See. ..."

Hardly the letter of the head of the church, if the people of Ireland had already been following the Roman religion happily since the time of Patrick.

---

33 Muchembled, RA. *A history of the devil: from the middle ages to the present*

But in the 19th century, the matter had still not ended. A 19th century Roman Catholic historian, O'Driscoll wrote in Volume II of *Views on Ireland* that the Council of Cashel left Irish religious belief and practice in a sorry state:

> "... This council put an end to the ancient Church of Ireland, and submitted it to the yoke of Rome. From the days of St. Patrick, to the council of Cashel, was a bright and glorious career for Ireland. From the sitting of this council to our time, the lot of Ireland has been universal evil, and all her history a tale of woe. ..."

Even worse assertions are made in the early 16th century, when the reformation threatens to loosen any hold that Rome might have in Ireland and sadly can be seen until recent times as the rationale for the continued struggle against British control. The Bishop of Mentz sent this letter from Rome to the Irish rebel leader Shane O'Neill on April 28, 1528:

> "My dear son O'Neill, thou and thy fathers are all along faithful to the Mother Church of Rome. His Holiness Paul III, now Pope, and the Council of the Holy Fathers there, have lately found a prophecy of one Saint Lazerianus Bishop of Cashel, wherein he saith that the Mother Church of Rome falleth, when in Ireland the Catholic Faith is overcome. Therefore for the glory of the Mother Church, the honour of St. Peter, and your own secureness suppress heresy and His Holiness' enemies, ..."[34]

So much for a flourishing Roman Church and the peace and love of Jesus; in the late nineteenth century, when talking about his world travels, John Lawson Stoddard had some interesting comments about religion in the second of his lectures on Ireland.

> "During the sixth, seventh, and eighth centuries, especially, this farthest boundary of the Continent held aloft and kept aflame the torch of Christian faith, and glittered like a star upon the dark horizon of the western world. Its hills and valleys were adorned with countless churches and monastic institutions, from which enthusiastic missionaries, burning with the zeal and rapture of new converts, crossed the seas, and preached the Gospel to the pagan tribes of Scotland, England, Germany, and Gaul. Churches were founded by Irish monks in the Black Forest, at Schaffhausen in

---

[34] Mant, R. *History of the Church of Ireland*

Switzerland, and at Wurzburg in Bavaria; and of the students who received their education in the Irish monasteries, free of cost, thousands on returning to their native lands brought back with them the influence and learning of this "Island of the Saints." Even so cautious and reliable an historian as Green, in his "Short History of the English People," says: "For a time it seemed as if the course of the world's history was to be changed; as if that older Celtic race which the Roman and German had swept before them had turned to the moral conquest of their conquerors; as if Celtic and not Latin Christianity was to mould the destinies of the Church of the West.""[35]

Not only did Stoddard find the influence of Celtic Christianity had been strongest in Ireland, he had found evidence of its greater influence in his travels through France, Germany and Switzerland.

In many parts of Europe, we find the same story, that Catholic Christianity was not readily and lovingly adopted and most of its conversions were achieved under severe duress... commonly the threat of death. In Europe, paganism remained strong for nearly a thousand years, especially in the vast remote rural areas where people were determined to hang on to their traditional ways and beliefs. Indeed, paganism flourished to varying degrees right through to the 18th and 19th centuries. Even the priesthood lacked dedication to the Christian faith and this has been exposed by the fact that inside many rural churches, pagan images and statues have been found which stood alongside the Catholic ones. Remarkably, the garden of the Prince-Archbishop in Salzburg, built in 1613 has to this day a small pagan grotto dedicated to Herne the Hunter.

Gnosticism likewise continued in the more remote areas, mainly in eastern Europe. The third Ecumenical Council of Constantinople was still discussing how to deal with the Mysteries of Dionysus — still being practised in the Balkans — as late as the end of the 7th century. The number of Gnostic followers must have been quite substantial because large numbers of Gnostic gospels and writings continued to be in wide circulation right into the 8th century. Despite all the attempts to confiscate and burn them, they continued to flourish. In the middle-east, the Paulicians, preserving the original teachings of Paul, continued to flourish into the 10th century, to the extent that the name Paulician became the generic name for Gnostics.

Inevitably, when philosophy strives to win over brute force, the battle is destined to be lost. It was nevertheless a long one and the struggle to survive

---

[35] Stoddard, J L. *Stoddard's Lectures — Ireland*

continued, which perhaps illustrates the determination of humans faced with preserving an important truth from destruction by an *evil empire*. Covert Gnosticism must have continued within the towns and cities, but numbers would have dropped quite quickly, for once the teachers were lost — whether their deaths were natural or un-natural — the secrets of the inner mysteries would have been lost too.

The new world created by the Catholic Church had no place for intellectuals or intellectual pursuits. There would be no more great centres-of-learning, no philosophical and scientific academies for such places were the breeding grounds of dangerous free-thinkers, liberals and subversives. Science was viewed with great suspicion for its findings normally challenged the belief-system of the Church. It threatened to undermine it, so men of science had to work in secrecy, fearing their heretical *devil's work* would see them burnt at the stake. In fact the Church strove to dismantle the human civilisation that had grown from Egypt, Greece and Rome.

The consequence of the Roman Church's ridding itself of men of learning and teachings that respected individuality and even health and fitness, was that the Romans' lifestyle rapidly declined. In Roman towns, cleanliness had been next to godliness, but the new religious masters in an attempt to put godliness first, pulled down the temples and called the public bathhouses immoral and sinful. The end of the daily Roman bath signalled the start of illness and disease. Church Father Tertullian even found shaving offensive to God, no attempt should be made to improve on what the Creator had designed![36]

The great cities which had been built of finely-carved stone and marble and well-made bricks, crumbled in disrepair; stones where looted from the great edifices and temples to patch up lesser structures. The fresh-water aqueducts, channels and pipes fell into neglected ruin, water coming in flooded grassy areas instead, so that disease-bearing insects could breed and the sewage system failed to remove the effluent. The tall multi-storied buildings that had once been Roman shopping malls and apartment blocks were neglected until they fell. Some patched-up buildings survived and became hovels; new structures were of wood, mud and plaster. The knowledge and skills of concrete and glass making, tile manufacture and even brick making were lost and would not reappear until the 16th century, even then stone was too expensive and reserved for the construction of churches.

Rome's fine roads, aqueducts and sewers too, were left unrepaired and eventually fell into disuse. Without the lavatories and sewers, raw sewage and garbage were thrown into and flooded the streets, encouraging rats and

---

[36] op. cit. Gibbon, E.

the diseases they carried. Theatres and other places of entertainment disappeared as frivolity found no favour with a Church which considered them immoral. As the bathhouses and nudity were banned, so were the gymnasia and fitness became ungodly. Roman health had long been linked with fitness — *Mens sana in corpore sano* — mental as well as physical; now physicians and their medical knowledge were soon discarded as superstition took their place. Diseases were not the result of dirty water or poor sanitation but the direct result of sin that allowed malevolent spirits to enter the body and in the words of St Ignatius, "There is only one Physician, Jesus Christ."

Trade withered, wealth diminished, many skilled trades disappeared, the *dangerous* learned classes — philosophers, orators, writers, poets, doctors, architects, engineers, mathematicians, scientists and astronomers — had no teachers and academies, so they literally died out. In the east, Byzantium kept the fading torch of civilisation flickering, but it was bedevilled by the restrictions of its own brand of Christianity, Eastern and later Greek Orthodox, and was a shadow of what had once been. Within a relatively short time Christianity had brought down the civilised world and in its place the Catholic Church offered nothing but poverty, hardship, aggression, oppression and dictatorship. Peace and Love were sold out for now.

Despite the best efforts of the Catholic Church, Gnosticism, holed up in inaccessible places, struggled on through the centuries and surfaced from time to time. Remarkably, in 1211 CE, it was rumoured that a sect known as the Bogomils, was practising the Hellenic Mystery rites of Dionysius in Constantinople and the adjacent region of Anatolia.[37] The Bogomils are believed to have formed out of a group of Paulicians who were resettled out of Asia Minor into Macedonia around 872 CE. Despite persecutions, the resilient Bogomils survived in the Balkan region until the 15th century.

The successful Bogomil resistance had earlier inspired a Gnostic revival in western Europe and reputedly inspired the Cathars, mentioned in connection with the Knights Templar in Chapter 19. The heretical Cathars' name came from the Greek word *katharai* meaning pure ones. They were also known as the Albigensians from the city of Albi near Toulouse, where an inclusive debate between Catholic priests and a group of Cathars once took place. The Cathars were proliferative in south–west France in the Languedoc region, but there were also active 'Cathar' conclaves in northern Spain, south–western Germany and northern Italy, where they were known as the Patarenes. The earliest known Gnostic Cathars can be traced to a heretic sect in Cologne around 1143 CE; this sect claimed that they were part of a wider movement of Christian clergy

---

[37] Stoyanov, Y. *The Hidden Traditions in Europe*

and monks who had secretly retained their true religion from the earliest times.

In the following few years, their heresy had spread into southern France and northern Italy, where it quickly became predominant. The Languedoc region, then known as Occitania, was independent of France and was ruled by various noblemen, the foremost being the Count of Toulouse. The area was regarded as a region of free-thinkers and troublemakers and as such, an ever present thorn in the side of the kings of France. How connected to the Bogomils the Cathars were is not absolutely certain, but there are certain eastern elements which can be traced to eastern thought and practice — the Cathar ritual of Lyon was very close to the Slavonic rituals — however it is absolutely clear that the Cathars were Gnostics; their spiritual beliefs and practices confirm this.[30]

Languedoc provided a particularly fertile ground for Cathar thoughts to grow and flourish. Like Provence, at that time it was ethnically and culturally different from the rest of France, not part of the kingdom; these regions were vassals to the king but nevertheless autonomous. Languedoc had links to the Muslim world just over the Pyrenees in Spain, from which it would have benefited from Arabic learning and its refined culture with its love of the arts and poetry.

Early European poetic works tended to recount the heroic deeds of warriors as described in the Saxon *Beowulf* and the Franks *Song of Roland,* but from Languedoc developed the vernacular lyric poetry that contributed to courtly love. The foundations were already laid for its popularity since the Languedoc's aristocracy had developed a court culture, whereas elsewhere culture was dominated by the church and thus starkly sombre and religious in tone. This court culture gave rise to the courteous and refined appreciation of women that was to influence the new age of chivalry, which Europe later adopted.

This prevalent chivalrous ethic was even to effect warfare, though it remained as brutally bloody as before. After the 12th century, it was subject to a new *gentlemanly* form of conduct that embraced the laws of God into a code of warfare. As the new fashion for chivalrous behaviour and manners spread, it helped raise the profile and worth of women in a Christian world that had long demeaned women as being worthless and witless stooges whom Satan used to tempt men away from God. So this region, with its enlightened and liberal society would have been open to a religion that rebuked the suffocating dominance of the corrupt Catholic Church. For the women of Languedoc, who had already benefited from living in a more

---

38 Frassetto, M ed. *Heresy and the Persecuting Society in the Middle Ages*

woman–friendly society, the religious and social equality that Gnosticism offered them attracted a great many followers.[39]

This new form of Christianity which rejected Jehovah, the Judaic Bible and the validity of Rome's New Testament, which was peace loving and against warfare, which promoted education, which encouraged a spiritual self–fulfilment and which granted equality to women, attracted converts in huge numbers. The Cathar black–robed missionaries, known as the *Perfecti*, roamed the countryside in pairs, finding more and more willing followers who wished to throw off the harsh and restrictive shackles of Catholicism. As Catharism began to spread across borders, the papal authorities began to tremble in fear. This was no schismatic sect of Christianity, it was an alternative religion, one that did not recognise the authority of the Church of Rome — but worse it did not believe in a historical Jesus. The Cathars believed that 'Christ' became manifest through the words of Paul.

By 1167, the spread of Catharism had grown enough for the leaders to hold an ecclesiastical council. Surprisingly, it was sixty years later before the Vatican finally felt compelled to act against this threat that had grown too great. Its response was extreme: Pope Innocent III — an ironic name for him who conceives the *Holy Inquisition* — called for a Christian crusade to obliterate the Cathar heresy. Perversely, Catholic religious leaders recognised the gentle loving piety and morals of the Cathars, but sentiment must not interfere with the preservation of orthodox Christianity, power and wealth. There was to be no leaving the people to make their own choice of which religion to follow.[40]

In Chapter 19, I mentioned that the Cathars were perceived as pure in thought and deed; the founder of the Cistercian Order, St Bernard of Clairvaux stated

> "No sermons are more Christian than theirs, and their morals are pure. ... If you interrogate them, no one could be more Christian. As to their conversation, nothing can be less reprehensible and what they speak they prove by deeds. As for the morals of the heretics, they cheat no one, they oppress no one, they strike no one."

This glowing praise sounds more like an endorsement, than a damning indictment and clashes distinctly with the charges of heresy. Even Pope Innocent III acknowledged the piousness of the Cathars, though he still called for their extermination as he understood the danger posed by these heretics. That any group or individual should hold a different view of God

---

39 Jaeger, C. S. *The Origins of Courtliness*
40 Barber, M. *The Cathars*

from that of the Catholic Church was not to be tolerated and this was made plain by Pope Innocent's brutal pronouncement that "anyone who attempted to construe a personal view of God, which conflicted with Church dogma must be burned without pity."[41] Pope Innocent formed the Holy Inquisition specifically to tackle the Cathar heretic problem. His *holy men* applied themselves to the task with a zeal that was merciless and barbarous: both witnesses and suspects were tortured using methods of perverted ingenuity, whilst rape was used for personal pleasure; if the guilty survived the torture, both adults and children were burnt alive at the stake.

Knights and soldiers, mainly from northern Europe, answered the call to arms. It was probably not so much the attraction of participating in a crusade, nor the promise of indulgences and eternal salvation made by the Vatican, but rather the gifting of Cathar land and property that motivated the volunteers. The Church had sanctified looting, theft, rape and murder on a massive scale. From 1209 CE, for thirty-five years, the terrible persecutions against the Cathars began, operating under the shameful travesty of a *Holy Crusade*. The Catholic Christian crusaders, be they clergy, commanders or common soldiers, were filled with a crazed blood-lust that knew no mercy. Bernard Gui, one of the Holy Inquisitors, demanded that no attempt be made to take heretic prisoners, so that they might repent, but instead the crusader should "thrust his sword into the man's belly as far as it will go".[42]

After tens of thousands had been slaughtered the Cathar *final solution* was enacted on March 16, 1244 CE, with the fall of their last stronghold at Montségur and the execution by burning of 200 *Perfecti*.

Of course this was not the last of the Cathars. Many did escape. Numerous Templars had estates in Languedoc and they had declined to participate in the crusade against the Cathars. The Templars gave sanctuary and protection to the fleeing Cathars. The Templars were wise enough to accept the realities of their situation and though they were a large and powerful force, they were not big enough to overcome the armies that the Vatican could raise to defend Christendom, so they continued to hide their true beliefs and did what they could to conceal and aid the overwhelmed Cathars.

Away from the whole-scale extermination that befell the towns, in the rural areas many Cathars saved themselves by converting to Catholicism. These converts, however, were never trusted by the Church and to identify them in public, *reformed* Cathars were forced to wear a yellow cross sewn

---

[41] Ellerbe, H. *The Dark Side of Christian History*
[42] ibid.

onto their clothes — a ghastly precursor to the marking-out of Jews in more recent times.

For many years, Cathars fled eastwards to the Balkans, where the Bogomils still thrived. The journey was hazardous, because the Inquisition and their informers were ever vigilant for the heretics. In 1325 CE Pope John XXI determined a final solution. The captured Cathars — these pious peace-loving people — were put into ovens, not to be gassed, but having first been liberally smeared with grease to be roasted alive.[43]

If this be the behaviour of Christians, were they following the example of their Jesus the son of God? Who were the real heretics, who were more deserving of the title Anti-Christ? A thousand years had been spent in the Roman Church's open repression of the Christian message in Europe. This tragic and barbarous episode in history may have ended with the destruction of the Cathar dream to resurrect Gnosticism and end the lie of Literalist Christianity. Catholicism had won the final great battle against the Gnostic *heresy*, but another battle was all that it was. Though the Church in Rome threw its dark blanket over the Truth, Gnostic thought could not be stifled; the light struggled out and the war raged on.

---

43 op. cit. Stoyanov, Y.

THE GREATEST LIE EVER TOLD

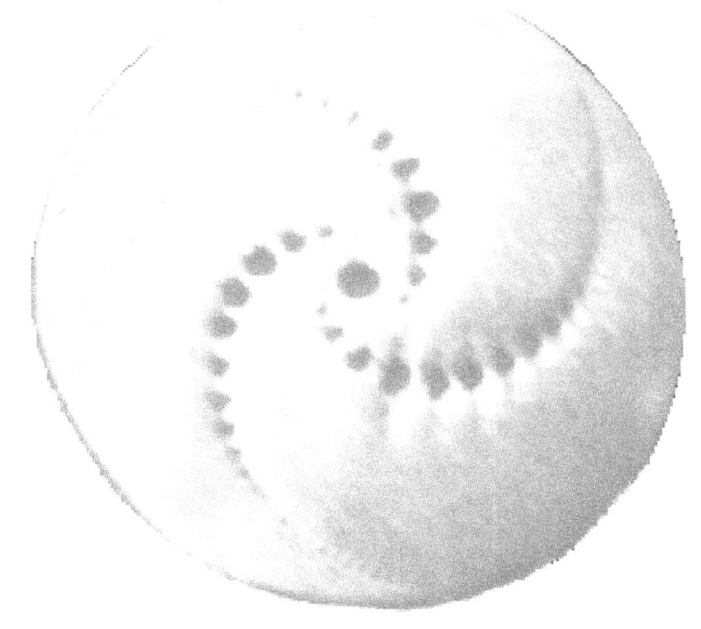

Part Four

The Truth, The Way, The Light — The Future

Chapter 28

From Inquisition to Inspiration

"There will be no end to the troubles of states, or of humanity itself, till philosophers become kings in this world, or till those we now call kings and rulers really and truly become philosophers, and political power and philosophy thus come into the same hands."

Plato

After its ruthless eradication of the Cathar movement, the iron fist of the Catholic Church held Europe in its murderous grip. The Vatican had determined that the spectre of Gnosticism would never again rise to haunt it and by 1255 the Inquisition rushed in to interrogate suspects in Sicily, Aragon, Lombardy, France, Burgundy, Brabant and Germany.[1] Mention of the Inquisition conjures images of witches and devil-worshippers in many minds, but that was only the sideshow; one which gave the Inquisition a useful facade. What the Inquisition really hoped to find were heretics, who might be attempting to resurrect Gnosticism, accusing them of devil worship avoided the need to reveal the dangerous truth: that it was hunting the real Christians. In most cases persecution of witches was done not by the Inquisition, but over-enthusiastic secular authorities and local courts who felt they were proving their own good Christian credentials by discovering, trying and executing the followers of Satan.

In 2003, the Vatican opened its archives to carefully-scrutinised researchers, provided they knew which document they wanted to view. In 2009, a Belgian researcher was allowed to *browse* for the first time, with certain restrictions on the date of documents — nothing after 1939.[2] For hundreds of years no-one could freely research these important records of the effects of Roman Christianity on the people it subjected to its influence. Oddly, in 1998, Cardinal Ratzinger, now the current Pope, opened up a small section of the archives that held documents and letters concerning the *Spanish* Inquisition. According to the documents available, the bloody

---

[1] Douais, C. *L'Inquisition. Ses Origines. Sa Procedure*
[2] Van den Heuvel, P. *The Vatican Secret Archives*

reputation was undeserved. The Catholic Church had executed only one per cent of the accused heretics that had been tried. Most people charged as heretics were dealt with by 'non–church tribunals' though there is no mention of how they were found or punished or by whom exactly, as the Church was neither responsible nor in charge. I strongly suspect that the Vatican, with its poor track record at truth–telling, has been manipulating the evidence in an attempt to conceal it.

Even with the Inquisition as the ultimate deterrent, the Vatican could not maintain total control. It is impossible to keep a firm grip on anything all of the time, sooner or later the effort wears you out and you release the pressure. Once it loosens, even slightly, there will always be an external force eager to usurp the space. Over the centuries, despite continued vigilance, the Church authorities couldn't always act as they wanted — they found powerful rulers hard to control and the recalcitrant king or count needed cautious handling. Nearly two hundred years before the Cathar threat erupted, the Normans had been one such headache for the Vatican.

The Normans were descendants of the Vikings that settled in northern France, giving their name to Normandy 'the land of the Norsemen'. Like their ancestors, the Normans remained a fierce warrior class and warfare was still their way of life — both to indulge their favourite pastime of fighting and to make their fortune. In mainland Europe, they found the best of both worlds and as a consequence, they hired out their skill as mercenaries.

Hoping to seek adventure, many Normans made the pilgrimage southwards into Italy and on to Jerusalem. *En route,* large groups of Normans were tempted by the lucrative opportunities afforded them in the employ of needy rulers like the Lombard princes of Salerno and Capua and the Byzantine Viceroy at Bari. Inevitably, having realised that a greater profit lay in keeping the spoils of war for themselves than in protecting it for their paymasters, these rapacious Norman warlords began to function independently.

The most formidable amongst the Norman *entrepreneurs* were the twelve brothers of Hauteville. The most fearsome of the brothers was Robert, given the apt Norman epithet Wiscard — rendered Guiscard in French — to denote his cunning. The brothers based themselves at Melfi, a strategic choice from which to make raids against Lombard and Byzantine territories. Their attacks on nearby Benevento, which was under papal protection, caused Pope Leo IX to form a military alliance against the Norman raiders. The outcome was a defeat for the Pope and his supporters at the Battle of Civitate in 1053; made worse by the capture of Pope Leo.

Suffering defeat at the hands of the Normans brought the threat they posed sharply into focus: not only the loss of land and wealth, but also the threat to the papacy itself. After the death of Pope Leo in 1054, his successor Nicholas II conferred the Lombard principality of Capua on Richard of Aversa, Robert Guiscard's brother–in–law and the Byzantine territories of Apulia, Calabria and the Muslim–held island of Sicily, on Robert himself. These lands were given in return for the promise of Norman protection for the papacy — some of the lands were not even under Vatican control, but that was no impediment as the Normans just conquered them and moved in.[3]

Effectively, the Vatican had bought the dangerous Norman incomers, thereby preserving its own position and gaining powerful allies. It is unlikely that either side had any real liking for each other, but it was an exchange that suited both parties. In typical disingenuous fashion, Amato di Monte Cassino a chronicler at the Abbey founded by St Benedict, reported Robert's conversion:

> "Duke Robert repented of his past sins and guarded against present and future sins and thus he began to love the priests".

Clearly this was a politically–motivated acclamation on Robert's part. Robert remained a rapacious warlord with an eye for the main chance. The Normans' reputation went before them and the lands of southern Italy wisely offered little resistance when their time came for conquest. The surrender of the Byzantine city of Bari in 1073 saw the culmination of the campaign. Needless to say, the Vatican was relieved and delighted to witness the Byzantines with their rival Church removed from its doorstep.

The task of invading Sicily was handed to Robert's youngest brother, Count Roger. Sicily had always been at the hub of trading in the Mediterranean. As early as the 8th century BCE, both the Phoenicians and the Greeks made use of its central position, and then centuries later Rome seized control from the Greeks and the Carthaginians. Following the fall of Rome and its empire to the barbarians, Emperor Justinian sent out a fleet from Constantinople to capture the island in 535 CE. By the 7th century CE, the Arabs began raiding and in the 9th century CE Sicily fell to their invasion. Under Arab control, the island flourished, the land was fertile and benefited from newly–introduced crops, trading between east and west, and north and south Europe boomed. Islamic glass, metalwork and textiles were found throughout Italy and Slavic Eunuchs brought from the Italian states to the Sicilian capital of Palermo were a prized commodity throughout Muslim lands.

---

3   Norwich, JJ. *The Normans in the South, 1016-1130*

In the early 11th century the Byzantines made a serious effort to recapture the island, but having secured a strong bridgehead at Messina, they failed to break out and after nearly twenty years of trying, in 1041 CE, they gave up and withdrew. In 1061 CE, in stark contrast to the efforts of the large Byzantine army, Count Roger and a modest-sized force of Norman adventurers, captured Messina. Two years later he defeated the army of the Emir of Palermo at Cerami, then in 1072 he captured the capital and effectively the whole island. As if to make plain the unstoppable military prowess of the Normans and the consequent threat they posed, not least to the Vatican, Count Roger's invasion force comprised barely a thousand men.[4]

Count Roger chose to ignore the frequent squabbles that took place amongst his Norman kinsmen in southern Italy and focussed his attentions on bringing stability to Sicily but when he died he left two very young sons. His wife's political skill enabled the children to grow up until the younger, named after his father, took control. Roger II proved himself to be not only a man of civilised tastes, but also an enlightened ruler. He was knighted when he attained his majority and later crowned king. His court was open in attitude and thus became cosmopolitan in nature. Sicily was mostly Muslim, so the court reflected this within its household. The sizeable Greek population was significant and Roger chose Greeks to run his administrative affairs and preferred the learned Greeks as his ministers. Latin immigrants moved in from Italy in steadily increasing numbers, hoping to benefit from the Norman conquest, but their numbers always remained small.

Roger's interest in literature caused him to import many works, especially from Constantinople. He had books translated from their original Greek and Arabic into Latin, thereby giving westerners access to a wide range of philosophical and scientific writings. Books that were considered heretical by Rome, works by authors such as Plato, Aristotle, Euclid and Hero were much sought after. Tragically Roger would only have access to the remnants that had survived the purges undertaken by the Christian zealots half a millennium earlier; the majority of scientific and philosophical works had been cast on the bonfires.

Fortunately the Arabs recognised the worth of the sciences and mathematics and had thus preserved much from earlier ages. The Christian Church deemed such things dangerous works of the Devil; luckily the Arabs understood the contents and extended the learning. It is to the enlightened Norman rulers of Sicily that we owe our thanks for saving and promoting these priceless treasures of human civilisation. Both Count Roger and his son Roger II, though they were Catholic, encouraged the building of

---

4   Angold, M. *Byzantium*

monasteries for the Greek Orthodox Church and were tolerant towards the Islamic Faith within their kingdom.[5]

Not surprisingly, by the end of Roger II's reign, the cosmopolitan openness within Sicily began to fade. For a short time, it seemed that perhaps the intellectual, tolerant and harmonious example might have reversed the flow of history and created a new age of enlightenment, but the divisions between the Holy Roman Empire, Byzantium and Islam were too entrenched. Nevertheless, there was still a degree of political and religious tolerance, a pragmatic stand–off, which largely held between the three great powers. However the thin veneer began to crack and within thirty years of Roger II's death, the real divisions started to show.

Increasing rivalries inevitably led to the open hostilities that would culminate in the Crusades, which not only sought to capture the Holy Lands from the Muslims, but also caused the sacking of Constantinople *en route* to Palestine. This assault upon fellow Christians, albeit of a different Church, considerably weakened Byzantium and led to its eventual fall to the invading Islamic Ottoman Turks. The collapse of the eastern Christian empire meant that the Byzantine counterbalance which had kept the Roman Popes to some extent in check, was lost and Roman Christianity then, as the Vatican had long wished, became supreme — at least for a time.

In the mid–15th century an enormous development took place that was to undermine the Vatican's stranglehold over what men were allowed to know, and prise loose its grip on what they could think. Johann Gutenberg and Johann Fust, two German goldsmiths residing in Mainz, developed a movable type for use in a printing press. The Gutenberg Bible was the first book printed and was available for purchase in 1455. The Germans recognised the potential of the printing press and immediately sought to exploit the market for books, particularly Bibles and other religious works, reference books and the very rare works of classical antiquity. The first Bible to be translated into the vernacular, in this case German for the layman to read, was printed in 1461 in Strasbourg.

Until this time, the Vatican forbade possession of the Bible by the laity and the Inquisition enforced the ban. A limited number of lay church members were permitted to own the *Breviary*, the *Psalter* and the *Book of Hours of the Virgin Mary* but these were written in Latin. Translation into the vernacular was a ground–breaking daring defiance of the Church. The ban had originally been enforced when the Inquisition attempted to stop Cathar

---

5 ibid.

Perfecti distributing hand-written versions of the New Testament in the language of the locality.

By 1470 Nuremberg had become the European centre for printing books. A printer named Anton Koberger had 24 presses working to fulfil the orders which came in from the scholars in his international contact-network. This innovative printing process spread quickly to other countries and each produced books and pamphlets in the country's own language, relegating Latin as an antiquated literary-language. The Italians had a strong scribal tradition as well as experience in block-printing and a large paper-making industry, so Italy soon became the leader of this new groundbreaking technological advance. Mass production of the printed word arrived at a critical time, at a period in history when the shackles imposed upon intellectual development were being broken. The rapid and widespread dissemination of information and knowledge ensured that the Church could not extinguish the escaping light of revelation.

The wide distribution of the Bible was disastrous, for the first time ever the educated layman could read it for himself, but more crucially it afforded scholars unrestricted time to analyse its contents and then to challenge them. That scholarly exposure of the lie of Christianity remained largely muted for several centuries more is an indicator of the power of the Church to dispense terrible punishment on the perpetrators of heretical dissent. Nevertheless, the suffocated challenges to the Church and especially to papal authority had reached the surface and were finding air.

As much as the Church managed to keep control, over the centuries, there were always those interested in philosophy and the sciences, who refused to be bowed. They risked facing torture and death for pursuing what were deemed to be 'dangerous heretical activities'. The Vatican viewed science as a Pandora's Box out of which all kinds of evils would flow to undermine the Church. The Church's threats and restrictions made the return to some semblance of enlightened times painfully slow and fragmented. The Dark Ages did not end suddenly — the light flickered slowly and painfully into a spluttering flame. The more people who saw it, the more who wanted to keep the torch of learning ablaze. The age of enlightenment started with the Renaissance, a period of transition between the Mediæval epoch when Europe was Christendom and the modern age of freedom with its associated diversity and conflict.

The Renaissance saw the shackles of hell and damnation cast aside, finally allowing science, philosophy and literature to flourish without undue fear. This process was itself still gradual and throughout the Renaissance period those men who were determined to push the boundaries still risked the wrath and punishment of the Church. A comparable modern-day period of change took place in the 1980s. The initial low-key swell of pressure exerted by the Czechoslovakian intellectuals, broke the grip already weakened by Polish trade–union resistance to bring the Communist hold over Eastern Europe to an end.

When the infant printing phenomenon was yet to launch the learned world into a new paradigm, a star was already shining in the academic firmament that would illuminate the revival from antiquity of sceptical scholarship and with it the critical freedom to confront authority. Lorenzo Valla (1402–57) was a gifted scholar who employed a painstaking and exact approach to study and made use of his quarrelsome nature in his specialised subject of rhetoric. He put his analytical talent to use lecturing at Padua, Rome and Naples, whilst his proficiency at polemic was honed in the court of Alfonso of Aragon, the King of Naples. Valla's studious arguments were crucial in the clashes between the secular and ecclesiastical camps. These disputes largely centred upon the papal rights of temporal dominion over the land ruled by kings and princes and Valla naturally spoke on the side of his royal employer.[6]

This on–going clash of opinions caused Valla to study the core document upon which the Vatican based its legal authority, the *Constitutum Constantini* or Constantine's 'Donation' as Valla chose to call it. The *Constitutum Constantini* was alleged to be a record of the conversations concerning Constantine's ceding to Pope Sylvester I (314–335 CE) and all his successors a number of principalities, giving him secular dominion over Rome and all its provinces and civitates in Italy and over all the Western regions, as well as making the Pope primate over all churches and clergy. The document also recorded that Constantine offered Sylvester the imperial crown of the west — a most suspect gift, if one knew anything of the Emperor Constantine.

Monarchs who sought political independence from the Roman Church had long contested these papal rights, but no–one had ever thought to have the document properly examined. Valla, an avid student of classical Latin, subjected the document to careful scrutiny and discovered that the clumsy vernacular Latin text was written in the 8th century, four centuries after Constantine's death: he exposed the document as a deliberate forgery. In 1440, Valla documented his investigations in *De Falso Credita et Ementita Constantini Donatione Declamatio*.

Valla had already courted trouble with the Church for his criticism of the dialectical teaching methods employed at universities by friars belonging to the Church. Valla argued that it was the duty of the rhetorician to teach, to please and to move the listener; the dialectician only did the first. Valla had the audacity to suggest that the Church should forsake its temporal

---

[6] Nauta, L. *In Defense of Common Sense*

power and devote itself to a single role as a spiritual institution. This last statement was the last straw for the Vatican following his attacks on the Church and the exposure of the fraudulent *Constantini Donatione;* in 1444 it summonsed Valla to face the Inquisition. Fortunately Valla was saved by the intervention of King Alfonso.[7]

Somewhat unexpectedly, in 1448, Valla accepted the post of apostolic secretary to the new Pope, Nicholas V. This was the beginning of a period of enlightenment and within the Vatican itself there were members of the clergy who were interested in the classics. Valla's versions of Herodotus, Xenophon and Thucydides would have found favour amongst them. It was Valla's lead, not least for his critical comparison of the Vulgate with the Greek original *New Testament*, which induced a growing band of scholars to follow his sceptical, critical and irreverent approach to scholarship. His style held an obvious appeal to students, especially those in the colleges specialising in the philosophy and sciences that were to characterise the Renaissance.

It can be argued that the Renaissance had its beginnings with the early Norman kings of Sicily and those kings' passion for acquiring books of learning was to be repeated in England. On the death of Henry V in 1422, his one-year-old son, Henry VI was too young to rule and Humphrey, Duke of Gloucester was made regent with the title of Lord Protector. Duke Humphrey was a poor leader and his mismanagement led to the loss of sovereignty over the lands in France and eventually to the English Wars of the Roses.

Despite his inability to display strong leadership, the Duke had some success as the patron of Renaissance learning in England. He was a collector of Greek and Latin classical works, including those of Plato and Aristotle, with an interest in newer and contemporary works from such masters as Dante, Petrarch and Boccaccio. He bequeathed his collection to Oxford University and it became the nucleus of the future Bodleian Library. Henry VI took the throne aged fifteen, he too had Duke Humphrey's ineptitude at leadership but likewise proved to be a pious and generous man with academic inclinations. The 1420s and 30s saw the founding of many colleges. Henry VI founded Eton College and King's College Cambridge and helped and encouraged the establishment of many more, including All Souls College Oxford, his patronage giving England its great reputation for learning.

Whilst Henry VI established the foundation of learning in England, another avid collector of classic and forbidden books put much of his family's vast banking fortune to developing art and literature in Florence —

---

7   Johnson, P *The Renaissance*

his name was Cosimo de' Medici. Cosimo's early education took place in the monastery of *Santa Maria degli Angeli* where he became proficient in Latin, French and German and learnt some Greek, Hebrew and Arabic. Later in Florence, he was educated by the eminent scholar Roberto de Rossi, from whom he acquired a passion for the classics and in particular Plato.

Around 1440 Cosimo began to build his book collection, which grew steadily to a sizeable library. At this time Italy was fragmented with small city–states under the control of numerous powerful families. The relationship between the families was generally one of undeclared warfare. The only thing that bound them together was their subservience to the Pope in Rome. Italy was a hornet's nest of intrigue and feuds, with the Pope attempting to manipulate each and everyone. The election of a Pope had more to do with which family was the most ruthless, had the deepest purse and the sharpest daggers. Rising out of this cauldron of self–seekers emerged Cosimo de' Medici a financier, statesman, philanthropist and scholar.[8]

The family name Medici meant 'doctors' but when the name was first recorded in the 12th century it was amongst the aristocracy. By the 13th the family had great wealth and through their banking industry, the beginnings of political power. Unlike other powerful and rich men, his motive in sponsoring the arts was not to disguise any ruthless shortcomings, but because Cosimo was a genuine scholar.[9]

The Medici gift, not only to Florence but also to the whole of Italy and Europe, was cultural, sponsoring the arts, sciences and scholarship. It embraced both classical antiquity and new ideas. Cosimo was to be *Pater Patriae*, the founding father of the Medici dynasty that was to dominate Florentine public affairs right though to the 18th century. His grandson, Lorenzo 'the Magnificent', continued what Cosimo had started and he was, in the words of Machiavelli: "the greatest patron of literature and the arts that any prince has ever been". The likes of Leonardo da Vinci, Michelangelo, Raphael and Donatello all flourished under Medici patronage.

Though he had no formal or legal authority, Cosimo's political influence became quite significant as his banking business not only made him extremely wealthy but enabled him to underwrite many important people, amongst them the Cardinals in the Vatican. When the increasingly isolated eastern emperor in Constantinople appealed to the Pope to send aid to fend off the Ottoman Turks, Pope Eugenius IV called a Great Council to be held

---

[8] Hibbert, C. *The House of Medici*
[9] Fremantle, R *God and Money*

in Italy. Cosimo offered to pay all expenses plus a generous loan to the Vatican if the council were to be held in Florence. Cosimo recognised the enormous glory to be derived from this, especially if it resulted in reconciling Eastern Orthodox and Western Catholic churches.

Accompanying the Byzantine delegation, were the great scholars, Bessarion and Gemistos Plethon, an authority on Plato. Cosimo persuaded them to stay in Florence.[10] Repeatedly hearing the great neo-pagan philosopher Gemistos Plethon delivering lectures on Plato led Cosimo to establish a Platonic Academy at the Villa Montevecchio where his great library was to be housed. By this period, the works of Plato had slowly started to gain some acceptance within the Catholic Church. It was the chink in the Vatican armour that Cosimo exploited, though he was wary to bang the drum of enlightenment too soon.[11]

Cosimo waited 25 years and his adopted son, Marsilio Ficino, himself a passionate and brilliant scholar and poet, became the Medici Academy's first director. One of his missions was to try to integrate Platonic philosophy into Christian teaching. For a while some in the Church took an interest in Plato, but eventually came a realisation that Plato was not compatible with Christianity. To Plato, ultimate reality was found in ideas or eternal forms that were only understood through reflection and reason, Aristotle's ultimate reality lay in physical objects that could be understood through experience. Plato's insistence on the necessity for independent reflection and reason in order to gain true knowledge had too many echoes of Gnosticism. The works of Aristotle, on the other hand, included classification of things according to identifiable physical attributes, which was much more acceptable; so Aristotle became the Church's 'approved' Greek sage — as long as his sagacity didn't conflict with the Bible.

In 1460, a Tuscan monk entered Florence, he had with him a donkey laden with books. Leonardo du Pistoia was returning from Byzantium, having just completed yet another book-finding mission for his master, Cosimo de' Medici. Each time Leonardo returned carrying books banned by the Church, with which Cosimo stocked his great private library in Florence. Amongst the works that Pistoia had brought back to Florence, were some that Cosimo had longed for him to find — Cosimo's sublime treasure. They were the fabled works of knowledge purportedly written by the Egyptian god of wisdom and knowledge Thoth. The Greeks had renamed him Hermes and he was now generally referred to as Hermes Trismegistus — Thrice Great Hermes — possibly because he calls himself Philosopher, Priest and King in his writings. The original source for these

---

[10] op. cit. Hibbert, C.
[11] Hankins, J. "Cosimo de' Medici and the 'Platonic Academy'"

works attributed to the god is not known, but the *Corpus Hermeticum* that Cosimo acquired was written in the first and second centuries CE by Gnostics. Many of these texts took the form of a discourse between Thoth–Hermes and a pupil, in the manner of the Egyptian texts offering advice from "Father" to "Son", but they sadly contained only superficial references to ancient Egyptian myth and religion. Some of these texts were also found amongst the hidden Gnostic library discovered at Nag Hammadi.[12]

What Cosimo had in his possession were texts translated out of Egyptian and into Greek. Immediately, Cosimo stopped his team of translators from working on Plato and eagerly set them to translating this rare intellectual gem. Within a year the translation was completed for Cosimo to read and this work became known famously as the *Hermetica*.

How authentic the books that came into Cosimo's possession were, we cannot know. The great library of Alexandria and most of its books and maps had been burnt by the Christian mob, so what Cosimo had could have been no more than a few copies of surviving fragments. Clement of Alexandria had described a procession of Egyptian priests, which he states, was led by a singer who carried two books of music and hymns by Thoth–Hermes. Next came the Horoscopus who carried four books on the stars. Altogether, there were 42 books, of which 36 contained the whole philosophy of Egypt and the other six books were on medicine.[13] Inspired by such reports, scholars searched untiringly for this collection of priceless jewels.

In 1463, Ficino completed a further Hermetic translation, which he entitled *Pimander* — the name for the universal mind. Pimander derives from the Greek Poimadres, which itself is derived from the Egyptian *Peim-n-Ra*, meaning Knowledge of Ra. Later a further book appeared which is called *Asclepius* the Hermetic book of Egyptian religious magic, which concerns itself with the practice of drawing down cosmic powers from the stars into inanimate objects such as statues and talismans.

The publishing of these Hermetic books inspired many people — scholars had been starved of knowledge about science and philosophy for many centuries — and an underground Hermetic movement swiftly developed. Scholars of the *Hermetica* came to despise the ancient philosopher Aristotle largely because he was 'approved' by the Church in Rome. The Hermetic movement became widespread and appears even to have permeated the Church, for in Siena Cathedral there is a floor, completed in 1488, depicting mythological scenes. One of these portrays a bowing Biblical–looking figure, assumed to be Moses, receiving a book from Thoth–

---

[12] Mahé, J-P. *Hermès en Haute Egypte*
[13] Yates, F *The Rosicrucian Enlightenment*

Hermes. On the front of the book is written, "Take up thy letters and laws Egyptians"; the plaque under the figures says, "Hermes Mercurius Trismegistus, the contemporary of Moses". This does not imply that the Catholic Church had adopted the *Hermetica* but indicates that there was a small and significant faction within the Vatican that followed its teachings and the teachings of Platonic philosophers.

In the mid 16th–century Cardinal Francesco Patrizzi, a neo–Platonist scholar, even went so far as recommending to Pope Gregory XIV, that the Hermetic works should replace Aristotle as the basis of Christian philosophy.[14] The significant influence this would have had on modern Christianity was never to come about as the fundamentalists within the Vatican eventually woke up to the danger within their walls. The realisation that the *Hermetica* would inevitably mean that people could once more choose what to think and whom to listen to, scared the fundamentalists, who knew that their power was vested in them not by God, but by their ability to cause fear and thus to control. The grip, nevertheless, was loosening, but scholars who had escaped the Vatican stranglehold still needed to be wary, for the Inquisition had not lost its extremely dangerous teeth. In 1600 the brilliant monk Giordano Bruno was burnt as a heretic for his enthusiastic support of Hermetic teachings.

Despite the *Hermetica*'s obvious Gnostic roots, it is clear that underpinning it all is the religion of ancient Egypt. When the Egyptian religion was absorbed into the Hellenist and replaced by the Roman socio–religious influence, much knowledge was lost, though thankfully some survived. The covert devotees seeking to resurrect this lost knowledge took what they still possessed and remodelled it so that it could be understood and accepted in a form that would suit their times. As a philosophical work, the Hermetica might appear to have little to do with ancient Egyptian religion, however this assumption would be incorrect. There is often a misconception that the ancient Egyptians were magnificent engineers and builders but primitive in all other ways — a view that stems from a lack of knowledge of the vast range of Egyptian beliefs and practices. Plato transmits a very different opinion when he relates the fable of Thoth and Amun in *Phaedros*. Following the death of Socrates, Plato spent thirteen years studying in Heliopolis. There is little to suggest that this time was spent studying civil engineering and much to show that, like Pythagoras, what he learned was Egyptian philosophy. Though modern scholars seem reluctant to accept it, the ancient Greeks say the source of their philosophy was Egypt.[15]

---

[14] ibid.
[15] Schwaller de Lubicz, R. *Sacred Science*

Hermetic teachings, as those of the Gnostics, Rosicrucians and later the early Freemasonry movement, encouraged followers to work for the improvement of all mankind. As part of this duty, they were to replicate the cosmos–heaven as the Egyptians had aspired to, even if the effort would be fruitless. The rationale within the teachings was that to make the attempt and fail was better than to do nothing at all. This led to the belief that temples and monuments should be meticulously constructed in design and dimensions which corresponded to solar and geodetic alignments. Hermetic literature places an importance upon the building of 'special' cities and the *Asclepius* talks of a city of God that would be aligned to the westward setting sun. The idea was mentioned in the ancient *Pyramid Texts* and *Book of the Dead*. Much later, in the seventeenth and eighteenth centuries the concept was to occupy the minds of influential people in London, Paris and the fledgling United States of America. In France the inspiration continued through the time of Napoleon up to modern times.

Amongst certain later Gnostic sects and certainly amongst the Bogomils and Cathars, there was a belief that both man and the Earth are corrupt and evil: a belief known as 'Dualism'. Dualism meant that an evil god ruled over the Earth and mankind's plight was to struggle free from this oppression and return to the higher cosmic state. Hermetic followers did not share this gloomy notion, but instead thought that man was prone to corruption. They believed that when the soul descends into the human body, the increasing weight of the physical body gradually causes a relinquishing of its contact with the Cosmic soul. So eventually the human child loses not only his early psychic abilities, but also his memory of higher things and thereby becomes corrupt. Man's saviour is his power of reason and by seeking knowledge he can fend off wickedness and strive to rediscover the truth, and thus he can return to the immortal state.

The *Asclepius* states that the 'divine' part of man consists of 'mind, intellect, reason and spirit', and it advises that Gnosis cannot be acquired merely through being 'taught', but that it must come from oneself, from one's own mind: enlightenment through self–experience.[16] The Egyptian god Sia who attends Ra on the Solar Barque's journey through the Netherworld, is the personification of intelligence; in Spell 237 of the Coffin Texts, the deceased soul, ready to embark upon its own journey, states 'I know what Sia knows and a path is open to me.'[17] Even from very early times, the Egyptians considered that man could not return to the cosmic soul without having knowledge.

---

[16] Copenhaver, B P. *Hermetica*
[17] Buck, de A. *The Egyptian Coffin Texts*

Early Gnostics and Hermetics considered that rather than man being imprisoned within an evil body as the Dualists thought, man needed a physical body to attend to physical work in the service of a higher cosmic cause, but man retained the link with the higher–self through his mind. Ma'at was the personification of harmony, order and balance, the antithesis of chaos. The 'thinking' man through his search for knowledge and truth and his achievement of personal Ma'at, must then be prepared to abandon his body in order to return to the cosmos in a non–physical form. Building a holy city — a place of beauty and harmony for people not only to live in, but where they could be at peace to study and attain enlightenment more easily — was seen as fundamental for everyone in order to achieve Ma'at. It is from these ideas that the notion of a 'New Jerusalem' was born — Egyptian–Gnostic philosophy disguised in Christian clothes.

Cosimo de' Medici had poked a significant hole into the Christian dam and he was probably the only man who could have done so. So great was Cosimo de' Medici's power and influence that he was a great king in all but name. Francesco Guicciardini, a Florentine historian, describes Cosimo as having had 'a reputation such as probably no private citizen has ever enjoyed from the fall of Rome to our own day'.

After Cosimo's puncture, Hermetic and philosophical books leaked out and Ficinio's development of the Platonic Academy ensured that knowledge flowed strongly, yet the Church was surprisingly slow to recognise the danger. Perhaps centuries of being unassailable had left it overconfident and allowed its vigilance to slip. Ficinio too was to exert a tremendous influence upon esoteric scholars and was the inspiration for future Hermetic magi–philosophers like Paracelsus, Dee and Fludd, whose influence I mention briefly below. Away from Florence, the Hermetic and Gnostic texts moved swiftly around Europe and were eagerly received, though with necessary discretion. It seems there were knowledgeable people who had been aware of the works' existence, people who risked persecution by the Inquisition but nevertheless ensured their rapid distribution. It would seem that there was an *invisible* organisation which acted as carrier for the Hermetic texts.[18]

In the second half of the 15th and through the 16th century, a large body of people started chipping away at the dam, in the wake of the distribution of the heretical texts. They were bound together like spiders secretly weaving a gigantic web across Europe, which continued in the new American colonies. Amongst these people were a number of prominent individuals.

---

[18] Eisenbichler, K. *The Cultural Politics of Duke Cosimo I de' Medici*

Copernicus (1473–1543) was born in Poland to German and Polish parents. He studied mathematics and optics at Kracow, then canon law at Bologna, lectured on astronomy in Rome and studied medicine in Padua before returning to eastern Germany. In the year of his death, his great treatise was published, on the 'Revolution of the Celestial Spheres', which challenged the Church's teaching of the Earth being the centre of the universe. Its publication was met with hostility and it was immediately placed on the Vatican's List of Banned Books.

Paracelsus (1493–1541) was born in Switzerland. He studied alchemy and chemistry at Basel University then studied the properties of metals and minerals in the mines of the Tyrol. He travelled widely around Europe studying and acquiring a vast store of facts. He returned to Basel and took the post of town physician and lectured at the university. His controversial views saw him exiled from Basel to Austria and he settled in Salzburg, where he became renowned as a medical healer and mystic. His legacy was the establishment of chemistry in medicine and his famous process of 'small doses of what makes someone sick, also cures' led to modern day homeopathy. His development of new chemical compounds encouraged research and experimentation that improved pharmacy and therapeutics, and revolutionised hidebound medical practices. He was supposedly a Hermetic alchemist and it has been speculated that he was a major inspiration for the Rosicrucians, a society based on a story of eight bachelor doctors who took an oath to heal the sick without payment and to find a replacement for themselves before they died.[19]

Dr John Dee (1527-1608) was born in London. He was a mathematician, geographer and alchemist and he was also astrologer and spymaster for Elizabeth I. He used the famous 007 glyph to sign his correspondence to the Queen. He was educated at St John's College, Cambridge and shortly following his graduation became a founding fellow of Trinity College.

Amongst Dee's seventy–nine works, dealing with subjects such as mathematics, geography, navigation, logic, astrology and alchemy, was the first English translation of Euclid. Dee travelled widely around Europe, searching libraries in his esoteric studies and allegedly uncovered some important documents, which may have included a copy of the *Book of Enoch*.[20]

---

[19] Gorceix, B. *La Bible des Rose-Croix*
[20] Peterson, J H. *John Dee's five books of mystery*

Dee devoted much of his time searching for the Northwest Passage over the Americas to the Far East. Using his vast knowledge of navigation and geography he provided maps and information that would aid the exploration. Dee also had a reputation as a sorcerer and alchemist, but his six–year association with the medium Edward Kelley brought him into disrepute, for spending so much time allegedly talking to angels and spirits. Dee was familiar with Hermetic teaching and is reputed to be the 'father' of the Rosicrucian movement. It is believed by some scholars that the birth of the Rosicrucians took place in Bohemia, when Dee was there in the 1580s.

Francis Bacon (1561-1626) was born in London. Educated at Trinity College, Cambridge, he then entered the legal profession at Grays Inn from where he was called to the Bar in 1582. He became a Member of Parliament in 1584. Bacon held a number of high positions including Attorney General and Lord Chancellor and was made Viscount St Albans in 1621. Bacon wrote many books and essays and some people think that he wrote the plays of Shakespeare. Bacon's philosophy is best demonstrated in his *Advancement of Learning* 1605, *De Augmentis Scientiarum* 1623 and *Novum Organum* 1621. He opposed the deductive logic of Aristotle and stressed instead the importance of experimentation to interpret nature and the proper regard for evidence that may run counter to any thesis. He taught that man is the servant and interpreter of nature, that truth is not derived from authority and that knowledge is the fruit of experience.

The impetus he gave to future scientific investigation is indisputable. Much of the language employed in his work shows distinct Rosicrucian thinking. His unpublished work entitled *New Atlantis* described his vision of a scientifically and spiritually–led society. His fictional Pacific land is almost certainly inspired by Plato's work and Bacon based it on the fledgling colony of Virginia — the name selected to refer to Isis not Elizabeth. Bacon, like the Rosicrucians, was known for his enthusiasm for the young American colonies. From his writings it seems that Bacon may have been a Freemason as well as a Rosicrucian.[21]

Michael Maier (1568–1622) was a German alchemist and philosopher. He worked in Prague as a personal physician to King Rudolph II of Bohemia. When the King died in 1612, Maier went to England. Whilst he was there Frederick of the Rhine–Palatinate lands married Elizabeth Stuart, James I's daughter. They returned home to Heidelberg, before moving to Prague as rulers of Bohemia.

---

[21] op. cit. Yates, F.

In England, Maier spent time in the company of Sir William Paddy, head of the London College of Physicians. He sent King James a personal Christmas greeting — now housed in the Scottish Records Office in Edinburgh — that depicts a large rose around which he wrote "Greetings to James, for a long time King of Great Britain. By your true protection, may the rose be joyful." With this clear reference to the Rosicrucian fraternity, Maier may have hoped to ensure James' future support. After its publication in England, Maier sent copies of his *Arcana Arcanissima* to prominent members of the new Virginia Company. His later *Atlantis Fugiens* was inspired by the Rosicrucian vision of America as the new Utopia.

Robert Fludd (1574-1637) was born in Kent, educated at Oxford and became a physician. He was a pupil of Dr Dee. Fludd was a mystic, Hermetic philosopher and Cabalist. In 1616, he published a treatise in defence of Rosicrucians — *Apologia Compendiaria Fraternitatem de Rosea Cruce*. Also influenced by Paracelsus, he recognised three cosmic elements — God archetypus, world macrocosmos and man microcosmos — and in 1618, he published two more Rosicrucian works, *History of the Macrocosm* and *History of the Microcosm*.

Giordano Bruno (1548-1600) was born in Nola near Naples. He became a Dominican monk, however his interest in reading heretical books, particularly Hermetic works, brought about charges of heresy; in anger, he lambasted his order and publicly defrocked himself. He then went on the run from the Inquisition travelling through Italy and eventually ended up in France where he was favoured by Henry III as a great Hermetic magus. From France, the zealous orthodox Aristotelians caused him to flee to London, where he stayed for two years. He gave numerous lectures in Oxford where he would have met with the English Rosicrucians. He travelled on through Germany and Bohemia before returning to Italy. In Venice, he was arrested by the Inquisition: he was imprisoned in Rome, questioned and tortured for eight years before being burned as an unrepentant heretic.[22]

Like other philosophers, Bruno embraced Neo–Platonism and Stoicism whilst fiercely rejecting the philosophy of Aristotle, which had been adopted by the Catholic Church. Bruno was also an avid supporter of Copernicus and often lectured upon the subject of the spheres, but promoting the idea in much stronger and less discreet terms by adding in his own scientific theories. By combining science with Hermetic intuition, he proclaimed that the universe was infinite, full of suns/stars, each with their own planetary

---

[22] Bruno, G et al. eds. *The Ash Wednesday Supper*

systems and populated by beings like mankind. To Bruno, the universe worked by a divine cosmic harmony, overseen by a supreme being and as a logical conclusion to this Bruno advised that Earth should be under the command of a solar monarch who would be advised by Hermetic philosopher–priests. Bruno had hoped that Henry of Navarre of France and then Elizabeth I of England — his earthly representation of Isis — could potentially be that monarch. Bruno's aim, he announced, was to reform the world out of its corruption and sought to revive the lost Egyptian solar-based religion: to bring the progression from multiplicity into Unity, from apparent chaos to universal participation in oneness.[23]

Galileo (1564–1642) was born in Pisa, he studied medicine and then mathematics, becoming a professor of mathematics at Pisa where his work attracted pupils from all over Europe. He disproved Aristotle's theory that the speed of a falling object depends on its weight, but his rejection of Aristotelian philosophy resulted in hostility and his forced resignation made him move to Florence. Galileo's series of astronomical investigations made him a great advocate of Copernicus; this brought him censure and the Inquisition forced his retraction through torture and he was sentenced to imprisonment. Pope Urban VIII commuted the sentence at the request of the Medici Duke of Tuscany. Galileo was transferred to a more pleasant house arrest in Sienna then finally Florence. Though losing his sight, he continued his great astronomical discoveries. The validity of his work was only formally recognised by the Vatican in 1993.[24]

Tommaso Campanella (1568-1639) was born in Calabria in southern Italy. At the age of fifteen, he joined the Dominican order, but ran away six years later. Like Bruno, he became a Hermetic magus–philosopher. He published his first philosophical work in 1591. This brought the wrath of the Church and though his writings failed to condemn him, the Inquisition, not to be cheated, found a demon familiar under a fingernail — sufficient to imprison Campanella for a few months. Upon his release, further false charges led to his arrest and torture by the Inquisition. In 1594, he was incarcerated in the same Roman dungeon as Bruno; it is unlikely that the two were allowed to meet, though it could have happened if the jailers had been offered bribes.

Eventually he was released and banished to Calabria, however he soon became embroiled in a plot to break Calabria free from the rule of Naples. Campanella preached about the rise of a new egalitarian republic led by a scientist–priesthood and the building of a city of God–Heaven–Sun. The

---

[23] ibid
[24] Fantoli, A. *Galileo: For Copernicanism and for the Church*

plot failed and Campanella was captured and tortured, but by feigning insanity under torture, this meant that the authorities could not burn him at the stake though he was to endure 27 years of imprisonment. It was from his dungeon, in 1623 that he managed to get his major work *Civitas Solis* — *The City of the Sun* — smuggled out to the Rosicrucians in Germany.[25]

Campanella was released in 1629. He spent the subsequent period in Rome, where he became acquainted with the French ambassador, who fortunately helped smuggled him into France when Campanella was falsely accused of being involved in a new revolt in the Naples region. Campanella's arrival in the French royal court was arranged by Cardinal Richelieu, who effectively ran the country at the time, and he recommended the magus–prophet to Queen Anne, wife of Louis XIII. Though Richelieu was a Catholic, he was a pragmatist and being a man of great intellect, he was well read and would have been familiar with the contents of even heretical works. Whereas it would be unseemly to have any link with organisations such as the Rosicrucians, Richelieu could fraternise with Campanella, who had 'renounced' the extremes of his heretical views to escape the Inquisition. Campanella too was a pragmatist and he clothed his heretical Hermetic philosophy in more acceptable Christian garments. Richelieu, as was common practice in that period of history, made great use of Campanella's astrological skills. The two had got on so well that Campanella dedicated several books to the cardinal, he also pressed Richelieu to assist him in constructing a Hermetic 'City of the Sun'.[26]

The French queen, Anne was concerned because there was no heir to the french throne — especially as the king no longer had any contact with his wife. Anne knew of Campanella's fabled abilities of prediction and asked him if there was any hope of a child. Despite the seeming insurmountable problems, Campanella predicted that the couple would have a son and that he would be a great solar–king ruling from a City-of-the-Sun. A chance thunderstorm, when the king was passing the queen's palace forced Louis XIII reluctantly to seek shelter there. Nine months later, on Campanella's seventieth birthday September 5th 1638, the future Louis XIV was born, the monarch who was to become known as the 'Sun King'. To Campanella, this unlikely birth was divinely contrived and he believed that this future king would bring about the great Hermetic revolution contained within a reformed Christian framework.

A secret and mysterious society emerged around this time, because of its secrecy it is difficult to know exactly when the Rosicrucians came into

---

[25] Campanella, T. *The City of the Sun*
[26] Headley, J M. *Tommaso Campanella and the Transformation of the World*

existence. Some scholars have suggested that it may have been founded in 1580 by Dr Dee, however I think that its true roots are probably much older and might be based in the 'Organization' — that secret resistance movement — that allegedly kept Gnosticism alive. Between 1607 and 1616, two anonymous documents appeared in Germany, lauding the efforts of a group of mystic–doctor–philosophers who wanted to bring about the "Universal Reformation of Mankind." *Fama fraternitatis Roseae Crucis oder Die Bruderschaft des Ordens der Rosenkreuzer* was published in 1614. In the following year the second book appeared in print *Confessio oder Bekenntnis der Societät und Bruderschaft Rosenkreuz*. Translations into English, *The Fame* and *The Confession*, took forty years but in the interim, the work caused a stir throughout Europe. The hero of these two tales is given the name Christian Rosenkreutz — in English Christian Rose Cross — in Latin "of the Rose Cross" becomes *Roseae Crucis*, from hence the name Rosicrucian.

Noted as magicians and alchemists, the Rosicrucians were clearly Hermetics, but whereas the Hermetics were seen as pagans by the Roman Catholics, the Rosicrucians were seen as part of the Reform movement and created a pseudo–Christian framework. Their adepts moved around Europe, mainly within the Protestant countries, discreetly promoting their philosophy whilst working as healers — their services were free, as those of the Cathar Perfects had once been. The Rosicrucian agenda promoted a revolution which would change the world, a new world in which man would be free from evil, a world free from the corruption of both the Papacy and Islam and when the time was right, the Rosicrucian store of knowledge would be revealed to all mankind.

In 1616, a third book was published on the activities of the fictional Christian Rosenkreutz, which was called *The Chemical Wedding*. It was an allegorical story of death and spiritual rebirth obtained through Gnosis. This story was a retelling of the ancient Mystery religion initiation, which clearly reveals the Rosicrucians' Gnostic roots. In his autobiography, the Lutheran pastor Johann Andreæ claimed that he wrote Chemical Wedding as a parody.[27] Andreæ's writing indicates that he was a Rosicrucian, but centuries of religious and political persecutions ensured that Rosicrucians made a point of blending invisibly into society. Andreæ promoted the Utopian city — one very similar to Campanella's description in *Civitas Solis*, which, when it was smuggled out from his prison cell, was taken to the town in Germany where Andreæ lived. This notion of a Utopian city–state of the sun was to reappear again in later times and one must assume that both Heliopolis the city of Ra the sun god, and Akhenaten's city dedicated to the Aten solar disc were the original inspirations.

---

[27] ibid.

From Inquisition to inspiration

The contents of Rosicrucian texts offer some intriguing questions. In *The Chemical Wedding of Christian Rosenkreutz*, there is a reference to the 'Father of Light' — a description never once used in the Christian Bible, but a common term used amongst Druids and Gnostics, who also defined themselves as the 'Sons of Light'. There is also a reference that seems to be taken from the *Egyptian Book of the Dead*, however this work was not translated for another 200 years, so how the Rosicrucians knew of it is quite a mystery. The book also mentions an enigmatic inscription which reads 'The height of Knowledge is to know Nothing' — a blatant echo of the beliefs pronounced by the Greek sages such as Pythagoras and Plato. Clearly the Rosicrucians knew a great deal about many things, which indicates that they had access to a most impressive library and source of knowledge.

Though I do not wish to delve excessively into the activities of Hermetics and Rosicrucians, it is necessary to outline certain events because it is important to show that the beliefs of the Gnostics had not died and that, despite the strenuous and bloody efforts of the Catholic Church, these beliefs were nurtured by one or more secret organisations, whose long-term aim was to reveal these beliefs and overthrow the heretical Catholic Church. The mathematicians, scientists and philosophers mentioned above and on the next few pages, all appear to be Hermetics, Rosicrucians or Freemasons, so it is evident that there was a *sub-rosa* network operating at the very highest levels in Europe and America.

The first major blow to the structure of the Catholic Church, was the rise of Protestantism in the early sixteenth century, led by Martin Luther's revolt against the corruption of the Vatican. Protestant austerity countered the Catholic love of lavish ornamentation, and demonstrated a distaste for Catholic corruption and religious practices, and for saints and holy relics. The Protestant movement was driven mainly by Lutherans and Calvinists. They had much in common with the Vaudois or Waldensians, a 12th-century reformist sect originating in Lyon, who were associated with the Cathars and persecuted as heretics.

Europe became split, roughly along a north–south divide, with the northern states becoming Protestant. In a few states loyalty to one side or another could waver. These were mainly the southern German states and Bohemia, though to a lesser extent, both England and France had their problems. The secret organisations that were seeking the overthrow of the Catholic Church naturally aligned themselves to the Protestants and worked amongst them as provocateurs, though it must be remembered that the Protestants themselves were still orthodox Christians. Groups like the Rosicrucians made use of the Protestants as either a tool or weapon that could be directed at the Papacy with its overthrow in mind. Individuals worked to cause dissent and to direct Protestant actions.

In 1623, eleven years before Campanella's arrival at the French court, two placards suddenly appeared in Paris announcing the presence in the city of the Brethren of the Rose Cross. The "Invisible College" was ready to enlighten people with the "most perfect knowledge of the Most High." The prospect of the rebirth of Europe, with a new age of intellectualism employing science and philosophy which would reform the world caused excitement amongst the population and panic amongst the Church.[28]

To paint the picture of the accelerating struggle to overthrow the Catholic Church, we need first to take a look at the political and religious strife that formed the 16th–century background. The Rosicrucians and other underground Gnostic groups became more ambitious, perhaps whilst scenting that a major breakthrough was at hand they grew impatient. They identified a new champion in the young French Protestant Prince, Henry of Navarre. Henry (1553-1610) was the son of Antoine de Bourbon and Jeanne d'Albret, heiress to the throne of Navarre in Spain. Navarre was under the rule of a rogue French Protestant dynasty at that time. Henry was born in Pau, Cathar country. After his father's death, his mother, a zealous Calvinist, ensured that Henry was carefully educated by Calvinist tutors.

The Catholic King Henry II spent his reign at war, externally with the Hapsburgs and internally with the Protestant Huguenots. Prior to Henry of Navarre's arrival, France had been unstable for many years. Henry II's wife was Catherine de' Medici — the orphaned daughter of Lorenzo — given in marriage by her uncle Guido de' Medici, by then Pope Clement VII. Catherine had three sons who were crowned successively after the death of their father. She ruled as co–regent with Francis II, Charles IX and Henry III through each of their brief reigns.

In the days of Charles IX, Henry of Navarre led the Protestant French Huguenot army to oppose the King and the Catholic League, which comprised the Vatican, France, Spain and the Germanic Hapsburgs, by tradition the rulers of the Holy Roman Empire. Hoping to broker a peace between the two sides, Catherine de' Medici offered her daughter Marguerite to Prince Henry. Whilst he was *en route* to his wedding in Paris in 1572, Henry's mother Queen Jeanne died so he arrived in Paris as the King of Navarre.

During the wedding celebration, attended by thousands of Huguenots, rumours of plots against the throne spread among the Catholics. They sought retaliation and attempted the assassination of a Huguenot leader, which then led the Huguenots to riot in protest. The resulting chaos caused

---

[28] ibid.

Charles IX to order the royal guards to attack the Huguenots. All Huguenots in the city were slaughtered in what was to become known as the infamous St Bartholomew's Day Massacre. Henry of Navarre was removed from the immediate situation, as he was held prisoner within the royal palace, primarily due to his refusal to attend the Catholic Mass. After three years, Henry feigned conversion and became a Catholic, then escaped back to Navarre and renounced the Catholic faith.

When Charles died his younger brother became Henry III. Henry was supposedly homosexual and though he married, sired no heir. On the death of the youngest of Catherine de' Medici's children, Francis Duke of Anjou, Henry of Navarre became the heir presumptive. The displeasure caused by Henry III recognising a Huguenot as his legitimate successor initiated a series of campaigns to rid France of the heir. In 1587 Henry of Navarre set up camp in the Protestant Huguenot stronghold of La Rochelle to oppose the forces of the Catholic League. However Henry III was also under pressure from within his own country, where some elements sided with the overtly ambitious Philip II of Spain. Philip's main goal was to secure the Netherlands against William of Orange and the Protestant insurgents, but he also planned to invade England to rid her of her Protestant queen, Elizabeth. Elizabeth was, of course, sending financial aid to Henry of Navarre and William of Orange.

As for the Vatican, things didn't work out quite as they hoped. The Catholic League was established supposedly to combat the Muslim threat in the Mediterranean and indeed won a crushing sea battle at Lepanto, but then the Netherlands' rebellion — driven by the tiny minority of zealot Calvinists — refocused the mind of Philip II. Philip's ambition to dominate Europe worried the Vatican, especially if he wanted to control its own affairs as well. Though the Catholics wished for a victory over the Protestants, they also wished for a strong and independent France that would act as a counterbalance to Spain. It would also please the Vatican to see Philip given a bloody nose by the Protestants if it kept him out of France.

In 1584, William of Orange died and the Dutch in despair turned to France. They invited Henry III of France to be their sovereign, as a way of keeping the Spanish out. In a desperate panic, Philip was driven to offer to sponsor his enemy Henry of Navarre if he undertook another civil war in France, which would divert Henry III's attention. Henry of Navarre dismissed Philip's offer and Henry III declined the Dutch throne since the pro–Spanish faction led by the Duke of Guise, the founder of the Catholic League, had disabled him politically.

By the summer of 1588, Philip had set into motion his plan to invade England and the Armada set sail from Cadiz. Henry III was enraged that his sovereignty was being usurped by the Spanish who expected to use the French channel ports to embark their invasion barges. His authority was also being flouted by the Duke of Guise. An uprising in Paris was sufficient to divert the king's attention at this critical time and prevent him from aiding England. Henry of Navarre too was occupied in Lorraine, trying to stop the Spanish forces heading northwards. The Spanish troop barges were attacked by fire-ships in Calais harbour and the Armada destroyed by the English fleet in the Channel putting an end to Philip's plan.

Under increasing pressure from Philip and his French allies led by the Duke of Guise, who was seeking to depose him, the harangued Henry III had the duke summoned to a council on Christmas Eve 1588. The duke was cut down in the king's antechamber and later his brother, the Cardinal of Guise, as well as the Cardinal of Bourbon were both arrested and subsequently murdered by their guards. This event led to outrage and the population turned against their king, who in the following spring was forced to flee Paris. In a secret deal with Henry of Navarre, the desperate French king offered him the succession if he helped him recapture Paris. Before they could mount the siege, Henry III was assassinated by a fanatical Jesuit monk and before he died, true to his word, Henry III proclaimed Henry of Navarre his legal successor.

Despite being a Catholic, Henry III's commitment had clearly not been sufficient for his Catholic allies to trust him, nor for all of his subjects to give him allegiance. Like his mother Catherine de' Medici, Henry III had been deeply interested in esoteric subjects such as astrology and Hermetic magic — as they were members of the Florence Medici family, this is hardly surprising. Whatever his reason, Henry III demonstrated his preference to leave his kingdom in the hands of a Protestant.

The majority of France felt differently and most of the cities held out against the new king unless Henry of Navarre converted to the Catholic faith. Having done it once before, Henry made the pragmatic conversion; if that was the only way to gain acceptance, bring peace to France and end its internal religious strife, then it was no big thing.

The Huguenots felt betrayed especially when Henry was slow in granting them the security they sought, though eventually he ensured that liberty of conscience was granted to the Protestants. As Henry IV, his rule was enlightened, he brought peace and a certain amount of religious reconciliation and his economic policies brought France new wealth. Alas, not everyone welcomed this French revival and Henry was assassinated by a fanatic in 1610. Henry's death was a severe blow to the Rosicrucians, who for a while had believed that the Catholic Church could be severely weakened and broken. They had already lost their one great hope, Elizabeth of England, who had finally succumbed to old age, and suspected the new king James I of having Catholic sympathies, despite being ruler of a Protestant country. Their hope had lain in King Henry — the catalyst for creating a Utopian society — and now, he was no more.

Disappointed, the Hermetics and Rosicrucians turned their hopes eastwards to Bohemia, where the people elected their kings. The person on whom they now rested their hopes was the young Prince Frederick, the Elector of the Palatine and Rhine, who had married Elizabeth Stuart, the daughter of James I of protestant England in 1613. The Palatine was seen as the Protestant states' bulwark against the Catholic League and Frederick was seen as their heroic figurehead. Frederick's close advisor was Prince Christian of Anhalt, a man who immersed himself in alchemy and esoteric magic, and who one can thus assume was probably a Rosicrucian. His close relative Prince Augustus published the earliest reference to the Rosicrucian brotherhood in 1605 — nine years before the appearance of the Rosicrucian manifesto.

The influence of Prince Christian encouraged many Rosicrucians to the royal court at Heidelberg and when, in 1619, the Bohemians invited Frederick to become their king, the Rosicrucian entourage decamped along with him to Prague. Many of Dr Dee's followers were also visitors to the court in Prague, including Robert Fludd. Prince Christian envisaged this as a springboard for Frederick from King to Emperor in order to replace the Hapsburg's Holy Roman Empire with a new Utopian state. Prince Christian was close to the Venetian statesman and anti–Catholic theologian Paulo Sarpi, who wanted Venice to become a Protestant city–republic and Sarpi was a close friend of Galileo. With such influence and desire the Utopian dream was in reach.

Sadly the great longing for Utopia was soon to be thwarted again. The Protestant princes became disunited and though Frederick was popular in England, James, with his Catholic sympathies would not assist with military aid, leaving Bohemia out on a limb. When the Hapsburg–led forces of the Catholic League moved against Bohemia, Frederick's army was defeated, though he managed to escape into exile. With brutal force, Bohemia became Catholic and its dream of being the catalyst of a new Hermetic–Gnostic Europe was painfully destroyed. Escaping from Bohemia, the Rosicrucian scholars headed west, most going to England, perhaps seen by them as the true birthplace of the brotherhood. One of Frederick's sons, Prince Rupert, became the famous Cavalier, commanding King Charles I's cavalry during the English Civil War. Though superficially a Calvinist, because of his family's affiliations Rupert must also have been steeped in Rosicrucian philosophies. When the monarchy was restored under Charles II, Rupert took a significant role in future events — most particularly in founding the Royal Society.

Rupert exerted tireless enthusiasm in his position as governor of the Hudson Bay Company: an indication of the Rosicrucians' hopes for the new North American continent. Francis Bacon, whose writings strongly indicate that he was a Rosicrucian, had a great eagerness for the new English colonies in America too. Michael Maier met Bacon during a visit to England, shortly after Bacon wrote the manuscript of New Atlantis. Bacon was also associated with the Virginia Company and was instrumental in drawing up a charter that was given the Royal seal. The charter gave the company the rights to govern the colonies, at that time centred on Virginia. Maier too was closely associated with members of the Virginia Company, which suggests that they were at the very least interested in Rosicrucian ideas. Maier had promoted a vision of a Utopian America in *Atalanta Fugiens* in 1618. In Germany, the Rosicrucian Lutheran pastor, Johann Andreæ became a member of what was called the Brotherhood of Antilia — a mediæval name for Atlantis — and their dream was to create the Hermetic Utopian society. The Brotherhood of Antilia had plans to buy an island in the Baltic, off Riga, but also had plans to move *en masse* to America. This Hermetic–Rosicrucian dream of creating a new reformed society in America was to influence the course of history.

This diverse group of seventeenth–century scholars, doctors and princes formed a brotherhood determined to overcome the religious and political opposition to intellectual enquiry that had removed individual freedom, slaughtered those who tried to demand it and kept moral and spiritual values in the dark. Although their aims were expressed in imaginary worlds, their intention was to reform values and society so that philosophers and scientists would lead Mankind into a wonderful new world.

It didn't all go according to plan.

Chapter 29

Isis Unveiled

"The pursuit of perfection, then, is the pursuit of sweetness and light."
Matthew Arnold

The 'Great Heresy' that had struggled to survive through one millennium into another, that had undergone numerous false dawns and dashed hopes, not only refused to perish, but pursued its mission to create an enlightened world. The cautious resurgence that began in the 16th century grew throughout the 17th and 18th and though remaining discreet, became increasingly confident and audacious. It would appear that through the covert networking of the Rosicrucians, influential people were made aware of and 'converted' to the cause. During the 17th century, the mysterious Rosicrucians suddenly faded back into the deep shadows and the movement that emerged into the dawning light between the Ages of Renaissance and Enlightenment, was Freemasonry. Perhaps the Rosicrucians had briefly put a toe in the water for the 'Organisation' — that deeply secret body, which from early Christian times, had striven to safeguard and resurrect the ancient Mysteries.

The link may seem unlikely, but the Freemasons have much about their practices that is Gnostic and Egyptian. Unfortunately, the need to encode the ancient teaching, combined with the requirement for secrecy from a hostile Church and society has muddied the waters of understanding. Originally membership of the Freemasons was exclusive, but over time it was opened up to men who no longer belonged to the academic hierarchy, especially in the 19th century when membership swelled rapidly. The real meaning encoded into Freemasonry has been lost to the rank–and–file members who probably have little interest in esoteric matters and remain very much like the outer initiates of the Mysteries. Whether those elevated to the higher degrees know the true secrets of their craft remains, to all intents and purposes, a mystery to its members. However, I would find it difficult to believe that no-one within Freemasonry's hierarchy is aware of the original purpose behind the craft. Yet if there is an inner movement, which is aware of its early goals, there is no external evidence of an attempt to develop gnosis amongst all of its lower-ranking members.

It would probably be accurate to state that the vast majority of Freemasons have little knowledge or interest in the real origins and aims. For most Freemasons their interest is motivated more by networking than learning a craft. Their hope is to enhance prospects for promotion and make financial gains through contact with other members, though in reality more deals are probably arranged on the golf course than within a Masonic Lodge. Sadly, the perceived secrecy, the seemingly odd rituals and the networking have cultivated a suspicion amongst the modern-day public, which is confirmed when members seriously abuse the contacts they have made amongst their brotherhood. This is, however, not a fault of the organisation but is a moral flaw of individual members of it. Freemasonry is no different from many other organisations whether political, financial or industrial; all at some time will suffer from the behaviour of corrupt individuals.

The obsessive conspiracy theorists and Evangelical Christians make unsubstantiated and bizarre accusations: Freemasons are variously described as Satanists, paedophiles and criminals, often controlled by an elite cabal of bankers and business leaders or even by shape-changing alien lizards. This paranoid and irrational condemnation is a reminder of the Literalist Christians of Ancient Rome: if you haven't a clue what an organisation represents, you must first assume that it is a force for evil.

According to some contemporary conspiracy-theorists the American Scottish Rite Freemasonry, which has counted fourteen American presidents amongst its members, is undertaking all manner of secret projects to control the world. Its stated aims reflect those of the Gnostics and its members' 'enlightenment' is also pursued through the teaching of ethics by allegory and philosophical debate.[1] One wonders what causes the

---

1 *Spes mea in deo est:* My hope is in God

The Scottish Rite seeks to strengthen the community and believes that each man should act in civil life according to his individual judgment and the dictates of his conscience.
A member of the Scottish Rite seeks to:
- Exalt the dignity of every person, the human side of his daily activities, and the maximum service to humanity.
- Aid mankind's search in God's universe for identity, for development and for destiny, and thereby produce better men in a better world, happier men in a happier world and wiser men in a wiser world.

conspiracy–theorists to form their conclusion as the aims are benign and it is clearly evident that for three hundred years, these Freemasons have been singularly unsuccessful in persuading the rest of the world to conform to their altruistic and benign beliefs.

Whatever Freemasonry might now be and regardless of how it is generally perceived as a movement, the fact that we can be sure of, is that it is an organisation whose purpose and ambitions are neither known nor understood. My own conclusion is that Freemasonry is a movement that is a conglomeration of Egyptian Hermetic, Judaic Cabalistic and Gnostic Christian systems and though it appears to source things back to Egypt, its attachment to the above systems strongly indicates that its knowledge and understanding of Egyptian religion and history is extremely limited. Its motives and aims are worthy, but unfortunately most people are in total ignorance of Freemasonry's agenda that promotes certain moral and philosophical ideals with the intention of benefiting and improving mankind. Neither is it widely known that Freemasonry had a profound effect upon the making of the modern world.

It is generally accepted that Freemasonry began in Scotland amongst some of the descendents of the outlawed Order of the Knights Templar, allegedly under the leadership of the Sinclair family and it is believed that Freemasonry evolved sometime around 1400. The first real evidence for Freemasonry appears on the wall of the family chapel built at Rosslyn near Edinburgh and completed in 1486. This engraving depicted a blindfolded kneeling man with a book in his hands and a noose held by a Knight Templar around his neck. This imagery matches that of the modern First–Degree Masonic Ceremony. Unfortunately, slovenly investigations by profit–driven theorists has embroiled Rosslyn Chapel in a modern–day myth linking it to the fictitious Ark of the Covenant.

Freemasonry spread from Scotland into England; lodges existed in England certainly by 1615, Robert Lomas provides evidence that members of the Edinburgh Lodge demonstrated two Masonic degrees to English Freemasons in York.[2] However, the Lodges maintained a low, even invisible profile, for though both Scotland and England were Protestant countries the Church and society would have considered Masonic beliefs heretical or

---

The Scottish Rite is a branch of Freemasonry designed to supplement and amplify the philosophical teachings of the first three degrees. The Scottish Rite claims to build upon the ethical teachings and philosophy of blue lodge Masonry through dramatic presentation. The Scottish Rite is sometimes called the "University of Freemasonry" because it uses extensive allegory and drama in its degrees to explore the philosophy, history, ethics and ultimate truths that guide Freemasons' lives. *Supreme Council, 33°, Ancient Accepted Scottish Rite Northern Masonic Jurisdiction*

[2] Lomas, R *Invisible College*

even pagan. Nevertheless, because its members included those from the very highest levels of society, the organisation's survival was ensured. Though the early Scottish Templar link is widely acknowledged the English kings Edward I and II had Templar connections as well, and offered the Templars discreet protection at times when the Popes attempted to coerce every country to persecute them. There is no reason to believe that subsequent kings were any less committed to the same ideals.

Freemasonry's first world-wide impact came in the aftermath of the English Civil War — a war that was both political and religious. Prior to the outbreak of the Civil War, the Rosicrucian fraternity had hoped to see England develop into is Utopian state and was striving vigorously for this to happen. Foremost amongst the Rosicrucians active in England were Samuel Hartlib an immigrant from German and Polish parents, who was an educationalist and philosopher; Theodore Haak another German immigrant, who had been exiled from the Palatinate to Poland and who worked as unofficial London diplomat for the Palatinate as well as the representative of the Bohemian Church of Unity of Brethren's Bishop Jan Komensky; and John Drury, the Scottish Minister and reformer who campaigned for the restoration of the Palatinate throne to Prince Carl-Louis, the eldest son of Frederick V and Elizabeth Stuart, the exiled monarchs of Bohemia. In 1641, Drury, Hark and Hartlib invited Bishop Komensky — known as Comenius — to England. The bishop was overjoyed, believing that he was in receipt of a mandate to build Francis Bacon's 'New Atlantis' in England as Parliament was in opposition to the crown. The following year, their optimistic dream of a peaceful shift to 'Utopia' was shattered with the outbreak of hostilities between Parliament and King Charles I.

The particularly brutal war, with the greatest mortality rate *per capita* of any war in history, deeply divided the nation and in many cases families — it also forced apart men who shared the same philosophical beliefs, but different political allegiances. At the outbreak of hostilities, the king left London and set up court in Oxford. The university city was noted for its great scholars and intellectuals and from out of these arose a group which were to designate themselves the 'Philosophical College', though more commonly they referred to themselves as the 'Invisible College'.

The Invisible College first formed in 1645 in London, but moved to Oxford three years later. From a letter, which emphasised the College's philosophical and humanitarian purpose, written by a founding member, the eminent physicist Robert Boyle, it was clear that the aspiration of the Invisible College was mankind's betterment, which it would promote through the expansion of knowledge and science. This aim echoes very closely the goals of the Rosicrucian's 'Invisible College' and it seems too large a coincidence for there to be no direct link between the two. Another strange coincidence linked two founder members to the Rosicrucians: Theodore Haak was a founder of the Oxford Invisible College, as was John Wilkins, a vicar who became Bishop of Chester, but whose previous post had been as the chaplain to Prince Carl–Louis of the Palatinate. Members of the Oxford Invisible College included the astronomer and architect Christopher Wren and the alchemist Elias Ashmole, who were both Freemasons.

In 1645 the Royalists were forced to surrender Oxford and the king was captured and eventually taken to London. For a while it seemed that a compromise would be agreed between the king and Parliament, but instead a second conflict erupted in 1648. The second conflict was brief and resulted in victory for the Parliamentary forces once more. The Parliamentarians were assured of retaining this victory when King Charles was tried for treason and executed in 1649. His son, the Prince of Wales was on the run in Scotland and took the title of King Charles II but had no constitutional rôle. Fleeing Britain, he went into exile in France, under the protection of the Sun King Louis XIV. England was transformed into the Commonwealth Republic of Free States, but the republican parliament was effectively sidelined under the dictatorship of Oliver Cromwell the 'Lord Protector'. Cromwell was a devout member of the strict Puritan church, but his interpretation of Christian teaching was selective, especially concerning degrees of meek and mild, showing love to one's neighbour and deciding exactly when 'thou shalt not kill'. The new regime enforced harsh Puritanical laws with brutal and bloody enthusiasm, particularly in Ireland, and the countries of Britain degenerated into joyless, bleak and spiritually-barren lands.

During these despotic times, the Invisible College decamped from Oxford and settled in Cambridge, where it maintained a secretive profile. Founder John Wilkins, who had been Warden of Wadham College Oxford, transferred too and became Warden of Trinity College Cambridge. In an ironic twist, Wilkins married the widowed sister of Oliver Cromwell, whose family home was in nearby Huntington. It seems probable that this was a marriage of convenience, one that allowed Wilkins to promote his educational agenda through his proximity to Cromwell.

In the years leading up to and during the royal exile, numerous men of significance spent time in France. These visits were extremely important and played a critical rôle in what was to take place in England on the king's return. Foremost amongst them was Robert Moray, a Scotsman and allegedly the first Freemason initiated in England.[3] Moray had spent time in

---

3   ibid.

France serving in the Scots Guard of Louis XIII and was promoted as its commander by Cardinal Richelieu in 1638. In the same year the 'Sun King' Louis XIV had been born and Richelieu had founded the *Academie Française*. The aim of the academy was to promote French as a language that could be understood by all. At that time French was a minority language within the country, which had several regional languages as well as 55 dialects and many more sub-dialects, so that the French had great difficulty in communicating with people from another part of the country. Richelieu might have had some idealistic Rosicrucian basis, but he also had a practical one.

Richelieu acted as patron to both Moray and Campanella, so it is highly unlikely that these two men did not meet and meet frequently. Had Moray been exposed to Rosicrucian teachings? The most probable answer is yes. In 1652 Moray married the daughter of the Earl of Balcarres Sir David Lindsay, a man who not only had a fascination with alchemy, but had also translated Rosicrucian works. In the same year Moray had sponsored the first English language edition of the Rosicrucian Manifestoes, which was published by Thomas Vaughan, a renowned alchemist and an ardent Rosicrucian. Clearly Moray had been *influenced* by the Rosicrucians and may well have been a *member*. In 1653 Moray was falsely charged with plotting to assassinate Charles II. In a letter Moray wrote to Charles to plead his innocence, he addressed him as 'Master Builder' revealing their Masonic connection. Later that year Moray was cleared of the charges against him as the political deceit was exposed. Clearly there was no doubt about Moray's innocence in the mind of the monarch and the fact that Moray had been a Royalist and he and Charles II were both Masons encouraged the close relationship that developed between them, which Moray took advantage of following the Restoration.

The diarist and horticulturalist John Evelyn was another influential man, who, at the outbreak of the Civil War, left for Paris and stayed there until 1652. He had married the daughter of the English ambassador and thus had circulated in the French court; it would seem likely that he had been exposed to Rosicrucian ideas. Despairing of Cromwell's unwillingness to promote scientific learning, Evelyn was to write in frustration to Robert Boyle in 1659, that the foundation of a mathematical college was not going to happen. He then expressed his hope that perhaps "some gentlemen whose geniuses, are greatly suitable, and who desire nothing more than to give a good example, preserve science and cultivate themselves, join together in a society."[4]

---

4   Spencer, C. *Prince Rupert*

During the royal exile in Paris, many of the Scots who attended the king were Freemasons from the Scottish Lodges. The eighteenth–century Masonic historian William Preston believed that Charles II was a Freemason and it appears that he was initiated at Scone in Scotland immediately before his exile. Prince Rupert of the Palatinate spent some time in Paris with the exiled court and his family background would make it reasonable to assume that he had strong Rosicrucian links that he renewed during his stay, though it is not known if he was a Mason. As Freemasons of this period were eager to study arcane knowledge, especially that of Egypt, it is logical therefore to conclude that they also would have been receptive to Rosicrucian ideas and particularly those concerning Campanella's vision for a Hermetic utopian world and a sacred City of the Sun. Certainly translating the latter into reality was to become central to Freemason activity.

Christopher Wren was a close friend of Rupert. During his childhood at the deanery at Windsor, Wren had known Rupert's elder brother, the boy–prince Carl–Louis of the Palatinate. In those early days Wren had been the protégé of John Wilkins, the private chaplain of Carl–Louis. Knowing his background and his friends, it seems likely that Wren would have been familiar with the Rosicrucian ideology. It is likely that he was initiated into Freemasonry in 1663, as we know that in 1685 he was Grand Master of English Freemasons. Today Wren is known as a great architect, however, he first pursued astronomy as a career and his great intellect rapidly gained him the position of Professor of Astronomy at Gresham College London. In 1661, after the Restoration, the king appointed Wren to the Savilian Chair of Astronomy at Oxford University. Wren's career change came suddenly following his escape from London's Great Plague of 1665, when he went to Paris. There he met the great Italian Baroque architect and sculptor, Gian Lorenzo Bernini, who had been invited by Louis XIV to design a façade for the Louvre Palace. Undoubtedly the meeting with Bernini had a profound effect upon Wren, but so too did events in Paris, where Louis had his greatest architects working to create the Sun City. When Wren returned to England, he brought with him a vision of how to transform London in similar fashion. Like the Egyptian astronomers, it seems that Wren now believed that his astronomical knowledge must to be translated on to the ground.

In the same year that Bernini and Wren arrived in Paris, so did two treasure troves found at two adjacent sites at Tournai. One was a tomb containing hundreds of golden items, which were attributed to the Frankish king Childeric, the other was Egyptian. Amongst the latter horde was a statue of Isis, the head of the sacred Apis bull — associated with Osiris and his later version as Serapis — and around 300 gold bees, which represented

405

divine solar rule. Even during the seventeenth century, scholars knew that bees were a symbol of the pharaohs and together with the long held belief that Paris was associated with Isis, the French concluded that the find indicated a link between the pharaohs and the early French kings. As we know, reports from earlier times tell of temples and statues of Isis in and around Paris.

It is most relevant to mention briefly what Bernini had been doing prior to his arrival at the French court. The call to Paris interrupted Bernini's creation of the great plaza that was to stand in front of St Peter's Basilica in Rome. The plaza had in its centre a gigantic Egyptian obelisk made from a single block of granite standing 25 metres high and weighing a massive 327 tonnes. This particular obelisk differed from other Egyptian obelisks because it did not bear any of the usual inscriptions that adorn the four sides of similar obelisks. This obelisk had once stood in Anu/Heliopolis, the 'Sun City'. Emperor Caligula had it brought to Rome in 37 CE and placed in the centre of his Vatican Circus that was used for chariot races. The redevelopment of the site for Constantine's great Christian Temple saw the demolition of both the Circus and the adjacent Temple dedicated to Mithras/Sol Invictus where the Basilica now stands. The construction worked around the giant obelisk, which, on completion, remained standing against the south wall of the new Basilica, penned into an alley–way by decaying tenements. A 14th century eye–witness account describes it having its pedestal covered by piles of rubbish.

In the 16th century, Pope Sixtus V — described as the last Renaissance pope — had a dream of redesigning Rome to make it the world's finest city.[5] It would have long wide avenues leading to spacious piazzas and churches, marked by four Egyptian obelisks, two of which stood at either end of the main west–east route from the Vatican, across the Tiber towards the rising sun behind the eastern hills. A new focus point would be marked in the centre of St Peter's Square, with the neglected Anu obelisk. Sixtus decided to retain the bronze globe that had been mounted on the obelisk's peak by Caligula and said to contain the ashes of Julius Cæsar, but added his family heraldic symbol of three small mountains surmounted by an eight–pointed, three–dimensional star, to the top of the sphere, over this he placed a golden cross.

In 1586, the Renaissance artist Domenico Fontana was given the arduous task of moving the obelisk. The *Guide to St Peter's Basilica 2003* tells us that this mammoth task required 907 men, 75 horses and 40 cranes and was started in April and finished in September. This of course raises the everlasting question of how the Egyptians managed to erect such obelisks in

---

5   Bacon, E N. *Design of Cities*

the first place without horses and cranes, for there are obvious constraints when you try to cram thousands of workers into an area which would leave them no room to move! Roman legend concerning the raising of the obelisk gives us a strange insight into Sixtus's motives. According to the story, Sixtus ordered the vast spectating crowd to remain silent under pain of death, but the ropes were seen to be too short by a sailor who shouted out, "Acqua alle funi!" By crying out for water on the ropes to lengthen them, he saved the obelisk from crashing down and breaking. Pope Sixtus V showed his gratitude by sparing the sailor's life instead of killing him for breaking the silence!

If the obelisk's placement were no more than an aesthetic adornment for the piazza, or even a vain–glorious posturing of the Church, then why the strange demand for total silence enforced by a death penalty. Some suggest it was for safety, but if it were, what is the point of silence if no–one is allowed to interrupt in the case of danger, as allegedly occurred. It seems more likely that the raising of the obelisk was a solemn ceremony with some profound mystical meaning. Once it was in place, a cardinal exorcised the obelisk to free it from any pagan influence or assaults of spiritual impurity; the exorcism was inscribed on the west and eastern faces of the base of the obelisk. It appears likely that two factions were at work here, with the overt Catholic group totally unaware of the *sub–rosa* group's clandestine activities.

It is an intriguing thought that Sixtus's three small mountains might actually represent the three Great Pyramids at Giza and the star represent Sirius, the star of Isis. Even stranger is the decision to surmount the obelisk with a cross, for in Egyptian hieroglyphs, which nobody supposedly could read in the 16th century, this very same hieroglyphic image of a cross over an obelisk represents the sacred sun city of Anu/Heliopolis. There is another symbol in the hieroglyph that represents Anu, which was missing at St Peter's in the time of Sixtus that of a circle or ellipse divided into eight segments. This eight–segment ellipse appeared about eighty years later, when Pope Alexander VII commissioned Bernini to redesign St Peter's Square. Bernini enclosed the square within an elliptical colonnade. This was the work that was interrupted by Bernini's visit to Paris, but then completed upon his return. The piazza was built in the design of a handsome eight–segment ellipse, which centred on the obelisk. So now the full hieroglyph, the name Anu, the sacred sun city of Ra was translated into St Peter's Square. It seems that the 'Organisation', perhaps via the Hermetic brotherhood or the Rosicrucians, had used figures of high authority within the Church to 'invisibly' engrave the name of the city of Ra into the sacred precincts at the very heart of Christianity — there to remain as long as the heretical Christian Church did.

Returning to Pre–Restoration England, the years of strict Puritan dictatorship had soured public support and left the people longing for a return to gaiety and freedom. The death of Oliver Cromwell and the failure of his son Richard to hold the regime together saw the country in turmoil and teetering on the brink of yet another civil war. Parliament attempted to reassert itself, however this brought it into confrontation with the Commonwealth army, which continued to support the new Lord Protector, Richard Cromwell. Despairing of the growing anarchy, General George Monck, who was commander of the Commonwealth Army controlling Scotland, saw that the only solution to avoid another civil conflict was to restore the monarchy. This may appear like a traitorous abandoning of political ideals, however Monck, the son of a Devonshire baronet who became a professional soldier, had fought on the Royalist side and was captured at the Battle of Nantwich. He had been imprisoned in the Tower for two years before he was persuaded to join the Commonwealth army.

Monck sent Sir John Grenville to France as an emissary to negotiate the terms by which he would offer his forces to support the king's return to England. These terms stipulated that the monarchy would uphold the Church of England against the Catholic Church, but also that the king would ensure his subjects the freedom to follow other faiths whilst Parliament would undertake all matters of state. In response Charles, who was now in Holland in an attempt to distance himself from the French and soothe English sensibilities, issued his 'Declaration of Breda', in which he further declared that there would be an equitable settlement to land disputes resulting from the war; a general amnesty to his previous enemies; and to keep the army sweet, he promised wage arrears would be honoured in full.

Monck marched down to London with his army, from his headquarters in Coldstream, to make the formal announcement that the monarchy would be restored. The presence of his army delivered a clear message that if challenged, he would use force to support his decision. On May 25th 1660, Monck was at Dover with a force of 20,000 troops to welcome Charles and escort him to London. At Blackheath, Charles reviewed Monck's elite troops, whom he later adopted. Monck used this military show not only to thwart any opposition, but also to make Charles aware that he would not survive without the military's backing.

The royal procession into London was unopposed, both soldiers and the populace gave the returning king a rapturous welcome — church bells pealed, the streets were carpeted with strewn flowers and a joyous party atmosphere gripped the nation. This was as much a response to the casting off of the unnatural Puritanical shackles, which had dulled the land for a decade, as it was a welcome for the King. When Cromwell's army was disbanded in 1671, Monck's regiment of Coldstreamers was the only regiment to remain and became the 2nd Regiment Coldstream Guards; the king's personal guards who had been with him in exile became the 1st Regiment Grenadier Guards.

Much was expected of the new king. The people wanted a real transformation in the country and in their lives and in particular they wished to see stability and peace within the land. External wars, if they were unavoidable, they could cope with; internal wars they could not. With the desire for reformation rife within the land, the Invisible College had the perfect opportunity to introduce itself to the world, to seize the moment and to take action. Just five months after the restoration, in November of 1661, twelve members of the Invisible College, including Boyle, Wren, Wilkins and Moray, held a meeting chaired by Haak at Gresham College. Directed by Moray they decided to found a new college whose intent would be the promotion of physico–mathematical experimental learning — this experimental learning was something that had long been promoted by Freemasonry. Moray also proposed that they should seek a Royal Charter to establish their acceptability.

King Charles had a special significance for the Invisible College. The Hermetic brotherhood followed the Egyptian philosophy believing that a king was necessary to achieve the state of Ma'at. Just as the Hermetics saw Louis XIV as the Sun King of France, in England the Sun King would be Charles II. The position of the Sun King was symbolic, but nevertheless, extremely important in much the same way that the Pharaoh in ancient Egypt was the personification or representative of God upon earth. From what we've learned of Akhenaten, we know that to achieve a perfect society, it must be in balance and harmony, and to maintain contact with the Creator the king becomes the golden apex of the earthly utopian pyramid.

The early Greeks philosophers had inherited this idea from the Egyptians but had interpreted it differently; Plato for instance envisaged a republic as the utopian state. This might suit a people who had tired of bad kings, but then humans, be they kings or commoners are flawed, and rule by neither senate nor parliament would ensure good government. The advantage of a king with a parliament beneath him was that the king could stand above mundane politics and offer continuity and stability impartially. Politicians, on the other hand, were self–promoting and career–obsessed, with their first loyalty to their political party rather than to the good of the people. Politicians' vision is always short–term and rarely looks beyond the next election, making their tenure transitory. As for presidents, they are unable to disassociate themselves from the political party they belong to and are therefore sectarian and are ever fearful of losing their 'throne' at the next election. In states where presidents have real political power rather than a rôle as a national figurehead, they are prone to becoming egotistical and dictatorial.

The republican system of multi–political parties rarely represents the needs and interests of the people, but rather it promotes the interests of the party's electoral sponsors, be they trade–unions, industrialists or bankers. In many so–called democratic elections, the government that comes to power has not received the majority of votes, yet it claims to have been given the right to speak for all the nation. Even worse when one considers that governments control the Justice system, they can manipulate laws to suit their own requirements or change them on whim without further consultation with their people. Too often we encounter republics where there is little or no real regard for either justice or morality.

Once a king is correctly enthroned he is above the mundane matters of government. When afforded power to influence and if necessary intercede, because he has no political allegiance, he can better assess the requirements of his people and what is best in the long–term for the state, and hereditary powers can ensure that the long–term plan is brought to fruition. The intellectuals of the 17th and 18th centuries were well aware of the short–comings of a republic and so both the Rosicrucians' and the Freemasons' esoteric philosophies projected their ideal of a democratic state with a king at its head.

The situation over this period of national flux left the academic world in a state of turmoil. During the years under Cromwell's rule, those scholars who had supported the Parliamentarian's cause were given high positions within the universities, but with the Restoration all except those employed by Gresham College were dismissed from their posts. Because there were numerous Freemasons within the Invisible College, they considered it a duty to give aid and employment to fellow members of the Craft. Following the meeting at Gresham College, Moray busied himself raising funds and used his influence with the king to promote the College's plan. In December 1661, Charles gave his approval to the founding of the Royal Society. The new Society then moved into Gresham College and set about drawing up a list of suitable members; amongst them were Evelyn and Ashmole, who along with Wren, were awarded prestigious positions by the king. After the Royal Charter was granted, Moray was appointed president of the Royal Society and granted a permanent residence in the royal court at Whitehall.

Some historians have proposed that the Royal Society was founded to address the various problems besetting the country, not least the threat of war against the Dutch. Certainly Moray, who though he had an interest in science was actually a soldier, was concerned with readying the country for a war and had particular concerns to equip the Royal Navy with whatever scientific advances would give an advantage to the nation. Though the possibility of war was of obvious concern, the weight of evidence clearly demonstrates that there was far more behind the society's founding than military disquiet.

It is interesting to see the parallels with what had and would occur in France. In 1638, Cardinal Richelieu the Prime Minister of France founded the *Académie Française*. At first the group of twelve academics met informally, but after receipt of the Royal Charter from Louis XIII, the membership expanded to forty. Just as the Invisible College transformed into the Royal Society, in the early 1640s, a number of French scientists held informal meetings in Paris; in 1666, under its patron Louis XIV, this elite group of scientists became the founding members of the *Académie des Sciences*.

The list of just a few of the early members of the Royal Society reads like a Who's–Who of the scientific world: Boyle, Wren, Hooke, Newton, Leibniz, Halley, Ashmole, Rooke and Wilkins. These founders of the Royal Society were men of science, drawn equally from both former–warring factions, men of opposing political and religious views, but the conflicts that might have driven them apart were never discussed, for the primary rule of the Society's meetings was passed on from the Invisible College: the discussion of politics or religion was never allowed. This unlikely coming–together of old enemies was marked by the Society's patron King Charles, who allowed the first meeting to be chaired by Oliver Cromwell's brother–in–law. Though the king had a deep hatred of Cromwell, whom he deemed responsible for the execution of his father, he was able to over–ride this loathing because they were both Freemasons; allegedly Cromwell himself had been a Mason. Many of the newly–chartered Royal Society's members were already linked across the old divide as brother Freemasons. Though Thomas Sprat, in *The History of the Royal Society,* wrote about "an unusual sight to the English nation, that men of disagreeing parties and ways of life have forgotten to hate, and have met in the unanimous advancement of the same works" without mentioning their links to Freemasonry and the Society's promotion of Masonic philosophy, the engraved frontispiece depicts Francis Bacon and the President either side of a bust of King Charles, surrounded by an abundance of Masonic symbolism.

Prince Rupert was one of the earliest members of the Royal Society. Though his fame came from his exploits as the cavalry commander for the Royalist cause during the Civil War and afterwards as a noted naval commander, he was also a mathematician and inventor. As we have seen, Rupert had close associations with the Rosicrucians and was almost certainly a member. Rupert was a close friend of the Chancellor, the Earl of Shaftesbury, who was a republican, but this seeming political and philosophical divide would be surmountable if they were both Rosicrucians. The hope for the future was that the old political and religious enmities would be set aside and that a new and more harmonious state would develop. This policy, which had been promoted through Freemasonry and the Invisible College was strictly adhered to by the Royal Society when it forbade political and religious discussion in its meetings. Though King Charles himself was keen to promote reconciliation and to forgive his old enemies, he could not bring himself to extend this to those who had played a part in the death of his father.

We need to be aware that this scientific community was not composed only of scientists with a narrow specialist focus as we might think of them today, many of the scientific elite, particularly Newton and Boyle, were also deeply interested in subjects that most modern scientists would scorn such as alchemy and astrology — subjects strongly associated with Hermeticism and the Rosicrucians. Allegedly, both Wren and Boyle had been Grand Masters of the Order of Rosicrucians.[6] The Church disapproved of subjects such as alchemy, so Newton and Boyle carried out their research and experiments in secret and Newton went so far as to encode all his research notes. During this period in history, the Church was loosening its stranglehold on society, but this did not mean that the members of the Royal Society were free to promote whatever ideas that they wished to. They avoided the wrath of the Church by making no attempt to destroy the notion that God could have caused Biblical miracles of nature, but did go as far as suggesting that these were special one-time-only events and promoted the opinion that the world and the universe now worked within a system of natural science; a view which appeared to placate the Church. Indeed members of the Royal Society had no objection to acknowledging that there was a Creator, but that after the creation, there were scientific explanations for everything that happened in the world. From the Royal Society came a deluge of scientific discoveries; the 'hole in the dam' was now unstoppable and led to a flood, which would change the world rapidly propelling it towards the modern day. Robert Lomas's book *The Invisible College* gives a compelling insight into the beginnings of the Royal Society.

Charles nurtured a dream to see London transformed into a splendid metropolis, a 'sun city' to rival the one that his cousin Louis XIV was proposing for Paris. Possibly inspired by Campanella's prediction in 1638 that Paris would become the new 'Egyptian City of the Sun', Louis had begun a huge building project which was to employ grandiose baroque and classical architecture and wide straight avenues: the esoteric nature of the ground plan and alignments was the most important aspect. Unlike the French king, Charles' ambitions were frustrated by the lack of public funds, kept in close check by a wary Parliament. By a strange chance, on

---

6   Gardner, L. *Bloodline of the Holy Grail*

September 2nd 1666, the Great Fire of London started, eventually to destroy around four fifths of the central area of London known as the 'City'. The old timber-framed buildings ignited easily and burnt rapidly in the raging inferno. The gothic cathedral of St Paul's was damaged irreparably. The king's standing amongst the populace rose as he manfully worked alongside the fire-fighters, as the fire spread finally consuming an area one and a half miles long and half a mile wide.

By coincidence the fire was sparked off in a bakery in Pudding Lane, allegedly by the carelessness of Thomas Farrinor who was the king's baker — Farrinor had neglected to douse the oven before retiring to his bed. Whether Charles had any involvement in the fire or not, he was suddenly presented with the opportunity to create his new city — and like the Ben-ben bird of Egypt, or as it is better known, the Phoenix, the 'sun city' could arise from out of the ashes.

Within a few days of the fire being extinguished, two new plans for the reconstruction for a new city were laid before the king. One came from Christopher Wren and the other from John Evelyn. Supposedly they had been drawn-up independently, but in fact they had many similarities and both contained esoteric designs within their ground plans for geometric streets and plazas which were aligned on the east-west axis of the rising and setting sun. The apparent readiness of these plans, which came from men who had been members of the Invisible College and were now members of the Royal Society, suggests that they had been drawn-up well before the fire.

Though the plans impressed the king, they could not be implemented, the fire had devastated too much of the city and now a volatile mass of people demanded new housing. Rapid construction of new houses for the many thousands of homeless Londoners became the immediate requirement — it was a priority if only to ensure the king's survival on the throne and expedient because Parliament held the purse strings and finances were limited. Rapid building on the old street plan, with certain safety modifications, was how it came to be. The great plans for London, with their Hermetic symbols like the octagon and the Sephirothic Tree — the 'Tree of Life' — in the street layouts were not implemented, the new 'City of the Sun' that was to rise like a Phoenix over the ancient site of Lugdunum, the 'Lightbringer's citadel' would never materialise. However the esoteric designs did not die, instead they reappeared just over a century later in the ground-plan for the new capital of a new 'utopian' country on the other side of the Atlantic Ocean.

Though it must have been considered painfully modest to Wren and Evelyn they did achieve something esoteric. Wren was at least given the opportunity to design the new cathedral. What he produced was a building of such radical design that nothing like it had ever before been seen in Britain — a structure whose 120 feet wide octagonal centre was capped by a magnificent dome on eight pillars. Both Wren and Evelyn had also proposed an east–west axis from the cathedral to a gigantic octagonal piazza, where the Knights Templar once housed their London headquarters. Today this area is still called the Temple and holds the 'Inns of Court', with the Inner and Middle Temples occupied primarily by members of the legal profession. The suppression of the Templars in 1307 saw the king, Edward II taking this area and its properties as a Crown possession. Five years later the buildings were given to the Knights Hospitallers until Henry VIII disbanded them and confiscated their property at the time of the Reformation. In 1609, James I finally handed over an Inn of Court by royal charter to the lawyer tenants.

Clearly to Wren and Evelyn this Templar site was of such great importance that it figured prominently in their plans. The Great Fire burnt itself out in front of the Temple Church, which though gothic in style had an unusual circular design. The Temple Church, perhaps not surprisingly, is dedicated to the Virgin Isis and the Templars considered it important enough to have transported the Patriarch of Jerusalem to consecrate it in 1185. To Wren and Evelyn too, the Templar Church represented Isis, whilst the rebuilt cathedral dedicated to Paul, the leader of Gnosticism the true Christianity, was the resurrected 'Sun Temple' for the new utopian city of the Sun.

The site of St Paul's was thought to be the *axis mundi* the sacred hub of the world, it was not at St Peter's Bascilica in Rome as the Catholics wished to believe nor the Temple of Jerusalem as the Jews would have it. From London would spring the new world order, offering the true religion and the scientific members of its Royal Society would become the fountain of knowledge to enlighten the world. Sadly, the cathedral was all that was ever to come of their plans, when the dream was thwarted once more. Nevertheless, the hopes and dreams expressed in these radical designs would be realised across the Atlantic in America.

Unwittingly, Charles II sowed a seed that flowered in the next century to his country's detriment. His father had owed a debt to Admiral Penn and this longstanding debt was eventually honoured by Charles II. Unwilling to part with money, of which there was too little to be had, in 1681 Charles II gave William Penn, the Admiral's son, a huge parcel of land in the American wilderness and encouraged Penn to build a community there. Charles II's motives were not entirely altruistic since Penn was the head of the Quaker Church and this church of radicals was deemed an unwanted nuisance in England. As a condition of the gift, Charles insisted that Penn established a province where Quakers and other non-conformists could relocate to enjoy freedom of worship and self-government. Penn happily accepted this heaven-sent gift with which he might attempt to create a utopian society. Charles named the state Pennsylvania after Admiral Penn and the woods and forests of the area. Pennsylvania's new city, named Philadelphia from the Greek for brotherly love, became the capital of America prior to the building of Washington DC. In the years leading up to the American Revolution, Philadelphia was a hotbed for rebellious agitators.

When Charles II died in 1685 without an heir, his brother, then King James VII of Scotland was invited to take the throne by the English Parliament and subsequently crowned James II of England. Unlike his elder brother, James was a devout Catholic, but as Charles had no legitimate children, Parliament had little choice but to accept him since the only alternative would be to revert to the highly unpopular republic once more. James claimed that Charles made a deathbed conversion to Catholicism — this could well have taken place, but only if James had badgered the dying king, who was suffering from dementia and hallucinations. These awful afflictions were the result of spending a lot of time towards the end of his life in the laboratory that Moray had made within the palace, where the king had been exposed to mercury vapours. The resulting dementia made the king vulnerable to James' fervent suggestions. Charles had never displayed any religious inclinations, but had played the field to his own advantage; he took the Covenant of the Presbyterians to gain the throne of Scotland whilst also accepting initiation into Freemasonry; he accepted the Anglican Church to gain the English throne and promised the king of France he would convert to Catholicism for as long as the king would give him gold. Clearly, if Charles had a religious belief, it was not one that bound him exclusively to any one sect.

Parliament's hopes that they could keep the new king's Catholicism in check were soon dashed, James II was deeply unpopular and a group of leading clerics and landowners gave a formal invitation to his Protestant nephew and son-in-law William of Orange to claim the throne. William invaded with an Anglo-Dutch army in 1688 and he and James II's daughter Mary became joint rulers. Abandoned by his ministers and the army, James was forced to escape into exile in France where Louis XIV welcomed him warmly. James made one major effort to regain his throne and raised a Catholic army in Ireland. His defeat at the Battle of the Boyne by 'King Billy' ended his ambitions but started the great sectarian feud amongst the Northern Irish that festers to this day.

As a Roman Catholic James was not a Freemason, but many of his close followers who went into exile with him were. James II's followers became known as 'The Jacobites' and Louis XIV settled them near Paris, in St

Germain–en–Laye where Louis had been born. It was at St Germain–en–Laye that the first French Masonic lodges appeared, after which further French lodges rapidly emerged. On the death of James II in 1701, Louis XIV proclaimed James' son Prince James Stuart as the new Pretender and the rightful king of England.

In 1702, William III died and Anne, the daughter of James II, was offered the throne. She was to become the last monarch of the Stuart line. Unlike her father, Anne was a staunch Protestant and had been a supporter of William III on his arrival in England, so Parliament considered her a safe choice to guard against the Catholic threat. During her reign the wars against France broke the French political predominance in Europe whilst enhancing the power of England and that of her army. On her deathbed in 1714, the queen was dissuaded from proclaiming her exiled Catholic brother as her successor and instead told to declare her German third cousin George — the son of Sophia the daughter of James I — who was the Elector of Hanover and a Protestant as king. Louis XIV died in 1715, leaving the would–be James III without his protector and sponsor. By the time James landed in Scotland to oppose George, his supporters' forces had been defeated at the battles of Sheriffmuir and Preston. His hope to be crowned King of Scotland was dashed when the elders of the Scottish Kirk refused to accept a Catholic as their king. With Hanoverian forces closing in, James retreated back to France.

The situation for George I, however, was far from secure. As a dour German who spoke no English, he did not endear himself to the populace, many of whom preferred the more charismatic Stuarts. With little interest in politics and a language problem, he did not attend Parliamentary meetings of Cabinet ministers and left the affairs of state to the Parliament who had given him the crown. This decision heralded the end of the monarch's attendance at Cabinet meetings. The Head of the Treasury, Sir Robert Walpole assumed the king's role as the Head of the Cabinet. His prominent position led people to call him the 'Prime Minister'.

Though not universally popular, George had the backing of the Protestants, but there were many who were Non–Catholics who wanted the restoration of the Stuarts. Scottish Freemasonry largely supported the Stuarts' cause — not unnaturally since the Stuart kings, apart from James II, had been Masons — and had raised money to buy arms for the Jacobites. This now meant that any Freemason with Jacobite sympathies was suspected as a traitor. In response to this, the worried London Masons acted to distance themselves from what were now their dangerous Scottish roots. On St John the Baptist's Day 1717 four London Lodges met and joined together to form a Grand Lodge of England.

The Masons, like the Knights Templar before them, give particular meaning to St John the Baptist and the date attributed to him. The Knights Templar attached great importance to what John the Baptist represented and the Freemasons still choose St John the Baptist's Day to hold significant events, linking it overtly to the Summer Solstice.[7] We see the solar representation of John in his Biblical utterance when stepping aside for Christ "He must increase, but I must decrease." The summer solstice starts the *decreasing* of the sun hence St John's Day is June 24th. Amongst Freemasons, the celebrations for St John's Day begin on the eve of the day itself, on June 23rd. This seemingly unimportant fact might appear odd or even an irrelevance but it is not, for it produces a date with which the world is familiar. In the early 18th century Britain still used the old Julian Calendar whilst elsewhere in Europe they employed the Gregorian Calendar introduced in 1582. Protestant Britain and its foreign colonies were reluctant to adopt the new calendar because they saw it as a Catholic device. The Julian Calendar, however, did not align itself accurately to the solar year and in practical terms the date of St John the Baptist's Day gradually slipped further away from the summer solstice. By the time that Britain and consequently America adopted the Gregorian calendar in 1752, the last Julian date of Wednesday September 2nd was followed by Thursday September 14th as the Julian calendar had lost eleven days. This meant that the important St John's Eve celebration of June 23rd 1752 in the Julian calendar became July 4th in 1753, according to the new Gregorian one. So when the American colonies, aided by the French, broke away from Britain, their official day for celebrating their independence was the 4th of July — the celebration of the Eve of St John the Baptist's Day.

In England too the date is important, English Masons consider that St John the Baptist's Day 1717 was the date when Freemasonry began. Nothing, for them, existed before this date; all connections to Scottish Freemasonry were severed and forgotten. This was probably the time when English Freemasonry abandoned its radical elements and philosophy — its leading lights had already succeeded with their aim to establish the Royal Society and were now distancing their new organization from Freemasonry, which was no longer seen as a vehicle that would create the utopian state in England. In its new *persona*, Freemasonry was transforming into the fraternal social club that is known today. Many of the extremely influential and powerful male Hanoverians saw the political advantage of accepting offers to become initiates as a means to ensure the loyalty of the Freemasons. It did not take long for senior members of the Hanoverian royal family to rise

---

7 Ward, H L Jr. *The Working Tools*

to the head of English Freemasonry, permanently ensuring that Freemasons would never again consider the restoration of a Stuart to the throne.

Despite their efforts, the Hanoverian dynasty came close to being short-lived with the 1745 Rebellion. In the reign of George II, a Jacobite army led by Charles Edward Stuart landed in Scotland from France and marched south to reclaim the throne. Bonnie Prince Charlie, as he was popularly known, reached the city of Derby before retreating back to Scotland. In the north of Scotland the Jacobites suffered a terrible defeat at Culloden, at the hands of the Hanoverian forces. It had not been an English–Scottish conflict, for there were a great number of Scots, from the Presbyterian majority who had no desire to see a Catholic on the throne who were on the Hanoverian side. Many of those Jacobites who were not killed went into exile, either voluntarily or by force. Charles Stuart escaped and ended up in exile in Florence living a dissolute life. His fame became widespread and has endured largely through sentimental romantic tales and distortions about the character of the man himself, but Bonnie Prince Charlie had no real effect upon history. Though he had an opportunity to, when America sought independence from England.

Just prior to the 1745 rebellion, another member of the English Freemasons appeared amongst the young French lodges. Unlike Charles Stuart this man is unknown to all but a few, but he was to play a significant role in changing the world — his name was Andrew Ramsay. Born a Scotsman, Ramsay was a member of the Royal Society and had been initiated into the Horn Lodge of London in 1730 by the Duke of Richmond. A little later, Ramsay moved to France and became tutor to the Jacobean exiles. Naturally, he was inducted into the fledgling French Freemasonry, where he quickly rose to a high position. As the Orator for the Grand Lodge of France, Ramsay delivered a pivotal speech in 1737.[8] Prior to this, initiations into Freemasonry gave candidates little idea of the aims and objectives of the organisation they were joining. This astonishing speech robustly defended the Knights Templar against the false charges which had been brought against them by the French king and the Pope, gave an allegorical account of the origins of Freemasonry, exhorted the members to take a pride in their Craft and proposed the ideals that would create a Heaven on earth were all men to follow them. On March 22, 1312, Clement V had published *Vox in excelsis* ordering the suppression of the Templars. Ramsey's oration was first delivered on the spring equinox, 425 years to the day after the papal bull had been issued. He visited numerous Lodges, delivering this famous oration to those members gathered for initiations. The oration clearly exposed the Egyptian/Greek/Gnostic ideals

---

8   Hancock, G and Bauval, R. *Talisman*

to which the Freemasons aspired and which sowed the seeds of the revolutionary movement, which was to shortly transform France and create the new republic of America.

During the 18th century, Europe was rife with various secret societies including Hermetics, Rosicrucians, Cabalists and a wide range of Masonic orders, and whilst these continued to provoke the severe disapproval of the Catholic Church, they also attracted the more liberal and esoterically minded members of the clergy. One such person was Antoine–Joseph Pernety, a Benedictine monk with an interest in alchemy, who left Holy Orders at the age of fifty to pursue unencumbered his devotion to the Hermetica. He founded the *Rite Hermetique* for an esoteric sect known as the *Illuminati d'Avignon*. Driven out by the Jesuits, Pernety was given sanctuary in Berlin by Frederick II of Prussia, who took a very different attitude to the activities of the ex–monk: Pernety was made curator of the Berlin Library and a member of the Prussian Academy of Science and Liberal Arts. The king was so amenable because he was a member of a Rosicrucian order named the 'Order of the Golden Rose Cross', which claimed it had been founded in Alexandria by an Egyptian sage called either 'Ormissus' or 'Ormus' — Frederick's initiation name had been 'Orimesus Magnus' — 'Ormus' was allegedly the second name of the Priory of Sion. Pernety undertook séances for Prussian aristocracy in which he communicated with 'angels' and 'spirits' — and as will see in the final chapter, which examines contemporary work by the Vatican in this field, Pernety's achievements may well have been real.[9]

With the exception of England, the Egyptian and Knights Templar roots underpinned the teachings of the majority of Masonic lodges. One of these, the 'African Architects', was founded by a Prussian military officer Frederick von Koppen in 1767 and sponsored by Frederick II, who built a splendid library for the order. Koppen wrote *Crata Repoa*, a Masonic tract, which supposedly contained authentic initiation rituals performed by Egyptian priests at Giza. Von Koppen's source is unknown and I suspect was probably largely invented, but it indicates how strongly the Egyptian link was seen as a necessary requirement for entry into the Craft. Carl Gothelff, also known as Baron von Hund founded another lodge with strong Egyptian roots. Gothelff had been initiated into one of the Templar orders of Freemasonry in Paris in 1743 and from this he founded *Die Strikte Observanz*, known in English as the rite of 'Strict Observance'. This order blended Egyptian, Hermetic, Rosicrucian, Masonic and neo–Templar ideology and flourished particularly in the Germanic states. The Masonic rites from *Zur Wohltätigkeit* lodge, into which Amadeus Mozart had been

---

9   ibid

initiated, laid the foundation for the composer's Egyptian–Masonic opera *The Magic Flute*.[10]

The *Illuminati von Bayern*, (Illuminati of Bavaria) was an off-shoot from *Die Strikte Observanz*. Originally called the Order of Perfectibilists they were founded in 1776 by Adam Weishaupt, a former Jesuit priest who became a Professor of Law at Ingolstadt. This famed order was known for its fiercely anti-clerical stance, which seems to continue the Rosicrucian crusade to overthrow the Church of Rome. Though today the name *Illuminati*, like *Freemasons*, conjures up horrors for conspiracy-theorists, the order aimed

> "... to attain the highest possible degree of morality and virtue and to lay the foundation for the reformation of the world by the association of good men to oppose the progress of moral evil"[11]

This certainly does not fit the modern-day profile of those to whom the conspiracy-theorists attribute the name *Illuminati*. These German orders had a strong effect on Freemasonry in the new American nation, particularly amongst those who attained the higher degrees. The American lodges exhibited more Egyptian influence than the Scottish and English lodges. Hancock & Bauval discuss this in some detail in *Talisman Sacred Cities, Secret Faith*.

This book will not attempt to consider the causes of the American Revolution in depth, but many immigrants had gone there to begin a new better and wealthier life, away from Europe, with its suffocating religious and political restrictions. Many followers of the Rosicrucian philosophy had settled there hoping to transform this new land into their utopia. Most of the new immigrants were Englishmen, the more influential of them spent their time in both their old and new homes and were in touch with the radical thinkers in England. Besides the English ex-patriots, there was also a large number of exiled Scottish Jacobites and the latter group had no love for the Hanoverian king. The final split came following the heavy-handedness of British Parliamentarian policy to their American colonies particularly concerning taxation. The Hanoverian king George III was removed from the reality of the situation and obstinately refused to intervene between his colonies and his Parliament. The subsequent loss of the colonies became inevitable due to the difficult trans-Atlantic logistics and a shortage of military manpower. The crucially decisive intervention of the French forces when the Americans were hard pressed, resulted from pressure exerted on the French king by the Marquis de Lafayette, who was a Freemason who

---

10   Ridley, J. *The Freemasons*
11   Mackey, A G. *The History of Freemasonry*

supported the American Freemasons' dream of creating a new utopian state.

The core of the American Revolutionary leaders were Freemasons connected to either the English or Scottish lodges; after the revolution of 1776, the lodges in America sought to break free from the control of London's Grand Lodge. A strong link had already been forged between American masons and lodges in France. One of the foremost leaders was the scientist Benjamin Franklin, who, like Thomas Jefferson America's 3rd president and Wren and Boyle was a Rosicrucian grand master. During a stay in France, Franklin became the Grand Master of the Parisian Nine Sisters Lodge and this bond generated support from the French lodges. Inspired by Franklin, the members of the Parisian lodges, such as the Marquis de Lafayette and John Paul Jones were drawn into the revolutionary cause to create the ideal state.

There is absolutely no doubt that the American Revolution was not just a protest against taxation, but an attempt by a small core of inspired men who were Freemasons to create the utopian land proposed by Campanella some 175 years earlier. Though the outcome of the revolution was a republic and the republic is normally linked to the utopian state, it must not be forgotten that amongst the Hermetics and Rosicrucians, as it had once been with the ancient Egyptians, to achieve the state of Ma'at, it was seen necessary to have a king — the pinnacle of the pyramid — as the symbolic head of state to link with the Creator.

Despite the popular idea that the American revolutionaries happily dispensed with a king, this in reality was not so. Twice they made a serious effort to obtain a monarch. During the War of Independence, a deputation from Boston went to Holland to meet with the exiled Prince Charles Edward Stuart, the Jacobite Pretender to the throne of England, to invite him to become the King of Virginia. The offer was declined. After the war, George Washington was offered the position of King of America, but felt unable to accept because he had no hereditary qualifications, making it difficult for him to gain acceptance for the title in Europe. At the end of 1782 George Washington sent four representatives to the San Clemente Palace in Florence for another audience with Prince Charles. The interview took place in the presence of Comtesse de Massillan, who became the Prince's second wife in 1765, the Honourable Charles Hervey–Townshend, British Ambassador to the Netherlands and John Stewart, the prince's secretary.[12] Once more, Charles was invited to become King of the Americans. For various reasons, but mainly because he did not have an heir to continue any new dynasty, Charles refused the offer. Another factor that

---

12   Petrie, C. *The Jacobite Movement*

may have concerned him was the possibility that without an heir, his death would allow the Hanoverians to make a legitimate claim on the vacant throne. I believe that the defeat of 1745 and the ill-feeling towards him by some of his own supporters, together with the fact that his claim to the English throne had not engendered the wide support he had expected, had taken away his enthusiasm and any stomach for any possible further conflict. In the wake of his failed rebellion, the Stuart propensity for dissolute living had also taken its toll upon him and left him wanting to spend the rest of his life in peace.

It was the hands of the Freemasons that literally laid the foundation stones of the American Republic — President George Washington wearing a Mason's apron gifted to him by the Marquis de Lafayette, laid the ceremonial cornerstone for the Capitol building. But this was not the only Masonic connection. The list of Egyptian/Masonic symbolism is significant and fundamental. The city of Washington was to be the new world's 'Sun City' and its geometric ground plan, which includes Templar octagons and the Sephirothic Tree of Life was drawn up by the French Freemason Pierre L'Enfant. The Washington monument is an obelisk and obelisks are linked to the Egyptian star Sirius. The axis of Washington's Pennsylvania Avenue aligns with the heliacal rising of Sirius. The eastern entrance in the Washington Memorial is designed like the entrance to an Egyptian temple and displays the solar disk, which contains the Sirius star and is guarded by a serpent. Benjamin Franklin and Thomas Jefferson designed the Great Seal, which displays a pyramid with the all-seeing eye of God. On modern-day dollar notes, there is an image of a truncated pyramid, symbolising that the 'work' is not yet complete.

The Statue of Liberty standing in the New York harbour, was designed by an Italian Freemason, built by a French Freemason and funded by Franco-American Freemasons. It is thought of as a representation of 'Liberty' and 'Reason' which are always linked to Isis and statues representing these virtues are generally modelled on Isis or her Greek/Roman counterparts. Bartholdi, the designer, called the statue Pharos, because he saw it as a new light giver, like the original Alexandrian lighthouse which was also linked with Isis and Sirius. George Washington Masonic Memorial lodge building in Alexandria, Virginia, the president's 'home' lodge, was constructed to look very like the Pharos lighthouse of Alexandria in Egypt. Just as in London and Paris, the Freemasons acquired an obelisk from Egypt and this was seen as a physical as well as spiritual link between the Freemasons and ancient Egypt. The one placed in New York, was the twin of the one in London, the pair constructed by Thutmose III stood outside the temple of Ra at Heliopolis.

Of course it is reasonable to choose a building style because of fashion or personal preference, so if the deliberate building of these structures is not sufficient to prove Freemasonry's deep link with ancient Egyptian religion, then one needs to find other clues. We discover that at George Washington's funeral, the Masonic mourners cast sprigs of acacia onto the coffin. The acacia traditionally symbolised Osiris's resurrection and when the Washington Memorial was dedicated, a prominent Mason finished his speech with these words

> "These minds enlightened with divine love, their hearts radiant with discovering pure love, their souls cherishing… like the ancient Egyptian worshippers of Osiris… the hope of immortality."

Not exactly the fundamentalist Christian sentiments that modern–day American politicians spout — but in those early years, the Freemason politicians were men who adhered scrupulously to a high moral code and believed passionately in their duty to deliver to the people a country of freedom, equality and compassion, and they appear to be men who understood the moral and spiritual philosophy of the ancient Egyptians.

A greed for power and financial gain, whilst controlling the people by a plethora of restrictive laws was not part of the original game–plan. Some historians of Freemasonry believe that 'Egyptian' Freemasonry was brought into France and then passed onto their American brothers by an Italian known as Count di Cagliostro, who arrived in Paris in 1785 and whose promotion of Egyptian Freemasonry rapidly won over many enthusiastic followers. This may have had some influence on the few American masons who visited France after they had won independence, but we have seen that there were much earlier and stronger Egyptian influences, which had inspired the Hermetics and Rosicrucians and can be traced back at least to the time of Cosimo de' Medici and the Renaissance.

The early hold of powerful Freemasons over the design and running of the new republic inspired the rapid spread of the brotherhood right across the new nation. Every city and large town became home to large impressive lodges, many had interiors that deliberately copied Egyptian temple designs. American Freemasonry blatantly gave the higher initiation degrees Templar titles, which their brother lodges in Britain had shied away from.

Unfortunately the ambitions of the American Freemasons were hit by an unexpected catastrophe in the early 19th century, when some masons were charged with the murder of a man they believed had betrayed lodge secrets. Their lodge was implicated in attempting a cover–up by exerting its political influence. The ensuing scandal, a bad press that inflated the incident into a national conspiracy and the unexpectedly ferocious public reaction, caused a sudden and dramatic fall from grace for all Freemasons throughout the country. In spite of later suggestions that the man had not been murdered at all, but had disappeared and created a conspiracy to ensure his book exposing Masonic secrets would a best-seller, many Masons resigned to preserve their reputations and numerous lodges closed down and were never reinstated.

Suddenly, this act of folly by members of one lodge, who probably knew too little about Freemasonry's higher ideals and standards of morality, unwittingly damaged the organisation that they were attempting to preserve. The hand of Freemasonry, guiding the way to a moral and compassionate life, was dashed aside and Christianity, in its unpleasant fundamentalist controlling guise, took its place. The idealism of the early republic is no longer discernible within the United States of America, through evangelical Christianity the modern country can only pay lip-service to the dreams of those early Freemasons, the *founding fathers* who created the Republic, but it has no comprehension of what their ambitions really were or why they held those dreams.

In France matters took a different course. A general assembly of all Masonic lodges within France in 1738 attempted to resolve the conflict of jurisdiction between the older Jacobite lodges who adhered to the Scottish Rite and the newer French lodges that followed the Grand Lodge of England. They elected a cousin of Louis XV, the Duke of Antin as the first French Grand Master. In 1772, a new Grand Master was elected — he was the Duke of Chartres, cousin to Louis XVI and the Grande Loge de France was altered to the Grand Orient de France. Under this new guise, French Freemasonry began to flourish, finding popularity amongst every strata of society including the clergy. The election of the new Grand Master was to affect the future of the nation and to a degree, the rest of Europe; the Duke of Chartres later became the Duke of Orleans and the major instigator of the French Revolution.

The Italian Giuseppe Balsamo, whom we have already heard of as the Count di Cagliostro for his alleged rôle in introducing Egyptian symbolism to America, was instrumental, albeit unwittingly, in what was about to unfold. When he left Italy, Cagliostro was skilled in medicine and alchemy and on his travels around Europe gained a reputation as a healer of some note as well as for his philanthropy. In 1776, he arrived in London via Malta and Spain carrying a batch of Masonic letters of recommendation from a Knight of Malta. In less than twelve months he attained the rank of Master Mason at London's Royal Tavern Lodge. Towards the end of 1777, Cagliostro was journeying to Bavaria and Saxony and when in Leipzig he met Pernety. It was probably whilst he was amongst the Egypto-Hermetic lodges that he adopted ideas found in Koppen's *Crata Repoa*. Whatever the source, Cagliostro moved on again promoting not only a very Egyptian–influenced form of Freemasonry, but his Egyptian Rite lodges for women, the first being in the Hague. Cagliostro eventually ended up in France where his exploits attracted many followers including Cardinal de Rohan whose sponsorship greatly aided his acceptance into the higher social circles. From every level of society he acquired followers, including many Masons who joined his Egyptian Rite; even the Duke of Orleans, the Grand Master of the French Freemasons had visited this new Egyptian lodge.

However, events that would change history suddenly swept Cagliostro into a scandal involving his mentor Cardinal de Rohan and Queen Marie–Antoinette. Louis XVI ordered the arrest of the Cardinal and Cagliostro was dragged in as a scapegoat. Such was the ill–feeling of the people and their outrage against the corrupt state and a pompous and weak king, that the pair were released to prevent violent protests. Cagliostro's popularity was so strong that around 8,000 people, of whom many were Masons, waited for their hero's release and cheered wildly as he exited the Bastille.

Many historians consider this to be the prelude to, or even the catalyst for the Revolution. Cagliostro then moved to the safety of England from where he published a letter to the French people in which he urged them to conduct a peaceful revolution, to destroy the Bastille and to replace it with a Temple of Isis. Cagliostro's Egyptian rite met with no success in England, so he left on his travels once more, but unfortunately made the same mistake as Giordano Bruno, he returned to Italy to be arrested as a heretic and potential revolutionary who might overthrow the Church. He was sentenced to burning at the stake, but fearing a public reaction, the death sentence was retracted and Cagliostro was incarcerated in a dungeon. He is thought to have died at the Fortress of Saint Leo in the region of Le Marche on the Adriatic coast.

The Grand Master of the French Freemasons, Philippe the Duke of Orleans, was a descendent of Frederick of the Palatinate and Elizabeth Stuart, the brief monarchs of Bohemia, whom the Rosicrucians had hoped to use in the creation of the new utopian anti–Catholic state. The Duke of Orleans was descended from other female members of the English house of Stuart too, as well as from Louis XIII and XIV. Philippe's strong English connections made him a staunch Anglophile and this obsession persuaded him to the idea of a parliament and constitutional monarchy. His opposition to his despotic uncle caused Louis XV to exile him to England in 1771. During that time, he became a close friend of the Prince of Wales the future George IV. He returned to France during the reign of Louis XVI and his hatred for his cousin was even stronger than it had been for his father. It is believed that he used his vast fortune to sponsor the revolutionary movement — amongst his followers there were many aristocrats who wished to see Louis gone — but their plan was to avoid violence and their goal was to declare Philippe the new king and constitutional monarch. Philippe is suspected of being the driving force behind the storming of the Bastille, which effectively started the French Revolution.

Unfortunately, things soon went badly wrong and the revolutionary fervour went unchecked. Unlike the American Revolution, there was no external enemy upon which to direct the energy and anger of the populace. Inevitably it turned in upon itself and the need to find someone to attack resulted in a manic witch-hunt and a bloodbath within its own people. At one point Philippe considered leaving for America, but decided to remain. Titles were outlawed so he took the ideological name of Philippe Egalité. Despite having been the *father* of the revolution, when in 1793, an arrest warrant was issued for Philippe's son Louis-Philippe and General Dumouriez because of their belief in constitutional monarchy, the two of them escaped to the Austrian army but Philippe himself was later arrested and executed. Louis-Philippe's exile lasted twenty-one years and in 1815 he returned. In 1830, he was elected as the Citizen King of France. The hopes of the Rosicrucians and Freemasons for a peaceful revolution and the installation of a new 'Sun king' were dashed completely.

The activities of Duke Philippe de Orleans show that the Rosicrucians and Freemasons were involved at the top level to create a state imbued with morality, equality and freedom. Those who had instigated the French Revolution also had another important motive and that was to bring an end to the corrupt and false Christian religion. Their plan was not the creation of an atheist state, but to replace the Christian Jehovah with the 'Supreme Being' to whom they would rededicate all cathedrals and churches. Robespierre introduced the Cult of the Supreme Being as the state religion.

Wresting control from the Church of Rome started in 1789 when the state confiscated Church property. The following year, the state put all the clergy on its payroll. By 1792, the state began to register all births, marriages and deaths and took charge of parish records. All the clergy, monks and nuns had been forced to renounce their Faith, which many, disenchanted with the corruption of the Church, happily did without any coercion. The revolutionary leaders promoted Isis and Egyptian symbols, which clearly indicates that they were Rosicrucians and Freemasons who followed the Egyptian Rite.

Throughout Paris Egyptian symbolism appeared quite suddenly. The front cover of the *Declaration of the Rights of Man and Citizen* — the forerunner of the Universal Declaration of Human Rights — showed the rays of a blazing sun emanating from a pyramid, within which was inscribed the all-seeing eye of the Supreme Being, an obvious reinterpretation of the Eye of Ra. As Cagliostro had proposed, there was a plan to build a pyramid on the site of the Bastille, using the dismantled remains of the fortress. The idea was only shelved because of a severe restriction on the country's hard-pressed funds. Another project went ahead in its place, though even that had to be modified to reduce the cost. Designed by the great artist and close friend of Robespierre, Jacques–Louis David, a large statue called the Fountain of Regeneration had water spurting from the nipples of a goddess into a large bath by her feet. Emblazoned on the bath was a winged solar disc, the emblem of the Egyptian pharaohs. The goddess was Isis and the statue was known by its popular name Isis of the Bastille. The statue was hurriedly constructed out of plaster and the permanent stone statue never got built, the temporary structure soon fell victim to the weather.

In the same year of 1793, a small pyramid dedicated to the Supreme Being, was constructed outside Paris's *Hotel de Ville*; two more pyramids were also built in the city. Joseph Lalande, an astronomer and prominent Freemason with the Nine Sisters lodge, introduced a new calendar for the republic, which was based on the Egyptian solar year.

According to Thomas Carlyle, in November and December 1793, following the death of Marie–Antoinette, the cult of the Goddess of Reason first appeared. Carlyle records priests abdicating in great numbers from Holy Order and marrying their nun–brides newly released from celibacy. He writes of a strange 'municipal procession' that takes place. The prominent political leader Pierre Gaspard Chaumette, later guillotined by Robespierre, started a fashion to process the Goddess Of Reason into churches in a torch–lit procession of dancing girls. Chaumette stormed *Notre Dame de Paris* with a Demoiselle Candeille of the Opera carried on a platform wearing a cloak in azure the colour of Isis, a red Phrygian cap and holding a torch.[13] That same image was gifted to the Americans by the French and is now known as the Statue of Liberty. The people marched from the Cathedral to the National Convention, the new French legislative assembly, and there it was decreed that henceforth the Cathedral of *Notre Dame* would be known as the Temple for the Goddess Reason.

The following year Charles Dupuis, another member of the Nine Sisters lodge, wrote a thesis stating that *Notre Dame*, which stands upon the island representing the barque of Isis, had originally been a temple dedicated to Isis before the Christians built over it. He also mentions 'Isis mother of the God of Light' — this term, 'God of Light' was not a Biblical term, but was one often used by Gnostics, then the Manicheans, later still the Cathars and employed again by Rosicrucians and Freemasonry.

On June 8th 1794, on what had formerly been the day of Pentecost, Robespierre, as the elected President of the National Convention, led a

---

13   Carlyle, T. *The French Revolution A History*

grand ceremony in front of the Louvre to celebrate the new religion of France, the Cult of the Supreme Being. After his oration, Robespierre set fire to a veiled effigy called 'Atheism'. As the veil burnt it revealed beneath it a stone statue of the goddess Sophia created by David. Sophia, also known as Wisdom was a representation of Isis. When Isis was unveiled, the statue, borne on a massive chariot pulled by eight oxen with gold painted horns was paraded through the centre of Paris.

Inevitably the whirlwind that had swept the revolution onwards, soon enough lost its momentum. The in-fighting increased, one faction against another in virulent dispute over ideology and Robespierre himself became a victim. As the new revolutionary assembly began to fall apart, anarchy increased — the ensuing power vacuum and the need to bring back law and order, laid the door open for a military take-over. Though the young general Napoleon had been a revolutionary he was also a historian and realised, that states can never become great without a strong military leader.

Napoleon saw the flaws in a republic run by a committee and had personal experience of the chaos that results from the lack of a strong leader after Robespierre's demise. Napoleon had been arrested for treason because of his earlier friendship with Robespierre; he was released due to the lack of evidence, whereas Robespierre lost his life. As his military career continued to rise so did his political career, his fame and the backing of the army gave France stability. No doubt his inspiration was Alexander the Great and it soon became clear that he would emulate Alexander's building of an empire, which would incorporate the ideals of fraternity and equality amongst his subjects. Unfortunately for Napoleon, other nations were reluctant to lose their independence and the new French emperor had to battle to fulfil his dream. Though his ambitions became increasingly egotistical and imperial, this may not have been a flaw, but a necessity if his great plan were to succeed.

Had Napoleon been a Mason? Academics still argue over the answer, but there is much that strongly suggests he was, if only that many lodges were named after him. The Grand Orient of France, the most influential and largest French Masonic Lodge, claimed that Napoleon and General Kleber, who commanded French forces for Napoleon in Egypt, undertook Egyptian Masonic initiation inside the Great Pyramid by a Coptic sage. I don't believe he would have done so simply because he happened to be in Giza, to take such a step, he must have already had a strong interest in Egypt and Freemasonry. I suspect that he had already been initiated, probably into Cagliostro's Egyptian Rite lodge. Certainly his ambition of a pan-european state had elements of the Rosicrucian and Freemasonry dream. We have at least to be thankful for Napoleon's having gone there and taken scholars of all academic disciplines too, because their visit led to the discovery of the Rosetta Stone and the subsequent successful deciphering of Egyptian hieroglyphics by Jean–Francois Champollion in 1822. Less successful was his attempt to persuade the Arabs of Egypt to abandon Islam in favour of the Supreme Being.

When Napoleon returned from Egypt, following the destruction of his fleet by the British under command of Admiral Nelson, he became increasingly fascinated, if not obsessed, by Isis. He was especially interested to discover if the 'Boat of Paris' found in the city's coat of arms might actually be the 'Boat of Isis'. To discover the truth behind the legend that Isis was the guardian deity of Paris, Napoleon established a special commission to investigate it and the following year its report confirmed that there was evidence that supported the legend. As a consequence, Napoleon ordered a change to the coat of arms; the image of an enthroned Isis be put into the boat, which would be led by Sirius her star and above the boat should be three golden bees to symbolise her divine solar rule. Napoleon also commissioned images of Isis for the facade of an inner doorway on the eastern side of the Louvre and for his grand monument, still under construction at the western end of the Champs–Elysees at a place which had long been called *L'Etoile* — the 'Star'. The *Place de L'Etoile*, now famous as a ten–deep roundabout, is exactly 120 metres diameter and has twelve roads radiating at equal angles from its centre. Twelve was the sublime number[14] represented in the zodiac constellations and twelve apostles.

The *Arc de Triomphe* was more than a superficial monument to the glory of Napoleon, it was his *star* monument and that star was Sirius. Paris's Historic Axis started at the Louvre then passed through the Tuileries Gardens. Napoleon commisioned his triumphal arc in 1806 and the route ends today at the Grande Arche de La Défense, in the city's business district. The grand avenue named Champs Elysées in 1709, was created by France's 'Sun King' Louis XIV to replicate the axis that ran through the solar temple complex at Thebes. Both axes are oriented to align with the setting sun on May 8th and August 6th, whilst at the easterly end, they align with the heliacal rising of Sirius. The two dates were adopted by Christians, May 8th is associated with the ascension of Christ and August 6th is the date for Christ's transfiguration. In 1836, shortly after the *Arc de Triomphe* was completed, an obelisk, one of an original pair that had stood outside the Luxor temple and brought to Paris by Louis XVIII, a Freemason, was

---

14 A *sublime* number has a *perfect* number of factors, including itself, so twelve has six factors 1, 2, 3, 4, 6 and 12 and they add up to 28, the next *perfect* number. *Perfect* numbers have factors which add up to themselves: $1+2+3=6$; $1+2+4+7+14=28$. There are actually only two known *sublime* numbers twelve and one that is so large that it has 76 digits.

erected along the Paris Axis in the Place de la Concorde. The Place de La Concorde itself emulated Bernini's design outside St Peter's Square in Rome. It was built as an octagon centred on the obelisk.

So even after the demise of Napoleon and the restoration of the monarchy, in France there was no real change to the *sub–rosa* interest in Egypt. In modern–day Paris, great monuments are still constructed and sited with Egyptian significance. In 1989, for the bi–centennial celebration of the Revolution, a glass pyramid was built in front of the Louvre. This somewhat controversial placement followed the centennial plan of 1889, which proposed but abandoned the construction of a baroque pyramid on this same site instead Paris got a 1000 foot iron tower on the other side of the Seine.

The modern colossus that is the Grande Arche also stands on the Axis. This too was part of the 1989 bi–centennial constructions and like the Louvre Pyramid is angled by 6.33 degrees and frames the setting sun on June 24th, St John's Day. Whatever it was that John the Baptist represented, it is still considered important to the ancestors of the Templars. Tommaso Campanella's prediction, made in 1638, that Paris would become the new Egyptian City of the Sun, began to take shape under the Sun King in 1665, was developed by the post–revolution Emperor and completed in 1989 by the President of the Republic. Campanella got the city of his dreams, but did not get his king.

The influence and idealism of Freemasonry did not end with the American and French revolutions, and though the French attempts ended disastrously, the ideals continued to inspire. One final revolution of sorts remoulded competing city–states into a united Italy. As in America and France, this minor revolution was led by patriots immersed in the ideology of Freemasonry. Camillo Cavour was the intellect behind the movement and Giuseppe Mazzini was the inspiring spirit, who recruited the young Giuseppe Garibaldi to provide the dynamic military leadership that their revolution needed. In 1870 when the Prussians besieged Paris, Garibaldi headed a force of Italian volunteers, who attempted to help the fledgling French Third Republic, which for the first time had a Freemason as its president. As his reward, Garibaldi was elected as a Member of the French National Assembly and later elected to high Masonic office.

There is little doubt that the early Freemasons who were initiated into the higher degrees, had some concept of their movement's beliefs and philosophical ideals, which new members of sufficient intellect would be taught to attain enlightenment. However, over time it becomes apparent that, as happened elsewhere, Freemasonry lost the truth and retained nothing more than incomprehensible ritual and rites. Even from the early days, pseudo–Christian motives were introduced. The nonsense of

Solomon's Temple provided a smokescreen of Christian credentials, which hid the true Egyptian and Gnostic roots.

There is much more that can be written about Freemasonry, but it is not the purpose of this book to detail the history of the organisation. It suffices to indicate that Freemasonry not only made efforts to keep Gnosticism alive and to promote its ideals, but it understood the ancient roots behind the Gnostic Mysteries and that Christianity, Judaism and Islam all began in Egypt, and all suffered at the hand of self-seeking men to become crude distortions of the truth.

THE GREATEST LIE EVER TOLD

Chapter 30

Quo Vadis?

"Better is the end of a thing than the beginning thereof."

Ecclesiastes 7:8

The End is Nigh! It seems that the Bible–Thumpers' claim is at last coming true. Not the end of mankind, as they might believe, but the end of their false religion. A constant stream of surveys tells us that the indigenous population of Europe and the United States is abandoning Christianity. The American Religious Identification Survey showed that up to 1990, 87% of Americans were Christian, by 2008 the figure was 76%.[1] They hadn't all become Buddhists and Scientologists, they had become secularists and abandoned religion altogether. According to the *Western Christian Encyclopedia*, there are 34,000 separate Christian groups representing one third of the world's religious adherents. Of these, around 1,000 claim to be the *true* religion. One can only assume that if the Christians are so divided, they must be bound to fall.

Many people say they belong to a faith and name which one, but they never attend any of its services other than a baptism, wedding or funeral, nor do they take any part in Christian community activities. When questioned, they will say that they have no interest in religion and feel Christianity is no longer relevant to the modern world. In Britain, the Church of England has systematically undertaken a path of self–destruction starting at a somnolent bumbling lethargic pace, then gathering speed with an awkward enthusiasm for being 'modern' and 'politically correct' — no time to display some Christian compassion, just a rush to update the image.

In northern Europe, the Non–Conformist churches offered strict morality and dour rules for how life should be lived. In the face of the 1960s

---

[1] Kosmin, BA & Keysar, A. *"American Religious Identification Survey 2008"*

popular–cultural revolution, which threw off the heavy shackles of control, these churches have withered though some survive.

The Catholic Church suffered deep wounds in the 1960s when the Vatican II turmoil challenged its authority. The commission created by Paul VI recommended that some form of contraception be allowed to married couples, the Pope did not agree with the commission's findings but the couples did and defiantly opposed his final veto. The outcry from priests insisting that the conscience of the individual, not the Pope, should have the last say on contraception was joined by the clamour from those who wished to marry and a large Exodus of intelligent thinking clergy ensued. Fifty years later, the Catholic Church blunders on. It has ordination rites for women[2] that date from before 500 CE, but it's stubborn resistance to their ordination in the 21st century has recently been over-shadowed by the furore over its failure to prevent and punish child–abuse.

Though Christianity is growing in the under–developed world, whilst it is rapidly fading away in the developed one, it is a false dawn, a false salvation. Missionaries might convert the poor and uneducated peoples of Africa, Asia and South America, but as they become wealthier and better educated, they will adopt the values of Europe and North America, demand freedom of thought and action and awaken to the irrelevance of an old–fashioned religion with its dubious authenticity.

The Christian Church has only itself to blame for its present perilous state. It attempted to control people, both their thinking and the way they lived, and for around a thousand years it was largely successful. This enslavement was inevitably bound to weaken and at some stage finally collapse. During the lifetime of the Church, a covert resistance movement has struggled on courageously, never abandoning its mission to bring down a false and corrupt religion, whilst maintaining its spiritual, philosophical and scientific aims. Though this underground resistance has ever been present and persistent like a terrier worrying its prey, it is the Church itself that must take responsibility for its demise. The Church has always been driven by one of two things, either by avarice or by fear of exposure. Its main concern has been self–preservation and so it created a religious dictatorship that would control the unthinking masses through unchallengeable dogma. To subdue dissent it created fear of eternal damnation in the next life and administered torture and painful death in this one.

Maintaining political–religious control was all that mattered; priests and monks could indulge their personal whims in this fictitious religion as long as they adhered to the dogma and rules, but the spiritual needs of the

---

[2] Schaff, P *Ante-Nicene Fathers*, Book III

masses were completely ignored. People needed to be kept in unthinking ignorance — but the human spirit could not be denied forever, people are naturally inquisitive and always wish to enquire and to learn. Once books were in circulation the intelligentsia could no longer be denied the answers that it sought. The defensive dam began to weaken and crumble and tiny leaks grew into a flood. The Church could perhaps have ameliorated the outcome, it could have been less dictatorial, more inclusive, more concerned about the spiritual needs of its followers. It could have slowly and subtly revised its religion, realigning it to the original Christianity of the Gnostics, but a greed for power and wealth, together with a paralysing fear of the consequences held the Church stubbornly in its vicious circle of ruthless power and outrageous lies.

The major hazard that grew in the path of the influence and standing of the Christian religion was science. The Church had approved of Aristotle and denounced Plato, it wasn't the science that was the danger, it was the thinking that could do it harm. Although many scientists were also priests, by the thirteenth century the Church had realised that Aristotle's rational science invited dangerous ideas too, people had started thinking about it and discussing it. In universities, science was getting beyond ecclesiastical control and so the Roman Church deemed certain ideas heretical. As a consequence, scientists or alchemists as they were originally known, were forced to do their work in secret to circumvent the attention of the Inquisition. Science was regarded as a Pandora's Box whose contents, if allowed to escape, would inflict great harm upon the Church; its long held fear was soon justified. Once the Royal Society was formed in Britain, scientific research flourished virtually unimpeded and scientists became men of great renown and much admired.

Ironically, science today has in some ways become the new religion of the modern world and too many scientists are eager to pick up the fallen mantle of the priesthood. Absolutely certain in their beliefs, they deliver pompous sermons declaring how the world and everything in it was created. Too often however, scientists convey theory as fact. The *Theory* of Evolution is still only a *theory* and there is much scientific research, which contradicts its premises. Research that supports the theory is often flawed, mostly because the researchers make assumptions that allow the facts to fit whatever the researcher is seeking to prove. The body of data that Darwin provided is not confirmed by that scientific research, which contradicts it, particularly that found in fossil records. Narrow-minded scientists see a simple dichotomy, Evolution or a supernatural being created us in a few thousand years. Surely an *unbiased* evaluation would find something in between the two, but scientists rarely seem to look *between* the two extremes. Most scientists follow the accepted line of thinking, few do as Darwin once had to, propose something new and face the ridicule.

When scientists consider evolution, they forget some of the basic principles of valid research and the most important of these is to define what it is you are trying to prove. Certain scientists refute God, but never tell us what it is they are refuting. Prof. Richard Dawkins, atheist and fervent flag-carrier for the Evolutionists, constantly attacks religious beliefs, wielding science as his sword, but in reality there is no substance to *his* beliefs for that is what they are and no scientific evidence to back them, as *beliefs* are not scientific. Prof. Stephen Hawking announced that science has proved that there is no God, but has no scientific evidence to support his claim and demonstrates an astonishing lack of logic. Making any pronouncement about the existence of God is exceedingly stupid — as the Ancients clearly understood. God is totally unknowable — one may not be able to prove that God exists, but to prove that God does not exist is impossible. Perhaps the self-appointed Emperors of 21st century Science need some new clothes more suited to 21st century thinking. To the Mathematician or Logician, their nakedness clearly shows.

Atheists too produce arguments that are flawed. Their basic premise lumps God and religion together and blames those who believe in God for the ills of the world. One can lay some of the blame against religions, but one can believe in a God without adhering to any religion, a concept that the atheist rarely considers and that many are wholly unaware of. Atheists make blanket accusations that God-believers heap the problems of the world onto God, on the bizarre assumption that *all* believers assume their creator has made a flawed and sick world. Those God-believers who *do* assume the latter then subjugate themselves to divine control and pray that the creator of the hell they experience will feel sorry for them and put things right. Such assumptions are banal. Certain religions may teach this and some of their followers believe it, but they know as little about God as the atheists appear to. It is quite possible for the Creator of the universe and those responsible for the flaws and weaknesses of mankind to be mutually exclusive, and thus for mankind to take responsibility for its own ills. The atheist arguments might be well-meaning, but they are ill-informed and for some reason always one-sided, showing no understanding of the wider possibilities.

Too many atheist scientists have allowed their egos to run away with them as they seek to mould themselves into 'priests' whose pronouncements are beyond dispute. Echoing the vanity of the Egyptologists and archaeologists, they display the same closed-mindedness of many religious leaders. It is of no surprise then, that they display the same form of defence:

to attack virulently anyone, be they peers or laymen, who dares to challenge the belief system that is fashionable within their particular discipline.

Fortunately there is a good number of scientists who are not afraid to buck the trend and who promote what they *know* to be right. One particular field of study, quantum physics, has threatened to turn traditional physics on its head by rewriting many of its laws and even presenting evidence that the impossible is sometimes possible; like the well replicated experiments of the photon that is in two places at the same moment.[3]

Quantum physicists believe that a universe can be created in a lab and that the orderly and comprehensible nature of the universe indicates the hand of a designer. If ours were created in such a manner, should we call that ancient scientist/alchemist God? The answer has to be no, because we cannot deduce the latter from the former. A massive creation does not indicate its creator was God, but simply that there was a creator. Indeed, some ancient texts state that the creators of worlds were not 'God' but were the first entities created by God.

So what might God be? It can only be speculation, but one proposal is that God was consciousness in a void, but unable to see itself and alone, so that the consciousness decided to create things from its consciousness. One could think of this God/consciousness, as pure intelligence, an intelligent energy like a brain but without material form. The consciousness could be considered as a mighty intelligent computer, which, in order to know itself, explodes into trillions of pieces so that when one piece sees the others, the computer can see itself. From all the trillions of parts of itself, the consciousness can experience trillions more sensations before eventually, they implode and return to the original source. So if God fragmented and became everything there is, each thing is just a small part of God and eventually each thing there is will return to God.

Where then, do we go from here, is the answer to be found in science and will we see the drawn–out sunset for Christianity? I believe the answer to both questions is yes. But the end to Christianity is not necessarily the end for the Church, provided it admits the truth and attempts to change and adapt. The change will need a religious revolution and will be painful, but if the Church can survive the upheaval, it will have something worthwhile to offer the world. Its new 'religion' can still maintain the core values of morality and of how life should be lived, but would no longer offer one single path to God. The main work of the Church would be to teach and encourage people to seek out their own individual path to enlightenment and reunification with God. Priests would no longer require unquestioning obedience, but would act initially as teachers for the

---

[3] Walther, P et al. 'De Broglie wavelength of a non-local four-photon state'

newcomers, facilitators for the initiates and comforters and confessors for those burdened by trouble or bad conscience.

Many people claim to have no interest in spiritual matters, but many others who were once Christians, seek alternative ways to fulfil their spiritual needs. The former, engrossed in a limited materialist world, will eventually seek some sort of benign, non-judgemental guidance when they find no happiness or satisfaction in material acquisitions and realise they do have spiritual needs. To fulfil the desires of both, Churches would need to offer contemplation and teaching in place of religious rituals and ceremonies. It may come as a shock to some hard-line Christians that Yoga is not an occult trick that lets the Devil into your life, it is a philosophy that can have great benefits to its practitioners both mentally and physically. Entrenched views of pagan practice will have to be dug out, but in its place a peace and harmony that benefits mankind can seed and grow. All it needs is an open mind and a spiritual commitment.

Even in its present form, the Christian Church offers a much-needed social service, which would be a great loss to communities and individuals. Churches bring people together regularly and they offer support and help in times of need. Although the main focus of the help may assist the Church's own members, most offer help to all who ask and no-one who asks is denied. Many countries levy a faith-based income tax and the faiths that receive the proceeds are responsible for providing social services within the country. Churches of all denominations provide the services but in Germany 98% of healthcare, education, advice clinics, old people and children's homes, social agencies and day-care centres are run by two church groups, one Catholic and one Protestant. In some areas of Germany, church institutions are the only service provider. The church could be ideally placed to take over this role in many more places and a more open approach to religious belief would also benefit those doctors, health and social workers in the countries where this system is already used; currently many of them feel compelled to go to church in order to stay in a job or get one.

Will the Christian Church have the courage to change? It is changing, but whether it will change enough to transform itself, this I cannot guess. However there have been two very significant, even profound, changes that have occurred quite recently in the Roman Catholic Church. The more surprising of these was the Vatican's announcement in 2008, that there might be extraterrestrial life. When one considers that the Vatican took 350 years to pardon Galileo and even Pope John Paul II spent thirteen years in personal deliberation prior to admitting that the Earth revolved around the sun, one must view this announcement as an enormous step forwards. One must also wonder why the public announcement on the possibility of extraterrestrials and why now?

There are two subjects that scientists shy away from and generally like to avoid discussing, one is religion and the other is extraterrestrials. They avoid the first because they like to believe that *they* know all the answers, that science can explain everything, and that creation did not involve God. The truth is that the more scientists have discovered, the more questions there are still to ask, so they are far from understanding how the universe and everything in it was created. They avoid the second subject, understandably to some extent, because they fear being associated with those who claim alien abduction or other spurious activity; nevertheless there are scientists and astronomers, Stephen Hawking amongst them, who know that the probability of alien life in our universe is almost certain.

But why did the Vatican feel it necessary to make a statement on this matter? A cynic might say they were covering their backs, just in case an alien craft landed, it would be very embarrassing to have denied the existence of intelligent life-forms elsewhere. Certainly there have been increasing reports of UFOs, many seen by credible witnesses and sometimes by large numbers of independent groups of people. These sightings are often coincident with banal denials by governments and the military, making the public wonder why there should be a deliberate cover-up. The Vatican has its own astronomers, so possibly they know something that they haven't yet revealed; the Vatican also have intelligent scholars who would be aware of the ancient texts, which told of extraterrestrial gods, and the different sources that mentioned Sirius as their home. If the ancients were correct in what they recorded, then perhaps the Vatican thinks their return is imminent, or maybe even knows that they are already arrived.

The other great change within the Vatican was revealed when it announced that it was acceptable for mediums to contact the spirit world. Though the Church naturally believed in the resurrection of souls who would live on in an eternal after-life, communicating with the dead was forbidden. I suspect that this ban was due in part to the fact that priests were *unable* to communicate with spirits and thus would be seen by the laity as having received fewer 'gifts' from God than mediums who could.

According to a survey by the UK public theology think tank Theo in 2009, 53% of people accept the existence of the afterlife, 70% believe in a soul and 27% in reincarnation.[4] It is strange then that the sceptics are always those who seem to rule the roost and whose voices crow the loudest. They employ propaganda and malicious rumour to denigrate and discredit

---

4 *The Telegraph* 13 Apr 2009

the work and character of their opponents claiming every medium is a charlatan — the same kind of behaviour displayed by the pharmaceutical companies to stifle alternate treatments, claiming homeopathy is a placebo. The sceptics have failed to disprove the existence of a single psychic phenomenon, failed to prove that life after death is non-existent, like they have failed to prove that homeopathy doesn't work.

There now is a mass of scientific evidence — evidence that the voluble sceptics refuse to acknowledge, most refuse to study, but more significantly refuse to challenge because the evidence is too solid to disprove. Hardcore sceptics, alas, will remain just that and never accept the evidence. After a presentation of the objective evidence for the afterlife by Victor Zammit, one of these closed-minded sceptics declared, "I would not believe in the afterlife even if you could prove it to me, Victor!"[5] Neither an intelligent nor scientific response, but yet these people expect us to have unquestioning belief in their opinions. One can trawl through history to see that many important scientific discoveries and inventions have been virulently attacked and ridiculed by the scientific sceptics and debunkers. This echoes the actions of the early Literalist Christians who refused to accept any evidence, no matter how sound, if it contradicted their beliefs.

Dr Dean Radin provides a rational and scientific understanding of psychic phenomena in his book listing meta-analyses of psychic experiments. He states

> "New discoveries in science are forcing an expansion to ideas of who and what we are, and that those who are most hostile to this topic know little or nothing about the evidence."[6]

In recent years there has been a great increase in the research into quantum physics — the study of characteristics and relationships between subatomic particles and energies — this ground-breaking study has already thrown-up many discoveries which are threatening to seriously undermine orthodox physics. Importantly, it shows that what have been termed paranormal phenomena are actually quite normal and that there is no real conflict between physics and the paranormal. A ground-breaking experiment took place at the University of Paris in 1982, which negated Einstein's long held tenet that no communication can travel faster than the speed of light. Physicists Aspect, Dalibard and Roger discovered that subatomic particles can communicate instantaneously with each other, regardless of the

---

[5] Zammit, V J., *A Lawyer Presents the Case for the Afterlife*
[6] Radin, D. *Entangled Minds*

distance separating them.[7] This led University of London physicist David Bohm to conclude that objective reality does not exist and that despite its apparent solidity, the universe is fundamentally a detailed hologram. Numerous physicists are converting to the view that rather than being made of inert matter and energy, the universe is essentially consciousness.

Radin, in his book, also gives the results of experiments using thought to affect the growth of cell cultures — exactly the type of activity that psychic healers claim to conduct. Not only 'New Age' practitioners perform such an act, but the Church would have us believe that Christ and his disciples did so too. Of course healing the sick is a Roman Catholic Church criterion for canonisation to sainthood. However the title Saint has not always been conferred on those who lived up to its meaning. The meaning is glaringly obvious to Latin or German linguists. From Latin and its derivatives Sanctus is translated into English as Holy. Holy comes to English from the Germanic root *Heilig*. *Sanctus* comes from *Sanus* meaning whole or healthy and *Heilig* comes from *heilen*, to heal. So in its original form the word saint or holy was used to refer to a healer.

Most old Celtic churches are situated by a well, most of these wells have particular healing properties attributed to them and to the saint whose name is associated with the place. The recognition of this healing property is still honoured today in Derbyshire where well blessings take place each spring under the current management, the Church of England. St John of Beverley, whom Bede recorded as a member of the old Celtic Church is still credited with healing that occurs in the town. If the church is to make a spiritual impact in the future, what better way than for its priests to become living healers as their Celtic and Pythagorean forefathers were.

Do we need religion? No. Will society and civilisation collapse without religion? No. Is there a useful purpose for religion continuing? Not in the format it has adopted. People today are generally more knowledgeable and open to new ideas, better educated, less superstitious and less reliant upon religion, but it is clear that many, probably most, require guidance. Certainly many seek enlightenment on the afterlife, some understand that our behaviour in this life will affect what is to happen to us in the next life and may decide whether we need to return to this physical earthly plain once again.

There is much talk of the world experiencing a spiritual transformation in the next few years — it may well do so, but there will no external cosmic force bringing such a thing about, no returning 'alien' gods to force a change, only mankind himself can effect such a thing. People need convincing proof, which is scientifically supported, then their behaviour will

---

[7] Aspect, A. et al., *Physical Review Letters*

improve and they will dispense with the selfishness, greed, corruption and violence that have caused mankind to spread a materialist plague over this beautiful and very wonderful planet Earth. The first step is for the Christian Church to confess to The Greatest Lie Ever Told.

Appendix 1

Islam — The Prophet Rolling in his Grave

Although this book is about the development of Christianity from the original concept to how it manifests in the twenty-first century, I feel that Islam deserves some comment because of its links to Judaism and Christianity. In just a few pages, it is impossible to do full justice to this subject, but I can outline some relevant aspects.

Like the original version of Christianity, Islam has its roots in a moral philosophy inspired by insights derived from the divine Higher-Self and like the original Christianity, it has also suffered from misrepresentation and corruption by fundamentalist fanatics. From without, the origins of Islam and its teachings are largely unknown yet draw opinion and derision. Within Islam also, there is an abundance of ignorance and a shortage of understanding of Mohammed's true teachings. Imams cherry-pick writings, overemphasise certain doctrine and ignore sayings which they do not like. Much is misinterpreted and distorted with the intention of controlling, subjugating and inflaming — just like the Catholic Christian Church once had done. In light of the modern world's present problems with Islamic fundamentalists, it is pertinent to look at the origins of Mohammedism and how it grew into Islam, especially as its beginning was intimately linked with Judaism and Christianity.

Mohammed was born in 570 CE, at Mecca in the Arabian Peninsula. At this period of history, Arabia was surrounded by the Byzantine Empire, which controlled Egypt and Palestine to the west and north, and the Persian Empire in the northeast. This meant that the religions of Christianity, Judaism and Zoroastrianism bordered and filtered into pagan Arabia, whilst further away across the Arabian Gulf, Hinduism and Buddhism from India were prevalent.

At that time, the Bedouin tribes of Arabia largely followed local tribal deities, though on the borders with Byzantium, numerous Arabic tribes had converted to Christianity; there were also several Jewish tribes, including the Qaynuqah, Qurayzah and Nadir, who had settled in the peninsula. Groups of Gnostic Christians had also retreated into Arabia to escape the persecutions of orthodox Christianity.

Arabia was largely a scorching desert waste, with its small population constantly living on the edge of starvation for the land offered little opportunity for agriculture and little in natural resources to benefit the people. The result of this bleak environment meant that those people who lived around Arabia considered it to be external to the civilised world and its people were dismissed as uneducated, illiterate primitives. Arab society was composed of family leaders, clan leaders and tribal chiefs, and because they would not tolerate overall leadership from a king, the lack of inter-tribal unity created a land wracked by continual feuding and warfare. This left outsiders to view the Arabs as violent savages. The Arabs were also mocked for their primitive pagan religious beliefs and sometimes derided as the only people who had never had a prophet.

Mecca was the only place where the Arabs touched civilisation. Controlled by the powerful Quraysh tribe, Mecca was the largest city in the peninsula and a thriving mercantile centre that traded with the surrounding countries. It was also the site of an ancient pilgrimage, where people from all over the peninsula came to circle the Kabah, a giant cube that contained a small black stone, possibly a meteorite — a link that connected earth to heaven.

The Kabah was officially sacred to the Nabatean deity, Hubal and though the shrine was surrounded by 360 idols of other deities, these were almost certainly representations of the days of the year — this number was common and widespread in early times. By Mohammed's time, the deity honoured at the Kabah was Al-Lah, meaning God. The northern Arabs who had converted to Christianity still made the pilgrimage to the Kabah at Mecca, which indicates that Al-Lah was considered to be the One-Creator-God, the same God worshipped by the monotheistic Jews and Christians, though the Jewish peninsula tribes did not acknowledge the significance of the site themselves.

The Quraysh tribe of Mecca were honour bound, as the guardians of this sacred site, to allow free passage and protect all pilgrims. Since all forms of quarrelling, disputes and violence were forbidden within the city and the surrounding countryside, this encouraged traders to come there without fear that they would be at the mercy of raiding Bedouin. Inter-tribal raiding was common because of the general deprivation, yet despite their primitive culture the raiding Bedouin tribesmen avoided killing, as it would have caused vendettas and further killings in reprisal.

The Quraysh became wealthy because of Mecca's trade, but with the wealth there inevitably followed a decline in traditional Bedouin virtues. People became self-centred and thought only of acquiring further riches; they also began to distance themselves from their poorer relatives, the smaller weaker clans within the Quraysh tribe and ignored the plight of the poor and needy.

This was the world into which Mohammed ibn Abdallah was born and as he grew into adulthood, he did not like what he saw. His tribe's obsession with wealth and materialism and its decline from the traditional caring society seemed to have deeply disturbed Mohammed. Legend has it that every year, Mohammed retreated to a cave on Mount Hira, just outside Mecca, to contemplate, pray and fast. In 610 CE, when he was forty years old, Mohammed received the first of the revelations that he would compile into the Qur'an, the Islamic Bible. Apparently, during his sojourn in his cave retreat, Mohammed awoke during the night and felt an overwhelming presence about him, which seemed to squeeze his body until a stream of words spilled from his mouth — words which revealed the first part of a new scripture defining how men should live their lives correctly.

Mohammed worried over the revelations and told only his wife Khadija, and a cousin Waraqu ibn Nawfal, who was a Christian. They encouraged him to preach, insisting that the words came from God. After two years, in 612 CE, Mohammed felt confident enough to begin preaching and gradually he gathered followers from amongst the poor people in the smaller, neglected clans of the Quraysh tribe. Many of those who were attracted to the new prophet's teachings, were women.

Mohammed did not offer a new religion, there were no new doctrines about God; the Quraysh already believed in Al-Lah as the One God who created the world and they believed that in the 'Last Days' when there would be a final judgement of mankind, echoing the beliefs of the Jews and Christians. What Mohammed was teaching, was that it was wrong to dedicate oneself to acquiring wealth, to build a private fortune was wrong; rather, if one had wealth, it was good and right to share it, thereby creating a society where the weak and vulnerable are looked after, rather than being looked down upon with contempt. What good would it be to have amassed earthly riches, when the day of judgement came, he riled, every one would be judged on their acts and whether they had helped the poor.

Mohammed warned that, as other societies had in the past, the Quraysh would fall if it did not mend its ways, for the people were violating the fundamental laws of existence. This was the core of Mohammed's teaching that was to make up the Qur'an. It seems that the Qur'an was gradually revealed verse by verse, over the next twenty years of his life up to his death, often in response to some crisis that was being experienced, or in response to a particular question which had been asked. Mohammed commented, 'Never did I receive a revelation, without thinking that my soul had been torn away from me.' Qur'an basically means 'recitation'; reciting the messages was necessary because the Arabs were almost entirely illiterate. The Arabs heard the teachings during public recitation of Mohammed's scriptures. The name 'Islam', which was later given to Mohammed's teaching, means 'surrender' to the will of God.

Predictably, the influential members of the Quraysh did not like what Mohammed was teaching. To begin with, his converts were small in number and were only from what was perceived as the unimportant down-and-outs. Over some four years, as the numbers began to grow, more attention was given to Mohammed's preaching which had the potential of stirring dissent amongst the poorer section of the populace and for the Quraysh, his position become increasingly untenable. Though Mohammed thought of himself as merely a preacher and a 'warner of things that could happen', with no political ambitions, the Quraysh leaders worried that one day the people would take their instructions from the one whom God spoke to rather than from them. Their growing persecution included a ban, which forbade trade with the Mohammedans and this included food. It is believed that the hardship encountered during the Quraysh persecutions caused the death of Mohammed's wife Khadija.

Matters became desperate in 619 CE when Mohammed's uncle died: since his parents had died when he was an infant, Mohammed's uncle had been his protector. In the violent Arabian society, everyone needed a patron, or protector to avenge him if he should be killed. Any man without a protector could be slain with impunity, for the perpetrators would be free from the vendetta which would otherwise ensue. Unsurprisingly Mohammed failed to find anyone in Mecca who to act as his new patron.

Fortunately for Mohammed, he received an offer from a delegation of chiefs from a place called Yathrib, which was 250 miles north of Mecca. Later, Yathrib became known as Medina. Medina was an agricultural settlement formed by a number of tribes who had abandoned their nomadic lifestyle. Unfortunately, because of the feuding culture of the Arabic Bendouin tribes, the tribes of Medina were constantly plagued by continual inter-tribal and inter-family fighting, which was tearing their community apart. A few of the Medina tribes were of Jewish descent and others had converted to Judaism, as monotheists their leaders saw in Mohammed a person who might bring their people unity and peace.

In 620 CE during their Hajj — the annual pilgrimage to the Kadah at Mecca — the Medina delegation of the tribes approached Mohammed. He agreed to their proposal and they converted to Mohammed's new religion and vowed that their tribes would never fight each other and would defend each other from their common enemies. By 622 CE, some seventy families who were followers of the Prophet, had left Mecca discreetly one by one, finally followed by Mohammed and his closest disciples. Mohammed was lucky to escape, for his new protector had died instigating an attempt upon his life.

The migration from Mecca to Medina is seen as the start of the Islamic era for then, free from the restrictions imposed by the Quraysh, Mohammed was able to implement fully the ideals for living that were encapsulated within the Qur'an. This migration also had another profound consequence, it broke down the traditional tribal notions of Arabic society. Up to that moment, it was totally unheard of, for anyone, any family, to abandon their blood–tribe. Such a heretical act enraged the leaders of Mecca and incited them into action; they felt it was their duty to annihilate Mohammed and his followers entirely. At Medina, Mohammed's confederation was not only new but deemed a threat, for it was not bound by blood ties, but by an ideology and no such thing had ever occurred before in Arabia. Despite binding the disparate tribes together into a new 'super–tribe' and extracting a solemn oath that they would never attack each other and always protect each other, Mohammed made no obligation on any person to convert to his new Islamic faith; he considered that both the Jews and Christians had no need to convert because they already possessed their own relevant religions.

Amongst the confederation of tribes at Medina there were tribes of Jews. Initially, Mohammed was extremely pleased by this and sought their company to learn more about Judaism. He incorporated certain elements into his own new religion with the intention of aligning the two faiths. Though he was accepted by some of the smaller Jewish clans, the three main tribes who had formed a powerful bloc within the confederation, resented Mohammed usurping their influence and his taking the role of overall leader. This resentment eventually led to these tribes betraying the confederation and deserting to re–align themselves with the Quraysh of Mecca; furthermore, they rejected Mohammed's claim of being a prophet, for the Jews the age of prophets had passed, so they could not accept him.

An important fact that Mohammed learnt from the Jews, was that there were major theological differences between the Jews and Christians — he had naively assumed that they had been different sects of the same religion; even much later, it is unlikely that he understood the full extent of the chasm between the two. Disappointed at what he must have seen as foolish religious sectarianism, he stopped thinking of his own religion as being the lesser younger brother and began to consider it as a new alternative, which

THE GREATEST LIE EVER TOLD

was returning to the original pure monotheism as promoted by Abraham and his son Ismail. A visible result of this rethinking came soon after his arrival in Medina; instead of having the faithful turn to Jerusalem to pray, he re-aligned them to Mecca, to the site of the Kabah, built by Adam and renovated by Abraham and Ismail. It was effectively an act of religious independence.

Because the confederation of tribes was of merchants rather than farmers like the natives of Medina and because there was little fertile land, the tribes resorted to raiding merchant caravans from rival tribes, which was the common age-old practice in Arabia. Inevitably this led to raids upon Meccan caravans and then open warfare between Mecca and Medina. The Islamic confederation, contrary to expectation, defeated the more powerful Meccan army. An unpleasant outcome from this conflict was the extermination of the powerful Jewish tribes, who had defected to Mohammed's enemies — a harsh punishment for their crime. Though a peace treaty was agreed Mecca quickly violated it, causing Mohammed — now the most powerful leader in Arabia — to march upon the city. Mohammed had attracted many new tribes to his confederacy and his army forced the bloodless surrender of Mecca. One of Mohammed's great attributes was that he never forced any of his new allies or defeated foes to convert to Islam. The choice of which religion to follow was left for each individual to decide upon.

In 632 CE, two years after his victory in Mecca, Mohammed died. Abu Bakr, one of Mohammed's closest companions, took control but many tribes left the confederacy, which led to his having to fight to regain control whenever one of numerous revolts broke out. By 644 CE the Muslim armies had invaded Syria, Iraq and Egypt and in their wake the Islamic religion spread with astonishing rapidity. The conversion of native populations was always achieved without coercion. Having captured Jerusalem, it became the third most important Islamic site and the Dome of the Rock laid the foundations for all subsequent mosque designs.

Though Jerusalem was now under control of the Muslims, the Jews and Christians were still allowed to live there, with the freedom to follow the religion of their choice with no kind of hindrance. The connection with Mohammed, who never actually travelled there, should be taken as symbolic, but inevitably, the myth was transformed into fact by the perverters of truth. In the hundred years following Mohammed's death, the struggle for power amongst various families and tribal factions increased and the leaders became far more political than religious in their priorities. Their political preference did not prevent them assuming grandiose religious titles, with one caliph designating himself as the 'Shadow of God upon Earth'. Mohammed did not assume self-glorifying and immodest titles and in his lifetime he was always addressed in an informal manner by his given name; such aggrandisement by his antecedents could easily be considered blasphemous.

During this period, both the arts and sciences flourished within the Arab and Islamic cultures, at centres such as Baghdad, Basra and Harran. They taught mathematics, science, medicine, astronomy and philosophy. Hellenic works were translated into Arabic, enabling Muslim scholars to develop the knowledge further. The study of Greek philosophy had a profound effect upon the intellectual Muslims. Sects developed which began to pursue a far more mystical path and where esoteric studies of the minute detail of the Qur'an led to believed secret meanings. Enlightenment through learning was a personal physical and spiritual experience, in the way that the initiates of the Mysteries experienced Sophia through Gnosis. But like their counterparts in the west, these Muslim mystic sects were forced to keep themselves secret, as Islamic leaders became less tolerant and more autocratic. In many ways, perhaps inevitably, after being exposed to Greek philosophy and mysticism, as well as Gnosticism, that there was a coming together and aspects of these Islamic mystics' practises seem close to those of the Mysteries.

Amongst the various esoteric movements was that of the Falsafah. They believed that wisdom should be sought and extracted from all sources, which for them meant that the Hellenic world was a rich mine to be worked. They were fascinated by the Greek philosophers and especially with the idea of reason. They believed that rationalism was the ultimate form of religion. They considered that the reasoning of intellectual humans was a reflection of the absolute reasoning of God; however there was a difference between the God of the Greek sages and that of their own God, the westerners' God was an abstract detached deity who had no interest in the activities of this world, whereas Allah, like the Jewish and Christian Jehovah, was ever concerned with the affairs of mankind. Nevertheless, the Falsafahs believed that by purifying the intellect so that one could live by reason and by dispensing with all that was unreasonable, they could ascend above the binding complexities of life and return themselves to the pure simplicity of the Godhead.

Abu Nasr al–Farabi, a member of the Sufi sect, who died in 950 CE, took an even stronger view of this subject and he was fundamental in establishing the Islamic tradition of rationalistic philosophy. He believed that philosophy was more important and should be placed at a higher level than that of the simplistic religion, which was no more than a social necessity, a simple vehicle that would make the teachings comprehensible for the unintelligent masses. Whilst Plato had stated that an orderly society required doctrines which the masses believed were divinely inspired so that they would feel bound to follow, the Islamic rationalists believed that men required stronger sanctions The unintelligent masses could not be swayed by reasoned and logical arguments, so Mohammed had reinforced the divine laws by warning of Hell's punishments for those who strayed. The Sufis took a very different attitude to religious belief from that of mainstream Islam, which was becoming increasingly less tolerant to anything other than total adherence to the writings within the Qur'an. The Sufis saw the validity of other religious beliefs, that there were many ways to communicate with God, even accepting that the pagan who worshipped a stone idol or a tree or a mountain, for God was in all things. Many Sufis were particularly attracted to Jesus, whom they regarded as a one of the great prophets by Islam and a true Sufi because of his preaching love.

The Sufis employed deep rhythmic breathing and fasting to enhance their powers of concentration; on occasions resulting in moods of ecstasy, so they were given the descriptive title of 'drunken Sufis'. This ecstatic state could be likened to the Mystery initiates' 'experiencing' God. The Sufis understood the concept of needing to rid the Self of its multi–layers of egotism, which confuses and denies man his perception of his real self and the ultimate truth that each man is God.

Were such an insight proclaimed publicly, it would not be understood, but would shock and scandalize and be punished by death for blasphemous heresy. The intellectual esoteric movements, albeit largely unknown to the rank–and–file Muslims, had transformed Islam onto a very different level, which was now more akin to the Mysteries. The probability is that if Mohammed had been there to witness this development, he would doubtless have been astonished. I believe too, that he would also have been fascinated and delighted that his attempts to provide a clear moral framework for his people had reached such spiritual heights, for he had been a thinking man himself, an untutored philosopher.

But all this was beyond the comprehension and needs of the masses, who merely required a practical form of religious devotion. In that way, the Qur'an became the Word of God, which had not been created until it had been delivered in the form of scriptures to his holy prophet, Mohammed. The masses needed some basic moral codes and someone to pray to and it came parcelled up in the Qur'an, just as the Jews had the Torah and the Christians their Bible Gospels. The Arab world was changing from how it had been in Mohammed's time and what was suitable for simple people living a basic and largely agrarian and semi–nomadic lifestyle, was inadequate to cover all kinds of matters which arose as the tribes became more settled.

The Islamic leaders did not believe, like Mohammed, that people should have just a few fundamental moral laws to use to get them through life, they considered that every aspect and practise of a man's daily life needed to be encoded in religious law. The problem was that Mohammed had not given them what they felt that they required, so the leaders decided to look back at Mohammed's life and try to discern how he would have acted in various situations and what he might have thought about all kinds of matters. To do this, they attempted to trace back stories relating to the prophet, relying for authenticity upon accounts given by 'eye witnesses' to an unbroken chain of devote Muslims and then to interpret from the prophet's actions what they wanted to know about how to behave.

When the deficiencies of this system became apparent, it was proposed that sacred law could be found by consensus, so if a traditional custom was adhered to by all Muslims, then it must be sacred because God would not allow it to be otherwise. To Muslims adherence to the *Shariah* — the way, the sacred laws derived from the Qur'an — rules their lives. So once again religious laws were being imposed upon people — surely the very antithesis of what God would want, for man to be free to make his own decisions, operating with his own laws received personally by his own conscience from God. If man understood that when stripped of all his illusory physical baggage, he would return himself to being God, then he would need no laws. Alas, as ever, there are men who elevate themselves into leaders and then seek to make religious laws with which they can control the rest of mankind, to make it into the unthinking obedient sheep.

It is important to consider the way Mohammed treated women, this is crucial in the light of their treatment in many parts of the modem Islamic world. If we look at the social norms of Arabia in the time of Mohammed, women had little or no status in society and men treated them as thy felt fit, so soften this was not too sympathetically. It was a society where men spent their time in the company of other men. Mohammed did not reflect the norm, he enjoyed the company of women and was happy to have them as his close companions. He also treated women with respect and as equals — so much so that his male disciples were often frequently aghast and dismayed at his allowing women to stand up to him and argue. He was very much an archetype of the 'modern man' feeling it his duty to assist with the everyday house–keeping tasks and did not consider it demeaning to undertake such womanly tasks as repairing his own clothing.

Polygamy was common practice, but during Mohammed's time at Mecca, according to most reports, he remained steadfastly monogamous, married only to his wife Khadija, who bore him numerous children until her death. Later, when he attained the position of leader of the confederation of tribes at Medina, at the age of fifty–two, he took a number of wives, as a great chief would be expected to. This action was partly necessitated by a compassionate moral duty, since many of these new wives were older, widowed women in need of a protector. However, Mohammed's main purpose in acquiring new wives was to bind his close companions by marrying their daughters. That way he would bring them into one family and so he also married the daughters of allied tribal chiefs to form unbreakable blood ties. Mohammed had no children by any of these wives, though he did form close companionable relationships with some of them. It would be totally wrong to assume that by acquiring a harem Mohammed was in anyway licentious and certainly not in the manner of later eastern potentates; everything that is known about Mohammed's simple lifestyle repudiates such notions.

What Mohammed did which was so radical in Arabian society and so opposed to what takes place today he demanded the emancipation of women, including the right to divorce their husbands and the right to inherit. There was no compulsion in the Qur'an for women to be either veiled or to be segregated, however these customs — possibly copied from Byzantium to align Islam with Christianity — were introduced some time after Mohammed's death. Though men and women were equal before God, as happened with patriarchal controlled Christianity, the male dominated world of Islam too soon ignored Mohammed's insistence upon female emancipation; no more than lip-service was given to this and the standing of women in society was reduced to virtual slavery with no real protection against abuse. This corruption of his ideals would have appalled Mohammed, but as so often happens, religion is highjacked and corrupted by men who are ambitious to use it to fulfil their own desires.

Today Islam is plagued by a great number of uneducated Muslims with no ability to rationalise let alone philosophize upon theology, who attempt to enforce selected Shariah laws upon all Muslims and forcefully convert the whole world to Islam. The original teachings within the Qur'an allowed people to follow freely whatever religion they chose; this promoted tolerance and non-violence. In some Islamic countries, the emancipation of females championed by Mohammed is not only ignored, but is vehemently condemned as contravening the teachings of the Qur'an and the subject even results in offended men resorting to extreme violence in their protestations. When people's religious beliefs are perceived to be threatened — whether or not they actually are — they become more hardline, more extreme and more zealous and so we end up with fundamentalism.

This unreasoning bigotry is not confined to Islam, but it is also rife in some Christian countries, particularly the United States of America. The heartlands of fundamentalism are generally found in conservative rural areas, usually amongst well meaning people, but those with little intellectual ability: people who perceive a threat to Christian values and are ripe for leadership by religious bigots and money-making conmen. When the

ISLAM — THE PROPHET ROLLING IN HIS GRAVE

circumstances are right, they spawn the Christian fundamentalist culture. The same thing happens with Muslims, especially in areas where the people are poor and have little education, they lay the blame for all their ills upon perceived enemies, either other Islamic sects or non–Muslims or both. Inevitably, such people are always ripe to be manipulated and readily led by men with silvery tongues who claim religious piety, whilst passionately spouting hatred and inciting violence and murder in the name of God. One of the great curses of the world is that the naïve are easily led and even worse, are too easily conned into becoming martyrs and mass murders.

The Taliban provide the worst example of this idiocy. A backward deprived people who have concocted grievances against the modern world, they see their solution in returning the Islamic society back to the primitive form it experienced before the time of Mohammed. They wish to embrace fully the brutal primitive world that existed in Arabia in the middle of the first millennium, where mutilations, stonings and beheadings were meted out to anyone deemed to be a lawbreaker. They then want to enforce the blasphemous rules invented by men after Mohammed's death that contravene their Prophet's teaching. Women are to be heavily veiled and segregated with severe limitations placed upon the things they are allowed and not allowed to do — effectively reducing women to slaves in opposition to the Prophet's practice and at the same time brain–washing them into believing it was written in the Qur'an because it was God's will. *Madrasah* is the name for a college of Muslim higher education, it is perversely ironic that the name Taliban means 'students of the *madrasahs*'. Despite their title, the Taliban demonstrate that they clearly know little of the Qur'an and its laws, for they violate the very core of Islamic teachings and bring Islam into disrepute, whilst blasphemously proclaiming they are doing Allah's sacred work.

Most members of the original Taliban belonged to the Pakhtum tribe and in the early days of their conflict against the Soviet backed Afghan government, were also fighting non–Pakhtum tribes, despite the Qur'an expressly forbidding inter–tribal fighting, chauvinistic ethnic behaviour and the harsh treatment of any minority groups. The Taliban's treatment of women flies in the face of what Mohammed practised and preached. The Qur'an insists that women and children should never be harmed, but the 'students of the *madrasahs*' missed classes the day that was taught. Their lust for the mass slaughter of innocent people, their encouragement of martyrs whom they promise exclusive entry into Heaven to receive a harem of young virgins would have truly horrified Mohammed and he would not have hesitated in condemning such callous perverts to eternal damnation.

Typical of fundamentalists regardless of their religion, the Taliban's version of theirs is highly selective. They cherry–pick bits that suit their own

453

prejudices, distort other parts and ignore totally a whole host of scriptures that do not suit, particularly those that recommend compassion, tolerance and understanding. These so-called religious 'scholars' have totally perverted their Islamic faith and turned good into evil. Whilst the Taliban, together with the al-Qa'eda terrorist organisation, are at the fundamentalist extreme, there are a great many others just beneath them who hold similar beliefs and are also ready to resort to violence whenever they see fit. Too many *Madrasahs*, these so-called religious colleges, discredit both the name of education and religion and are little more than bigoted recruitment centres to brainwash eager sheep. The reality of the education received at many *Madrasahs* is that it is solely aimed at mindlessly learning the 6,000 verses of the Qur'an. The Qur'an is written in Arabic, however most of the *Madrasahs* are in Pakistan where the language is Urdu. The Arabic script is virtually the same as the Urdu script so the students can read the script, but do not actually understand what the words mean. It is like an English speaker reading Italian, but not understanding the meaning of the words. The students, mainly from the poor uneducated classes, are expected to recite the verses over and over again until they memorise them, but they are not expected to understand what they mean — they are the words of God, and that is sufficient.

Only around forty percent of students succeed in this monumental task of memorisation and then just a few of these go on to study the hadith and sannah, the sayings and examples of the Prophet. The examples of the Prophet copy every action attributed to Mohammed in his life: students sit in a particular position upon the floor, with one leg tucked under the other, which is supposedly the way the Prophet sat. The farcical nature of this mimicry is lost upon Muslims, who seem to disregard the reality that the accounts of Mohammed's every physical action and every thought have to be viewed with deep suspicion: its authenticity cannot be verified. Ironically by acting like sheep these naïve Muslims are contravening the Prophet's command: the Qur'an 17:36 actually warns against such action "You shall not accept any information, unless you verify it for yourself. I have given you the hearing, the eyesight and the brain, and you are responsible for using them." This instruction from the Prophet is clearly being ignored. In practice, verification of information and rational thought with the brain is not required by the *Madrasah* teachers, but rather blind obedience, not least to the words of the Imams. Muslims would do well to consider the advice from the Buddha too, "Believe nothing, no matter where you read it or who said it — even if I have said it — unless it agrees with your own reason and your own common sense." Common sense and reason are rare in many people's lives and even less so when they cling mindlessly to religions of the fundamentalist variety. Blindly memorising the Qur'an without understanding what it says is an action of total lunacy and attempting to excuse it because it is the Words of God is nonsensical and unjustifiable. Mindless repetion with no requirement to understand is quite simply, brainwashing. The real intention is to remove free will, instil blind faith and obtain total obedience from the students. This continues into adult life and as a consequence, the fundamentalist leaders can incite their mindless mob to undertake any action they choose and blasphemously call it the 'Will of God'.

What is deeply disturbing and distressing is that like other religions, both leaders and laity are reluctant to act against their own. Too few Muslims condemn outright those violent lunatics who are perverting, blaspheming and committing heresy, yet too many Muslims are quick to protest at any perceived slight by non–Muslims. There is also an arrogant insistence that Islam is supreme, that all other religions are inferior, that all who oppose the formation of a world–wide Islamic state make themselves enemies of Islam. Effectively, this translates as, "All non–Muslims are rivals and enemies and therefore must convert or be eliminated." If Muslim leaders do not support this doctrine then they must say so both loudly and clearly and take real and positive action to rid Islam of this uncivilised, blasphemous and dangerous thinking. There should be no place within religion for a belligerent confrontational approach, but many Islamic religious leaders have it at the core of their teaching. The fundamental belief is that we are right and everyone else is wrong, this implies that you must give us everything we demand and we owe you nothing in return, because you are non–believing infidels. Indeed, how many times have we heard Imams not just *excusing*, but actually *condoning* the heretics who fail to adhere to the Qur'an and then applaud their evil actions. It's time for much rational thinking. I think it is not just Mohammed who is 'rolling in his grave' at the atrocity and perversion of his religion, but all right minders Muslims who have followed what he taught.

Though I have given a glimpse at Mohammed's life and teachings and what motivated the good work he did, I am interested also to find what influenced his writings. He appears to have claimed that he received all his revelations from God. We cannot avoid asking questions, which doubtless may offend unthinking Muslims, anymore than we can suppress the truth just because it might offend some people — I too am offended, offended by hypocrisy, intolerance, bigotry, ignorance, violence and domination. The revelations that make up the Qur'an did not all appear in one flood of communication, but over many years. I suspect that having been deeply concerned over the demise of traditional social care within his city's community, when Mohammed went to his retreat, he could have done nothing other than contemplate the problem and give great thought to how things could be resolved and how people ought to live in a moral caring society. In other words he philosophised, just as other concerned men such as Plato had done. After Plato's time, in the period immediately prior to and during the time of Mohammed, the Gnostics had their hermit–sages and mystics who isolated themselves so that they could contemplate without distraction and interruption, exactly as those mystics known as the Greek Oracles before Plato had done.

This does not to mean that 'divine' revelations did not occur, but rather than 'personal utterances from God', we should think of them as 'divine' inspirations received from the Psyche, or Higher–Self, that part of each of us that is in contact with God as the Universal Daemon or Universal Soul. The literal experience of Gnosis is one of the ways the initiates of the Mysteries 'received' philosophical inspirations and insights. If one believes that God delivered personally the divine revelations of one mystic–philosopher whilst denying those of others, one is being irrational, unreasonable and partisan. It certainly can never be proven that one man's revelations are genuine whilst the rest are not; but this is what religions do — insist that their man is the one and only genuine article, theirs is the sole earthly manifestation of the Word of God. Particularly ironic in the case of Islam, which considers God to be everything in existence, yet chooses to deny the bits of God that it doesn't like.

Whether Mohammed received any form of Gnostic teaching prior to his revelations, cannot now be known — early Muslims would have quickly suppressed any evidence of it — but it is surely significant that his cousin, in whom he first confided the revelations, was a Christian. It is highly unlikely that this cousin was the only Christian in Mohammed's clan, for it was unheard of to be a Christian in isolation. Later in his life, Mohammed had a concubine named Mariam, with whom he had a child who died in infancy; Mariam was also a Christian. It is possible that these were literal Christians who somehow had been baptised into the Byzantine Church, but this is highly unlikely What is far more probable is that they were Gnostic Christians. As a result of the persecutions suffered at the hands of the orthodox Church, many Gnostics fled eastwards and set up small communities, over the borders in little populated regions out of the imperial reach. Many Jews too fled the Roman retribution and had resettled in Arabia. If this is the case, it is hard to believe that as an orphan living amongst his wider family members, that Mohammed would not have been influenced to some level by the Gnostic beliefs and teachings of that same family.

It is more generally accepted that Mohammed's close contact with the Judaic faith and particularly his friendship with the smaller Jewish clans enabled him to learn something of Judaic scripture, which was to give the Arabs a legitimate place alongside the others followers of the monotheistic faith. From the Book of Genesis, Mohammed would have discovered the story that recounted how Abraham had two sons, the eldest from a concubine named Hagar. This son Ishmael, (or Ismail), together with his mother, had been forced out into the wilderness by Abraham, however God saved them and promised Ismail that he would be the father of a great nation, the Arabs. The next part of the story, probably an invention by the story-tellers of the exiled Jews, has Hagar and Ismail settled at Mecca and when Abraham came to visit them, they set about rebuilding the Kabah — the cube shaped shrine — which had originally been built by Adam, but had fallen into disrepair. This account would have pleased Mohammed, for it bestowed the Kabah with impeccable credentials linking the sacred site with the monotheistic God and proved that the Arab people had not been left out of the divine equation for mankind. Now the Arabs could hold up their heads and take their rightful place alongside the Jews and Christians.

In the early days when he was struggling against Mecca, whenever he called the people to prayer, Mohammed had the people kneel to make them understand their insignificance before God. For Arabs, it was generally deemed beneath them to prostrate themselves before anyone. He also had them turn towards Jerusalem to pray, for that seemed the most appropriate site to honour God. From 624 CE Mohammed had his followers turn to face Mecca when they prayed. This can be seen as both a sign of his own confidence that he would soon overcome the rulers of Mecca and it was also a declaration that the Muslim Arabs no longer needed to be subservient to Judaism and Christianity. In the Kabah at Mecca, they had their own holy shrine, rebuilt by Abraham and Ismail and originally built by Adam; it was their own direct link to God, to Allah.

At that time, Mohammed was probably not aware that Judaism and Christianity were separate religious faiths, since they shared so much, giving the impression that they were merely different sects. Because he could not read the competing scriptures for himself, from the fragment samples recounted to him from both Jew and Christian he would have been left with an incomplete picture; neither would he have had the time to immerse himself in theologies when he had his own work to do. Mohammed was no academic scholar, nor was he literate — Arabia had virtually no books and no academies and schools at all — but that is no bar to becoming a valid philosopher: clearly Mohammed was a man with a conscience, a moralist, a humanist, a social reformer, a man who was interested in other religions, in other words he was a great thinker. As we have seen throughout this book to know God, you must first be a great thinker.

Rather than viewing Mohammed as a great religious prophet, he should get his true recognition, as a philosopher who remoulded the religious beliefs already existent in Arabia, adopted appropriate aspects of Judaism and used the philosophical thinking of Gnosticism to form a base for his moralistic teachings. As a profoundly intelligent man, he would have realised that to effect a moral change within a society there is little chance of success if it is not presented within a religion, for that is the only way to get people to listen, but more importantly, to get them to adhere permanently to the teachings and moral code. Sadly history shows us that religion is far from an ideal vehicle to transport moral beliefs and practice, inevitably opportunists seeking power and wealth, politicians seeking to control and direct people, both will twist and pervert the teachings so that all religions become corrupt.

The major problem that seems to affect Islam in particular is that the religion was appropriate for the era in history within which it was born — a primitive age in a primitive country — but whether it is still relevant to the modern age is questionable. It has not adapted particularly well and it is not helped by the strong resistance to change shown by its adherents. It might be a religion, but all things evolve and things that do not accommodate change struggle to exist and eventually die. There is a sad irony as Islam has changed, but long ago in its early years, when it was perverted from Mohammed's original teachings. Those resistant to change now fiercely hang on to a teaching that is not even the original teaching of Mohammed.

How much credibility can we give to the Islamic faith? Well if one considers that truth be paramount and that God would not allow any untruth to be a part of religious teachings, then Islam immediately fails the test. It is a religion, even in its radical mystical forms, which believes in the fictional myth of Adam and Abraham and that Adam constructed the Kabah; this falsehood completely undermines any claim that it is a religion that is absolutely imbued with the Truth of God. The fact is that all religion is man–made and Islam is just another one and not necessarily the worse because of that, but no religion is perfect and without flaws, and the real truth is that none have been divinely sent by God. Because everybody has God within them, as long as it harms no one, every form of religious devotion is equally valid — and as the Sufi mystics confessed even the pagan worshipping a stone is communing with the God who created and is within all things.

As I was writing of this book, I was appalled to hear a radio news report that in the Jordanian capital of Amman, a Muslim gunman shot tourists in the back, killing one and wounding six, which included two women. Apparently, the gunman shouted "Allahu Akbar" — 'God is great' — as he ran away. To the great credit of the Jordanian people, who displayed a great sense of moral decency as well as heroism, a number of street hawkers tackled and captured the fleeing Palestinian gunman, after which they expressed their disgust by exclaiming "He was a dog," and "A true Jordanian would never do such a thing." I had the privilege of living in Jordan for a short while and I can say that there I saw the Islamic faith as Mohammed had intended it to be lived; with tolerance, compassion and understanding. I have never met more genuinely welcoming and friendly people, and they follow their faith with a sense of commitment, but also a semblance of rational restraint; they feel shame at terrorist acts, knowing that they have no part in their beliefs. Sadly, this kind of thinking is too often missing amongst Muslims — those who justify terrorist action have not rationalised their feelings. How would they feel if Christian fundamentalist terrorists blew up men, women and children in an Arab market place. They would be rightly horrified and believe it to be an act of evil… yet when Muslims do it, to many it is for the glory of God.

Pope Benedict XVI provoked a furore in 2006, when he quoted a Byzantine text that questioned Islam's use of violence to further its cause. The reaction was beyond reason: outraged Islamic political rulers and religious leaders demanded an apology and retraction, whilst the more fundamentally inclined Muslims, who doubtless had not even read the reported texts o the Pope's sppech, felt duty bound to take to the streets and protest by setting fire to effigies of the Pope and haranguing Christians, whilst the extremists set fire to churches and murdered. The Pope had asked a group of theologians, "Is the conviction that acting unreasonably contradicts God's nature merely a Greek idea, or is it always and intrinsically true?" He used a conversation recorded at the very end of the fourteenth century between "the erudite Byzantine emperor Manuel II Paleologus and an educated Persian on the subject of Christianity and Islam, and the truth of both" to make his point. Both the Pope and the emperor argue that actions should be based on reason, not the perceived understanding of a scripture.

The whole extremist reaction was totally out of proportion, intolerant and not least a deceitful political opportunity to claim the moral high ground, but it provided a perfect illustration of what the Pope had meant to say. Reacting to a medieval text that suggested the Muslims used violence to get their own way by saying it was an offensive lie and then going out and committing acts of violence, was self defeating and only proved the text to be accurate in its opinion — but alas too many Muslims proved themselves too stupid to see this obvious truth. The Pope quoted the Emperor's words ""Not to act reasonably (with logos) is contrary to the nature of God", said Manuel II, according to his Christian understanding of God, in response to his Persian interlocutor" and the Muslim outcry proved them both true.

I keep repeating the message that religious passions tend to extinguish reason. Any religion that condones, promotes, or gives its followers the notion that such behaviour is honourable and that religiously-motivated assassins will be rewarded in heaven, whose moderates limit themselves to muted verbal condemnations, can only be described as appallingly flawed. Any religion that has become so self-obsessed and full of its own rightness and the desire to shield the sensitivities of its followers is totally wrong — facts and the truth are far more important. For most of its life, the Christian Church sought to punish its shirkers, to silence its critics, to kill the heretics, convert the whole world and slaughter those who refused; but it has moved away from such lunatic and barbarous aims. Alas Islam appears to have chosen to follow the same misguided and immoral path and shows little indication of moving out of its own 'dark age'. Islam is deeply riddled with a cancer that is rapidly spreading and has made it desperately sick. If Islam is not active in seeking to cure itself by surgical removal of the evil cancer cells, its sickness will become its death. The patient is dying and its only doctor is itself. It is time for Mohammed to heal his sick.

Appendix 2

The Templars, Their Cathedrals and Their Cistercian Friends

The Templars' lasting legacy was their building of the great Gothic cathedrals. The word Gothic has nothing to do with the Scandinavian tribe who crossed the Baltic into Prussia, but derives from the Greek 'goetik', meaning 'magical' in the context of magical effect. These massive structures were unique in design and size and almost all were built within a hundred years in the late twelfth to early thirteenth century. Most of the stonemasons employed, belonged to a guild which was under the instruction of St. Bernard's order of Cistercians. The architectural designs had never been attempted before. Instead of solid walls and tiny windows, the ground–breaking engineering created a skeleton of curved stone columns which allowed vast interior spaces filled with 'illumination' from the specially crafted windows, and the incredible flying buttresses on the outside, seen in Le Mans and Notre Dame de Paris. These cathedrals are full of other more intriguing and enigmatic features, like the Pythagorean geometry often revealed in some of the floor designs.

A common feature of these cathedrals, found in the stone carvings on the walls and pillars, is the 'Green Man', which may seem bizarre, when we think of him as a well–known pagan nature god. Once we find out that the Green Man is also Osiris, who as the dying–resurrected god was linked to the natural growing cycle of seeding, growth and harvest and thus usually depicted with green skin, the Green Man's appearance in certain Christian buildings is no surprise.

Another unexplained oddity of these Cathedrals is a property of the original stained glass windows. Unlike glass that was manufactured in later times, it had the strange ability of seeming to hold the light; unfortunately many of these windows have been replaced and the original magic lost. Fortunately in Chartres Cathedral, 152 of the original 186 windows survive.

The Templar constructions were filled with details and symbols, which not only gave clues as to their roots but were meant to pass on knowledge — but only 'to those who have eyes to see'.

The position of the French Gothic cathedrals within northern France corresponds to an overlay of the brightest stars in the Virgo constellation onto the ground. The cathedrals of Chartres, Paris, Reims and Strasbourg also lie along the path of the sun as it moves through the constellation. This appears to be a deliberate link to the Virgin female goddess and Mary/Isis, to which the Notre Dame cathedrals are dedicated. The most sacred of these cathedrals is the one at Chartres. Reputedly, the altar was built upon *La Grotte des Druides,* a Druidic dolman which has been called the 'womb of the earth'. The site is considered so sacred, that unlike other cathedrals, there are no kings, bishops, dukes or bishops buried there. According to scientists, this ancient Druidic site is also a hub of tellueric earth currents — the potential energy of the earth's electrical current is particularly high at this site. Whether one believes that people at that time were aware of this, the fact is that Chartres in particular was deemed extremely important to them.

The Templars supplied the funds and the new technology to construct these cathedrals, which were clearly designed for a purpose other than the support of devout orthodox Christians. Within these structures the Templars deliberately encoded many things, which were meaningless to orthodox Christians, but could be understood by Gnostic initiates.

There is much to set the Templars apart from every other religious/political organisation, except for one — the Cistercians, the monastic order founded by their mentor Bernard of Clairvaux. The two organisations activities were so often inter–twinned, but whereas the Templars fell from grace, the Cistercians survived. During the Templar heyday, as they grew and expanded, so did the Cistercians, both in wealth and the number of their monasteries. Intriguingly, in Scotland the Cistercians reputedly integrated with the remnants of the Celtic Church, once more indicating that the Templars and Cistercians had more than a passing interest in Druidic and Gnostic beliefs. I suspect that after the fall of the Templars and the death of St Bernard, the Cistercian order hid, then finally relinquished their unorthodox activities.

Appendix 3

Holy Grail

In recent times there have been a number of suggestions that the Templars had encoded the blood line of Jesus within the story of the Holy Grail. The Grail, in this scenario, actually represented the womb of Mary Magdalene carrying Jesus' child. Previous stories had interpreted it as the chalice of the last supper. It is generally believed that Chretien de Troyes, a Templar who included a chalice in his version of the romances of King Arthur, first wrote the Grail story some time after 1180 CE. Chretien named his story *le Conte del Graal* and though it gives his version of the search for the Grail, he fails to define what the Grail actually was. As he was a Templar, this is probably a deliberate omission. Although we see the word Grail as the frequent translation of *Graal*, Chretien wrote it *graal* with a lower case *g*. I suspect he did this deliberately in order to show that it wasn't a significant object that the word represents. In 1190, an anonymous author wrote what has been called the First Continuation, which developed the story where Chretien had left off. In this version too, the Grail is undefined, but it seems to act like a servant, perhaps implying that it was the human shell in service to the spirit.

Ten years later, Robert de Boron wrote another version, which he claimed was from a different source — a book written by Christian clerics — so not surprisingly the Grail was now defined as the 'Holy Grail' and became the cup of the Last Supper, which later collected a few drops of Jesus' blood when he was taken to his tomb. Around 1200 CE, in Germany Wolfram von Eschenbach wrote his version of the Grail story, which he entitled 'Parzival'. In this tale the guardians were not Arthurian warriors, but the Knights Templar and the Grail was a small stone which had the power to heal and rejuvenate — this sounds very like the Egyptian Benben stone, with its Benben bird/Phoenix, which had the ability to regenerate and whose appearance heralded a new era. Another stone that healed was the Hermetic alchemists' 'philosopher's stone' and this too was probably based on the Benben.

The Grail story has it origins in Britain, in the region once known as the White Lands, which is now North Wales/Cheshire/Shropshire and allegedly once the heartland of the Druids, later the real historical Arthur and even later still an important site for the Cistercians and the Knights Templar. The Grail stories were exported verbally from here and written down in France, before returning to Britain. There is evidence for a historical Arthur in North Wales and Shropshire, a leader named Owain Ddantgwyn, whose battle title Bear is *Arth* in welsh. *Arth Gwyr,* which sounds very like Arthur means Bear Man. The original author of the Perceval Grail story was a descendent of Owain Ddantgwyn, a monk named Blayse from St Asaph in North Wales. Blayse went into the employ of the Peveril family in Shropshire. A thread, which runs through these individuals links things back to very ancient times in Britain.

In Celtic Britain, the magical cauldron of the gods could not only heal but revive the dead and can be viewed as the forerunner of the grail chalice. In the Grail stories, there are several holy items that make an appearance all had their origins with the early Celts — a sword, a spear, a bowl and a stone. Unsurprisingly, Christians contrived to equate these items with the sword that cut off John the Baptist's head, the spear which pierced the side of Christ, the cup of the Last Supper and the stone on which Jacob laid his head to sleep. The reality is that their origins are in the ancient Celtic legends, which state that when the Danaan gods landed upon earth from the heavens, they brought the supernatural sword and spear of Lugh, the cauldron of Dagda, which revived the dead, and the stone of destiny — Lia Fail. From my research, I have concluded that the ancients put familiar names upon the Danaan's tools and instruments, which they could not properly define.

The places in North Wales from which the Grail story might have originated present evidence of Templar activity. Quite by chance, I stumbled across a 17th century painting that depicted a father and son of a very influential family in the area. What should have been just an ordinary family portrait showed the young son in a very unusual pose — the identical posture given to John the Baptist, by painters who were reputed to have had Templar/Sion connections.

It will probably never be known for certain just what the Grail was meant to be, but looking at the wider evidence, the most likely answer would be that the Grail was nothing other than a symbol meant to preserve the true Christianity of the Gnostics, the more ancient Egyptian Mysteries and the ideals of the Druids of Britain and Gaul. From research into pre-history and ancient history, which I had undertaken before discovering the truth and lies of the Bible and Christianity, I felt that there was a common ancient heritage shared between the early true Druids and the priests of Ra in Egypt. It also became apparent that there were guardians of esoteric knowledge who passed some of this information on and eventually inspired the formation of the Priory of Sion and then the Knights Templar. What the ancients knew, filtered down to us through the Celtic legends, whilst in the Middle Ages further information was encoded into the Arthurian and Grail legends. From some of the things which I have discovered about the Templars and their activities in strangely remote places, it strongly suggest interests which have nothing to do with either money-making or religion, but it did involve keeping people well away from these areas, some of which have mysterious artefacts whose origins cannot even be guessed at. Hopefully in the future, after more extensive research, I will be able to expand more fully on some of these things.

An intriguing link connects the homelands of the Druids to Canaan. Sacred sites, which include springs, standing stones and stone circles are almost exclusively linked to the lands where Druids were known to have lived. Canaan too had standing stones and some stone circles, often attributed in local legends to the Nephilim and later the Hebrews adopted these places as sacred sites of their own. A stone circle site has been located in Upper Egypt where on the summer solstice the suns rays cast no shadow. The site is located on the Tropic of Cancer, its finding has caused quite a stir amongst academics as until recently it was thought that stone circles only occurred in western Europe. If there is one megalithic structure, then the odds are that there are, or were, more. The problems of finding them in this location are compounded by the vast amounts of sand likely to be on top of them. The Canaanite name for stone circles was gilgal and the Hebrews adopted the same, naming a town near Jericho, Gilgal. It was at this stone circle that Saul was supposedly crowned as the first king of the Israelites. According to Bible expert Professor SH Hooke, early tradition makes this Canaanite stone circle an important Israelite site where the Ark of the Covenant was first installed, the first Passover was celebrated after the entry into the Promised Land and where important Israelites were circumcised.

In Kings 18:30–35, there is a report of Elijah repairing a stone circle. It says that he took twelve stones — possibly an astrological reference to the twelve planets/houses — and built an altar to God, then about the altar he built a trench and filled it with water. This sounds very much like a stone circle with a surrounding henge ditch. This is a unique reference because no stone circles with surrounding henges have been found outside of the British

Isles. The purpose of the water filled ditches was to make astronomical measurements from the reflections.

The stone circles present a large and complex subject and their meaning and purpose are as difficult to discern as the origins and methods of those who built them. The Templar links to these and many obscure and remote sites are the subject of a further book. The search for the Holy Grail is much easier to accomplish once we know how to look, we find it where it has always been — within ourselves.

Appendix 4

Lessons from the Afterlife

Since time immemorial, man has asked the question, "Where will I go to when I die?" Few people had a truthful answer and many made one up. Foremost amongst the fiction was the familiar Heaven and Hell, erroneously alleged to be your final destination depending on whether you lived by or failed to comply with someone else's rules.

The Ancient Egyptians had a complicated Afterlife that gave you five attempts to get earthly life right. If after your five opportunities you failed, then you would be condemned to the realm of chaos. Socrates, Plato and Pythagoras all believed in reincarnation and it was central to the teachings of the *Hermetica*. Reincarnation thus became part of the early Christian belief, though Emperor Justinian put an end to it at an Ecumenical Council in 545 CE.

In Chapter 21, *Paul — Dangerous Heretic*, I mentioned Professor Raymond Moody's technique of mirror–gazing by which the bereaved could contact recently deceased family and friends. Not only could the living contact the dead, but the spirits materialised and presented themselves in audible and tangible form, so the bereaved could converse with and touch their loved ones. Some of these same procedures have been used elsewhere with quite amazing results.

In order to evaluate the application of a range of techniques for communicating with the spirits of the deceased, a group of lawyers collaborated to assess the evidence. This group of highly qualified and experienced professionals was comprised of open–minded sceptics who applied the legal benchmark of 'beyond reasonable doubt' when considering the credibility of witnesses and the strength of the evidence put before them.

The evidence they considered was obtained under controlled conditions. It included experiments with mediums, materialisation, mirror gazing and electronic voice phenomena. The latter using sophisticated electronic equipment, which records communications with spirits and compares these with recordings when the deceased was still alive. Voiceprints can be used to confirm the identity as they are as unique as fingerprints.

These contacts revealed that there is a spirit world, or in fact several as some spiritual religions claim. Communications gave a consistent message even when they originated in different locations around the world, in different societies with differing racial and ethnic backgrounds, different religious beliefs and social systems. The information concerning the afterlife and its format and structure was always the same. With Victor Zammit's permission, I include a summary of the messages from his book *A Lawyer Presents the Case for the Afterlife*.

Vital eyewitness messages from the afterlife

Vital messages from afterlife intelligences transmitted in different countries to us humans on this earth in the last few decades REPEATEDLY inform us that, (succinctly put):

- All humans survive physical death, irrespective of their beliefs.
- At the point of death we take our mind with all its experiences, our character and our etheric (spirit) body — which is a duplicate of the earth body. It comes out of the earth body on the point of death and is connected to the earth body by a silver chord. Death occurs when the silver cord is severed from the physical body. Silver Birch, a high Intelligence from the afterlife who has transmitted more than nine books, informs us that in the afterlife the etheric body and our surroundings will be just as solid as our world seems to us now.
- There is no such thing as heaven "up in the sky" or hell "down below": the location of the afterlife does not change from the earth plane. Just as there are different radio frequencies within the same room different worlds or "spheres" or "planes" inter–penetrate — from the highest vibrations to the lowest.
- There are different levels or "spheres" in the afterlife — from the lowest vibrations to the highest. On physical death we go to the sphere which can accommodate the vibrations we accumulated throughout our life on earth. Simplistically put, most ordinary people are likely to go to the "third" sphere — some people call it the "Summerland." The higher the vibrations, the better the conditions — this will take us to the higher spheres. We are informed that the higher spheres are too beautiful to even imagine. For those with very, very low vibrations, very serious problems do exist.
- Hell for eternity and eternal damnation were invented by men to manipulate the hearts and the minds of the unaware — they do NOT exist. Whilst there ARE lower spheres in the afterlife that are

- particularly dark, unpleasant and even horrific — some call them "hell" — ending down there is NOT for eternity. There is always help available for any soul willing to learn the lessons of kindness and unselfishness.
- Once you are freed from the body and enter the afterlife, you will experience a feeling of enormous lightness. Some communicators liken it to taking off a heavy diver's suit.
- The state of mind at the point of death is crucial. Some pass over consciously and are fully aware of the loved ones who come to welcome the new arrival; others are unconscious and are taken to a special place of rest.
- In the areas nearest to our world, the mind creates reality. So those who expect to find nothing may well stay in a deep sleep.
- Those people who have been ill for some time may need to be helped to change their mental picture of themselves and create with their minds a healthy etheric body. "Hospitals" exist for this purpose.
- Ordinary reasonable people are met by their loved ones — soul-mates are reunited. Higher Intelligences inform us that in the afterlife our appearance can regress to our best age — for most people, from the early to mid twenties.
- Atheists, agnostics and others may not be encumbered from passing on to the higher spheres — what they did in their lifetime and the motivation for what they did will be important, not what they believed in.
- Not participating in religious rituals, e.g. baptism and confessions, and non-belief in creeds and dogmas does NOT encumber anyone from attaining higher spirituality and the higher afterlife spheres.
- Soon after crossing over you will experience a life-review. In your life review you will experience all of your thoughts, words and deeds and effects they had on others. No-body judges you. You judge yourself by comparing the reality of your life and the effects it had on others with what you set out to do.
- Loved ones from the afterlife, recently arrived and others, do have the power to visit loved ones still living on earth and some of them may even become their "guides".
- In the afterlife communicating is done by telepathy. Communicating from and to the earthplane with those in the afterlife can be (and is being) done by telepathy.
- Recently arrived loved ones, usually within three months of transition, are permitted to transmit visually — by way of dreams or by apparition and other means — evidence that they are still alive. Many choose to attend their own funerals.

- Any physical disabilities people had on earth will disappear. Once they have adjusted mentally there will be no such thing as deformity, sickness, blindness or any other thing that adversely affected them on earth.
- The mind has enormous power in the afterlife. It can create matter there and can cause the body to travel at the speed of thought, e.g. you imagine you are at any place in the world and you are there instantly.
- Some people on earth have a much better transition to the afterlife than others. The more knowledge we have about the afterlife, the easier the transition. It also helps if you are able to control your mind, think positively and concentrate on one thing at a time.
- Some people get stuck "between the two worlds." Because they still feel themselves solid, they do not accept that they have actually died. Some are afraid of going to the light. Many get into mental confusion and could get lost for decades and even for thousands of years.
- In the afterlife, there is no need to eat or drink or go to sleep. There is no night–time, no rain or bad weather. All is light.
- You will have the opportunity to mix with others of the same vibrations and join with them in co-operative endeavors.
- You will usually find yourself in a house, often the exact replica of a favorite house from your life. Of if you have a clear mental picture of the house you have always wanted and you have earned it, you can create it.
- All animals also survive death. You can expect to be reunited with loved pets who are usually cared for by someone close to you until you arrive. Undomesticated animals continue to exist in their own spheres.
- You can continue to pursue your favorite interests. You can continue to read, enjoy art, music, attend concerts or play sports. Or you can do gardening.
- One can still learn spiritual lessons in the afterlife and progress to higher, even more beautiful spheres.
- You also will have the opportunity to go to the Halls of Learning, and continue to do spiritual work — helping those crossing over or helping others less informed. You may like to do rescue work — informing those lost in the darker realms and who qualify to be in the sphere of the light to come up towards the light. You can be creative in how you spend your time.
- Ultimately, there will come a time when you have to increase your vibrations by increased spirituality to continue to spiritually refine and graduate to a higher realm where circumstances would be much more beautiful and better than the one you were in before.

- This "transition" to the next sphere happens gradually and naturally. You find yourself going into a deep sleep and awaken on the next level.
- In the higher spheres, you will be able to recall and see any event in any period of your existence three dimensionally.
- Love, unconditional love, is the most powerful force known in the universe. It is the link with our loved ones in the afterlife.
- No one judges you or condemns you to the lower spheres. You condemn yourself to the lower horrific spheres ("hell") by the low vibrations (low spirituality) you acquired during life on earth.
- Those who were consistently evil are, on their transition, either left alone or are met by those others of the same very low vibrations and with the same very low spirituality. They are naturally attracted to the darker lower spheres.
- However the universal Law of Progress ensures that at some time in the future those with lower vibrations will eventually, even if it takes eons of time — centuries or even thousands of years — obtain higher vibrations and graduate to the higher spheres.
- Selfishness is one of the greatest transgressions against spirituality and is highly karmic.
- Energy — positive or negative — is a "boomerang." When you send out good energy towards someone, that good energy is returned sooner or later. If you send out negative energy by unfairly being dishonest against someone, or by cheating, lying, harassing, discrediting or causing harm to someone, that kind of negative energy will inevitably return to you.
- "You will reap what you sow" — the Law of Cause and Effect — is the recognized universal spiritual law. Karma means you will not get away with it. All negative deeds against others have to be experienced for the purpose of "continuous spiritual refinement."
- Selfishness, abuse of power and systematic harassment of others are two of the most karmic actions. Horrific karma awaits those whose task it was to protect society but themselves willfully abused their power, indulged in willful transgressions and caused harm and injury to others.
- You will NOT be excused for your evil behavior by claiming that you were just obeying orders.
- Cruelty – mental or physical against humans or animals – is highly karmic and is never justified.
- Those who consistently abused and harassed others will have to face their victims in the afterlife to ask for forgiveness. After the severest retribution, the transgressors will have to apologize and seek forgiveness by the victims before they are allowed to make any progress.

- Those who on earth are deeply caught in very strong addictions — drugs, alcohol, gambling, tobacco, or overindulgence in sex — can get caught on the astral level trying to satisfy them.
- A WARNING: Some hallucinogenic drugs have the potency to lift the duplicate out of the physical body. Seen by entities from the afterlife, drug takers "… have pathetic looks as if they had no soul … they are vacant behind the eyes. When out of the body, other lower entities try to enter the drug-taker's body — then you have possession."
- Deathbed conversion? We have been and we are repeatedly being informed by Higher Sources that immediately after we die our vibrations do not change — not even if one repents shortly before death. We take with us the accumulated vibrations (spirituality) we gained or lost during our whole lifetime on earth. Baptism as repentance is absolutely meaningless as a way of getting "a better deal" immediately after death.
- If you helped just one person to attain the true knowledge you would have justified your existence on earth — Silver Birch.
- Not everybody has to "reincarnate."
- You do not come into this world to have a dream run — without pain, suffering, without problems. The more varied your experience, the more learning from many mistakes, the more valuable your lifetime.
- Many of you will be cheated, maligned, unfairly harassed … but justice will be done… not in your world, maybe, but certainly in the world to come. The universal laws operate whether or not you are aware of them.
- There are some inherent dangers in communicating with entities from the afterlife. Those from the afterlife can sometimes read our minds and can put thoughts and ideas into our minds. Lower, mischievous entities can put negative thoughts and ideas and the positive more enlightened entities assist us with positive thoughts and ideas. A great deal is left to the exercise of free will.
- We are at liberty to call the powerful protectors from the afterlife to assist us in coping with our everyday problems, but they will not make decisions for us.
- Materialists and others spend too much time worrying about their last ten or twenty years on earth and do not spend a tiny fraction of their time thinking what's going to happen to them in the next ten, twenty thousand years, fifty thousand years … and much, very much longer.
- What will happen to a person who suicides will depend on a number of things. Motivation is always very important. For example, there will be a big difference if one commits suicide because of inevitable death and one who suicides to avoid responsibilities. Those who take their own

lives to avoid problems and responsibilities are likely to increase their problems and responsibilities in the afterlife.
- Consistent with the Law of Progress, eventually, even if it takes eons of time, all will progress to the higher spheres.
- Like attracts like in the afterlife. Unlike on the earth plane, those with lower vibrations cannot mix freely with those in the higher spheres.
- Self-responsibility — ultimately, you yourself are responsible for all acts and omissions during your time on the earth plane.
- The kind of life to be lived in the afterlife — the beauty, peace, light and love that await most decent people — is unimaginable.

Whatever our beliefs about the Afterlife, we can ensure a peaceful and enjoyable one by the kindness we display while we're on Earth.

The greatest lie ever told

Bibliography

Albright, W F., *The Biblical Period from Abraham to Ezra,* Harper & Row, 1949
—, *Archaeology and the Religion of Israel,* Westminster John Knox Press, 2006
Alford A F., *The Mystery of the Stones at Baalbek,* The Baldwins Challenge, Eridu Books, 2004
Alley, R B et. al., *Nature,* Abrupt Increase in Greenland Snow Accumulation at the End of the Younger Dryas Event, 1993
Angold, M., *Byzantium,* Phoenix Press, 2002
Angus, S., *Mystery Religions,* Dover, 1925
Aspect, A. et al. *Physical Review Letters* 49 'Experimental test of Bell's inequalities using time-varying analyzers,' 1982
Ayrton, E R., *Proceedings of the Society of Biblical Archaeology,* The Tomb of Thy, 1907
Bacon, E N., *Design of Cities,* Penguin Books, 1967
Bagatti, B., *Excavations in Nazareth,* Franciscan Print, 1969
Baigent, M. Leigh, R. and Lincoln, H., *The Holy Blood and the Holy Grail,* Jonathan Cape, 1996
Barber, M., *The Cathars: Dualist Heretics in Languedoc in the High Middle Ages,* Longman, 2000
Bauval, R and Gilbert, A., *The Orion Mystery: Unlocking the Secrets of the Pyramids ,* Three Rivers Press, 1995
Beard, M et. al., *Religions of Rome:* Volume 1, Cambridge University Press, 1998
Begg, E., *The Cult of the Black Virgin,* Penguin, 1996
Benson, B E., *Journal of Philosophy and Scripture Issue,* Vol 2,, Paul and the Knowledge that Puffs Up: A Taste for Idolatry, 2005
Black. M and VanderKam J C., *The Book of Enoch; or, 1 Enoch,* Brill, 1985
Brandon, S G F., *Religion in Ancient History,* George Allen & Unwin, 1969
Bregman, AJ., *Synesius of Cyrene: Philosopher Bishop,* University of California Press, 1982
Brier, B., *Archaeology,* How to Build a Pyramid, May/June 2007
Bright, J., *A History Of Israel,* 3rd edn., SCM, 1980

Brooke. R and C., *Popular Religion in the Middle Ages: Western Europe 1000–1300,* Thames and Hudson, 1984
Bruce, F F., *The Hittites and The Old Testament,* The Tyndale Press, 1947
Brugsch, H K., *Religion und mythologie der alten Aegypter,* J C Hinrichs, 1888
Bruno, G. Gosselin, E A and Lerner, L S eds., trans., *The Ash Wednesday Supper,* Renaissance Society of America, 2001
Buck, de A., *The Egyptian Coffin Texts, 7 volumes,* Oriental Institute Publications, 1961
Budge, E A W., *An Egyptian Hieroglyphic Dictionary,* Vol. 1, Harrison and Sons, 1920
—, *Egyptian Religion,* Bell Publishing, 1959
—, *The Gods of the Egyptians,* Methuen & Co.,1904
—, *The Book of the dead: the papyrus of Ani in the British Museum,* Dover Publications Inc., 1985
—, *Teaching of Amen-Em-Apt, Son of Kanekh,* Kessinger Publishing, 2003
Burkert, W., *The Orientalising Revolution,* Harvard University Press, 1992
C. Suetonius Tranquillus, *The Lives Of The Twelve Caesars,* , Project Gutenberg EBook, 2006
Calvin, J., *Traité Des Reliques,* Les Editions de Paris-Max Chaleil, 2008
Campanella, T., *The City of the Sun,* Cosimo Classics, 2007
Cantor, N., *The Civilization of the Middle Ages,* Harper Perennial, 1994
Carter, G F., *Earlier Than You Think: A Personal View of Man in America,* Texas A&M University, 1980
Charles, R., *Apocalypse of Baruch,* Kessinger Publishing, 2005
Charlesworth, J H., *Jesus and Archaeology,* William B Eerdmans Publishing Co., , 2006
Cohen, R., *Excavations At Kadesh-Barnea: 1976–1978,* Israel Department of Antiquities, 1980
Collins, A., *From The Ashes Of Angels: The Forbidden Legacy of a Fallen Race,* Bear & Company, 2001
—, *Gods Of Eden: Egypt's Lost Legacy and the Genesis of Civilization,* Bear & Company, 2002
Collins, A and Ogilvie-Herald, C., *Tutankhamun—The Exodus Conspiracy Mystery,* Virgin, 2000
Concetti, G., *Osservatore Romano,* 28 November, 1996
Connelly, J., *Saint Brigid,* www.kildare.ie/local-history/kildare/saint-brigid.htm, 2009
Coogan, M D ed., *The Oxford History of the Biblical World,* Oxford University Press, 2001
Coote, R B and Whitelam, K W., *The Emergence of Early Israel in Historical Perspective (Social World of Biblical Antiquity),* Continuum International Publishing Group, 1987

Copenhaver, B P., *Hermetica: The Greek Corpus Hermeticum and the Latin Asclepius in a New English Translation, with Notes and Introduction,* Cambridge University Press, 1995

Cremo, M A and Thompson, R L., *Forbidden Archeology,* Bhaktivedanta Book Publishing, 1998

Croke, B and Harries, J (eds.), *Religious Conflict in Fourth-Century Rome: A Documentary Study,* Macarthur Press, 1982

Cross, F L ed., *The Oxford Dictionary of the Christian Church,* Tübingen School, Oxford University Press, 2005

Dechend, von, H and de Santillana, G., *Hamlet's Mill: An Essay on Myth and the Frame of Time,* Gambit Incorporated, 1969

Deschner, K., *Kriminalgeschichte des Christentums 1 Die Frühzeit:Die Frühzeit: Von den Ursprüngen im Alten Testament bis zum Tod des hl. Augustinus (430),* Rowohlt Taschenbuch Verlag, 1996

Devereux, P., *Places of Power: Measuring the Secret Energy of Ancient Sites,* Cassell Illustrated, 1999

Diodorus Siculus, *The Library of History,* Loeb Classical Library, 1939

Diogenes Laertius, trans. Yonge, C.D., *The Lives and Opinions of Eminent Philosophers,* Henry G Bohn, 1853

Dobecki, T and Schoch, R., *Geoarchaeology,* Seismic Investigation in the Vicinity of the Great Sphinx of Giza, Egypt, 1992

Douais, C., *L'Inquisition. Ses Origines. Sa Procedure,* Plon-Nourrit, 1906

Dunn, C., *The Giza Power Plant: Technologies of Ancient Egypt ,* Bear and Company, 1998

Eisenbichler, K., *The Cultural Politics of Duke Cosimo I de' Medici,* Ashgate, 2001

Ellerbe, H., *The Dark Side of Christian History,* Morningstar Books, 1995

Ellis, P B., *A Brief History of The Druids.,* Robinson, 2002

Ellis, R., *Thoth, Architect of the Universe ,* Edfu Books, 1997

—, *K2 Quest of the Gods,* Edfu Books 2001

Emery, W B., *Archaic Egypt: Culture and Civilization in Egypt Five Thousand Years Ago,* Penguin, 1974

Eskenazi, T C., *In an Age of Prose: A Literary Approach to Ezra–Nehemiah,* Scholars Press, 1988

Eusebius, *The History of the Church,* Penguin Classics, 1965

Evans, J A S., *The age of Justinian: the circumstances of imperial power,* Routledge, 1996

Evans-Grubbs, J., *Abduction Marriage in Antiquity: A Law of Constantine (CTh IX. 24. I) and Its Social Context,* Society for the Promotion of Roman Studies, 1989

Evans–Wentz, W Y., *The Fairy–Faith in Celtic Countries,* Oxford University Press, 1911

Fantoli, A., *Galileo: For Copernicanism and for the Church*, Vatican Observatory Publications, 1996
Faulkner, R O., *The Ancient Egyptian Pyramid Texts 1910*, Kessinger Publishing, 2004
Favazza, A R., *Bodies Under Siege*, Johns Hopkins University Press, 1996
Fidler, D., *Jesus Christ, Sun of God*, Quest Books, 1993
Finkelstein, I and Piasetzky, E., *Science*, Comments on '14C Dates from Tel Rehov: Iron Age Chronology,Pharaohs and Hebrew Kings', 2003
Finkelstein, I and Silberman, N A., *The Bible Unearthed*, Free Press, 2001
Fisher, D J V., *The Anglo-Saxon Age*, Longman, 1973
Fleming, A., *World Archaeology*, The Myth of the Mother Goddess, 1969
Francino, G., *Maraviglose Dell Alma Citta di Roma*, Girolamo Francino, 1588
Fraser, P M., *Ptolemaic Alexandria*. Volume I of III, Oxford University Press, 1972
Frassetto, M ed., *Heresy and the Persecuting Society in the Middle Ages: Essays on the Work of R.I. Moore*, Brill, 2006
Frazer, J G., *The Golden Bough: A Study in Magic and Religion*, Papermac, 1995
Freke, T and Gandy, P., *Jesus and the Goddess*, Thorsons, 2001
—, *The Jesus Mysteries*, Thorsons, 1999
Fremantle, R., *God and Money: Florence and the Medici in the Renaissance: Including Cosimo I's Uffizi and its Collection*, Casa Editrice Leo S Olschki, 1992
Frere, S S., *Brittannia A History of Roman Britain*, Routledge & Kegan Paul, 1967
Gardner, L., *Bloodline of the Holy Grail: The Hidden Lineage of Jesus Revealed*, Element Books, 1996
Gaus, A., *The Unvarnished New Testament*, Phanes Press, 1991
Gauvin, M J., *Did Jesus Christ Really Live?*, Peter Eckler Pub. Co, 1925
Gibbon, E., *The History of the Decline and Fall of the Roman Empire*, Folio Society, The, 1995
Gilbert, A., *Signs in the Sky*, Bantam Press, 2000
Giles, J A., *Hebrew and Christian Records*, BiblioBazaar, 2009
Goneim, Z., *The Buried Pyramid*, Longmans, Green, 1956
Gorceix, B., *La Bible des Rose-Croix*, PUF, 1998
Grant, M., *The History of Ancient Israel*, Orion Publishing Group, 2002
Graves, R., *The Greek Myths: Complete Edition*, Penguin, 1993
—, *The White Goddess: A Historical Grammar of Poetic Myth*, Faber and Faber, 1999
Grimal, N., *A History of Ancient Egypt*, Wiley-Blackwell, 1994
Hadas-lebel, M., *Flavius Josephus Eyewitness to Rome's first-century conquest of Judea*, Simon and Schuster, 2001
Hancock, G and Bauval, R., *Talisman*, Michael Joseph, 2004
—, *The Message of the Sphinx*, Crown Publishers, 1996

Hankins, J., *Journal of the Warburg and Courtauld Institutes Vol 53*, Cosimo de' Medici and the 'Platonic Academy', 1990
Hari, R., *New Kingdom Amarna Period: the Great Hymn to Aten*, Brill, 1985
Harnam, D., *The Real Moses and His God*, Jahkhepri, 2007
Harper, RF., *The Code of Hammurabi King of Babylon*, University Press of the Pacific, 2002
Hawass, Z., *The Pyramids of Ancient Egypt*, Carnegie Museum of Natural History, 1990
Headley, J M., *Tommaso Campanella and the Transformation of the World*, Princeton University Press, 1997
Helms, R M., *Who Wrote The Gospels*, Millennium Press, 1997
Hengel, M., *Jews, Greeks and Barbarians*, SCM Press, 1980
Herodotus, Marincola, J M ed. De Selincourt, A trans., *Herodotus: The Histories*, Penguin Classics, 1996
Hibbert, C., *The House of Medici: Its Rise and Fall*, Penguin, 2001
Hoffman., M A, *Egypt Before the Pharaohs*, Alfred A. Knopf Inc, 1984
Hoffman, R J., *Celsus on the True Doctrine*, Oxford University Press, 1987
Hogan, J., *Nature*, Quantum trick may multiply CD capacity, 2004
Hoover, R eds. Copan, P, Craig, W L, Lüdemann, G and Tacelli, RK., *Jesus' Resurrection: Fact of Figment? A Debate Between William Lane Craig and Gerd Lüdemann*, InterVarsity Press, 2000
Hussein, F and Harris, J E., *Fifth International Congress of Eryptology*, Abstract Papers, 1988
Hutton, R., *The Pagan Religions of the Ancient British Isles*, Oxford, 1991
Ibach, R D Jr., *Archaeological Survey of the Hesban Region: Catalogue of Sites and Characterization of Periods*, O S La Bianca ed., Andrews University Press, 1987
Jaeger, C S., *The Origins of Courtliness: Civilizing Trends and the Formation of Courtly Ideals 939-1210*, University of Pennsylvania Press, 1985
John Paul II, Pope, *Bild Zeitung*, Das Leben nach dem Tod, 1998
Johnson, P., *The Renaissance*, Phoenix Press, 2001
Jones, B W., *The Emperor Domitian*, Routledge, 1992
Jones, H L., *The Geography of* Strabo Vol VI, Book 14, William Heinemann, 1960
Josephus, F., *Antiquities of the Jews*, Project Gutenberg EBook, 2001
Josephus, F tr Whiston, W et. al., *The Works of Flavius Josephus*, John E. Beardsley, 1895
Julius Caesar author, Edwards, H J trans., *Caesar, I, The Gallic War*, Loeb Classical Library, 1917
Julius Firmicus Maternus, *The Error of Pagan Religions*, Paulist Press, 1970
Justin Martyr and Bullock K O., *The Writings of Justin Martyr*, Broadman & Holman Publishers, 1999

Kasser, R et. al. eds., *The Gospel of Judas*, National Geographic, 2008
Kenyon, K M., *Digging Up Jericho*, Ernest Benn, 1957
—, *Archaeology in the Holy Land*, Ernest Benn, 1960
Kingsland, W., *The Gnosis*, Phanes Press, 1937
Kingsley, P., *Ancient Philosophy, Mystery and Magic*, Oxford University Press, 1995
Knight, C and Butler, A., *Civilization One*, Watkins Publishing, 2004
Knight, C and Lomas, R., *Uriel's Machine*, Century Books, 1999
Knight, P., *Ancient Stones of Dorset*, Power Publications, 1996
Kosmin, BA & Keysar, A. "*American Religious Identification Survey 2008*", Trinity College, Hartford, Connnecticut, 2008
Lane-Fox, R., *Pagans and Christians*, Penguin Books, 1986
Latner, H., *The Everything Jewish Wedding Book: The complete guide to planning the ceremony and celebration-from traditional to contemporary-for the most important day of your life*, Adams Media Corporation, 1997
Le Roy Ladurie, E. ed., *Autour de Montaillou - un village occitan; histoire et religiosité d'une communauté villageoise au Moyen Âge*, L'Hydre, 2001
Lee, T E., *Anthropological Journal of Canada* , Canada's National Disgrace, 1964
Lehner, M and Hopkins, R., *Secrets of Lost Empires*, Pyramid, BBC, 1992
Lemche, N P., *The Old Testament: Between Theology and History*, John Knox Press, 2009
Levine, E., *Shofar: An Interdisciplinary Journal of Jewish Studies*, How the Bible Became a Book: Textualization in Ancient Israel, 2006
Lévy, S and O., *The Pentateuch According to Rashi, Exodus*, Fondation Samuel et Odette Levy, 1990
Lietzmann H., *The History of the Early CHurch*, Lutterworth Press, 1961
—, *The History of the Early Church Vol 3*, Lutterworth Press, 1961
Liguori, A., *The Glories of Mary*, Liguori Publications , 2000
Lomas, R., *The Invisible College*, Hodder Headline, 2002
Long, B., *Planting and Reaping Albright: Politics, Ideology, and Interpreting the Bible*, Pennsylvania State University Press, 1997
Luckenbill, D D., *The Annals Of Sennacherib*, University of Chicago Press, 1924
Lüdemann, G, *Heretics*, SCM Press, 1995
—, quoted in Sanders, E P ed. , *The Shaping of Christianity in the Second and Third Century*, The Successors of Pre–70 Jerusalem Christianity: a critical evaluation of the Pella–tradition, SCM, 1980
Macalister, R A S ed. and tr., *Lebor Gabála Érenn: Book of the Taking of Ireland Part 1-5*, Irish Texts Society, 1941
Mack, B L., *The Lost Gospel*, Element Books, 1993
MacMullen, R., *Enemies of the Roman Order*, Oxford University Press, 1966

Mahé, J–P., *Hermès en Haute Egypte: Le fragment du discours parfait et les définitions hermetiques armeniennes*, Peeters Publishers, 1982
Mant, R., *History of the Church of Ireland*, John W Parker, 1840
Marrou, H-I and Momigliano, A ed., *The Conflict of Paganism and Christianity in the Fourth Century*, Clarendon Press, 1963
Massey, G A., *Ancient Egypt - The Light of the World: A Work of Reclamation and Restitution in Twelve Books*, NuVision Publications, 2008
—, *Book of the Beginnings, Part 1*, Kessinger Publishing, LLC, 2002
—, *Book of The Beginnings Vol 2*, Black Classic Press, 1995
Mathews, SA., *History of New Testament Times in Palestine, 175 B.C.-70 A.D.*, Macmillan, 1908
Mathieu, B., *Le Bulletin de l'Institut français d'archéologie orientale* , 'Chantiers archéologiques et programmes de recherche. Etudes égyptologiques et papyrologiques. 1. Abou Rawash' , 2000
Matthews, J F, Binns J W ed., *"The Letters of Symmachus" in Latin Literature of the Fourth Century*, Routledge and Kegan Paul, 1974
Maxwell Miller, J., *The Biblical Archaeologist*, Old Testament History and Archaeology, 1987
Mc Carthy, DP., *Celtica 24*, On the shape of the Insular tonsure, School of Celtic Studies, 2003
Mead, G R S., *Fragments of a Faith Forgotten*, Theosophical Publishing Society, 1906
Metzger, B M., *The Canon of the New Testamanent*, Oxford University Press, 1987
Moody, R and Perry, P., *Reunions: Visionary Encounters With Departed Loved Ones*, Ivy Books, 1994
—, *Reunited: How to Meet Loved Ones Again Who Seem Lost to Death*, Rider & Co, 2006
Moran, W L., *The Armana Letters*, John Hopkins University Press, 1992
Muchembled, R., *A history of the devil: from the middle ages to the present*, Polity Press, 2003
Na'aman, N., *Bulletin of the American School of Oriental Research*, The Contribution of the Amarna Letters to the Debate on Jerusalem's Political Position in the Tenth Century B.C.E., 1996
Nauta, L., *In Defense of Common Sense: Lorenzo Valla's Humanist Critique of Scholastic Philosophy*, Harvard University Press, 2009
Naville, E., *The Times*, 1914
Newberry, P E., *The Journal of Egyptian Archaeology*, Vol. 15, No. 1/2, 'The Shepherd's Crook and the So-Called "Flail" or "Scourge" of Osiris', Egypt Exploration Society, May 1929
Nicholson, P and Shaw, I., *The British Museum Dictionary of Ancient Egypt*, British Museum Press, 1997

Norman, A F trans., *Libanius: Selected Works,* Loeb Classical Works, 1977
Norwich, J J., *The Normans in the South, 1016-1130,* Longmans, 1967
Noth, M., *The Deuteronomistic History,* Sheffield Academic Pr, 2002
Oren, Eliezer D., *Gerar,* The Anchor Bible Dictionary 2, Doubleday, 1992
Origen, *Origen Against Celsus,* Kessinger Publishing, 2004
Otto, W F., *Dionysos Myth and Cult,* Spring Publications, 1965
Owen, R., *Times,* Vatican plots against 'Da Vinci Code', 2005
Pagels, E., *The Gnostic Gospels,* Vintage Books, 1979
—, *The Gnostic Paul,* Trinity Press International, 1975
—, *The Origin of Satan: How Christians Demonized Jews, Pagans, and Heretics,* Vintage, 1996
Peterson, J H., *John Dee's five books of mystery: original sourcebook of Enochian magic,* Weiser Books, 2008
Petrie W M F., *Tell el–Amarna,* London, 1894
—, *The Pyramids and Temples of Gizeh,* Field and Tuer, 1883
—,, *Researches in Sinai*, John Murray, 1906
Phillips, G., *The Search for the Grail,* Century, 1995
Philo Judeaus, *De vita contemplativa,* Loeb Classical Library, 1941
Pinkham, M A., *Guardians Of The Holy Grail: The Knights Templar, John The Baptist, And The Water of Life,* Adventures Unlimited Press, 2005
Pinot, N., *Vaincre,* 'An Interview with Pierre Pantard de Saint–Clair, 1989
Pirie, V., *The Triple Crown,* G P Putnam's Sons, 1936
Plutarch, *Plutarch's Lives,* Vol. VII, 'Alexander', Loeb Classical Library, 1928
Porphyry, *Against Christians,* www.ccel.org/ccel/pearse/morefathers/files/porphyry_against_christians_02_fragments.htm, 2004
Pritchard, J B and Hyatt, J P eds., *The Bible in Modern Scholarship,* Culture and History, Abingdon Press, 1966
Radin, D., *Entangled Minds,* Paraview Pocket Books, 2006
Ralls, K., *The Templars & the Grail: Knights of the Quest,* Quest Books, 2003
Rawson, E., *Cicero: A Portrait,* Duckworth Publishers, 2009
Redford, D B., *Egypt, Canaan, and Israel in Ancient Times,* Princeton University Press, 1993
Richardson, A and Bowden, J eds., *The Westminster Dictionary of Christian Theology,* Westminster John Knox Press, 1983
Richardson, R., *Gnosis,* The Priory of Sion Hoax, 1999
Robinson, J M., *The Nag Hammadi Library,* Harper One, 1990
Rolleston, T W., *Myths And Legends Of The Celtic Race,* George G Harrap, 1911
Rowe, F., *The Lord's My Shpeherd, I'll Not Want,* Scottish Psalter, 1650
Russell, J C., *Late Ancient and Medieval Population,* American Philosophical Society, 1958

Sabbah, M and Sabbah, R., *Secrets of the Exodus,* Thorsons, 2000
Sader, H. ed., *Baalbek 1898-1998: Rediscovery of the Ruins,* Steiner, 1998
Sallustius, *Concerning the Gods and the Universe,* Cambridge University Press, 1984
Scarre, C., *Chronicle of the Roman Emperors: the reign-by-reign record of the rulers of Imperial Rome,* Thames & Hudson, 1995
Schäfer, P., *The History of the Jews in the Greco-Roman World,* Routledge, 2003
Schaff, P. Menzies, A ed. *Ante–Nicene Fathers,* Book III, T&T Clark, 1893
Schaff, P., *Nicene and Post–Nicene Fathers Series 2, Volume 3, Theodoret, Jerome, Gennadius, Rufinus, Jerome: The Principal Works of St. Jerome,* Cosimo, 2007
Schoch, R M and McNally, R A., *Voices of the Rocks ,* Harmony Books, 1999
Schoch, R M and West, J A., *Geological Society of America abstracts,* 'Redating the Great Sphinx of Giza, Egypt', American Association for the Advancement of Science, 1991
Scholem, G., *Jewish Gnosticism, Merkabah Mysticism, and Talmudic Tradition,* The Jewish Theological Seminary of America, 1965
Schwaller de Lubicz, R A., *Sacred Science,* Inner Traditions, 1982
—, *The Temple in Man,* Inner Traditions Bear and Company, 1982
Schweitzer, A., *The Quest of the Historical Jesus,* Augsburg Fortress Publishers, 2001
Scott, J., *An Early History of Glastonbury,* Boydell Press, 1981
Seidel, M and Seidel A G., *Das Grab der Nacht: Kunst und Geschichte eines Beamtengrabes der 18. Dynastie in Theben–West,* Das Schöne Fest vom Wüstental, Zabern, 1991
Selim Hassan, *Excavations at Giza* Vol 6 Part 1, Government Printing Office, 1933
Skinner, J., *The Confession of Saint Patrick and Letter to Coroticus,* Image, 1998
Smallwood, E M., *Classical Philology ,* 'Domitian's attitude towards the Jews and Judaism', 1956
Smith, J L., *Patrick of Ireland Not a Romanist,* Associated Printing Co, 1924
Spence, L., *The Myths of Mexico and Peru,* Dover Publications, 1995
Spencer, C., *Prince Rupert,* Wiedenfeld and Nicholoson, 2007
St Augustine, Bettenson, H tr., *City of God,* Penguin, 1972
Stanton, G., *Gospel Truth,* Harper Collins, 1995
Stecchini, L C., *A History of Measures,* www.metrum.org/measures, 1960
Stoddard, J L., *Stoddard's Lectures — Ireland,* Geo L Schuman & Co, 1909
Stoyanov, Y., *The Hidden Tradition in Europe,* Penguin, 1994
Strange, J., *Anchor Bible Dictionary,* Nazareth, Doubleday, 1992
Strohmeier, J and Westbrook, P., *Divine Harmony: The Life and Teachings of Pythagoras,* Berkeley Hills Books, 2003
Stuller, J., *Smithsonian,* 'Cleanliness has only recently become a virtue', 1991
Tacitus, *The Annals of Imperial Rome,* Penguin Classics, 1956

Tacitus and Hadas, M ed., *The Annals & The Histories, Annals Book 15,* Modern Library, 2003
Tappy, R E., *The Archaeology of Israelite Samaria,* Scholars Press, 1992
Taylor, T trans., *Iamblichus: Life of Pythagoras,* Kessinger Publishing, 1998
Teeter, E and Brewer, D J., *Egypt and the Egyptians,* 'Religion in the Lives of the Ancients', Cambridge University Press, 2002
The Telegraph, 'Most people believe in life after death, study finds',13 Apr 2009
Tertullian, *Apologeticum, 50,* Loeb Classical Library, 1931
Thompson, E A., *Saint Germanus of Auxerre and the End of Roman Britain,* Boydell Press, 1988
Turcan, R., *Cults of the Roman Empire,* Blackwell, 1996
Ucko, P J., *Anthropomorphic Figurines of Predynastic Egypt and Neolithic Crete,* A. Szmidla, 1968
Ulansey, D., *The Origins of the Mithraic Mysteries: Cosmology and Salvation in the Ancient World,* OUP USA, 1991
Van den Heuvel, P., *The Vatican Secret Archives,* VDH Boooks, 2009
Van Seters, J., *Abraham in History and Tradition,* Yale University Press, 1987
Walker, G S M., *Letters of Columbanus,* CELT: Corpus of Electronic Texts, 2008
Wallis, R T., *Neoplatonism and Gnosticism,* State University of New York Press, 1992
Walther, P et al. *Nature* 429, 'De Broglie wavelength of a non-local four-photon state', 2004
Weinfeld, M., *Anchor Bible 5,* Deuteronomy, Book of, Doubleday, 1991
Wells, G A., *Did Jesus Exist?,* Pemberton Publishing Company, 1975
Wheless, J., *Forgery in Christianity: A Documented Record of the Foundations of the Christian Religion,* Kessinger Publishing, LLC, 1992
Wightman, G J., *Bulletin of the American School of Oriental Research,* The Myth of Solomon, 1990
Williams, R., *Conspiracy Theories Don't Match Up to the Truth of the Gospel,* Easter Address, www.archbishopofcanterbury.org/671?q=Easter+2006, 2006
Willoughby, H R., *Pagan Regeneration,* University of Chicago Press, 1929
Wilson, I., *Jesus, The Evidence,* Weidenfeld and Nicholson, 1984
Wilson, K A., *The Campaign of Pharaoh Shoshenq I into Palestine,* Mohr Siebeck, 2005
Wright, C., *Deuteronomy New International Bible Commentary,* Hendrickson, 1996
Yaqut, Jwaideh W, ed./trans., *The Introductory Chapters of Yaqut Mu'Jam Al-Buldan,* Brill, 1988
Yates, F A., *The Rosicrucian Enlightenment,* Routledge & Kegan Paul , 1972
Zammit, V J., *A Lawyer Presents the Case for the Afterlife,* Gammell Pty Ltd, 2006

Index

Aaron, 36
Abraham, 3-6, 7, 11, 13-17, 20-24
 becomes Father of Jews, 65, 75
 encoding of Egyptian link, 25-27, 29-30, 32, 34
 Exodus from Babylon, 82
 hiding religious message, 95
 Pools of, 29-30
Abu Roash, 112
Abydos, 101, 109, 116, 118, 136
 and Osiris Mysteries, 188
 decline in influence, 208
Académie Française, 413
Acts of the Apostles, 257
Adam and Eve, 145, 150, 156
Adam Weishaupt, 422
Adonay
 first altars established, 26-27
 shared God, 62, 70-73
 changed to Yahweh, 77, 79, 83
 link to Aten, 165, 168
Adonis, 188, 192
 Mystery cult of Galilee, 214
 in Tarsus, 262
 see Bethlehem
Aesath, 34

Agbar the Great, 30
Agrippa, 235
Ahab, 69
Ahaz, 63
Aidan, 349
Akenaten, 19, 133, 135-138, 140-143
 appearance and lifestyle, 145-149, 157-158
 exile after death of, 161-163, 167
 see Adam and Eve
 androgenous nature of god, 191
 Utopian city-state, 392
Akhet-Aten, 143
 reburial of Akenaten, 146
 abandonment of, 161-162, 164, 166-167, 189
Akkadian, 10, 11
Albigensians, 365
Alexander, 234
 Jannaeus, 89
 the Great, 84
  Ra initiation, 199
  religious legacy, 207
  influence on Robespierre, 430
Alexandria, 84, 87
 Bishop of, 8
 Library of, 8, 201

INDEX

see Clement of
intellectual and religious influence, 207-210
annexation Temple of Bacchus, 330
dark shadow of Christianity, 332-334
Hermetica, 383
Allah, 211
Amarna Letters, 167
Ambrosius, 341
Amen, 97, 100
Amenhotep, 132
Amenhotep II, 129
Tomb of, 146
Amenhotep III, 80
Amenhotep IV, 132-135
America, 60
building special cities, 385
Rosicrucian vision of, 389
secret organisations, 393
Utopian, 398
American Revolution, 417
influence of Freemasons, 422-423
unlike French, 428
Americans, King of the, 424
Ammonius, 332
Amon, 97, 100
Amorite, 39
migration, 14-15
Amun, 81, 97
in Thebes, 100-101
creation story, 104
Hatshepsut and, 128-130, 132, 135-138, 142-143
decline of, 208
Anatolia, 155
Andreæ, Johann, 392
angels, 105
Anglesey, 339
Annu, 99, 141
Antiochus Epiphanes, 87
Antipater, 91
Antonines, 310
Antoninus Pius, 291
Anthony, Saint 307
Apollo, 314
aspect of Ra, 359
Apostle, 257, 260
Apostolic Succession, 340, 343
Apuleius, 200, 202

Arad, 39
Aram, 63
Aramaic, 209
Archaic Period, 120
Arians, 334
Arianism, 320-322, 342
Aristotle, 311, 321
and Hypatia, 333
Arius, 308, 320
Ark of the Covenant, 36,
lost, 243
Arnaud, 252
Aristobulus, 86
Aristotle, 85-86,
and Eleusian Mysteries, 190
and Druids, 193
and Alexander, 199-200
heretical works, 376
Bodleian Library, 380
Church approval, 382-384
opposition by Francis Bacon, 388-390
Artemis, 241
Arthurian legends, 338
Asclepius, 280
Ficino translation, 383
enlightenment through self-experience, 385
Ashmole, Elias, 405
Assyria, 63-64, 77-78
attack on Egypt, 189
Assyrian, 26-27
destruction of Israel, 63-64
Judean autonomy, 69-71
decline, 73, 75
Rayi, 156
see Watchers
astronomy, 189
Aswan, 138
Aten, 80
Trinity, 106
solar manifestation, 130-132
and Akhenaten, 133-143
after death of Akhenaten, 161-168,
and Ra, 190-191,
depicted as sun's rays, 197
city dedicated to, 392
see Lugh Lamfada
Atenism, 164-167
Aten-Tjehen, 132

486

Atheists, 438
Attis, 188
  in Tarsus, 262
  and Claudius, 298
Atum, 99-100, 105-106
Atum-Ra, 99, 106, 136, 140
Augustine, 265
  sent to Britain, 347-349
Augustus, 262-263
  initiated at Eleusis, 289
  civilisation peak, 309
Avebury, 196
axis mundi. See St Paul's
Ay, 162- 168

Baal, 192
Ba'albek, 110
Babylon, 4, 77, 80, 82-83
Babylonian, 77
Babylonians, 32, 67
Bacchus, 188
  in Tarsus, 262
  Julius Cæsar revokes ban on, 289
  followers at hands of Christian mob, 330
Bacon, Francis, 388
  American colonies, 397
  New Atlantis, 404
  Royal Society, 413
barque of Isis. *See* Isis
Bast, 99
Bartholomew's Day Massacre, 394
Bede, 349
Bedouin, 36, 38
Beersheba, 26
Behdet, 138-139
Benben, 105-106, 140
Benjamin,
  tribe of, 61, 67, 82
Bennu, 140
Bent and Red, 28
Bernard of Clairvaux, 252-253
  morals of Cathars, 367
Benjamin Franklin, 423-424
Bernini, Gian Lorenzo, 407-409, 432
Bethel, 26, 66, 73-74
Bethlehem, 84
  sanctuary to Adonis, 214

Beautiful Feast of the Desert Valleys, 279
Béziers, 252
Bible, 303
Bicheris, 112
Black Madonna, 253
Boat of Paris, 431
Bodleian Library, 380
Bogomils, 365-366, 368
  Dualism, 385
Boniface, 352
Bonnie Prince Charlie, 420
Boyle, Robert 151, 404
book burning, 331
  edicts of Theodosius, 334
Book of Judges, 45
Book of the Dead, 279
Book of the Heavenly Luminaries, 151
  see Book of Enoch
Book of Revelation of St John, 212
Brigid, 356
Bruce, James, 151
Bruno Giordano, 384, 389
Buddha, 245

Cadwaladr, King of Gwynedd, 353
Cagliostro, 425-427
  Paris pyramid plan, 429
  and Napoleon, 431
Cain, 150
Calvin, John, 242
Calvinist, 393
Cambridge Colleges, 380, 387-388
Camiño de Santiago, 253
Campanella, Tommaso, 390
  Richelieu's patronage, 406-407
  Louis XIV, 414
  American Revolution, 423
  Paris, 432
Canaan, 13, 25, 33, 36- 39, 41-44
  divided kingdoms of, 61, 67
  Josiah's control, 73, 79
  arrival of Aten priests, 165
Canaanites, 25, 32-34
Canis Major, 30
  Minor, 30
Capernaum, 84
Capernicum, 216
Carolus Magnus. See Charlemagne

487

INDEX

Catal Huyuk, 10
Cathars, 9, 251-252, 254
  Pope Joan as spiritual ancestor, 355
  early evidence of, 365-369
  Normans, 373-374
  ban on written New Testament, 378
  Dualism, 385
  healers, 392
  Luther and, 394
Catholic League, 397
Celestine, 340
Celsus, 230
  Mithraism and Christianity, 263
  Asclepsius v Jesus, 280
  Christians' mutual scorn, 303, 305-306
Celtic Christians, 153, 156, 193
Celts, 338
  opposition to Roman Church, 340
  rule in Western Europe, 343
  maintain power in Britain, 346-347
  resistance post Synod of Whitby, 353
Champs Elysées, 431
Charlemagne, 324
  hopes of Roman Church, 344-345
  Celtic dispute of successors, 354
Charles I, 404
Charles II, 405
Chemical Wedding, The, 392
Chief Astronomer, 29
Chi-Rho, 315
Christianity, 29
  allegorical teachings, 101, 104
  Egyptian roots, 122
  Gnosis and Aten link, 134, 136-137
  Pyramid Texts and, 185, 188
  misunderstood myth of, 192-193
  Roman slaves and, 206, 284
  Glastonbury fiction, 338
  conversions under duress, 363
  decline in numbers, 435
  individual sects, 435
  social benefit, 440
    church as provider, 440
    faith-based income tax, 440
Christians, 60, 150, 154
  see Roman Christians
  see Celtic Christians
Christian Church,
  criticism of Mysteries, 210, 213

Chosen People, 82
Cicero, 262
  promotion of Mysteries, 289
City of the Sun, 407
  Paris and London, 414-415
  Paris completed, 432
Civil War, 404
  effect on scientific learning, 406
  turmoil after, 413
Civitas Solis, 392
Claudius, Emperor, 234
  fortification of Jerusalem, 281
Clement V, Pope, 252
Clement of Alexandria, 8
  Gnostic, 307
Cleopatra, 207
Columba, 350, 353
Columbanus, 350-352
Comenius. *See* Komensky
Commandments
  Egyptian source, 270
  ignored by Christians, 328
Constantine, 60
  population at time of, 154
  biographer of, 308
  control of Empire, 309
  as leader, 311-317
  Rome as Christian capital, 319-322
  pagan persecution post, 327-329
  unenforceable edits of, 338
Constantinople, 320, 322-324
Copernicus, 386
  influence on Bruno and Galileo, 389-390
Coptic, 151
Corpus Hermeticum, 383
Cosmos, 97
Council of Troyes, 254
Council of Nicæa, 315, 320
Crata Repoa, 421
Creator, 97-99, 101-105, 107
Cromwell, Oliver, 405, 410, 413
Crotona, 189
Cybele, 241
Cyngen, 353-355
Cyprian, 290, 293, 295
Cyril, Patriarch of Alexandria, 332-333
Cyrus, 81

488

Dagon, 214
Dahshur, 28, 113
Daniel, 86
Danu, 360
David, 17, 61, 63, 65-66, 68, 75, 88-89
David, 233, 237
    Jewish nostalgia, 211-212,
    New Testament lineage, 214
    irrelevance of lineage, 225
Da Vinci Code, The, 239-242, 249
Dead Sea Scrolls, 79, 150- 152, 157
Decius, 292- 294, 295
Dee, John, 387
Demeter, 190- 192
    Black Madonnas, 241, 246-247
Derinkuyu, 154
Deuteronomy, 73, 75
Didcot. *See* Grail
Dionysus, 46, 132, 188
    link to Serapis, 209, 217
    Mysteries, 247
        prohibition, 289
        resurge in popularity, 298
        in the Balkans, 363
Disciples, 257
Divine Father, 162-163, 165, 168
    see Ay
Djedefre, 112
Domitian, 293, 295, 298
Dream Stele, 129
Druids, 97, 152, 186, 193- 195, 197-198
    Colleges, 195
    and Templar beliefs, 251
    support of Gnostic Christianity, 338-340
    spiritual interest, 341
    development of Celtic Church, 350-351
    Brigid, St, 356
    Patrick, St, 358
    Sons of Light, 393
Dualists, 386
Duat, 99
Dynastic period, 98

Easter, 210
    calculation of, 351, 353

Eastern church, 31
Edessa, 29
Edom, 39, 80
Egyptian, 79
    Council of Antiquities, 108
    priesthood, 186
    Rite, 427-428
        Napoleon, 431
Egyptian Book of the Dead, 393
Egyptologists, 96, 98, 106-121, 123,125
Elephantine, 100, 138-139
Eleusis, 190, 202, 204
    Mystery of Serapis, 209
    destruction of Temple, 334
Eleusian Mystery, 84, 188, 190, 192
El, 157
Elijah, 31, 252
Elizabeth I, 387, 390
Elohim, 156- 159
Ennead, 101, 104-105
Enoch, 105, 149- 153, 155-159
    Book of, 149- 153, 155, 157
    see Bruce
Ephesus, 321
Eros, 246
Essenes, 149-150, 152-153, 155
    Damascus and, 272
Eternal God, 32
Ethiopia, 151
Euclid, 376-387
Eunapius, 329
Eusebius, 210
    criticism of Jews, 230
    forgery by, 236
    false description of Domitian, 293
    number of martyrs, 296
    biographer of Constantine, 308
    voice of God, 312
    conversion of Constantine, 314
    baptism of Constantine, 316
    Arian heretic, 320-321
Exodus, 24
    dating of, 33
    Moses, 35-36
    evidence of Sinai occupation, 38-39
    Joshua's conquest, 41-44, 47
    Laws of Moses, 73, 75
    Atenist priests, 163, 167-168
Eye,

of Horus, 102
of Ra, 102
Ezra, 78, 82

Fergal. *See* Virgil
Ficino, Marsilio, 382
Flood, 150, 153
Fludd, Robert, 389
France,
  King of, 151
Frederick of the Rhine-Palatinate, 388
Freemasonry,
  links with Royal Society, 151
  improvement of all mankind, 385
  sub-rosa network, 393
  emergence of, 401-404
  Wren, 407
  Invisible College, 411
  Royal Society, 413-414
  European developments of, 419-424
  high ideals of, 425-427, 430-431
  God of Light, 430
French Revolution
  French Grand Master, 426, 428-429

Galilee, 25, 84, 89, 91
  political and religious influences, 214, 216
Galileo, 390
  Utopian dream, 397
Garden of Eden, 10, 24
Garibaldi, 432
Gematria, 198, 212
Genesis, 75, 150, 156
Gentiles, 84, 89
Geologists, 28
Geometer, The. *See* Virgil
George I, 418
George III, 422
Germanus, 341, 358
Germany, 59
Giza, 9
  plan of Orion's Belt, 27-28, 31, 253
  Heliopolis and, 99, 101, 106
  dating Great Pyramids, 109, 113-115, 118-120, 122
  uncovering of Sphinx, 133-134, 136, 141

Hall of Records and, 147
Ra priesthood and, 149
Glastonbury, 338
Gnosis, 134
Gnostics
  Corpus Hermeticum, 383
  improvement of mankind, 385-386
  Sons of Light, 393
Gnosticism, 134,
  edicts to end, 331-334
Gnostic Jews, 242
God of Light, 429
Goddess of Reason, 429
Goebbels, 59
Golden Ass, 202
Gospel of Judas, 220-222
Gospel of Luke, 132
Gospel of Mark, 185
Gospels,
  authenticity, 219- 229
  mathematical encoding, 212-213
Grail, 338
Great Fire of London, 415
Great Pyramids, 9, 27, 106, 109-113, 115, 118-119, 196
  of Khufu, 197
Great Sphinx, 133-134
Greek Empire, 211
Guiscard, Robert, 374
Gutenberg, 377

Haak, Theodore, 404
Hadrian, 262-263
  refusal to punish Christians, 291
Hall of Records, 141, 147
Harnesses, 33
Hanoverian dynasty, 420
Harran, 82
Hartlib, Samuel, 404
Hasmodean, 45
  fall of Greek Empire, 211
Hasmonean, 74, 88-91
Hatshepsut, 128-129, 161
Hawking, Stephen, 438, 441
Head of the Treasury, 418
Hebrew, 35-36
  language source, 75, 79
  epithets for God, 103

Massai, 163-165, 167
  decline in language use, 209
Hebron, 26, 66
Heh, 35, 80, 164
Helen, 245-246
Helena (Mother of Constantine), 316-319
Heliodorus, 206, 210
Heliopolis, 29
  sanctuary for Judahite priests, 81
  and Primeval Mound, 99-101, 105-106
  Hysos and Ra priesthood, 127-128
  Thutmosis IV and, 130, 132-133
  religion of, 135-136, 138, 141, 188-189, 195, 200-201
  Akenaten and, 147, 158
  decline in influence, 208
  Plato and, 384
  Utopian city-state, 392
Helios, 314
Helios Mysteries, 313
Hell, 208, 217
Hellenised, 84, 87, 89
Henry of Navarre, 394
Hermes, 8
Hermetica, 8
Hermes, 382-384
Hermes Trismegistus, 382
Hermetica, 383-385, 421
Hermippus, 86
Herod, 91
  date of reign, 225
Herodotus, 85
  Valla and, 380
Heshbon, 39
Hetepheres, 111
Hezekiah, 64-65, 71-75, 84
hieratic, 106
hieroglyphs, 97, 100
Historic Axis, 429
Higher Self, 247
  Eusebius, 210
Hittite/s, 43, 165
Holy Blood and the Holy Grail, The, 239, 241-243, 251
Holy Land, 253
Homer, 85
Honorius, 340
Hor-aha, 98

Horemakhet, 102
Horemheb, 166-167
Horus, 99, 101-102, 105
  Hatshepsut and, 128-129, 131
  son of Ra, 136, 141
  Trinity, 192
Hosea, 69
Huguenots, 394
Hyades, 30
Hyksos, 9, 32-33, 36
  New Kingdom Era, 101
  immigration, 127-128
Hymn to Aten, 143
Hypatia, 333

Iamblychus, 213
Illuminati d'Avignon, 421
Illuminati von Bayern, 420
in hoc signo vinces, 314
  see Constantine
Innocenti III, Pope, 252
  see Inquisition
Inns of Court, 416
Inquisition, 367-369, 373-374
  possession of *Bible*, 377
  Valla and, 380
  danger of Hermetic teaching, 384
  invisible organisation, 386
  science and, 389-391
Invisible College, 403-405, 411-415
Iona, 349-350
Ireland, 339, 349-350, 352, 354, 356-359, 361-363
Isis, 360
Inquisition, 252-253
Irenaeus, 229
Isaac, 13
Isis, 99, 101-102, 105
  consort of Osiris, 136
  and Demeter, 190,
  sites dedicated to, 239-241
  Queen of Heaven, 243-245
  and Cistercians, 250, 254-255
  and Serapis, 263
  sailors cutting hair, 267
  barque of, 429
  Boat of, *See* Boat of Paris
Islam, 104, 122

491

INDEX

Israel, 25-27, 31, 33
Israelites, 25-26, 33, 37-45

Jacob, 13, 26, 31, 34
    Ladder, 31
    Staff, 31
Jacobites, 418, 420, 422
James, 257, 259
James I, 388
James II, 417-418
Jamina, 216
Jawbone of an ass, 30
Jefferson, Thomas, 423-424
Jehoiakim, 77
Jehovah, 35, 43
    worship of Jesus, 137
    Messiah sent by, 212
Jeremiah, 77, 80
Jericho, 10, 40, 43-44
Jeroboam, 66-67, 69
Jerusalem, 26
    fall to Babylon, 77-78
    Greek influence, 81-82, 84- 86
    Roman assault, 90-91
    Temple, 14
Jesus, 35
    see Jehovah, 137
    Pagan Mystery stories, 187-188
    Philo and, 206
    origin of sayings, 278
Jezebel, 69
Joan, Pope, 255
John, 224-228, 242-243, 245, 247
    Revelation of, 257, 259
    Celtic Imperial claims, 354-356
John Drury, 404
John Evelyn, 406
John the Baptist
    Importance to Templars and Masons, 419
    Grande Arche and Louvre Pyramid, 432
John VIII, Pope. See Joan, Pope
John Crysostom, 230
John the Baptist, 31
    Orion constellation, 249, 252-255
Jordan, 81, 89
Joseph, 26, 32-34
    link to David, 225
Joseph of Arimathea, 227, 338
Josephus, 236
    Essenes, 272
    bandits and Messiahs, 281
Joshua, 36, 40-45, 88-89
    ben Nun, 40
        Alexandrian Jewish Mystery, 188
    relevance of name, 212, 214
Josiah, 65-66, 68, 72- 75, 77-78, 88-89
Judah, 26, 45
Judahite/s, 71, 136
    see Judean
Judaism, 35, 104, 125
    links to Massai, 164
Judas Maccabeus, 87-88
Jude, 257, 259
Judea, 26, 60
    fall to Babylon, 77-78
    Greek influence, 80-91
    Pagan Mysteries, 189
    after Alexander, 208
    Hellenisation of, 211-212
    Gospels and, 215
Judean, 25- 27, 32, 34, 59, 61, 63- 75, 95
    scribes, 3, 59, 61, 65, 67, 70, 95
Judges, 45
Julian, 320- 322
Julius Cæsar, 194
    and Tarsus, 262
    revokes ban on Mysteries, 289
        subsequent popularity, 298
    title, 309
Julius Firmicus Maternus, 327
Justin Martyr, 229-230
Justinian, Emperor, 240
    Pythagorean, 323
    ban on thinking, 334
Justus of Tiberias, 237

Kabbalah, 29
Kadesh-barnea, 38-39
Kamose, 128
Khafre, 109, 112, 116-119
Khepri, 99
Khnum, 99-100
Khufu, 111-112, 114, 116, 119
king list, 113

King's Chamber, 32
Kiya, coffin and canopic jars, 146
Knights Templar, 9
  Book of Enoch, 151
  and Green Man, 202
  bloodline of Christ, 243
  Priory of Sion, 249-250, 254, 337
  sanctuary for Cathars, 356, 365, 368
  origins of Freemasonry, 403
  Inns of Court, 416
  John the Baptist's Day, 419-421
Komensky, Bishop Jan, 404
Koppen, Frederick von, 421
Kurdistan, 148

Laban, 31
Lafayette, Marquis de, 423
Lake Marenotis, 209
Lake Van, 9- 11
Lamech, 157
Leo, 30-31, 114
Leo IX, 374
Libanius, 330
Library,
  National of Paris, 151
  Bodleian, 151
  see Alexandria
Lightbringer, 135
Lights of Israel, 209
Lindisfarne, 349, 353
Lot, 26
Louis XIV, 391
  see Sun King
Louvre, 407, 430-432
Lucifer, 360
Lugh Lámfada, 197, 250
  Patrick, 358-361
  Michael, 360
  see Celtic Christianity, Lucifer, Lightbringer
Luke, 223, 225-228, 257
Luther, 329, 393

Ma'at, 102, 105
  in building of cities, 140
  and Alexander's capital, 207
Maccabean Revolt, 150, 153

religious intolerance, 281
Machpelah, 66
Madonnas, Black. See Virgins, Black
Magnus Maximus, 341, 353
Maier, 388-398
Malkata, 131-132
Manasseh, 65, 72
Mandaeans, 9
Manetho, 114
Marcion, 273
Marcionites, 334
Mark, 222-229
  list of disciples, 257
  spikenard, 244
Marcus Aurelius, 310-311, 321
Mark Anthony, 89-90
Martyrs, 217
Mary, 192
  Magdalene, 193
    John crucifixion story, 227-228
    as fallen woman, 239-247
    Templars and, 249-251
  of Bethany, 244-245, 247-248
  Virgin, 254
    grave, 321
    Danu, 360
Massai, 163-164
Matthew, 223, 225- 227
  Orion Elijah, 253
  list of disciples, 257
Medici, Cosimo de'
  patronage, 381-382
  reputation, 386
  Egyptian influence in Renaissance, 425
  Catherine de', 394
Medici Academy, 382
Megalithic Yard, 196
  weights and measures, 151
  see Thom, Alexander
Megiddo, 77
Meidum, 111
Mellitus, 347-349
Memphis, 99-100, 127, 129
  religion of, 136, 188
  transfer of government to, 162-163
  decline in influence, 208
Menes, 98
Men-Kau-Ra, 101

Menkaure, 112
  megalithic measure, 197
    see Megalithic Yard
Mercury. *See* Lugh
Merovingian, 243, 251
Meses-ay, 163
  see Massai
Mesopotamia, 63, 67, 146, 148, 157
Mesopotamians, 26
Messiah, 91
  political rôle, 211
  link to Christ, 214-215
Methuselah, 153
Migdol, 38
Milky Way, 29, 31, 253-254
Milvian Bridge, 314
Minoan, 196
mirror-gazing, 266-267
Mithras, 188
  and Christian inner initiates, 217
  rival cult to Christianity, 298-299
  threat to Imperial stability, 313
  Temple demolition, Constantine 319
Mnevis, 136
Mohammed, 35
Mohammedans, 103
Monck, 410-411
Montu, 100
Moody, Raymond, 266
Moray, Robert, 406
Moses, 24, 35-36, 39-40, 43, 46-47, 61, 71, 73, 75
  return of priests from Babylon, 81-82
  inventor of Greek ideas, 86
  abuse of Laws, 89-90
  behind the fiction, 95
  pre-Moses history of Egypt, 104
  Exodus of Atenists, 167
  Egyptian laws, 270-271
  Hermetica, 384
Mount
  Horeb, 73
  Nebo, 40
  Sinai, 73
Muslim, 154
  support of religious tolerance, 211
Mystery, ...ies, 84, 89, 134, 145, 159
  Alexander and, 207
  Bacchus, 289
  city religions, 262-263
  common themes, 187-192,
  export of Egyptian, 198
  famous initiates, 200-206
  Gospel stories, 219-220
  Jesus, 233
  Jewish, 206, 209- 214, 216
  Pagan, 187
  see Eleusian, Osiris
  Dionysian, 277

N
adab, 69
Nag Hammadi, 220
  initiate of Paul, 268
  monastery founded, 307
  Organization, 337
  Corpus Hermetica, 383
Napoleon, 430-432
Nazarene, 237, 251
Nazareth, 233, 237
Nazarite, 267
Nazi, 59-60
Nebuchadnezzar, 77
Nefertiti, 138, 191
  see Smenkhare, 161
Neo-Platonism, 333, 389
Nephilim, 157
  and Celtic legend, 352
Nepthys, 99
  personification of duality, 192
  see Set
Nero, Emperor, 215, 234-235
  strife after death of, 281
  troubles with Jews, 294
Netjerikhet, 111
Netjeru, 105, 140-141, 147
Nevali Cori, 10
New Atlantis, 388-398
New Kingdom, 101, 113
New Testament, 96, 219, 222-223, 229-231, 245, 247, 378, 380
Newton, Isaac, 151, 413-414
Nicæa, 308
  Synod of, 320
Nicene Creed, 315
Nile, 36, 39, 46, 138
Nimrod, 7, 29-31
Noah, 11, 29, 150, 153-154, 157

Normans, 346, 374-376
Notre Dame. *See* Isis
Notre Dame de Sion, 250
Novatians, 334
Nubia,
  Massai migration, 163
Nun, 214

Obelisk, Egyptian, 406-409
  America and London, 424-425
  Paris, 432
Octavian, 289, 309
Old Testament, 45, 78, 88, 90, 95-96, 150, 152
Order of the Golden Rose Cross, 421
Orestes, 332-333
Orion, 25, 27- 32, 157
  Belt of, 31, 196, 253
Origen, 231
  Asclepsius v Jesus, 280
  Gnostic academy, 307-308
Orion, 249, 253, 255
Osireion, 101, 109, 113, 116
Osiris, 29, 46, 99- 102, 105-106, 109, 132, 136-137
  married god and goddess, 192
  as teacher of mankind, 197-198
  change to Dionysus, 201-202, 206
  Mystery of, 29, 137, 158, 159, 188-190
    demise of, 208
    and Serapis, 263
    Negative Confession, 270
    Domitian, initiate of, 298
    Mysteries abandoned, 277
  as Good Shepherd, 279-280
  as teacher, 359
  Passion of, 202
Oswy, 353,
  see Synod of Whitby
Othniel, 46
Owain Ddantgwyn, 341
Oxford, 380, 389

Pachomius, 307
Palestine, 84- 87, 91, 127
pantheon, 97
Parabolani, 332-333

Paracelsus, 387, 389
Parisii. *See* Isis
Parmenides, 198
Patriarchs, 13-15, 25
  Orion and, 249
Patrick, 357-358, 361

Priory of Sion, 337, 356
Pythagorean
Pythagorean, 339
Paul, 222, 224, 261-275
  death of Christ, 227
  non-Jewish Jesus, 230
  Gnostic heretic, 245
  disciple, 257, 260
  forged letters, 288
  fictitious death of, 294
  relic of, 318
  Gnostic evidence, 338-340
  Columbanus, 351
  Cathars and, 367
Paulicians, 334, 363
Pelagians, 255
Pelagius, 340, 357
Pella, 216
Penn, William, 416
Pentecost, 209
Perfecti, 378
Persephone, 246
Persia, 157
  Judea as vassal state, 211
Persian Empire, 199
Persians, 29, 81, 83-84
  School of, 8
Peter, 257-260
  arrival in Rome, 288, 294
  execution, 318-319
  Papal succession, 324
Pharaoh, 35- 37, 39, 42
  Merneptah, 33
  see Amenhotep, Hatshepsut, Ramesses, Menkaure, Netjerikhet, Tosothros, Thutmosis
  see king list
Pharisees, 89
Philae, 240
Philip IV, 252
Philistines, 20, 44-46
Philo,

495

INDEX

and Therapeutae, 209-210
awareness of Jesus, 237
Helenised Dionysian Mysteries, 277
start of Christianity, 323
Phoenicia, 192, 199
Phoenician, 79
Pi, 113, 118
Pilate, 318
Pimander, 383
Pi-Rarnesses, 33
Plantagenets, 250
Plantard, 249
Plato, 85, 86, 186
   Eleusian Mysteries, 190, 198
   Egypt, 200-201, 203
   Paul, 266, 272
   Marcus Aurelius, 311
   Emperor Julian, 321
   Hypatia, 333
   heretical works, 376
   Renaissance influence, 380-384
   New Atlantis, 388
   Rosicrucian link, 393
Platonic Academy, 334
Pliny, 290-291
Platonism, 254
Platonists
   and Hellenic Jews, 209
Pliny, 285
Pompey, 89-91
   and Tarsus, 261-262
Pontius Pilate
   Gospel accounts, 226, 230
   according to Philo, 234-237
Porphyry, 285
   critique of Christianity, 316
Prime Minister, 418
Primeval Mound, 99-100, 104-105
Promised Land, 36, 40-41, 45, 82
Propaganda, 59-61, 63, 66, 69, 72, 75
Prophets, 66, 69
Protestant, 393
Provence, 244
Priory of Sion, 249-255
Proverbs, 280
Psalm 23, 279
Psalms, 278, 280
Psyche, 246
psychic phenomena, 442

psychomanteum, 267
Ptah, 100
Ptolemy, 87
Ptolemy II, 207-209
Puritan, 405, 410
Pyramid. *See* Giza,
   Red and Bent, 113, 196
   Texts, 185, 188
Pythagoras, 84, 118
   in Egypt, 188-191
   and Druids, 193,
   development of Eleusian Mysteries
   200-201
   teachings of Paul, 272
   Plato and, 384
   Rosicrucian link, 393
Pythagoreans
   and Hellenic Jews, 209, 211-212
   Templar link, 254
   Essenes, 272
   Anthony, Saint, 307
   Justinian, 323

Qedarite Arabs, 39
quantum physics, 439, 442
Queen of Heaven, 240, 243
Qumran, 149-151,
   Damascus and, 272
Queen of Heaven, 250, 254-255

Ra, 97-102, 105-106, 127-132-134
   and Ay, 162
   and Massai, 164
   priests of, 147, 149, 158, 166, 195
   and Aten, 190
   and Lugh Lamfada, 197
   and Alexander, 199, 200-201
   temple falling into disuse, 208
   Pimander, 383
   Solar Barque, 385
   Utopian city, 392
Ra-Horakhty, 99, 102
Ra Temple, 29, 81
   and foreign students, 188, 189, 200
Rameses I, 166
Rameses II, 33, 36, 42
Rameses IX, 146
Ramsay, Andrew, 420

Rayi, 156
  see Watchers
Ratzinger, 373
Red Sea, 36-37
Reformation, 392
relics, 317-318
  big business from, 329
religion, 95-96, 104, 106-107, 122, 125
Regina Coelis. See Queen of Heaven
Rehoboam, 61, 67
Renaissance
  start of, 378
  Norman kings and books, 380
  emergence of Freemasonry, 401
  Pope, last, 408-409
  Egyptian influence from, 425
Revelation. *See* Book of St John
Richelieu, Cardinal, 391
  patron of Moray and Campanella, 406
  Académie Française, 413
Roger, Count 375-377
Roger II. *See* Count Roger
Roman Christians, 60
Rome, 87, 89-91
  invasion of Judea, 209-211
  Nero & Jewish revolt, 215-217
Rosenkreutz, Christian, 392
Rosicrucians
  improvement of mankind, 385
  early influence, 387-394
  ambitions, 396-397
Rosmerta, 250
Rostau, 99
  place of the First Time, 141
Royal Society, 151
Rupert, Prince, 397, 407, 413

Sabbath, 209
Sabian, 8-9
St Christopher, 31
  and Orion, 253
St Paul's, 415-416
Sainte Baume, La, 242
Saintes-Maries-de-la-Mer, Les, 241
  see Mary Magdalene
saints. *See* relics
Sacred Geometry, 254
Samaria, 45

Samaritan, 69, 89
Samos, 188
Samson, 30-31
Sanhedrin, 216
Santiago Compostela, 253-254
Santorini, 37
Saqqara, 109-110
Sarah, 242
Sargon, 46, 64
Sarsen, 197
Satan, 101
  Literalist excuse for sin, 217
  political evolution of, 360
  use to demean women, 366
Saul, 61
Schoch, 28
Schwaller, 28
Schweitzer Albert, 233
Scottish Rite, 402-403, 426
Sekhemket, 111
Sekhmet, 99, 192
Sennacherib, 64
Sep Tepi, 105, 119, 140
Sepphoris, 283
  see Tree of Life
Serapis, 188,
  combined Osiris and Dionysus, 209
  development of Jewish Mysteries, 210, 217
  and Paul, 262-263, 268
  and Vespasian, 298
  destruction of Temple, 331
Set, 101-102
  personification of duality, 192
  see Nephthys
Seti, 109
Shamgar, 45
Shasu, 80
Shechem, 26
Shemsu-hor, 105, 141, 149
Shepherd Kings, 32
Shishak, 67-68
Sicily, 373
  Norman invasion, 375-377
  Renaissance beginnings, 380
sign of the fish, 213
  see vesica pisces
Silbury, 196
Simeon, 45

497

Simon Magus, 245
  heretic, 261
Sinai, 36-38, 167
Sinclair, 403
Sixtus, 408-409
Smenkhkare, 161, 166
Socrates, 85
  initiate of Eleusian Mysteries, 190
  charge of heresy, 198, 200
  Cosmos, 201, 204
  philosophy and subversion, 287
  Marcus Aurelius, 311
  Plato in Egypt, 384
Sokar, 100
Soleb, 80
Solomon, 14, 17, 19, 22, 61, 63, 65-68, 88
  Jewish hope for new leader, 211
  omitted from Joseph's ancestors, 225
Son of God, 186-188
Sophia, 246, 248
Sphinx, 101, 106, 108-109, 114-119, 122-123, 127, 129-132
  Orion's Belt and, 253
Star,
  Chamber, 29, 133
  Room, 29
Star of the Sea. *See* Queen of Heaven
Stella Maris. See Queen of Heaven
Stoicism, 389
Stonehenge, 193, 196-197
Strabo, 261-262
Strikte Observanz, Die, 421
Suetonius, 234-235
Sufism, 254
Sumeria, 156
Sumerian, 196
Summer Solstice, 419
Sun King, 405-406, 411, 431-432
Supreme Being, 428-431
Supreme Council of Antiquities, 28, 115-116
Symmachus, 328
Syncellus, 151
Synesius, 333-334
Syria, 37, 42-43, 87, 90, 127
Synod of Whitby, 353, 358, 361

Tacitus, 235-236
  and Christian fanatics, 285
Talmud, 167
  Yeshu in, 237
Tammuz, 192
Tatian, 229
Taurus, 30-31
Teacher of Righteousness, 150
Telesterion, 204
Tell el-Amarna, 167
Temple/s, 67, 74
  Valley and Sphinx, 101, 108,
Temu, 99
Ten Commandments, 73, 164
Tertullian, 230
  becomes Gnostic, 292
  earlier lies, 296, 298
  fantasy history, 318
  and the sin of shaving, 364
Thebes, 81, 100-101, 128, 130-132, 135, 138-139, 146, 162, 166
  diminishing importance of, 208
Theodosius, 154
  end of Arian sect, 320
  Emperor, 322
  religious ban, 325
  pagan Holocaust, 328, 330-334
  edicts ignored by Celts, 338
  acceptance of pagans, 351
  defeat of Magnus Maximus, 354
Therapeutae, 209-210, 212,
  and Essenes, 272
  and Matthew, 277
Thom, Alexander, 196
Thoth, 28, 105, 122, 359
  Hermes, 382-384
Thutmosis II, 128
Thutmosis III, 128-129
Thutmosis IV, 129-131, 141
Tiberius, Emperor, 235
Timotheus, 209
Titus Antoninus Pius, 310
Torah, 61, 95, 167
Trajan, 290-291
Tree of Life, 415, 424
  see Sepphoris
Trinity,
  Egyptian Divine, 192
True Cross, 242

Twelve Tribes of Israel, 31
Tutankhamun, 146, 148, 162, 165-166

Ubaid, 148
Uffington, 196
Underworld, 246
Universal Reformation of Mankind, 392
University of Tel Aviv, 13
Ur of the Chaldees, 4, 7, 82
Urhay, 29, 31
Urshu, 105, 156
Utopia, 398

Valentinian II, 328
Valentinians, 334
Valla, Lorenzo, 379
Valley of the Kings, 146
   Beautiful Feast of the Desert Valleys, 280
Valley of the shadow, 279
Vatican, 251
   Peter's grave, 319
   threat from Britain, 350
   Celtic Church and, 354, 356-361
   Cathar suppression, 367-368
   archives, 373
   suppression of enlightenment, 373-382
   Hermetica, 384
   Banned Books, 387
   Galileo and, 390
   Reformation, 393-395
   Circus, 408
   Vatican II, 436
   extraterrestial life, 440
   spirit contact, 441
Vau, 35, 80
vesica pisces, 213
Vespasian, Emperor, 236
   return to Rome, 281
Virgins, Black, 241
Virginia, 388-389, 398

Walpole, Robert, 418
Watchers, 105
   in various cultures, 153, 156-157
Wilfred, Bishop, 353
William of Orange, 417
Wisdom text, 280
Wren, Christopher, 405
Washington, George, 423-425

Yahu, 80
Yahweh, 79-80, 83, 89-90
   Paul's view of, 269
Yehud, 81, 83
YHWH, 35, 43, 79-80
Yod, 35, 79
Yod-Heh-Vau-Heh, 79

Zadok, 150
Zaphenath-paneah, 34
Zedekiah, 77
zodiac, 31
Zoser, 110

Map of Middle East

*the places shown indicate their relative geographic position,
the names used were not contemporary with one another*

Neolithic Age	Bronze Age 3000 – 1000 BCE					
Egypt	Dynastic	Old Kingdom	Intermediate & Middle Kingdoms	Second Intermediate	New Kingdom 18th Dynasty	19th Dynasty
Catal Huyuk, Nevali Cori and Jericho	Canaans' urban civilisation declines, move to highlands, Mari Kingdom in Syria			Hyksos settle in Egypt, Canaanite urban revival	Ahmose retakes Egypt Hyksos expelled routed in Canaan, highland villages disappear, era of Thutmosis to Akhenaten & Aten	Rameses Philistines settle in Canaan; Proto-Hebrews & other Canaanites, monotheism appears
6500–3000 BCE	3100–2137 BCE		2137–1780	1780–1575	1575–1320 BCE	1320–1087 BCE

Early Iron Age 1000 BCE				Iron Age ends 500 BCE	
Pharoah Shishak destroys Southern Canaan				Pythagoras brings Mystery religion out of Egypt	cultural advance started by Alexander, Hellenisation of countries from Libya to India spread
supposed time of David & Solomon	Judah and Israel/Samaria are rivals	Assyria destroys Israel, Hezekiah buys back Jerusalem	Josiah's religious reforms Babylonians invade, Jerusalem priests exiled	Jerusalem destroyed by Zedekiah later temple reconstructed	Dionysus Mystery stories; Library of Alexandria flourishes
1000 BCE	900–722 BCE	772 BCE	639–597 BCE	587–516 BCE	330–50 BCE

Roman control around most of Mediterranean	Roman Empire expansion includes Britain		Hadrian, Trajan and Marcus Aurelius civilisation peaks	Decius, Valerian & Diocletian oppression	Constantine capital to Constantinople	Magnus Maximus Western Emperor, Theodosius
Romans adopt Mysteries of Bacchus and Mithras, Alexandrian Jews develop Mysteries of Jesus	Paul of Tarsus Greek Mission, Gnostic teaching expands around Med	Romans destroy Jerusalem, Jews killed, dispersed & enslaved in Rome taking Mysteries of Jesus	Roman Christianity ignores Gnostic teaching; Christianity and pagan Mysteries equal status in Roman Empire; Gnostics write Acts of Apostles	Roman subjects punished for refusal to sacrifice incense; Gnostic/Literalist rift widens	Literalists compile New Testament; Nicene Council gives Emperor say on Christianity; Pelagius leads Celtic Christians refutes Rome	St Anthony founds first Christian Monastery; 'Barbarian' Invasions, Arian Christians rule Gaul, Western Empire falls; Theodosius bans all pagan religions Hypatia killed in Alexandria 414
30 BCE — 50 CE		70–100 CE	100–200 CE	250–1 CE, 257–9 CE, 303–5 CE	307 CE –>	350 CE –>
447 CE Council of Toledo invents Devil and issues description	500 CE last Isis temple handed to Christians	664 CE Synod of Whitby bans Celtic Christianity	800 CE Charlemagne		late 10th century Bogomils	999 Normans arrive in Italy
1022 Pope bans marriage of priests	1115 Bernard founds Abbey of Clairvaux 1128 founds Knights Templar		12th–13th century Cathars strong in France, eliminated by Pope, Inquisition created		14th century –> Medicis printing, philosophy, art and Plato	16th century –> science, mathematics, new worlds and new freedoms

www.ingramcontent.com/pod-product-compliance
Lightning Source LLC
Chambersburg PA
CBHW060102170426
43198CB00010B/744